D1878656

A CATALOGUE

OF THE

TAMIL BOOKS

IN THE

LIBRARY

OF THE

BRITISH MUSEUM

A CATALOGUE
OF THE
TAMIL BOOKS
IN THE
LIBRARY
OF THE
BRITISH MUSEUM

COMPILED BY
L. D. BARNETT
G. U. POPE

IN TWO VOLUMES
VOL-I

GYAN

Published by

GYAN

Gyan Publishing House
5, Ansari Road
Daryaganj, New Delhi-110002
Phone: 011-47034999, 9811692060
E-mail: books@gyanbooks.com

Distribution Network
gyanbooks.com
India, USA, Canada, UK, Australia, France

© Publisher
All rights reserved. No part of this work may be reproduced, stored, adapted, or transmitted in any form or by any means, electronic, mechanical, photocopying, micro-filming, recording or otherwise, or translated in any language, without the prior written permission of the copyright owner and the publisher.

ISBN : 978-81-212-3195-4 (Set)
ISBN : 978-81-212-4657-6 (PB)
First Published, London, 1909

2nd Impression 2020

Printed at: Gyan Press, Delhi.

The book is sold subject to the condition that it shall not, by way of trade or otherwise, be lent, resold, hired out, or otherwise circulated without the prior publisher's written consent.

A Catalogue of the Tamil Books in the Library of the British MuseumVol. I
Compiled by : L. D. Barnett

PREFACE.

Of all the literatures of India, with the single exception of the Sanskrit, the Tamil is the richest, the oldest, and the most various. It is thus most completely representative of that ancient Dravidian culture which preceded the civilisation of the conquering Aryan immigrants, and doubtless contributed much to the literary and social development of the latter. Hence the oldest surviving works of Tamil literature bear a peculiar character; though it would perhaps be too bold to assert them to be wholly independent of Sanskritic influences, they are both in vocabulary and in literary form distinctly different from the typical products of the classical Sanskrit literature.

The Hindu tendency to construct arbitrary and exaggerated systems of chronology is fully shared by the Tamils, who assign the beginnings of their culture to a fabulous antiquity, and trace the progress of their literature through three successive Saṅghams or Academies. For the first two of the latter no historical basis can be found. As to the third, works are still extant which bear the names of several writers traditionally associated with it; but there seems to be no sufficient ground to accept the legend which has grouped together their names as those of contemporaries, especially as Nakkīra Dēvar, the most prominent poet of the Third Saṅgham, can hardly be assigned to a date earlier than the fifth or sixth century, whilst there are reasons for believing that the Kuṟaḷ, the famous collection of ethical and erotic verses attributed to the somewhat legendary "Tiru-vaḷḷuvar" (popularly believed to have been a Paraiyar priest, but possibly a Jain), may have been composed some three centuries earlier.

Tradition traces back the origin of extant Tamil literature and science to the sage Agastyar (Agattiyar), who plays a prominent part in ancient Sanskrit mythology. A grammar of the Tamil language bearing his name, the Agattiyam, was formerly extant, which apparently was based upon the Pāṇinian school of Sanskrit grammar. It has long since been superseded by the Tol-kāppiyam, of which the author (reputed to have been a disciple of Agastyar) followed the principles of the Aindra Sanskrit grammarians. Upon the Tol-kāppiyam was based the Nan-nūl of Pavaṇandi, apparently a Jain; this is an aphoristic compendium of grammar composed about the beginning of the thirteenth century.* Around these two works has arisen a copious grammatical literature. Mention may be made likewise of the Vīra-ṣōḻiyam, a grammar by Buddha-mitran

* The author of the ancient commentary upon the Nan-nūl, traditionally believed to have been a disciple of Pavaṇandi, states that the latter wrote his work under the orders of a king Ṣīya Gaṅgan in Ṣanagai, who is evidently identical with the prince of that name who is shown by inscriptions to have been a vassal of Kulōttuṅga III. (see *South-Indian Inscriptions*, vol. iii., p. 122, and *Epigraphia Indica*, vol. vii., Appendix, p. 135).

(towards the end of the 11th century),* the commentary upon the latter by Perun-dēvanār,† who is believed to have been Buddha-mitran's disciple, the treatises upon the art of poetry by Nāṟ-kavi-rājar ‡ and Aiyanār-idanār, and Amirta-sāgaran's Yāpp'-aruṅgalam, a manual of prosody, with its commentary by Guṇa-sāgaran (before the 13th century); all these writers were apparently Jains. In the allied department of lexicography the earliest known work is probably the Divākaram of Divākarar, whose son Piṅgalar supplemented his father's collection in his Piṅgalandai (8th century or later, and quoted by Pavaṇandi). Another ancient lexical work is the Nēmi-nātham of the Jain Guṇa-vīrau. Of considerable importance also is the Chūḍāmaṇi-nighaṇṭu of Vīra-maṇḍalavar (about the end of the 9th century)§.

Classical grammar is the norm (*ilakkaṇam*) for classical literature (*ilakkiyam*). Among the most interesting and characteristically Dravidian products of the latter are the Pattu-pāṭṭu or "Ten Poems," which with the exception of the first (Nakkīra Dēvar's Tiru-mṟug'-āṟṟu-paḍai, a poem to a deity) are brilliant pictures of romantic scenes of love and war. Some of them may possibly be as early as the second century. To the same type and period belong the Eṭṭu-togai, eight collections of verses by various poets, and the eighteen *Kīṟ-kaṇakku* poems, among which are classed the Kuṟaḷ of Tiru-vaḷḷuvar, the Nāl-aḍiyār, a Jain anthology compiled about the eighth century,‖ and Poygaiyār's Kaḷa-vaṟi.¶ In this classical literature the Jains again took an active part from early times; five or six *Kīṟ-kaṇakku* poems, if not more, are by Jains, as likewise are the five *Kāvyams*, romances in verse, of which the most famous are Ṣāttan's Maṇi-mēkhalai, Iḷaṅ-gōv-aḍigaḷ's Ṣilapp'-adhikāram, and Tiru-takka Dēvar's Jīvaka-chintāmaṇi. The Maṇi-mēkhalai and Ṣilapp'-adhikāram have been assigned to the second century; the Jīvaka-chintāmaṇi is probably not earlier than the tenth.** To the same period apparently belongs the Bhāratam, a version of the Sanskrit epic in *veṇ-bā* metre by Perun-dēvanār.††

In poetry of the *Kāvyam* type the most admired work of medieval and modern times is Kamban's adaptation of Vālmīki's Rāmāyaṇam, with the appended Uttara-kāṇḍam by Oṭṭa-kūttar. The poetical abridgment of the Mahā-bhāratam by Villiputtūrar and

* See *Epigraphia Indica*, vol. vi., p. 334 foll., and Seshagiri Sastri's *Report* for 1893-4, p. 113.

† This writer must be distinguished from the epic poet Perun-dēvanār, on whom see below. By an oversight the entries for the works of these two authors have been included under one heading in col. 70 of this Catalogue, where also the date assigned to Kulōttuṅga's reign should be corrected to 1073—1118.

‡ I take this opportunity to supply an omission: the edition of Nāṟ-kavi-rājar's Aga-poruḷ-viḷakkam published in 1878, which is catalogued on col. 213 below, contains also Poyyā-moṟi Pulavar's Tañjai-vāṇan-kōvai.

§ See *Indian Antiquary*, vol. 36 (1907), p. 288. Both the Divākaram and the Piṅgalandai are quoted in the Chūḍāmaṇi-nighaṇṭu.

‖ See *Madras Government Epigraphist's Report*, 1907, p. 68.

¶ King Ṣeṅgaṇṇān, the hero of this poem, lived before the 7th century; he is mentioned in the Dēvāram The poem itself, however, may be later.

** See *Indian Antiquary*, vol. 36 (1907), p. 285 foll.

†† He mentions as his patron a Pallava king who gained a victory at Teḷḷ'-āṟu; this is apparently Nandi-varma or Nandi-pōtt'-araiyar, late in the 8th century (see *Epigraphia Indica*, vol. vii., Appendix, pp. 108-9, ibid., vol. viii., pt. 5, Appendix II., p. 20; *Madras Government Epigraphist's Report*, 1907, p. 65).

Pugaṟēndi's poem on the legend of Nala are also much esteemed.* To the same period belongs Jayaṅ-goṇḍāṉ's Kaliṅgattu Paraṇi, a poem on the conquest of Kaliṅga by Kulōttuṅga I (1073—1118). In most of these authors the influence of Sanskrit literature is apparent, as is also the case with the writings of Ativīra-rāma Pāṇḍiyan, believed to have been a king of Madura, whose date is assigned variously to the 12th and the 16th centuries.† The latter is the reputed author of the Naiḍadam (a version of the epic story of Nala), some poems on religious legends and cult, and the Veṯṯi-vēṟ kai, a little moral tract in prose.

In religious poetry Tamil literature is remarkably rich. The worship of Ṣiva seems to have been indigenous to the South, though doubtless it has been locally influenced in various degrees by the Ṣaiva cults of the North. The oldest extant Ṣaiva poems in Tamil are the hymns ascribed to Ñāna-sambandhar, Appar (Tiru-nāvukk'-araṣu), and Sundara-mūrtti,‡ collectively known as the Dēvāram, and the fine lyrics (Tiru-vāchakam) of Māṇikka-vāchakar,§ which form part of the Tiru-muṟai, a collection of Ṣaiva poems codified by Nambiy-āṇḍār Nambi about the eleventh century.|| Of fairly ancient date is likewise the Kanda-purāṇam by Kachiy-appar of Kāñchi, which is said to have been composed in Ṣaka 700. Still more popular is the Periya-purāṇam of Ṣēkkiṟār, a voluminous poetical hagiology, which is apparently based upon Nambiy-āṇḍār Nambi's Toṇḍar-tiruv-antādi, the third of his hymns in the Tiru-muṟai.¶ The scholastic theology of this church seems to have taken its classical form (whether directly or indirectly is not clear) under the influence of the Ṣaiva schools of Kashmir. According to tradition, the following great authors formed an unbroken spiritual

* There is much uncertainty as to the chronology of these poets. Popular tradition makes them all contemporaries, but can hardly be correct. It may be provisionally inferred from the data of tradition and fact that Kamban's period is about 1100, and this date is supported by the legend of his connection with the theologian Nātha Muni (11th century). Oṭṭa-kūttar seems to be later. Pugaṟēndi may be earlier, if any confidence may be placed in the legend that he was patronised by Vara-guṇa Pāṇḍiyan (9th century). Villiputtūrar again seems to be considerably later; but all that is certain in his case is the information derivable from the verses bearing the name of his son Varandaruvār, which are prefixed to his poem. We learn thence that Villiputtūrar was later than the three poets of the Dēvāram (*circa* 7th—9th century), and that he found a patron in Āṭ-koṇḍāṉ, a Koṅga prince who rendered valuable service to a Chola king Kaṇḍan; but neither of the latter personages have yet been traced in historical records.

† He may be identical with the king of that name whose reign began in 1562-3 (*Epigraphia Indica*, vol. vii., p. 16).

‡ Ñāna-sambandhar appears to belong to the 7th century, Sundara-mūrtti to the 8th or 9th. See Sundaram Piḷḷai, *Some Mile-stones in the History of Tamil Literature*; also *Madras Christian College Magazine*, vol. xiv., no. 5 (1896), p. 286 foll., *Epigraphia Indica*, vol. iii., p. 277-8, *Indian Antiquary*, vol. 25, pp. 113 foll., 164, *South-Indian Inscriptions*, vol. ii., pt. 2, p. 152 f.

§ His date is somewhere between 800 and 1000 A.D. He apparently is later than Sundara-mūrtti, and he twice mentions a king Vara-guṇa Pāṇḍiyan, who is either the Vara-guṇa Varma who ascended the throne in 862-3, or his grandfather; on the other hand, his Tiruv-em-bāvai is quoted in an inscription of 1056-7. See *Epigraphia Indica*, vol. viii., pt. 8, p. 319, vol. ix., pt. 2, pp. 88-9; *Madras Government Epigraphist's Report*, 1907, p. 64 foll., 1908, p. 66; *South-Indian Inscriptions*, vol. ii., p. 384.

|| See *Madras Christian College Magazine*, vol. xiv., no. 5 (1896), p. 286 foll.

¶ The Periya-purāṇam was written under the patronage of Anapāya Chōḷan. An attempt has been made to identify this king with Kulōttuṅga Chōḷan I., who reigned A.D. 1073—1118. See *Madras Review*, 1904, p. 366 f.; *Indian Antiquary*, vol. 36 (1907), p. 288; *South-Indian Inscriptions*, vol. ii., pt. 2, p. 153 f.

lineage: Mey-kaṇḍa Dēvar (author of the Ṣiva-ñāna-bōdham, about 1223 A.D.), Aruṇandi (author of the Ṣiva-ñāna-siddhiyār, etc.), Maṟai-ñāna-sambandhar (author of the Ṣaiva-samaya-neṟi, etc.), and Koṭṭavangudi Umā-pati (whose Saṅkaṟpa-nirākaraṇam is dated Ṣaka 1235, or A.D. 1313). A still higher antiquity is claimed for Tirukaḍavūr Uyya-vandar, who is said to have flourished about Ṣaka 1100. Of other medieval Ṣaiva writings perhaps the most important are the Tiru-viḷaiy-āḍaṟ-purāṇam, a poetical account of the Ṣaiva legends of Madura by Parañ-jōdi (born at Tiru-maṟai-kāḍu or Vēdāraṇyam in the 16th or 17th century, and said to have been patronised by Ati-vīra-rāman), and the devotional poems of Paṭṭaṇattu Piḷḷai (perhaps of the tenth century), "Ṣiva-vākyar," and Tāyumāṇavar (about 1650). Paṭṭaṇattu Piḷḷai and Ṣiva-vākyar are remarkable for the enlightened spirit of piety and disregard for orthodox ritualism to which they occasionally give expression. The modern lyrics of Rāma-liṅga Piḷḷai are also very popular. The most influential of modern Ṣaiva theologians is perhaps Ṣiva-ñānar of Tiruvāvaḍuduṟai (died 1785 A.D.), whose disciple Kachiy-appar of Tiru-taṇigai wrote several poems on religious legends.

The Vaishṇava church is likewise of great importance in the South. Its characteristic doctrine of *Viṣishṭādvaitam*, "qualified monism," is best known from the Sanskrit works of the famous Rāmānuja, said to have been born in the month Chaitra of Ṣaka 939, who has been followed by a large number of theologians writing both in Sanskrit and in the peculiar form of sanskritised Tamil which in its extreme form is known as *maṇi-pravāḷam.* The church, however, traces its doctrines back through Rāmānuja to a series of earlier apostles, the *Āṟvārs*, for some of whom it claims extreme antiquity;* to them is ascribed the devotional literature codified in the Nāl-āyira-prabandham.

Ethical poetry holds an important place in Tamil literature. Among the oldest classics are works of this nature; and the moral tracts in prose and verse attributed to the somewhat legendary poetess Auvaiyār (traditionally believed to have been the sister of Tiru-vaḷḷuvar)† have long been extremely popular. A favourite modern poem of similar character is the Nīti-neṟi-viḷakkam of Kumara-guru-parar, a Ṣaiva monk.

In these and in many other departments the development of Tamil literature has been copious and vigorous. In modern times it has been reinforced by influences from without—Hindu, Muhammadan, and European. The latter class includes the specifically Christian literature founded by the great Jesuits De' Nobili and Beschi, which is continually being increased by the various Catholic and Protestant communities of Southern India, and the abundant supply of modern educational works, fiction, and poetry which is based more or less directly upon European and especially English models.

* Namm'-āṟvār and Tirumaṅgai-āṟvār perhaps belong to the 8th century or thereabouts. See *Madras Government Epigraphist's Report*, 1908, p. 69; *Epigraphia Indica*, vol. viii., p. 294.

† Verses ascribed to Auvaiyār are found in the Puṟa-nāṉūṟu and other anthologies of the oldest period. On the other hand, v. 40 of the Nal-vaḻi attributed to her speaks of the *mūvar tamiṟum*, i.e., the Dēvāram, and hence is not earlier than the 8th century. Evidently, then, there were at least two writers with the title "Auvaiyār."

The first steps towards the preparation of a catalogue of the large and representative collection of Tamil printed books in the British Museum were taken some twenty years ago, when the late Dr. G. U. Pope was commissioned by the Trustees to describe them. Circumstances, however, prevented him from bringing his task to completion. I have accordingly revised or re-written his descriptions, and catalogued the numerous works acquired during the last fifteen years, whereby the original number of titles has been fully trebled. The titles for the books lithographed in the "Arvī," or modification of Arabic character commonly used for the dialect of Tamil Muhammadans, have been prepared by Mr. A. G. Ellis, until recently Assistant in this Department.

In the following pages the primary sounds of the Tamil language are thus transliterated :—

—	அ a	ஆ ā	இ i	ஈ(இ) ī	உ u	ஊ ū	எ e	ஏ ē	ஐ ai	ஒ o	ஓ ō	ஔ au
க் k	க ka	கா kā	கி ki	கீ kī	கு ku	கூ kū	கெ ke	கே kē	கை kai	கொ ko	கோ kō	கௌ kau
ங் ṅ	ங ṅa	ஙா ṅā	ஙி ṅi	ஙீ ṅī	ஙு ṅu	ஙூ ṅū	ஙெ ṅe	ஙே ṅē	ஙை ṅai	ஙொ ṅo	ஙோ ṅō	ஙௌ ṅau
ச் ṣ*	ச ṣa	சா ṣā	சி ṣi	சீ ṣī	சு ṣu	சூ ṣū	செ ṣe	சே ṣē	சை ṣai	சொ ṣo	சோ ṣō	சௌ ṣau
ஞ் ñ	ஞ ña	ஞா ñā	ஞி ñi	ஞீ ñī	ஞு ñu	ஞூ ñū	ஞெ ñe	ஞே ñē	ஞை ñai	ஞொ ño	ஞோ ñō	ஞௌ ñau
ட் ṭ	ட ṭa	டா ṭā	டி ṭi	டீ ṭī	டு ṭu	டூ ṭū	டெ ṭe	டே ṭē	டை ṭai	டொ ṭo	டோ ṭō	டௌ ṭau
ண் ṇ	ண ṇa	ணா ṇā	ணி ṇi	ணீ ṇī	ணு ṇu	ணூ ṇū	ணெ ṇe	ணே ṇē	ணை ṇai	ணொ ṇo	ணோ ṇō	ணௌ ṇau
த் t	த ta	தா tā	தி ti	தீ tī	து tu	தூ tū	தெ te	தே tē	தை tai	தொ to	தோ tō	தௌ tau
ந் n	ந na	நா nā	நி ni	நீ nī	நு nu	நூ nū	நெ ne	நே nē	நை nai	நொ no	நோ nō	நௌ nau
ப் p	ப pa	பா pā	பி pi	பீ pī	பு pu	பூ pū	பெ pe	பே pē	பை pai	பொ po	போ pō	பௌ pau
ம் m	ம ma	மா mā	மி mi	மீ mī	மு mu	மூ mū	மெ mo	மே mē	மை mai	மொ mo	மோ mō	மௌ mau
ய் y	ய ya	யா yā	யி yi	யீ yī	யு yu	யூ yū	யெ ye	யே yē	யை yai	யொ yo	யோ yō	யௌ yau
ர் r	ர ra	ரா rā	ரி ri	ரீ rī	ரு ru	ரூ rū	ரெ re	ரே rē	ரை rai	ரொ ro	ரோ rō	ரௌ rau
ல் l	ல la	லா lā	லி li	லீ lī	லு lu	லூ lū	லெ le	லே lē	லை lai	லொ lo	லோ lō	லௌ lau
வ் v	வ va	வா vā	வி vi	வீ vī	வு vu	வூ vū	வெ ve	வே vē	வை vai	வொ vo	வோ vō	வௌ vau
ழ் ṛ	ழ ṛa	ழா ṛā	ழி ṛi	ழீ ṛī	ழு ṛu	ழூ ṛū	ழெ ṛe	ழே ṛē	ழை ṛai	ழொ ṛo	ழோ ṛō	ழௌ ṛau
ள் ḷ	ள ḷa	ளா ḷā	ளி ḷi	ளீ ḷī	ளு ḷu	ளூ ḷū	ளெ ḷo	ளே ḷē	ளை ḷai	ளொ ḷo	ளோ ḷō	ளௌ ḷau
ற் ṟ†	ற ṟa	றா ṟā	றி ṟi	றீ ṟī	று ṟu	றூ ṟū	றெ ṟe	றே ṟē	றை ṟai	றொ ṟo	றோ ṟō	றௌ ṟau
ன் n‡	ன na	னா nā	னி ni	னீ nī	னு nu	னூ nū	னெ ne	னே nē	னை nai	னொ no	னோ nō	னௌ nau

The sound ஃ is transliterated by the rough breathing, as பஃரொடி, *pa'roḍi.* The sign ௲ is used to indicate our "etcetera."

As these are the only signs in ordinary use to express the variety of sounds in the language, transliteration is attended with some difficulty. For example, க in Tamil words can represent according to its position either *k* or *g*, and in Sanskrit words it has to do duty also for *kh*, *gh*, and even *h*. I have therefore generally transliterated Tamil words

* The compound ச்ச is transliterated by *ch*.

† The compound ற்ற is transliterated by *ṯṯ*.

‡ In transliteration no distinction is made between this sound and the pure dental ந, as the latter only occurs initially and in combination with other dentals, where the ன is never found.

CATALOGUE

OF

TAMIL PRINTED BOOKS

[Words enclosed in square brackets are added by the compiler. Titles or other additions are included in parentheses when taken from some source other than the main title-page; thus the parenthesis alone denotes that the words are taken from the wrapper, an asterisk in the parenthesis that they are from a second or half title-page, and a dagger that they are from some other place within the book. Omission of words at the beginning of a title is indicated by three small circles, omission in the middle of a title by three dots.]

'ABD ALLĀH, *Maulavī.* See VĀLAI-BĀVA SĀHIB. தொழுகைஅகீகத்துவிளக்கம். [Toṛugai-ḣakīkat-viḷakkam. An adaptation of the Ḣakīkat al-ṣalāt of 'Abd Allāh.] [1862.] 8°. **14173. b. 33.**

'ABD ALLĀH ibn 'ABD al-KARĪM, *of Bangalore.* ஆன்றோர் அனுபோக கைவல்லிய வைத்திய சங்கிரகம். [Vaidya-saṅgraham. A treatise on the medical art, chiefly in verse. Arranged for singing by A. Amirta-vāchaka Dāsar, and edited by T. Ratna-sāmi Piḷḷai.] pp. 4, viii. 88. பெங்களூர் [*Bangalore,* 1900.] 8°. **14170. i. 72.**

'ABD al-ḲĀDIR, *Maulānā Maulavī, Sāḣib 'Ālim, of Tinnevelli-pet.* ஈமானுண்மை இசுலாநன்மை என்னும், ஹக்கீசத்துல் இஸ்லாம். [Ḣakīkat al-Islām, also called Īmān-uṇmai Islām-nanmai. A treatise on the principles of Islām.] pp. 174. சென்னை கஅகஅ [*Madras,* 1898.] 8°. **14173. b. 5.**

'ABD al-ḲĀDIR, *Āmūr Vālai-bāva.* இரத்நமுகம்மது காரணசரித்திரம். [Ratna-Muḣammad-kāraṇa-charitram. The history of a Muhammadan saint, compiled from Persian sources by 'Abd al-Ḳādir. Edited by his son, 'Abd al-Wahhāb.] pp. 64. கஅஅஉ [*Madras,* 1882.] 8°. **14173. b. 19.**

'ABD al-ḲĀDIR ibn MADĀR. فتوحات السلام فى النصايح والاحكام [Futūḣāt al-salām. A compendium of Muhammadan law, according to the Ḣanafī and Shāfi'ī schools.] pp. viii. 604, 32. البمبئى ١٣٠٧ [*Bombay,* 1890.] 8°. **14173. c. 8.**

'ABD al-ḲĀDIR ibn MUḢAMMAD MUḢYI al-DĪN, *al-Ḳādirī.* فتح الصمد فى مسائل التودد [Fatḣ al-ṣamad. The story of the learned slave-girl Tawaddud and her examination by the 'Ulamā before the Caliph Hārūn al-Rashīd. Adapted from the Arabian Nights.] pp. 336, *lith.* ١٣٢٠ بمدراس [*Madras,* 1902.] 8°. **14170. k. 4.**

'ABD al-ḲĀDIR ibn MŪSĀ, *al-Jīlānī.* [*Life.*] See MUḢAMMAD GHAUṢ, *al-Shāfi'ī al-Madrāsī.* [Naṣr al-jawāhir.] **14173. c. 7.**

'ABD al-ḲĀDIR NAYINĀR, *Shaikh, of Kayalpatnam.* See 'UMAR, *Poet.* சீறா [Ṣīṟā. Edited by 'Abd al-Ḳādir.] [1885.] 8°. **14173. b. 20.**

—— இஃது சித்திரகவி முதலிய பலபாடற்றிரட்டு [Chitra-kavi-mudaliya pala-pādaṯ-ṯiraṭṭu. Poems, several of them in very elaborate metres, upon worthies and doctrinal topics of the Muhammadan Church.] vol. i. pp. xxxiv. 376; 1 *plate.* சென்னை தருகரு [*Madras*, 1896.] 8°. **14173. b. 35.**

'ABD al-MAJĪD, *of Vellore.* تلقين فى مهمات الدين لأولاد المسلمين [Talkīn fī muhimmāt al-dīn. A catechism of religious instruction for Muhammadan children. Translated from the Hindustani.] pp. iv. 132, *lith.* مدراس ۱۳۲۱ [*Madras*, 1904.] 8°. **14173. b. 27.(1.)**

'ABD al-RAHMĀN, *'Arabī.* [*Panegyric.*] *See* PAVĀNI PULAVAR. இஸ்து அப்துறகுமானறபிச்சதகம். ['Abd al-Rahmān 'Arabi ṣatakam.] [1895.] 8°. **14173. b. 26.**

'ABD al-RAHMĀN, *Nelliguppam.* *See* MUHAMMAD ibn MUHAMMAD, *al-Ghazzālī.* கீமியாஎ ஸஆதத்து. [Kīmiyā i sa'ādat. Translated by 'Abd al-Rahmān.] 1906, *etc.* 8°. **14173. b. 10.**

'ABD al-WAHHĀB, called BANDAH. *See* BANDAH.

'ABD al-WAHHĀB ibn 'ABD al-KĀDIR. *See* 'ABD al-KĀDIR, *Ā.V.* இரத்நமுகம்மது காரணசரித்திரம். [Ratna - Muhammad - kāraṇa - charitram. Edited by 'Abd al-Wahhāb.] [1882.] 8°. **14173. b. 19.**

'ABD al-WAHHĀB ibn MUHAMMAD HĀDI, *al-Āturī.* اسرار الصلوات على خير البريات [Asrār al-salawāt 'ala khair al-bariyāt. A treatise on prayer for Muhammad.] pp. xxiv. 424, *lith.* بمدراس ۱۳۱۹ [*Madras*, 1901.] 12°. **14173. a. 3.**

ABRAHAM (B.). *See* DIOGNETUS. தியோக்னேது என்பவருக்கு எழுதின நிருபம். The Epistle to Diognetus. A translation by B. Abraham. 1893. 8°. **14170. c. 24.(8.)**

ABRAHAM (ISAAC). [*Life.*] *See* PĀṆḌIYAN (T. B.). The life of . . . I. Abraham, *etc.* 1906. 12°. **14170. bbb. 11.**

ABŪ al-HASAN, *al-Shāzilī.* *See* 'ALĪ ibn 'ABD ALLĀH (ABŪ al-HASAN).

ACADEMIES, etc.

GERMANY.

Deutsche Morgenlaendische Gesellschaft.

Zeitschrift, *etc.* *Leipzig*, 1846, *etc.* 8°. **Ac. 8815/2.**
In progress.

ACADEMIES, etc.

LONDON.

Oriental Translation Fund of Great Britain and Ireland.

Miscellaneous translations from Oriental languages. Vol. i. [Including the Sahādēvan-ṣāstram and Vētāla-kathai.] *London*, 1831. 8°. **14003. d. 5.**

MADRAS.

Ṣennai-ṣen-damir-urai-saṅgham.

University of Madras. Exhaustive notes on the Matriculation Tamil text for 1900 . . . by the Chennai Sendamilurai Sangham, *etc.* 1900. 8°. *See* below: *University of Madras.* **14172. bb. 6.(4.)**

University of Madras.

See JAGA-RĀU MUDALIYĀR. University of Madras. The Tamil Text Examiner for the Matriculation Examination, 1898. 1898. 8°. **14172. b. 16.(2.)**

See MRUGA-DĀSA SVĀMI. University of Madras. F.A. Examination—1903. Pulawar Puranam, *etc.* 1901. 8°. **14172. bb. 3.(4.)**

See RUDRA-KAṆṆANĀR. University of Madras. B.A. Examination of 1906 . . . Pattinappalai, *etc.* 1906. 8°. **14172. b. 37.(2.)**

See ṢELVA-KĒṢAVA-RĀYA MUDALIYĀR, *T.* Tiruvalluvar, *etc.* (University of Madras. First Examination in Arts—1905. Tamil prose, *etc.*) 1904. 12°. **14171. d. 2.**

The Nalavenba and Nanmanikadigai, with . . . notes, &c., for the use of Matriculation Examination, 1879. By C. Rajagopala Pillai, *etc.* 1879. 12°. *See* PUGAḌĒNDI. **14172. a. 22.**

Notes on the Tamil text for the Matriculation Examination of 1888. Bharata Venba [annotated] by . . . T. E. Srinivasa Raghavacharyar . . . Pazhamozhi, &c. [annotated] by K. Srinivasaraghavacharyar. ('Kalatarangini' Supplement Series. No. 2.) 6 pts. *Madras*, 1888. 12°. **14172. a. 41.**

The University of Madras. The First in Arts Examination—1892. The Tamil text, poetry, with copious notes by the late C. Rajagopaul Pillai . . . and . . : P. Vasudeva Mudelliar. [Comprising Ativīra-rāma Pāṇḍiyan's Kūrma-purāṇam, bk. 12, his Tiru-karuvai-kali-tuṟai, and Villiputtūrar's Mahā-bhāratam, Ṣalya-parvam, with commentary.] pp. ii. 12, 328, 60. *Madras*, 1891. 8°. **14172. bb. 4.**

Copious notes on the Tamil text-book for the Matriculation Examination, 1898 [viz. (1) Pugaẓēndi's Naḷa-veṇ-bā, Kali-doḍar-kāṇḍam, (2) Pañcha-tantram ii., (3) Jayaṅ-goṇḍān's Kaliṅgattu-paraṇi, Rāja-pāramparyam and Avatāram, (4) Perun-dēvanār's Bhāratam, Udyōga-parvam, (5) Tamil-English glossary to Hitōpadēṣam i., with the original texts of nos. 1 to 5 in Tamil and English], by Vithvan P. Krishnasawmy Mudaliyar. pp. 120, 72, 18. *Madras*, 1898. 8°. **14172. b. 16.(1.)**

லீலாவதி-சுலோசனையுரை. (F.A. Tamil Text 1899. Full notes on Lilavati-Sulochana, *etc.*) 1898. 8°. *See* Rāma-sāmi Aiyaṅgār, *Ṣarukkai.* **14172. bb. 6.(1.)**

University of Madras. F.A. Examination 1900. Tamil poetry—the prescribed portions in Naladyar and Bharatam; and explanatory notes . . . By C. M. Swaminatha Iyer. 1899. 8°. *See* Nāl-aḍiyār. **14172. b. 37.**

The Tamil text for the Matriculation Examination of the University of Madras, December, 1900. [Comprising Perun-dēvanār's Bhāratam, Udyōga-parvam; part of the Aṟattu-pāl of Pāṇḍi-turai Dēvar's Pan-nūṯ-ṯiraṭṭu; and portions of the prose Rāmāyaṇam and Dāmōdaram Piḷḷai's Chūḷā-maṇi.] pp. 70. *Madras*, 1899. 8°. **14172. bb. 6.(7.)**

University of Madras. Matriculation Examination, 1900. Copious notes on the Tamil text-book [viz. Perun-dēvanār's Bhāratam, Pāṇḍi-turai Dēvar's Pan-nūṯ-ṯiraṭṭu, Rāmāyaṇam, and Chūḷā-maṇi, with vocabularies.] By Vithvan P. Krishnasawmy Mudaliar. [With the Tamil texts and English translations by the latter and V. Veṅkaṭa-ṣrīnivāsan.] pp. 140, 16, 4, 27. *Madras*, 1900. 8°. **14172. bb. 6.(2.)**

Copious annotations on the Matriculation Tamil text for 1900 [scil. Perun-dēvanār's Bhāratam, Pāṇḍi-turai Dēvar's Pan-nūṯ-ṯiraṭṭu, Rāmāyaṇam, and Chūḷā-maṇi] by V. M. Satakoparamanujachariar . . . and S. Krishnamachariar . . . With a complete English translation by T. E. Venkatachariar. pp. ii. 108, 92, 44. *Madras*, 1900. 8°. **14172. bb. 6.(3.)**

ACADEMIES, etc.

Madras (*continued*).

University of Madras (*continued*).

University of Madras. Exhaustive notes on the Matriculation Tamil text for 1900 [viz. the Udyōga-parvam of Perun-dēvanār's Bhāratam, Pan-nūṯ-ṯiraṭṭu, and Rāmāyaṇam]. With . . . explanations and hints on prosody and rhetoric, &c., &c., by the Chennai Sendamilurai Sangham, with complete English translation [of the above texts and the Chūḷā-maṇi] by T. R. Ramanatha Aiyar. pp. 4, 119, 69. [*Madras*,] 1900. 8°. **14172. bb. 6.(4.)**

University of Madras. F.A. Examination of 1901. Tamil poetry, containing Bharatham and Naladiyar, with copious annotations and notes on Alvargal Charitram and Chulamani, by V. M. Satakoparamanujachariar . . . and S. Krishnamachariar . . . Also comprising an English translation of Naladiyar by an experienced graduate. pp. 212, 52, 42, 6, 31, 5. *Madras*, 1900. 8°. **14172. bb. 6.(5.)**

The Chūḷā-maṇi is wanting in this edition.

University of Madras. B.A. Examination of 1901, Dec. A Tamil text-book, part 1, containing Thirukkural [stanzas 701-800, with commentary based on that of Parimēl-aẓagar], Kandapuranam [in the version of Kachiy-appar], and Surpanakaippatalam of Kambaramayanam, with copious annotations and notes on [Sāmināth'-aiyar's] Buddhacharitram, by V. M. Satakoparamanujachariar . . . and S. Krishnamachariar. *Madras*, 1900. 8°. **14172. bb. 6.(6.)**

Each part is separately paginated.

University of Madras. F.A. Examination of 1903. Full notes on Pulavar Puranam, Bhoja Raja Charitram, and Bhartruhari, by V. M. Satakoparamanujachariar . . . and S. Krishnamachariar . . . with an English translation of Naladiyar [xvi.-xx.]. pp. 50, 53. *Madras*, 1903. 8°. **14172. hh. 19.**

University of Madras. B.A. Degree Examination 1905. Purapporul Venbamalai, *etc.* 1905. 8°. *See* Aiyanār-idanār. **14172. bb. 21.(1.)**

University of Madras. B.A. Examination of 1906. Jivakachintamani, *etc.* 1905. 8°. *See* Tiruttakka Dēvar. **14171. bb. 21 (2.)**

ACADEMIES, etc.

MADURA.

செந்தமிழ். [Ṣen-damiṟ. A monthly journal of literature and science, published by the Tamiṟ-saṅgham of Madura. Edited by R. Rāghav'-aiyaṅgār.] *Madura*, 1902, *etc.* 8°. **14172. i. 1.**

In progress.

["Ṣen-damiṟ" supplement, comprising works published in the "Ṣen-damiṟ," with separate pagination.] 1902, *etc.* **14172. i. 1*.**

In progress.

PARIS.

Bibliothèque Nationale.

Manuscrits tamouls. [Proof sheets of a catalogue of the Tamil MSS. in the Bibliothèque Nationale, compiled by E. H. J. Vinson.] ff. 49. [*Paris*, 1880?] Fol. **14172. k. 1.**

École Spéciale des Langues Orientales Vivantes.

Mélanges Orientaux. Textes et traductions publiés par les professeurs de l'École Spéciale des Langues Orientales Vivantes à l'occasion du Sixième Congrès International des Orientalistes réuni à Leyde, Septembre 1883. (*Publications de l'École des Langues Orientales Vivantes, iie série—volume ix.) pp. lv. 577, i.; 6 *plates.* *Paris*, 1883. 8°. **14003. i. 16.**

Nouveaux Mélanges Orientaux. Mémoires, textes et traductions publiés par les professeurs de l'École Spéciale des Langues Orientales Vivantes à l'occasion du septième Congrès International des Orientalistes réuni à Vienne, Septembre, 1886. (*Publications de l'École des Langues Orientales Vivantes, iie série—volume xix.) pp. xiv. 598, i.; 5 *plates.* *Paris*, 1886. 8°. **14003. i. 18.**

Recueil de Textes et de Traductions, publié par les professeurs de l'École des Langues Orientales Vivantes à l'occasion du viiie Congrès International des Orientalistes tenu à Stockholm en 1889. 2 vols. *Paris*, 1889. 8°. **14003. i. 23.**

ĀNANDA-RAṄGA PIḶḶAI. Les Français dans l'Inde. Dupleix et Labourdonnais. Extraits du journal d'Anandarangappoullé, courtier de la Compagnie Française des Indes, 1736-1748. Traduits du tamoul par Julien Vinson. (*Publications de l'École des Langues Orientales Vivantes, iiie série—volume xv.) pp. i. lxxix. 339. *Paris*, 1894. 8°. **14003. i. 32.**

ACHALĀMBIKAI AMMĀḶ, *daughter of Iraṭṭaṇai Perumāḷ Aiyar*, and **KUṞANDAI-VĒLU PIḶḶAI**, *Viṟupuram Kāṭṭa-perumāḷ.* மேலசேவூரென்று வழங்குந் திருவிடையூர்த்தலபுராணம். [Tiru-viḍaiyūr-tala-purāṇam. A metrical account of the legends of the Ṣaiva sanctuary at Melsevur. Pt. i. by Achalāmbikai Ammāḷ, pt. ii. by Kuṟandai-vēlu Piḷḷai.] pp. viii. ix. 128. கூடலூர் [*Kudalur*,] 1899. 8°. **14170. ee. 61.**

ĀCHĀN PIḶḶAI, *Nāyanār, son of Periyav-āchān Piḷḷai.* ∘ ∘ ∘ ముక్తిభోగావళి [Mukta-bhōgāvaḷī. A treatise upon the Vaishṇava doctrine of salvation. Edited by P. Anantāchārya Svāmi.] pp. 24. *Conjeeveram*, 1901. 12°. **14170. d. 46.(3.)**

ĀDI-CHUVAḌI. ஆதிச்சுவடி. [Ādi-chuvaḍi. A first Tamil reader, for the use of Catholic schools.] pp. 44. புதுவை ௲௮௱௪௰௪ [*Pondicherry*, 1844.] 12°. **14172. h. 10.**

—— [Another copy of the same edition, bound up with Beschius' Paramārtha-guruvin kathai and other extracts, in a wrapper dated 1862.] pp. 91. புதுவை ௲௮௱௬௰௨ [*Pondicherry*, 1862.] 12°. **14172. h. 58.(3.)**

ĀDI-MŪLA MUDALIYĀR, *Tirukaṟukunṟam.* *See* AUVAIYĀR.—*Supposititious Works.* ∘ ∘ ∘ திருக்குறள்மூலம். [Tiru-kuṟaḷ-mūlam. Edited by Ādi-mūla.] [1882.] 16°. **14172. a. 10.(3.)**

—— *See* TĀYUMĀNAVAR. தாயுமான சுவாமிகள்... திருப்பாடற்றிரட்டு. [Tiru-pāḍaṯ-ṯiraṭṭu. Edited by Ādi-mūla.] 1885. 8°. **14172. b. 32.**

ĀDI-NĀRĀYAṈ'-AIYĀ, *V. B.* ஜனமனோல்லாஸினி [Jana-manōllāsini.] . . . A funny farce in five and one acts. A merry and cheerful companion to a railway traveller. By V. B. Audinarayaniah. pp. 98. *Madras*, 1896. 8°. **14170. l. 32.(3.)**

ĀDIY-APPANĀR, *Kaḷandai.* ∘ ∘ ∘ திருக்களர்ப்புராணம். [Tirukaḷar-purāṇam. The sacred legends of the Ṣaiva sanctuary of Tirukalar. Edited with introduction by Pinnattūr A. Nārāyaṇa-sāmi Aiyar.] pp. 30, 74, 12. கும்பகோணம் [*Kumbakonam*,] 1902. 12°. **14170. ee. 55.**

ADIYĀRKKU-NALLĀR. *See* ILAṄ-GŌV-ADIGAḶ. ∘ ∘ ∘ சிலப்பதிகார மூ [Silapp'-adhikāram. With commentary by Adiyārkku-nallār.] 1892. 8°. **14172. d. 13.**

ADLEY (WILLIAM). *See* NEGRO. The Negro Servant, *etc.* [Translated by W. Adley.] 1844. 12°. **14170. b. 1.(34.)**

—— The Pearl of Great Price ... ஆணிமுத்து. [A Christian tract. Second edition.] pp. 8. *Jaffna*, 1843. 12°. **14170. b. 1.(7*.)**

ADVAITĀNANDA. *See* BĀDARĀYAṆA. The Brahma Sutra Artha Deepika, or The Brahma Sutras . . . with ... extracts from the glossaries of ... Brahmavidyabharana, *etc.* 1904, *etc.* 4°. **14170. fff. 5.**

AESOP. Aesop's Fables, containing instructive morals, translated into Tamil by A. Theroovengada Pillay [together with the English text] ... and revised by C. Rajah Soobboroya Moodeliar (*கட்டுக்கதைகள்). pp. ii. ii. iii. iii. 260. *Madras*, 1853. 8°. **14170. k. 32.**

ĀGAMAS. *See* SABHĀ-PATI YŌGI. ∘ ∘ ∘ சகலாகமத்திரட்டு. [Sakalāgama-tiraṭṭu. A compendium of Āgamik teaching.] 1894. 16°. **14170. d. 14.**

—— ஸ்ரீமத் ஸகலாகமஸார ஸங்க்ரஹம். [Sakalāgama-sāra-saṅgraham. A Sanskrit digest of the Āgamas in their bearing upon everyday ritual. Edited with Tamil introduction by K. Shaṇmukha-sundara Mudaliyār. Second edition.] pp. xlviii. 148. சென்னை சார்வரி [*Madras*, 1900.] 8°. **14033. aa. 11.**

—— ஸ்ரீமத் காமிகாகமம் மூ [Kāmikāgamam. In Sanskrit. With Tamil commentary and glossary to every verse of the first volume.] 2 vols. சென்னை விளம்பி—விகாரி [*Madras*, 1898-1899.] 4°. **14033. d. 23.**

In progress? Vol. i. *has two title-pages; the first states that the printing was begun Nov.* 1888 *and ended Dec.* 1898, *while the second is dated Dec.* 1889.

—— ஸ்ரீமத் பூர்வகாரணாகமம் மூலம். (*உத்தர காரணாகமம்.) [Kāraṇāgamam. In Sanskrit. Edited with Tamil introduction *etc.* by K. Shaṇmukha-sundara Mudaliyār.] 2 vols. சென்னை விகாரி—ப்லவ [*Madras*, 1900-1902.] 8°. **14033. aa. 8.**

—— ∘ ∘ ∘ பௌஷ்கராகமம் த்ராவிடடீகையுடன [Paushkarāgamam. An *upāgama* of the Pāramēṣvara, the 26th of the Ṣaiva *āgamas*. 8 chapters in Sanskrit, with Tamil word-for-word interpretation and commentary by K. Shaṇmukha-sundara Mudaliyār.] pp. xviii. 780. சென்னை விக்ருதி [*Madras*, 1890.] 12°. **14028. b. 65.**

AGAPPEY SIDDHAR. அகப்பைசித்தர்பாடல். [Pādal. Ṣaiva verses.] pp. 12. *See* SIDDHARGAḶ. ∘ ∘ ∘ பெரியஞானக்கோவை [Periya-ñāna-kōvai.] 1899. 12°. **14170. ee. 33.**

—— —— pt. i., pp. 68-80. 1906. 12°. **14170. dd. 12.**

AGASTYAR. [For the Pura-poruḷ-veṇ-bā-mālai, containing stanzas exemplifying the rules of poetical composition laid down in the Poruḷ-paṇṇ'-iru-paṭalam ascribed to Agastyar's disciples:] *See* AIYANĀR-IDANĀR.

—— [For the various poems or *ñānam* under the name of Agastyar contained in the Periya-ñāna-kōvai:] *See* SIDDHARGAḶ.

—— [For editions of the Dēvāram in the recension ascribed to Agastyar.] *See* TIRU-MUṞAI.

—— ∘ ∘ ∘ அகஸ்தியமாமுனிவர் திருவாய்மலர்ந்தருளிய பஞ்சகாவியங்களில் . . . வாதகாவியம் ஆயிரம். (*ஞானகாவியம் ஆயிரம், பூரணகாவியம் ஆயிரம், *etc.*) [Vāta-kāvyam, Ñāna-kāvyam, Pūraṇa-kāvyam, Lakshaṇa-kāvyam, and Māntriya-kāvyam. Five poems ascribed to Agastyar, each containing about 1000 stanzas, on theosophy, Yoga, Ṣaiva doctrine, pseudo-philosophy, pseudo-science, *etc.* Edited by K. V. Kanda-sāmi Mudaliyār.] 5 vols. சென்னை ௧௮௯௫ [*Madras*, 1895]-1903. 8°. **14170. e. 70-74.**

—— ∘ ∘ ∘ நாலுகாண்ட வயித்தியகாவியம் ௲௨௱. [Nālu-kāṇḍa-vaidya-kāvyam. A treatise on medicine in 4 books (1200 verses), ascribed to Agastyar. Edited by K. V. N. Aiyā-sāmi Mudaliyār and Kanda-sāmi Mudaliyār.] pp. 8, 192. சென்னை [*Madras*,] 1896. 8°. **14170. i. 48.**

—— ∘ ∘ ∘ வயித்தியரத்தினச்சுருக்கம் ௩௱௬௰. [Vaidya-ratna-ṣurukkam. An abridgment, in 360 verses, of the Vaidya-ratnam, a treatise on medicine, attributed to Agastyar. Edited by T. Āṟumuga Svāmi.] pp. iv. 60. பிரமாதி [*Madras*, 1879.] 8°. **14172. c. 20.**

—— ∘ ∘ ∘ வாதகாவியத் திறவுகோலாகிய வாதசௌமியம், ௲௨௱. [Vāta-saumyam. An introduction in 1200 stanzas to the Vāta-kāvyam, which forms one of the five poems ascribed to Agastyar. Edited by K. Āru-muga Ñāniyār.] pp. iv. 291. சென்னை [*Madras,*] 1893. 8°. **14170. e. 52.**

AGATTIYAR. *See* AGASTYAR.

AGHŌRA DĒVAR. ° ° ° வேதாரணிய புராணம். [Vēdāraṇya-purāṇam. The sacred legends of the Ṣaiva shrine at Vēdāraṇyam in Tanjore, in verse. Followed by the Dēvāram, a series of hymns by Ñāna-sambandhar, Appar, and Sundara-mūrtti. Edited with notes by K. Vēr Piḷḷai.] pp. vii. 457, 20, i. i. சென்னபட்டணம் [*Madras,*] 1898. 8°. **14170. e. 65.**

AGNES, *Saint.* இன்னேசகன்னியெனப் பெயர்வழங்கும் அகினேசகன்னி அம்மானை. [Agnēskanni-ammānai. A Catholic poem on St. Agnes.] pp. 46. யாழ்ப்பாணம் [*Jaffna,*] 1893. 8°. **14170. c. 24.(9.)**

AGYĀNAM. அக்கியானம் ஆ [Agyānam. A tract against paganism, by the Danish Missionaries.] pp. 64. தரங்கன்பாடி தனடை [*Tranquebar,* 1733.] 12°. **14170. b. 16.(1).**

AḤKĀM. இஃது அஹ்காமுஸ்ஸியாம். [Aḥkām al-ṣiyām. A treatise on Muhammadan fasts. Edited by Muḥammad Kamāl al-Dīn.] pp. 48, i. வேலூர் [*Vellore,*] 1905. 8°. **14173. b. 28.(6.)**

AḤMAD ibn 'ABD al-LAṬĪF, *al-Sharjī al-Yamanī.* *See* AḤMAD ibn AḤMAD, *al-Sharjī al-Zabīdī.*

AḤMAD ibn AḤMAD, *al-Sharjī al-Zabīdī.* هذا كتاب الفوائد والصلاة والعوائد ترجمة بلسان الاروى . . . ويليها طب الابدان وكتاب الراش المضمر بالرضوان وكتاب الفال نامة المضمون آيات القران [Al-Fawā'id fi al-ṣalāt wa'l-'awā'id. A work on prayers and pious charms, translated by 'Uthmān ibn Muḥammad. Together with several other works on like themes.] pp. xviii. 446, *lith.* المنبئى ١٢٩٧ [*Bombay,* 1880.] 8°. **14173. c. 3.**

AḤMAD ibn ḲĀDIR MUḤYI al-DĪN. ° ° ° திருநடை வழியலங்காரம். கிழக்கரை. [Tiru-nadai-vaṛiy-alaṅkāram. Muhammadan verses panegyrising Saiyid Ibrāhīm Auliyā.] pp. ii. 8. கொழும்பு [*Colombo,*] 1895. 8°. **14173. b. 28.(5.)**

AḤMAD ibn MUḤAMMAD ḤASAN, *al-Matabatanī.* هذه درة المفاخر فى هداية الحاير الخ [Durrat al-mafākhir. A compendium of Muhammadan religious instruction.] pp. 64, *lith.* كلمب ١٣١٠ [*Colombo,* 1893.] 8°. **14173. b. 36.**

AḤMAD ibn MUḤAMMAD ibn SHAIKH TĪKĀ. *See* SĀM SHIHĀB al-DĪN. مظهر الاحكام [Maẓhar al-aḥkām. Edited by Saiyid Aḥmad.] [1901.] 8°. **14173. b. 27.(3.)**

AHŌBILĀCHĀRYAR, *Vātsya Rāghava.* *See* VARADĀCHĀRYAR, *Vātsya Dēva-rāja.* ° ° ° ப்ரபன்னபாரிஜாதம் ஆ [Prapanna-pārijātam. Edited with Tamil interpretations and commentary by Ahōbil-āchāryar.] [1895.] 8°. **14028. d. 55.**

'AIDARŪS. *See* SHĀH al-ḤAMĪD ibn 'AIDARŪS.

AIYA-KANNU NĀYAKAR, *T.* Vannikula Vilakkam. A treatise [in English] on the Vanniya Caste [with copious extracts from Sanskrit and Tamil authorities]. pp. i. 5, 43, 10. *Madras,* 1891. 8°. **14170. g. 19.**

AIYANĀR-IDANĀR. புறப்பொருள் வெண்பாமாலை [Puṟa-poruḷ-veṇ-bā-mālai. A series of verses exemplifying the poetical treatment of external emotion, based on the Poruḷ-pann'-iru-paṭalam ascribed to Agastyar's disciples.] *See* TĀṆḌAVA-RĀYA MUDALIYĀR. இலக்கணப்பஞ்சக ஆ [Nan-nūl, *etc.*] pp. 60-119. [1835.] 8°. **14172. e. 3.**

—— ° ° ° புறப்பொருள்வெண்பாமாலை மூலமும் உரையும். [Puṟa-poruḷ-veṇ-bā-mālai. Edited with preface, glossary, and indices by U. V. Sāminātha'-aiyar.] pp. vi. ix. ii. i. 155, xix. ii. சென்னை [*Madras,* 1895.] 8°. **14172. f. 21.**

—— Extracts from the Tamil "Purra-poruḷ Veṇbā-Mālai," and the "Purra-nānnūrru" [in English]. By . . . G. U. Pope. (Journal of the Royal Asiatic Society of Great Britain and Ireland for 1899, pp. 225-269.) *London,* 1899. 8°. **Ac. 8820/3 & 2110. e, f.**

—— University of Madras. B.A. Degree Examination 1905. Purapporul Venbamalai. The first four padalams [on themes of 4 kinds of warriors' crowns] with ancient commentary and explanatory notes by V. Saminatha Aiyar. pp. 4, 68. *Madras,* 1905. 8°. **14172. bb. 21.(1)**

AIYĀ-SĀMI MUDALIYĀR, *Beṅgaḷūr Ā.* *See* VĒṄKAṬĀRYA YAJVA. உலககுணக்கண்ணடி ஆ [Teyva-guṇa-veḷicham. A prose rendering, by Aiyāsāmi, of Vēṅkaṭārya's Viṣva-guṇādarṣa.] 1906. 8°. **14171. e. 13.**

AIYĀ-SĀMI MUDALIYĀR, *Kumbhamaṅgalam V. N.* See AGASTYAR. ∘ ∘ ∘ நாலுகாண்ட வயித்தியகாவியம் குஉரா. [Nālu-kāṇḍa-vaidya-kāvyam. Edited by Aiyā-sāmi.] 1896. 8°. **14170. i. 48.**

AIYĀ-SĀMI PIḶḶAI. See MAYAN. ∘ ∘ ∘ சிற்பநூலென்னும் மனையடிசாஸ்திரம் [Manaiy-aḍi-śāstram. Collected and enlarged by Rāma-krushṇa and Aiyā-sāmi.] [1885.] 8°. **14172. c. 30**

AIYĀVU PIḶḶAI, *Ṣ., of St. Michael's College, Coimbatore.* See CHIDAMBARA KAVI-RĀYAR. உசிதசூடாமணி நிகண்டு. (†" Oositha Soodamani Nigandu," *etc.*) [Edited by Aiyāvu Piḷḷai.] 1903. 12°. **14172. ee. 10.**

AKHILĒṢA PIḶḶAI, *Trikōṇamalai V.* See KARAIṢAI. திருக்கரைசைப்புராணம் மூல [Tiru-karaiṣai-purāṇam. Edited by Akhilēṣa.] [1890.] 8°. **14170. e. 38.**

AḶAKĒṢA-KATHAI. See NĀLU-MANTRI-KATHAI.

ĀLĀLA-SUNDARAM PIḶḶAI, *Kāñchi E.* See KĀMĀKSHI. காமாக்ஷி லீலா பிரபாவம். [Kāmākshi-līlā-prabhāvam. Translated by Ālāla-sundaram.] 1906. 8°. **14170. eee. 20.(2.)**

—— காஞ்சி க்ஷேத்திர மஞ்சரி. [Kāñchi-kshētra-mañjari. An account of the cults (chiefly Ṣaiva) of Conjevaram.] pp. xii. 38, 2. சென்னை [*Madras,*] 1906. 8°. **14170. eee. 20.(1.)**

ĀḶAVANDĀR, *Vaishṇava writer.* See YĀMUNĀCHĀRYAR.

ĀḶAVANDĀR, *Virai.* ∘∘∘ஞானவாசிட்டவமலராமாயணம் தமிழ்மூலமுமுரையும். [Ñāna-vāṣiṭṭav-amala-rāmāyaṇam. A poem on the Vedantic philosophy, freely adapted and abridged from the Sanskrit Yōga-vāsishṭha-rāmāyaṇam. With commentary by Aruṇāchala Svāmi and others.] pp. iv. iv. 527. சாதாரண [*Madras,* 1851.] 4°. **14170. fff. 2.**

—— ∘ ∘ ∘ ஞானவாசிட்டவமலராமாயணம் மூல [Ñāna-vāṣiṭṭav-amala-rāmāyaṇam. With the commentary of Aruṇāchala Svāmi. Edited by Pēṟai Jega-nātha Piḷḷai.] 2 vols. சென்னை [*Madras,*] 1890. 8°. **14172. b. 41.**

—— ∘ ∘ ∘ ஞானவாசிட்ட வமலராமாயணவசனம். [Ñāna-vāsiṭṭav-amala-rāmāyaṇam. A prose summary. Edited by P. Teyva-ṣikhāmaṇi Mudaliyār.] pp. ii. 411. சென்னை [*Madras,*] 1902. 8°. **14170. ee. 53.**

'ALĪ ibn 'ABD ALLĀH (ABŪ al-ḤASAN), *al-Shāẕilī.* [*Life.*] See NŪḤ ibn 'ABD al-ḲĀDIR, *al-Ḳāhirī.* [Nafaḥāt al-'anbar.] **14173. c. 10.**

—— الوظيفة المباركة [Al-Waẓīfat al-Shāẕilīyah. A prayer-book, in Arabic, with a paraphrase in Tamil.] See NŪḤ ibn 'ABD al-ḲĀDIR, *al-Ḳāhirī.* نفحات العنبر الخ [Nafaḥāt al-'anbar.] pp. 222-244. [1902.] 8°. **14173. c. 10.**

ALMANACKS. See EPHEMERIDES.

AMADUZZI (GIOVANNI CRISTOFANO). Alphabetum Grandonico-malabaricum sive Samscrudonicum. [Compiled from materials supplied by Clemens Peanius.] pp. xxviii. 100 ; 9 *plates.* *Romae,* 1772. 12°. **621. b. 5.(2.)**

AMARA-SIṀHA. अमरकोशम्॥ Amarakosa. With Tamil and English explanation of words . . . By K. R. Anantarama Sastri. *Srirangam,* 1905, *etc.* 12°. **14092. a. 30.**
In progress.

AMBALA-VĀṆA KAVI-RĀYAR. ∘ ∘ ∘ சதுரகிரி அறப்பளீசுரசதகம். [Aṟapaḷīṣura-ṣatakam. 100 stanzas in praise of Ṣiva as worshipped in the temple of Arapalisuram on the Chaturagiri.] pp. 62. *Madras,* 1897. 16°. **14170. d. 48.(1.)**

—— ∘ ∘ ∘ சதுரகிரி அறப்பளீசுரசதக மூல [Aṟa-paḷīṣura-ṣatakam. With paraphrase and notes by K. Rāma-sāmi Nāyuḍu.] pp. 4, 152. சென்னை [*Madras,*] 1905. 12°. **14172. a. 56.**

—— ∘ ∘ ∘ அறப்பளீசுரசதகம். [Aṟapaḷīṣura-ṣatakam.] pp. 61. 1906. See RĀMA-SĀMI NĀYUḌU, *K.* சதகத்திரட்டு. [Ṣataka-tiraṭṭu.] pt. i. 1905-1906. 12°. **14170. dd. 10.**

AMBALA-VĀṆA NĀVALAR, *Vaṭṭukoṭṭai Ā.* See APPAYA DĪKSHITAR. பிரமதருக்கஸ்தவம். [Brahma-tarka-stavam. Translated by Ambala-vāṇa.] 1895. 8°. **14170. e. 69.**

—— See ĀRĀVA-MUD'-ĀCHĀRYAR. திருச்சுழியற்புராணம். [Tiruchuṟiyaṟ-purāṇam. Edited by Ambala-vāṇa.] [1901.] 8°. **14170. ee. 56.**

—— See GAṆA-PATI NĀYUḌU, *K.M.S.* ∘ ∘ ∘ சண்முகஷடாக்ஷரப்பதிகம். [Shaṇmukha-shaḍāksha-ra-padigam. Edited by Ambala-vāṇa.] 1898. 12°. **14170. d. 45.(3.)**

—— See GAṄGAI-MUTTU PIḶḶAI. நடநாதிவாத்தியரஞ்சனம். [Naṭa-nādi-vādya-rañjanam. Edited by Ambala-vāṇa.] 1898. 8°. **14170. i. 58.**

AMBALA-VĀṆA PILLAI, Ṣ. *See* PERIODICAL PUBLICATIONS.—*Perak.* தேஜோபிமானி. Thajobimani. [Edited by Ambala-vāṇa.] [1896]-1897. Fol. **14172. l. 1.(2.)**

AMBIKĀ-PATI, *son of Kamban.* ∘∘∘ அம்பிகாபதிகோவை [Ambikā-pati-kōvai. A series of mystical Ṣaiva poems of erotic form. With preface by Ṣiva-ñāna Svāmi.] pp. iv. 100. திருநெல்வேலி [*Tinnevelli,*] 1899. 8°. **14172. bb. 5.**

AMIRTA KAVI-RĀYAR. ∘∘∘ நாணிக்கண்புதைத்தல் என்னும் ஒருதுறைக்கோவை. [Orudurai-kōvai, or Nāṇi-kaṇ-pudaittal. 400 stanzas on panegyrical and sentimental themes. Edited, with biography, by K. Rāma-sāmi Nāyuḍu and K. Knppu-sāmi Mudaliyār.] pp. viii. 57. சென்னை [*Madras,*] 1905. 12°. **14172. a. 55.**

Forms no. 3 *of the* Tamiṟ-kavi-mālai.

AMIRTA-SĀGARAN. ∘∘∘ காரிகை மூலமும் . . . விருத்தியுரையும். [Kārikai, or Yāpp'-aruṅ-gala-kārikai. A metrical compendium of the art of prosody. With the commentary of Guṇa-sāgaran. Edited by K. Vēda-giri Mudaliyār.] pp. 103. சென்னபட்டினத்து விரோதிகிருது [*Madras,* 1851.] 8°. **14172. e. 36.**

AMIRTA-VĀCHAKA DĀSAR, *A.* *See* 'ABD ALLĀH ibn 'ABD al-KARĪM. ஆன்ரோர் அனுபோக கைவல்லிய வைத்திய சங்கிரகம். [Vaidya-saṅgraham. Arranged for singing by Amirta-vāchaka Dāsar.] [1900.] 8°. **14170. i. 72.**

AMMAṆI AMMĀḶ. ∘∘∘ அற்புதகோலமஞ்சரி. [Aṟpuda-gōla-mañjari. Decorative patterns and pictorial designs for use in girls' schools.] pp. 48, *lith.* சென்னை [*Madras,*] 1897. 8°. **14170. i. 51.**

AMMŪVANĀR. நெய்தல். [Neydal. Erotic verses.] *See* KŪḌALŪR-KIṞĀR. ∘∘∘ ஐங்குறுநூறு ஞூ [Aiṅ-guṟu-nūṟu.] pp. 33-61. 1903. 8°. **14172. c. 48.**

AMURTA-LIṄGA TAMBIRĀN. திருமயிலைத்தலபுராணம். [Tiru-mayilai-tala-purāṇam. A poem on the legends of the Ṣaiva sanctuary at Mailapur. With commentary by Kāñchīpuram Sabhā-pati Mudaliyār. Edited by Purasai Ashṭāvadhānam Sabhā-pati Mudaliyār.] pp. ii. 168, 64; 20 *plates.* சென்னை நந்தன [*Madras,* 1893.] 8°. **14170. e. 60.**

ĀNAIY-AIYAR. *See* KAVI-KUÑJARA BHĀRATI.

ĀNANDA-GIRI. *See* BĀDARĀYAṆA. The Brahma Sutra Artha Deepika, or The Brahma Sutras . . . with . . . extracts from the glossaries of Anandagiri, *etc.* 1904, *etc.* 4°. **14170. fff. 5.**

ĀNANDA-RAṄGA PIḶḶAI. Les Français dans l'Inde. Le Journal d'Ânandarangappoullé, 1736-1761. (*Par Julien Vinson.) *See* ACADEMIES, *etc.*—Paris.—*École Spéciale des Langues Orientales Vivantes.* Recueil de Textes et de Traductions, *etc.* tom. i., pp. 335-382. 1889. 8°. **14003. i. 23.**

—— Les Français dans l'Inde. Dupleix et Labourdonnais. Extraits du journal d'Anandarangappoullé, courtier de la Compagnie Française des Indes, 1736-1748. Traduits du Tamoul par Julien Vinson. 1894. 8°. *See* ACADEMIES, *etc.*—Paris.—*École Spéciale des Langues Orientales Vivantes.* ĀNANDA-RAṄGA PIḶḶAI. **14003. i. 32.**

—— The Private Diary of Ananda Ranga Pillai, Dubash to Joseph François Dupleix . . . A record of matters political, historical, social, and personal, from 1736 to 1761. Translated from the Tamil by order of the Government of Madras, and edited by Sir J. Frederick Price . . . assisted by K. Rangachari. *Madras,* 1904, *etc.* 8°. **14171. e. 4.**

In progress.

ĀNANDA-TĪRTHA (MADHVĀCHĀRYAR). *See* SANDHYĀ-VANDANAM. யஜுர்வேத ஸந்த்யாவந்தநம் ஞூ [Sandhyā-vandanam, *etc.* With extracts, in a Tamil translation, from the commentaries of Ānanda-tīrtha.] 1901. 8°. **14033. aa. 27.**

—— *See* UPANISHADS. ∘∘∘ நூற்றெட்டு உபநிஷத்துகள். [Nūṭṭ'-eṭṭu Upanishattugaḷ. With extracts from the commentaries of Ānanda-tīrtha, translated into Tamil.] 1887. 8°. **14010. dd. 2.**

ANANTA BHĀRATI. ஸ்ரீமத் வேதாந்ததேசிக வைபவப்பிரகாசிகைக் கீர்த்தனை. [Vēdānta-dēṣika-vaibhava-prakāṣikai-kīrttanai. Songs in honour of the Vedantist teacher Vēṅkaṭa-nātha, called Vēdānta-dēṣika. Edited by Pēṟai Jega-nātha Piḷḷai.] pp. 81. செங்கற்பட்டு விக்ருதி [*Chengalpat,* 1890.] 8°. **14172. c. 37.**

ANANTĀCHĀRYA SVĀMI, *Prativādi-bhayaṃkara, of Conjevaram.* *See* ĀCHĀN PIḶḶAI. ∘∘∘ ముక్తాభోగావళి. [Mukta-bhōgāvaḷī. Edited by Anantāchārya.] 1901. 12°. **14170. d. 46.(3.)**

ANANTĀCHĀRYA SVĀMI, *Prativādi-bhayaṃkara, of Conjevaram (continued).* See NAÑ-JĪYAR. ० ० ० ఆత్మవివాహం మొ॥ [Ātma-vivāham, *etc.* Edited by Anantāchāryar.] 1893. 8°. **14170. ee. 40.**

ANANTA-RĀMA ṢĀSTRI, *K.R., of National High School, Trichinopoli.* See AMARA-SIṂHA. अमरकोशः ॥ Amarakosa. With Tamil and English explanation . . . By K. R. Anantarama Sastri. 1905, *etc.* 12°. **14092. a. 30.**

ANANTA VAIDYA-NĀTHA ṢIVAN. See PERIODICAL PUBLICATIONS.—*Tiruvadi.* சிவபக்திசந்திரிகை. [Ṣiva-bhakti-chandrikai. Edited with translations by Ananta Vaidya-nātha Ṣivan.] 1890-1893. 8°. **14033. bb. 35.**

ANAVARATA-VINĀYAKAM PIḶḶAI, *Ṣ.* See PURĀṆAS.—*Matsya-purāṇam.* ० ० ० மச்சபுராணம். [Matsya-purāṇam. With introduction by Anavarata-vināyakam.] 1900. 8°. **14170. ee. 43.**

—— See VIṢĀKHA PERU-MĀḶ AIYAR. அணியிலக்கணம். [Aṇiy-ilakkaṇam. Edited by Anavarata-vināyakam.] 1906. 12°. **14172. g. 3.(3.)**

—— See VIṢĀKHA PERU-MĀḶ AIYAR. யாப்பிலக்கணம். [Yāpp'-ilakkaṇam. Edited by Anavarata-vināyakam.] 1906. 12°. **14172. g. 3.(2.)**

ĀṆḌĀL (ṢŪḌI KOḌUTTA NĀCHIYĀR). [For editions of the Tiru-pāvai and Tiru-moḻi of this poetess included in the editions of the whole or parts of the Nāl-āyira-prabandham:] See ĀḺVĀRGAḶ.—*Nāl-āyiram.*

AṆḌA-PIṆḌA-VYĀKHYĀNAM. அண்டபிண்டவியாக்கியானம். [Aṇḍa-piṇḍa-vyākhyānam. A work on physical science, translated into Tamil by "Periya Sañjīvi-nātha Svāmi," an Italian Catholic missionary to Ceylon in the 18th century. Followed by Ulaga-pramāṇa-ṣāstram, a tract by the same on the dimensions of the world, *etc.* Edited by R. Ñāna-prakāṣa-nātha Svāmi.] pp. viii. i. 186, 27, ii.; 2 *plates.* சென்னபட்டணம் [*Madras,*] 1874. 12°. **14170. i. 11.**

ANDHAKA-KAVI. See VĪRA-RĀGHAVA MUDALIYĀR.

ANDRĒS PILLAI. அன்னை அருங்கல் ஒப்பாரி. [Annai-aruṅgal oppāri. Elegies on the Virgin Mary as *Mater Dolorosa.* A Catholic tract.] pp. 32. யாழ்ப்பாணம் [*Jaffna,*] 1893. 16°. **14170. a. 57.(3.)**

AṄGA-MUTTU MUDALIYĀR, *Kaḷattūr.* See ṢUKA. Sugarnadi Sothidam, *etc.* [Edited by Aṅga-muttu.] 1895. 8°. **14170. i. 36.**

—— சிரோரத்னவயித்தியபூஷணம். [Ṣirō-ratna-vaidya-bhūshaṇam. A handbook of medicine.] pp. xii. viii. 192. *Madras,* 1896. 8°. **14170. i. 44.**

AṄGA PIḶḶAI, *Bhavāni N.* முருகப்ப நவரச சிலேடை. [Mṛug'-appa-nava-rasa-ṣilēḍai. A poem, addressed to V. Ṣ. Mṛug'-appa Chetti, and illustrating the 9 poetical emotions, followed by Charama-kavigaḷ, epitaphs by Aṅga Piḷḷai and others upon Kanniy-ammāḷ, wife of the former.] pp. 12, 8. கோயமுத்தூர் [*Coimbatore,*] 1894. 8°. **14172. b. 44.(4.)**

ANGLO-TAMIL READER. A Vade Mecum of all Anglo-Tamil Readers. [With preface by D. E. Kēṣava-rāu.] pp. i. 94. *Madras,* 1896. 8°. **14172. hh. 12.**

AṆṆĀ-MALAI MUDALIYĀR, *Āraṇi.* மதுரை வெண்பாமாலை. (Madooray Venba Malei [a series of panegyrical verses,] with certain grammatical rules bearing on poetry, on P. M. Madooray Pillay, Esq., composed by Arni Annamalay Moodaliar.) pp. 41. *Rangoon,* 1891. 8°. **14172. c. 21.**

AṆṆĀ-SĀMI AIYAR, *Chidambaram.* See CHIDAMBARAM. சிதம்பர மஹாத்மியம் [Chidambara-māhātmyam. Translated by Aṇṇā-sāmi.] [1897.] 8°. **14170. ee. 11.**

AṆṆĀ-SĀMI PIḶḶAI, *A.* See GŌVINDA-RĀJU MUDALIYĀR, *V.*, and AṆṆĀ-SĀMI PIḶḶAI, *A.* மனோரம்மிய சிங்காரபதம். [Manō-ramya-ṣiṅgāra-padam.] 1893. 16°. **14172. a. 44.**

AṆṆĀVIYĀR, *Ativīra-rāman-paṭṭiṇam.* ஸ்ரீ மகாபாரத அம்மானை [Mahā-bhārata-ammānai. A poetical paraphrase of the Mahā-bhāratam. Edited by Karundiṭṭāṅguḍi Ashṭāvadhānam K. Rāma-sāmi Piḷḷai. Vol. ii., the Yuddha-kāṇḍam.] pp. viii. 368. தஞ்சை [*Tanjore,*] 1903. 8°. **14172. c. 49.**

ANTHONY PILLAY. See ANTŌNI PIḶḶAI.

ANTŌNI-KUṬṬI AṆṆĀVIYĀR. ० ० ० கிறிஸ்து சமய கீர்த்தனம். [Kiṟīstu-samaya-kīrttanam. Catholic devotional poems. Edited by T. A. Innāṣi-tambi.] pp. i. 102. *Jaffna,* 1891. 8°. **14170. c. 38.**

ANTŌNI - NĀTHAR. பதிதமத்தேசு தூஷண மறுத்தலாகிய தர்க்கக்கும்மி. [Tarka-kummi. A controversial song for native women, in which Roman Catholic doctrines are stated and defended.] pp. iii. 60. புதுவை தூஅச்சாகூடு [*Pondicherry,* 1865.] 16°. **14170. a. 34.(3.)**

ANTŌNI PILLAI (Thomas). The English, Tamil, Telugu and Hindustani Sonmalai, or An easy way of learning to speak four languages. Compiled by T. Anthony Pillay, and revised by C. Venkataswamy Naidoo, and Tanjore Samathanum Daniel Pillay, Poet. (*சொன் மாலை.) pp. i. 45. *Madras,* 1880. 8°. **14172. e. 10.**

ANTŌNIS (*V. S., Don* John). ∘∘∘ அர்ச. அன்னம்மாள் திருப்பதியில் . . . பிரசங்க வியாக்கியானக் கும்மி. [A *kummi* poem by Don John Antōnis founded on a sermon preached by the Rev. C. Bonjean at the church of St. Anne of Talaivillu.] pp. 10. யாழ்ப்பாணம் [*Jaffna,*] 1885. 12°. **14170. b. 34.(2.)**

ANTONY (S.), *O.M.I.* *See* Muller (A.). சுகுணகமருந்தின் கைத்துணை. Homœopathic Guide. Translated . . . by Rev. S. Antony. 1892. 12°. **14170. i. 70.(2.)**

—— *See* Muller (A.). மின்சாரச்சுகுணகமருந்தின் கைத்துணை. (*A Guide to . . . Mattei's Electro-Homœopathic Medicines. Translated . . . by . . . S. Antony.) 1892. 12°. **14170. i. 70.(3.)**

ANTONY, *Saint.* அர்ச். அந்தோனியார் பேரில் புலம்பல். [Pulambal. Elegies addressed to St. Antony.] pp. 11. யாழ்ப்பாணம் [*Jaffna,*] 1893. 12°. **14170. a. 35.(9.)**

—— சந்தந்தோனியார் அம்மானை. [Sant'-antōniyār-ammānai. The legends of Saint Anthony, in easy verse.] pp. 56. யாழ்ப்பாணம் [*Jaffna,*] 1892. 8°. **14170. c. 24.(5.)**

APPĀJĪ. இராயர் அப்பாசிகதை. [Rāyar-appāji-kathai. Tales of the minister Appājī and his king.] *See* Kathā-chintāmaṇi. The Katháchintámani, *etc.* pp. 34-60. 1875. 8°. **14170. k. 27.**

—— இராயர் அப்பாஜி கதை. [Rāyar-appāji-kathai.] *See* Pūrṇa-liṅgam Pillai, *M.S.* Witty Stories, *etc.* pp. 33-56. 1897. 12°. **14171. a. 6.(2.)**

APPĀJĪ (*continued*). Kings and Ministers. [Tales of Appājī, in English.] *See* Robinson (E. J.). Tales and Poems of South India, *etc.* pp. 320-336. 1885. 8°. **14170. k. 63.**

—— The Tales of Royar Appaji the Prime Minister. [Translated] by K. R. Sesha Iyer. pp. i. 19. *Madras,* 1903. 12°. **14171. d. 1.(1.)**

APPAṆA NĀYAKKAR, *Karaḍi-vāvi Kammavār Kulōttuṅga.* Vanasuranatakum. வாணாசுரநாடகம். [A drama on the story of the demon Vāṇan overthrown by Vishṇu. Edited by G. Aruṇāchala Mudaliyār.] pp. vii. 456; 8 *plates.* சென்னை [*Madras,*] 1890. 8°. **14170. l. 29.**

APPAN SVĀMI, *Doḍḍāchāryapuram.* *See* Purāṇas. திருமலைமஹாத்மியம். [Tirumalai-māhātmyam. Compiled by Appan.] [1878.] 8°. **14170. e. 2**

APPA-PILLAI (James T.). தமிழ் இலக்கண தீபிகை . . . Tamil Grammar. Part first. Orthography: for use in Standard vi. pp. vii. 76. *Batticaloa,* 1891. 12°. **14172. e. 16.**

APPAR. *See* Tiru-nāvukk'-araṣu.

APPĀ-SĀMI MUDALIYĀR, *Puduvai.* *See* Yādava-giri. ∘∘∘ சதுர்வேதி சரித்திர சங்கீர்த்தனை. [Chatur-vēdi-charitra-saṅkīrttanai. Edited by Appā-sāmi.] 1900. 8°. **14170. ee. 35.(4.)**

APPĀ-SĀMI PILLAI, *C.* Anglo-Tamil Manual, or Phrase Book, based on the plan of Forbes' Hindustani Manual. . . . Compiled, arranged and translated by C. Appasawmy Pillay. Second edition. pp. vi. 218. *Madras,* 1884. 8°. **14172. hh. 10.**

—— Third edition. pp. viii. 244. *Madras,* 1894. 8°. **14172. hh. 8.**

—— A Translation Guide. Or Exercises in general English with translations for the use of the Middle School Department (*the Matriculation & Upper Secondary Classes, the candidates for Translation Test, *etc.*) . . . English and Tamil . . . By C. Appasawmy Pillai. 3 vols. *Madras,* 1890-1895. 8°. **14172. h. 61.**

Vol. i. (1895) *is of the third edition, vol.* ii. (1893) *is of the second; vol.* iii. *is an "improved and enlarged edition," and appeared in* 1890.

APPĀ-SVĀMI PIḶḶAI. நவநீதசாரம். [Nava-nīta-sāram. A catechism of Vedantic philosophy.] pp. iv. 80. சித்தாத்திரி [*Madras*, 1859.] 8°. **14170. e. 16.**

—— நவநீதசாரம். [Nava-nīta-sāram. Edited by K. Vaḍi-vēlu Cheṭṭi.] pp. 2, i. i. 149. சென்னை [*Madras*,] 1903. 12°. **14170. d. 87.**

APPĀ-TURAI PIḶḶAI, *M.* மருதடி அந்தாதி. [Marud'-aḍi-antādi. A hundred quatrains in honour of Ṣiva.] pp. 16. யாழ்ப்பாணம் விசிர்தி [*Jaffna*, 1891.] 12°. **14172. a. 45.(1.)**

APPĀVU CHEṬṬI, *Pallavapuram*. *See* Sōmā-sundara Nāyakar. சித்தாந்தரத்நாகரம். [Siddhānta-ratnākaram. Edited by Appāvu.] 1906, *etc.* 8°. **14170. eee. 14.**

APPĀVU MUDALIYĀR, *Muḍichūr*. *See* Āṟvārgaḷ.—Nāl-āyiram.—*Tiru-vāy-moṟi*. ० ० ० திருவாய்மொழி ௸ [Tiru-vāy-moṟi. With commentary. Edited by Appāvu.] [1859.] 8°. **14172. c. 18.**

APPĀVU PIḶḶAI, *Pāmban*. *See* Kumara-guru-dāsa Svāmi.

APPĀVU PIḶḶAI, *Bookseller, of Trichinopoli*. *See* Pugaṟēndi. ० ० ० அபிமன்னன் சுந்தரிமாலை [Abimannan-sundari-mālai. Edited by Appāvu.] 1884. 8°. **14172. b. 29.**

APPĀVU PIḶḶAI, *Tiruṣirapuram Tirumalai* (Muttu-sāmi Piḷḷai). ० ० ० சித்திராங்கிவிலாசம் [Chitrāṅgi-vilāsam. A comedy on the story of the marriage of the prince Chitrāṅgan. Edited by Tāyumāna Mudaliyār.] pp. iii. 168. சென்னை [*Madras*,] 1886. 8°. **14170. l. 19.**

—— நன்னெறி சத்தியபாஷா அரிச்சந்திரவிலாசம். [Nan-neṟi-satya-bhāsha-hariṣchandra-vilāsam. A drama, founded on the legend of Hariṣchandra. Edited by P. Kalyāṇa-sundara Mudaliyār. Second edition.] pp. iii. xiii. ii. vi. xxvi. 572; 20 *plates*. சென்னை [*Madras*,] 1890. 8°. **14170. l. 23.**

—— நூதன பவழேந்திரிசபா. [Nūtana-pava-ṟēndiri-sabhā. A drama. Revised by P. Māṣilāmaṇi Mudaliyār.] pp. 84; 4 *plates*. சென்னை [*Madras*,] 1893. 8°. **14170. l. 39.**

APPAYA DĪKSHITAR, *son of Raṅga-rāja*. பிரமதருக்கஸ்தவம். [Brahma-tarka-stavam. A Ṣaiva theological poem with prose commentary. Translated from the Sanskrit by V. Ā. Ambala-vāṇa Nāvalar.] pp. ii. iv. 108. *Tinnevelly*, 1895. 8°. **14170. e. 69.**

—— குவலயாநந்தம். [Kuvalayānandam. A treatise on the art of rhetoric. Translated from the Sanskrit, in verse and prose, by Ṣaṅkara-nārāyaṇa Ṣāstri of Ettayapuram and Mugavūr Mīnākshi-sundara Kavi-rāyar, and published under the superintendence of Tirumalai Īchambāḍi Ṣrīnivāsāchāryar and Ānūr Ṣiṅgāra-vēlu Mudaliyār.] pp. 5, viii. 291, v. சென்னை [*Madras*,] 1895. 8°. **14170. i. 40.**

APPAYA DĪKSHITAR, *Pattamaḍai*. பாலபோதினி [Bāla-bōdhinī. A Tamil treatise in 6 books, in catechetical form, with Sanskrit quotations, forming a digest of Advaita-Vēdāntam teachings.] pp. 128, i. பாளையங்கோட்டை [*Tinnevelli*,] 1897. 8°. **14048. cc. 14.**

AP-PIḶḶAI, *disciple of Aṟagiya-maṇavāḷa Perumāḷ*. வாழித்திருநாமம். [Vāṟi-tiru-nāmam. A Teṅgalai Vaishṇava devotional poem, including praises of the heads of the Church.] pp. 11. *See* Aṟagiya-maṇavāḷa Peru-māḷ. ஸ்ரீ . . . உபதேசரத்தினமாலை ௸ [Upadēṣa-ratna-mālai, *etc.*] [1836.] 8°. **14172. b. 3.**

—— வாழித்திருநாமம். [Vāṟi-tiru-nāmam.] *See* Āṟvārgaḷ.—Nāl-āyiram.—*Selections*. ० ० ० நித்யாநுஸந்தானம் ௸ [Nityānuṣandhānam.] pp. 122-133. 1886. 8°. **14170. ee. 14.**

—— తిరునక్షత్ర, శ్లో॥ [Vāṟi-tiru-nāmam, with Tiru-nakshatra-ṣlōkaṅgaḷ.] *See* Āṟvārgaḷ.—Nāl-āyiram.—*Selections*. ० ० ० నిత్యానుసంధానము శ్లో॥ [Nityānusandhānam.] pp. 681-717. 1906. 8°. **14170. eee. 21.**

APPU MUDALIYĀR, *Ṣ.G.* (Gōvinda-svāmi Mudaliyār), *of Chintadripet*. *See* Hari. ஸ்ரீஹரிநாமஸ்தோத்திரப்பா ௸ [Hari-nāma-stōtram, *etc.* Edited by Appu.] 1887. 8°. [*Tukārām-svāmigaḷ-charitram*.] **14170. ee. 34.**

ARABIAN NIGHTS. *See* 'Abd al-Kādir ibn Muhammad Muhyi al-Dīn. فتح الصمد [Fatḥ al-ṣamad. The story of Tawaddud. Adapted from the Arabian Nights.] [1902.] 8°. **14170. k. 4.**

—— Arabian History. Thousand Nights . . . அராபிக் கதை. [Arābi-kathai. A translation of the Arabian Nights' Entertainments, based upon the edition published by Ṣokka-linga Mudaliyār, and revised by Āṛu-muga Dēṣikar.] 3 vols. [*Madras*,] 1888. 8°. **14171. a. 41.**

—— படிக்கத் தகுந்த பக்காக் கதை. [Pakkā-kathai. The stories of the hunchback, the broker, the Bagdad merchant, the Jewish doctor, the tailor, and the barber and his brothers, forming Nights xxiv.-xxxii.] pp. 144. சென்னை [*Madras*,] 1906. 8°. **14171. e. 12.**

AṚAGAR-ĀCHĀRYAR, *Ṣ., of Nahalnagar, Dindigal.* விகாரிவருஷத்திற்குரிய விநோதக்கும்மி. [Vinōda-kummi. A *kummi* poem disproving current prognostications of evil for the year Vikāri, A.D. 1899-1900.] pp. 12. திண்டுக்கல் [*Dindigal*,] 1900. 8°. **14172. b. 44.(7.)**

AṚAGIYA-MAṆAVĀḶA-DĀSAR. *See* PIḶḶAI PERU-MĀḶ AIYANGĀR.

AṚAGIYA-MAṆAVĀḶA MĀ-MUNI. *See* AṚAGIYA-MAṆAVĀḶA PERU-MĀḶ.

AṚAGIYA-MAṆAVĀḶA PERU-MĀḶ, called MAṆAVĀḶA MĀ-MUNI, PERIYA-JĪYAR, and RANGA-NĀTHAN. *See* ĀṚVĀRGAḶ.—Nāl-āyiram.—*Iyaṟ-pā.* ∘∘∘ இராமாநுச நூற்றந்தாதி. [Rāmānuja-nūṯṯ'-antādi. With commentary by Periya-jīyar.] [1905.] 8°. **14170. ee. 6.(6.)**

—— *See* ĀṚVĀRGAḶ.—Nāl-āyiram.—*Mudal-āyiram.* ∘∘∘ முதலாயிரம் ௸ [Mudal-āyiram. With commentaries by Periya-jīyar, *etc.*] 1880-1885. 8°. **14170. f. 9.**

—— —— ∘∘∘ ముదలాయిరము ॥ [Mudal-āyiram. Another edition of the preceding, in Telugu characters.] 1881-[1886.] 8°. **14170. f. 8.**

—— *See* GŌPĀLA-KRUSHṆA PIḶḶAI, *T.* ஆசாரிய ஹ்ருதயசாரசங்க்ரஹம். [Āchārya-hṛudaya-sāra-saṅgraham. A digest of Aṛagiya-maṇavāḷar's commentary Āchārya-hṛudayam on the Tiru-vāy-moṛi.] 1892. 8°. **14170. e. 61.**

—— *See* PIḶḶAI LŌKĀCHĀRYAR. ∘∘∘ முமுக்ஷுப்படி ௸ [Mumukshu-paḍi. With the commentary Tiru-mantrārtham by Periya-jīyar.] 1889. 8°. **14170. f. 17.**

—— *See* PIḶḶAI LŌKĀCHĀRYAR. ∘∘∘ முமுக்ஷுப்படி ௸ [Mumukshu-paḍi. With the Tiru-mantrārtham of Periya-jīyar.] 1890. 8°. **14170. f. 18.**

AṚAGIYA-MAṆAVĀḶA PERU-MĀḶ, called MAṆAVĀḶA MĀ-MUNI, PERIYA-JĪYAR, and RANGA-NĀTHAN (*continued*). *See* PIḶḶAI LŌKĀCHĀRYAR. Mumukshuppaḍi, *etc.* [With Periya-jīyar's commentary.] 1905, *etc.* 8°. [*Viṣishtâdvaitin.*] **14170. eee. 11. (vol. 1, &c.)**

—— *See* PIḶḶAI LŌKĀCHĀRYAR. ప్రపన్నజనకూ-సరరాజ శ్రీపిళ్ళైలోకాచార్యస్వామి . . . తత్త్వత్రయము ॥ [Tattva-trayam. With commentary by Aṛagiya-maṇavāḷar.] [1875.] 8°. **14170. f. 24.**

—— *See* PIḶḶAI LŌKĀCHĀRYAR. ప్రపన్నజనకూ-సరరాజ శ్రీపిళ్ళైలోకాచార్యస్వామి . . . తత్త్వత్రయము ॥ [Tattva-trayam. With commentary of Aṛagiya-maṇavāḷar.] [1904.] 8°. **14170. ff. 11.**

—— *See* PIḶḶAI LŌKĀCHĀRYAR. ஸ்ரீ . . . ஸ்ரீவசநபூஷணம் ௸ [Vachana-bhūshaṇam. With commentary by Aṛagiya-maṇavāḷar.] 1879. 8°. **14172. b. 10.**

—— *See* VĒNKAṬA-RANGA RĀMĀNUJA-DĀSAR. ஸ்ரீ மந்மணவாளமாமுநிகள் திருவந்தாதி. [Maṇavāḷa-mā-munigaḷ-tiruv-antādi. A poem on Aṛagiya-maṇavāḷar.] [1869.] 8°. **14172. b. 23.(2.)**

—— ஸ்ரீ . . . உபதேசரத்தினமாலை. திருவாய்மொழிநூற்றந்தாதி. ஸ்ரீ ஆர்த்திப்பிரபந்தம் ௸ [Upadēṣa-ratna-mālai, Tiru-vāy-moṛi-nūṯṯ'-antādi, and Ārtti-prabandham. Three Vaishṇava poems by Aṛagiya-maṇavāḷa Peru-māḷ. Followed by the Kaṇṇinuṇ Ṣiṟu-tāmbu of Kōyil Kandāḍaiy Aṇṇan, the Ṣrīṣaila-vaibhavam of Para-vādi-kēsari, the Amalan-ādi-pirān Ṣrī-pādādi-kēṣa-mālai of Prativādi-bhayankara Aṇṇan, the Sampradāya-chandrikai of Ap-piḷḷār, and the Vāṛi-tiru-nāmam of Ap-piḷḷai, a series of short devotional poems by disciples of Aṛagiya-maṇavāḷa Peru-māḷ, and by the Tiru-nakshatra-mudaliyavaigaḷin Vivaram and Tiru-muḍiy-aḍaivu, tracts on the chronology of the heads of the Vaishṇava church. Edited by Tirumalai Īchambāḍi Ṣrīnivāsa Rāghavāchāryar.] 7 pts. துன்முகி [*Madras*, 1836.] 8°. **14172. b. 3.**

—— உபதேசரத்தினமாலை (†திருவாய்மொழிநூற்றந்தாதி, ஆர்த்திப்பிரபந்தம் *etc.*) [Upadēṣa-ratna-mālai, Tiru-vāy-moṛi-nūṯṯ'-antādi, Ārtti-prabandham, and Ñāna-sāra-ṣlōkangaḷ. Vaishṇava theological and devotional poems, the last being a Sanskrit paraphrase of Aruḷ-āḷa Peru-māḷ's

Ñāna-sāram.] *See* ĀṞVĀRGAḶ.—Nāl-āyiram.—*Selections.* ◦◦◦ நித்யாநுஸந்தாநம் ஶ்ரீ [Nityānusandhānam.] pp. 72-118. 1886. 8°. **14170. ee. 14.**

—— ఉపదేశరత్నమాల (తిరువాయ్మొழినూற்றந்தாதி *etc.*) [Upadēṣa-ratna-mālai, Tiru-vāy-moṟi-nūṯṟ'-antādi, Ārtti-prabandham, and Ñāna-sāra-ṣlōkaṅgaḷ. With Telugu word-for-word interpretation, paraphrase, *etc.*] *See* ĀṞVĀRGAḶ.—Nāl-āyiram.—*Selections.* ◦◦◦ నిత్యానుసంధానము శ్రీ [Nityānusandhānam.] pp. 471-641. 1906. 8°. **14170. eee. 21.**

—— ஶ்ரீ . . . ஶ்ரீமதார்த்தி ப்ரபந்தத்துக்கு ப்ரதிபதம். [Ārtti-prabandham. A devotional Vaishṇava poem. With a *pratipadam* or explanatory paraphrase. Edited by Tirumalai Nallān Chakravartti Krushṇam-āchārya Svāmi.] pp. 36. சென்னை [*Madras,*] 1893. 8°. **14170. ee. 6.(1.)**

—— ◦◦◦ யதிராஜவிம்ஶதி. [Yati-rāja-viṃṣati. Twenty Sanskrit stanzas in praise of Rāmānuja. With a commentary in Tamil by Piḷḷai Lōkam-jīyar. Edited by Jīyar-sannidhi Tirumalāchāryar and Araṣāṇipālai Kandāḍai Vijaya-rāghavāchāryar.] pp. 50. திருவல்லிக்கேணி கஅஅச [*Triplicane,* 1884.] 12°. **14028. b. 63.(1.)**
The Sanskrit text is printed in the Telugu character.

—— ◦◦◦ యతిరాజవింశతి. [Yati-rāja-viṃṣati. With the Tamil commentary of Piḷḷai Lōkam-jīyar and some other devotional verses, Sanskrit and Tamil. Edited with a Telugu literal interpretation of the 20 stanzas and epitome of the commentary, by Māḍabhūshi Rāmānujāchāryar.] pp. 64. చెన్నై క్రొత [*Madras,* 1904.] 8°. **14028. c. 86.**

AṞAGIYA-MAṆAVĀḶA RĀMĀNUJA-JĪYAR SVĀMI, *Kāñchi Vādi-kēsari.* *See* YĀMUNĀCHĀRYAR. తత్త్వభూషణమ్. [Tattva-bhūshaṇam. Edited by Aṟagiya-maṇavāḷar.] 1902. 8°. **14170. ee. 6.(2.)**

AṞAGIYA ṢOKKA-NĀTHA PIḶḶAI, *Tirunelvēli.* *See* RĀMĀYAṆAM. இராமாயணக்கொம்மி. [Rāmāyaṇa-kommi. Edited by Aṟagiya Ṣokka-nātha.] [1870.] 8°. **14172. a. 25.**

AṞAGIYA-VARADA MUNI. *See* VĀNA-MĀ-MALAI RĀMĀNUJA-JĪYAR.

AṞAGU-MUTTU PULAVAR. ◦◦◦ ஶ்ரீமெய்கண்ட வேலாயுத சதகம். திறப்புகழ். [Mey-kaṇḍa-vēlāyudha-ṣatakam and Mey-kaṇḍa-tiṟa-pugaṟ. Hymns in glorification of the god Kumāra. Edited, with preface and life of the poet, by G. Sadā-ṣivam Piḷḷai.] pp. 112. தஞ்சை சார்வரி [*Tanjore,* 1900.] 12°. **14170. d. 66.**

ARAṢA-KĒSARI, *of Nallur, Jaffna.* *See* KĀLIDĀSA. இரகுவம்மிசம். [Raghu-vaṃṣam. A translation into Tamil verse by Araṣa-kēsari.] 1887. 8°. **14172. b. 33.**

ARAṢAN SHAṆMUKHANĀR, *Ṣōṟavandānūr.* *See* TOL-KĀPPIYANĀR. தொல்காப்பியச் சண்முகவிருத்தி ஶ்ரீ [Tol-kāppiyam. With commentary styled Shaṇmukha-vrutti by Araṣan-Shaṇmukhanār.] 1905, *etc.* 8°. **14172. e. 43.**

ĀRĀV'-AMUD'-ĀCHĀRYAR, *Tiruchuṟiyal.* திருச்சுழியற்புராணம். [Tiruchuṟiyaṟ-purāṇam. A poem on the Ṣaiva cult of Tiruchuliyal. Edited by Ambala-vāṇa Nāvalar.] pp. ii. vi. 103. சென்னபட்டணம் பிலவ [*Madras,* 1901.] 8°. **14170. ee. 56.**

ARDEN (ALBERT HENRY). A Progressive Grammar of Common Tamil. (*A Companion Reader to Arden's Progressive Tamil Grammar, vol. i. The Panchatantra in Tamil, with notes and translation, being volume ii. of Arden Tamil Reader.) 3 vols. *London, Madras,* 1891-1893. 8°. **12907. c. 38.**

AREEVANUNDUM PILLAY. *See* AṞIV'-ĀNANDAM PIḶḶAI.

ARI. *See* HARI.

ARIEL (E.). *See* TIRU-VAḶḶUVAR. Kuṟaḷ . . . fragments traduits . . . [by E. Ariel]. 1848, 1852. 8°. **Ac. 8808 (4e série, tom. 12, 19).**

ARIṢIL-KIṞĀR. எட்டாம் பத்து. [Decade viii. Ten poems on the Chera king Peruñ-chēral Irumboṟai.] *See* PADIṮṮU-PATTU. ◦◦◦ பதிற்றுப்பத்து ஶ்ரீ [Padiṭṭu-pattu.] pp. 119-137. 1904. 8°. **14172. bb. 14.**

ARITHMETIC. பாலகணிதம். An elementary Arithmetic, combining many of the peculiarities of the European and Tamil systems. pp. 179. *Jaffna,* 1849. 16°. **14172. h. 44.(1.)**

AṞIV'-ĀNANDAM PIḶḶAI (JOHN). Laws of Tamil Composition. Part i.: Syntax. வாசக இலக்கணம் . . . By John Areevanundum Pillay. pp. i. ii. ii. 185. *Madras,* 1866. 8°. **14172. h. 78.**

ĀRIYAN, *Pseud.* பேதவாத திரஸ்காரம் . . . Bhêdavâda Tiraskaram. [A digest of texts, chiefly

Sanskrit, in defence of monism, with Tamil dissertations and explanations, in refutation of the arguments of Ṣendināth'-aiyar.] pp. ii. 98, ii. சென்னை [*Madras*,] 1897. 8°. **14048. cc. 13.**

—— தத்துவவாதம். [Tattva-vādam. Articles on the Vedantic philosophy, reprinted from Tamil newspapers.] pp. 52. சென்னை [*Madras*,] 1889. 8°. **14170. e. 31.(1.)**

—— வேதாந்ததீபிகை. Vêdânta Deepika. [A treatise on Vedantic philosophy.] pp. ii. 82. சென்னை [*Madras*,] 1898. 8°. **14170. ee. 28.(3.)**

ARNDT (Johann). Joannis Arndtii . . . Libellus Precum religiosissimarum, dictus Hortulus Paradisiacus . . . Ex germanico in tamulicum convertit Beniamin Schulzius (ஞான மந்திர செலவபூங்காவனம்). 4 pts. *Halae Magdeburgicae*, 1749-1750. 12°. **14170. bbb. 7.**

Pts. 1 and 2 have distinct title-pages, pagination, and registers. Pts. 3 and 4 have a common title-page and a continuous pagination.

—— Joannis Arndtii . . . de Vero Christianismo liber primus. Ex germanico in tamulicum convertit Beniamin Schulzius (ஞானக்கண்ணாடி). pp. v. 399. *Halæ Magdeburgicæ*, 1751. 8°. **G. 19,737.**

ARNOLD (*Sir* Edwin). *See* Gautama. The story of the life of Buddha . . . as depicted by Sir E. Arnold in his 'Light of Asia,' *etc.* 1897. 12°. **14171. aa. 6.**

ARNOLD (J. R.), also called Aruṇāchalam Sadāṣivam Piḷḷai. [*Life.*] *See* Arnold (S. T.). ஸ்ரீ . . . Life of . . . Mr. J. R. Arnold, *etc.* 1897. 12°. **14171. a. 17.**

—— *See* Gāṅgēyar. உரிச்சொல்நிகண்டு மூல [Uri-chol-nighaṇṭu. Edited by J. R. Arnold.] 1889. 12°. **14172. ee. 9.(2.)**

—— இல்லற நொண்டி. (*Illara Nondy. The Husband and Wife. A poem on domestic life.) pp. viii. 72. *Jaffna*, 1887. 16°. **14172. a. 37.**

—— கீர்த்தனசங்கிரகம் . . . Keertana Sangraha. A collection of songs [on Christian religious subjects] composed by J. R. Arnold. pp. 80. *Manippay*, 1890. 12°. **14170. b. 53.**

—— நன்னெறிக் கதா சங்கிரகம். (*Nannery Kathasangrakam: or A collection of moral tales in Tamil. Second edition.) pp. iv. 328. *Jaffna*, 1893. 12°. **14171. a. 3.**

ARNOLD (J. R.), also called Aruṇāchalam Sadāṣivam Piḷḷai (*continued*). Pavalar Chariththira Theepakam, or The Galaxy of Tamil Poets (*பாவலர் சரித்திர தீபகம்). pp. viii. 268. *Jaffna*, 1886. 8°. **14172. b. 25.**

—— சாதாரண இதிகாசம். (*A Compend of Universal History, with a chronological table of particular events.) pp. xiv. 480. *Jaffna*, 1858. 12°. **14172. h. 59.**

—— வானசாஸ்திரம். . . . A Compend of Astronomy, *etc.* pp. ii. 71. *Jaffna*, 1861. 12°. **14172. h. 65.**

—— வெல்லை அந்தாதி . . . Vellai Anthathy, a poem on Christ intended for Christian schools & children. pp. 16. *Manippay*, 1890. 12°. **14170. b. 34.(4.)**

ARNOLD(Sadā-ṣivam Tamb'-aiyā). ஸ்ரீமத். ஜே. ஆர். ஆனல்ட் ஆசிரியர் அவர்களின் ஜீவியசரித்திரம். . . . Life of the late Mr. J. R. Arnold, author, editor, poet, and Tamil scholar. Edited [*i.e.* composed] by his son, S. T. Arnold. pp. 48; 1 *plate*. *Jaffna*, 1897. 12°. **14171. a. 17.**

ĀRŌGYAM PILLAI, *Triṣirapuram Dhairyam*. *See* Durai-sāmi Mudaliyār, *T. Ṣ.* வேதபுரியந்தாதி. [Vēda-puriy-autādi. Edited by Ārōgyam.] [1868.] 8°. **14170. c. 32.**

AROOLAPPEN. *See* Aruḷ-appan.

ARPUDAM, *Ṣavēriyā-kuṭṭiy-uḍaiyār*. Leçons faciles de Français et de Tamoul, suivant la méthode de T. Robertson, par Arpoudam fils de Savériakouttyodéar . . . பிராஞ்சு தமிழ்ப் பாஷையின் எளிதானபாடங்கள். pp. 7, 147. புதுவை தூஅார்றெய [*Pondicherry*, 1850.] 12°. **14172. h. 5.**

ĀRŪḌHA-ṢĀSTRAM. ◦ ◦ ◦ ஞானப்ரதீபிகை என்னும் ஆருடசாஸ்திரம் மூல [Ārūḍha-ṣāstram, or Ñāna-pradīpikai. A Sanskrit astrological treatise, here ascribed to Jaimini. With a Tamil commentary by K. Ṣorna-ṣāstri and V. R. Ṣrīnivāsāchāryar, entitled Bhāva-prakāṣikai. Edited by V. Krushṇa Ṣāstri of Devakota.] pp. 2, ii. 144. சென்னை விகாரி [*Madras*, 1899.] 8°. **14053. ccc. 27.**

ARUḶ-ĀḶA PERU-MĀḶ EM-BERUMĀNĀR. ஞானஸாரமும் . . . ஜ்ஞானஸாரப்லோகங்களும் (†பிரமேயஸாரம்). [Ñāna-sāram, 40 stanzas on Vaishṇava theology, with Sanskrit paraphrase by Maṇavāḷa Mā-muni, and Pramēya-sāram, a like work in 10 verses.] *See* ĀṞVĀRGAḶ.—Nāl-āyiram.—*Selections*. ००० நித்யாநுஸந்தாநம் ஸ்ரீ [Nityānusandhānam.] pp. 108-120. 1886. 8°. **14170. ee. 14.**

According to tradition, this writer was originally an Advaita-vādi and known as Yajña-mūrtti, but was converted and instructed by Rāmānuja.

—— జ్ఞానసారము (ప్రమేయసారము). [Ñāna-sāram and Pramēya-sāram. With Telugu word-for-word interpretation, paraphrase, *etc.*] *See* ĀṞVĀRGAḶ.—Nāl-āyiram.—*Selections*. ००० నిత్యానుసంధానము ॥ [Nityānusandhānam.] pp. 617-648. 1906. 8°. **14170. eee. 21.**

ARUḶ-APPAN (JOHN CHRISTIAN). *See* MORTIMER (F. L.). The Peep of Day. Translated into Tamil, by J. C. Aroolappen, *etc.* 1852. 12°. **14170. b. 32.**

—— The Scripture Mirror, or Index of the Bible. Containing the principal words, alphabetically arranged. சத்திய வேதக் கண்ணாடி. pp. 258. *Madras*, 1846. 12°. **14170. b. 25.**

ARUḶ-APPA NĀVALAR, *of Jaffna* (BHŪ-LŌKA-SIṂHA MUDALIYĀR). திருச்செல்வர்காவியம். [Tiru-chelvar-kāvyam. A biographical poem on the life of Tiru-chelva-rāyam, a Roman Catholic devotee. Edited with explanations and paraphrases by N. Tyāga-rāja Piḷḷai.] pp. xiii. 263. யாழ்ப்பாணம் [*Jaffna*,] 1896. 8°. **14170. bb. 6.**

ĀṞU-MUGA DĒŚIKAR. *See* ARABIAN NIGHTS. Arabian History, *etc.* [Revised by Āṟu-muga.] 1888. 8°. **14171. a. 41.**

ĀṞU-MUGAM PIḶḶAI, *Ādi Pūlāru-sāmi.* சோடசப் பிரபந்தம். [Shōḍaṣa-prabandham. Sixteen religious poems, chiefly on the Ṣaiva cult.] pp. x. i. v. 261. சென்னை [*Madras*,] 1899. 8°. **14172. b. 5.**

ĀṞU-MUGA MUDALIYĀR, *Kalattūr Vēda-giri.* *See* NAṬA-RĀJAR, *K.* சாதகாலங்காரம். [Jātakālaṅkāram. Edited by Āṟu-muga.] [1867 ?] 8°. **14170. i. 9.**

—— *See* PAVAṆANDI. நன்னூல் ஸ்ரீ [Nan-nūl. With commentary. Edited by Āṟu-muga.] [1875.] 8°. **14172. f. 9.**

—— *See* RĀVAṆAN. சகஸ்திரமுகராவணன் கதை ஸ்ரீ [Sahasra-mukha-rāvaṇan-kathai, *etc.* Edited by Āṟu-muga.] [1874.] 8°. **14172. b. 24.**

ĀṞU-MUGA ÑĀNIYĀR, *of Melakaveri, Kumbakonam.* *See* AGASTYAR. ००० வாத . . . சௌமியம், ஞஉா. [Vāta-saumyam. Edited by Āṟu-muga.] 1893. 8°. **14170. e. 52.**

ĀṞU-MUGA NĀVALAR, *of Nallur, Jaffna.* *See* AUVAIYĀR.—*Two or More Works*. ००० ஆத்திசூடி ஸ்ரீ [Ātti-ṣūḍi and Konṟai-vēndan. With commentaries by Āṟu-muga.] [1893.] 12°. [*Bāla-pāṭham.*] **14172. h. 92. (pt. 1.)**

—— *See* MEY-KAṆḌA DĒVAR. ००० சிவஞானபோத ஸ்ரீ [Ṣiva-ñāna-bōdham. Edited by Āṟu-muga.] [1885.] 12°. **14170. d. 1.**

—— *See* ÑĀNA-SAMBANDHAR. சைவசமயநெறி. [Ṣaiva-samaya-neṟi. With commentary by Āṟu-muga.] [1875.] 12°. **14172. a. 14.**

—— *See* PAVAṆANDI. ००० நன்னூல் ஸ்ரீ [Nan-nūl. With commentary of Ṣaṅkara Namaṣ-ṣivāyar. Edited by Āṟu-muga.] [1851.] 8°. **14172. f. 2.**

—— —— [1887.] 8°. **14172. e. 12.**

—— —— [1903.] 8°. **14172. e. 39.**

—— *See* PAVAṆANDI. நன்னூற்காண்டிகையுரை. [Nan-nūl. With commentary. Edited and augmented by Āṟu-muga.] [1880.] 8°. **14172. e. 28.**

—— *See* PURĀṆAS.—*Skanda-purāṇam.* கந்தபுராணம். [Kanda-purāṇam. Edited by Āṟu-muga.] [1869.] 8°. **14170. f. 3.**

—— *See* ṢEKKIṞĀR. பெரியபுராணம் ஸ்ரீ [Periya-purāṇam. A summary by Āṟu-muga.] [1852.] 8°. **14170. e. 10.**

—— *See* SUBRAHMAṆYA DĪKSHITAR. ००० பிரயோகவிவேகம் ஸ்ரீ [Prayōga-vivēkam. Edited by Āṟu-muga.] [1882.] 8°. **14170. e. 22.**

—— *See* TIRU-MUṞAI.—*Two or More Sections.* ००० தேவாரத்திரட்டு. [Dēvāram, *etc.* Edited by Āṟu-muga.] [1880.] 8°. **14172. b. 8.**

—— —— [1885.] 8°. **14172. b. 35.**

—— *See* TIRU-VAḶḶUVAR. ००० தமிழ்வேதமாகிய திருக்குறள் ஸ்ரீ [Kuṟaḷ. With commentary Edited by Āṟu-muga.] [1861.] 8°. **14172. d. 7.**

—— —— [1875.] 8°. **14172. d. 8.**

ĀṞU-MUGA NĀVALAR, *of Nallur, Jaffna (continued)*. *See* TOL-KĀPPIYANĀR. தொல்காப்பியம் ஆ [Tol-kāppiyam (Ṣoll'-adhikāram.) With commentary. Edited by Āṟu-muga.] [1868.] 8°. **14172. e. 6.**

—— *See* UMĀ-PATI ṢIVĀCHĀRYAR. கோயிற்புராணம். [Kōyiṟ-purāṇam. With commentary by Āṟu-muga.] [1868.] 12°. **14170. d. 13.**

—— *See* VĪRA-MAṆḌALAVAR. சூடாமணிநிகண்டு ஆ [Chūḍāmaṇi-nighaṇṭu. Edited by Āṟu-muga.] [1867.] 8°. **14172. f. 11.**

—— —— 1880. 8°. **14172. e. 29.**

—— —— [1894.] 8°. **14172. e. 17.**

—— இலக்கணச்சுருக்கம். [Ilakkaṇa-churukkam. An abridged grammar.] pp. i. 237. சென்னபட்டணம் பவ [*Madras*, 1874.] 12°. **14172. h. 30.**

—— இலக்கணவினுவிடை. [Ilakkaṇa-vinā-viḍai. A catechism of Tamil grammar.] vol. ii. pp. 70. சென்னபட்டணம் யுவ [*Madras*, 1875.] 16°. **14172. h. 34.**

—— சைவவினுவிடை. [Ṣaiva-vinā-viḍai. A catechism of the Ṣaiva religion. Followed by a series of hymns, called Tōttira-tiraṭṭu.] vol. ii. pp. ii. 193. சென்னபட்டணம் யுவ [*Madras*, 1875.] 16°. **14170. d. 16.**

ĀṞU-MUGA PIḶḶAI, *Uḍuppiṭṭi C.* கிறிஸ்துசமயபேதம். [Kiṟistu-samaya-bhēdam. A controversial tract against Christianity.] pp. 10. யாழ்ப்பாணம் விரோதி [*Jaffna*, 1889.] 16°. **14170. d. 10.(1.)**

—— நெற்கொழு வைரவர்பதிகம். [Neṟ-koṟu-vairavar-padigam. 10 stanzas to the god Vairavan, as a song for sifters of rice.] pp. 14. யாழ்ப்பாணம் விரோதி [*Jaffna*, 1889.] 32°. **14170. d. 10.(3.)**

—— விவிலிய நூல் வரலாறு. [Viviliya-nūl-varal-āṟu. An anti-Christian tract upon the origin of the Bible.] pp. 14. யாழ்ப்பாணம் விரோதி [*Jaffna*, 1889.] 16°. **14170. d. 10.(2.)**

ĀṞU-MUGA SVĀMI, *Tirukōvalūr.* ◦ ◦ ◦ நிஷ்டானுபூதிமூலம் . . . உரையுடன். [Nishṭhānubhūti. A work, purporting to be lectures by Ṣiva to Pārvati, on the Ṣuddhādvaita Vedantic system. With a commentary by Muttu-kṛushṇa Brahmam.] pp. xiii. 134. சென்னபட்டணம் நளஎச [*Madras*, 1852.] 8°. **14172. c. 23.**

Pp. 131-2 are missing.

ĀṞU-MUGA SVĀMI, *Tiruveṅgāḍu.* [For works edited by Āṟu-muga Svāmi, see under the following headings:]

AGASTYAR. PAÑCHA-TANTRAM.
DICTIONARIES. PAVAṆANDI.
DIVĀKARAR. TĀṆḌAVA-RĀYA-MŪRTTI SVĀMI.
MĀRIY-AMMAN. VĪRA-SVĀMI, *Madurai.*

ĀṞU-MUGA TAMBIRĀN SVĀMI, *Tiruvaṇṇāmalai.* *See* ṢEKKIṞĀR. சேக்கிழார் . . . செய்த . . . பெரியபுராணம் ஆ [Periya-purāṇam. Edited with interpretation by Āṟu-muga.] [1885]-1898. 8°. **14170. f. 1.**

ĀṞU-MUGA UPĀDHYĀYAR, *M., of Jaffna.* ஆறும் புத்தகம். [A Sixth Reader for schools.] pp. 84. யாழ்ப்பாணம் விய [*Jaffna*, 1886.] 12°. **14172. h. 70.**

—— சிறுத்தொண்டநாயனார்புராணம். [Ṣiṟu-tonḍa-nāyanār-purāṇam. A legend of a Ṣaiva saint, in prose and verse, based upon the Periya-purāṇam of Ṣēkkiṟār.] pp. 22, 8, ii. கொக்குவில் ஜய [*Kokkuvil*, 1894.] 8°. **14170. ee. 4.(1.)**

ARUṆĀCHALA AIYAR, *Tiruvaṇṇāmalai.* *See* ELL'-APPA NĀVALAR. ◦ ◦ ◦ அருணுசலபுராணம் ஆ [Aruṇāchala-purāṇam. Edited by Aruṇāchala.] [1875.] 8°. **14170. e. 18.**

ARUṆĀCHALA KAVI-RĀYAR, *M.R., of Settur.* *See* KAMBAN. ஸ்ரீ . . . ராமாயணம் ஆ [Kamba-rāmāyaṇam, Āraṇya-kāṇḍam. Edited by Aruṇāchala.] 1900. 8°. **14172. d. 25.**

—— *See* KANAKA-SABHAI PIḶḶAI, *K.* வருண சிந்தாமணி. [Varṇa-chintāmaṇi. Edited by Aruṇāchala.] 1901. 8°. **14170. g. 22.**

—— *See* NIRAMBAV-AṞAGIYA DĒṢIKAR. திருப்பரங்கிரிப் புராண ஆ [Tiru-paraṅ-giri-purāṇa-vachanam. A prose version, by Aruṇāchala, of Nirambav-aṟagiyar's poem. Followed by Tiru-paraṅ-giri-piḷḷai-tamiṟ, a devotional composition by Aruṇāchala on the childhood of the god Kumāra.] [1899.] 12°. **14170. d. 70.**

—— *See* TRIKŪṬA-RĀJ'-APPAR. இது திருக்குற்றலத்தலபுராண ஆ [Tiru-kuṭṭāla-tala-purāṇa-vachanam. Rendered in prose by Aruṇāchala.] 1906. 12°. **14170. dd. 13.**

ARUṆĀCHALA KAVI-RĀYAR, *M.R., of Settur (continued)*. *See* VENṞI-MĀLAI KAVI-RĀJAR. திருச்செந்-தூர்த்தலபுராண ஞூ [Tiruchendūr-tala-purāṇa-vachanam. A prose version by Aruṇāchala. Followed by Pagaṟi-kūttar's Tiruchendūr-piḷḷai-tamiṟ, edited by the same.] [1899-1900.] 12°. **14170. d. 59.**

—— சேதுபர்வதவர்த்தனியம்மை பிள்ளைத்-தமிழ். [Sētu-parvata-vartaniy-ammai-piḷḷai-tamiṟ. A poem on the stages in the childhood of the consort of the god Rāma-nātha-mūrtti worshipped at Ramesvaram. Followed by Tōttira-ṣeyyuṭkaḷ, or stanzas on the local cult of Ramesvaram.] pp. i. 13, 52, 3, i. மதுரை [*Madura*,] 1906. 8°. **14172. bb. 23.**

ARUṆĀCHALA KAVI-RĀYAR, *Ṣīrkāḻi*. இராம-நாடகம். [Rāma-nāṭakam. A drama on the epic history of Rāma. Edited by Tirutoṭṭikalai Vaiyā-puri Mudaliyār, on the basis of the edition of T. Vēṅkaṭāchala Mudaliyār and P. Rāma-sāmi Nāya-kar. Preceded by Rāmāyaṇa-ōr-aḍi-kīrttanai, appropriate devotional verses by Paṭṭūr Rāja-ṣēkhara Mudaliyār.] pp. 8, 16, 377; 1 *plate*. பிரபவ [*Madras*, 1867.] 8°. **14170. l. 3.**

—— இராமநாடகம். [Rāma-nāṭakam. An edition based upon that of Vēṅkaṭāchala Mudaliyār and Rāma-sāmi Nāyakar, with Rāja-ṣēkhara's Rāmāyaṇa-ōr-aḍi-kīrttanai.] pp. 24, 378, i. யுவ [*Madras*, 1875.] 8°. **14170. l. 11.**

—— ∘ ∘ ∘ இராமநாடகம். [Rāma-nāṭakam. Preceded by Rāja-ṣēkhara's Rāmāyaṇa-ōr-aḍi-kīrt-tanai. Revised by N. Aruṇāchala Mudaliyār.] pp. 403. விக்கிரம [*Madras*, 1880.] 8°. **14170. l. 2.**

—— ∘ ∘ ∘ இராமநாடகம் ஞூ [Rāma-nāṭakam. With Rāja-ṣēkhara's Rāmāyaṇa-ōr-aḍi-kīrttanai. Revised by T. Tyāga-rāya-svāmi.] pp. 403. சித்திரபானு [*Madras*, 1883.] 8°. **14170. l. 10.**

—— ∘ ∘ ∘ இராம நாடகம் ஞூ [Rāma-nāṭakam. Preceded by the Rāmāyaṇa ōr-aḍi-kīrttanai, *etc*. Edited by Vīrā-sāmi Nāyuḍu.] pp. iv. viii. xvi. 380, i.; 24 *plates*. *Madras*, 1893. 8°. **14170. l. 36.**

—— இராமநாடகமென்று வழங்குகின்ற குச-லவநாடகம். [Kuṣa-lava-nāṭakam, or Rāma-nā-ṭakam. A drama on the epic legend of Rāma and his sons. Revised by G. Aruṇāchala Muda-liyār, on the basis of Vēṅkaṭāchala Mudaliyār's edition. Seventh edition.] pp. 171, i. பிரமாதி [*Madras*, 1870.] 8°. **14170. l. 5.**

ARUṆĀCHALAM, *P*. *See* TIRU-MUṞAI.—*Tiru-vā-chakam*. A few hymns of Manikka Vachaka and Tayumanavar. Translated by P. A[ruṇāchalam], *etc*. 1897. 8°. **14170. ee. 12.(2.)**

—— Studies and translations from the Tamil [viz. from the poems of Mudi-nāka-rāyar, Māṇikka-vāchakar, and Tāyumānavar]. By P. A[ruṇā-chalam]. pp. i. 62. *Madras*, 1898. 8°. **14170. ee. 12.(3.)**

ARUṆĀCHALAM PIḶḶAI, *Panḍaṇa-Nallūr*. *See* SAṄGĪTAM. Tamil Sungeatha Surabooshany, *etc*. [Translated by Nārāyaṇa-dās and Aruṇāchalam.] 1900. 8°. **14170. i. 68.**

ARUṆĀCHALA MUDALIYĀR, *Gōkulāpuram*. [For works edited by Aruṇāchala Mudaliyār, see under the following headings :]

APPAṆA NĀYAKKAR.
ARUṆĀCHALA KAVI-RĀYAR, Ṣ.
AUVAIYĀR.—*Two or More Works*.
MAHĀ-BHĀRATAM.
MUHAMMAD KĀDIRĪ.
VAIYĀPURI PIḶḶAI.
VAḶḶIY-AMMAN.
VIKRAMĀRKA CHARITAM.
VĪRA KAVI-RĀYAR.

—— *See* BHĪMA KAVI-RĀYAR. ∘ ∘ ∘ ஸ்ரீராமர் அஸ்-வமேதயாக ஞூ [Ṣrī-rāmar-aṣva-mēdha-yāgam, *etc*. With occasional verses by Aruṇāchala.] [1875.] 4°. **14172. dd. 1.**

ARUṆĀCHALA MUDALIYĀR, *Nāyar*. *See* ARUṆĀ-CHALA KAVI-RĀYAR, Ṣ. ∘ ∘ ∘ இராமநாடகம். [Rāma-nāṭakam. Revised by Aruṇāchala Mudaliyār.] [1880.] 8°. **14170. l. 2.**

ARUṆĀCHALA NĀYANĀR, *Eḍuttukūṭṭi*. *See* PU-RĀṆAS.—*Bhāgavata-purāṇam*. அவதூதசம்வாத ஞூ [Avadhūta-saṃvādam. With commentary by Aruṇāchala.] 1888. 12°. **14172. a. 35.(1.)**

ARUṆĀCHALA SVĀMI, *Piṟaiṣai*. *See* ARUṆĀCHALA SVĀMI, *Piṟaiyāṟu*.

ARUṆĀCHALA SVĀMI, *Piṟaiyāṟu, disciple of Tiru-nāgai Aruṇāchala*. *See* ĀḶAVANDĀR. ∘ ∘ ∘ ஞான-

வாசிட்ட ஞூ [Ñāna-vāsiṭṭav-amala-rāmāyaṇam. With commentary by Aruṇāchala.] [1851.] 4°. **14170. fff. 2.**

—— *See* Āḻavandār. ○ ○ ○ ஞானவாசிட்ட ஞூ [Ñāna-vāsiṭṭav-amala-rāmāyaṇam. With commentary of Aruṇāchala.] 1890. 8°. **14172. b. 41.**

—— *See* Śiva-prakāṣa Dēṣikar. வேதாந்தசூளாமணி ஞூ [Vēdānta-chūḷāmaṇi. With commentary by Aruṇāchala.] 1861. 8°. **14170. e. 14.**

—— *See* Tāṇḍava-rāya-mūrtti Svāmi. கைவல்யநவநீதம் ஞூ [Kaivalya-nava-nītam. With commentary by Aruṇāchala.] [1864.] 8°. **14172. c. 17.**

—— *See* Tattva-rāya Svāmi. ○ ○ ○ சசிவன்னபோதம் ஞூ [Ṣaṣi-varṇa-bōdham. With Aruṇāchala's commentary.] [1895.] 12°. **14170. d. 39.**

ARUṆĀCHALA SVĀMI, *Tiruninṟavūr.* *See* Kāriya Nāyanār. கணக்கதிகாரம். [Kaṇakk'-adhikāram. Edited by Aruṇāchala.] [1860.] 8°. **14172. f. 5.**

ARUṆĀCHALA UPĀDHYĀYAR, *Kāyalpaṭṭaṇam.* சுப்பிரமணியர் ஆசிரியவிருத்தம். [Subrahmaṇyar-āṣiriya-vṛuttam. A Ṣaiva hymn.] *See* Sāmba-ṣiva Kavi-rāyar. ○ ○ ○ துங்கம்பாக்கம் ஞூ [A series of hymns.] pp. 43-47. 1867. 12°. **14170. d. 25.(1.)**

ARUṆA-GIRI-NĀTHA SVĀMI, *Tiruvaṇṇāmalai.* ○ ○ ○ திருப்புகழ். [Tiru-pugaṛ. Praises of deities connected with Ṣaiva shrines in South India, in four series of 100 songs each.] 4 pts. *Madras,* 1889-விகுர்தி [1890]. 16°. **14172. a. 36.**

Pt. i. *is of the second edition.*

—— ○ ○ ○ திருப்புகழ். [Tiru-pugaṛ. Edited by Tirupādiri-puliyūr Ṣiva-chidambara Mudaliyār.] 2 vols. சென்னபட்டணம் [*Madras,*] 1894-1901. 8°. **14172. b. 51.**

—— வேல்விருத்தம். மயில்விருத்தம். [Vēl-vṛuttam and Mayil-vṛuttam. Hymns on the god Skanda's javelin and peacock-car respectively.] pp. 18. *See* Sundara Mudaliyār, *T.* ○ ○ ○ திருமுருகாற்றுப்படை ஞூ [Tiru-mṛug'-āṯṯu-paḍai, *etc.*] pt. ii. [1890.] 16°. **14172. a. 32.(2.)**

—— ○ ○ ○ கந்தரலங்கார மூலமும் . . . பதவுரையும். [Kandar-alaṅkāram. A series of devotional quatrains addressed to the god Skanda. With interpretation by the editors of the Vidyā-vinōdini.] pp. 64. சென்னை [*Madras,*] 1892. 8°. **14172. c. 39.(3.)**

Forms part of the Vidyā-vinōdini Series. *Apparently unfinished.*

—— ○ ○ ○ கந்தரநுபூதி உரையுடன். [Kandar-anubhūti. Poems on the revelation of the god Kandar or Skanda. With a commentary.] pp. i. 18, iv. சென்னை வியய [*Madras,* 1887.] 12°. **14172. a. 6.(3.)**

—— ○ ○ ○ கந்தரனுபூதி. [Kandar-anubhūti. Fourth edition.] pp. 14. சென்னை [*Madras,*] 1889. 16°. **14172. a. 7.(5.)**

ARUṆANDI DĒVA-NĀYANĀR, *Tiruturaiyūr.* சிவஞானசித்தியார்பரபக்கம். (†சிவஞானசித்தியார்சுபக்கம், இருபாவிருபது.) [Ṣiva-ñāna-siddhiyār-parapakkam, Ṣiva-ñāna-siddhiyār-supakkam, and Iru-bāv-iru-badu. Three works on the Ṣaiva-Siddhāntam. With commentaries (i.) on the first by Tattva-prakāṣa-tambirān Svāmi, (ii.) on the second by Subrahmaṇya Dēṣikar, (iii.) on the third by Namaṣ-ṣivāya Tambirān.] *See* Mey-kaṇḍa-ṣāttiram. மெய்கண்டசாத்திரம் ஞூ [Mey-kaṇḍa-ṣāttiram.] pp. 211-598. 1897. 8°. **14170. ff. 3.**

Said to have been written in Ṣaka 1175.

—— சிவஞானசித்தியார் ஞூ [Ṣiva-ñāna-siddhiyār-parapakkam, Ṣiva-ñāna-siddhiyār-supakkam, and Iru-bāv-iru-badu.] pp. 141, 8. *See* Mey-kaṇḍa-ṣāttiram. ○ ○ ○ சைவசித்தாந்த ஞூ [Ṣaiva-siddhānta-ṣāttiram.] [1899.] 12°. **14170. d. 53.**

—— சிவஞானசித்தியார் சுவபக்கத்துக்கு . . . வியாக்கியானம். [Ṣiva-ñāna-siddhiyār-supakkam. With commentary of Ñāna-prakāṣar. Edited by I. Naṭa-rāja Aiyar.] pp. 288, vi. திருப்பற்றூர் சர்வஜித்து [*Tirupatur,* 1888.] 8°. **14170. ee. 10.**

—— Sivagnana Siddhiyar. *etc.* [Translated by J. M. Nalla-sāmi Piḷḷai.] 1897, *etc.* *See* Periodical Publications.—*Madras.* The Light of Truth, *etc.* Vol. i., no. 1, *etc.* 1897, *etc.* 4°. **14170. fff. 4. (vol. i., etc.)**

In progress.

—— Widerlegung des Buddhistischen Systems vom Standpunkte des Sivaismus. [Translated from the Ṣiva-ñāna-siddhiyār.] (†Von K. Graul.) 1854. *See* Academies.—Germany.—*Deutsche Morgenlaendische Gesellschaft.* Zeitschrift, *etc.* Bd. viii., pp. 720-738. 1846, *etc.* 8°. **Ac. 8815/2 (Bd. 8.)**

ĀṞVĀRGAḶ. [*Lives.*] [For editions of the Guru-paramparā-prabhāvam, or histories of the Fathers of the Church, compiled by the Tṛutīya Brahma-tantra-svatantra-svāmi:] *See* BRAHMA-TANTRA-SVATANTRA-SVĀMI.

—— *See* GŌVINDĀCHĀRYAR, *A.* The Holy Lives of the Âzhvârs, *etc.* 1902. 8°. **14170. eee. 2.**

—— *See* NAMM'-ĀṞVĀR. ∘ ∘ ∘ நம்மாழ்வார்தாலாட்டு. [Namm'-āṟvār-tālāṭṭu.] 1900. 8°. **14170. ee. 35.(8.)**

—— [For editions of Pinb'-aṟagiyar's Guru-paramparā-prabhāvam, or histories of the Fathers of the Church:] *See* PINB'-AṞAGIYA PERU-MĀḶ JĪYAR.

—— *See* ṢAṬHAKŌPA-DĀSAR, *K.* ∘ ∘ ∘ அரிசமயதீபம் ஸ்ரீ [Hari-samaya-dīpam.] 1904. 8°. **14170. ee. 58.**

—— *See* ṢAṬHAKŌPA-RĀMĀNUJĀCHĀRYAR, *V. M.* ஆழ்வார்கள் சரித்திரம். [Āṟvārgaḷ-charitram.] [1898.] 8°. **14170. ee. 35.(7.)**

—— [For editions of the Tiru-muḍiy-aḍaivu, or chronicle of the Vaishṇava Church Fathers:] *See* TIRU-MUḌIY-AḌAIVU.

—— ஆழ்வாராசாரியர்கள் திருநக்ஷத்திரமுதலியவைகளின் விவரம். [Āṟvār-āchāryargaḷ-tiru-nakshatra-mudaliyavaigaḷin vivaram. A chronology of the Āṟvārs.] *See* AṞAGIYA-MAṆAVĀḶA PERU-MĀḶ. ஸ்ரீ . . . உபதேசரத்தினமாலை ஸ்ரீ [Upa-dēṣa-ratna-mālai, *etc.*] [1836.] 8°. **14172. b. 3.**

NĀL-ĀYIRAM.

ENTIRE CANON.

திராவிடவேதமாகிய நாலாயிரப்பிரபந்தத்துள் . . . முதலாயிரம் (பெரியதிருமொழி, திருவாய்மொழி, இயற்பா). [Nāl-āyira-divya-prabandham. The canonical Scriptures of the Tengalai Vaishṇavas, in 4000 verses, attributed to the saints known as Āṟvārs. In 4 parts, styled Mudal-āyiram, Periya-tiru-moṟi, Tiru-vāy-moṟi, and Iyaṟ-pā. Edited by K. Ṣrīnivāsa Mudaliyār.] 4 pts. சென்னை [*Madras*, 1861.] 8°. **14172. c. 16.**

The work, as presented in this edition, consists of the following:—

I. Mudal-āyiram, comprising
1. Tiru-moṟi (Tiru-pall'-āṇḍu, etc.) of Periy-āṟṟār.
2. Tiru-pāvai of Āṇḍāl.
3. Tiru-moṟi " "
4. Tiru-moṟi of Kula-ṣē-kharar.
5. Tiru-chanda-vṛuttam of Tiru mariṣai.
6. Tiru-mālai of Toṇḍar-aḍi-poḍi.
7. Tiru-pall'y-eṟuchi of Toṇḍar-aḍi-poḍi.
8. Ama'an-ādi-birān of Tiru-pāṇ.
9. Kaṇṇi-nuṇ-ṣiṟu-tāmbu of Madhura Kavi.
II. Periya-tiru-moṟi of Tiru-maṅgai.
III. Tiru-vāy-moṟi of Namm'-āṟvār.
IV. Iyaṟ-pā, comprising
1. Tiruv-antādi of Poigaiy-āṟvār.
2. Tiruv-antādi of Pūdatt'-āṟvār.
3. Tiruv-antādi of Pēy-āṟvār.
4. " " of Tiru-mariṣai.
5. Tiru-vṛuttam of Namm'-āṟvār.
6. Tiruv-āṣiriyam of Namm'-āṟvār.
7. Periya-tiruv-antādi of Namm'-āṟvār.
8. Tiruv-eṟugūtt'-irukkai of Tiru-maṅgai.
9. Ṣiṟiya-tiru-maḍal of Tiru-maṅgai.
10. Periya-tiru-maḍal of Tiru-maṅgai.
11. Rāmānuja-nūṟṟ'-antādi of Tiruv-araṅgatt'-amudanār.
12. Iyal-ṣāttu (conclusion).

∘ ∘ ∘ தமிழ்வேதமாகிய நாலாயிரதிவ்யப்ரபந்தம். [Nāl-āyira-divya-prabandham. Edited with notes, prefaces, and appendices by Araṣāṇipālai Kandāḍai Kṛushṇam-āchāryar. Second edition.] 4 pts. சென்னை [*Madras*,] 1890. 8°. **14172. c. 38.**

The Iyaṟ-pā is here printed as the third section, and the Tiru-vāy-moṟi as the fourth, the Rāmānuja-nūṟṟ'-antādi appearing at the end of the latter. A list of the 108 Vaishṇava sanctuaries is appended.

∘ ∘ ∘ தமிழ்வேதமாகிய நாலாயிரதிவ்யப்ரபந்தம். [Nāl-āyira-divya-prabandham. Edited with notes, indices, *etc.*, by C. K. Tiru-vēṅkaṭāchāryar.] pp. 534. சென்னை ஹெவிளம்பி [*Madras*, 1898.] 8°. **14172. d. 20.**

The arrangement is the same as in the Madras edition of 1890.

దివ్యప్రబన్ధవ్యాఖ్యాన రత్నావళి. [Divya-prabandha-vyākhyāna-ratnāvaḷī. The Nāl-āyiram, with commentary by Periya Parakāla-svāmi and Gōpāla Dēṣikar, glosses, *etc.*] Edited by Srisailatata-charya. pts. 1-3. pp. 80. *Conjeeveram*, 1901, *etc.* 8°. **14170. ff. 9.**

Apparently no more has been published. The above contains only the Tiru-pall'-āṇḍu.

See KUMARA-GURU-DĀSA SVĀMI. ∘∘∘ நாலாயிரப்பிரபந்தவிசாரம். [Nāl-āyira-prabandha-vichāram. A criticism of the Nāl-āyiram.] 1905. 12°. **14170. dd. 7.**

SELECTIONS.

నిత్యానుసంధానము [Nityānusandhānam. A ritual of daily devotions compiled from the Nāl-āyiram. Edited by K. Kēṣavāchāryulu.] pp. vi. 124. చెంగల్పట్టు [*Chingleput*, 1862.] 12°. **14170. d. 22.**

నిత్యానుసంధానము. [Nityānusandhānam.] pp. 72. [*Madras*,] 1864. 8°. **14170. e. 12.**

∘ ∘ ∘ நித்யாநுஸந்தாநம் ஸ்ரீ [Nityānusandhānam. Followed by Maṇavāḷa Mā-muni's Upadēṣa-ratna-mālai, Tiru-vāy-moṟi-nūṟṟ'-antādi, Ārtti-prabandham, and Ñāna-sāra-ṣlōkaṅgaḷ; Aruḷ-āḷa

Peru-māḷ's Ñāna-sāram and Pramēya-sāram; Viḷāñjōlai Piḷḷai's Sapta-gāthai; Ap-piḷḷai's Vāṟi-tiru-nāmam; and Tiru-nakshatra-ṣlōkaṅgaḷ, in Sanskrit. Edited by Yadugiri Jīyar-sannidhi Tirumalāchāryar.] pp. 133, 19; 1 *plate.* திருவல்லிக்கேணி [*Triplicane,*] 1886. 8°. **14170. ee. 14.**

The Nityânusandhânam Series . . . with word-for-word meaning, a free paraphrase in the vernacular [*i.e.* Tamil], and English translation [and introductions] . . . Edited by M. B. Srinivasa Aiyangar. (*நித்தியாநுஸந்தானம்.) *Madras,* 1898, *etc.* 8°. **14170. ff. 4.**
In progress.

நித்தியாநுஸந்தானம். [Nityānusandhānam. Another edition of the preceding, in Tamil only.] சென்னை [*Madras,*] 1898, *etc.* 8°. **14170. ff. 5.**
In progress.

The Nityânusandhânam Series. . . . With word-for-word meaning, a free paraphrase in the vernacular [*i.e.* Kanarese], and English translation. Kanarese language. Edited by M. B. Srinivasa Aiyangar. *Bangalore,* 1898, *etc.* 8°. **14176. b. 49.**
In progress.

ನಿತ್ಯಾನುಸನ್ಧಾನವು ವ॥ [Nityānusandhānam. The Tamil text in Kanarese characters, edited with Kanarese glossaries, paraphrases, and notes by M. B. Ṣrīnivāsa Aiyaṅgār.] ಬೆಂಗಳೂರು [*Bangalore,*] 1898, *etc.* 8°. **14176. b. 48.**
In progress.

The Nityânusandhânam Series . . . [Tamil text] with word-for-word meaning, a free paraphrase in the vernacular [*i.e.* Telugu], and English translation. Telugu language. Edited by M. B. Srinivasa Aiyangar. *Madras,* 1898, *etc.* 8°. **14174. b. 51.**
In progress.

నిత్యానుసన్ధానమ్. [Nityānusandhānam.] *See* NITYA-KARMA. పఞ్చకాలప్రకాశః [Pañcha-kāla-prakāṣa.] [1904.] 8°. **14033. bbb. 26.**

○ ○ ○ నిత్యానుసన్ధానము. సంపూర్ణాంధ్రప్రతిపదటీకాతాత్పర్యసహితము. [Nityānusandhānam. Followed by the same texts as in the edition of 1886, and some additional poems. With Telugu word-for-word interpretation, paraphrase, biographical notes, *etc.*, by R. L. Ṣrīnivāsa Rāmānuja-dāsar. pp. viii. 717, iv.; 1 *plate.* *Madras,* 1906. 8°. **14170. eee. 21.**

IYAṞ-PĀ.

இயற்பா . . . திருவாசிரியம். (*பெரியதிருவந்தாதி, திருவெழுகூற்றிருக்கை.) [Iyaṟ-pā. The sections Tiruv-āṣiriyam, Periya-tiruv-antādi, and Tiruv-eṟugūṯṯ'-irukkai. With the commentary of Periyav-āchān Piḷḷai, and glosses, together with paraphrases *etc.* by Māḍabhūshi Rāmānujāchāryar. Edited by the latter and C. Muttu-kṛushṇa Nāyuḍu.] 3 pts. சென்னப்பட்டணம் சோபக்ருத்-குரோதி. [*Madras,* 1903-1904.] 8°. **14170. eee. 4.**

○ ○ ○ இராமாநுச நூற்றந்தாதி. [Rāmānuja-nūṯṯ'-antādi. Verses ascribed to Tiruv-araṅgatt'-amudanār, and forming bk. xi. of the Iyaṟ-pā. With commentary by Periya-jīyar. Followed by the Iyal-ṣāttu-vyākhyānam, or commentary on the concluding verses of the Nāl-āyiram, of Piḷḷai Lōkam-jīyar. Edited by Māḍabhūshi Rāmānujāchāryar and C. Muttu-kṛushṇa Nāyuḍu.] pp. ii. 117. சென்னப்பட்டணம் விஶ்வாவஸு [*Madras,* 1905.] 8°. **14170. ee. 6.(6.)**

○ ○ ○ பெரிய திருமடல். [Periya-tiru-maḍal. Devotional verses, ascribed to Tiru-maṅgaiy-āṟvār, and forming bk. x. of the Iyaṟ-pā. With the *maṇi-pravāḷam* commentary of Periyav-āchān Piḷḷai and glosses. Edited by Māḍabhūshi Rāmānujāchāryar and C. Muttu-kṛushṇa Nāyuḍu, with a commentary by the former.] pp. 76. சென்னப்பட்டணம் க்ரோதி [*Madras,* 1905.] 8°. **14170. ee. 6.(5.)**

○ ○ ○ சிறிய திருமடல். [Ṣiṟiya-tiru-maḍal. Devotional verses, ascribed to Tiru-maṅgaiy-āṟvār, and forming bk. ix. of the Iyaṟ-pā. With the *maṇi-pravāḷam* commentary of Periyav-āchān Piḷḷai and glosses. Edited by Māḍabhūshi Rāmānujāchāryar and C. Muttu-kṛushṇa Nāyuḍu, with a commentary by the former.] pp. 68. சென்னப்பட்டணம் க்ரோதி [*Madras,* 1905.] 8°. **14170. ee. 6.(4.)**

○ ○ ○ திருவிருத்தம். [Tiru-vṛuttam. 100 *antādi* stanzas (bk. v. of Iyaṟ-pā), ascribed to Namm'-āṟvār. Edited with critical and historical prefaces, notes, and commentary by V. M. Ṣaṭhakōpa-rāmānujāchāryar.] pp. iv. 190, xvi. சென்னை விகாரி [Madras, 1899.] 8°. **14170. ee. 35.(5.)**

MUDAL-ĀYIRAM.

○ ○ ○ முதலாயிரம் மூலமும் . . . வ்யாக்யாநமும். [Mudal-āyiram. The first section of the Nāl-āyiram, ascribed to Periy-āṛvār. With commentaries by Periya-jīyar (Aragiya-maṇavāḷar), Periyav-āchān Piḷḷai, and Piḷḷai Lōkam-jīyar. Edited by C. K. Tiru-vēṅkaṭāchāryar and A. K. Krushṇam-āchāryar.] 4 pts. சென்னபட்டணம் [Madras,] 1880-1885. 8°. **14170. f. 9.**

Pt. 2 is a second edition, and is dated 1885 ; *pt.* 3, *dated* 1882, *is a third edition ; pt.* 4 *is dated* 1885.

○ ○ ○ ముదలాయిరమూలమున్ . . . వ్యాఖ్యానమున్. [Mudal-āyiram. Another edition of the preceding, in Telugu characters.] 4 pts. తిరువల్లిక్కేణి [Triplicane,] 1881-౧౮౮౬ [1886]. 8°. **14170. f. 8.**

Imperfect.

○ ○ ○ తిరుమల్లేదరాచార్య నాలాయిరదివ్యప్రబన్ధత్తిల్ ముదలాయిరమ్. [Mudal-āyiram. Edited by M. K. Tirumalāchāryar and Tiru-nagari Rāmānuja-dāsar.] pp. 182. *Madras*, 1889. 8°. **14170. e. 33.**

○ ○ ○ திருமாலைக்கு ப்ரதிபதம் [Tiru-mālaikku pratipadam. Text, with a word-for-word prose interpretation, of Toṇḍar-aḍi-poḍi's Tiru-mālai, preceded by an account of the author.] pp. 32. சென்னை [Madras,] 1906. 8°. **14170. eee. 19.**

○ ○ ○ திருப்பல்லாண்டு ௵ [Tiru-pall'-āṇḍu. A hymn from the Tiru-moṛi of Periy āṛvār. With commentary by Periyav-āchān Piḷḷai, and glosses. Edited by Āttān Krushṇam-āchāryar.] pp. 107, ii. பிரமோதூத [Madras, 1870.] 8°. **14170. e. 15.**

○ ○ ○ திருப்பள்ளியெழுச்சி . . . திருப்பாவை ௵ [Tiru-paḷḷiy-eṛuchi and Tiru-pāvai. Two poems from the Mudal-āyiram, ascribed respectively to Toṇḍar-aḍi-poḍi and Āṇḍāḷ.] pp. 48. சென்னை [Madras,] 1899. 32°. **14170. d. 68.**

○ ○ ○ ஸ்ரீ ஆண்டாள் அருளிச்செய்த திருப்பாவை. [Tiru-pāvai. Edited, with a commentary, by Kāñchi Rāma-sāmi Nāyuḍu and A. L. Ṣrīnivāsa Tātāchārya Svāmi.] pp. ii. 56 ; 1 *plate*. சென்னை [Madras,] 1902. 12°. **14170. d. 76.**

PERIYA-TIRU-MOṚI.

○ ○ ○ பெரியதிருமொழி . . . மூலமும் . . . வ்யாக்யாநமும் ௵ [Periya-tiru-moṛi, or section ii. of the Nāl-āyiram, ascribed to Tiru-maṅgaiy-āṛvār. Decades 1-3, with commentaries of Nañ-jīyar, Piḷḷai Lōkam-jīyar, and Periyav-āchān Piḷḷai, and glosses and interpretations. Edited by C. K. Tiru-vēṅkaṭāchāryar and A. K. Krushṇam-āchāryar.] pp. iv. ii. viii. 608 ; 1 *plate*. திருவல்லிக்கேணி [Triplicane,] 1881. 8°. **14170. f. 7.**

Pp. 1-2 *are wanting.*

○ ○ ○ திருக்குறுந்தாண்டகம், திருநெடுந்தாண்டகம், மூலமும் . . . வ்யாக்யாநமும் ௵ [Tiru-kuṛun-dāṇḍakam and Tiru-neḍun-dāṇḍakam. The last two poems in the Periya-tiru-moṛi. With commentaries by Periyav-āchān Piḷḷai and Piḷḷai Lōkam-jīyar, glossaries, and interpretations. Edited by C. K. Tiru-vēṅkaṭāchāryar.] pp. 269. சென்னை [Madras,] 1888. 8°. **14172. d. 4.**

TIRU-VĀY-MOṚI.

See GŌPĀLA-KRUSHṆA PIḶḶAI, *T.* ஆசார்ய ஹ்ருதயசாரசங்க்ரஹம் [Āchārya-hrudaya-sāra-saṅgraham. A digest of Aragiya-maṇavāḷar's commentary Āchārya-hrudayam on the Tiru-vāy-moṛi.] 1892. 8°. **14170. e. 61.**

○ ○ ○ திருவாய்மொழிக்கு வியாக்கியானம். [Tiru-vāy-moṛi. Section iii. of the Nāl-āyiram, ascribed to Namm'-āṛvār. With commentary. Edited by M. Appāvu Mudaliyār, Rāmānujāchāri, and K. Rāja-gōpāla Piḷḷai.] pp. ii. xvi. ii. 234, vi. காளயுக்தி [Madras ? 1859.] 8°. **14172. c. 18.**

○ ○ ○ நம்மாழ்வாருடைய பகவதநுபவபரீவாஹரூபமானத்ராவிட வேதஸாகரஸாரமாகிய திருவாய்மொழி. மூலமும் . . . பதவுரையும். [Tiru-vāy-moṛi. With complete glossary to every verse by Kāñchīpuram Rāma-sāmi Nāyuḍu. Edited by Addaṅgi-tirumalai Lakshmī-nrusiṃha Ṣrīnivāsa Tātāchārya Svāmi.] pp. iv. 476, 52. சென்னை விளம்பி [Madras, 1899.] 8°. **14170. ff. 8.**

○ ○ ○ తిరువాయ్మొழி. [Tiru-vāy-moṛi. With glosses and commentaries in Telugu, based on the works of Periyav-āchān Piḷḷai and others, by Māḍabhūshi Rāmānujāchāryar.] pp. xvi. 536. చెన్నపట్టణమందు [Madras,] 1902. 8°. **14170. ff. 10.**

ஹமவத்விஷயம். பகவத்விஷயம். [Bhagavad-vishayam. Being the Tiru-vāy-moṛi together with a series of commentaries—viz. Tiru-kurugai-pirān Piḷḷān's Āṛ'-āyira-paḍi, Vēdānta-rāmānuja's Iru-batti-nāl-āyira-paḍi, Raṅga-rāmānuja's Dramidōpanishad-bhāshyam or On-badin-āyira-padi (in Sanskrit), Periya Parakāla-svāmi's Dramida-ṣruti-tattvārtha-prakāṣikai or Padin-enn'-āyira-padi—and the Vēdānta-dēṣikar's Dramidōpanishat-tātparya ratnāvali and Dramidōpanishat-sāram (in Sanskrit), with commentaries by Vēṅkaṭēṣā-chāryar and Ṣrīnivāsa Dēṣikar respectively, and preceded by various memorial verses and introductions. Edited by A. Krushnam-āchāryar and K. Ṣ. Varada-vēdāntāchāryar.] காஞ்சீ கும்பகோணம் ஞானாந—குரோதி [*Conjevaram, Kumbakonam*, 1883-1904.] 4°. **14170. fff. 3.**

Imperfect, containing only decades 1-4 *and* 10.

The Divine Wisdom of the Drâvida Saints. [Selections from the Bhagavad-vishayam, translated into English] by Alkondavilli Govindâchârya. pp. 13, 2, xxiii. 215. *Madras*, 1902. 8°. **14170. ee. 64.**

ĀṚVĀR TIRUMALAI AYYAṄGĀR, *M.A.* *See* PILLAI LŌKĀCHĀRYAR. ప్రసన్నజనాగ్రేసరౌ శ్రీపిళ్ళై-లోకాచార్య . . . తత్త్వత్రయము ॥ [Tattva-trayam. Edited by Āṛvār Tirumalai Ayyaṅgār and others.] [1875.] 8°. **14170. f. 24.**

ĀRYA-MUTTU PILLAI, V. *See* RĀMA-SĀMI PILLAI, *Bh. K.* சகாநாடி ஜூ [Jōdida-ṣikhāmaṇi. Edited with commentary, *etc.*, by Ārya-muttu.] 1897. 8°. **14170. i. 52.**

ASBURY (ROBERT O. D.). A History of Tamil Literature. . . தமிழ்ப் பாஷை வைபவம். pp. 12. *Jaffna*, 1886. 12°. **14172. h. 71.**

—— A collection of Tamil proverbs, *etc.* (†பழமொழிகள்.) pp. 8. *Madras*, 1887. 8°. **14171. a. 38.(2.)**

A proof-sheet, with author's MS. corrections.

ASHTON (JOHN PERKINS). An English Grammar for Tamil Youth. Compiled by the Rev. J. P. Ashton . . . with the aid of his Munishi Parippakam Muniappa Muthaliar . . . இங்கிலீஷ் இலக்கணம். pp. 108. *Madras*, 1862. 16°. **14172. h. 45.**

ĀṢIRVĀD'-APPA PIRIṢĀR. *See* BRISARD (B.).

ASTRONOMY. Astronomy. சோதிசாஸ்திரம். [A school-book.] pp. 40. *Madras*, 1862. 16°. **14172. h. 42.**

AṢVA-GHŌSHA. Vajra Suchi; the Needle of Adamant; or The original divine Institution of Caste. Examined and refuted by the Budhist Pundit Ashwaghosha. English and Tamil versions [the former by W. Morton, the latter by P. Percival,] of the Sanscrit original. (*வச்சிரசூசி.) pp. 41. *Jaffna*, 1851. 12°. **14028. c. 25.**

ATIVĪRA-RĀMA PĀṆḌIYAN. *See* PURĀṆAS.—*Kūrma-purāṇam.* ° ° ° கூர்மபுராண ஜூ [Kūrma-purāṇam. In the metrical version of Ativīra-rāma.] 1898-1899. 8°. **14170. ff. 6.**

—— *See* PURĀṆAS.—*Kūrma-purāṇam.* கூர்மபுராணம். [Kūrma-purāṇam. Bk. 12.] 1891. 8°. [*University of Madras: First in Arts Examination*, 1892.] **14172. bb. 4.**

—— *See* PURĀṆAS.—*Skanda-purāṇam.* காசிகாண்டம். [Kāṣi-khaṇḍam. An adaptation in verse, attributed to Ativīra-rāma.] 1884. 8°. **14170. e. 24.**

—— *See* PURĀṆAS.—*Skanda-purāṇam.* ° ° ° காசிகண்டம். [Kāṣi-khaṇḍam.] 1892, *etc.* 8°. **14170. f. 20.**

—— ° ° ° மாகபுராணம். [Māgha-purāṇam. A series of metrical Ṣaiva legends, in 28 chapters. Edited by Rāma-liṅga Guru.] pp. viii. 200. சென்னை [*Madras*,] 1904. 8°. **14170. eee. 3.**

—— நைடதம் மூலமும் உரையும். [Naiḍadam. A poem adapted from the Sanskrit Naishadha-charitam of Ṣrī-harsha. With a commentary on cantos 1-5 by Ṣara-vaṇa Peru-māḷ Aiyar, and on cantos 6-28 by K. A. Kumāra-svāmi Dēṣikar, T. Ṣ. Kanda-svāmi Aiyar, and others.] pp. x. ii. ii. 600. சுபகிருது [*Madras*, 1842.] 8°. **14172. b. 58.**

—— நைடதம் மூலமும் உரையும். [Naiḍadam. Edited with interpretation and paraphrase by Kaḷattūr Vēda-giri Mudaliyār.] pp. 556. சித்தார்த்தி [*Madras*, 1859.] 8°. **14172. c. 3.**

—— ° ° ° நைடதம் ஜூ [Naiḍadam. With commentaries by Ṣara-vaṇa Peru-māḷ Aiyar, Kanda-svāmi Aiyar, and Vēda-giri Mudaliyār. Edited by Taṇḍalam Subba-rāya Mudaliyār.] pp. i. 488. பவ [*Madras*, 1875.] 8°. **14172. b. 59.**

—— ° ° ° நைடதம் மூலமும் உரையும். [Naiḍadam. With the commentaries of Ṣara-vaṇa Peru-māḷ Aiyar, Kumāra-svāmi Dēṣikar, Kanda-svāmi

Aiyar, *etc.* Edited by Tirumayilai Mṛugēṣa Mudaliyār.] pp. i. 269, 354. சென்னபட்டணம் [*Madras,*] 1881. 8°. **14172. b. 14.**

—— திருக்கருவைக்கலித்துறையந்தாதி. [Tiru-karuvai-kali-tuṛaiy-antādi. A panegyric in 100 stanzas upon the Ṣaiva sanctuary at Karuvai. With commentary.] *See* ACADEMIES, *etc.*—Madras.—*University of Madras.* The University of Madras. The First in Arts Examination, *etc.* 1891. 8°. **14172. bb. 4.**

—— [For the text of the Veṭṭi-vēṛ-kai in both Tamil and English, with and without commentary, published in the various editions of the "Tamil Minor Poets":] *See* TAMIL MINOR POETS.

—— The Proverbs, or Sententious Sayings [*i.e.* the Veṭṭi-vēṛ-kai] of Athivira-ramen [in English]. *See* TAYLOR (W.). Oriental Historical Manuscripts, *etc.* Vol. ii., Appendix, pp. 21-24. 1835. 4°. **14171. c. 5.**

ĀTMA-NĀTHA BHĀGAVATAR, *Tiruperunduṛai M.* *See* KALYĀṆA-NĀṬAKAM. கலியாணநாடகம். [Kalyāṇa-nāṭakam. Edited by Ātma-nātha.] 1900. 8°. **14170. l. 37.(3.)**

ĀTMA-NĀTHAN. *See* JESUS CHRIST. கிருஸ்து போன்ற ஒழுக்க முறை நூல் (The Imitation of Christ. [Translated by] Atmanathan.) 1905, *etc.* [*Vāṇī-vilāsinī.*] **14172. m. 1. (vol. 1, etc.)**

ĀTMA-VĀSAM. ஆத்மவாசவிவரணம் [Ātma-vāsa-vivaraṇam. A first book on human physiology for the use of schools.] pp. 38, i. *Madras,* 1858. 16°. **14170. i. 2.(1.)**

AUDINARAYANIAH. *See* ĀDI-NĀRĀYAṆ'-AIYĀ.

AUGSBURG CONFESSION. *See* EVANGELICAL LUTHERAN CHURCH. Concordia . . . VI. [*sic*] Confessio Augustana. V. Apologia Confessionis, *etc.* 1872-1880. 8°. **14170. c. 2.**

AUVAIYĀR. [*Life.*] *See* GAṄGĀDHARA MUDALIYĀR. ஔவை சரித்திரம். [Auvai-charitram.] [1890.] 16°. **14172. h. 87.**

—— *See* SUBRAHMAṆYĀCHĀRYAR, *S.* ஔவையார் சரித்திரம் [Auvaiyār-charitram.] 1902. 8°. **14171. a. 53.(1.)**

—— *See* VĪRĀ-SĀMI CHEṬṬIYAR. Vinodarasa-manjari . . . To this are added the life of Auviyar, *etc.* 1891. 8°. **14170. k. 56.**

AUVAIYĀR (*continued*).

TWO OR MORE WORKS.

—— *See* MṚUGĒṢA MUDALIYĀR. நீதிமஞ்சரித்தருப்பணம். [Nīti-mañjari darpaṇam. Interpretations of ethical works of Auvaiyār and others.] 1881-1883. 16°. **14172. a. 8.**

—— Short Lessons and Moral Maxims of the Singalese and Malabars, taken from the Malabar Book, [Ātti-ṣūḍi and] Connevendam. (†Sayings of a Female Sage.) *See* FELLOWES (R.). The History of Ceylon, *etc.* pt. i., pp. 315-321. 1817. 4°. **152. h. 13.**

—— வாக்குண்டாம். நல்வழி. நன்னெறி. [Vākk'-uṇḍām or Mūd'-urai, and Nal-vaṛi. Two ethical poems. Followed by Ṣiva-prakāṣar's Nanneṛi. With commentaries by Ṣara-vaṇa Peru-māḷ Aiyar. Fourth edition.] pp. 79. பிலவ [*Madras,* 1841.] 16°. **14172. a. 1.**

—— ○ ○ ○ வாக்குண்டாம் . . . நல்வழி . . . நன்னெறி ஆ [Vākk'-uṇḍām, Nal-vaṛi, and Nanneṛi. With commentaries by Ṣara-vaṇa Peru-māḷ Aiyar. Edited by T. Kuppan Aiyaṅgār.] pp. 70. சித்தார்த்தி [*Madras,* 1859.] 16°. **14172. a. 12.**

—— ஆத்திசூடி. [Ātti-ṣūḍi, Konṛai-vēndan, Mūd'-urai, and Nal-vaṛi.] *See* TAMIL MINOR POETS. Tamil Minor Poets, *etc.* pp. 1-9, 16-25. 1864. 16°. **14172. a. 17.**

—— —— pp. 1-11, 19-34. 1868. 16°. **14172. a. 18.**

—— ஆத்திசூடி. [The same works. With commentary.] *See* TAMIL MINOR POETS. Tamil Minor Poets, *etc.* pp. 1-32, 57-88. 1865. 16°. **14172. a. 16.**

—— ஆத்திசூடி. [Ātti-ṣūḍi and Konṛai-vēndan. With commentary.] *See* TAMIL MINOR POETS. Tamil Minor Poets. First Book, *etc.* pp. 1-32. 1865. 16°. **14172. h. 35.(2.)**

—— ○ ○ ○ வாக்குண்டாம் . . . நல்வழி . . . நன்னெறி ஆ [Vākk'-uṇḍām, Nal-vaṛi, and Nanneṛi. With commentaries by Ṣara-vaṇa Peru-māḷ Aiyar. Edited by G. Aruṇāchala Mudaliyār.] pp. 64. [*Madras,*] 1882. 16°. **14172. a. 11.(1.)**

—— ஆத்திசூடி ஆ [Ātti-ṣūḍi and Konṛai-vēndan.] *See* HARI. ஹரிச்சுவடி ஆ [Hari-chuvaḍi.] pp. 37-44. [*n.d.*] 16°. **14172. h. 35.(3.)**

AUVAIYĀR (*continued*). ◦ ◦ ◦ ஆத்திசூடி கொன்றைவேந்தன். [Ātti-ṣūḍi and Konṟai-vēndan. With commentaries by Āṟu-muga Nāvalar.] [1893.] *See* JAFFNA.—*Ṣaiva-prakāṣa-sabhai.* பால பாடம். [Bāla-pāṭham.] pt. i. [1893-1894.] 12°. **14172. h. 92. (pt. 1.)**

—— நீதிச்சொல். Anthesoody, Konraiventhen. [Ātti-ṣūḍi and Konṟai-vēndan, here collectively entitled Nīti-chol. With English interpretations.] pp. 47. *Madras,* 1895. 16°. **14172. a. 43.**

—— Attisudi. (†Konraiventhan, Muthurei, Nalvali.) [Translated into English.] *See* TAMIL MINOR POETS. Tamil Minor Poets, *etc.* pp. 1-12, 19-29. 1872. 12°. **14172. e. 6.**

—— Muthuray. (†Attisudi, Conday-vēnthan.) [In English verse. Preceded by a life of Auvaiyār.] *See* ROBINSON (E. J.). Tamil Wisdom, *etc* pp. 70-86. 1873. 12°. **14170. k. 62.**

—— The Revered Mother. [The legends concerning Auvaiyār and a metrical translation of the Mūd'-urai, Ātti-ṣūḍi, and Konṟai-vēndan.] *See* ROBINSON (E. J.). Tales and poems of South India, *etc.* pp. 150-180. 1885. 8°. **14170. k. 63.**

SINGLE WORKS.

—— (†முதுமொழி.) [Ātti-ṣūḍi, called here Mudu-moṛi.] pp. 16. [*Manepy?* 1835?] 16°. *No title-page.* **14172. h. 1.(2.)**

—— Attisudi. Expurgated edition ... ஆத்திசூடி உரைபாடம். [With commentary.] pp. 16. *Madras,* 1865. 16°. **14172. a. 10.(1.)**

—— Aweiar's Kalwiorhuckam [*i.e.* Kalviyoṛukkam] oder Sittensprüche aus tamulischen Palmblättern übersetzt, mit Bemerkungen über indische Gelehrsamkeit, von J. C. C. Rüdiger. pp. 28. *Halle,* 1791. 12°. **14172. a. 40.**

—— ◦ ◦ ◦ கொன்றைவேந்தன் ௸ [Konṟai-vēndan. Edited with explanatory notes by K. N. Īṣvar'-aiyar.] (No. 2. The "Literary Sun" Press Series.) pp. 22. *Coimbatore,* 1894. 16°. **14172. a. 10.(4.)**

—— ◦ ◦ ◦ மூதுரை உரைபாடம். [Mūd'-urai, or Vākk'-uṇḍām. Ethical verses.] pp. 16. *Madras,* 1865. 16°. **14172. a. 10.(2.)**

AUVAIYĀR (*continued*).

SUPPOSITITIOUS WORKS.

—— ◦ ◦ ◦ விநாயகர் அகவல் ௸ [Vināyakar-agaval and Vēṟa-mugam, two religions poems, and Ulaga-nīti, ethical verses, ascribed to Auvaiyār. Edited by T. Kanda-svāmi Aiyar.] pp. 16. சென்னை [*Madras,*] 1889. 16°. **14172. a. 33.**

—— விநாயகர் அகவல். [Vināyakar-agaval and Vēṟa-mugam.] *See* NAKKĪRA DĒVAR. ◦ ◦ ◦ விநாயகர் திருஅகவல் ௸ [Vināyakar-agaval, *etc.*] pp. 9-16. 1903. 16°. **14170. d. 31.(3.)**

—— ◦ ◦ ◦ திருக்குறள் மூலம். [Tiru-kuṟaḷ-mūlam. Philosophic and moral verses in *kuraḷ* metre. Edited by T. Ādi-mūla Mudaliyār.] pp. 32. சித்திரபானு [*Madras,* 1882.] 16°. **14172. a. 10.(3.)**

—— ஔவை குறள் ௸ [Auvai-kuṟaḷ. Edited by M. Ṣ. Pūrṇa-lingam Piḷḷai.] pp. iv. 27. சென்னை [*Madras,*] 1899. 12°. **14172. a. 50.(2.)**

—— [Occasional verses, ascribed to Auvaiyār. With interpretation.] *See* TANI-PĀḌAL. (†தனிப்பாடற்றிரட்டு) [Tani-pāḍaṯ-ṯiraṭṭu.] pp. 90-121. [1892, *etc.*] 8°. **14172. e. 39.(5.)**

ĀVIḌAI AMMĀḶ, *of Shenkotta.* வேதாந்தப்பள்ளு. [Vēdānta-paḷḷu. A ballad on Vedantic philosophy, in the popular *paḷḷu* metre.] pp. 16. திருவாதி [*Trivadi,*] 1896. 16°. **14170. d. 33.(2.)**

AVIRŌDHIY-ĀṞVĀR. திருநூற்றந்தாதி ௸ [Tiru-nūṯṯ'-antādi. A century of Jain devotional verses, with interpretation.] pp. 48. 1903. *See* ACADEMIES, *etc.*—*Madura.* ["Ṣen-damiṟ" supplement.] no. 4. 1902, *etc.* 8°. **14172. i. 1.* (no. 4.)**

AVVAIYĀR. *See* AUVAIYĀR.

ÂZHVÂRS. *See* ĀṞVĀRGAḶ.

BABINGTON (BENJAMIN GUY). *See* BESCHI (C.G.E.). பரமார்த்தகுருவின கதை. The Adventures of the Gooroo Paramartan ... accompanied by a translation and vocabulary ... by B. Babington. 1822. 4°. **14170. k. 70.**

—— *See* VĒTĀLA-PAÑCHA-VIṂṢATI. The Vedàla Cadai ... Translated by B. G. Babington. 1831. 8°. [*Oriental Translation Fund; Miscellaneous Translations.*] **14003. d. 5.**

BĀDARĀYAṆA. *See* ṢIVA-PRAKĀṢA DĒṢIKAR. வேதாந்தசூளாமணி ஸ்ரீ [Vēdānta-chūḷāmaṇi. A theological treatise adapted from the Brahma-sūtram.] 1861. 8°. **14170. e. 14.**

—— శ్రీ . . . శ్రీమద్భాష్యార్థసంగ్రహం. [Brahma-sūtram. With Ṣrīmad-bhāshyārtha-saṅgraham, an epitome of Rāmānuja's Ṣrī-bhāshyam, and ascribed to the latter, rendered into Tamil in the *maṇi-pravāḷam* style by Kārakuruchi Vēṅkaṭa-rāghavāchāryar. Edited by Īchambāḍi Ṣrīnivāsa Svāmi.] pp. 304. చెన్నపురి ముద్రిత [*Madras*, 1890.] 8°. **14048. c. 69.**

—— The Brahma Sutra Artha Deepika, or The Brahma Sutras of Sri Vedavyasa, with the commentaries of Sri Saukaracharya and extracts from the glossaries of Anandagiri, Ramananda, Brahmavidyabharana &c., in Tamil. Published by :— A. Siva Row . . . பிரம்மசூத்திரார்த்ததீபிகை [*sic*], *etc. Madras*, 1904, *etc.* 4°. **14170. fff. 5.**
In progress.

—— சங்கர ராமாநுஜ நீலகண்ட பாஷ்யங்களை அநுசரித்த பதவுரைகூடிய ப்ரஹ்மஸூத்ர த்ராவிடபாஷ்யம். [Brahma-sūtra-drāviḍa-bhāshyam. The Brahma-sūtram in Sanskrit, with a triple Tamil commentary based upon the works of Ṣaṅkara, Rāmānuja, and Nīla-kaṇṭha respectively. Compiled by Māḍabhūshi Rāmānujāchāryar. Edited by Sītā-rāma Ṣāstri.] pp. 8, 256, 53, 15. சென்னை [*Madras*,] 1905. 8°. **14049. bb. 8.**

BADR al-DĪN, *Pulavar.* முகியித்தீன் புராணம். [Muhyi-al-dīn-purāṇam. A poem on the life and work of the saint Muhyi al-Dīn. Edited by K. P. Shaikh Tambi Pāvalar.] 2 pts. *Madras*, 1901-1903. 8°. **14172. bb. 1.**

BĀLA-BŌDHAM. ஸ்ரீபாலபோதம். [Bāla-bōdham. An epitome of monist Vedantic philosophy, with a commentary. Translated by V. Kuppu-svāmi Rāju.] pp. vi. viii. ii. 330; 1 *plate.* சென்னை [*Madras*,] 1902. 12°. **14170. d. 78.**

BĀLA-DĒṢIKA NĀYANĀR, *P. V., disciple of Mārimuttu Dēṣikar. See* ṢISHṬA-DĒṢIKAR. குருஸ்தோத்திரகதம்பம் ஸ்ரீ [Ṣishṭa-dēṣika-dvaya-paddhati, *etc.* Edited by Bāla-dēṣikar.] 1903. 12°. **14170. d. 86.**

BĀLA-KṚUSHṆA DĪKSHITAR, *Kumbhaghōṇam Ṣarjveṅgaṭṭa-rāma. See* TIRUKADAVUR. திருக்கடவூர் புராணம். [Tirukaḍavūr-purāṇam. Summarised by Bāla-kṛushṇa.] 1905. 12°. **14170. dd. 4.**

BĀLA-KṚUSHṆA MUDALIYĀR, *V., of Haidarabad. See* MAHĪ-PATI. ஸ்ரீ . . . பக்தமால ஸ்ரீ [Bhakta-māla-vachanaṁ. A Tamil prose version by Bāla-kṛushṇa of the Bhakta-māla, a Telugu *tōrā* poem by himself paraphrasing the legends in Mahī-pati's Marathi poems.] 1907, *etc.* 8°. **14170. e. 17.**

—— *See* MAHĪ-PATI. ००० பிபாஜிராஜன் சரித்திரம். [Pipājī-rājan-charitram. Taken from Bāla-kṛushṇa's Bhakta-māla, with Tamil translation and commentary by the same.] 1900. 8°. **14170. ee. 35.(6.)**

BĀLAR. (†பாலர்சுவடி.) [Bālar-ṣuvaḍi. A Tamil primer.] pp. 16. [*Pondicherry, n.d.*] 8°. **14172. h. 84.**
No title-page or imprint.

BALA-RĀMA AIYAR, *N., of Kadalur.* தாமரை நாண்மலர். (The Fresh Lotus. A collection of Tamil poems. First budding.) pp. 72, i. *Madras*, 1901. 12°. **14172. a. 50.(4.)**
Forms "Pendant" 4 in the series "The Girdle of the Tamil Muse."

BĀLA-SUBRAHMAṆYA AIYAR, *T. K., of Srirangam. See* PERIODICAL PUBLICATIONS.—*Srirangam.* ஸ்ரீ வாணீ விலாஸினீ. (Sri Vani Vilasini.) [Edited by Bāla-subrahmaṇya.] 1905, *etc.* 8°. **14172. m. 1.**

BĀLA-SUBRAHMAṆYA BRAHMA-SVĀMI, *Paramahaṁsa, of Madura. See* MAHĀ-BHĀRATAM. பகவத்கீதா தாத்பரிய தீபிகை. [Bhagavad-gītā. Edited with Tamil version by Bāla-subrahmaṇya.] 1900. 32°. **14068. a. 10.**

—— *See* UPANISHADS.—*Separate Upanishads.* ஈசாவாஸ்யோபநிஷத் ஸ்ரீ (Isavasyopanishad. With [Tamil] commentaries [by] . . . Bala Subrahmania Brahma Swamy.) [1899.] 8°. **14010. b. 21.**

—— *See* UPANISHADS. கேநோபநிஷத்தீபிகை ஸ்ரீ [Kēnōpanishad. With the commentary Kēnōpanishad-dīpikai of Bāla-subrahmaṇya, in Tamil.] 1900. 12°. **14007. b. 13.(1.)**

BĀLA-SUBRAHMAṆYA KAVI-RĀYAR, *Tiruvāviṉaṅguḍi, son of Periyavan Kavi-rāyar.* பழனித்தல புராண மூலம். [Paraṇi-tala-purāṇam. A poem on legends of the Ṣaiva sanctuary on the Palni Hills. Edited by Īrōḍu Daṇḍa-pāṇi Svāmi.] pp. 112, i. *Coimbatore,* விஜய [1893.] 8°. **14170. e. 57.**

——— ∘ ∘ ∘ பழநித் தலபுராணம் . . . பொழிப்புரையுடன். [Paṟani-tala-purāṇam. Edited with preface and paraphrase by N. Kadirai-vēr̲ Piḷḷai.] pp. ii. ii. x. 528. சென்னை [*Madras,*] 1903. 12°. **14170. d. 80.**

BĀLA-SUBRAHMAṆYA MUDALIYĀR, *Kāñchīpuram Sabhā-pati.* *See* ṢIVA. சிவபூசைதிரட்டு ஞ். [Ṣiva-pūjai-tiraṭṭu, *etc.* Edited by Bāla-subrahmaṇya.] [1875.] 12°. **14170. d. 11.**

——— *See* TIRU-MUṞAI.—*Dēvāram.* ∘ ∘ ∘ திருவேகம்பத்தேவாரப்பதிகங்கள். [Tiru-ēkamba-dēvāra-padigaṅgaḷ. Edited by Bāla-subrahmaṇya.] [1875.] 16°. **14170. d. 12.**

BĀLA-SUBRAHMAṆYA NĀṬṬĀR, *Ā. P. Pichāṇḍi Nāḍan.* *See* PONNU-SĀMI NĀḌĀR. பாண்டியகுல விளக்கம். [Pāṇḍiya-kula-viḷakkam. Edited by Bāla-subrahmaṇya.] 1899. 12°. **14170. g. 17.(2.)**

BĀLA-SUBRAHMAṆYA PIḶḶAI, *Tirupādiri-puliyūr Nāgaliṅgam.* ∘ ∘ ∘ ஆக்னேயபுராண சாரமென்னும் வன்னியநாடகம். [Vanniya-nāṭakam, or Āgnēya-purāṇa-sāram. A drama founded upon the Agni-purāṇam. Edited by T. Ṣiva-chidambara Mudaliyār.] pp. 231. சென்னை [*Madras,*] 1902. 8°. **14170. l. 58.**

BĀLA-SUNDARA MUDALIYĀR, *Taṇḍālam.* *See* PONNU-SĀMI PIḶḶAI, *T. M.* Kamalatchi . . . with an introduction . . . by . . . Balasundara, *etc.* 1903. 8°. **14171. a. 50.(2.)**

BĀLA-SUNDARA NĀYAKAR, *of Wesleyan Mission College.* இராமலிங்க பிள்ளைபாடல் ஆபாசதர்ப்பணம். அல்லது மருட்பா மறுப்பு. [Rāma-liṅga-piḷḷai-pāḍal-ābhāsa-darpaṇam, or Maruṭ-pā-maṟuppu. Critical essays on Rāma-liṅga Piḷḷai's religious poems.] pp. 163. *Madras,* 1904. 12°. **14172. g. 6.**

BALAVĒNDRAM, *Rāy'appan.* A short Bible History . . . by the Rev. R. Balavendrum (*சத்திய வேதச்சரித்திரசாரம்.) pp. 37. *Penang,* 1887. 8°. **14170. b. 55.**

BĀL'-AYYĀ. *See* RĀMA-LIṄGA GURU.

BANDAH ('ABD al-WAHHĀB). قصائد بنده [Ḳaṣā'id i bandah. A series of Muhammadan religious poems.] pp. 32, *lith.* مدراس ۱۳۱۴ [*Madras,* 1897.] 8°. **14173. c. 5.**

BARNES (A.), *of the American Mission, Madura District.* *See* DUTHIE (J.). Homiletics, *etc.* [Translated by A. Barnes.] 1865. 12°. **14170. b. 6.**

——— *See* WAYLAND (F.). Wayland's Moral Science, *etc.* [Translated by A. Barnes.] [1859.] 12°. **14172. h. 11.**

BARRIGUE de FONTAINIEU (G. DE). *See* TIRU-VAḶḶUVAR. Le Livre de l'Amour . . . traduit . . . par G. de Barrigue de Fontainieu. 1889. 12°. **14172. a. 38.**

BARTH (CHRISTIAN GOTTLOB). A brief History of the Church of Christ, from the German of the Rev. C. G. Barth. Translated [into Tamil by J. A. Regel] from the English. (*கிறிஸ்து சபையின் சரித்திரச் சுருக்கம்.) pp. 656. *Madras,* 1845. 16°. **14170. a. 4.**

BAYLIS (FREDERIC). *See* MACDUFF (J. R.). The Footsteps of St. Paul . . . A Tamil translation . . . by . . . F. Baylis, *etc.* 1863. 12°. **14170. b. 45.**

——— *See* PERIODICAL PUBLICATIONS. — *Madras.* தேசோபகாரி . . . Désópakári, *etc.* [Edited by F. Baylis.] 1861-1870. 8°. **14172. i. 5.**

BERTOLDI (CHARLES MICHEL). ஞானமுயற்சி. [Ñāna-muyaṟsi. A Roman Catholic manual of spiritual exercises.] pp. viii. 267. புதுவை குஅராசமடம் [*Pondicherry,* 1843.] 12°. **14170. a. 21.(1.)**

The author of this work, who is known only as "Ñāna-prakāsa Svāmi" (i.e. *Père Louis*), *is not known with certainty. Backer ascribes it to Bertoldi* (Bibliothèque de la Compagnie de Jésus, i. 1392, v. 34), *Murdoch to J. V. Bouchet* (Catalogue of Tamil Printed Books, *p.* 53): *cf. Revue de Linguistique, tom.* 35, *p.* 276.

BESCHI (COSTANZO GIOSEFFO EUSEBIO). [For the Ñānav-uṇarttudal ascribed to Beschi:] *See* ÑĀNAV-UṆARTTUDAL.

——— *See* TIRU-VAḶḶUVAR. திருவள்ளுவநாயனார் . . . திருக்குறள். The 'Sacred' Kurraḷ . . . With . . . C. J. Beschi's and F. W. Ellis' versions, *etc.* 1886. 8°. **14172. c. 40.**

——— பேதகமறுத்தல். [Bhēdaka-maṟuttal. A rejoinder to the pamphlet of the Tranquebar

Lutheran Mission in answer to Beschi's Vēda-viḷakkam.] pp. 139. புதுவை தரங்கம்பாடி [Pondicherry, 1842.] 12°. 14170. b. 9.(2.)

—— [Another edition.] pp. 121. புதுவை தரங்கம்பாடி [Pondicherry, 1868.] 12°. 14170. b. 10.(2.)

—— இஃது வீரமாமுனிவர்செய்த சதுரகராதி. [Chatur-agarādi. A fourfold dictionary of high Tamil, giving (1) meanings, (2) synonyms, (3) classes, (4) rhymes. Edited by Tāṇḍava-rāya Mudaliyār and Rāma-chandra Kavi-rāyar.] pp. i. ii. 179, 33, 20, 86, 31, 36, ii. 139, ii. vi. சென்னை [Madras, 1824.] 4°. 14172. f. 13.

—— [Another copy.] 14172. f. 19.

—— ... சதுரகராதி. [Chatur-agarādi. With an appendix. Edited by T. Kuppu-sāmi Mudaliyār.] pp. 416, 30. ௲௮௱ [Madras, 1880.] 8°. 14172. f. 8.

—— Clavis Humaniorum Litterarum sublimioris Tamulici Idiomatis . . . Printed for [and with a prefatory note by] A. Burnell. pp. viii. 171. Tranquebar, 1876. 8°. 14172. f. 17.

—— லுத்தேரினத்தியல்பு [Luttērin att'-iyalpu. A tract against Luther and Lutheranism.] pp. 38, i. புதுவை தரங்கம்பாடி [Pondicherry, 1842.] 12°. 14170. b. 9.(3.)

—— [Another edition.] pp. 32. புதுவை தரங்கம்பாடி [Pondicherry, 1847.] 12°. 14170. b. 12.(1.)

—— [Another edition.] pp. 33. புதுவை தரங்கம்பாடி [Pondicherry, 1868.] 12°. 14170. b. 10.(3.)

—— பரமாறதகுருவின கதை. The Adventures of the Gooroo Paramartan: a tale in the Tamul language: accompanied by a translation and vocabulary, together with an analysis of the first story. By Benjamin Babington. pp. xii. i. 243. London, 1822. 4°. 14170. k. 70.

—— பரமார்த்தகுருவின் கதை. [Paramārtha-guruvin kathai.] pp. 34. புதுவை தரங்கம்பாடி [Pondicherry, 1859.] 12°. 14171. a. 39.

—— [Another copy.] 14171. a. 40.

—— பரமார்த்தகுருவின் கதை. [Paramārtha-guruvin kathai. Followed by extracts from the Tēm-bāv-aṇi.] See Ādi-chuvaḍi. ஆதிச்சுவடி. [Ādi-chuvaḍi.] pp. 45-89. [1862.] 12°. 14172. h. 58.(3.)

—— Strange surprising Adventures of the venerable Gooroo Simple, and his five Disciples, Noodle, Doodle, Wiseacre, Zany, and Foozle. [Freely rendered from B. G. Babington's version by "Grey Goosequill."] Adorned with fifty illustrations, drawn on wood, by Alfred Crowquill [i.e. A. Forrester]. pp. 223. London, 1861. 12°. 14170. k. 64.

—— Aventures du Gourou Paramarta. See Dubois (J. A.). Le Pantcha-Tantra, etc. pp. 231-338. 1826. 8°. 14170. k. 67.

—— —— 1872. 8°. 14170. k. 68.

—— Aventures du Gourou Paramarta. Conte drôlatique indien. [Translated by the Abbé J. A. Dubois.] Orné de nombreuses eaux-fortes par Bernay & Cattelain. [With a preface by F. Sarcey.] pp. ix. 184; 8 plates. Paris, 1877. 8°. 12315. h. 3.

—— Fahrten und Abenteuer Gimpels und Compagnie. Ein tamulisches Reise- und Scherzmärchen. Nacherzählt von Dr. Johann Georg Theodor Grässe. Mit 6 colorirten Bildern. pp. 81. Dresden, [1856?] 12°. 14170. k. 72.

—— தேம்பாமாலை. [Tēm-bā-mālai. Being (1) devotional poems from the Tēm-bāv-aṇi, with commentary, and (2) other hymns by Beschi, separately published in the Tiru-pāv-aṇi.] pp. iv. 244. புதுவை [Pondicherry, 1865?] 8°. 14170. b. 24.

—— தேம்பாவணி. [Tēm-bāv-aṇi. An epic poem on the legends of St. Joseph and the Gospel narratives. With an interpretation by the author. Edited by the Abbé Dupuis.] 3 vols. புதுவை தரங்கம்பாடி [Pondicherry, 1851-1853.] 8°. 14170. c. 9.

Beschi was aided in the composition of this work by Supradīpa Kavi-rāyar.

—— தேம்பாவணி விருத்தியுரை. [Tēm-bāv-aṇi. Edited with interpretation and commentary by A. S. Jaga-rāu Mudaliyār.] vol. i. pp. 804. Madras, 1901. 8°. 14170. cc. 8.

—— See Dupuis (L. S.). Notice sur la Poésie Tamoule, le Rév. P. Beschi et le Tembavani, etc. 1851. 8°. 14172. c. 7.

BESCHI COSTANZO GIOSEFFO EUSEBIO) (*continued*). தேம்பாவணி ஆ [Tēm-bāv-aṇi, books i.-iv. and part of v., with a commentary.] புதுவை தூஅ௱௬௬ [*Pondicherry*, 1866.] 8°. **14170. c. 4.**

Incomplete, breaking off at p. 160.

—— திருப்பாவணி. [Tiru-pāv-aṇi. Hymns to the Virgin Mary, forming the last section of the Tēm-bāv-aṇi.] pp. 46. புதுவை தூஅ௱ரு௬ [*Pondicherry*, 1856.] 12°. **14170. b. 11.**

—— ஐந்திலக்கணத் தொன்னூல்விளக்கம் மூலமும் உரையும். [Ton-nūl-viḷakkam. A grammar, ascribed to Beschi, and founded on older native works. Edited by Ṣrīnivāsa Rāghavāchāryar, with a life of the author in Tamil by G. Mackenzie Cobban. Second edition.] pp. viii. 268, 6. சென்னை தஅகூக [*Madras*, 1891.] 8°. **14172. f. 16.**

—— வேதவிளக்கம். [Vēda-viḷakkam. A compendium of theology.] pp. v. 324, ii. புதுவை தூஅ௱சம௨ [*Pondicherry*, 1842.] 12°. **14170. b. 9.(1.)**

—— [Another edition.] pp. iv. i. 281. புதுவை தூஅ௱௬அ [*Pondicherry*, 1868.] 12°. **14170. b. 10.(1.)**

—— வேதியர் ஒழுக்கம். [Vēdiyar-oṛukkam,] or Instructions to Catechists, in twenty chapters; with an appendix of eight chapters. [Preceded by a biography of Beschi in English and Tamil.] pp. xiii. 91. *Madras*, 1844. 8°. **14170. c. 23.**

Abridged and adapted to the use of Protestant Missions.

—— [Another edition, with biography in Tamil only.] pp. vii. 232. *Madras*, 1849. 12°. **14170. a. 43.**

—— வேதியரொழுக்கம். [Vēdiyar-oṛukkam.] pp. viii. 199. புதுவை தூஅருஅ [*Pondicherry*, 1858.] 12°. **14170. b. 29.(1.)**

BESCHIUS. *See* BESCHI.

BHADRA-GIRIYĀR. பத்திரகிரியார் மெய்ஞ்ஞானப் புலம்பல் ஆ [Mey-ñāna-pulambal. Ṣaiva religious elegies on the vanity of the world. With a biography of the poet and prose paraphrase of the verses by M. Vaḍi-vēlu Mudaliyār.] pp. 4, 56. *See* PAṬṬAṆATTU-PIḶḶAI. பட்டணத்துபிள்ளையார் பாடல் ஆ [Pāḍal, *etc.*] 1899. 12°. **14170. d. 46.**

BHADRA-GIRIYĀR (*continued*). மெஞ்ஞானப்புலம்பல். [Meñ-ñāna-pulambal. With short life of the poet.] pp. 16. *See* SIDDHARGAḶ. ◦ ◦ ◦ பெரிய ஞானக்கோவை [Periya-ñāna-kōvai.] 1899. 12°. **14170. ee. 33.**

—— —— pt. ii. 1906. 12°. **14170. dd. 12.**

—— பத்திரகிரியார்புலம்பல். [Pulambal.] *See* PAṬṬAṆATTU PIḶḶAI. ◦ ◦ ◦ திரு . . . பாடற்றிருமுறை ஆ [Pādaṯ-ṯiru-muṟai.] pp. 142-155. 1906. 8°. **14170. ff. 16.**

BHĀGYA-NĀTHA SVĀMI, *Rāyapuram*. *See* LITURGIES.—Rome, *Church of*. நித்திய சீவனம். [Nitya-jīvanam. Edited by Bhāgya-nātha.] 1901. 32°. **14170. a. 55.**

BHAKTA-VATSALAM, *T.* *See* ṢIṢIRA-KUMĀRA GHŌSHA. ஸ்ரீக்ருஷ்ண சைதன்ய . . . சரித்திரம் ஆ (Sri Krishna Chaitanya . . . [Translated] by T. Bhaktavatsalam, *etc.*) 1902. 8°. **14170. ee. 51.**

BHARTṚU-HARI. *See* ACADEMIES, *etc.*—Madras.—*University of Madras*. University of Madras. F.A. Examination of 1903. Full notes on . . . Bhartrnhari, *etc.* 1903. 8°. **14172. hh. 19.**

BHĀSKARA, *son of Mudgala, Laugākshi*. தருக்ககௌமுதி. [Tarka-kaumudi. A manual of Vaiṣēshika logic. Translated by V. Kuppu-svāmi Rāju. Followed by an excursus on the categories of the Nyāya.] pp. iii. 54, 6. சென்னை விளம்பி [*Madras*, 1898.] 12°. **14170. i. 57.**

BHĀSKARA MIṢRA BHAṬṬAR. *See* SANDHYĀ-VANDANAM. யஜுர்வேத ஸந்த்யாவந்தநம் ஆ [Sandhyā-vandanam, *etc.* With extracts, in a Tamil translation, from the commentaries of Bhāskara.] 1901. 8°. **14033. aa. 27.**

BHAṬṬAR-PIRĀN. *See* PERIY-ĀṚVĀR.

BHIKSHU ṢĀSTRI. *See* ULAGA-NĀTHA-SVĀMI.

BHĪMA KAVI-RĀYAR. ◦ ◦ ◦ ஸ்ரீ ராமர் அஸ்வமேதயாகமும் . . . உத்தரகாண்டமும் ஆ [Ṣrī-rāmar-aṣva-mēdha-yāgam. A prose paraphrase by Bhīma of an episode in the Uttara-kāṇḍam of the Rāmāyaṇam. Followed by a short paraphrase of the Uttara-kāṇḍam, styled Mahā-vindam, by V. Gōvinda Piḷḷai. With occasional verses (*vruttam*) by G. Aruṇāchala Mudaliyār. Edited, on the basis of the edition of Aruṇāchala Aiyar, by P. A. Muni-sāmi Mudaliyār.] pp. iv. 180. யுவ [*Madras*, 1875.] 4°. **14172. dd. 1.**

—— ஸ்ரீராமர் அஸ்வமேதயாகம். [Ṣrī-rāmar-aṣva-mēdha-yāgam.] *See* KAMBAN. ஸ்ரீராமாயண வசனம் ரு [Rāmāyaṇa-vachanam.] pp. 89-422. 1903. 8°. **14172. d. 27.**

BHŌJA-RĀJA PAṆḌITAR (TĒNUVARAI PERU-MĀḶ). சரசோதிமாலை மூலம். [Chara-jōdi-mālai. A poetical manual of astrology. Edited by N. Ch. Raghu-nāth'-aiyar and N. Ṣ. Naṭa-rāj'-aiyar.] pp. vii. 119. யாழ்ப்பாணம் கர [*Jaffna*, 1892.] 8°. **14170. i. 23.**

BHŪ-LŌKA-SIṂHA MUDALIYĀR. *See* ARUḶ-APPA NĀVALAR.

BIBLE.

COMPLETE BIBLES.

Biblia Damulica, seu quod Deus Omnipotentissimus semetipsum ex sua æternitate clarius manifestaturus de cœlo est locutus Veteris Testamenti pars prima, in qua Mosis libri quinque, Josuæ liber unus atque liber unus Judicum, studio & opera Bartholomæi Ziegenbalgii . . . in linguam damulicam versi continentur. (*Pars secunda, in qua libellus Ruth, Samuelis liber . . . Regum liber . . . Chronicorum liber . . . liber Esræ, liber Nehemiæ, liber Esther, liber Jobi, liber Psalmorum . . . liber Proverbiorum, liber Ecclesiastæ, et liber Cantici Canticorum studio & opera Bartholomæi Ziegenbalgii & Benjamini Schultzii . . . versi continentur. Pars tertia, in qua Prophetæ Majores . . . Prophetæ Minores . . . studio & opera Bartholomæi Ziegenbalgii & Benjamini Schultzii . . . versi continentur. Libri apocryphi . . . studio & opera Bartholomæi Zigenbalgii & Benjamini Schultzii . . . versi.) [Pt. v.–vi., translated by Ziegenbalg and Gründler.] (*பாராபாவஷத்து வானவா . . . வெதபொஷததகததின முதலாம வகுபபு *etc.*) 6 pts. *Tranquebariæ*, தரளமச [1714]-1728. 4°. **3068. g. 6.**

Pt. v.-vi., *containing the New Testament, were printed in* 1714, *pt.* v. *being in a larger type; both are without Latin title-pages. Pt.* i. *was printed in* 1723, *pt.* ii. *in* 1726, *pt.* iii. *in* 1727, *and pt.* iv. *in* 1728.

—— [Another copy of pt. i., without title-page.] **466. b. 17.**

The Old Testament in Tamil, *etc.* [Revised by C. T. E. Rhenius, with J. P. Rottler and others, from the version of Fabricius.] (*சத்தியவேத-மெனஇற பழைய உடம்படிக்கை) (*The New Testament [translated into Tamil by C. T. E. Rhenius] . . . புதிய ஏற்பாடு.) 5 vols. *Madras Auxiliary Bible Society: Madras*, 1827-1833. 8°. **3068. c. 21.**

Vols. 1 (1827), 3 (1830), *and* 4 (1831) *are of the fourth edition.*

—— [A separate copy of pp. 511-580 (Corinthians i.-ii.), and 590-627 (Galatians—Philippians).] **3070. bb. 18.**

[Another edition of the whole Bible.] [*Madras*, 1840?] 8°. **1109. d. 6.**

Wanting title-page.

The Holy Bible, containing the Old and New Testaments: translated out of the original tongues: and with the former translations diligently compared and revised [chiefly by P. Percival, together with M. Winslow, L. Spaulding, and T. Brotherton], under the auspices of the British and Foreign Bible Society. (*பழைய புதிய உடன்படிக்கைகள் அடங்கிய வேதபுத்தகம்.) pp. 1253. *Madras Auxiliary Bible Society: Madras*, 1850. 4°. **3070. d. 26.**

This translation is that known as the "Union Bible."

—— [Another copy.] **3070. e. 7.**

The Old Testament [in the version of Fabricius] . . . with references, contents of the chapters and chronology, from the English . . . பழைய ஏற்பாடு. (*The New Testament [in Rhenius' version] . . . with contents of the chapters and chronology.) pp. 1302. *Madras Auxiliary Bible Society: Madras*, 1860. 4°. **3068. e. 10.**

The printer's note at the end bears the date 1861.

The Holy Bible . . . translated out of the original tongues into Tamil [on the basis of Fabricius' version, revised by H. Bower and others] . . . under the auspices of the British and Foreign Bible Society. (*சத்தியவேதம்.) pp. i. 1209. *Madras Auxiliary Bible Society: Madras*, 1877. 4°. **3070. g. 10.**

—— [Another edition.] pp. 951, 315. *Madras Auxiliary Bible Society: Madras*, 1883. 12°. **3070. ee. 2.**

The Holy Bible. In Tamil. The Old Testament, translated from the original by the Rev. J. P. Fabricius; the New Testament, by the Rev.

C. T. E. Rhenius, and revised by the Committee of the Madras Auxiliary Bible Society. [With the headings and chronology of the English version translated by M. Winslow.] (*சத்தியவேதம்.) pp. 1105, 388. *Madras Auxiliary Bible Society: Madras*, 1844. 8°. **3070. i. 1.**

A poetical version in Tamil of the Holy Scriptures. Part i. Genesis and Exodus xx. Edited by the Rev. C. C. Macarthur. திருவாக்குப்புராணம். pp. 200. *Jaffna*, 1866. 8°. **3070. dd. 17.**

Pp. 193-200 are specimen pages of a version of the Gospels and Acts.

ABRIDGMENTS AND SELECTIONS.

Historiæ e Scriptis Sacris Veteris et Novi Testamenti selectæ, in usum iuventutis Tamulicæ. (*சததிய வேததததின பிறதானசரிததிரஙகள.) Editio secunda. pp. 252. *Trankenbariae*, 1816. 8°. **14170. c. 10.**

Scripture Extracts ... வேதவாக்கியங்கள். Second edition. pp. 44. *American Mission Press: Jaffna*, 1844. 12°. **14170. b. 1.(33.)**

தினபோதம். [Dina-bōdham.] . . . The Daily Monitor: containing a text from Holy Scripture and a verse of sacred poetry for every morning and evening in the year. [Third edition.] pp. 324. *Jaffna Religious Tract Society: [Jaffna,]* 1849. 32°. **14170. a. 1.**

The first edition (1837) was edited by P. Percival, the second (1843) by L. Spaulding.

Chants. Consisting mostly of selections from the sacred Scriptures adapted to appropriate music. சங்கீதங்கள். *See* Hymnals. Tamil Hymns in English metre, *etc.* pp. 119-146. 1853. 8°. **14170. c. 5.(2.)**

ஃஃஃ சத்திய வேதப்பொழிப்பு. [Satya-vēda-porippu. A compendium of Scripture. Fourth edition.] 2 pts. pp. i. 339, 206. *Jaffna*, 1857. 16°. **14170. a. 14.**

வேத சரித்திரம். [Vēda-charitram. A translation by A. Blomstrand of Zahn's Biblische Geschichten. With catechism appended. Third edition.] 2 vols. *Tranquebar*, 1871-1873. 12°. **14170. b. 26, 27.**

The catechism is of the second edition.

OLD TESTAMENT.

Librorum Sacrorum Veteris Testamenti pars prima (*secunda—quarta) . . . editio secunda correctior. [Revised by J. P. Fabricius, from the version of Ziegenbalg and Schultze.] (*சததியவெதம) 4 pts. *Trangambariæ*, 1777-1796. 4°. **3068. g. 10.**

The Old Testament in Tamil. [Translated by Fabricius.] (*சத்தியவேத புஸ்தகம். பழைய ஏற்பாடு.) pp. 900. *Tranquebar*, 1893. 8°. **14170. c. 48.**

Contains only pt. i., the Historical Books.

The Old Testament in Tamil ... பழைய ஏற்பாடு. [Translated by J. P. Fabricius.] New edition. pp. i. 1568. *Tranquebar*, 1898. 8°. **14170. bb. 7.**

A reprint, as far as the historical books are concerned, of the edition of 1893.

Pentateuch.

The First Book of Moses called Genesis. [Ch. i.-ix., in English and Tamil, being a specimen of Rhenius' translation.] pp. 69. *Colombo Auxiliary Bible Society: Colombo*, 1819. 16°. **T. 2070.(1.)**

சத்தியவேதப் பழைய ஏற்பாட்டின் . . . ஆதியாகமம். [Genesis. Translated from the Vulgate by a Catholic missionary, with notes.] pp. 201. *Coimbatore*, 1899. 8°. **14170. cc. 7.**

Psalms.

[For editions of the Book of Psalms as contained in the Book of Common Prayer:] *See* Liturgies.—England, *Church of.*

Liber Psalmorum Davidis Regis et Prophetæ, ex originali textu in linguam damulicam versus opera & studio Benjamin Schultze. (*தாவீதென-திறவா எழுதிவைதத ஞானசசஙகிதஙகளுடைய பொஸ்ததகம) pp. iv. 255. *Tranquebariæ*, 1724. 12°. **3090. ccc. 6.**

தாவீதின் சங்கீதங்கள். Psalms. [The version of the Union Bible.] pp. 274. *Jaffna Auxiliary Bible Society: Jaffna*, 1861. 16°. **3089. aa. 27.**

சங்கீத புஸ்தகம். [Psalms. A revised version.] *See* below: *New Testament.* The Tamil Testament, *etc.* pp. 333-413. 1868. 12°. **3070. ee. 4.**

The Book of Psalms. சங்கீத புஸ்தகம். pp. 110. *See* below: *New Testament.* The New Testament, *etc.* pt. 2. 1887. 12°. **3070. de. 37.**

The Psalms of David, metrically arranged in Tamil by the Rev. J. Gillings. தாவீதின் சங்கீதங்கள். pp. v. 257. *Madras*, 1891. 12°. **3090. aaa. 14.**

BIBLE.

Psalms (*continued*).

Book of Psalms. [In Fabricius' version.] ஞான சங்கீதங்களின் புஸ்தகம். [Third edition.] pp. 242, iv. *Tranquebar*, 1898. 12°. **14170. a. 62.**

Proverbs.

சாலொமோனின் நீதிமொழிகள். Proverbs of Solomon. pp. 148. *American Bible Society: Jaffna*, 1845. 16°. **3068. a. 39.**

NEW TESTAMENT.

Novum Jesu Christi Testamentum, ex originali textu in linguam damulicam versum opera & studio Bartholomæi Ziegenbalgii & Joh. Ernesti Gründleri. Editio secunda. (*எசுககிறிஸததுநாதாானவா . . . வெதபொஸததகம) pp. xv. 1048. *Tranquebariæ*, 1722. 12°. **1410. g. 1.**

Het Nieuw Testament, ofte Alle de Boeken des Nieuwen Verbonds van onsen Heer Jesus Christus. Door Last van de Hooge Overheid deeses Eilands uit de oirspronglyke Grieksche Taal in de Tamulsche Spraak overgezet, en naar Kerken-order behoorlyk overzien. [Translated chiefly by Philippus de Melho. With preface in Dutch and Tamil by S. A. Brousveld and J. J. Fybrands.] (*புதிய ஏறபாடு) *Colombo*, 1759. 4°. **1411. k. 16.**

There is no continuous pagination. Each part is numbered by folios.

This translation was a revision of the preceding versions. Philippus Baldaeus had translated Matthew, and Adrianus de Mey the whole New Testament; and on the basis of these and the Tranquebar version Adolphus Cramer completed in 1740 his revised Matthew. Continuing this work, Johannes Philippus Wetzelius printed in 1742 a revised version of the other Gospels, and in 1750 a translation of the rest of the Testament as far as Ephes. iii. 6. In the latter work he was aided by de Melho. In 1757 de Melho was appointed, with Simon de Zilva, to complete this revision; and in 1759 the whole Testament as revised by him was published, after having been approved by a committee consisting of Frans Jansz, Pieter de Zilva, and J. J. Fybrands.

Besides the above-mentioned sources, there had been printed in 1739 at Colombo a version of the four Gospels by Willem Konijn, with a preface by J. P. Wetzelius (second edition 1780).

The Tamul New Testament of our Lord and Saviour Jesus Christ . . . புது ஏறபாடு. [In Fabricius' version. Third edition.] pp. v. 921. *Church Mission Press*: செனனபபடடணததில அசசு [*Madras*, 1824.] 8°. **1105. d. 1.**

—— [New Testament, comprising Gospels and Acts in Rhenius' version and the remainder in a reissue of Fabricius' version, with the title-page of the 1824 edition.] **1410. h. 3.**

—— [Another copy.] **1110. f. 16.**

° ° ° புதிய ஏற்பாடு. (*The New Testament.) [In Fabricius' version.] pp. 16, vii. 516. *Tranquebar*, 1878. 8°. **3068. dd. 24.**

The New Testament in Tamil [in Fabricius' version] . . . புதிய ஏற்பாடு . . . Revised edition. pp. vi. i. 560. *Tranquebar*, 1906. 8°. **14170. bbb. 9.**

The New Testament of our Lord and Saviour Jesus Christ, in the Tamil language . . . புதிய ஏற்பாடு. [Translated by C. T. E. Rhenius.] pp. 670. *Jaffna Auxiliary Bible Society: Jaffna*, 1843. 8°. **1106. c. 13.**

New Testament . . . புதிய ஏற்பாடு. [In Rhenius' version.] pp. 750. *Madras Auxiliary Bible Society: Madras*, 1857. 12°. **3070. ee. 1.**

The New Testament . . . with references, contents of the chapters and chronology, from the English . . . புதிய ஏற்பாடு. [In Rhenius' version.] pp. 563. *Madras Auxiliary Bible Society: Madras*, 1859. 8°. **3070. g. 6.**

The New Testament . . . translated into Tamil from the original Greek . . . புதிய ஏற்பாடு. [A new revision, by H. Bower and others. Second edition.] pp. i. 437. *Madras Auxiliary Bible Society: Madras*, 1867. 8°. **3070. h. 40.**

The Tamil Testament and Psalms . . . புதிய ஏற்பாடு. [The same recension.] pp. 413. *Madras Auxiliary Bible Society: Madras*, 1868. 12°. **3070. ee. 4.**

The New Testament . . . translated into Tamil from the original Greek. [The same recension.] . . . புதிய ஏற்பாடு. (*The New Testament and Psalms.) pp. 476, 110. *Madras Auxiliary Bible Society: Madras*, 1887. 12°. **3070. de. 37.**

The New Testament of our Lord Jesus-Christ. Translated into Tamil from the Latin Vulgate with annotations by the Rev. J. B. Trincal, of the Society of Jesus, and carefully revised by several Fathers of the same Society. (*யேசுக்கிறீஸ்துநாதருடைய பரிசுத்த புதிய ஏற்பாடு.) Third & revised edition. pp. i. i. 703. *Trichinopoly*, 1906. 8°. **14170. cc. 10.**

BIBLE (*continued*).

Gospels and Acts.

Quatuor Evangelia et Acta Apostolorum, ex originali textu in linguam damulicam versa, in usum gentis malabaricæ. Opera & studio Barth. Ziegenbalg, & Jo. Ern. Grundler. (*எசுகதிரீஷதது நாதாானவா . . . அஞசுவெதபொஷதநகமல.) pp. v. 494. *Tranquebaræ,* 1714. 4°. **2. a. 4.**

A duplicate of pt. v. of the complete Tamil Bible catalogued above, with a Latin title-page.

Gospels.

சுவிசேஷ விரித்துரை. [Suvișēsha-viritt'-urai, *i.e.* the "Explicação dos Evangelhos Dominicaes e Festivaes" of Jacome Gonçalves. Being the texts from the Gospels for the Christian Year with Gonçalves' expositions.] pp. vii. 301, iii. ii. யாழ்ப்பாணம் ௧௮௯௧ [*Jaffna,* 1891.] 8°. **14170. c. 31.**

[*Harmonies.*] Harmony of the Gospels (†follows almost exclusively the chronological order of Greswell). சுவிசேஷ சம்பந்த அட்டவணை. [By A. F. Caemmerer.] pp. 44. *Nagercoil,* 1854. 12°. **14170. b. 14.(2.)**

[*Matthew.*] Evangelium Matthaei de Domini Nostri Jesv Christi. [In Ziegenbalg and Gründler's version.] . . . Editio tertia. (*மததேயி யெனபவனொழுதிவைதத சுவிசேஷததாகமம.) pp. 110, ii. *Trangambariae,* 1739. 12°. **Grenville 20,059.**

—— Het Heylige Evangelium onzes Heeren en Zaligmakers Jesu Christi, na de Beschryvinge van . . . Mattheus, uyt de oorspronkelyke Griekse, in de mallabaarse Tale overgebragt [by Adolphus Cramer ?], en behoorlyk na Kerken ordre gerevideert. (* மத்தெவுசு எழுதிவைத்த . . . யெசுஸகிறிஸத்துஸவுடைய சுத்தமானசுவிசெஷம்.) ff. ii. 59. *Colombo,* 1741. 4°. **466. b. 16.**

—— A brief commentary on the Gospel according to Saint Matthew. [With the text of Fabricius.] பரி. மத்தேயு எழுதின சுவிசேஷத்தின் சுருக்க வியாக்கியானம் . . . [by] Rev. K. Ihlefeld, *etc.* pp. v. 197. *Tranquebar,* 1891. 8°. **14170. c. 37.(1.)**

BIBLE.

Gospels (*continued*).

—— Sermon on the Mount (A paraphrase) . . . இயேசுநாதர் மலையின்மேற் சொன்ன பிரசங்கத்தின் விஸதரிப்பு. Third edition. pp. 24. *Jaffna,* 1843. 12°. **14170. b. 1.(40.)**

—— Our Blessed Lord's Sermon on the Mount . . . in English . . . in Tamil . . . in Malayâ̱lam . . . in Kanarese . . . and in Telugu; in the Anglo-Indian character, with a vocabulary, minute grammatical praxis and inflexional tables; by the Rev. G. U. Pope. pp. ii. iv. 38, 84, xxii. *Madras,* 1860. 8°. **3068. cc. 11.**

—— Specimens of South-Indian Dialects, consisting of versions of the Parable of the Sower . . . Collected by A. C. Burnell. No. 4. In the dialect of Tami̱l spoken at Tanjore, from the Vulgate. pp. 12. *Tranquebar,* 1876. 16°. **C. 40. b. 38.**

[*Mark.*] *See* Ihlefeld (K. A. A.). A brief Commentary on the Gospel according to Saint Mark, *etc.* 1893. 8°. **14170. c. 37.(2.)**

—— St. Mark's Gospel. மாற்கு என்பவர் எழுதின சுவிசேஷம். [In Rhenius' version.] pp. 125. *Madras Auxiliary Bible Society: Madras,* 1859. 16°. **3068. a. 35.**

—— St. Mark's Gospel. [In Fabricius' version.] மாற்கு எழுதின சுவிசேஷம். pp. 84. *Tranquebar,* 1893. 16°. **14170. a. 54.(1.)**

[*Luke.*] *See* Ihlefeld (K. A. A.). A brief Commentary on the Gospel according to St. Luke, *etc.* 1896. 8°. **14170. c. 37.(3.)**

—— லூக்கா என்பவன் எழுதின சுவிசேஷம். Luke's Gospel. [In the text of the 1850 "Union Bible."] pp. 169. *Manepy,* 1862. 12°. **3068. a. 11.**

—— The Gospel of Luke. லூக்கா எழுதின சுவிசேஷம். [In English and Tamil, the latter in the same text as the revised Bible of 1877.] pp. 137, 137. *Madras Auxiliary Bible Society: Madras,* 1884. 16°. **3070. aa. 62.**

BIBLE.

Gospels (*continued*).

—— St. Luke's Gospel. [In Fabricius' version.] லூக்கா எழுதின சுவிசேஷம். pp. 148. *Tranquebar*, 1900. 16°. 14170. a. 54.(2.)

[*John.*] St. John's Gospel. [In Fabricius' version.] யோவான் எழுதின சுவிசேஷம். pp. 107. *Tranquebar*, 1901. 12°. 14170. a. 54.(3.)

Acts.

The Acts of the Apostles. [In Fabricius' version.] அப்போஸ்தலர் நடபடிகள். pp. 132. *Tranquebar*, 1905. 16°. 14170. a. 54.(4.)

Epistles.

See WINKEL (E.). A brief Commentary . . . on St. Paul's Epistle to the Galatians. 1891. 8°. 14170. c. 36.

St. Paul's Epistle to the Ephesians, with introduction and notes explanatory and practical, by the Rev. J. Lazarus. (அப்போஸ்தலனாகிய பவுல் எபேசியருக்கு எழுதின நிருபமும் . . . குறிப்புகளும்) pp. xxiii. 211 ; 1 *plate*. *Madras*, 1903. 12°. 14170. bbb. 2.

CONCORDANCES.

Concordance to the Tamil New Testament. புதிய ஏற்பாட்டின் ஒத்த வாக்கிய அகராதி. [Compiled by J. Gritton, and revised by A. Dibb and D. Fenn.] pp. vii. 1060. *Palamcottah*, 1878. 4°. 3104. aaa. 8.

APPENDIX.

[*Complete Bibles.*] *See* ARUL-APPAN (J. C.). The Scripture Mirror, or Index of the Bible, *etc.* 1846. 12°. 14170. b. 25.

—— *See* BALAVENDRAM (R.). A short Bible History, *etc.* 1887. 8°. 14170. b. 55.

—— *See* BOGATZKY (C. H. VON). பரமண்டலங்களிலதங்கள . . . ஆபறணப்பெட்டி [The Golden Treasury.] [1800.] 8°. 14170. c. 26.

—— —— Golden Treasury. 1876-1878. 8°. 14170. c. 1.

—— *See* MORTIMER (F. L.), *Mrs.* The Peep of Day, *etc.* 1852. 12°. 14170. b. 32.

BIBLE.

APPENDIX (*continued*).

—— *See* PACHECO (G.). தேவப்பிரஜையின் திருக்கதை. [Dēva-prajaiyin tiru-kathai.] [1880-1886.] 8°. 14170. bb. 2.

—— The Bible and Ancient Monuments. அருளாகமமும் ஆதிசின்னங்களும். (†Based chiefly on "Recent Archæology and the Bible," by Professor Nicol.) pp. i. 110. *Religious Tract and Book Society: Madras*, 1901. 12°. 14171. a. 45.

[*Old Testament.*] (†பிள்ளைகளிடத்திற்கேட்கும் கேள்விகள்.) [Questions on the Pentateuch for children.] vol. i. pp. 270. [*n.d.*] 12°. 14170. b. 22.

Wanting title-page. Apparently a part of an uncompleted series.

[*New Testament.*] *See* SCHULTZE (B.). Historia Passionis Jesu Christi, *etc.* 1723. 16°. 14170. a. 24.

—— *See* WARD (F. D. W.). Practical Expositions of the Parables of Christ, and of the briefer Similes, employed by the Divine Teacher, *etc.* 1844. 12°. 14170. b. 47.

—— The Last Judgment . . . a description, taken from different parts of the word of God, of the solemnities of the last Judgment . . . நியாயத்தீர்ப்பு. Second edition. 1844. 12°. *See* SPAULDING (L.). 14170. b. 1.(39.)

—— An Analysis of the New Testament . . . புதியேற்பாட்டு ஆகமங்களின் பொருளடக்கம். [Compiled by A. F. Caemmerer, on the model of the work of W. H. Pinnock.] 2 pts. pp. ii. 402, 67. *Palamcottah*, 1854-1855. 12°. 14170. b. 44.

—— Questions in New Testament History. Tentative edition. புதியேற்பாட்டு வினாவிடை. pp. 59. *South India Christian School Book Society: Madras*, 1856. 12°. 14170. b. 4.

BLOMSTRAND (ANDERS). *See* BIBLE.—*Abridgments and Selections.* வேத சரித்திரம். [Vēda-charitram. A translation by Blomstrand of Jahn's Biblische Geschichten.] 1871-1873. 12°. 14170. b. 26, 27.

BLOMSTRAND (Anders) (*continued*). *See* Evangelical Lutheran Church. Concordia, *etc.* [Translated by Blomstrand.] 1872-1880. 8°. **14170. c. 2.**

—— *See* Graul (K. F. L.). ∘ ∘ ∘ போதக வித்தியாசம். [Bōdhaka-vittiyāṣam. Translated by Blomstrand.] 1870. 12°. **14170. b. 3.**

—— —— 1882. 12°. **14170. b. 31.**

—— *See* Luther (M.). மார்த்தின் லுத்தர் . . . வினு விடைகள். [Martin Luther enbavarin ñā-nōpadēṣa-kuripp'-idattai vistarikkum vinā-vidai-gaḷ. Revised by Blomstrand.] 1872. 12°. **14170. b. 20.**

—— திருச்சபைசரித்திரம். [Tiru-sabhai-charitram. A history of the Christian Church, based chiefly upon that of J. H. Kurtz.] 2 vols. *Tranquebar*, 1867-1869. 8°. **14170. c. 13, 14.**

BOGATZKY (Carl Heinrich von). பரமணடலஙகளிலதஙகள பொககிஷம உணடெணடிருக்கிற பராபரனுடையபிளளைகளின ஆபறணபபெட்டி [The Golden Treasury. Comprising texts, hymns, and prayers for every day in the year. Translated into Tamil by Daniel Pillai.] pp. 732. வேபபேரியில தஅா [*Vepery*, 1800.] 8°. **14170. c. 26.**

—— Golden Treasury . . . New edition [revised by J. M. N. Schwarz] . . . ஞானாபரணப்பெட்டி. 2 pts. pp. iv. 365, 372. *Tranquebar*, 1876-1878. 8°. **14170. c. 1.**

BONAVIA (Emanuel). Dr. Bonavia's Date Palm in India, chapters 11 and 12. இந்தியாவிலே ஈச்சமரம் பயிராதல் ௲ [Signed by C. D. Macleane as official translator.] pp. 16. *Madras*, [1894 ?] 8°. **14170. i. 50.**

BONJEAN (Christophe), *Roman Catholic Archbishop of Colombo*. *See* Antōnis (*V.S., Don* J.). ∘ ∘ ∘ அர்ச். அன்னம்மாள் . . . கும்மி. [A *kummi* poem by Don J. Antōnis founded on a sermon by C. Bonjean.] 1885. 12°. **14170. b. 34.(2.)**

—— மகாகனம்பொருந்திய கிறிஸ்தோப்பர் போஞ்சின் அதிமேற்றிராணி ஆண்டவரவர்கள் தேகவியோகத்தின்பேரிலெபற்றிய பிரலாபகவிதை. Elegics on the death of his Grace the Archbishop of Colombo. pp. 14. *Jaffna*, 1892. 8°. **14170. c. 24.(6.)**

BONNAND (Clément), *Roman Catholic Bishop of Drusipara*. இலத்தினிலக்கணநூற்சுருக்கம். [I-lattīn-ilakkaṇa-nūṟ-ṣurukkam. A short Latin Grammar.] pp. 3, 224, iii. புதுவை தஅாசமடு [*Pondicherry*, 1845.] 12°. **14172. e. 1.**

BOWER (Henry). *See* Bible.—*Complete Bibles*. The Holy Bible . . . [revised by H. Bower], *etc.* 1877. 4°. **3070. g. 10.**

—— —— 1883. 12°. **3070. ee. 2.**

—— *See* Bible.—*New Testament*. The New Testament, *etc.* [A new revision, by H. Bower, *etc.*] 1867. 8°. **3070. h. 40.**

—— *See* Bible.—*New Testament*. The New Testament . . . [as revised by H. Bower], *etc.* 1887. 12°. **3070. de. 37.**

—— *See* Mahā-bhāratam. The Bhagavad-gita . . . translated into English and Tamil by . . . H. Bower. 1889. 8°. **14065. c. 44.**

—— *See* Pavaṇandi. Introduction to the Nannul . . . By . . . H. Bower. 1876. 16°. **14172. h. 37.**

—— A Biblical and Theological Dictionary, *etc.* (*வேத அகராதி.) pp. iv. 556. *Madras*, 1841. 8°. **14170. c. 15.**

The English equivalent is given to each Tamil heading.

—— Caste as it exists among Hindus and Native Christians. [With an appendix containing passages on caste from the Ṛig-vēda in Sanskrit and Tamil.] (*சாதி வித்தியாச விளக்கம்.) pp. viii. 155. *Madras*, 1857. 12°. **14170. b. 54.**

—— History of Christianity in India. (*கிறிஸ்துமார்க்கம் இந்துதேசத்தில் விருத்தியான சரித்திரம்.) pp. x. i. i. 328. *Madras*, 1879. 12°. **14170. b. 2.**

—— Prasanga Ratnávali. Four series of sermons on Scripture subjects, with an introduction on the character and office of the Christian preacher. (*பிரசங்க ரத்நாவளி.) pp. xxxv. 252. *Madras*, 1875. 12°. **14170. b. 40.**

—— A Vocabulary, English and Tamil, comprehending terms, relating to Christian theology, and the religion, philosophy, and mythology, of the Hindus (†second part) . . . பதமஞ்சரி. pp. i. 100. *Madras*, 1852. 8°. **14170. c. 18.**

BRĀHMA SAMĀJ. வேதாந்தசூரியோதயம் ஃ (Vedhanta Sooryothaiah, or An Appeal to the Citizens of Coimbatore, &c. By the members of the Coimbatore Brahmo Samaj.) pp. 18, 44, 24. *Coimbatore,* 1882. 16°. **14170. d. 19.**

—— வேதம். [Vēdam. A tract asserting the right of non-brahmans to chant the Vedas, issued by the Southern Brāhma Samāj.] pp. 25. *Madras,* 1894. 12°. **14170. d. 44.**

BRAHMA-TANTRA-SVATANTRA SVĀMI, *Tṛutīya.* குருபரம்பராப்ரபாவம் [Guru-paramparā-prabhāvam. A prose history of the leaders of the Śrī-vaishṇava church, beginning with the Āṟvārs. With appended summaries, *etc.* Edited by Tirukuḍandai Taṭṭai Kṛushṇam-āchāryar.] pp. ii. 167. பிங்கள [*Madras,* 1857.] 8°. **14170. e. 8.**

—— ∘ ∘ ∘ குருபரம்பராப்ரபாவம். [Guru-paramparā-prabhāvam. Edited by Kiḍāmbi Raṅgāchārya Svāmi.] pp. i. 159. சென்னபட்டணம் விரோதி [*Madras,* 1890.] 8°. **14170. e. 37.**

BREN (Robert). The Test of Religions, or Hinduism and Christianity contrasted and examined. The former . . . proved to be erroneous, and the latter . . . shown to be from God. (*சமயபரீட்சை) pp. ii. 463. *Jaffna,* 1858. 12°. **14170. b. 38.**

BRISARD (Benoît). காணாவிஷக்கடிக்கு மருந்து. [Kāṇā-visha-kaḍikku marundu. A Catholic tract against Protestantism.] pp. 224. புதுவை ௲அ௱௬௯ [*Pondicherry,* 1869.] 16°. **14170. a. 31.**

—— கரும்பாம்பின் விஷக்கடிக்கு மருந்து. [Karum-bāmbin visha-kaḍikku marundu. A controversial work against Protestantism.] pp. 66, ii. புதுவை ௲அ௱௬அ [*Pondicherry,* 1868.] 16°. **14170. a. 34.(2.)**

—— கரும்பாம்பின் விஷக் கடிக்குத்தயிலம். [Karum-bāmbin visha-kaḍikku tailam. A controversial work against Protestantism.] pp. iv. 92. புதுவை ௲அ௱௬அ [*Pondicherry,* 1868.] 16°. **14170. a. 34.(6.)**

BRITO (Christopher). ஒன்பதாம் பத்திநாத பாப்பரசர் சரித்திரம். [Life of Pope Pius IX.] pp. 111. யாழ்ப்பாணம் [*Jaffna,*] 1892. 8°. **14170. c. 44.**

BRONSVELD (Sigisbert Abrahamsz). See Bible.—*New Testament.* Het Nieuw Testament, *etc.* [With preface by S. Bronsveld and J. J. Fybrands.] 1759. 4°. **1411. k. 16.**

—— *See* Heidelberg Catechism. Catechismus, ofte Onderweyzing in de Christelicke Leere . . . overgezet . . . door S. A. Bronsveld. 1754. 8°. **14170. b. 62.**

—— —— 1769. 8°. **14170. b. 63.**

—— Kort Begryp der Christelyke Religie, voor die zig willen begeven tot des Heeren heilig Avondmaal; ten dienste der Kerken en Schoolen, in de Tamulsche Spraak overgezet . . . door Sigisbertus Abrahamsz Bronsveld. (*கிறிஸ்தவர்களுடைய் வெதபபடி பதினையின சுருககமானதொகை.) pp. xii. 22. *Colombo,* 1754. 12°. **14170. b. 15.**

—— Tamulsch Kinder-Catechismus . . . Ten dienste der Schoolen in een vervolg geschikt en uitgegeven door Sigisb : Abrah : Bronsveld . . . nu met den derde Druk, verbeetert en van veele fouten gezuyvert door M. I. Ondaatje. (*தமிடபாஷையிற சிறுபிளளைககதெகிஸமு) pp. iv. 56. *Colombo,* ௲எ௱அ௰அ [1788.] 12°. **14170. a. 36.**

BROTHERTON (Thomas). *See* Bible.—*Complete Bibles.* The Holy Bible . . . revised [by T. Brotherton,] *etc.* 1850. 4°. **3070. d. 26.**

—— —— [Another copy.] **3070. e. 7.**

—— *See* Pavaṇandi. Grammatica Tamuliensis, or An English version of the . . . Nunnool . . . revised . . . by . . . T. Brotherton. 1848-1851. 8°. **14172. f. 10.**

—— —— [Another copy.] **14172. f. 20.**

BUDDHA. *See* Gautama.

BUDDHA-MITRAN, *Prince of Ponbaṯṯi.* ∘ ∘ ∘ வீரசோழியம். [Vīra-ṣōṟiyam. A Tamil grammar composed under Vīra-ṣōṟan or Kulōttuṅga I (reigned between 1064 and 1113 A.D.). With a commentary by Perun-dēvanār. Edited by Ṣ. V. Dāmōdaram Piḷḷai.] pp. xxxvi. 192, ii. சென்னபட்டணம் விசு [*Madras,* 1881.] 8°. **14172. f. 12.**

—— [Another edition.] pp. xxxvi. 200. சென்னை [*Madras,*] 1895. 8°. **14172. e. 21.**

BUKHĀRĪ, *Saiyid.* *See* Pavāni Pulavar.

BULWER, afterwards **BULWER LYTTON** (Edward George Earle Lytton), *Baron Lytton*. *See* Sundaram Piḷḷai, *Ā.P.* மனோன்மணீயம். (Manônmanîyam. A play . . . [based on "The Secret Way," one of Lytton's "Lost Tales of Miletus."]) 1891. 8°. **14170. l. 31.**

BUNYAN (John). The Pilgrim's Progress from this World to that which is to come: delivered under the similitude of a Dream . . . ஒருபரதேசி இநதலோகததைவிடடுமேறுமைககு நடநதேறினது சொறபனம் ௲ [English and Tamil text of part i.] pp. 137. *Vepery*, 1793. 4°. **14170. cc. 1.**

—— The Pilgrim's Progress . . . பரதேசி மோட்சபிரயாணம். [Translated by L. Spaulding.] 2 pts. pp. 361, ix. யாழ்ப்பாணம் ௲அ௱௫௩ [*Jaffna*, 1853.] 12°. **14170. b. 19.**

BURNELL (Arthur Coke). *See* Beschi (C. G. E.). Clavis Humaniorum Litterarum sublimioris Tamulici Idiomatis . . . Printed for [and with a prefatory note by] A. Burnell. 1876. 8°. **14172. f. 17.**

—— *See* Bible.—New Testament.—*Gospels*. [*Matthew*.] Specimens of South-Indian Dialects . . . Collected by A. C. Burnell, *etc.* 1876. 16°. **C. 40. b. 38.**

BUTLER (James), *R. C. Archbishop of Cashel*. ஞான உபதேசம் [Ñāna-upadēsam. A Roman Catholic catechism for the use of Tamils, slightly modified from Butler's "Catechism for the Instruction of Children." Translated by Māṇikkam Rāy'-appa Svāmi. Preceded by Morning and Evening Prayers, *etc.*] pp. 110. *Madras*, 1839. 16°. **14170. a. 6.**

BUTTERWORTH (Alan). *See* Madras, *Government of*. A collection of the inscriptions . . . in the Nellore district. Made by A. Butterworth . . . and V. Venugopaul Chetty. 1905. 8°. **14058. c. 11.**

C. (M.). *See* Collins (M.).

CAEMMERER (Augustus Frederick). *See* Bible.—New Testament.—*Gospels*. [*Harmonies*.] Harmony of the Gospels, *etc.* [By Caemmerer.] 1854. 12°. **14170. b. 14.(2.)**

—— *See* Bible.—*Appendix*. [*New Testament*.] An Analysis of the New Testament, *etc.* [Compiled by Caemmerer.] 1854. 12°. **14170. b. 44.**

CAEMMERER (Augustus Frederick) (*continued*). வேதாகமத்தில் கிறிஸ்துநாதருக்கிடப்பட்டிருக்கிற நாமங்களை . . . உணர்த்திக்காட்டிய செபத்தியானங்கள். [Kiristu-nāthar-nāmangaḷ. The titles of Christ, with explanations and prayers.] pp. 24. *Palamcottah*, 1854. 12°. **14170. b. 14.(3.)**

CANKERGOLD. Mr. Cankergold. சொன்னராயனுக்கும் சருவலோக இராசனுக்கும் உண்டான வியாச்சியம். pp. 36. *Jaffna*, 1857. 16°. **14170. a. 33.(4.)**

No. 2 of the New Series of the Jaffna Religious Tract Society.

CARROLL (D.), also known as D. C. Visva-nātha Piḷḷai. சுப்பிரதீபம். [Ṣubhra-dīpam. A reply to the attacks made by the Ṣaivas of Jaffna upon Christianity.] pp. viii. 60. *Jaffna*, 1857. 12°. **14170. b. 12.(2.)**

CASIE CHITTY (S.). *See* Chitty (S. C.).

CASTE. *See* Madras, *City of*. Minute of the Madras Missionary Conference . . . on . . . Caste, *etc.* 1850. 8°. **14170. c. 22.**

CATECHISM. *See* Bronsveld (S. A.). Tamulsch Kinder-Catechismus, *etc.* [1788.] 12°. **14170. a. 36.**

—— [For the Catechism of the Church of England:] *See* England, *Church of*.

—— [For editions of the Heidelberg Catechism:] *See* Heidelberg Catechism.

—— [For the Catechismus of Martin Luther:] *See* Luther (M.).

—— [For the Wesleyan Methodist Catechism:] *See* Wesleyan Methodists.

—— Ordo Salutis Methodo Catechetica, pro diverso Catechumenorum captu trifaria forma exhibitus, & notis quibusdam . . . instructus. (ரெக்ஷ சித்துதவின [*sic*] ஒழுங்கு) pp. 72. *Trangambariæ*, 1730. 16°. **14170. a. 29.**

This is different from the "Heilsordnung" (இரட்சிப்பின் ஒழுக்கம்) *by Ziegenbalg, which also exists in Portuguese under the title* A Ordem da Salvaçaõ ou A Doutrina Christaã (*Tranquebar*, 1712, 16°).

—— Tamil and English First Catechism . . . வேதோபதேச முதல் வினாவிடை. pp. 36. *Madras*, 1860. 16°. **14170. a. 16.**

—— Tamil First Catechism. முதலாம் வேதோபதேச வினாவிடை. pp. 16. *Madras*, 1865. 16°. **14170. a. 33.(6.)**

CATECHISM (*continued*). (†சின்ன கேள்வி மறு-மொழியின் விஸ்தாரம்.) [Ṣinna-kēḷvi-maṟumoḻiyin vistāram. An enlargement of the Lesser Catechism.] pp. 64. [*Jaffna, n.d.*] 12°. 14170. b. 16.(3.)
No title-page.

—— [For Butler's Catechism:] *See* BUTLER (J).

—— [For editions of the Roman Catechism included in devotional collections:] *See* LITURGIES.—Rome, *Church of.*

—— வாலர் பொக்கிஷம். [Vālar-pokkisham. Morning and evening prayers of the Roman Church, service for hearing the Mass, and the shorter and longer Catechisms.] pp. 266; 6 *plates.* புதுவை தூ அாசுக [*Pondicherry,* 1861.] 32°. 14170. a. 32.

—— ○ ○ ○ ஞானஉபதேசச் சுருக்கம். [Ñāna-upadēṣa-churukkam. A Larger Catechism for the use of Tamil Catholics, preceded by the Morning and Evening Prayers.] pp. ii. 126. புதுவை தூஅசுக [*Pondicherry,* 1861.] 16°. 14170. a. 23.

—— ○ ○ ○ சுகிர்தமந்திரங்களும் ஞானோபதேசக் குறிப்பிடமும் [Ñānōpadēṣa-kuṟipp'-iḍam. The Shorter Catechism for the use of Tamil Catholics, preceded by the Morning and Evening Prayers.] pp. 34; 1 *plate.* புதுவை தூ அாசுரு [*Pondicherry,* 1865.] 16°. 14170. a. 34.(5.)

—— படங்களால் விளக்கப்பட்ட ஞான உபதேசம். [Ñāna-upadēṣam. The Roman Catholic Catechism illustrated by pictures. Text only.] pp. 21. புதுவை [*Pondicherry,* 1863 ?] 12°. 14170. b. 34.(1.)

CATHOLIC SCHOOLS. First Book of Lessons for the use of Catholic Schools. [In English, Sinhalese, and Tamil.] pp. 21. *Colombo,* 1876. 8°. 14165. l. 4.(1.)

CAVELLY VENKATA RAMASAWMY. *See* VEṄKAṬA-RĀMA-SVĀMI, *K.*

CEYLON. இலங்கைப் பூமிசாஸ்திரம். [Laṅkai-bhūmi-ṣāstram. A geography of Ceylon for Roman Catholic schools.] pp. 96. யாழ்ப்பாணம் [*Jaffna,*] 1891. 12°. 14172. h. 68.(2.)

—— *Department of Public Instruction.* Extracts from the Code for Aided Schools, 1892 . . . புது ஒழுங்குச் சட்டம், 1892. [Signed by J. B. Cull.] pp. 24. *Colombo,* 1892. 8°. 14172. hh. 6.

CEYLON (*continued*). [Another edition.] pp. 24. *Colombo,* 1893. 8°. 14172. hh. 7.

—— *Province of Jaffna.* [For the Dēṣa-vaṟamai of the Province of Jaffna:] *See* JAFFNA, *Province of.*

—— *Railways.* Ceylon Government Railways. இலங்கை அரசாட்சியாரின் றெயில்வே. [The Rules and Regulations of the Ceylon Government Railways, in force since January 13th, 1892. Translated from the English by Samuel Crossett.] pp. 111. *Colombo,* 1892. 12°. 14172. i. 15.

CEYLON CATHOLIC ALMANACK. *See* EPHEMERIDES.

CHAITANYA. *See* ṢIṢIRA-KUMĀRA GHŌSHA. ஸ்ரீ க்ருஷ்ண சைதன்ய . . . சரித்திரம் ஆ (Sri Krishna Chaitanya: His Life and Teachings, *etc.*) 1902. 8°. 14170. ee. 51.

CHĀMA-RASA. [For the Prabhu-liṅga-līlai of Ṣiva-prakāṣar, adapted from Chāma-rasa's Kanarese poem of the same name:] *See* ṢIVA-PRAKĀṢA DĒṢIKAR.

CHANDLER (JOHN SCUDDER). *See* HYMNALS. Tamil Christian Lyrics . . . Enlarged and edited . . . by . . . J. S. Chandler. 1902. 12°. 14170. b. 30.

CHANDRA-ṢEKHAR, *Tañjai Ṣ.* சுதேச வைத்தியரத்னம். (The Swadesa Vaidyaratnam, or Common Medical Plants of India, by S. Chandrasegar.) pp. xii. 156. *Tanjore,* 1906. 12°. 14171. g. 7.

CHANDRA-ṢEKHARA KAVI-RĀJA PAṆḌITAR, *Tillaiyambūr.* ○ ○ ○ வருஷாதி நூற் சித்தாந்த விளக்கமும் . . . அறுபதுவருஷபலனும். [Varshādi-nūṟ-siddhānta-viḷakkam. A work on astrology. Followed by the Aṟu-badu-varsha-phalan, ascribed to Iḍai-kāḍar.] pp. viii. 246. சென்னபுரி [*Madras,* 1875.] 16°. 14171. f. 2.

CHANDRA-ṢEKHARA SVĀMI, *disciple of Govinda.* வேதாந்தசாரம். [Vēdānta-sāram. A catechism of the Vedanta.] pp. 114. [*Madras,*] 1862. 8°. 14170. e. 3.
Printed on pink and yellow paper.

CHARBONNAUX (ÉTIENNE-LOUIS), *Roman Catholic Bishop of Jasso.* கன்னியரநுசாரம். [Kanniyar-anusāram. Rules and prayers for nuns in the province of Mysore.] pp. 80. புதுவை தூ அாசுரு [*Pondicherry,* 1865.] 16°. 14170. a. 34.(4.)

CHAUCER (Geoffrey). The Canterbury Tales. Chaucer's Life and the Clerk's Tale, or The Tale of Crisild the Chaste. Tamil translation. [By] M. S. Natesa Aiyar. (*காண்டர்பரிக் கதைகள் சாஸரின் சரித்திரமும் . . . பண்டிதன் கதை எனப்படும் கற்பிற் சிறந்த கிரிசில்டின் கதையும்.*) pp. ix. 58. *Madras*, 1904. 12°. **14171. d. 1.(2.)**

CHĒDI-RĀYAR. [For the hymns of this author contained in the Tiruv-iṣai-pā :] *See* Tiru-muṟai.

CHĒKKIṞĀR. *See* Ṣekkiṟār.

CHELLAIYĀ. *See* Ṣell'-aiyā.

CHELVAKESAVARAYA. *See* Ṣelva-kēṣava-rāya.

CHĒNDANĀR. *See* Ṣendanār.

CHENNAI SENDAMILURAI SANGHAM. *See* Academies, *etc.* — Madras. — *Ṣennai-ṣen-damiṟ-urai-saṅgham.*

CHEYYAPPA. *See* Ṣeyy'-appa.

CHIDAMBARA KAVI-RĀYAR, *of Tinnevelli.* *உசிதசூடாமணி நிகண்டு.* († "Oositha Soodamani Nigandu" [*i.e.* Uchita-chūḍāmaṇi-nighaṇṭu] . . . a Suitable Coronal-Gem like Vocabulary of Simile, History, &c., of Gods, men &c. in verse . . . a *Vade Mecum* to the Puranas, Itigasas, and Kavias.) [Edited with notes by C. Malaiya Gauṇḍar, Ṣ. Naṭēṣa Piḷḷai, and Ṣ. Aiyāvu Piḷḷai.] pp. vii. i. iv. 104. *Coimbatore*, 1903. 12°. **14172. ee. 10.**

CHIDAMBARAM. *சிதம்பர மஹாத்மியம்* [Chidambara-māhātmyam. An account of the sacred legends of the Ṣaiva sanctuary at Chidambaram. Translated from the Sanskrit by Chidambaram Aṇṇā-sāmi Aiyar. Second edition.] pp. 86. *நடுக்காவேரி ஹேவிளம்பி* [*Nadukkaveri*, 1897.] 8°. **14170. ee. 11.**

Pp. 81-84 *are wanting.*

—— *சிதம்பரத்தில் வேதபாராயணம்.* [Chidambarattil vēda-pārāyaṇam. An appeal for funds to maintain Vedic studies in Chidambaram.] pp. 8. *சிதம்பரம்* [*Chidambaram,*] 1890. 16°. **14170. d. 31.(1.)**

CHIDAMBARAM PIḶḶAI, *Māvaḍi.* *See* Mut-tamiṟ-kavi-rāyar. ∘ ∘ ∘ *சுசீந்திர ஸ்தல புராணம்.* [Ṣuchīndra-sthala-purāṇam. Edited by Chidambaram.] 1894. 8°. **14170. e. 58.**

CHIDAMBARAM PIḶḶAI, *Māvaḍi* (*continued*). *See* Sundara Svāmi. ∘ ∘ ∘ *நிஜானந்தவிலாசம்.* [Nijānanda-vilāsam. Edited by Chidambaram.] 1904. 8°. **14170. eee. 9.**

CHIDAMBARA MUNIVAR, *Kāñchipuram.* ∘ ∘ ∘ *க்ஷேத்திரக்கோவைப்பிள்ளைத்தமிழ்.* [Subrahmaṇya-kaḍavuḷ-kshētra-kōvai-piḷḷai-tamiṟ. Hymns on the sanctuaries of Subrahmaṇya, in *piḷḷai-tamiṟ* style.] pp. 27. *See* Sambandha-ṣaraṇālaya-svāmi. *கந்தபுராணச்சுருக்கம்.* [Kanda-purāṇa-churukkam.] [1906.] 8°. **14170. eee. 10.**

CHIDAMBARA-NĀTHA KAVI-RĀJAR, *Kallaḍai-kuṟichi.* *See* Kamban. ∘ ∘ ∘ *ஸ்ரீமத்கம்பராமாயணம் ௵* [Kamba-rāmāyaṇam. Book v. Edited by Chidambara-nātha.] [1870.] 8°. **14172. c. 4.**

CHIDAMBARA-NĀTHA MUNIVAR, *Ilakkaṇam, of Pillaiyarpalayam, Conjevaram.* *See* Umā-pati Ṣivāchāryar. ∘ ∘ ∘ *சிவப்பிரகாசம் ௵* [Siddhāntāshṭakam. Comprising the Ṣiva-prakāṣam, *etc.*, with commentaries founded upon those of Chidambara-nāthar and others.] [1895.] 12°. **14170. d. 37.**

—— *See* Umā-pati Ṣivāchāryar. *சிவப்பிரகாசம்.* [Siddhāntāshṭakam, viz. Ṣiva-prakāṣam, with commentary of Chidambara-nāthar, *etc.*] 1897. 8°. [*Mey-kaṇḍa-ṣāttiram.*] **14170. ff. 3.**

—— ∘ ∘ ∘ *திருப்பாதிரிப் புலியூர்ப் புராணம்.* [Tirupādiri-puliyūr-purāṇam. The sacred legend of the Ṣaiva shrine at Tirupapuliyur, near Cuddalore, in verse, with prose epitomes by Chidambaram M. Sāmināth'-aiyar. Edited by Ṣiva-shaṇmukha Mey-ñāna Ṣivāchārya Svāmi.] pp. iii. iii. ii. 235, 2. *சென்னை* [*Madras,*] 1896. 12°. **14170. d. 40.**

CHIDAMBARA PIḶḶAI, *Paruttituṟai N.* ∘ ∘ ∘ *வயிரவக்கடவுள் கீர்த்தனம்* [Vairava-kaḍavuḷ-kīrttanam. Hymns to Bhairava. Revised by K. Kand'-appa Upādhyāyar.] pp. 8. *வல்வை சர்வசித்து* [*Valvai*, 1887.] 16°. **14170. d. 5.(1.)**

CHIDAMBARA SVĀMI, *Kōyilūr.* *See* Ṣaṅkarāchāryar. [*Doubtful and Supposititious Works.*] *ஸ்ரீ . . . இலக்ஷணாவிர்த்தி ௵* [A collection, comprising Lakshaṇā-vṛutti, metrically translated by Chidambara Svāmi, *etc.*] [1888.] 16°. **14170. d. 28.**

CHIDAMBARA SVĀMI, *Tiruporūr*. See KAṆṆ'-UḌAIYA VAḶḶAL. ∘ ∘ ∘ ஒழிவிலொடுக்க மூலம் [Orivil odukkam. With commentary by Chidambara Svāmi.] 1875. 16°. **14170. d. 17.**

—— See KAṆṆ'-UḌAIYA VAḶḶAL. ∘ ∘ ∘ ஒழிவிலொடுக்கம். [Orivil odukkam. With Chidambara Svāmi's commentary.] 1906. 16°. **14170. dd. 14.**

—— ஸ்ரீ . . . திருப்போரூர்ச் சந்நிதிமுறை மூலம் [Tiruporūr-sannidhi-murai. A poem on the cult of the Ṣaiva sanctuary of Tiruporur, near Madras. With commentary and interpretation by T. K. Subba-rāya Chetti.] pts. i.-ii. pp. 96. சென்னை நகரம் [*Madras*, 1892.] 8°. **14170. f. 19.**

—— ∘ ∘ ∘ வேதகிரியீஸ்வரர்பதிகம். [Vēdagiriy-īṣvarar-padigam. A Ṣaiva poem on the god of Vedagiri.] pp. 7. See SUNDARA MUDALIYĀR, *T.* ∘ ∘ ∘ திருமுருகாற்றுப்படை மூலம் [Tiru-mrug'-āttu-padai, *etc.*] pt. iv. [1890.] 16°. **14172. a. 32.(4.)**

CHIDAMBARA-TAMBIRĀN SVĀMI, *Tiruvāvaḍuḍurai*. See UYYA-VANDA DĒVA-NĀYANĀR, *Tiruviyalūr*. திருவுந்தியார் மூலம் [Tiruv-undiyār. With commentary by Chidambara-tambirān, *etc.*] [1896.] 12°. **14170. d. 65.**

—— See UYYA-VANDA DĒVA-NĀYANĀR, *Tiruviyalūr*. திருவுந்தியார். [Tiruv-undiyār. With commentary by Chidambara-tambirān.] 1897. 8°. [*Mey-kaṇḍa-ṣāttiram*.] **14170. ff. 3.**

CHID-GHANĀNANDA GIRI. ஸ்ரீ . . . நியாயப்பிரகாசம். [Nyāya-prakāṣam. A treatise on logic. Translated from the Hindi by P. Nāga-ratna Nāyakar. Edited by V. Mṛugēṣa Mudaliyār.] சென்னை [*Madras*,] 1906, *etc.* 8°. **14170. ff. 21.**
In progress.

CHILDREN. New Children's Series. [Tamil tracts for children, published by the Jaffna Religious Tract Society.] no. 1-28. [*Jaffna*, 1842-1848 ?] 16°. **14170. a. 15.**
No title-pages or Tamil headings.

CHINDURAYELOO. See SINDHU-RĀYALU.

CHINNA. [For names beginning with this word:] See ṢINNA.

CHIṮṮ'-AMBALA-NĀḌIGAḶ. See ṢIṮṮ'-AMBALA-NĀḌIGAḶ.

CHITTY (SIMON CASIE). See KAḌAVUṆ MĀ-MUNI. The sixth chapter of the Tiruvathavur Purana . . . Translated . . . by S. C. Chitty. 1861. 8°. **Ac. 8830. (vol. i., no. 2.)**

—— The Tamil Plutarch, containing a summary account of the lives of the poets and poetesses of Southern India and Ceylon, from the earliest . . . times, with select specimens of their compositions. pp. v. 122. *Jaffna*, 1859. 8°. **14172. b. 49.**

CHRISTIANS, *South Indian*. See INDIAN CHRISTIANS.

CLARKE (*Mrs.* T.). தாய்மாருக்கு உபதேசம். [Tāymārukku upadēṣam. A Christian tract addressed to the mothers of Southern India.] pp. 51. *Madras*, 1860. 12°. **14170. b. 16.(2.)**

CLOUSTON (WILLIAM ALEXANDER). See NĀLU-MANTRI-KATHAI. The King and his Four Ministers . . . translated . . . by . . . Natesa Sastri . . . With notes and introduction, by W. A. Clouston. 1888. 12°. **14170. k. 48.(1.)**

—— A group of Eastern Romances and Stories, from the Persian, Tamil, and Urdu. With introduction, notes, and appendix by W. A. Clouston. pp. xl. 586. *Glasgow*, 1889. 8°. **14003. h. 21.**

COBBAN (G. MACKENZIE). See BESCHI (C. G. E.). ஐந்திலக்கணத் தொன்னூல்விளக்கம் மூலம் [Tonnūl-viḷakkam. With life of the author by G. M. Cobban.] [1891.] 8°. **14172. f. 16.**

COLLETT (CHARLES). A Manual of the Law of Torts, and of the Measure of Damages . . . Translated into Tamil by Puducotai Sami Iyer. (டார்ட்டெஸ் . . . சங்க்ஷேபபுஸ்தகம்.) Second edition. pp. i. ii. 252. *Madras*, 1872. 8°. **14170. g. 10.**

COLLINS, afterwards **COOK** (MABEL). மார்க்க விளக்கம். [Mārga-viḷakkam, *i.e.* "Light on the Path," a theosophical tract] . . . written down by M. C. . . . Translated [into Tamil] by S. Ramaswamier. pp. 28. *Madras*, 1885. 16°. **14170. d. 6.**

COLOMBO.—*Ṣaiva-prakāṣa-sabhai*. புராணம். [Purāṇam. A tract on the Ṣaiva religious books.] pp. 14. யாழ்ப்பாணம் [*Jaffna*,] 1891. 8°. **14170. e. 41.(3.)**

COLTON (JOHN), *of the American Mission, Madura*. Description of Madura. மதுரைச்சீமைவிருத்-

தாந்தம். [A geographical and historical account.] pp. i. 85; 2 *plates*. *Palamcotta*, 1863. 12°. **14172. h. 66.**

CONDASVÁMI PULAVER. *See* KANDA-SĀMI PULAVAR.

CONFESSIO AUGUSTINA. *See* AUGSBURG CONFESSION.

COOMÁRASWÁMY. *See* KUMĀRA-SVĀMI.

COOPPOOSWAMY AIYAR. *See* KUPPU-SĀMI AIYAR.

CORNELIUS NĀḌĀR (J. S.). Indian Antiquities. Amarar Puranam, being the antiquities of the gods of India, as described in the Sacred Writings of the Hindus, treated historically. அமரர் புராணம் என்னும் தேவர் குலவிளக்கம். pp. vii. 500. *Salem*, 1901. 8°. **14170. k. 52.**

CRAMER (ADOLPHUS). *See* BIBLE.—New Testament.—*Gospels.* [*Matthew.*] Het Heylige Evangelium . . . na . . . Mattheus . . . in de mallabaarse Tale overgebragt [by A. Cramer?], *etc.* 1741. 4°. **466. b. 16.**

CROSSETT (SAMUEL). *See* CEYLON. Ceylon Government Railways, *etc.* [Translated by S. Crossett.] 1892. 12°. **14172. i. 15.**

CULL (J. B.). *See* CEYLON.—*Department of Public Instruction.* Extracts from the Code for Aided Schools, *etc.* [Signed by J. B. Cull.] 1892. 8°. **14172. hh. 6.**

—— —— 1893. 8°. **14172. hh. 7.**

CUNDASAWMY PILLAY. *See* KANDA-SĀMI PILLAI.

CUTTER (CALVIN). ∘ ∘ ∘ அங்காதிபாத சுகரணவாத உற்பாலனநூல். (*Anatomy, Physiology, and Hygiene.) [A treatise by S. F. Green, mostly translated from the work of Cutter bearing the above English title.] Second edition. pp. 204. *Madras*, 1857. 12°. **14172. h. 55.**

CUŸLENBURG (ARTHUR VAN). Arithmetic. Standard IV. நான்காந்தரக் கணிதம். pp. 74. *Batticaloa*, 1889. 12°. **14172. h. 47.**

CYRIACUS A SANCTO ELISEO. *See* PACHECO (G.). தேவப்பிரசையின் திருக்கதை. [Dēva-prajaiyin tiru-kathai. Edited by Cyriacus.] [1880-1886.] 8°. **14170. bb. 2.**

DAIRIYA-NĀTHA-SVĀMI. *See* BESCHI (C. G. E.).

DAIVA-ŞIKHĀMAṆI MUDALIYĀR. *See* TEYVA-ŞIKHĀMAṆI MUDALIYĀR.

DAJJĀL. دجّالنامه پنگبر کتاب [Dajjāl-nāmah. Traditions relating to "al-Masīh al-dajjāl," or Antichrist, collected and translated from the Arabic.] pp. 32, *lith.* مدراس ١٣٢٤ [*Madras*, 1906.] 8°. **14173. b. 27.(2.)**

DALYELL (ROBERT ANSTRUTHER). *See* MADRAS, *Presidency of.* — *Board of Revenue.* சென்னை ரவினியுசசபாஸ்தியமாநாறு சாசநங்கள் ஸ்ரீ [The Standing Orders of the Madras Board of Revenue from 1820 to 1866. Compiled by R. A. Dalyell.] [1868.] 8°. **14170. g. 6.**

DĀMŌDARA AṚAGIYA-ŞIṄGAR ĀCHĀRYAR, *B.A.* *See* PIḶḶAI LŌKĀCHĀRYAR. ప్రపన్నజనకూటస్థ శ్రీపిళ్ళైలోకాచార్యస్వామి . . . తత్త్వత్రయము॥ [Tattva-trayam. With commentary. Edited by Dāmōdara Aṛagiya-şiṅgar.] [1875.] 8°. **14170. f. 24.**

DĀMŌDARAM (D. V.). *See* TRIMMER (G. J.). "Stewards of the Mysteries of God" . . . an ordination charge delivered at the ordination of the Rev. D. V. Thamotheram, *etc.* 1892. 16°. **14170. a. 57.(1.)**

DĀMŌDARAM PIḶḶAI, *Şiruppiṭṭi Vairava-nātha, Rāu Bahādur.* [*Life.*] *See* RĀJA-RATNAM PIḶḶAI, *T. A.* The Life of . . . Thamotharam Pillai, *etc.* 1902. 12°. **14170. k. 44.**

—— *See* BUDDHA-MITRAN. ∘ ∘ ∘ வீரசோழியம். [Vīra-şoṛiyam. Edited by Dāmōdaram.] [1881.] 8°. **14172. f. 12.**

—— —— 1895. 8°. **14172. e. 21.**

—— *See* IṚAIYANĀR. இறையனாரகப்பொருள் [Iṛaiyanār-aga-poruḷ. With commentary. Edited by Dāmōdaram.] [1883.] 8°. **14172. e. 25.**

—— *See* KACHIY-APPAR, *Tirutaṇigai.* ஸ்ரீ . . . தணிகைப்புராணம். [Taṇigai-purāṇam. Edited by Dāmōdaram.] [1883.] 8°. **14170. e. 64.**

—— *See* NALLANDUVANĀR. ∘ ∘ ∘ கலித்தொகை. [Kali-togai. Edited by Dāmōdaram.] 1887. 8°. **14172. b. 38.**

—— *See* TŌLĀ-MOṚI DĒVAR. ∘ ∘ ∘ சூளாமணி. [Chūḷāmaṇi. Edited by Dāmōdaram.] 1889. 8°. **14172. b. 39.**

DĀMŌDARAM PIḶḶAI, *Şiruppiṭṭi Vairava-nātha, Rāu Bahādur* (*continued*). See TŌLĀ-MOḺI DĒVAR. ○○○ திவிட்டகுமாரன்கதை ஞூ [Vachana-chūḷāmaṇi. The story of the Chūḷāmaṇi rendered into prose by Dāmōdaram Piḷḷai.] 1898. 12°. **14171. a. 31.**

——— *See* TOL-KĀPPIYANĀR. தொல்காப்பியம் ஞூ [Tol-kāppiyam. With commontary. Edited by Dāmōdaram.] 1885-[1892.] 8°. **14172. e. 13.**

——— *See* VAIDYA-NĀTHA DĒŞIKAR. ○○○ இலக்கண-விளக்கம் ஞூ [Ilakkaṇa-viḷakkam. Edited by Dāmōdaram.] [1889.] 8°. **14172. e. 24.**

——— *See* VAIDYA-NĀTHA DĒŞIKAR. இலக்கண-விளக்கப்பதிப்புரைமறுப்பு. [Ilakkaṇa-viḷakka-padipp'-urai-maṟuppu. A criticism of Dāmōdaram Piḷḷai's commentary on the Ilakkaṇa-viḷakkam.] 1894. 8°. **14172. f. 22.**

——— *See* VAIDYA-NĀTHA DĒŞIKAR. ○○○ இலக்கண-விளக்கம். செய்யுளியல். [Şeyyuḷ-iyal. Edited by Dāmōdaram.] 1900. 8°. **14172. e. 35.**

——— சூளாமணி. அரசியல். [Chūḷāmaṇi. Araş'-iyal, or the section on Royalty.] *See* ACADEMIES, *etc.*—Madras.—*University of Madras.* The Tamil text, *etc.* pp 49-70. 1899. 8°. **14172. bb. 6.(7.)**

——— Chulamani. Government. [Translated into English by V. Veṅkaṭa-şrīnivāsan.] *See* ACADEMIES, *etc.*—Madras.—*University of Madras.* University of Madras. Matriculation Examination, 1900, *etc.* 1900. 8°. **14172. bb. 6.(2.)**

——— Chulamani. Royalty. [In English, with Tamil notes.] *See* ACADEMIES, *etc.*—Madras.—*University of Madras.* Copious annotations, *etc.* 1900. 8°. **14172. bb. 6.(3.)**

——— Chulamani. Royalty. [In English.] *See* ACADEMIES, *etc.*—Madras.—*University of Madras.* University of Madras. Exhaustive notes, *etc.* 1900. 8°. **14172. bb. 6.(4.)**

DAṆḌA-PĀṆI SVĀMI, *Īrōḍu.* *See* BĀLA-SUBRAHMAṆYA KAVI-RĀYAR. பழனித்தல புராண ஞூ [Paṟani-tala-purāṇam. Edited by Daṇḍa-pāṇi.] [1893.] 8°. **14170. e. 57.**

DANIEL (E.). The Conversation. A dialogue between a Christian and a follower of Mohammed . . . சமவாதம். Second edition. pp. 12. *Jaffna,* 1844. 12°. **14170. b. 1.(23.)**

DANIEL PIḶḶAI, *of Tranquebar.* *See* BOGATZKY (C. H. VON). பரமண்டலங்களிலதங்கள . . . ஆபரணபெட்டி [The Golden Treasury. Translated by Daniel Piḷḷai.] [1800.] 8°. **14170. c. 26.**

——— *See* BOGATZKY (C. H. VON). Golden Treasury . . . New edition, *etc.* 1876-1878. 8°. **14170. c. 1.**

DANIEL PIḶḶAI, *Tañjai Samādhānam.* *See* ANTŌNI PIḶḶAI. The English, Tamil, Telugu and Hindustani Sonmalai . . . revised by . . . Daniel Pillay, *etc.* 1880. 8°. **14172. e. 10.**

DĀŞARATHI CHEṬṬI, *Tirupaṯṯūr Kōdaṇḍa-rāman,* and **MĀṆIKKAM PIḶḶAI,** *Tirupaṯṯūr Rāma-sāmi.* Vithyabivirthi Sambashanam, or A dialogue on the improvement of education . . . New edition. (வித்யாபிவிர்த்தி சம்பாஷணம்.) pp. ii. 44. *Bangalore,* 1895. 8°. **14172. hh. 11.**

DAVID (CHRISTIAN). *See* LITURGIES.—England, *Church of.* The Tamul Translation [by C. David] of the Book of Common Prayer, *etc.* 1818. 8°. **14170. b. 51.**

DEFOE (DANIEL). The Life and Adventures of Robinson Crusoe. Translated into Tamil by V. Visvanatha Pillai. (ருபின்ஸன் குரூசோ சரித்திரம்.) New edition. pp. 471; 1 *plate.* *Madras,* 1906. 12°. **14171. d. 8.**

DE NOBILI (R.). *See* NOBILI (R. DE').

DE RIEMER (W. E.). *See* RIEMER (W. E. DE).

DĒŞIKĀCHĀRYAR, *Āḍūr Ichambāḍi.* *See* PARĀŞARA. பராசரஸ்ம்ருதி. [Parāşara-smṛuti. Edited with Tamil translation by Dēşikāchāryar.] 1902. 8°. **14039. b. 30.**

DĒŞIKĀCHĀRYAR, *K.* *See* PURĀṆAS.—*Kalki-purāṇam.* ஸ்ரீ . . . கல்கிபுராணம். [Kalki-purāṇam. Translated by Dēşikāchāryar.] [1902.] 8°. **14170. ee. 50.**

DĒVĀṄGAR. ○○○ தேவாங்கபுராணம். [Dēvāṅga-purāṇam. The sacred legends of the Dēvāṅga or weaver caste, translated from the Sanskrit. Versified by Māmbaṟa Kavi-şiṅga Nāvalar from the version of Sadā-şiva Svāmi and Doḍḍaya Dēşikar. With a commentary by R. Sabhā-pati Piḷḷai.] pp. ii. ii. 350. சென்னை [*Madras,* 1893.] 8°. **14170. e. 55.**

DĒVAṆṆA BHAṬṬAR. [For editions of the Vyavahāra-sāra-saṅgraham, abridged from the Smṛuti-chandrikā of Dēvaṇṇa :] *See* KANDA-SĀMI PULAVAR, *Madurai.*

DĒVA-RĀJA KAVI-RĀYAR, *Kalavai Puraṣai.* *See* KAUṢIKAR. The Kowseegasindamony . . . written [*i.e.* edited] by K. P. Thavaraja Pundit. 1895. 8°. **14170. i. 35.**

—— *See* MUNI-SĀMI MUDALIYĀR, Ṣ. இ௸து சோதிட பிரமாண்டசேகரம் [Jōdiḍa-brahmāṇḍa-ṣēkharam. Compiled by Muni-sāmi, as transmitted by Dēva-rāja.] [1898.] 8°. **14170. i. 66.**

DĒVA-SAHĀYAM, *E. Ārōgyam, Bāla-kavi, of Bangalore.* அர்ச் : பார்ப்பரம்மாள் அம்மானை. [Archya-barbarammāḷ-ammānai. A poem on the legend of St. Barbara.] pp. iv. 88. பெங்களூர் [*Bangalore,*] 1897. 8°. **14170. bb. 8.(2.)**

DĒVA-SAHĀYAM PIḶḶAI. *See* MUTT'-AIYĀ PULAVAR. வேதசாக்ஷியாகிய தேவசகாயம்பிள்ளை வாசகப்பா. [Dēva-sahāyam-piḷḷai-vāchaka-pā. A drama on the martyrdom of Dēva-sahāyam.] 1894. 8°. **14170. l. 42.**

—— வேதசாட்சியான தேவசகாயமபிள்ளை சரித்திரம. [Dēva-sahāyam-piḷḷai-charitram. A life of Dēva-sahāyam, a native Christian martyr.] pp. iii. 72, ii. புதுவை ௲அ௱௫அ [*Pondicherry,* 1858.] 16°. **14170. a. 12.**

The author seems to be L. Saint-Cyr, S.J.

—— தேவசகாயசிகாமணிமாலை. [Dēva-sahāya-ṣikhāmaṇi-mālai. A Christian poem on the story of Dēva-sahāyam.] pp. 56. யாழ்ப்பாணம் [*Jaffna,*] 1897. 8°. **14170. bb. 8.(3.)**

DĒVĒNDRA. ००० ௰௨ மாநுப்ரேக்ஷையென்கிற ஜீவஸம்போதனை. [Jīva-sambōdhanai, or Dvādaṣānuprēkshai. A metrical version of a Jain Sanskrit treatise purporting to contain answers by the Gaṇadhara Gautama to the questions of Ṣrēṇika on 12 cardinal topics of Jain doctrine. With prose interpretation.] pt. i.-ii. pp. 36, i. 12. சின்னகாஞ்சிபுரம் சுபானு [*Little Conjeveram,* 1883.] 8°. **14170. e. 21.**

Apparently no more has been published.

DEVÈZE (GÉRARD). *See* RĀMA-CHANDRA KAVI-RĀYAR, *N.* Çakuntalâ. Traduction [by G. Devèze], *etc.* 1886-1887. 8°. **P.P. 4964. d. (tom. 19-20).**

DHAIRYA-NĀTHA-SVĀMI. *See* BESCHI (C. G. E.).

DHANVANTARI. ००० தண்டக கலை க்ஞானம்சுரா. [Daṇḍaka-kalai-ñānam. A medical work of Yogic tendency, in six hundred metrical sections, attributed to Dhanvantari. Edited by T. Vēṅkaṭāchala Mudaliyār.] pp. 94. பவ [*Madras,* 1874.] 8°. **14170. i. 12.**

—— ००० பாலவாகடமென்னும் சிமிட்டுரத்தினசுருக்கம் நடாசுய. [Ṣimiṭṭu-ratna-ṣurukkam, or Bāla-vāhaṭam. A medical work in 361 stanzas, attributed to the legendary Dhanvantari, and apparently based on Vāg-bhaṭa's Bāhaṭam. Edited by T. Subba-rāya Mudaliyār.] pp. ii. 86. பவ [*Madras,* 1874.] 8°. **14172. c. 19.**

DIALOGUE. A Dialogue between a Protestant Christian and a Càsi Pandáram . . . Edited and published by Vathamuthoo Francis Thomas. (*ஒரு கிறிஸ்தவருக்கும் . . . ஒரு காசிப்பண்டாரத்துக்கும் நடந்தசம்பாஷணைகள்.) pp. xi. 536. *Madras,* 1857. 8°. **14170. c. 20.**

The wrapper bears the date 1859.

DIBB (ASHTON). *See* BIBLE.—*Concordances.* Concordance to the Tamil New Testament, *etc.* [Revised by A. Dibb.] 1878. 4°. **3104. aaa. 8.**

DICTIONARIES. A Manual Dictionary of the Tamil Language. Published by the Jaffna Book Society. (*பெயரகராதி.) pp. iv. 771, xxii. *Jaffna,* 1842. 8°. **14172. e. 19.**

The work was commenced by J. Knight, and completed after his death by native assistants supervised by L. Spaulding.

—— பேரகராதி. [Pēr-agarādi. A second edition of the preceding, revised with additions by Kāñchīpuram Rāma-sāmi Nāyuḍu.] pp. i. 948, 68, 32, 114. சென்னை [*Madras,*] 1893. 8°. **14172. f. 15.**

—— தமிழ்ப் பேரகராதி. [Tamiṟ-pēr-agarādi. Another edition of the same work, enlarged by N. Kadir-vēṟ Piḷḷai.] pp. vii. 948, 287. சென்னை [*Madras,*] 1899. 8°. **14172. f. 24.**

—— A Polyglot Vocabulary in the English, Teloogoo, and Tamil Languages; to which are appended . . . dialogues; with selections and a glossary of Revenue terms . . . arranged . . . and . . . translated, by a late student of Mr. Lewis

. . . with the assistance of T. M. Kistnasawmy Pillay. pp. iv. 262, iii.; 1 *plate*. *Madras*, 1851. 8°. **14172. h. 21.**

—— A Vocabulary [in English and Tamil] of Technical Terms as used in Logic and Metaphysics. pp. 12, 17. *Jaffna*, 1860. 12°. **14172. h. 67.**

—— இங்கிலிஷும் தமிழுமாகிய ஒக்கபுலேரியும் டையலாக்சும். [English-Tamil vocabulary and dialogues, the English words being written in the Tamil character. Edited by T. Āṟu-muga Svāmi.] pp. 72. கஅஅக [*Madras*, 1881.] 16°. **14172. h. 46.**

—— English and Tamil grammatical vocabulary. Useful words and idiomatic sentences. Series of vocabularies, no. iii. pp. 76. *Madras*, 1881. 16°. **14172. h. 31.**

DIETRICH (Johann Konrad). ஞான உபதேச விஸ்தரிப்பு. [Ñāna-upadēṣa-vistarippu. A catechetic exposition of Lutheran theology. Translated into Tamil by K. A. A. Ihlefeld.] pp. 275. *Tranquebar*, 1880. 12°. **14170. b. 33.**

DIOGNETUS. தியோக்னேது என்பவருக்கு எழுதின நிருபம். The Epistle to Diognetus. A translation by B. Abraham. pp. 12. *Madras*, 1893. 8°. **14170. c. 24.(8.)**

DIVĀKARAR. சேந்தன்திவாகரம் மூலபாடம். [Divākaram. A metrical dictionary in twelve parts. Edited by Tāṇḍava-rāya Mudaliyār.] pp. 204. ஈசுவர [*Madras*, 1877.] 12°. **14172. e. 4.**

Composed at the instance of a certain Ṣendanār (sometimes identified with Ṣendan of Ambarnagar, mentioned by Auvaiyār), and often passing under his name.

—— ००० திவாகரம் ௸ [Divākaram. Bk. i., or names of gods (Teyva-peyar-togudi). Edited by T. Kuppan Aiyaṅgār.] pp. 24. சித்தார்த்தி [*Madras*, 1859.] 16°. **14172. ee. 9.(1.)**

—— சேந்தன் திவாகரம் . . . தெய்வர்பெயர்த்தொகுதி ௸ [Divākaram. Bk. i. Edited by T. Āṟu-muga Svāmi.] pp. 24. கஅஅ0 [*Madras*, 1880.] 16°. **14172. ee. 8.**

DODDAYA DĒṢIKAR, *Kalappadi*. See Dēvāṅgar. ००० தேவாங்கபுராணம். [Dēvāṅga-purāṇam. Versified from the version of Sadā-ṣiva and Doḍḍaya.] [1893.] 8°. **14170. e. 55.**

DODD'-AYYAṄGĀR, *Ṣuddha-sattvam*. See Piḷḷai Lōkāchāryar. ००० முமுக்ஷுப்படி ௸ [Mumukshu-paḍi. With glosses by Doḍḍ'-ayyaṅgār.] 1890. 8°. **14170. f. 18.**

DODDRIDGE (Philip). The Rise and Progress of Religion in the Soul . . . Abridged and altered. [In English and Tamil.] (*மெய்ஞ்ஞானஜெதயவிருத்தி.) pp. 339. *Jaffna*, 1848. 12°. **14170. b. 36.**

DREW (William Hoyles). See Tiru-vaḷḷuvar. The Cural . . . with the commentary of Parimelaragar, an amplification . . . by Ramanuja Cavi-Rayar, and an English translation of the text by . . . W. H. Drew. 1840-1852. 8°. **14172. b. 48.**

DUBOIS (Jean-Antoine), *Abbé*. See Beschi (C. G. E.). Aventures du Gourou Paramarta . . . [Translated by J. A. Dubois], *etc*. 1877. 8°. **12315. h. 3.**

—— Le Pantcha-Tantra, ou Les Cinq Ruses, fables du Brahme Vichnou-Sarma ; Aventures de Paramarta, et autres contes, le tout traduit pour la première fois sur les originaux indiens ; par M. l'Abbé J.-A. Dubois. pp. xvi. 415. *Paris*, 1826. 8°. **14170. k. 67.**

—— [Another edition, typographically identical with the above, with 13 engravings by Léonce Petit.] *Paris*, 1872. 8°. **14170. k. 68.**

DUMAST (A. P. F. de). See Guerrier de Dumast.

DUPUIS (Louis-Savinien), *Abbé*. See Beschi (C. G. E.). தேம்பாவணி. [Tēm-bāv-aṇi. Edited by Dupuis.] [1851-1853.] 8°. **14170. c. 9.**

—— இல்லறவொழுக்கம். [Ill'-aṟav-udyānam. Rules for conjugal and domestic life.] pp. iv. 540. புதுவை க௲அசுஎ [*Pondicherry*, 1867.] 12°. **14170. a. 51.**

—— Notice sur la Poésie Tamoule, le Rév. P. Beschi et le Tembavani, par un membre de la Congrégation des Missions-Étrangères. pp. 81. *Pondichéry*, 1851. 8°. **14172. c. 7.**

DURAI-SĀMI AIYAR, *T. S.* See Periodical Publications.—*Trichinopoli*. சுபோத பாரிஜாதம் ௸ [Subōdha-pārijātam. Edited by Durai-sāmi.] 1907, *etc*. 8°. **14172. i. 12.**

DURAI-SĀMI MUDALIYĀR, *Tirukuḍandai Ṣ.* வேதபுரியந்தாதி. [Vēda-puriy-antādi. A Catholic devotional poem. Edited successively by T. Dh. Ārōgyam Piḷḷai and M. Vēda-nāyakam Piḷḷai.] pp. 13. புதுவை ௲௮௱௬௮ [*Pondicherry*, 1868.] 8°. **14170. c. 32.**

DURAI-SĀMI MŪPPANĀR, *Kavitalam* (Rāmabhadran). கங்காயாத்ராப்ராபவம். [Gaṅgā-yātrā-prābhavam. An account of a pilgrimage to the Ganges, and the appropriate legends.] pp. v. 132, 2. சென்னை ஸர்வஜித்து [*Madras*, 1889.] 8°. **14172. b. 36.**

—— ராமபத்திரீயம். [Rāmabhadrīyam. Essays on religious and ethical themes, from a Vaishṇava standpoint.] pp. 30, iv. 113. கும்பகோணம் [*Kumbakonam*,] 1896. 12°. **14171. a. 15.**

DUTHIE (James). Homiletics . . . பிரசங்க இலக்கணம். [Translated into Tamil by A. Barnes.] pp. ii. 92. *Palamcottah*, 1865. 12°. **14170. b. 6.**

DVITA-MATA-TIRASKĀRI, *Pseud.* (†முதற்குறள்வாதம்.) [Mudar-kuraḷ-vādam. A tract on the interpretation of the first verse of the Kuraḷ.] pp. 16. சென்னை [*Madras*,] 1897. 8°. **14170. ee. 32.(1.)**

No title-page. The List of Books Registered (1897, iii., p. 72) *gives the name of the author as Vaḍi-vēlu Cheṭṭi.*

—— ○○○ முதற்குறளுண்மை அல்லது முதற்குறள்வாத நிராகரணசததூஷணி. [Mudar-kuraḷ-uṇmai, or Mudar-kuraḷ-vāda-nirākaraṇa-ṣata-dūshaṇi.] The Truth of the First [verse of the] Kural, or Exposition of one hundred fallacies in the criticism on the discursive treatise on the First Kural. pp. 16, 236. சென்னை [*Madras*,] 1900. 8°. **14170. ee. 29.**

DWIGHT (Timothy). *See* Rhenius (C. T. E.). Summary of a Body of Divinity . . . [abridged from the works of Pictet and Dwight], *etc.* 1838. 12°. **14170. b. 42.**

—— —— 1845. 12°. **14170. b. 43.**

EDMONDSON (Jonathan). Five Sermons on the Nativity,—the Crucifixion,—the Resurrection,—and the Ascension of Jesus; and the Descent of the Holy Spirit . . . Translated into Tamil:—from the two volumes of short Sermons by . . . J. Edmondson, *etc.* pp. 12, 16, 12, 12, 11. சென்னபட்டணத்தில் [*Madras*,] 1831. 8°. **T. 2124.(6.)**

EDWARD VII., *King of Great Britain and Ireland. See* Krushṇam-Āchāryar, V. His Most Excellent Majesty King-Edward VII. A biographical sketch with an account of the great Coronation, *etc.* 1902. 8°. **14170. k. 51.**

ĒKĀMBARA MUDALIYĀR, *Señji. See* Sahādēvan. ○○○ பாச்சிகைசாஸ்திரம் ஞ [Pāchikai-ṣāstram, *etc.* Edited and recast, with paraphrase, by Ēkāmbara.] 1905. 8°. **14171. g. 12.**

—— *See* Vīra-brahmēndriya Svāmi. Arputha Kalakgiyana Manchari Vachanakaviam, *etc.* [Edited by Ēkāmbara.] 1897. 8°. **14170. i. 73.**

—— சோதிடகோட்சாரசிந்தாமணி. மூலமும், உரையும். [Jōdiḍa-gōṭ-chāra-chintāmaṇi. A metrical manual of astrology, with commentary.] pp. 120. *Madras*, 1902. 8°. **14171. g. 1.**

—— ஸ்ரீ மகாபாரதத்தில் பதினேழாம்போர் என்னும் கர்னமகாராஜன் நாடகம். [Karṇa-mahārājan-nāṭakam. A drama on the epic legend of the 17th day of battle between the Kauravas and Pāṇḍavas. Edited by Puduvai Subrahmaṇya Piḷḷai.] pp. 80. *Madras*, 1904. 8°. **14170. l. 61.**

—— மதுரைவீரஅலங்காரம். [Madurai-vīra-alaṅkāram. A poem on the heroic legend of Vīra-svāmi of Madura.] pp. 8. [*Madras*,] 1892. 8°. **14172. b. 44.(2.)**

—— மயிலிராவணன்நாடகம். [Mayil-irāvaṇan-nāṭakam. A lyrical drama upon a legend of the Rāmāyaṇam. Edited by Puduvai Subrahmaṇya Piḷḷai.] pp. 222. சென்னை [*Madras*,] 1904. 8°. **14170. l. 62.**

—— ○○○ நூதனமனைக்குறிசாஸ்திரம். [Nūtana-manai-kuri-ṣāstram. Rules and rites for the acquisition and use of building sites, in verse, with commentary.] pp. 20. சென்னை [*Madras*,] 1894. 8°. **14172. b. 44.(5).**

—— சர்வவிஷ முறிப்பு மூலமும் - உரையும். [Sarva-visha-murippu. A tract in 61 stanzas on remedies for poisons, compiled with a prose paraphrase by Ēkāmbara.] pp. 24. சென்னை [*Madras*,] 1905. 8°. **14171. g. 11.**

ĒLA-PĀṬṬU. Yêlappâṭṭu, chant de trait ou de halage. [A religious-philosophic poem, in the form of a ballad for sailors or workmen. Translated by J. Vinson.] (Revue de Linguistique et de Philologie Comparée. Tome xxxv., pp. 234-240.) *Paris*, 1902. 8°. **PP. 4964. d. (vol. 35.)**

ELL'-APPA NĀVALAR. *See* SUBRAHMANYA AIYAR, *D.G.* திருவிரிஞ்சைப்புராணவசனம். [Tiru-viriñchai-purāṇa-vachanam. A prose epitome of Ell'-appar's Tiru-viriñchai-purāṇam.] [1897.] 12°. **14170. d. 51.**

—— அருணாசலபுராணமும் அருணாசலேசுரர் தோத்திரப்பிரபந்தத்திரட்டும். [Aruṇāchala-purāṇam. A poem on the sacred legends of the shrine at Arunachalam (Tiruvannamalai), with paraphrastic commentary by Maṟavai Mahā-liṅg'-aiyar. Preceded by several religious poems and introductory matter in prose, and followed by Aruṇāchalēṣurar-tōttira-prabandha-tiraṭṭu, poems by Ell'-appar and other Ṣaiva writers upon the holy places about Arunachalam, including Ell'-appar's Tiruv-aruṇaïy-antādi and Tiruv-aruṇai-kalambakam, Ṣiva-prakāṣa's Sōṇa-ṣaila-mālai, *etc.*] pp. xciv. ii. xii. 428; 15 *plates. Madras*, 1898. 12°. **14170. d. 52.**

—— அருணாசலபுராணம் மூலம் [Aruṇāchala-purāṇam. Another edition of the preceding, with some additional verses.] pp. 624; 16 *plates. Madras*, 1902. 12°. **14170. d. 75.**

—— அருணாசலபுராணம் மூலம் [Aruṇāchala-purāṇam. Another edition, with some additional verses.] pp. 704; 16 *plates.* சென்னை [*Madras*,] 1903. 12°. **14170. d. 83.**

The third edition, according to the 'Catalogue of Books Registered,' 1903, iv., p. 116.

—— [Another edition.] pp. 676, xiv.; 15 *plates.* சென்னை [*Madras*,] 1903. 12°. **14170. d. 84.**

—— ◦◦◦ அருணாசலபுராணம் மூலமும் உரையும். [Aruṇāchala-purāṇam. With interpretation. Edited by T. Aruṇāchala Aiyar.] pp. ii. 168. யுவ [*Madras*, 1875.] 8°. **14170. e. 18.**

The interpretation is practically the same as that of Mahā-liṅg'-aiyar. The book is crudely illustrated.

—— *See* TIRU-VEṄKATĀCHALA KAVI-RĀYAR. ◦◦◦ வல்லாளமகாராசன்கதை [Vallāla-mahā-rājan-kathai. A story illustrative of Ell'-appar's Aruṇāchala-purāṇam, ch. vii.] [1879.] 8°. **14170. k. 13.**

—— ◦◦◦ திருவருணைக் கலம்பக மூலமும் . . . விருத்தி யுரையும். [Tiruv-aruṇai-kalambakam. With commentary by N. Kadirai-vēṟ Piḷḷai.] pt. i. pp. 24. சென்னை [*Madras*,] 1902. 8°. **14172. c. 47.**

ELLIS (FRANCIS WHYTE). *See* TIRU-VAḶḶUVAR. (†அறப்பால *etc.*) [Kuṟaḷ. Edited by F. W. Ellis.] [1816?] 4°. **14172. c. 5.**

—— *See* TIRU-VAḶḶUVAR. திருவள்ளுவநாயனார் . . . திருக்குறள். The 'Sacred' Kurral . . . With . . . Beschi's and F. W. Ellis' versions, *etc.* 1886. 8°. **14172. c. 40.**

—— *See* TIRU-VAḶḶUVAR. [Extracts from the Kuṟaḷ, with F. W. Ellis' explanation.] 1906. 8°. [*Brief Biographies of Twelve Standard Tamil Poets.*] **14171. e. 9.**

ELYATAMBI. *See* IḶAIYA-TAMBI.

EMBĀV-AYYAṄGĀR, *Ṣuddha-sattvam. See* PIḶḶAI LŌKĀCHĀRYAR. ◦◦◦ முமுக்ஷுப்படி மூலம் [Mumukshu-paḍi. With glosses by Embāv-ayyaṅgār.] 1890. 8°. **14170. f. 18.**

—— *See* PIḶḶAI LŌKĀCHĀRYAR. ◦◦◦ முமுக்ஷுப்படி மூலம் [Mumukshu-paḍi. With gloss by Embāv-ayyaṅgār.] 1889. 8°. **14170. f. 17.**

EM-BERUMĀNĀR. *See* RĀMĀNUJA.

ENGLAND, *Church of.* The Thirty-nine Articles of Religion, with Scripture references and short explanations. இதில் வேதமார்க்கப்பிரமாணங்கள் மூலம். pp. 59. *Madras*, 1862. 12°. **14170. b. 13.(2.)**

—— The Church Catechism . . . ஞானோபதேசவினாவிடை. pp. 17. *Madras*, [1860?] 12°. **14170. b. 13.(3.)**

ENGLISH. First Lessons in English and Tamul: designed to assist Tamul youth in the study of the English language. 2 pts. pp. 64, 96. *Manepy*, 1835-1836. 16°. **14172. h. 1.(5.)**

—— English-Tamil First Book. pp. 72. *Madras*, 1865. 16°. **14172. h. 23.**

—— (†Vocabulary of words in Second Book.) [In English and Tamil.] pp. 24. [*Madras*, 1865?] 12°. **14172. h. 26.**

No title-page.

ENGLISH IRREGULAR VERBS. இங்கிலீஸ் முறையில்கிரியாமாலை. Exercises on the English Irregular Verbs explained in Tamil. Together with a supplement explaining some English idioms in daily use. pp. vi. 57. *Madras*, 1844. 8°. **14172. f. 18.**

EṆ-ṢUVAḌI. நெடுங்கணக்கென்னும் எண்சுவடி. [Eṇ-ṣuvaḍi. A school arithmetic with various lists of names, figures, *etc.* Edited by T. Kuppan Aiyaṅgār.] pp. 54. சித்தார்த்தி [*Madras*, 1859.] 16°. **14172. h. 44.(2.)**

EPHEMERIDES. நெடுநாட்பஞ்சாங்கம். [Neḍu-nāṭ-pañchāṅgam. A perpetual calendar of Roman Catholic Church festivals.] pp. 64. புதுவை ௲௮௱௪௰௪ [*Pondicherry*, 1844.] 16°. **14170. a. 34.(1.)**

—— The Ceylon Catholic Almanac, 1890 (*1891, 1893) . . . இலங்கைச் சத்தியவேத பஞ்சாங்கம். 3 pts. யாழ்ப்பாணம் [*Jaffna*,] 1890-1893. 12°. **14170. a. 35.(4.)**

—— ∘ ∘ ∘ நந்தன (*விஜய, மன்மத, துன்முகி) வருஷ வாக்கிய பஞ்சாங்கம் . . . Tamil Calendar for 1892-93 (*1893-94, 1895-96, 1896-97, 1897-98). [Calculated for 1892-93 and 1893-94 by C. Raghu-nāth'-aiyar; for 1895-96 and 1896-1897 by V. Sabhā-pati Aiyar; and for 1897-98 by R. Ṣiva-rāma-liṅg'-aiyar.] 5 pts. யாழ்ப்பாணம் கர-துன்முகி [*Jaffna*, 1891-1896.] 8°. **14172. i. 11.**

—— Universal Encyclopedic Calendar, giving . . . information for several centuries . . . and on a large variety of matters astronomical and astrological . . . by T. Streeneevasa Row. pp. viii. 96. *Madras*, 1892. 8°. **759. h. 8.**

—— ஜந்திரி. [Jantri. An almanack showing in parallel columns the Tamil and the European dates of every day from A.D. 1807 to 1901. Compiled by Sēlam Māriy-appa Mudaliyār.] pp. 570. சேலம் [*Salem*,] 1893. 12°. **14172. i. 14.**

—— ∘ ∘ ∘ ஏவிளம்பிவர்ஷ . . . வாக்கிய பஞ்சாங்கம் . . . Tamil Calendar for 1897-98. [Calculated by T. P. Vēṟ Piḷḷai.] pp. 80. யாழ்ப்பாணம் துன்முகி [*Jaffna*, 1897.] 8°. **14172. i. 16.(1.)**

—— விளம்பிவர்ஷ . . . வாக்கிய பஞ்சாங்கம். [Calendar for 1898-99. Calculated by T. M. Muttu-kumāra-svāmi and Ṣ. Subrahmaṇya Ṣāstri.] pp. 84. யாழ்ப்பாணம் [*Jaffna*,] 1897. 8°. **14172. i. 16.(2.)**

—— ஜந்திரி. Jantri. 1805-ம் ௵ முதல் 1926-ம் ௵ வரை. Edited by K. Ramanathaiyar. pp. 126. *Trichinopoly*, 1899. 8°. **14172. i. 9.**

EPHEMERIDES (*continued*). Tamil Calendar.—A.D. 1849. திரியாங்கம். ௲௮௱௪௯-ம் ஆண்டு... Published by the Jaffna Religious Tract Society. pp. 48. *Jaffna*, 1849. 12°. **14172. i. 17.**

—— Tamil Almanac, for the year of our Lord 1858. புதுப்பஞ்சாங்கம். ௲௮௱௫௮-௵. pp. 28. *Madras*, 1857. 8°. **14170. k. 31.**

ESSOOF RAWUTHER. *See* Yūsuf Rauttar ibn Madār Sāhib.

ETERAJOOLOO NAIDOO. *See* Yati-rājulu Nāyuḍu.

EṬṬU-TOGAI. [For works forming part of the Eṭṭu-togai which are separately registered in this Catalogue, see under the following headings:]

Kūḍalūr-kiṟār. Padiṯṯu-pattu.
Nallanduvanār. Puṟa-nānūṟu.

—— Cameos from Tamil literature († mostly from the collection of poems called எட்டுத்தொகை). [In Tamil and English.] 1897, *etc.* *See* Periodical Publications. — *Madras*. The Light of Truth, *etc.* vol. i., no. 4, *etc.* 1897, *etc.* 4°. **14170. fff. 4.**

In progress.

EUCLID. கேத்திரகணிதம். (The Elements of Euclid in Tamil. Book I. 1-15 . . . By D. C. Valooppillai.) pp. ii. 32. *Jaffna*, 1888. 8°. **14170. i. 20.**

EUROPE. ஐரோப்பாவின் தேசங்கள். [Airōp-pāvin dēṣaṅgaḷ. A school manual of European geography.] pp. 97. யாழ்ப்பாணம் ௧௮௮௬ [*Jaffna*, 1886.] 12°. **14172. h. 73.**

EVANGELICAL LUTHERAN CHURCH. Concordia (*ஒருமிப்பு.) Libri Symbolici Ecclesiae Evangelicae Lutheranae. Pars Prima. I-III. Symbola Oecumenica. VI [*sic*]. Confessio Angustana V. Apologia Confessionis. VI. Articuli Smalcaldici. (*Pars Secunda. VII. Catechismus Minor. VIII. Catechismus Major. IX. Formula Concordiæ.) [Translated by A. Blomstrand.] 2 vols. pp. vii. 417, viii. 455. *Tranquebar*, 1872-1880. 8°. **14170. c. 2.**

—— Abridgment of the Book of Concord. மெய்ப்போதக சாரம். pp. 24. *See* Graul (K. F. L.). Graul's Distinctive Doctrines, *etc.* 1882. 12°. **14170. b. 31.(2.)**

EVILS. Evils of Comedies ... நடனநட்டம். [A Christian tract.] Second edition. pp. 12. *Jaffna,* 1842. 12°. **14170. b. 1.(46.)**

—— On the Evils of Drunkenness ... வெறி-விலக்கல். [A Christian tract.] pp. 8. Second edition. *Jaffna,* 1844. 12°. **14170. b. 1.(19.*)**

EVVALUR. திருஎவ்வளூர்மான்மியம். [Tiru-evvaḷūr-māṉmiyam. The legends of the Vaishṇava sanctuary at Evvalur, in prose, with some verses appended.] pp. 24. சென்னை ஜெய [*Madras,* 1895.] 12°. **14170. d. 45.(1.)**

FABRICIUS (Johann Philipp). *See* Bible.—*Complete Bibles.* The Old Testament, *etc.* [Revised from the version of Fabricius.] 1827-1833. 8°. **3068. c. 21.**

—— —— —— [1840 ?] 8°. **1109. d. 6.**

—— —— *Complete Bibles.* The Holy Bible ... The Old Testament, translated ... by ... J. P. Fabricius, *etc.* 1844. 8°. **3070. i. 1.**

—— —— *Complete Bibles.* The Old Testament [in the version of Fabricius], *etc.* 1860. 4°. **3068. e. 10.**

—— *See* Bible.—*Old Testament.* Librorum Sacrorum Veteris Testamenti ... editio, *etc.* [Revised by J. P. Fabricius.] 1777-1796. 4°. **3068. g. 10.**

—— —— *Old Testament.* The Old Testament, *etc.* [Translated by Fabricius.] 1893. 8°. **14170. c. 48.**

—— —— *Old Testament.* The Old Testament ... [Translated by Fabricius.] 1898. 8°. **14170. bb. 7.**

—— —— —— *Psalms.* Book of Psalms. [In Fabricius' version], *etc.* 1898. 12°. **14170. a. 62.**

—— *See* Bible.—*New Testament.* The Tamul New Testament ... [In Fabricius' version.] [1824.] 8°. **1105. d. 1.**

—— —— *New Testament.* [New Testament, comprising Gospels and Acts in Rhenius' version and the remainder in a reissue of Fabricius' version.] **1410. h. 3.**

—— —— *New Testament.* ... புதிய ஏற்பாடு. (*The New Testament.) [In Fabricius' version.] 1878. 8°. **3068. dd. 24.**

FABRICIUS (Johann Philipp) (*continued*). *See* Bible.—*New Testament.* The New Testament ... [in Fabricius' version], *etc.* 1906. 8°. **14170. bbb. 9.**

—— —— *New Testament.—Gospels.* [*Matthew.*] A brief commentary ... [With the text of Fabricius], *etc.* 1891. 8°. **14170. c. 37.(1.)**

—— —— —— *Gospels.* [*Mark.*] St. Mark's Gospel. [In Fabricius' version], *etc.* 1893. 16°. **14170. a. 54.(1.)**

—— —— —— *Gospels.* [*Luke.*] St. Luke's Gospel. [In Fabricius' version], *etc.* 1900. 16°. **14170. a. 54.(2.)**

—— —— —— *Gospels.* [*John.*] St. John's Gospel. [In Fabricius' version], *etc.* 1901. 12°. **14170. a. 54.(3.)**

—— —— —— *Acts.* The Acts of the Apostles. [In Fabricius' version], *etc.* 1905. 16°. **14170. a. 54.(4.)**

—— [For later editions of the Bible in translations based upon that of Fabricius :] *See* Bible.

—— *See* Hymnals. Hymnarium Tamulicum ... secundum versionem correctiorem ... Fabricii, *etc.* 1807. 8°. **14170. c. 8.**

—— *See* Hymnals. German Tunes to Fabricius' Hymnbook, *etc.* 1878. 12°. **14170. b. 57.(2.)**

—— *See* Hymnals. Hymnologia Germano-tamulica ... Fabricius' Hymnbook. 1881. 12°. **14170. b. 57.(1.)**

FACTS. Facts in Fiction. மூடின முத்து. [Six Christian stories and dialogues.] pp. i. 99. *Madras,* 1896. 16°. **14171. aa. 1.**

FĀSĪ. *See* Muḥammad ibn Muḥammad.

FELLOWES (Robert). The History of Ceylon, from the earliest period to the year MDCCCXV ... by Philalethes, *etc.* 2 pts. *London,* 1817. 4°. **152. h. 13.**

FENN (David). *See* Bible.—*Concordances.* Concordance to the Tamil New Testament, *etc.* [Revised by D. Fenn.] 1878. 4°. **3104. aaa. 8.**

FERGUSON (Alastair Mackenzie), *the Younger.* "Ingē Vā !" or The Sinna Durai's Pocket Tamil Guide. pp. i. i. i. 66. i. *Colombo,* 1878. 12°. **12906. aaa. 21.**

FERGUSON (Alastair Mackenzie), *the Younger* (*continued*). "Ingē Vā!"... Second edition. Revised and greatly enlarged. pp. ii. ii. ii. 160. ii. *Colombo*, 1883. 12°. **14172. e. 18.**

—— Third edition. Completely revised. pp. ii. ii. 156. *Colombo*, 1892. 12°. **12907. aaa. 54.**

FERNANDO KAṆAKKA-PIḶḶAI, *Xavier-Cruz.* ஞானச் சவுந்தரியம்மாள் நாடகம். [Ñāna-saundariy-ammāḷ-nāṭakam. A drama, founded on the history of a Christian devotee.] pp. 130. *Ramnad*, 1889. 8°. **14170. l. 37.(2.)**

FLEURY (Claude). Questions et Réponses du Petit Catéchisme Historique de Fleury, avec quelques leçons supplémentaires par un membre de la Congrégation des Missions-Étrangères. சரித்திராத்துக் கடுத்த ஞான உபதேசச்சுருக்கத்தின் வினாவிடை. [In French and Tamil.] pp. 72. புதுவை தூஅாருஅ [*Pondicherry*, 1858.] 12°. **14172. h. 9.**

FONTAINIEU (Barrigue de). *See* Barrigue de Fontainieu.

FOUCHER D'OBSONVILLE ( ). *See* Purāṇas.—*Bhāgavata-purāṇam.* Bagavadam, *etc.* [Edited by Foucher d'Obsonville.] 1788. 8°. **279. d. 21.**

—— —— 1789. 8°. **14016. c. 1.**

FOULKES (Thomas). *See* Nija-guṇa Yōgi. A Synopsis of Hindu Systems and Sects. Translated ... by ... T. Foulkes. 1860. 8°. **14170. e. 36.(3.)**

—— *See* Sabhā-pati Mudaliyār, *K.* A Catechism of the Shaiva Religion ... Translated ... by ... T. Foulkes. 1863. 8°. **14170. e. 36.(6.)**

—— *See* Ṣānta-liṅga Svāmi. Eclectic Vedantism ... translated ... by ... T. Foulkes. 1860. 8°. **14170. e. 36.(2.)**

—— *See* Ṣeshādri Ṣivanār. The Elements of the Vedantic Philosophy, translated ... by T. Foulkes. 1860. 8°. **14170. e. 36.(1.)**

—— *See* Ṣiva. Siva-prakasha Kaṭṭaḷai ... Translated ... by ... T. Foulkes. 1863. 8°. **14170. e. 36.(5.)**

—— *See* Tattva-rāya Svāmi. Sasivarna-potham ... Translated ... by ... T. Foulkes. 1862. 8°. **14170. e. 36.(4.)**

FRENCH GRAMMAR. 'பிராஞ்சிலக்கண நூற்சுருக்கம். [Pirāñṣ'-ilakkaṇa-nūṟ-ṣurukkam. A compendium of French grammar.] pp. 30, 175. புதுவை தூஅாசுரு [*Pondicherry*, 1865.] 12°. **14172. h. 12.**

FRERE (Mary). Old Deccan Days; a collection of Hindu fairy tales in Tamil, newly adapted [from the English] and edited by V. Krishnamacharyar. தக்காணத்துப்பூர்வகதைகள். pp. 354. *Madras*, 1880. 12°. **14170. k. 10.**

FREYLINGHAUSEN (Johann Anastasius). Theologica Thetica, in qua omnia dogmata ad salutem cognoscendam necessaria perspicua methodo tractantur ... ad propagationem Evangelii Christi inter gentes orientales in lingua tamulica scripta a missionariis danicis Bartholomaeo Ziegenbalg et Johanne Ernesto Gründler. Editio secunda. (வேதசாஸ்திரம்.) pp. xii. i. 354. *Halis, Lipsiae* [printed], 1856. 8°. **3559. c. 13.**

FYBRANDS (Johannes Joachim). *See* Bible.—*New Testament.* Het Nieuw Testament, *etc.* [With preface by S. Bronsveld and J. J. Fybrands.] 1759. 4°. **1411. k. 16.**

GALLAUDET (Thomas Hopkins). The Class Book of Natural Theology. ... தத்துவ வேதம். pp. 267. *Madras*, 1846. 8°. **14170. b. 35.**

GAṆA-PATI NĀYUḌU, *Kōyiṟpaṭṭi M.Ṣ.* ஸ்ரீகாந்திமதியம்பாள் திருவிழா அலங்காரம். [Kānti-matiy-ambāḷ-tiru-viḻā-alaṅkāram. Verses on the cult of Kāntimati-ambāḷ, a form of Umā.] pp. 15. திருநெல்வேலி [*Tinnevelli*,] 1897. 16°. **14170. d. 31.(2.)**

—— ... சண்முகஷடாக்ஷரப் பதிகம் [Shaṇmukha-shaḍākshara-padigam. A hymn in praise of Skanda and his cult at Tiruchendur, with special reference to the Ṣaiva *mantra* of 6 letters. Followed by a similar poem in *aḍi-maḍakku* style. Edited by V. Ā. Ambala-vāṇa Nāvalar.] pp. 11. திருநெல்வேலி [*Tinnevelli*,] 1898. 12°. **14170. d. 45.(3.)**

—— எட்டயபுரம் மக-ா-ா-ஸ்ரீ மானேஜர் வெங்கிட்டராயரவர்கள் படுகளச்சிந்து [Veṅgiṭṭa-rāyar-avargaḷ-paḍugaḷa-chindu. A series of elegies upon a religious riot at Tinnevelli which caused the death of E. Veṅgiṭṭa Rāyar and others.] pt. i. pp. 21. திருநெல்வேலி [*Tinnevelli*,] 1895. 8°. **14172. b. 52.**

GAṆA-PATI SUBB'-AIYAR. *See* MADHURA-KAVI BHĀRATI.

GAṆĒṢA ṢĀSTRI, *Maruvūr.* *See* PURĀṆAS.—*Padma-purāṇam.* கீதைரத்தினம்... ஸ்ரீசிவகீதை ௵ [Ṣiva-gītā. With Tamil interpretation by Gaṇēṣa.] 1906, *etc.* 8°. **14049. b. 40.**

GAṄGĀDHARA DĒVAR, *Pāṇḍēṣuram Vēṅkaṭa-sāmi.* *See* VĀG-BHAṬA. அஷ்டாங்கஹ்ருதயம் ௵ [Ashṭāṅga-hṛudayam. The Ṣārīra-sthānam, translated by Gaṅgādhara.] 1898. 8°. **14170. i. 56.**

GAṄGĀDHARA MUDALIYĀR, *Āṭṭupākkam Aṇṇāmalai.* ஔவை சரித்திரம். [Auvai-charitram. The history of the poetess Auvaiyār.] pp. ii. 124. பெங்களூர் ௲அ௱௯௰ [*Bangalore,* 1890.] 16°. **14172. h. 87.**

GAṄGAI-MUTTU PIḶḶAI, *of Tinnevelli.* நடநாதிவாத்தியரஞ்சனம் [Naṭa-nādi-vādya-rañjanam. A manual of the arts of dancing, singing and instrumental music. Edited by V. Ā. Ambala-vāṇa Nāvalar.] pp. viii. ii. 2, 120, i. திருநெல்வேலி [*Tinnevelli,*] 1898. 8°. **14170. i. 58.**

GĀṄGĒYAR. உரிச்சொல் நிகண்டு ௵ [Uri-chol-nighaṇṭu. A Tamil dictionary of epithets in *veṇ-bā* metre with commentary. Edited by A. Sadā-ṣivam Piḷḷai, *i.e.* J. R. Arnold.] pp. 110. யாழ்ப்பாணம் [*Jaffna,*] 1889. 12°. **14172. ee. 9.(2.)**

—— ◦ ◦ ◦ உரிச்சொல்நிகண்டு. [Uri-chol-nighaṇṭu. With a commentary. Edited by V. T. Ṣivan Piḷḷai and T. K. Subba-rāya Cheṭṭi.] pp. ii. 131. சென்னை விகுர்தி [*Madras,* 1890.] 12°. **14172. e. 15.**

GAṆI-MEDHĀVIYĀR. திணைமாலை நூற்றைம்பது ௵ [Tiṇai-mālai nūṭṭ'-aim-badu. Erotic verses of the 5 classes, with commentary, forming no. 8 of the 18 *kīṟ-kaṇakku* poems.] pp. 50, i. 1904. *See* ACADEMIES, *etc.*—*Madura.* ["Ṣen-damiṟ" supplement.] no. 13. 1902, *etc.* 8°. **14172. i. 1*. (no. 13.)**

GARTHWAITE (LISTON). First Reader, Tamil ... Part i. Edited by Walter Joyes ... நூலாதாரம் ... Second edition. pp. 104. *Madras,* 1879. 12°. **14172. h. 25.**

GAUḌA-PĀDA ĀCHĀRYAR. கௌடபாதகாரிகா [illegible]: [Kārikāḥ. The Sanskrit text. With the commentary of Ṣaṅkara in Tamil, Tamil glosses, *etc.*] *See* UPANISHADS. ◦ ◦ ◦ தசோபநிஷத்த்ராவிடபாஷ்யம். [Daṣōpanishad-drāviḍa-bhāshyam.] pt. i., pp. 246-320. [1897]-1898. 8°. **14010. dd. 14.**

GAUTAMA, called BUDDHA. The story of the life of Buddha, describing the Great Renunciation, Mahabhinishkramana, as depicted by Sir Edwin Arnold in his 'Light of Asia.' Reprinted from the Viveka Chintamani. புத்தரது திவ்வியசரித்திரம் ௵ (*The Viveka Chintamani Series.) pp. viii. i. i. 146, ii. *Madras,* 1897. 12°. **14171. aa. 6.**

GAUTAMANĀR, *Pālai.* மூன்றும்பத்து. [Decade iii. Ten poems on the Chera king Kuṭṭuvan or Pal-yānai-chel-keṟu-guṭṭuvan.] *See* PADIṬṬU-PATTU. ◦ ◦ ◦ பதிற்றுப்பத்து ௵ [Padiṭṭu-pattu.] pp. 24-43. 1904. 8°. **14172. bb. 14.**

GEOGRAPHY. பூமிசாஸ்திரச் சுருக்கம். [Bhūmi-ṣāstra-churukkam. A compendium of geography, with information on history, theology, and chronology, for use in Catholic missionary schools.] pp. vi. 575. புதுவை ௲அ௱௬௰௩ [*Pondicherry,* 1863.] 12°. **14172. h. 8.**

—— Élémens de Géographie, avec un précis de Cosmographie. [In Tamil and French.] . . . பூமிசாஸ்திர நூலாதாரம். pp. iv. 216. புதுவை ௲அ௱௬௰௪ [*Pondicherry,* 1864.] 12°. **14172. h. 16.**

—— ◦ ◦ ◦ பூமிசாஸ்திர நூலாதாரம். [Bhūmi-ṣāstra-nūl-ādhāram. The Tamil text of the preceding work.] pp. 368. புதுவை ௲அ௱௬௰௪ [*Pondicherry,* 1864.] 32°. **14172. h. 3.**

—— பூமிசாஸ்திரச் சங்க்ஷேபம். [Bhūmi-ṣāstra-saṅkshēpam. A compendium of geography.] pp. ii. 64. புதுவை ௲அ௱௬௰௯ [*Pondicherry,* 1869.] 16°. **14172. h. 43.**

—— Geography of Europe and Africa. ஐரோப்பா, ஆபிரிக்கா பூகோளசாஸ்திரம். pp. i. 114; 12 *plates.* *Madras,* 1906. 12°. **14172. g. 8.**

—— Geography of Asia, with introductory subjects. ஆசியா பூமிசாஸ்திரம். pp. iv. i. 102. *Madras,* 1906. 12°. **14172. g. 7.**

GHAZZĀLĪ. *See* MUHAMMAD ibn MUHAMMAD, *al-Ghazzālī.*

GHULĀM 'ALĪ ibn MUHAMMAD AMĪN al-DĪN, *Āṟugāḍu.* விவேகவிளக்கம். [Vivēka-viḷakkam.

Wise sayings of prophets, sages, and kings from the Persian Tārīkh i Guzīdah and other works. Compiled and translated into Hindi by Ghulām 'Alī, and thence rendered into Tamil by Muhammad Mastān.] pp. iv. 43. சுக்கில [*Madras*, 1870.] 8°. **14173. b. 39.**

GILLINGS (J.). *See* BIBLE.—Old Testament.—*Psalms.* The Psalms of David, metrically arranged ... by ... J. Gillings, *etc.* 1891. 12°. **3090. aaa. 14.**

GNANAMANI. *See* ÑĀNA-MAṆI NĀḌĀR.

GNANAMUTHOO NADAR. *See* ÑĀNA-MUTTU NĀḌĀR.

GNANAPRAGASA, *Moodeliar.* *See* ÑĀNA-PRAKĀŞA MUDALIYĀR.

GONÇALVES (JACOME). *See* BIBLE.—New Testament.—*Gospels.* சுவிசேஷ விரித்துரை. [Suviṣēsha-viritt'-urai, *i.e.* the "Explicação dos Evangelhos Dominicaes e Festivaes" of Gonçalves.] [1891.] 8°. **14170. c. 31.**

—— வியாகுல பிரசங்கம். [Vyākula-prasaṅgam. Nine sermons on the Passion of Jesus Christ.] pp. 4, 96. யாழ்ப்பாணம் [*Jaffna*,] 1886. 8°. **14170. c. 25.**

GOOSEQUILL (GREY), *Pseud.* *See* BESCHI (C. G. E.). Strange surprising Adventures of ... Gooroo Simple ... [Freely rendered from Babington's version by "Grey Goosequill"], *etc.* 1861. 8°. **14170. k. 64.**

GŌPĀLĀCHĀRYA SVĀMI. *See* YĀDAVA-GIRI-MĀHĀTMYAM. ००० சதுர்வேதி சரித்திர சங்கீர்த்தனை. [Chatur-vēdi-charitra-saṅkīrttanai. Translated on the basis of Gōpālāchārya's rendering.] 1900. 8°. **14170. ee. 35.(4.)**

GŌPĀLA DĒŞIKĀCHĀRYAR, *N. Araṣānipālai.* *See* VIŞVA-NĀTHA SŪRI, *K.* ००० மணிப்ரவாள விராட-பர்வம். [Maṇi-pravāḷa-virāṭa-parvam. Edited with notes by Gōpāla Dēşikāchāryar.] 1905. 8°. **14172. bb. 16.**

GŌPĀLA DĒŞIKAR. *See* ĀṞVĀRGAḶ.—Nāl-āyiram.—*Entire Canon.* దివ్యప్రబన్ధవ్యాఖ్యాన రత్నావళి. [Divya-prabandha-vyākhyāna-ratnāvalī. The Nāl-āyiram, with commentary by Gōpāla], *etc.* 1901, *etc.* 8°. **14170. ff. 9.**

GŌPĀLA-KṚUSHṆA AIYAR, *Ānaidāṇḍāpuram Bhārati.* பெரியபுராணம் ... நந்தனார்சரித்திரக்-கீர்த்தனை. சிதம்பரக்கும்மி. [Nandanār-charitra-kīrttanai. Lyrics upon the history of Nandanār, nicknamed Nāḷai-pōvār, a Şaiva devotee celebrated in the Periya-purāṇam, and based upon the latter work. Followed by Chidambara-kummi, a devotional poem for women in *kummi* form. Edited by G. Aruṇāchala Mudaliyār.] pp. 144. சித்திர-பானு [*Madras*, 1882.] 8°. **14170. e. 9.**

—— ००० நந்தனார்சரித்திரக்கீர்த்தனை மூ [Nandanār-charitra-kīrttanai, with Chidambara-kummi. Edited by T. V. Sundara Mudaliyār.] pp. 154; 4 *plates.* சென்னை [*Madras*,] 1899. 8°. **14170. ee. 25.**

GŌPĀLA-KṚUSHṆA AIYAR, *Nattam S.* ஹிந்துஸ்தானி பாஷா மஞ்சரி. Hindustani Basha Manjary. [A Hindustani-Tamil vocabulary and phrase-book, the Hindustani being printed in Tamil characters.] pp. 169. மதுரை [*Madura*,] 1898. 12°. **14172. ee. 5.**

GŌPĀLA-KṚUSHṆA AIYAR, *V.A.* குணசீலன் மூ (Gunasîlan. A Tamil novel. ... With an introduction by V. G. Suryanarayana Sastriar.) pp. ix. 124. சென்னை [*Madras*,] 1900. 8°. **14170. k. 50.(2.)**

—— நீதிபாலன். ஒரு தமிழ் நவீனகம். (Nithipalan. A Tamil novel.) pp. i. i. i. i. 132. *Madras*, 1905. 8°. **14171. e. 1.(2.)**

Forms no. 2 of the "Hanumadwajam Series."

GŌPĀLA-KṚUSHṆA-DĀSAR. ००० எம்பிரான் சதகம். [Em-birān-ṣatakam. A century of Vaishṇava verses.] pp. 31. 1906. *See* RĀMA-SĀMI NĀYUḌU, *K.* சதகத்திரட்டு. [Ṣataka-tiraṭṭu.] pt. 6. 1905-1906. 12°. **14170. dd. 10.**

GŌPĀLA-KṚUSHṆAM-ĀCHĀRYAR, *Vaittamānidhi Muḍumbai.* *See* PINB'-AṞAGIYA PERU-MĀḶ JĪYAR. ००० குருபரம்பராப்ரபாவம் மூ [Guru-param-parā-prabhāvam. Edited by Gōpāla-kṛushṇam-āchāryar.] [1906.] 8°. **14170. ff. 22.**

GŌPĀLA-KṚUSHṆA PIḶḶAI, *Tirumaṅgai-mannan.* ஆசார்ய ஹ்ருதயசாரசங்க்ரஹம். [Āchārya-hṛudaya-sāra-saṅgraham. A digest of Aṟagiya-maṇavāḷar's commentary Āchārya-hṛudayam on the Tiru-vāy-moṟi. Preceded by Taniyan and Āmōda-padyaṅgaḷ, Sanskrit devotional verses commemorating the heads of the Şrī-vaishṇava Church, *etc.*; and followed by the Sanskrit passages quoted in the Āchārya-hṛudayam, with Tamil interpretation.] pp. xviii. iv. 242; 1 *plate*. சென்னை [*Madras*,] 1892. 8°. 14170. e. 61.

GŌPĀLA TĀTĀCHĀRYAR, *T., disciple of Krushṇa Tātayāryar*. *See* VEṄKAṬA-NĀTHA VĒDĀNTĀCHĀRYAR. ஸ்ரீ . . . ஸ்ரீரஹஸ்யத்ரயஸாரம்: [Rahasya-traya-sāra. Edited by Gōpāla.] 1889. 8°. 14048. c. 68.

GORIS (A.). *See* LOUIS [GONZAGA], *Saint*. திருச்சிறுப்பள்ளி . . . அமலோற்பவபொக்கிஷம் [Amalōrbhava-pokkisham. A manual, comprising rules signed by A. Goris, *etc.*] 1906. 32°. 14170. a. 45.

GOUZIEN (PAUL). Manuel Français-Anglais-Tamoul de Conversation à l'Usage du Médecin. A Hand-book of Conversation for Doctors in French, English and Tamil. பிரான்சு - இங்கிலீஷ் - தமிழ் சம்பாஷணைச் சுருக்கம் வைத்தியர்களின் உபயோகத்திற்காக. pp. xii. 231; 1 *plate*. *Paris*, 1904. 8°. 14172. f. 25.

GOVER (CHARLES E.). The Folk-songs of Southern India, [translated] by Charles E. Gover. *London, Madras* [printed], 1872. 8°. 14170. k. 71.

GŌVINDĀCHĀRYAR, *Āḻkoṇḍavilli*. *See* ĀRVĀRGAḶ.—Nāl-āyiram.—*Tiru-vāy-moṟi*. The Divine Wisdom of the Drâvida Saints. [Selections translated] by A. Govindâchârya. 1902. 8°. 14170. ee. 64.

—— *See* PERIODICAL PUBLICATIONS.—*Srirangam*. The Viṣishtâdvaitin. Edited by A. Govindacharya, *etc*. 1905, *etc*. 8°. 14170. eee. 11.

—— The Holy Lives of the Âzhvârs, or The Drâvida Saints. [In English.] pp. i. ii. lxxvii. 226. *Mysore*, 1902. 8°. 14170. eee. 2.

—— The Life of Râmânujâchârya, the Exponent of the Viṣishṭâdvâita philosophy (†and others). [In English.] pp. 250, ii.; 2 *plates*. *Madras*, 1906. 8°. 14170. eee. 26.

GŌVINDA-DĀSAR, *P.C.S., of Chennanguppam, Gudiyettam*. ஸ்ரீ துக்காராம்சுவாமிகள் சரித்திரக்கீர்த்தனை. [Tukārām-svāmigaḷ-charitra-kīrttanai. Lyrics on the life of the Marathi religious poet Tukā-rām, with prose paraphrase.] pp. iii. 205. செங்கல்பட்டு [*Chingleput*,] 1905. 8°. 14172. bb. 18.

GŌVINDA PIḶḶAI, *Tuṟaiyūr Muttu-vīram*. *See* RAṄGA-NĀTHA KAVI-RĀYAR. மகாபாரதம். [Mahābhāratam. Edited by Gōvinda.] [1903.] 8°. 14172. b. 9.

GŌVINDA PIḶḶAI, *V., of Trichinopoli*. மகாவிந்தம். [Mahā-vindam. A prose abstract of the Uttara-kāṇḍam of the Rāmāyaṇam.] *See* BHĪMA KAVI-RĀYAR. ००० ஸ்ரீ ராமர் அஸ்வமேதயாகம் ஓ [Śrī-rāmar-aṣva-mēdha-yāgam.] pp. 173-180. [1875.] 4°. 14172. dd. 1.

—— மகாவிந்தம். [Mahā-vindam.] *See* KAMBAN. ஸ்ரீ ராமாயண வசனம் ஓ [Rāmāyaṇa-vachanam.] pp. 423-436. 1903. 8°. 14172. d. 27.

GŌVINDA-RĀJU MUDALIYĀR, *V.*, and **AṆṆĀ-SĀMI PIḶḶAI**, *A*. மனோரம்மிய சிங்காரப்பதம். [Manō-ramya-ṣiṅgāra-padam. Songs of love, by various authors.] 2 pts. சென்னை [*Madras*,] 1893. 16°. 14172. a. 44.

GŌVINDA-SĀMI UPĀDHYĀYAR and **PONNU-SĀMI PIḶḶAI**, *V. A*. ००० சல்லாப லாவணி. Sallapa Lavany. [Lyrics appropriate to the festival of the god of love.] pt. i. pp. 16. சிங்கப்பூர் நந்தன [*Singapore*, 1893.] 8°. 14170. e. 47.(2.)

GŌVINDA-SVĀMI MUDALIYĀR. *See* APPU MUDALIYĀR.

GRAESSE (JOHANN GEORG THEODOR). *See* BESCHI (C. G. E.). Fahrten und Abenteuer Gimpels und Compagnie . . . Nacherzählt von Dr. J. G. T. Grässe. [1856?] 12°. 14170. k. 72.

GRAMMAR. (†இலக்கணசுருக்கம்.) [Ilakkaṇa-ṣurukkam. A brief Tamil grammar.] pp. 36. [*Manepy?* 1835?] 16°. 14172. h. 1.(3.)

No title-page.

—— இலக்கண நூற் சுருக்கம். Abridgement of Tamil grammar. pp. 43. *Jaffna*, 1848. 16°. 14172. h. 38.

—— இலக்கண நூலாதாரம். [Ilakkana-nūl-ādhāram. Compiled by a missionary of the Society for the propagation of the Faith. Second edition.] pp. 79. புதுவை தூஅாசுடு [*Pondicherry*, 1865.] 12°. 14172. h. 7.

—— An introduction to the study of Tamil Grammar, specially intended for primary schools.

முதலிலக்கணம். pp. iv. 88. *Madras*, 1897. 16°. **14172. h. 40.(2.)**

According to the official Catalogue of Books printed in Madras Presidency, 1897, ii., *p.* 44, *the authors are C. Munisāmi Nāyuḍu and T. A. Pārtha-sārathi Aiyaṅgār.*

GRAUL (KARL FRIEDRICH LEBERECHT). Die tamulische Bibliothek der evang. luth. Missionsanstalt zu Leipzig. 1853-1857. *See* ACADEMIES, *etc.*—Germany.—*Deutsche Morgenlaendische Gesellschaft.* Zeitschrift, *etc.* Bd. vii., pp. 558-568, viii., pp. 720-738, xi., pp. 369-395. 1846, *etc.* 8°. **Ac. 8815/2. (Bd. 7-11.)**

—— Bibliotheca Tamulica, sive opera praecipua Tamuliensium, edita, translata, adnotationibus glossariisque instructa a Carolo Graul. 4 vols. *Leipzig*, 1854-1865. 8°. **14170. e. 42.**

For the Tamil works contained in this collection, see under the following headings:—

Sāyaṇāchāryar.
Tāṇḍava-rāya-mūrtti Svāmi.
Tiru-vaḷḷuvar.

—— ◦◦◦ போதக வித்தியாசம். [Bōdhaka-vittiyāṣam. The differences in doctrine between the Evangelical Lutherans and other Christian communions. Translated by A. Blomstrand.] pp. 111. *Tranquebar*, 1870. 12°. **14170. b. 3.**

—— Graul's Distinctive Doctrines. With an abridgment of the Book of Concord. போதக வித்தியாசம் ஜ [Translated by A. Blomstrand. Second edition.] pp. iv. 99, 24. *Tranquebar*, 1882. 12°. **14170. b. 31.**

—— Indische Sinnpflanzen und Blumen, zur Kennzeichnung des indischen, vornehmlich tamulischen, Geistes. [Poems and translations.] pp. xxi. 227. *Erlangen*, 1865. 16°. **14172. a. 39.**

GREEN (HENRY WATKINS). A Primer of Agriculture . . . Being an adaptation [and translation into Tamil] of the Agricultural Class-book by W. R. Robertson . . . கிருஷிகா சாஸ்திரம் ஜ. pp. 137. *Colombo*, 1885. 12°. **14172. h. 52.**

—— Second edition. pp. 137. *Colombo*, 1887. 12°. **14171. f. 5.**

GREEN (SAMUEL F.). *See* CUTTER (C.). ◦◦◦ அங்காதிபாத சுகரணவாத உற்பாலன நூல். (*Anatomy, Physiology, and Hygiene.) [A treatise by S. F. Green, mostly translated from the work of Cutter.] 1857. 12°. **14172. h. 55.**

GRITTON (JOHN). *See* BIBLE.—*Concordances.* Concordance to the . . . New Testament. [Compiled by J. Gritton.] 1878. 4°. **3104. aaa. 8.**

GRUENDLER (JOHANN ERNST). *See* BIBLE.—*Complete Bibles.* Biblia Damulica, *etc.* [Pt. v.-vi., translated by Ziegenbalg and Gründler.] [1714]-1728. 4°. **3068. g. 6.**

—— *See* BIBLE.—*New Testament.* Novum . . . Testamentum . . . in linguam damulicam versum opera & studio B. Ziegenbalgii & J. E. Gründleri. 1722. 12°. **1410. g. 1.**

—— *See* BIBLE.—New Testament.—*Gospels.* [*Matthew.*] Evangelium Matthaei . . . [In Ziegenbalg and Gründler's version], *etc.* 1739. 12°. **Grenville 20,059.**

—— [For editions of the translation of the Bible as revised by Fabricius and subsequent translators on the basis of Ziegenbalg and Gründler's version:] *See* BIBLE.

—— *See* FREYLINGHAUSEN (J. A.). Theologia Thetica . . . in lingua tamulica scripta a . . . B. Ziegenbalg et J. E. Gründler. 1856. 8°. **3559. c. 13.**

GUERRIER DE DUMAST (AUGUSTE PROSPER FRANÇOIS), *Baron.* *See* INDIA. Fleurs de l'Inde, *etc.* [With extracts from the Kuṛaḷ, by P. G. de Dumast.] 1857. 8°. **14085. d. 4.**

—— *See* TIRU-VAḶḶUVAR. Maximes traduites . . . par P. G. de Dumast. 1854. 8°. **14172. b. 47.**

—— —— 1857. 8°. **14085. d. 4.**

GUHA-DĀSAR, *Kokkuvil.* சீவான்ம பேதம். [Jīvānma-bhēdam.] Life and Soul. [A Ṣaiva tract on psychology.] pp. 31. கொக்குவில் நந்தன [*Kokkuvil*, 1893.] 16°. **14170. d. 35.(2.)**

GUṆA-SĀGARAN. *See* AMIRTA-SĀGARAN. ◦◦◦ காரிகை ஜ [Kārikai. With commentary of Guṇasāgaran.] [1851.] 8°. **14172. e. 36.**

GUṆA-VĪRA PAṆḌITAR. ◦◦◦ நேமிநாதமூலமும் உரையும். [Nēmi-nātham. A metrical treatise on Tamil orthography and orthoepy, with a commentary. Edited by R. Rāghav'-aiyaṅgār.] pp. iv. 98, ii. iii. மதுரை [*Madura*,] 1903. 8°. **14172. e. 42.**

Forms no. 6 *of the* Ṣen-damiḻ-prachuram.

GUṆA-VĪRA PAṆḌITAR (*continued*). [Another copy, with preface, &c.] *See* ACADEMIES, *etc.*—*Madura*. ["Ṣen-damiẕ" supplement.] no. 6. 1902, *etc.* 8°. **14172. i. 1.* (no. 6.)**

—— வச்சணந்திமாலையென்னும் வெண்பாப்பாட்டியல் . . . வரையறுத்தபாட்டியல் ஸ்ரீ [Veṇ-bā-pāṭṭ'-iyal, or Vachaṇandi-mālai, and Varaiy-aṟutta-bāṭṭ'-iyal. Two metrical tracts, the former by Guṇa-vīran, upon the composition of *veṇ-bā* and *varaiy-aṟutta* verses, with prose commentary.] pp. 51. சென்னை [*Madras*,] 1900. 12°. **14172. ee. 7.**

GURU-PĀDA-DĀSAR. ◦ ◦ ◦ திருப்புல்வயல் குமரேசசதகம். [Kumarēṣa-ṣatakam. 100 verses on the cult of Kumarēṣa at Tirupulvayal.] pp. 62. 1905. *See* RĀMA-SĀMI NĀYUḌU, *K.* சதகத்திரட்டு. [Ṣataka-tiraṭṭu.] pt. 2. 1905-1906. 12°. **14170. dd. 10.**

GURU-SĀMI MUDALIYĀR, *C. Tāta.* *See* MANU. மநுதரும சாத்திரம். [Manu-dharma-ṣāstram. Edited with Tamil translation by Guru-sāmi. Followed by the Vyavahāra-sāra-saṅgraham, in Tamil, edited by the same.] 1896. 8°. **14039. b. 23.**

—— சாமுத்திரிக லக்ஷண சாஸ்திரம். [Sāmudrika-lakshaṇa-ṣāstram. A work on the art of reading characters and fortunes from bodily features. Pt. i. containing Varāha-mihira's Bṛuhat-saṃhita, ch. 68-70, in Sanskrit, with Tamil version by Īgai Varadāchāryar and English version by P. A. Lakshmaṇa Piḷḷai. Pt. 2, the Purusha-sāmudrikam and Strī-sāmudrikam ascribed to the god Ṣiva.] pp. 178, 2, 80. *Madras*, 1892. 8°. **14170. i. 26.**

GURU-ṢUKRA-NĀḌI. ◦ ◦ ◦ கருணாநந்தசித்தர் சரித்திரம். [Karuṇānanda-siddhar-charitram. A poetical biography, in 113 stanzas, of Karuṇānanda Siddhar, a legendary teacher of medicine, purporting to be from the Guru-ṣukra-nāḍi. With a prose rendering by Ṣ. M. Sāmināth'-aiyar.] pp. 24, 84. சென்னை [*Madras*,] 1906. 12°. **14171. d. 6.**

ḤABĪB MUḤAMMAD, *al-Bakrī al-Ḳāhirī.* *See* ḲUR'ĀN. فتوحات الرحمانية الخ [Kur'ān. With an interlineary translation and commentary in Tamil, together entitled al-Futūhāt al-raḥmānīyat, by Ḥabīb Muḥammad.] [1879-1884.] Fol. **14507. e. 4.**

ḤABĪB MUḤAMMAD, *al-Bakrī al-Ḳāhirī* (*continued*). بشرى الكريم وفوائد القرآن العظيم [Bushra al-karīm. A work on the interpretation of dreams, and the mystic virtues of the Koran.] pp. iv. 137, *lith.* البمبئى ١٣٠٧ [*Bombay*, 1890.] 8°. **14173. c. 4.**

—— تنبيه الانام فى تعبير المنام [Tanbīh al-anām. A treatise on the interpretation of dreams.] pp. iv. 132, *lith.* ١٢٩٩ [*Bombay*, 1882.] 8°. **14170. i. 22.**

ḤABĪB MUḤAMMAD ibn NAINĀ MUḤAMMAD, *Ḥājī 'Ālim Ṣāḥib.* ஞானதீபசம்காரம். [Ñāna-dīpa-saṃhāram. A tract on the doctrines of Islām.] pp. 34. கொழும்பு [*Colombo*,] 1893. 8°. **14173. b. 28.(4.)**

HAEGHEN (PHILIPPE VAN DER). Maximes Populaires de l'Inde Méridionale. Traduites et expliquées par Ph. van der Haeghen. [In Tamil and French.] *Paris, Bruxelles, Leipzig* [printed], 1858. 8°. **14170. k. 73.**

HAEMMERLEIN (THOMAS), *à Kempis.* [For the *De Imitatione Christi* ascribed to this writer:] *See* JESUS CHRIST.

ḤĀMID, *Ṣāḥib-durai, of Galle.* ஞானப் பெண் கும்மி [Ñāna-peṇ-kummi. Religious songs for Muhammadan women. Edited by K. V. Muḥammad Muḥyi al-Dīn.] pp. 14. *Galle*, 1892. 12°. **14173. a. 8.(1.)**

ḤAMĪD PULAVAR, *Shāh.* *See* SHĀH al-ḤAMĪD ibn MĪRĀN ṢĀHIB.

HARI. ஹரிச்சுவடி ஸ்ரீ [Hari-chuvaḍi. A Tamil primer and reading-book of easy verses, *etc.*] pp. 48. [*Madras, n.d.*] 16°. **14172. h. 35.(3.)**

—— ஸ்ரீ ஹரிநாமஸ்தோத்திரப்பா ஸ்ரீ [Hari-nāma-stōtram and Hari-nāma-saṅkīrttanam. A series of Vaishṇava hymns and anthems, translated from the Marathi by Jauḷi-kaṟār Muni-svāmi Mudaliyār, and edited by Ṣ. G. Appu Mudaliyār.] pp. 76. 1887. *See* MAHĪ-PATI. ◦ ◦ ◦ ஸ்ரீமத்துக்காராம் . . . சரித்திரம். [Tukārām-svāmigaḷ-charitram.] pt. ii. 1898, *etc.* 8°. **14170. ee. 34.**

HARI-HARA-PUTRA, *Poygaipākkam.* *See* VIVĒKA-CHINTĀMAṆI. ◦ ◦ ◦ விவேகசிந்தாமணி [Vivēka-chintāmaṇi. According to the recension of Hari-hara-putra.] 1871. 16°. **14172. a. 13.(2.)**

HARI-KṚUSHṆA PAḌAIYĀCHI, *V.* The Tamil Short-hand. தமிழ் சுருக்கெழுத்து. Part i. . . . New edition. (*Key to the Tamil Short-hand, part 1.) pp. 12, 16. *Kumbakonam*, 1898. 12°. **14172. h. 95.**

HARIṢCHANDRA, *King of Ayodhya.* Arichandra, the Martyr of Truth: a Tamil drama, translated into English [partly from the Hariṣchandra-vilāsam or dramatic version of the story ascribed to Raṅga Piḷḷai] by Mutu Coomàra Swàmy, Mudeliàr. pp. xxiii. 262. *London*, 1863. 12°. **14170. l. 33.**

HARIṢCHANDRA, *Bābū, son of Gōpāla-chandra, of Benares.* मानसोपायन *etc.* (The Intellectual Offering, or A Collection of poems in honour of the visit of His Royal Highness the Prince of Wales, to this country, written by several gentlemen in various languages. Compiled by the late Babu Harishchandra.) *Bankipur*, 1889. 8°. **14076.d.52.**

Separate pagination for each language.

HARSHA-DĒVA, *King of Thanesar.* நாகானந்தம். (Nagananda. A Tamil version [in prose] by M. C. Sadagopa Chariar . . . With an [English] introduction by V. Venugopaul Chetty.) pp. 10, 107. *Madras*, 1900. 8°. **14170. l. 24.(1.)**

ḤASAN 'ALĪ PULAVAR, *Ṣīruḍaiyārpuram*, otherwise called KANDA PULAVAR. இ ு சங்கீதசிந்தாமணி. [Saṅgīta-chintāmaṇi. A collection of Muhammadan devotional lyrics by Shāh al-Ḥamīd, Ḥasan 'Alī Pulavar, *etc.*] [1897.] 8°. *See* SHĀH al-ḤAMĪD ibn MĪRĀN ṢĀḤIB. **14173. b. 12.**

HEIDELBERG CATECHISM. Catechismus, ofte Onderweyzing in de Christelicke Leere, die in de Hervormde Kerken en Schoolen geleerd word . . . in de Tamulsche Spraak overgezet, en . . . in 't Licht gegeven, door Sigisbertus Abrahamsz Bronsveld. (*கததகஙிசுமுஸ . . . கிறீஸததமானதெவாாாதனையின உபதெசம.) pp. vi. xxxv. 144. *Columbo*, 1754. 8°. **14170. b. 62.**

—— Twede Druk. pp. xlii. 128. *Columbo*, 1769. 8°. **14170. b. 63.**

HEILSORDNUNG. [For the catechetical Heilsordnung:] *See* CATECHISM.

HERRE (WILHELM). *See* HYMNALS. Spiritual Songs, *etc.* [With musical notation edited by W. Herre.] 1867. *obl.* 16°. **14170. a. 9.**

HERRICK (D. S.). *See* POPE (G. U.). A first Catechism of Tamil Grammar . . . with an English translation by . . . D. S. Herrick, *etc.* 1895-1905. 8°. **12906. m.**

ḤIKĀYĀT i LAṬĪF. மனோரஞ்சிதத்திரட்டு. [Manō-rañjita-tiraṭṭu. A series of tales, translated by Muḥammad Ṭambi ibn Zain al-Dīn from the Hindustani version of the Ḥikāyāt i laṭīf, a Persian story-book.] pp. 52, 16. சென்னை [*Madras*,] 1901. 8°. **14173. b. 38.**

HINDU, *Pseud.* மாயாவாதசைவசண்டமாருதம். [Māyā-vāda-ṣaiva-chaṇḍa-mārutam. An essay upholding the Ṣaiva-Siddhāntam in reference to the Vedantic theory of cosmic illusion.] pp. 194. சென்னை [*Madras*,] 1895. 8°. **14170. e. 62.**

HINDU - MATAM. († இந்துமதமேஉண்மை.) [Hindu-matamē uṇmai. A Ṣaiva tract in Tamil and English on the impression made by Hinduism abroad.] pp. 12. யாழ்ப்பாணம் [*Jaffna*,] 1894. 12°. **14170. d. 25.(2.)**

No title-page.

HIPPOLYTE (J.), *O.M.I.* அர்ச்சியசிஷ்ட பதுவை அந்தோனியார் கோடியற்புதரும் வழியவர்களின் அன்னதாதாவும். [The life and miracles of St. Antony of Padua. With appended prayers, *etc.*] pp. 130. யாழ்ப்பாணம் [*Jaffna*,] 1896. 16°. **14170. a. 39.(2.)**

HOBBS (STEPHEN), *Archdeacon of Mauritius.* ◦ ◦ ◦ பூர்வீகசரித்திரசுருக்கம். An Outline of Ancient History . . . to the birth of the Lord Christ. pp. viii. i. 205. *Palamcottah*, 1851. 12°. **14172. h. 17.**

HOISINGTON (HENRY R.). *See* MEY-KAṆḌA DĒVAR. சிவஞானபோதம். Siva-gnâna-pōtham . . . Translated . . . with an introduction and notes. By . . . H. R. Hoisington. 1854. 8°. **Ac. 8824. (vol. 4.)**

—— *See* PARA-HITAM. சோதிசாத்திரம். The Oriental Astronomer . . . with a translation [by H. R. Hoisington], *etc.* 1848. 8°. **14170. i. 8.**

—— *See* ṢĒSHĀDRI ṢIVANĀR. தத்துவக்கட்டளை. Tattuva-kaṭṭaḷei . . . translated . . . with notes. By . . . H. R. Hoisington. 1854. 8°. **Ac. 8824.(vol. 4.)**

—— *See* UMĀ-PATI ṢIVĀCHĀRYAR. சிவபிரகாசம். Siva-pirakâsam . . . translated . . . with notes. By . . . H. R. Hoisington. 1854. 8°. **Ac. 8824.(vol. 4.)**

HOISINGTON (Henry R.) (*continued*). Syllabus of the Siva-gnána-pótham, one of the sacred books of the Hindús. (Journal of the American Oriental Society. Vol. ii., pp. 135-151.) *Boston*, 1851. 8°. **Ac. 8824.(vol. 2.)**

HOOLE (Elijah). *See* Liturgies.—England, *Church of*. Dureisâni-tamil-puttagam . . . Containing the Morning and Evening Services . . . in romanized Tamil . . . with . . . grammar and vocabulary by E. Hoole. 1859. 8°. **3408. d. 23.**

HORNE (Thomas Hartwell). *See* Rhenius (C. T. E.). வேதவுதாரணத்திரட்டு. [Vēdav-udāraṇa-tiraṭṭu. A work partly based upon Horne's "Introduction to the critical Study of the Holy Scriptures."] 1835. 8°. **14170. c. 16.**

—— —— 1852. 12°. **14170. b. 41.**

HOUSEHOLD WORDS. Tamil Household Words, with their corresponding English ones. pp. 12. *Tiruvadi, Tanjore* [printed], 1898. 12°. **14171. a. 34.**

HULTZSCH (Eugen). *See* India.—*Archaeological Survey*. South-Indian Inscriptions . . . Edited . . . by E. Hultzsch. 1890, *etc*. Fol. **1710. b. 9, 10, etc.**

HURMUZ. ஹுர்முஜ்கதை. [Hurmuz-kathai. A Muhammadan romance. Translated by Nāgūr Taḷavāy M. Ṣinnavāppu Maraikkāyar from the Hindustani.] pp. 2, 2, 279. *Singapore*, 1904. 8°. **14173. b. 41.**

HUTTER (Leonhard). Hutter's Compend of Theology. தேவசாஸ்திரப் பொழிப்பு. pp. iv. 276. *Tranquebar*, 1881. 12°. **14170. b. 21.**

HYMNALS. [For Wesley's Hymns:] *See* Wesley (J.).

—— Hymnologia Damulica, sive ex Germanico in Damulorum idioma, observatis usque et melodiis et rhythmis odarum, translatorum centum et sexaginta Hymnorum Spiritualium fasciculus: in gratiam juventutis damulicæ æque ac Ecclesiæ hujus gentis . . . exhibita a Benjamin Schultze (*ஞானபபாடடுகளினபொஸ்ததகம). pp. viii. 200. *Tranquebariæ*, 1723. 12°. **14170. b. 17.**

—— Hymnologia Tamulica, sive ex germanico, partim etiam latino sermone, nec non e textu sacro in tamulicum idioma translatorum ducentorum et nonaginta Hymnorum Spiritualium fasciculus: quos in gratiam Ecclesiæ Tamulicæ . . . successive collegerunt Missionarii Danici. Editio quarta. (*ஞானப பாடடுகள அடஙகியிருககிற பொஸ்தகம.) pp. ii. 315, xvi. *Trangambariæ*, 1733. 12°. **Case 27. e. 6.**

—— [Fifth edition, without Latin title, containing 295 hymns, and an appendix of 13.] pp. x. 315, xxv. தரஙகனபாடியிலே தரளாருகு [*Tranquebar*, 1756.] 12°. **14170. b. 39.**

—— Hymnarium Tamulicum, seu Collectio hymnorum selectiorum in usum Ecclesiæ Christianæ Tamulicæ e lingua germanica translatorum, secundum versionem correctiorem beati I. Ph. Fabricii ... Editio nova. pp. 13, 297, ix. *Trankenbariæ*, 1807. 8°. **14170. c. 8.**

—— Spiritual Songs, from the German adapted to the Tamil tongue. இனிமையான ஞானப்பாட்டுகள். [Hymns selected by Hugo Schanz, with the musical notation edited by W. Herre.] pp. 37. *Tranquebar*, 1867. *obl.* 16°. **14170. a. 9.**

—— ஞானப்பாட்டுமாலை. [Ñāna-pāṭṭu-mālai. Tamil hymns from the German, with tunes.] pp. iv. 134. *Tranquebar*, 1871. 8°. **14170. a. 27.**

—— German Tunes [*i.e.* musical notation] to Fabricius' Hymnbook. ஞானப்பாட்டுகளின் இராகப்புஸ்தகம். pp. vi. 48. *Tranquebar*, 1878. 12°. **14170. b. 57.(2.)**

—— Hymnologia Germano-tamulica. Editio tertiadecima. ஞானப்பாட்டுகளின் புஸ்தகம். Fabricius' Hymnbook. Seventh edition. pp. viii. 430. *Tranquebar*, 1881. 12°. **14170. b. 57.(1.)**

This is the seventh edition after the additions and improvements introduced by Fabricius.

—— Tamil Hymns, selected and original, adapted for public, private, and social worship. (*ஞானகீதசஙகிரகம்.) pp. xvi. ii. 420, xcii. *Jaffna Religious Tract Society: Jaffna*, 1846. 16°. **14170. a. 5.**

—— [Another copy of the same edition on larger paper.] pp. xiv. 420, cxxiii. *Jaffna*, 1846. 8°. **14170. c. 3.(1.)**

—— Tamil Hymns. ஞானப் பாட்டுக்கள். pp. i. iii. iii. 476, xx. i. மானிப்பாய் கஅகுசு [*American Mission Press: Manippay*, 1854.] 12°. **14170. b. 50.**

HYMNALS (*continued*). (†சங்கீதலக்கணம்.) [Saṅgīta-lakkaṇam. A treatise on European music, followed by Gīta-saṅgraham, *i.e.* the notation of 53 hymn-tunes.] pp. 68. 8°. **14170. i. 49.**

No title-page. Apparently a publication of the American Mission, probably printed at Madras or Jaffna.

—— Hymns for Schools. பள்ளிக்கூடத்திற்குரிய ஞானப்பாட்டுகள். pp. 89. *Madras Tract and Book Society: Madras,* 1848. 16°. **14170. a. 8.**

—— Tamil Hymn Book. ஞானப்பாட்டுப் புத்தகம். pp. 188. *Tinnevelly Tract and Book Societies: Nagercoil,* 1848. 12°. **14170. b. 18.**

—— தேவாராதனையிலே பாடுகிற ஞானப்பாட்டுகள் அடங்கிய சங்கீதத்திரட்டு. A Tamil Hymn Book. pp. xii. 136. *Madras Tract and Book Society: Madras,* 1848. 16°. **14170. a. 7.**

—— Tamil Hymns in English metre. ஞானப்பாட்டுகள். (*Chants. Consisting mostly of selections from the sacred Scriptures adapted to ... music.) pp. xviii. 146. *American Madura Mission: Madras,* 1853. 8°. **14170. c. 5.(1.)**

—— சேலம் ஞானப்பாட்டுகளும், கீர்த்தனைகளும். The Salem Hymnal and Lyrics, arranged by William Robinson. (*The Fifty Lyrics; for public and social worship.) 2 parts. *London Missionary Society: Salem, Tirupatur* [printed], 1901. 8°. **14170. bbb. 3.**

Without pagination.

—— Tamil Christian Lyrics. ஞான கீதங்கள். Enlarged and edited, from the lyrical compilations of the Rev. E. Webb and the Rev. G. T. Washburn, D.D., by the Rev. J. S. Chandler. pp. xxxii. 373. *Religious Tract and Book Society: Madras,* 1902. 12°. **14170. b. 30.**

IAGO PILLAI, *M. Ṣ.* *See* NOBILI (R. DE'). ஞானோபதேச ஞூ [Ñānōpadēṣam. Edited by Iago Pillai.] 1907. 8°. **14170. bb. 9.**

IBN 'AIDARŪS. *See* SHĀH al-ḤAMĪD ibn 'AIDARŪS.

IDAI-KĀDAR, *Siddhar.* அறுபதுவருடபலன் [Aṟu-badu-varuḍa-phalan. A metrical tract on the sixty cyclic years, ascribed to Idai-kādar.] *See* CHANDRA-ṢEKHARA KAVI-RĀJA PAṆḌITAR. ∘∘∘ வருஷாதி நூற்சித்தாந்த விளக்கம் ஞூ [Varshādi-nūṟ-siddhānta-viḷakkam.] pp. 233-246. [1875.] 16°. **14171. f. 2.**

IDAI-KĀDAR, *Siddhar* (*continued*). இடைக்காட்டுச்சித்தர்பாடல். [Pāḍal. Ṣaiva verses.] pp. 12. *See* SIDDHARGAḶ. ∘∘∘ பெரிய ஞானக்கோவை [Periya-ñāna-kōvai.] 1899. 12°. **14170. ee. 33.**

—— —— pt. i., pp. 56-67. 1906. 12°. **14170. dd. 12.**

IGNATIUS [LOPEZ DE RECALDE, *de Loyola*], *Saint.* சேசுசபையை ஸ்தாபித்தவரான அர்ச். லொயோலா இஞ்ஞாசியார் சரித்திரம். [Archya-ṣishṭa-loyōlā-iññāṣiyār-charitram. A life of Loyola, by a member of the Jesuit Order.] pp. 535; 4 plates. *Trichinopoly,* 1906. 12°. **14170. bbb. 12.**

IHLEFELD (KONRAD ADOLPH ANTON). *See* BIBLE.—New Testament.—*Gospels.* [*Matthew.*] A brief commentary on the Gospel according to Saint Matthew ... [by] Rev. K. Ihlefeld, *etc.* 1891. 8°. **14170. c. 37.(1.)**

—— *See* DIETRICH (J. K.). ஞான உபதேச விஸ்தரிப்பு. [Ñāna-upadēṣa-vistarippu. Translated into Tamil by K. Ihlefeld.] 1880. 12°. **14170. b. 33.**

—— A brief Commentary on the Gospel according to Saint Mark. பரி. மாற்கு எழுதின சுவிசேஷத்தின் சுருக்க வியாக்கியானம் ... [by] Rev. K. Ihlefeld, *etc.* pp. iv. 48. *Tranquebar,* 1893. 8°. **14170. c. 37.(2.)**

—— A brief Commentary on the Gospel according to Saint Luke. பரி. லூக்கா எழுதின சுவிசேஷத்தின் சுருக்க வியாக்கியானம் ... [by] Rev. K. Ihlefeld, *etc.* pp. vi. 115. *Tranquebar,* 1896. 8°. **14170. c. 37.(3.)**

ILAIYA-TAMBI (S.). *See* STICKNEY (D.). போதகாபிஷேகபிரசங்கம். A sermon at the ordination of Rev. S. Elyatamby, *etc.* 1888. 16°. **14170. a. 39.(1.)**

ILAṄ-GŌV-ADIGAḶ. ∘∘∘ சிலப்பதிகாரமூலமும் அடியார்க்குநல்லாருரையும். [Ṣilapp'-adhikāram. A metrical romance, forming one of the 5 classical epics. With a commentary by Aḍiyārkku-nallār. Edited with prolegomena and notes by V. Sāmināth'-aiyar. Followed by Ṣilapp'-adhikāra-arum-padav-urai, an anonymous glossary to the text, edited by the same.] pp. i. lxvi. ii. 497, 76, ii. ii. சென்னை [*Madras,*] 1892. 8°. **14172. d. 13.**

—— Le Silappadigaram. [A French epitome.] *See* VINSON (E. H. J.). Légendes Bouddhistes et Djainas, *etc.* vol. i., pp. 111-175. 1900. 12°. **14171. aa. 4.**

INCANTATIONS. Incantations. மந்திரம். [A Christian tract.] *See* VĒDA-NĀYAKA ṢĀSTRI, *T.D.*, and WINSLOW (M.). Blind Way, *etc.* pp. 118-122. 1852. 32°. **14170. a. 3.**

INDIA. Fleurs de l'Inde, comprenant . . . plusieurs . . . poésies indoues, *etc.* [With extracts from the Kuṛaḷ of Tiru-vaḷḷuvar, *etc.*, by P. G. de Dumast.] pp. x. ii. 266, i. *Paris, Nancy* [printed], 1857. 8°. **14085. d. 4.**

—— *Archæological Survey.* Archæological Survey of India. [Old Series.] 24 vols. *Simla, Calcutta,* 1871-1887. 8°. **2354. g.**

—— [New Imperial Series of the Reports.] *London, Madras, etc.* 1874, *etc.* 4° & Fol. **1710. b. 1, etc.**

In progress. The above title was adopted in order to embrace the "New" Series of Reports of the 3 surveys of Northern, Southern, and Western India, etc.

—— South-Indian Inscriptions, Tamil and Sanskrit . . . Edited and translated by E. Hultzsch. 1890, *etc.* *See* above : *Archæological Survey.* [New Imperial Series.] vols. ix. x. xxix., *etc.* 1874, *etc.* 4° & Fol. **1710. b. 9, 10, etc.**

—— Epigraphia Indica, and Record of the . . . Survey . . . Edited by J. Burgess, *etc.* (*Vol. iii., *etc.*, published . . . as a supplement to the "Indian Antiquary." Vol. iv., *etc.*, edited by E. Hultzsch.) 1892, *etc.* Fol. & 4°. **1710. b. 13, 14.**

In progress.

—— *Legislative Council.* *See* MADRAS, *Presidency of.—Board of Revenue.* உப்புசம்பந்தமாய் . . . சட்டங்கள் ௸ [Rules, *etc.*, for the administration of the Salt Acts.] [1867.] 8°. **14170. g. 5.(1.)**

—— சிவில் புரோசிடியூர் கோட். Act no. viii. of 1859, *etc.* [The Civil Procedure Code. Edited with notes by V. K. Rāghavāchāryar.] pp. 143. சென்னபட்டணம் ௧௮௭௦ [*Madras*, 1870.] 8°. **14170. g. 5.(2.)**

—— Acts of the Government of India . . . Act no. ix. of 1871. ௧௮௭௧ ௵த்து-௯-வது ஆக்ட்டு. The Indian Limitation Act, 1871. ௧௮௭௧ ௵த்திய இந்துதேசத்துக்காலநிர்ணயச்சட்டம். (*Viyavaharatharunghinee. Supplement. December 1871.) pp. 80. *Madras*, 1871. 8°. **14170. g. 2.(2.)**

INDIA (*continued*). Acts of the Government of India . . . Act no. viii. of 1871. ௧௮௭௧ ௵த்து-௮-வது ஆக்ட்டு. The Indian Registration Act, 1871. ௧௮௭௧ ௵த்திய இந்தியன் ரிஜிஸ்திரேஷன் ஆக்ட்டு. (*Viyavaharatharunghinee. Supplement. May, 1872.) pp. 68. *Madras*, 1872. 8°. **14170. g. 2.(1.)**

—— The Indian Evidence Act. Or Act i. of 1872, as amended by Act xviii. of 1872. இந்துதேசத்துச் சாட்சி ஆக்ட்டு. pp. viii. 83. *Madras*, 1872. 8°. **14170. g. 7.**

—— The Indian Penal Code. Containing Acts no. xlv. of 1860, no. vi. of 1864, and no. xxiv. of 1870. இந்தியன் பினல் கோட் ௸. pp. ii. 125. *Madras*, 1872. 4°. **14170. g. 8.(1.)**

—— Act no. xix. of 1872. ௧௮௭௨ ௵த்து-௧௯-வது ஆக்ட்டு. p. i. [*Madras*, 1872.] 8°. **14170. g. 8.(2.)**

—— Act no. x. of 1872. The Code of Criminal Procedure. குற்றவிசாரணைச்சட்டம் என்னும் ௧௮௭௨ ௵த்து-௧௦-வது ஆக்ட்டு. pp. 229, xiv. 83 ; 1 *plate.* *Madras*, 1873. 8°. **14170. g. 9.**

—— The Indian Contract Act. இந்து தேசத்துக் கந்திராக்ட்டு ஆக்ட்டு. Or Act no. ix. of 1872, *etc.* pp. 134. *Madras*, 1874. 8°. **14170. g. 1.**

—— (†Act no. iii. of 1873 . . . The Madras Civil Courts' Act, 1873. ௧௮௭௩ ௵த்திய சென்னபட்டணம் சிவில் கோர்ட்டு ஆக்ட்டு.) pp. 24. [*Madras*, 1874 ?] 8°. **14170. g. 5.(3.)**

No title-page.

—— நீதிவிவாதமஞ்சரி எனும் தமிழ்சட்ட புஸ்தகம். [Nīti-vivāda-mañjari. Various acts, in Tamil, edited with commentaries and examples by Ṣ. S. Veṅkaṭa-ramaṇa Aiyar.] *Madras*, 1901, *etc.* 8°. **14170. g. 23.**

In progress?

—— *Post Office.* *See* POSTAL GUIDE. Postal Guide, *etc.* 1904. 8°. **14172. i. 23**

INDIAN CHRISTIANS. Sketches of South Indian Christians. Lives of [14] Tamil, Telugn, and Malayalam Christians. இந்திய கிறிஸ்தவர்களின் ஜீவிய சரித்திரச் சுருக்கம். [Translated by Joseph David from the English.] pp. 86. *Madras*, 1896. 12°. **14171. a. 14.**

INDIAN CHRISTIANS (*continued*). Sketches of Indian Christians. இந்திய கிறிஸ்தவர்களின் ஜீவிய சரித்திரச் சுருக்கம். pp. vi. 264. *Madras,* 1897. 12°. **14171. a. 22.**

INNĀṢI-TAMBI, *Trikōṇamalai A.* See ANTŌNI-KUṬṬI AṆṆĀVIYĀR. ∘∘∘ கிறீஸ்துசமயகீர்த்தனம். [Kiṟistu-samaya-kīrttanam. Edited by Innāṣi-tambi.] 1891. 8°. **14170. c. 38.**

INQUIRIES. Devout Inquiries. A conversation between a convert to Christianity and his minister . . . பத்திநாட்டம். Second edition. pp. 12. *Jaffna,* 1842. 12°. **14170. b. 1.(41.)**

INSTRUCTION. Good Instruction . . . நற்புத்தி. [A Christian tract.] Second edition. pp. 12. *Jaffna,* 1844. 12°. **14170. b. 1.(26.)**

IṞAIYANĀR. [For works current under the name of Pēr-āṣiriyar, sometimes identified with Iṟaiyanār:] See PĒR-ĀṢIRIYAR.

—— இறையனாரகப்பொருள் [Iṟaiyanār-agaporuḷ. A treatise upon the art of erotic poetry. With a commentary ascribed to Nakkīranār. Edited by Ṣ. V. Dāmōdaram Piḷḷai.] pp. iii. i. 180. சென்னபட்டணம் சுபானு [*Madras,* 1883.] 8°. **14172. e. 25.**

IRAṬṬAIYAR. [12 occasional verses, with interpretation.] See TANI-PĀḌAL. (†தனிப்பாடற்றிரட்டு) [Tani-pāḍaṭ-ṭiraṭṭu.] pp. 210-216. [1892, *etc.*] 8°. **14172. c. 39.(5.)**

IRATTINAVĒLU. See RATNA-VĒLU.

IRSHĀD al-'IBĀD. இர்ஷாது... இறுசாதுல் இபாத். [Irshād al-'ibād. A treatise on the Muhammadan faith, translated from the Arabic by Muḥyi al-Dīn Sulṭān Piḷḷai.] pp. viii. 152. சென்னை [*Madras,*] 1901. 8°. **14173. b. 6.**

ISIDORE, *Saint.* அர்ச்சியசிஷ்ட இசிதோர் சரித்திரம். [Life of St. Isidore.] pp. 36. யாழ்ப்பாணம் [*Jaffna,*] 1898. 16°. **14170. a. 39.(3.)**

ĪṢVAR'-AIYAR, *K.N.* See AUVAIYĀR. — *Single Works.* ∘∘∘ கொன்றைவேந்தன் மூ [Konṟai-vēndan. Edited by Īṣvar'-aiyar.] 1894. 16°. **14172. a. 10.(4.)**

ITIHĀSA-MAÑJARI. Ithihasa Manjari Series. [A collection of works on epic and religious legends, in prose versions by Shaṇmukham Piḷḷai.] (வேதோபபிருங்கணமாகிய புராணேதிகாசமஞ்சரி.) சென்னை கஅஅஅ [*Madras,* 1888]-1894. 8°. **14172. d. 11.**

The works published in this series are separately catalogued under the headings:—

Kamban.
Mahā-bhāratam.
Purāṇas.—Skanda-purāṇam.

The Tamil title given above is that printed on the wrapper of the fascicules.

IYĀGA PIḶḶAI. See IAGO PIḶḶAI.

JACOLLIOT (LOUIS). Théatre Indou. La Devadassi, Bayadère. Comédie (†attribuée à un certain Parasourama), en quatre parties, traduite du tamoul [?] par Louis Jacolliot. pp. 46. *Paris, Bruxelles* [printed], 1868. 8°. **14170. l. 34.**

—— Le Pariah dans l'Humanité. [Followed by a translation of portions of the Kuṟaḷ.] pp. 347, ii. *Paris,* 1876. 8°. **10058. cc. 1.**

JAENICKE (DAVID). The life of Rev. R. Sathianaden of Tanjore. தஞ்சாவூர் பூர்வீக சத்தியநாதஐயர் ஜீவிய சரித்திரச் சுருக்கம். pp. ii. 60. *Tranquebar,* 1893. 8°. **14170. bb. 4.**

JAFFNA. யாழ்ப்பாண வைபவம். [Yārpāṇa-vaibhavam. An account of the history of Jaffna. Followed by Laṅkai-bhūmi-ṣāstra-saṅgraham, a brief geographical sketch of Ceylon. Edited by V. V. Sadā-ṣiva Piḷḷai.] pp. ii. 71. *Madras,* 1884. 12°. **14171. d. 4.**

—— A new edition of the Thesawaleme [*i.e.* Dēṣa-vaṟamai], or, The Laws and Customs of Jaffna, together with the decisions of the various courts on the subject . . . up to 1861. The English translation of the Seventy-two Orders. The Ordinances no. 18 of 1806 and no. 1 of 1842. Mr. Atherton's edition of the Thesawaleme, with original notes. And an appendix, including the Tamil version of the Thesawaleme, the Tamil version of the Seventy-two Orders, and a Tamil translation of the most important Schedule & Pre-emption Cases. By Henry Francis Mutukisna. pp. iv. vii. xix. iv. ii. xlviii. 736, vii. 104. *Colombo,* 1862. 8°. **14170. g. 3.**

—— The Tésawaḷamai; or, The Laws and Customs of the Malabars of Jaffna. Promulgated by the Dutch Government of Ceylon in the year 1707 . . . Reprinted from the edition . . . by Advocate H. F. Mutukisna. pp. 30. *Colombo*, 1891. 8°. **05319. k. 3.**

—— *Church Missionary Society.* The ninth (*eleventh) Annual Report of the Jaffna C.M.S. Native Missionary Association for 1891-92 (*1893-94) . . . அறிக்கைப்பத்திரம். 2 pts. *Jaffna*, 1892-1894. 12°. **14170. a. 49.(3.)**

—— *Kiristu-mata-khandana-sabhai.* கடிதம். [Kadidam. A letter from the Anti-Christian Society of Jaffna to the Christian Missionaries.] pp. 12. யாழ்ப்பாணம் சர்வசித்து [*Jaffna*, 1887.] 16°. **14170. a. 40.(1.)**

—— —— மாமிச போசன விலக்கு [Māmsa-bhōjana-vilakku. A tract against the use of animal food, giving opinions of English authors.] pp. 10. யாழ்ப்பாணம் விரோதி [*Jaffna*, 1889.] 16°. **14170. i. 1.**

—— *Mlēchchha-mata-khandana-sabhai.* ००० மிலேச்சமதகண்டனசபா காகலகோஷம். [Mlēch-chha-mata-khandana-sabhā-kākala-ghōsham, or Kiristu-mata-tūla-vātūlam. An anti-Christian tract, addressed to the Theistic Hindu-mata-khandana-sabhai.] pp. 12. யாழ்ப்பாணம் விகிர்தி [*Jaffna*, 1891.] 12°. **14170. a. 49.(2.)**

—— *Native Evangelical Society.* Forty-seventh Annual Report of the Jaffna Native Evangelical Society. 1893 . . . அறிக்கைப்பத்திரம். pp. 36. *Manippay*, 1894. 12°. **14170. a. 49.(6.)**

—— *Ṣaiva-paripālana-sabhai.* சிவத்துரோக கண்டன திக்கார தண்டனம். [Ṣiva-drōha-khandana-dhikkāra-dandanam. An answer to the tract entitled Ṣiva-drōha-khandanam by Vetti-vēr Pillai.] pp. 13. சென்னை துர்முகி [*Madras*, 1896.] 16°. **14170. d. 57.**

—— *Ṣaiva-prakāṣa-sabhai.* பாலபாடம். [Bāla-pāṭham. A series of readers for schools, issued by this Society, and comprising:—pt. i. (fasc. 2), Auvaiyār's Ātti-ṣūḍi and Konrai-vēndan; pt. ii., a reader by T. Kailāsa Pillai; pts. iii. and v., readers by K. V. Vēlu Pillai.] pts. 1-3, 5. நந்தன-விஜய [*Jaffna*, 1893-1894.] 12° & 8°. **14172. h. 92.**

—— —— சைவதூஷணபரிகாரம். [Ṣaiva-dūshaṇa-parihāram. Answers to Christian adversaries of the Ṣaiva system, republished in Madras.] pp. ii. 72. சென்னபட்டணம் கஅகூo [*Madras*, 1890.] 8°. **14170. e. 40.**

JAGA-NĀTHA NĀYUḌU, *M.* வைத்ஜகல்பம் . . . Hindu Pharmacopœia. Compiled from various ancient standard works of reputation, with an index of diseases and remedies . . . by M. Jaga-natham Naidu. Second edition. pp. xvi. 52, 310. *Madras*, 1906. 8°. **14171. g. 9.**

JAGA-RĀU MUDALIYĀR, *Rāyapuram A.Ṣ., of St. Mary's College, Madras.* See BESCHI (C. G. E.). தேம்பாவணி ஷூ [Tēm-bāv-aṇi. Edited with interpretation by Jaga-rāu.] 1901. 8°. **14170. cc. 8.**

—— University of Madras. The Tamil Text Examiner for the Matriculation Examination, 1898. pp. i. 128, xii. *Madras*, 1898. 8°. **14172. b. 16.(2.)**

JAGGAIYĀ PILLAI (C. P.). Olichittira Naya-num, or Practice of Photography, in Tamil. ஒளிச்சித்திர நயனம். pp. 2, 3, 53. *Madras*, 1884. 8°. **14170. i. 13.**

JAIMINI. [For the Ārūḍha-ṣāstram or Ñāna-pradīpikai, ascribed to Jaimini:] See ĀRŪḌHA-ṢĀSTRAM.

—— ஜயமுனிவாக்கியம் ஷூ [Jaya-muni-vākyam, or Jaya-muni-sūtra-moẓi-peyarpu. A book on astrology, professing to be a translation of the Aphorisms of "Jaya Muni," *i.e.* Jaimini. Edited by U. Vaidi-linga Jōdishar.] pp. 66. பவ [*Madras*, 1874.] 8°. **14172. b. 20.**

JANANĒNDRIYAṄGAḶ. சனனேந்திரியங்கள். [Jananēndriyaṅgaḷ. A Christian tract on sexual abuses.] pp. 24. யாழ்ப்பாணம் ஆனந்த [*Jaffna*, 1854.] 12°. **14170. i. 5.**

JANĀRDANAM PILLAI. See JENĀRTTANAM PILLAI.

JAYA MUNI. See JAIMINI.

JAYAṄ-GOṆḌĀN. சயங்கொண்டான் அருளிச்செய்த கலிங்கத்துப்பரணி. [Kaliṅgattu paraṇi. A poem on the conquest of Kalinga by the Chālu-kya king Rāja-kēsari Varma, or Kulōttuṅga Ṣoẓa Dēva I. Edited with introduction by V. G. Sūrya-nārāyaṇa Ṣāstri.] pp. 31, 130, i. *Madras*, 1898. 12°. **14172. a. 49.**

No. 1 of the Kalai-mayil-kalāpam.

JAYAṄ-GOṆḌĀN (*continued*). The Kalingattu Parani. [Extracts with English analysis by V. Kanaka-sabhai Piḷḷai.] 1890. *See* PERIODICAL PUBLICATIONS.—*Bombay*. The Indian Antiquary, *etc.* vol. xix., pp. 329-345. 1872, *etc.* 4°. **14096. e. (vol. 19.)**

—— *கலிங்கத்துப்பரணி.* [Kaliṅgattu paraṇi, the Rāja-pāramparyam and Avatāram. In Tamil and English, with Tamil commentary, *etc.*] *See* ACADEMIES, *etc.*—Madras.—*University of Madras*. Copious notes, *etc.* 1898. 8°. **14172. b. 16.(1.)**

JAYA-RĀMA CHEṬṬIYĀR, Ṣ. *See* MADRAS, *Presidency of.* *சென்னை ரைவிநியாசசபாஸ்திய்யமா-நாறு சாசநங்கள் ௸* [The Standing Orders of the Madras Board of Revenue. Translated by Jaya-rāma.] [1868.] 8°. **14170. g. 6.**

JEGA-NĀTHA PIḶḶAI, *Pēṟai, Daṣāvadhānam.* *See* ĀḶAVANDĀR. ∘∘∘ *ஞானவாசிட்ட ௸* [Ñāna-vāṣiṭṭav-amala-rāmāyaṇam. Edited by Jega-nātha.] 1890. 8°. **14172. b. 41.**

—— *See* ANANTA BHĀRATI. *ஸ்ரீ . . . கீர்த்தனை.* [Vēdānta-dēṣika-vaibhava-prakāṣikai-kīrttanai. Edited by Jega-nātha.] [1890.] 8°. **14172. c. 37.**

JEGA-RĀU MUDALIYĀR. *See* JAGA-RĀU MUDALIYĀR.

JENĀRTTANAM PIḶḶAI, *Kaḷambūr Nāga-nātham.* ∘∘∘ *ஸ்ரீ சந்திரஹாசக் கட்டியம்.* [Chandra-hāsa-kaṭṭiyam, also styled Poṟāmai-veṭṭi. Verses on the legend of Chandra-hāsan.] pp. ii. 27. *வேலூர்* [*Vellore*,] 1893. 12°. **14172. a. 35.(2.)**

JENSEN (HERMAN). A practical Tamil Reading Book for European beginners. [In Tamil, with English notes.] pp. 4, 162, 2. *Madras*, 1882. 8°. **14172. h. 77.**

—— A Classified Collection of Tamil Proverbs, [with translation, explanations, and indices,] by the Rev. Herman Jensen. pp. xxiv. 499. *London, Madras* [printed], 1897. 8°. **14171. b. 2.**

—— [Another copy, with a different title-page.] *London*, 1897. 8°. **2318. h. 12.**

Forms part of "Trübner's Oriental Series."

JEREMIAH (S. S.), called also C. ṢINNA-TAMBI PIḶḶAI. Jubilee Songs, composed for the occasion of the celebration of Her Most Gracious Majesty the Queen Empress Victoria's accession to the throne, *etc.* († *இராணிநாயகியார் அரசியற்றிய ஐம்பதாம்வருட மகோற்சவ வாழ்த்து.*) pp. 16. *Manippay*, 1887. 8°. **14172. c. 28.(2.)**

—— *விசிட்ட வாசகம் ௸* [Viṣiṭṭa-vāchakam.] (*Tamil Senior Reader, first part . . . Second edition.) pp. viii. 120. *Jaffna*, 1886. 12°. **14172. h. 72.**

—— *தமிழ் ஐந்தாம் புத்தகம்.* Tamil Fifth Reader. pp. 116. *Jaffna*, 1892. 12°. **14172. h. 88.**

JĒSU-DĀS (DANIEL). The Tamil Tutor, or Támil Grammar & Language. Containing various information on the study of the language, arranged and adapted for use in Lower Secondary Classes . . . New edition. (**தமிழ் ஆசிரியன் அல்லது தமிழ் இலக்கணமும் பாஷையும்.*) pp. ii. 248, 38. *Trichinopoly*, 1901. 12°. **14172. ee. 12.**

The numeration begins with p. 9; there are no pp. 1-8.

JĒSU-DĀSAN PIḶḶAI (C.). *See* KEENE (H. G.). Persian stories . . . translated into Tamil by C. Jesudasen Pillay. 1840. 12°. **14172. e. 2.**

JESUS CHRIST. *இயேசுநாயகர் திருச்சதகம்.* [Iyēṣu-nāyakar-tiru-ṣatakam] . . . A poem of one hundred stanzas on the character of Christ, *etc.* pp. 114. *Manepy*, 1850. 32°. **14170. a. 2.**

—— De Imitatione Christi. *கிறீஸ்துநாதர் அநுசாரம்.* [Ascribed to Thomas à Kempis. Translated from the Latin by Ṣ. Ñāna-prakāṣa-nāthar.] pp. 390. *புதுவை ௲௮௱௬௩* [*Pondicherry*, 1863.] 16°. **14170. a. 20.**

—— *கிருஸ்துபோன்ற ஒழுக்க முறை நூல்.* (The Imitation of Christ. [Translated by] Atmanathan.) 1905, *etc.* *See* PERIODICAL PUBLICATIONS.—*Srirangam.* *ஸ்ரீ வாணீ விலாஸினீ.* (Sri Vani Vilasini.) vol. i., *etc.* 1905, *etc.* 8°. **14172. m. 1. (vol. 1, etc.)**

In progress.

JOHANNAS. *See* JONAS.

JONAS, *T.C.R.* *See* SINDHU-RĀYALU, *T.*, and JONAS, *T.C.R.* Baradha Sungeeta Swayabodini, *etc.* 1895. 12°. **14170. i. 45.**

JONES (J. P.). *See* THEOLOGY. Outlines of Systematic Theology, *etc.* [Edited and revised by J. P. Jones.] 1901. 8°. **14170. bbb. 1.**

JOSEPH (A.). A Cummi Poem on Coffee Planting, with English translation. (கோப்பிக் கிருஷிக் கும்மி.) pp. i. 71, 22. *Jaffna*, 1869. 8°. **14172. b. 31.**

JOSEPH (PUVIMANNA-ṢIṄGA MUDALIYĀR). *See* PUVIMANNA-ṢIṄGA MUDALIYĀR JOSEPH.

JOSEPH MUNSHI (A.). *See* MUNSHI (A. J.).

JOYES (WALTER). *See* GARTHWAITE (L.). First Reader . . . Edited by W. Joyes, *etc.* 1879. 12°. **14172. h. 25.**

—— *See* PAVAṆANDI. Grammatica Tamuliensis, or An English version of the . . . Nunnool . . . By W. Joyes and S. Samuel Pillay, *etc.* 1848-1851. 8°. **14172. f. 10.**

—— —— [Another copy.] **14172. f. 20.**

—— Second Reader, Tamil . . . இரண்டாம்பாடபுஸ்தகம். pp. xii. 183. *Madras*, 1878. 16°. **14172. h. 27.**

JUBILEE. Jubilee Tract. Jaffna Bible Society—1853 († designed to show . . . the extensive operations of the British and Foreign Bible Society, the great difference between the Bible and the sacred books of the Hindus, *etc.*). வேதாகமசங்கத்தின் மகோற்சவத்தைப்பற்றியபுத்தகம். pp. 24, iv. *Jaffna*, 1853. 12°. **14170. b. 28.**

JUDSON (ADONIRAM). The Life of Dr. Judson. . . . ஜட்ஸன் போதகரின் சரித்திரச் சுருக்கம். pp. 91. *Madras*, 1879. 16°. **14170. a. 26.**

KACHI ṢĀSTRI, *Vaḷavanūr*. *See* PURĀṆAS.—*Brahmāṇḍa-purāṇam.* எயினனூர் . . . ஆதிபுரதலபுராணம். [Ādipura-tala-purāṇam. Metrically adapted, on the basis of the version of Kachi Ṣāstri.] [1896.] 8°. **14170. ee. 8.**

KACHIY-APPAR, *Kāñchi Kāḷattiy-appar.* *See* PURĀṆAS.—*Skanda-purāṇam.* கந்தபுராணம். [Kanda-purāṇam. Adapted into Tamil verse by Kachiy-appar.] [1869.] 8°. **14170. f. 3.**

—— *See* PURĀṆAS.—*Skanda-purāṇam.* கந்தபுராணம் [Kanda-purāṇam. In the metrical version of Kachiy-appar.] 1896, *etc.* 8°. **14170. f. 23.**

—— *See* PURĀṆAS.—*Skanda-purāṇam.* ஸ்ரீ கந்தபுராண ஞ [Kanda-purāṇa-churukkam. A prose epitome of Kachiy-appar's Kanda-purāṇam.] 1907. 8°. **14170. e. 28.**

KACHIY-APPAR, *Kāñchi-Kāḷattiy-appar* (*continued*). *See* PURĀṆAS.—*Skanda-purāṇam.* கந்தபுராணம். [Kanda-purāṇam, Tāraka-vadha-paṭalam. In the version of Kachiy-appar. With life of the latter and commentary.] 1900. 8°. [*University of Madras; B.A. Examination.*] **14172. bb. 6.(6.)**

—— *See* PURĀṆAS.—*Skanda-purāṇam.* ∘∘∘ கந்தபுராணம் ஞ [Teyvayānaiy-ammai-tiru-maṇa-paṭalam. From the Skanda-purāṇam as translated by Kachiy-appar.] [1889.] 8°. **14170. e. 30.**

—— *See* PURĀṆAS.—*Skanda-purāṇam.* கந்தபுராணம் ஞ [Vaḷḷiy-ammai-tiru-maṇa-paṭalam. From the Skanda-purāṇam as translated by Kachiy-appar.] [1886.] 8°. **14170. e. 25.**

—— *See* PURĀṆAS.—*Skanda-purāṇam.* கந்தபுராண ஞ [Kanda-purāṇa-vachanam. The Kanda-purāṇam, done into prose.] 1890-1891. 8°. [*Itihāsa-mañjari Series.*] **14172. d. 11.**

KACHIY-APPAR, *Tirutaṇigai, disciple of Ṣiva-ñānar, of Tiruvāvaḍuduṛai.* *See* PURĀṆAS.—*Vināyaka-purāṇam.* பார்க்கவபுராணம் ஞ [Vināyaka-purāṇam, or Bhārgava-purāṇam. A metrical version by Kachiy-appar.] 1899. 8°. **14170. f. 15.**

—— *See* PURĀṆAS.—*Vināyaka-purāṇam.* பார்க்கவ புராணம் ஞ [Vināyaka-purāṇam, or Bhārgava-purāṇam. A prose paraphrase of the metrical version by Kachiy-appar.] 1899. 8°. **14170. ee. 19.**

—— ∘∘∘ காஞ்சிப்புராணம். [Kāñchi-purāṇam. The local Ṣaiva legends of Conjevaram. The first part by Ṣiva-ñānar, and the second part by his disciple Kachiy-appar. Edited with commentary by T. K. Subba-rāya Cheṭṭi.] [1891, *etc.*] 4°. *See* ṢIVA-ÑĀNA SVĀMI, *Tiruvāvaḍuduṛai.* **14170. f. 14.**

—— ஸ்ரீ . . . தணிகைப்புராணம். [Taṇigai-purāṇam. A series of poems upon the sacred legends of Taṇigai (Tirutani). Edited by Ṣ. V. Dāmōdaram Piḷḷai.] pp. iv. ii. 426. சென்னபட்டணம் சுபாஜு [*Madras*, 1883.] 8°. **14170. e. 64.**

KADAVUṈ MĀ-MUNI, *Tiru-chiṭṭambalam.* திருவாதவூரர்புராணம். [Tiruvādavūrar-purāṇam. A poetical account of the legends relating to the Ṣaiva poet Māṇikka-vāchakar. Edited by N. C.

Tamb'-aiyā Piḷḷai.] pp. 75. யாழ்ப்பாணத்து விஜய [*Jaffna*, 1893.] 8°. **14171. a. 9.**

—— மாணிக்கவாசகரென்னும் திருவாதவூரர் புராணம். [Tiru-vādavūrar-purāṇam, or Māṇikka-vāchakar-purāṇam. With a paraphrase by Kāñchīpuram Kumāra-svāmi Dēṣikar. Edited by Tiruv-aruṇai Sabhā-pati Svāmi.] pp. 232; 10 *plates*. சென்னை [*Madras*,] 1896. 12°. **14171. a. 10.**

—— ००० திருவாதவூரடிகள்புராணமும் . . . திருவெம்பாவையும். [Tiruvādavūr-aḍigaḷ-purāṇam. Followed by the Tiruv-em-bāvai of Māṇikka-vāchakar. Edited by M. K. Vēṟ Piḷḷai.] pp. 66, 4. ஏவிளம்பி [*Jaffna*, 1897.] 8°. **14171. a. 16.**

—— திருவாதவூரர்புராணவசநம் [Tiruvāda-vūrar-purāṇa-vachanam. The Tiruvādavūrar-purāṇam, rendered into prose by P. Vāsudēva Mudaliyār.] See TIRU-MURAI.—*Tiru-vāchakam*. ००० திருவாசகம் ஆ [Tiru-vāchakam.] 1897. 8°. **14172. b. 57.**

—— (†மாணிக்கவாசகசுவாமிகள் புராணவசனம்.) [Māṇikka-vāchaka-svāmigaḷ-purāṇa-vachanam. A prose version of the Vādavūrar-purāṇam.] pp. 184. [*Madras?* 1870?] 16°. **14170. d. 90.**
Without title-page.

—— The sixth chapter of the Tiruvathavur Purana, entitled "The Vanquishing of the Buddhists in Disputation." Translated . . . by Simon Casie Chitty. (Journal of the Ceylon Branch of the Royal Asiatic Society. 1846-7. Vol. i., no. 2, pp. 63-83.) *Colombo*, 1861. 8°. **Ac. 8830.(vol. i., no. 2.)**

KADIRAI-VĒṞ PIḶḶAI, *N., of Melai-Puloli, Jaffna*. See BĀLA-SUBRAHMAṆYA KAVI-RĀYAR. ००० பரணித்தலப்புராணம் ஆ [Paraṇi-tala-purāṇam. Edited with paraphrase by Kadirai-vēṟ Piḷḷai.] 1903. 12°. **14170. d. 80.**

—— See DICTIONARIES. தமிழ்ப் பேரகராதி. [Tamiṟ-pēr-agarādi. Enlarged by Kadirai-vēṟ Piḷḷai.] 1899. 8°. **14172. f. 24.**

—— See ELL'-APPA NĀVALAR. ००० திருவருணைக் கலம்பக ஆ [Tiruv-aruṇai-kalambakam. With commentary by Kadirai-vēṟ Piḷḷai.] 1902. 8°. **14172. c. 47.**

—— See PURĀṆAS.—*Kūrma-purāṇam*. ००० கூர்மபுராண ஆ [Kūrma-purāṇam. In the version of Ativīra-rāma Pāṇḍiyan. With commentary by Kadirai-vēṟ Piḷḷai.] 1898-1899. 8°. **14170. ff. 6.**

—— See VARADA-RĀJA PAṆḌITAR, *K. R.* ஏகாதசி புராணம். [Ēkādaṣi-purāṇam. Edited and annotated by Kadirai-vēṟ Piḷḷai.] 1898. 12°. **14170. ee. 21.**

—— See VARADA-RĀJA PAṆḌITAR, *K. R.* ००० சிவராத்திரி புராண ஆ [Ṣiva-rātri-purāṇam. Edited with commentary by Kadirai-vēṟ Piḷḷai.] 1902. 8°. **14170. ee. 59.**

—— சுப்பிரமணிய பராக்கிரமம். [Subrahmaṇya-parākramam. An account of the myths of the various manifestations of the god Subrahmaṇya.] pp. xvi. 414, ii.; 90 *plates*. சென்னை பரபவ [*Madras*, 1906.] 12°. **14170. dd. 9.**

KADIRA-VĒṞ PIḶḶAI, *of Tambalagamam, Trincomali*. கோணேசர்பதிகம் [Kōṇēṣar-padigam. Hymns to Ṣiva as worshipped at Trincomali.] pp. 12. வல்வை விரோதி [*Valuvettiturai*, 1889.] 16°. **14172. a. 4.(2.)**

ḲĀDIRĪ (MUḤAMMAD). See MUḤAMMAD ḲĀDIRĪ.

ḲĀDIR ṢĀḤIB, *S.P.S.K., of Penang*. ஹாஸ்ய மஞ்சரி. [Hāsya-mañjari. 9 humorous tales.] pp. 17. பினாங்கு [*Penang*,] 1898. 12°. **14171. a. 6.(3.)**

ḲĀDIR ṢĀḤIB, *Tēraḷandūrī*. See MUḤAMMAD 'ABD al-ḲĀDIR ibn ĀDAM.

KADIR-VĒL KAVI-RĀJA PAṆḌITAR. See SUBBA-RĀYA MUDALIYĀR, *V.*, MUTTI-RĀMA KAVI-RĀYAR, *G.*, and KADIR-VĒL KAVI-RĀJA PAṆḌITAR. ஸ்ரீ மஹாபாரதக்கீர்த்தனை ஆ [Mahā-bhārata-kīrttanai.] [1905.] 8°. **14172. bbb. 1.**

KADIR-VĒLU NĀḌĀR, *K.Ṣ.* பகையதமென்னும் படுதோஷி விலாசம். [Paḍu-dōshi-vilāsam, or Pagaiyadam. A satiric lyrical drama.] pp. 2, 182. சென்னை [*Madras*,] 1905. 8°. **14171. k. 1.**

KĀGANĀR. See VIḶAMBIYA NĀGANĀR.

KAILĀSA PIḶḶAI, *T., of Jaffna*. See JAFFNA.—*Ṣaiva-prakāṣa-sabhai*. பாலபாடம். [Bāla-pāṭham. Pt. ii., a reader by Kailāsa Piḷḷai.] [1893-1894.] 12° & 8°. **14172. h. 92.(pt. 2.)**

KĀḶA-MĒGHAM. ஸ்ரீ . . . காளமேகப்புலவர் . . . பாடியவை. [174 occasional verses. With interpretation.] *See* TANI-PĀḌAL. (†தனிப்பாடற்றிரட்டு) [Tani-pāḍaṯ-ṯiraṭṭu.] pp. 1-89. [1892, *etc.*] 8°. **14172. c. 39.(5.)**

KĀLIDĀSA. அபிஜ்ஞானசாகுந்தலம். [Abhijñāna-ṣākuntalam. An abstract in Tamil, with occasional translations.] *See* SUNDARA-RĀJA ṢARMĀ, *D.* வ்யாஸ ... பார்யாதருமம். (Vyasa and Vatsyayana's Bharyadharmam, *etc.*) pp. 179-197. 1901. 12°. **14085. b. 44.**

—— ००० சாகுந்தல நாடகம். [Ṣākuntalam. Translated by N. Vēdāchalam Piḷḷai.] pp. 4, 146. 1907. *See* PERIODICAL PUBLICATIONS.—*Madras.* ००० ஞானசாகரம். [Ñāna-sāgaram.] vol. ii., no. 1—vol. iii., no. 12. 1902, *etc.* 8°. **14172. i. 10.(vol. 2-3.)**

—— மேகதூதக்காரிகை. [Mēgha-dūta-kārikai. A metrical version by Ṣ. A. Kumāra-svāmi Piḷḷai, preceded by a life of Kālidāsa and glossary.] pp. xiv. 20. கொக்குவில் துர்முகி [*Kokkuvil,* 1897.] 8°. **14170. l. 32.(4.)**

—— இரகுவம்மிசம். [Raghu-vaṃṣam. A translation into Tamil verse by Araṣa-kēsari of Jaffna. Edited by Nallūr Ṣ. Ponn'-ambala Piḷḷai.] pp. i. ii. 310, i. யாழ்ப்பாணம் [*Jaffna,*] 1887. 8°. **14172. b. 33.**

—— இரகுவம்ச வசனம். [Raghu-vaṃṣam. Translated into Tamil prose, with introduction, by Ṣ. M. Naṭēṣa Ṣāstri, and edited by V. M. Ṣaṭhakōpa-rāmānujāchāryar.] *Madras,* 1901, *etc.* 8°. **14172. bb. 2.**
In progress.

—— ரகுவம்ஶம் - முதலாவது - ஸர்க்கம் [Raghu-vaṃṣam. Canto i., in Sanskrit, edited with literal interpretations and paraphrase in Tamil, styled Bāla-sad-guru-bōdhikā, by Ṣiṟugaḷattūr Rāma-svāmi Ṣāstri.] pp. iv. 98. திருவாதி தாரண [*Tiruvadi,* 1884.] 8°. **14070. c. 44.**

KAḶḶA-PIRĀN PIḶḶAI, *Ṣ. V.* *See* SHAKSPERE (W.). வெனிஸ் வர்த்தகன் (Shakespeare's Merchant of Venice, in Tamil, by S. V. Kallapiran Pillai.) 1904. 12°. **14171. i. 1.(2.)**

KALYĀṆA-NĀṬAKAM. கலியாணநாடகம். [Kalyāṇa-nāṭakam. An operatic play on marriage-practices. Edited by M. Ātma-nātha Bhāgavatar.] pp. 94. தேவகோட்டை [*Devakota,*] 1900. 8°. **14170. l. 37.(3.)**

KALYĀṆA-SUNDARAM PIḶḶAI, *Mudukuḷatlūr Ashṭāvadhānam V.* ००० மெய்யரிச்சந்திர நாடகம். [Meyy'-arichandira-nāṭakam. A drama on the legend of the truthful Hariṣchandra.] pp. 773. *Madura,* சென்னை [*Madras* printed], 1905. 8°. **14171. k. 5.**

KALYĀṆA-SUNDARA MUDALIYĀR, *Ashṭāvadhānam Pūvai.* *See* RĀMA-LIṄGA SVĀMI, *Tiruv-aruṭ-prakāṣa-vaḷḷalār.* ००० திருவருட்பா ஐ [Tiruv-aruṭ-pā-tiru-muṟai-tiraṭṭu. Revised by Kalyāṇa-sundara.] 1892. 8°. **14172. d. 14.**

—— *See* TIRUVĒṞKĀṬṬU. திருவேற்காட்டுப்புராணம். [Tiruvēṟkāṭṭu-purāṇam. Edited by Kalyāṇa-sundara.] 1903. 8°. **14170. ff. 14.**

—— *See* UMĀ-PATI ṢIVĀCHĀRYAR. சிவப்பிரகாசம். [Eight works—viz., Neñju-viḍu-dūdu, with commentary of Kalyāṇa-sundara, *etc.*] 1897. 8°. [*Mey-kaṇḍa-ṣāttiram.*] **14170. ff. 3.**

—— சித்தாந்தக் கட்டளை. [Siddhānta-kaṭṭaḷai. A compendium of the Ṣaiva-Siddhāntam. Second edition.] pp. 37. சென்னை [*Madras,*] 1890. 16°. **14170. d. 33.(1.)**

—— சித்தாந்தவசனபூஷணம். [Siddhānta-vachana-bhūshaṇam. A dialectic exposition of the Ṣaiva religious philosophy.] pp. iv. 325, ii. சென்னை சுபகிருது [*Madras,* 1902.] 12°. **14170. d. 3.**

KALYĀṆA-SUNDARA ṢĀSTRI, *Ṣāttanūru.* *See* NĪLAKAṆṬHA DĪKSHITAR. ஸ்ரீ... கலிவிடம்பநம் [Kali-viḍambanam. With Tamil translation by Kalyāṇa-sundara.] 1904. 16°. **14070. a. 9.**

KĀMĀKSHI. காமாக்ஷி லீலா பிரபாவம். [Kāmākshi-līlā-prabhāvam. An account of the legends of the goddess Kāmākshi and her cult in Conjevaram. Translated by K. Ē. Ālāla-sundaram Piḷḷai and M. Bhairava Ṣivāchāryar.] pp. ii. vi. 104, i. சென்னை [*Madras,*] 1906. 8°. **14170. eee. 20.(2.)**

KAMALĀKARA BHAṬṬAR, *son of Rāma-kṛushṇa.* ஶூத்ரகமலாகராக்யஶூத்ரதர்மதத்த்வம் [Ṣūdra-kamalākara, or Ṣūdra-dharma-tattva. Part ix. of the Dharma-tattva, treating of the religious duties of the fourth caste. In Sanskrit, edited with a commentary called Ṣūdra-sarvasva and Tamil translation by Ṣrīnivāsa Dīkshitar.] 1901, *etc.* *See* PERIODICAL PUBLICATIONS.—*Chi-*

dambaram. ப்ரஹ்மவித்யா *etc.* [Brahma-vidyā.] vol. xv., no. 1, *etc.* 1886, *etc.* 4°.
14096. dd. 3.(vol. 15, etc.)
In progress!

KAMALA MUNI. ... சாமுத்திரிகாலட்சண-மென்னும் இரேகைசாஸ்திரம். [Rēkhai-śāstram, or Sāmudrikā-lakshaṇam. A metrical treatise on palmistry, in 7 chapters. Edited by P. Mārga-liṅga Nāyanār.] pp. 238. பிரமாதி [*Madras,* 1879.] 16°. **14172. a. 19.**

KAMBAN. [For editions of Bhīma Kavi-rāyar's prose version of the Rāmar-aśva-mēdham :] *See* BHĪMA KAVI-RĀYAR.

—— *See* ŚELVA-KĒŚAVA-RĀYA MUDALIYĀR, *T.* Kambar. 1902. 8°. **14171. a. 53.(2.)**

—— *See* VINSON (É. H. J.). Littérature Tamoule Ancienne . . . Le Ramayana de Kamban', *etc.* [An essay on the poem, with translation of extracts.] 1861. 8°. **14172. b. 26.**

—— ஸ்ரீமத் கம்பராமாயணம் ஆரணியகாண்டம் ௸ [Kamba-rāmāyaṇam, Āraṇya-kāṇḍam. With exegetical commentary by M. R. Kanda-sāmi Kavi-rāyar and Ś. Veṅkaṭa-rāyalu Nāyuḍu. Edited by M. R. Aruṇāchala Kavi-rāyar.] pp. viii. 556. சென்னை [*Madras,*] 1900. 8°.
14172. d. 25.

—— கம்பராமாயணம். [Kamba-rāmāyaṇam, Śūrpaṇakhai-paṭalam, from the Āraṇya-kāṇḍam. With life of the poet and commentary.] pp. 127. *See* ACADEMIES, *etc.* — Madras.—*University of Madras.* University of Madras. B.A. Examination, *etc.* 1900. 8°. **14172. bb. 6.(6.)**

—— ஸ்ரீமத்கம்பராமாயணம் ௸ [Kamba-rāmāyaṇam, Ayōdhyā-kāṇḍam. With paraphrase and commentary by T. Shaṇmukham Piḷḷai.] pts. i.-iv. pp. 1-192. சென்னை [*Madras,*] 1896. 8°.
14172. d. 17.

—— ஸ்ரீமத்கம்பராமாயணம். அயோத்தியா-காண்டம் ௸ [Kamba-rāmāyaṇam, Ayōdhyā-kāṇḍam. With commentary by T. K. Shōḍaśāva-dhānam Subba-rāya Cheṭṭi.] pp. 374, 89. [*Madras,*] 1904. 8°. **14172. bb. 12.**

—— ... ஸ்ரீமத்கம்பராமாயணம் . . . சுந்தர-காண்டம். [Kamba-rāmāyaṇam, Sundara-kāṇḍam. Edited by K. Chidambara-nātha Kavi-rājar.] pp. 171. திருநெல்வேலி சுக்கில [*Tinnevelli,* 1870.] 8°. **14172. c. 4.**

—— Kamba Ramayanam. Edited [with a summary of the story] by Pandit P. R. Krishnam-achariar [and with an English preface by T. K. Bāla-subrahmaṇyam]. Sundarakandam (சுந்தர-காண்டம்). (Sri Vani Vilas Tamil Series no. 1.) pp. i. xxxvi. cii. 279. ஸ்ரீரங்கம் [*Srirangam,*] 1907. 12°. **14172. a. 62.**

—— ஸ்ரீமத் கம்பராமாயண வசனம் ௸ [Kamba-rāmāyaṇam, Bāla-kāṇḍam to Yuddha-k°. Rendered into prose by Shaṇmukham Piḷḷai.] 2 vols. 1891-1893. *See* ITIHĀSA-MAÑJARI. Ithihasa Manjari Series. [1888]-1894. 8°. **14172. d. 11.**

—— ஸ்ரீராமாயண வசனம். சப்தகாண்டங்களின் சுருக்கமும் . . . ஸ்ரீராமர் அஸ்வமேதயாகமும் . . . மகாவிந்தவசனமும் ௸ [Rāmāyaṇa-vachanam. Comprising a prose summary of Kamban's Rāmāyaṇam with Oṭṭa-kūttar's Uttara-kāṇḍam, Bhīma Kavi-rāyar's Rāmar-aśva-mēdha-yāgam, and Mahā-vinda-vachanam by V. Gōvinda Piḷḷai. Edited by Puduvai Nārāyaṇa-dāsar.] pp. 436 ; 16 *plates.* சென்னை [*Madras,*] 1903. 8°.
14172. d. 27.

—— இதிஹாசசிரேஷ்டமாகிய ஸ்ரீமத் கம்பராமாயண வசனம். [Kamba-rāmāyaṇa-vachanam. A prose version of the poem of Kamban, and also of the Uttara-kāṇḍam of Oṭṭa-kūttar. Revised by Pālūr Vēlu Dēśikar.] 2 vols. *Madras,* 1903. 8°. **14172. d. 2.**

—— ... ஸ்ரீமத்கம்பராமாயணக்கருப்பொருள். [Kamba-rāmāyaṇa-karu-poruḷ. An epitome of the Rāmāyaṇam, in 100 stanzas. Edited with interpretation and notes by K. Purushōttama Mudaliyār.] pp. ii. i. iv. ii. 121. சென்னபட்டணம் [*Madras,*] 1882. 12°. **14172. a. 24.**

—— ... சரஸ்வதியந்தாதி மூலபாடம். [Sarasvatiy-antādi. An artificial poem in honour of the goddess Sarasvatī.] pp. 14. சென்னை [*Madras,*] 1887. 16°. **14172. a. 7.(2.)**

—— [66 occasional verses, ascribed to Kamban. With interpretation.] *See* TANI-PĀḌAL. (†தனிப்-

பாடற்றிரட்டு) [Tani-pāḍaṭ-ṭiraṭṭu]. pp. 126-155. [1892, *etc.*] 8°. **14172. c. 39.(5.)**

KĀMIL WALĪ DAIKKĀ. *See* [Addenda] 'ABD al-KĀDIR LEBBAI.

KANAKA-SABHAI PIḶḶAI, *Kūḍalūr.* வருணசிந்தாமணி. [Varṇa-chintāmaṇi. A dissertation on the Hindu caste-system. Preceded by divers commendatory verses. Edited by M. R. Aruṇāchala Kavi-rāyar.] pp. lvi. 528. சென்னை [*Madras,*] 1901. 8°. **14170. g. 22.**

KANAKA-SABHAI PIḶḶAI, *V.* Tamil Historical Texts [with translation. Comprising Poigaiyār's Kaḷa-vaṟi, Jayaṅ-goṇḍān's Kaliṅgattu parani, the Vikrama-chōṟan-ulā, *etc.*] 1889, *etc.* *See* PERIODICAL PUBLICATIONS.—*Bombay.* The Indian Antiquary, *etc.* vol. xviii., *etc.* 1872, *etc.* 4°. **14096. e. (vol. 18, etc.)**

In progress?

KANAKA-SABHAI PIḶḶAI, *V., of Chidambaram.* காணூர் செல்வியம்மன்பதிகம். [Kāṇūr-ṣelliyamman-badigam. A hymn in 10 stanzas on the goddess Ṣelli Amman of Kanur.] pp. 8. சிதம்பரம் பாரபவ [*Chidambaram,* 1906.] 16°. **14170. d. 36.(6.)**

KANAKA-SABHĀ PIḶḶAI, *Uḍuvil A.* பூகோளசாத்திரம். (The Student's Manual of Geography ... Part i. Asia. Part ii. Europe.) 2 pts. *Manippay, Madras,* 1887-1890. 16°. **14172. h. 50.**

KANDA PIḶḶAI, *Vēlanai.* *See* TATTVA-PRAKĀṢA SVĀMI. ००० தத்துவப்பிரகாசம் ஸ்ரீ [Tattva-prakāṣam. Edited by Kanda Piḷḷai.] [1893.] 8°. **14170. e. 46.**

KAṆḌAR-ĀDITTAR. [For the hymns of this author contained in the Tiruv-iṣai-pā :] *See* TIRU-MUṞAI.

KANDA-SĀMI AIYAR, *Tirutaṇigai Ṣara-vaṇa Perumāḷ.* *See* ATIVĪRA-RĀMA PĀṆḌIYAN. நைடதம் ஸ்ரீ [Naiḍadam. With commentary on cantos 6-28 by Kanda-sāmi, *etc.*] [1842.] 8°. **14172. b. 58.**

—— *See* ATIVĪRA-RĀMA PĀṆḌIYAN. ००० நைடதம் ஸ்ரீ [Naiḍadam. With commentaries by Kanda-sāmi, *etc.*] [1875.] 8°. **14172. b. 59.**

—— *See* ATIVĪRA-RĀMA PĀṆḌIYAN. ००० நைடதம் ஸ்ரீ [Naiḍadam. With commentaries of Kanda-sāmi, *etc.*] 1881. 8°. **14172. b. 14.**

KANDA-SĀMI AIYAR, *Tirutaṇigai Ṣara-vaṇa Perumāḷ (continued).* *See* AUVAIYĀR. — *Supposititious Works.* ००० விநாயகர் அகவல் ஸ்ரீ [Vināyakar-agaval, *etc.* Edited by Kanda-sāmi.] 1889. 16°. **14172. a. 33.**

KANDA-SĀMI KAVI-RĀYAR, *Uḍumalaipēṭṭai M. Rāma-sāmi, of Settur.* *See* KAMBAN. ஸ்ரீ . . . ராமாயணம் ஸ்ரீ [Kamba-rāmāyaṇam, Āraṇya-kāṇḍam. With commentary by Kanda-sāmi and Veṅkaṭa-rāyalu.] 1900. 8°. **14172. d. 25.**

—— *See* SHAṆMUKHAM PIḶḶAI, *Ṣ.A.* ००० மாலைமாற்றுமாலை ஸ்ரீ [Mālai-māṭṭu-mālai. Edited with commentary by Kanda-sāmi.] 1903. 8°. **14172. bb. 3.(5.)**

KANDA-SĀMI KAVI-RĀYAR, *V.* *See* KANDA-SĀMI PIḶḶAI, *V. Ṣ.*

KANDA-SĀMI MUDALIYĀR, *Kaḷattūr Vēda-giri.* *See* AGASTYAR. ००० அகஸ்திய . . . வாதகாவியம் ஸ்ரீ [Vāta-kāvyam, *etc.* Edited by Kanda-sāmi.] [1895]-1903. 8°. **14170. e. 70-74.**

—— *See* AGASTYAR. ००० நாலுகாண்ட வயித்தியகாவியம் கூஉா. [Nālu-kāṇḍa-vaidya-kāvyam. Edited by Kanda-sāmi.] 1896. 8°. **14170. i. 48.**

—— *See* SIDDHARGAḶ. ००० ஆத்மரக்ஷாமிர்தம் ஸ்ரீ [Ātma-rakshāmirtam. Edited by Kanda-sāmi.] [1874.] 8°. **14170. i. 42.**

KANDA-SĀMI PIḶḶAI, *of Andar Street, Trichinopoli.* A Manual of Practical Cattle Chintamani. By Cundasawmy Pillay. (மாட்டின் அனுபோக வயித்தியசிந்தாமணி.) pp. i. iv. 152. *Madras,* 1895. 8°. **14170. i. 33.**

KANDA-SĀMI PIḶḶAI, *Madurai Āṟu-mugam.* அல்லியரசாணி நாடகம். [Alliy-araṣāṇi-nāṭakam. A play on the legend of Arjuna's marriage with the princess Alli of Madura.] pp. 168. *Madras,* 1902. 8°. **14170. l. 59.**

—— விகட சுந்தரி ஸ்ரீ (Vigata Sundari.) [A romance based on Shakspere's "Taming of the Shrew."] pp. 78, ii. *Madras,* 1906. 8°. **14171. e. 8.**

No. 2 of "M.N.C. Series."

KANDA-SĀMI PIḶḶAI, *Pālakāḍu Muttu-kaṟu.* *See* [Addenda] BĀLA-SUBRAHMAṆYA KAVI-RĀYAR. பறணித் தலபுராண வசனம். [Paṟani-tala-purāṇa-vachanam. A prose paraphrase by Kanda-sāmi of the Paṟani-tala-purāṇam.] 1905. 12°. **14170. dd. 2.**

KANDA-SĀMI PIḶḶAI, *Vīrākshimaṅgalam Ṣinna-karuppana, Kavi-rāyar.* மரபாள புராணம் என்னும் வேளாள புராணம். [Vēḷāḷa-purāṇam, or Marapāḷa-p°. A poem on the origins and religious traditions of the Vēḷāḷar or farmer caste. With an account of the author by N. Muttu-sāmi Upādhyāyan, and introductory verses *etc.* by divers writers.] pp. viii. 16, 208. ஈரோடு [*Erode,*] 1907. 8°. **14172. bb. 7.**

KANDA-SĀMI PULAVAR, *Madurai.* தருமநூல். மிருதிசந்திரிகை. விவகாரசாரசங்கிரகம். (* An abridgment, in the Tamil language, of the Smriti Chandricá, a treatise [by Dēvaṇṇa Bhaṭṭar] on the municipal law of the Hindus. By Madura Condaswámi Pulaver.) [Vyavahāra-sāra-saṅgraham. Edited by Veṅkaṭ-rāya Ṣāstri.] pp. ii. i. i. 325, ii. iii. *Madras,* 1826. Fol. **14170. g. 15.**

—— Vyavahara-sara-sangraha, Abrégé substantiel de Droit, d'après la Smriti-tchandrika ou Exposé de Loi. (* Legislation Hindoue, publiée sous le titre de Vyavahara-sara-sangraha ou Abrégé substantiel de Droit . . . Traduite du Tamil par F.-E. Sicé.) pp. xii. 251. *Pondichéry,* 1857. 8°. **14170. g. 14.**

The first title-page is a translation of that prefixed to the Madras edition of 1826.

—— விவகாரசாரசங்கிரகம். [Vyavahāra-sāra-saṅgraham. Edited by Ṣ. Ṣ. Ṣiva-rāma Mudaliyār.] pp. xvi. ii. 121, vi. சென்னை [*Madras,*] 1894. 8°. **14170. g. 16.**

KANDA-SĀMI PULAVAR, *Tirupūvaṇam.* ००० திருப்பூவணநாதருலா. [Tirupūvaṇa-nāthar-ulā. 469 Ṣaiva devotional verses to the local deity. Edited by U. V. Sāmināth'-aiyar.] pp. ii. 3, 40. சென்னபட்டணம் [*Madras,*] 1904. 8°. **14170. eee. 8.**

KANDA-SVĀMI AIYAR. *See* KANDA-SĀMI AIYAR.

KAṆṆ'-AḤMAD MAKHDŪM MUḤAMMAD. *See* MAKHDŪM MUḤAMMAD ibn MAKHDŪM PIḶḶAI.

KANN'-AIYA-DĀSAR, *Vēlūr.* *See* MAHĀ-BHAKTA-VIJAYAM. ००० ஸ்ரீமகா பக்தவிஜயம் [Mahā-bhakta-vijayam. Vol. iii., iv., translated by Kann'-aiya-dāsar.] 1905. 4°. **14170. ff. 18.**

KANN'-AIYA NĀYUḌU, *Vēlūr.* *See* MAYAN. உ . . . சர்வார்த்த சிற்பசிந்தாமணி. [Sarvārtha-ṣirpa-chintāmaṇi. Edited by Kann'-aiya.] 1905. 8°. **14171. g. 5.**

KANN'-AIYA NĀYUḌU, *Vēlūr (continued).* கீசகவிலாசம். [Kīchaka-vilāsam. A drama upon the epic story of Kīchaka's attempt to seduce Draupadī.] pp. 62. *Madras,* 1897. 8°. **14170. l. 47.**

KAṆṆANĀR, *Kumaṭṭūr.* இரண்டாம் பத்து. [Decade ii. Ten poems on the Chera king Neḍun-Chēralādan.] *See* PADIṮṮU-PATTU. ००० பதிற்றுப்பத்து ஷ [Padiṯṯu-pattu.] pp. 1-23. 1904. 8°. **14172. bb. 14.**

KAṆṆAN AYYA, *Tirukuḍandai Purōhita Ṣen-dāmarai.* ००० పరమవిలక్షణ తిరువారాధన క్రమసంగ్రహము. [Tiruv-ārādhana-krama-saṅgrahamu. A book of hymns, offices, *etc.*, for the liturgies of the Rāmānujī. Vaishṇavas, in Sanskrit, Telugu, and Tamil. Edited by Māḍabhūshi Tarka-tīrtha Rāmānujāchāryar.] pp. ii. 96; 1 *plate.* చెన్నపట్టణము [*Madras,*] 1902. 12°. **14033. a. 46.**

KANN'-AYYA. *See* KANN'-AIYA.

KAṆṆ'-UḌAIYA VAḶḶAL, *Ṣīgāḻi, disciple of Ñāna-sambandhar.* மாயாப்பிரலாபம். [Māyā-pralāpam. A Ṣaiva Vedantic poem. Edited by T. Shaṇmukham Piḷḷai.] pp. 19. சென்னை விபவ [*Madras,* 1869.] 16°. **14170. d. 8.(1.)**

—— ००० ஒழிவிலொடுக்க மூலமும் . . . உரையும் [Oḻivil oḍukkam. A work on Vedantic philosophy. With a commentary by Tirupōrūr Chidambara Svāmi. Edited by T. Mṛugēṣa Mudaliyār.] pp. v. 404. சென்னபட்டணம் [*Madras,*] 1875. 16°. **14170. d. 17.**

—— ००० ஒழிவிலொடுக்க மூலம். [Oḻivil oḍukkam. Edited by A. Rāma-sāmi Svāmi.] pp. ii. 44. சென்னை [*Madras,*] 1888. 12°. **14170. d. 29.**

—— ००० ஒழிவிலொடுக்கம். [Oḻivil oḍukkam. With Chidambara Svāmi's commentary, and an exposition by Chidambaram Rāma-liṅga Svāmi of the *ṣiṟappu-pāyiram* or prefatory stanza. Edited by Ṣ. Anavarata-vināyakam Piḷḷai.] pp. xiv. i. 419. சென்னை [*Madras,*] 1906. 16°. **14170. dd. 14.**

KAPĀLA-MŪRTTI PIḶḶAI, *Ā. Nayana-paṇḍitar.* ००० ஸ்ரீ சிவசுப்பிரமணியக்கடவுள் திருமுகவுலா, சித்திரக்கவிப்புஞ்சம் இதனோடு கம்பை வழிநடைக்கும்மியுஞ் சேர்ந்திருக்கின்றது. [Ṣiva-subrahmaṇya-kaḍavuḷ-tiru-mukhav-ulā, Chitra-kavi-puñjam, and Kambai-vaḻi-naḍai-kummi. Poems on the cult of Ṣiva-Subrahmaṇya at Rangoon.

With other religious verses.] pp. 16, 52 ; 1 *plate.* வேலூர் [*Vellore,*] 1902. 8°. **14172. bb. 9.**

KAPILAR. கபிலரகவல். [Kapilar-agaval. A poem, forming one of the pure classics, on various moral themes, especially on character as against caste. Followed by the *veṇ-bā* verses attributed to Kapilar and his brothers and sisters when abandoned by their parents.] pp. 20. சென்னை [*Madras,*] 1887. 16°. **14172. a. 7.(1.)**

—— Cabilar-agaval. [In English verse. Preceded by a life of Kapilar.] *See* ROBINSON (E. J.). Tamil Wisdom, *etc.* pp. 94-100. 1873. 12°. **14170. k. 62.**

—— The Professor of Madura. [With a translation of Kapilar's Agaval into English metre.] *See* ROBINSON (E. J.). Tales and Poems of South India, *etc.* pp. 181-191. 1885. 8°. **14170. k. 63.**

—— The Song of Kapila: being a translation in blank verse of the Tamil poem known as Kapilar Agaval, by R. Sivalingam Pillay. pp. 9. *Coimbatore,* 1901. 8°. **14172. bb. 3.(1.)**

See also the translation in the Siddhanta Deepika, *vol.* i., *pp.* 284-5.

—— குறிஞ்சிப்பாட்டு. [Kuriñji-pāṭṭu. An erotic idyll, being no. 8 of the Pattu-pāṭṭu. With Nachinārkk'-iniyar's commentary.] *See* PATTU-PĀṬṬU. பத்துப்பாட்டு ஆ [Pattu-pāṭṭu.] pp. 261-288. 1889. 8°. **14172. d. 10.**

—— Kurinjippáṭṭu. [Translated into English.] *See* KUMĀRA-SVĀMI (P.). A Half-hour with two ancient Tamil Poets, *etc.* 1895. 8°. **Ac. 8830. (vol. 13, no. 45.)**

—— குறிஞ்சி. [Kuriñji. A like poem.] *See* KŪḌALŪR-KIṞĀR. ∘∘∘ ஐங்குறுநூறு ஆ [Aiṅguṟu-nūṟu.] pp. 62-93. 1903. 8°. **14172. c. 48.**

—— ஏழாம்பத்து. [Decade vii. Ten poems on the Chera king Ṣelva-kaḍuṅ-gō Vāṛiyādan.] *See* PADIṬṬU-PATTU. ∘∘∘ பதிற்றுப்பத்து ஆ [Padiṭṭu-pattu.] pp. 100-118. 1904. 8°. **14172. bb. 14.**

KĀPPIYANĀR, *Kāppiyāṭṭu.* நான்காம் பத்து. [Decade iv. Ten poems on the Chera King Nārmuḍi Chēral.] *See* PADIṬṬU-PATTU. ∘∘∘ பதிற்றுப்பத்து ஆ [Padiṭṭu-pattu.] pp. 44-59. 1904. 8°. **14172. bb. 14.**

KARAIṢAI. திருக்கரைசைப்புராணம் ஆ [Tirukaraiṣai-purāṇam. The legends of the sanctuary of Ṣiva at Karaiṣai on the Mavaligaṅgaikarai, near Trincomali in Ceylon. With interpretation by Kumāra-sāmi Piḷḷai. Edited by T. V. Akhilēṣa Piḷḷai.] pp. i. 49. யாழ்ப்பாணம் வித்தி [*Jaffna,* 1890.] 8°. **14170. e. 38.**

KARA-PĀTRA YŌGĪṢVARA, *Indra-pīṭham.* சாம்பிரதாய சிந்தனைகள். [Sāmpradāya-chintanaigaḷ. A catechism of the Vedantic doctrine of Ṣaṅkara's school.] *See* MĀṆIKKA SVĀMI, *A.M.* ஸ்ரீ . . . ஸ்ரீமதாதிசங்கராசாரிய . . . சரித்திரச்சுருக்கம் ஆ [Ādi-ṣaṅkarāchārya-charitra-churukkam.] pp. 1-277. 1901. 12°. **14170. ee. 44.**

KĀRIYA NĀYANĀR, *Koṟukkaiyūr.* கணக்கதிகாரம். [Kaṇakk'-adhikāram. A treatise on arithmetic in verse and prose. Edited by T. Aruṇāchala Svāmi.] pp. 74. சித்தாத்திரி [*Madras,* 1860.] 8°. **14172. f. 5.**

KARUṆĀNANDA SIDDHAR. [*Life.*] *See* GURU-ṢUKRA-NĀḌI. ∘∘∘ கருணாநந்தசித்தர் சரித்திரம். [Karuṇānanda-siddhar-charitram.] [1906.] 12°. **14171. d. 6.**

KARUṆĀNANDA SVĀMI, *Chidambaram.* *See* MADANA-KĀMA-RĀJAN. மதனகாமராஜன்கதை ஆ [Madana-kāma-rājan-kathai. Edited by Karuṇānanda.] [1880.] 8°. **14170. k. 22.**

—— *See* MUTTU-TĀṆḌAVAR, *Ṣīrkāḻi.* சிதம்பரம்... கீர்த்தனம் ஆ [Kīrttanam. Edited by Karuṇānanda.] [1870.] 8°. **14170. k. 20.**

—— *See* PUGAṞĒNDI. ∘∘∘ பவளக்கொடிமாலை. [Pavaḷa-koḍi-mālai. Edited by Karuṇānanda.] [1885.] 8°. **14172. b. 27.**

KARUPP'-AIYĀ PĀVALAR, *Koṭṭāmbaṭṭi M.* ∘∘∘ மெய்ஞ்ஞானத்திருப்பாடற்றிரட்டு. [Mey-ñāna-tiru-pāḍaṭ-ṭiraṭṭu. Followed by the Tiru-kōṭṭāṭṭu-kalambakam, Muhammadan poems by Karupp'-aiyā. Edited by the latter.] [1898.] 8°. *See* MUḤYI al-DĪN MALUK MUDALIYĀR, *Kōṭṭāṟu, the Elder.* **14173. c. 2.(1.)**

—— *See* MUḤYI al-DĪN MALUK MUDALIYĀR, *Kōṭṭāṟu, the Younger.* ∘∘∘ மெய்ஞ்ஞானவிளக்கம். [Mey-ñāna-viḷakkam. Edited by Karupp'-aiyā.] [1898.] 8°. **14173. c. 2.(2.)**

KARUTTA-MUTTU PILLAI, *Ā., of Ettayapuram.* [*Life.*] *See* Ṣiva-ñāna Yōgi, *V.* ००० ஆ. கருத்தமுத்துப்பிள்ளை . . . சரித்திரம். [Karutta-muttu-piḷḷai-charitram.] 1897. 12°. **14171. aa. 5.**

KARUVŪRĀR. கருவூரார்பூஜாவிதி. [Karuvūrār-pūjā-vidhi. A poem on the worship of Ṣiva.] pp. 10. *See* Siddhargaḷ. ००० பெரிய ஞானக்கோவை [Periya-ñāna-kōvai.] 1899. 12°. **14170. ee. 33.**

—— —— pt. i., pp. 27-35. 1906. 12°. **14170. dd. 12.**

KARUVŪR-DĒVAR. [For the hymns of this author contained in the Tiruv-iṣai-pā :] *See* Tiru-muṟai.

KĀṢI-VIṢVANĀTHA MUDALIYĀR, *Ṣaidāpuram.* டம்பாசாரி விலாசம். [Ḍambhāchāri-vilāsam. A comedy satirising coxcombry. Fourth edition, revised and expurgated.] pp. iv. xx. 301. சென்னை [*Madras,*] 1879. 8°. **14172. b. 17.**

—— ००० கொம்மிப்பாட்டு. [Kommi-pāṭṭu. A song embodying an account of the visit to India of the Duke of Edinburgh, with a hymn and an English translation.] pp. 12, 4, 8. *Madras,* சக்கில [1870.] 12°. **14172. a. 23.**

—— கூலிக்குமாரடிக்கும், கூத்தாடிச்சிகள் நடிப்பு. [Kūlikku mār-aḍikkum kūttāḍichigaḷ-naḍippu. A drama satirising hired mourning-women and dancers.] pp. 22. *Madras,* சக்கில [1870.] 12°. **14170. l. 1.(1.)**

KATHĀ-CHINTĀMAṆI. The Katháchintámani. A series of narratives in Tamil. Edited for the use of the members of the Civil Service by Pundit A. Santiagopulle Chandrewarnam, Mudaliyar. pp. viii. 162, i. *Colombo,* 1875. 8°. **14170. k. 27.**

KĀTTĀN (Varṇa-kulādittan). (†காத்தான் என்கிற இயற்பெயருடைய வருணகுலாதித்தன்மடல்.) [Varṇa-kulādittan-maḍal. An erotic poem.] pp. 36. [*Madras, n.d.*] 8°. **14172. b. 18.**
Without title-page.

KAUDAMANĀR. *See* Gautamanār.

KAUṢIKAR. The Kowseegasindamony . . . கௌசிகசிந்தாமணி [Kauṣika-chintāmaṇi, or Tarka-jōdiḍam. A metrical treatise on astrology.] . . . Thoroughly examined and written [*i.e.* edited] by K. P. Thavaraja Pundit (*by Margalinga Astrologer). 2 vols. pp. 76, 188. *Madras,* 1895. 8°. **14170. i. 35.**
Vol. 1 is of the second edition, vol. 2 of the first.

KAVI-KUÑJARA BHĀRATI (Ānaiy-aiyar). கவிகுஞ்சர பதங்கள். [Kavi-kuñjara-padaṅgaḷ. Erotic verses.] *See* Vijaya-raṅga Mudaliyār, *P.* ००० கவி . . . பதங்கள். [Padaṅgaḷ.] pp. 1-36. 1886. 8°. **14172. c. 33.**

KEARNS (James F.). *See* Ṣaṅkarāchāryar. Ātma bōdʻa prakāśika . . . text, [English] translation [of the text] and [of the Tamil] commentary . . . By . . . J. F. Kearns. 1867. 12°. **14048. b. 8.(1.)**

KEENE (Henry George), *the Elder.* Persian Stories, illustrative of Indian manners and customs, translated [into English by H. G. Keene, and thence] into Tamil by C. Jesudasen Pillay. [With the English text in parallel columns.] (†பெர்ஷியன்கதைகள்.) pp. 104, i. *Madras,* 1840. 12°. **14172. e. 2.**

KEMPIS (Thomas à). *See* Haemmerlein (T.), *à Kempis.*

KĒṢAVĀCHĀRYULU, *Kāṭrambākam.* *See* Āṟvārgaḷ.—Nāl-āyiram.—*Selections.* నిత్యానుసంధానము [Nityānusandhānam. Edited by Kēṣavāchāryulu.] [1862.] 12°. **14170. d. 22.**

KĒṢAVA MUDALIYĀR, *Tirutoṭṭikalai Kṛushṇa-svāmi.* மதுரை-அறுபத்துநான்குதிருவிளையாடற்சற்குருமாலை. [Madurai-arubattu-nāngu-tiru-viḷaiy-āḍaṟ-saṟ-guru-mālai. An abstract in prose and verse of the legends of Madura concerning the 64 miracles of Ṣiva. Edited by Puraṣai Sabhā-pati Mudaliyār.] pp. viii. 65; 68 *plates.* *Madras,* 1862. 8°. **14170. e. 26.**

KĒṢAVA-RĀU, *D. E.* *See* Anglo-Tamil Reader. A Vade Mecum, *etc.* [With preface by Kēṣava-rāu.] 1896. 8°. **14172. hh. 12.**

KILNER (John). *See* Wesley (J.). A collection of Hymns . . . Translated into Tamil [by J. Kilner and others]. 1881. 12°. **14170. bbb. 10.**

KINDERSLEY (Nathaniel Edward). Specimens of Hindoo Literature: consisting of translations, from the Tamoul language, of some Hindoo works of morality and imagination, with explanatory

notes: to which are prefixed introductory remarks on the mythology, literature, &c. of the Hindoos. pp. xiii. i. 335; 3 *plates*. *London*, 1794. 8°.
980. k. 19.

For works translated in this volume, see:—
Nalan.
Tiru-valluvar.

KINGSCOTE (GEORGIANA), *Mrs.*, and **NATĒSA ŚĀSTRI**, *Saṅgēndi Mahā-liṅgam*. Tales of the Sun, or Folklore of Southern India. Collected by Mrs. Howard Kingscote and Paṇḍit Naṭêśa Śastrî. pp. xii. 308. *London*, 1890. 8°. **12431. c. 40.**

KIṞISTU - MATA - KHAṆḌANA - SABHAI. *See* JAFFNA.

KĪṞ-KAṆAKKU. [For editions of works belonging to this class, see under the following headings:]

GAṆI-MĒDHĀVIYĀR. PERU-VĀYIN MUḶḶIYĀR.
MĀṞAN PORAIYANĀR. POYGAIYĀR.
MUN-ṞUṞAIY-ARAIYAR. PŪDAÑ-ṢĒNDANĀR.
NĀL-AḌIYĀR. TIRU-VAḶḶUVAR.
NALLĀḌANĀR. VIḶAMBIYA NĀGANĀR.

KIRUSHṆA. [For names beginning with this word:] *See* KṚUSHṆA.

KISTNASAWMY PILLAY. *See* KṚUSHṆA-SĀMI PIḶḶAI.

KNIGHT (JOSEPH). *See* P., *Philip*. Renunciation of Evil Ways, *etc.* [Translated by J. Knight.] 1844. 12°. **14170. b. 1.(31.)**

KNIGHT (W.) and **WINSLOW** (MIRON). Spiritual Lamp. [A Protestant catechism.] (†ஞான தீபிகை.) pp. 36. *Jaffna*, 1854. 16°. **14170. a. 33.(2.)**

No. 72 of the General Series of the Jaffna Religious Tract Society.

KŌDAṆḌA-PĀṆI TAÑJA-RĀYAR, Ṣ. *See* PERIODICAL PUBLICATIONS.—*Manakudi*. கிராமாதிகாரி ஸ்ரீ [Grāmādhikāri. Edited by Kōdaṇḍa-pāṇi.] 1900–1901. 8°. **14172. i. 20.**

KŌḌAṄGI-MĀLAI. கோடங்கிமாலை. [Kōḍaṅgi-mālai. A tract on astrological divination.] pp. 38. ஈரோடு [*Erode*,] 1901. 8°. **14170. i. 55.(3.)**

KOHLHOFF (JOHN CASPAR). *See* SATYA-NĀTHAN (R.). Translation [by J. C. Kohlhoff] of a sermon . . . preached by Sattianaden, *etc.* 1792. 4°. **115. h. 9.**

KŌNĒRIY-APPAN AIYAṄGĀR. சீரங்கநாயகியார் ஊசற்றிருநாமம். [Ṣiraṅga-nāyakiyār-ūṣaṭ-ṭiru-nāmam. A swinging-song for the service of Lakshmī at the temple of Srirangam.] *See* PIḶḶAI PERU-MĀḶ AIYAṄGĀR. திருவரங்கத்தூசற்றிருநாமம் ஸ்ரீ [Tiruv-araṅgatt'-ūṣaṭ-ṭiru-nāmam.] pp. 15-20. [1875.] 16°. **14172. a. 20.(7.)**

KOṄGANA NĀYANĀR. வாலைக்கும்மி. [Vālai-kummi. A Ṣaiva poem]. pp. 16. *See* SIDDHARGAḶ. ○ ○ ○ பெரிய ஞானக்கோவை [Periya-ñāna-kōvai.] 1899. 12°. **14170. ee. 33.**

—— —— pt. ii. 1906. 12°. **14170. dd. 12.**

KOṄGU-DĒṢAM. Translation of the Kongu-desa-rajakal. By the Rev. William Taylor. (Madras Journal of Literature and Science. Vol. xiv., pt. 1, pp. 1-66.) *Madras*, 1848. 8°.
Ac. 8829.(vol. 14.)

See also the Journal of the Royal Asiatic Society of Great Britain and Ireland, vol. 8. The genuineness of this document is doubtful (Indian Antiquary, vol. xxx., p. 201).

KORAN. *See* KUR'ĀN.

KOSTĪN (DAVID), *son of Juan Kostīn, of Mandai.* பூதத்தம்பி விலாசம். [Pūdā-tambi-vilāsam. A play founded on the actual history of Pūda-tambi of Jaffna, occurring some two centuries ago. Revised and edited by Mayiliṭṭi Nall'-aiyā Piḷḷai.] pp. 82. [*Jaffna*,] 1888. 8°. **14170. l. 17.**

KOVILADI. History of the Kovilady Charities in the then Tiruvadi and now Tanjore Taluk, of the Tanjore District. Founded in the year 1818 by Rai Roya Rai R. Vencat Row, Dewan of Travancore and the Native Assistant to the Commissioner of Mysore. [In English and Tamil.] pp. 32, ii. *Madras*, 1899. 12°. **14171. a. 35.**

KRISHṆA. [For Tamil names beginning with this word:] *See* KṚUSHṆA.

KRISHṆA PĀLA. [*Life.*] *See* WARD (W.). The Salvation of the Soul . . . a translation of the . . . tract Krishna Pal, *etc.* 1844. 12°. **14170. b. 1.(37.)**

KRISHNASAWMY. *See* KṚUSHṆA-SĀMI.

KṚUPAI SATYA-NĀTHAN, *Ammāl.* Kamala: a story of Hindu life. By Mrs. S. Satthianadhan . . . A translation [from the English original]. கமலம். [Preceded by a short biography of the authoress, abridged from Mrs. H. B. Grigg's "Introductory Memoir" to the English original.] pp. xiii. 230; 1 *plate*. *Madras*, 1896. 12°. **14171. a. 5.**

KRUPAI SATYA-NĀTHAN, *Ammāḷ (continued).* Sagunâ : a story of native Christian life, by Mrs. S. Satthianádhan . . . A translation [from the English original]. சகுணா ஓ. pp. v. i. 276. *Madras,* 1898. 12°. **14171. a. 29.**

KRUSHṆA BHĀRATI, *Tirunayam Vēṅkaṭa-rām'-aiyar.* See PURĀṆAS.—*Śiva-purāṇam.* அன்பி-லாலந்துறை . . . மான்மியம் [Prēmapuri-sthala-mānmiyam. In a Tamil paraphrase by Nara-simha and Kṛushṇa.] [1895.] 12°. **14170. d. 42.**

——— திருவிளையாடல் நாடகம். [Tiru-viḷaiy-āḍal-nāṭakam. A lyrical drama on the subject of the Tiru-viḷaiy-āḍar-purāṇam. With biography of the poet.] pp. 6, 412. மசூலிபட்டணம் [*Ma-sulipatam,*] 1899. 8°. **14170. l. 49.**

Kṛushṇa Bhārati was born A.D. 1791.

KRUSHṆ'-AIYAR, *Mayilāḍupuram.* See VIṢVA-BRAHMA-PURĀṆAM. விஸ்வபிரமபுராணம் [Viṣva-brahma-purāṇam. With paraphrase by Kṛushṇ'-aiyar.] 1894. 8°. **14170. f. 16.**

KRUSHṆA JŌSYĀR, *Mūnāmbaṇṇai, of Nanguneri.* ஜோதிஷகணிதசாஸ்திரம் . . . பஞ்சாங்ககண-னம் (*சாரகணனமும் . . . ஸ்புடகணனமும், கிர-ஹணகணனமும் . . . அகணனமும்) [Jōdisha-gaṇita-ṣāstram. A handbook of astronomy and guide to almanack-making, in 5 sections, called Pañchāṅga-gaṇanam, Chāra-gaṇanam, Sphuṭa-gaṇanam, Grahaṇa-gaṇanam, and Agaṇanam.] 3 vols., 5 pts. திருநெல்வேலி [*Tinnevelli,* 1897.] 16°. **14171. f. 1.**

KRUSHṆAM-ĀCHĀRYAR, *Arasāṇipālai Kandāḍai.* See ĀṚVĀRGAḶ.—Nāl-āyiram.—*Entire Canon.* ० ० ० தமிழ்வேதம் ஓ [Nāl-āyira-divya-prabandham. Edited by Kṛushṇam-āchāryar.] 1890. 8°. **14172. c. 38.**

——— See ĀṚVĀRGAḶ.—Nāl-āyiram.—*Mudal-āyi-ram.* ००० முதலாயிரம் ஓ [Mudal-āyiram. Edited by Kṛushṇam-āchāryar.] 1880-1885. 8°. **14170. f. 9.**

——— ——— ० ० ० ముతలాయిర ను॥ [Another edition, in Telugu characters.] 1881-[1886.] 8°. **14170. f. 8.**

——— See ĀṚVĀRGAḶ.—Nāl-āyiram.—*Periya-tiru-moṛi.* ० ० ० பெரியதிருமொழி ஓ [Periya-tiru-moṛi. Edited by Kṛushṇam-āchāryar.] 1881. 8°. **14170. f. 7.**

KRUSHṆAM-ĀCHĀRYAR, *Arasāṇipālai Kandāḍai (continued).* See ĀṚVĀRGAḶ.—Nāl-āyiram.—*Tiru-vāy-moṛi.* భగవద్విషయ ॥ [Bhagavad-vishayam. Edited by Kṛushṇam-āchāryar.] [1883-1904.] 4°. **14170. fff. 3.**

——— See PIḶḶAI LŌKĀCHĀRYAR. ० ० ० அஷ்டா-தசரஹஸ்யங்கள். [Ashṭādaṣa-rahasyaṅgaḷ. Edited by Kṛushṇam-āchāryar.] 1889. 8°. **14170. f. 12.**

——— See PIḶḶAI LŌKĀCHĀRYAR. ००० முமுக்ஷுப்-படி ஓ [Mumukshu-paḍi. Edited by Kṛushṇam-āchāryar.] 1889. 8°. **14170. f. 17.**

——— See PIḶḶAI LŌKĀCHĀRYAR. ప్రపన్నజనాగ్రేస-రరాజ శ్రీపిళ్లైలోకాచార్యర్ . . . తత్త్వత్రయము ను॥ [Tat-tva-trayam. Edited by Kṛushṇam-āchāryar.] [1875.] 8°. **14170. f. 24.**

——— See PIḶḶAI LŌKĀCHĀRYAR. ஸ்ரீ . . . ஸ்ரீவ-சநபூஷணம் ஓ [Vachana-bhūshaṇam. Edited by Kṛushṇam-āchāryar.] 1879. 8°. **14172. b. 10.**

——— See PINB'-AṚAGIYA PERU-MĀḶ JĪYAR. ஸ்ரீ . . . வார்த்தாமாலை. [Vārttā-mālai. Edited by Kṛush-ṇam-āchāryar.] 1882. 8°. **14172. d. 3.**

——— See VIḶĀÑ-JŌLAI PIḶḶAI. ० ० ० ஸப்தகாதை ஓ [Sapta-gāthai. Edited by Kṛushṇam-āchāryar.] [1882.] 16°. **14172. a. 9.**

KRUSHṆAM-ĀCHĀRYAR, *Āttān.* See ĀṚVĀRGAḶ.—Nāl-āyiram.—*Mudal-āyiram.* ० ० ० திருப்பல்-லாண்டு ஓ [Tiru-pall'-āṇḍu. Edited by Kṛush-ṇam-āchāryar.] [1870.] 8°. **14170. e. 15.**

KRUSHṆAM-ĀCHĀRYAR, *Īchambāḍi R.* See PURĀ-ṆAS.—*Bhavishyōttara-purāṇam.* ஸ்ரீ . . . ப்ரஸந்நவேங்கடேசமாஹாத்ம்யம் [Prasanna-veṅkaṭēṣa-māhātmyam. Edited with Tamil translation by Kṛushṇam-āchāryar.] 1906. 8°. **14016. dd. 18.**

KRUSHṆAM-ĀCHĀRYAR, *P. R.* See KAMBAN. Kamba Ramayanam. Edited by . . . Krishnam-achariar. Sundarakandam. 1907. 12°. **14172. a. 62.**

——— See MAHĀ-BHĀRATAM. பகவத்கீதை ஓ (Bhagavad Gita Venba.) [Edited by Kṛushṇam-āchāryar.] 1906-1907. 16°. **14172. a. 59.**

KRUSHṆAM-ĀCHĀRYAR, *Ṣ., of Wesleyan Mission College, Madras.* See ACADEMIES, *etc.*—Madras.—*University of Madras.* Copious annotations on the Matriculation Tamil text for 1900 by V. M. Satakoparamanujachariar . . . and S. Krishnamachariar, *etc.* 1900. 8°. **14172. bb. 6.(3.)**

—— See ACADEMIES, *etc.*—Madras.—*University of Madras.* University of Madras. F.A. Examination. Tamil poetry . . . with . . . notes . . . by V. M. Satakoparamanujachariar . . . and S. Krishnamachariar, *etc.* 1900. 8°. **14172. bb. 6.(5.)**

—— See ACADEMIES, *etc.*—Madras.—*University of Madras.* University of Madras. B.A. Examination of 1901 . . . A Tamil text book . . . with . . . annotations . . . by V. M. Satakoparamanujachariar . . . and S. Krishnamachariar. 1900. 8°. **14172. bb. 6.(6.)**

—— See ACADEMIES, *etc.*—Madras.—*University of Madras.* University of Madras. F.A. Examination of 1903. Full notes . . . by V. M. Satakoparamanujachariar . . . and S. Krishnamachariar, *etc.* 1903. 8°. **14172. hh. 19.**

—— See PAVAṆANDI. நன்னூற் காண்டிகையுரை. (Nannul kandikai. [Being the Nan-nūl with a commentary] by V. M. Satakoparamanujachariar, and S. Krishnamachariar, *etc.*) [Third edition.] 1900. 8°. **14172. e. 32.**

—— —— [Fourth edition.] 1903. 8°. **14172. e. 37.**

—— See PINB'-AṚAGIYA PERU-MĀḶ JĪYAR. ००० குருபரம்பராப்ரபாவம் ஆ [Guru-paramparā-prabhāvam. Edited by Kṛushṇam-āchāryar.] [1906.] 8°. **14170. ff. 22.**

KṚUSHṆAM-ĀCHĀRYAR, *Ṣiruvaḷūr Āsūri Bhāshyam.* See VEṄKAṬA-NĀTHA VĒDĀNTĀCHĀRYAR. ००० சில்லரை ரஹச்யங்கள் - கள [Ṣillarai-rahasyaṅgaḷ. Edited by Kṛushṇam-āchāryar.] [1900.] 8°. **14170. ee. 36.**

KṚUSHṆAM-ĀCHĀRYAR, *Tirukuḍandai Taṭṭai.* See BRAHMA-TANTRA-SVATANTRA-SVĀMI. குருபரம்பராப்ரபாவம் [Guru-paramparā-prabhāvam. Edited by Kṛushṇam-āchāryar.] [1857.] 8°. **14170. e. 8.**

—— See VEṄKAṬA-NĀTHA VĒDĀNTĀCHĀRYAR. ஸ்ரீ . . . வைபவஸாரஸங்கிரகம் ஆ [Nigamānta-mahādēṣikan-vaibhava-sāra-saṅgraham, *etc.* Edited by Kṛushṇam-āchāryar.] [1894.] 12°. **14170. d. 46.(2.)**

KṚUSHṆAM-ĀCHĀRYAR, *Vēlāmūr.* திருப்புல்லைத் திரிபந்தாதி. (*திருவெவ்வுளூர்த் திரிபந்தாதி, திருக்குருகூர் யமகவந்தாதி, *etc.*) [Tiru-pullai-tirib'-antādi, Tiruv-evvuḷūr-tirib'-antādi, Tiru-kurugūr-yamakav-antādi, Tiru-nāgai-t°., Tiruv-ariya-kuḍi-t°., Tiruv-ariyai-ṣilēḍai-veṇ-bā-mālai, and Ariya-kuḍiyalar-mēn-maṅgai-piḷḷai-tamiṛ. Vaishṇava devotional poems.] 7 pts. சென்னை [*Madras*,] 1902. 12°. **14170. d. 82.**

KṚUSHṆAM-ĀCHĀRYAR, *Vembākkam, Dīvān Bahādur.* See FRERE (M.). Old Deccan Days . . . newly adapted and edited by V. Krishnamacharyar, *etc.* 1880. 12°. **14170. k. 10.**

—— See MṚUGA-DĀSA SVĀMI. ००० புலவர்புராணம் . . . Metrical Biographies of Tamil Poets . . . with an introductory note by the editor [V. Kṛushṇam-āchāryar], *etc.* 1901, *etc.* 8°. **14172. c. 41.**

—— See MṚUGA-DĀSA SVĀMI. University of Madras . . . Pulawar Puranam . . . Edited . . . by . . . V. Krishnama chariar. 1901. 8°. **14172. bb. 3.(4.)**

—— The Maharani's Greetings for the Festive Season, *etc.* [6 New-Year's cards in Tamil and English issued to subscribers of the "Mahārāni," a Tamil and Telugu magazine published in Madras, and edited by Kṛushṇam-āchāryar.] [*Madras*, 1891.] *s.sh.* 4°. **14172. k. 6.**

—— Travels to other Countries. A Trip through Europe, with map-pictures . . . நாநாதேச யாத்திரை சரித்திரம். ஐரோப்பா கண்டம். (The Maharani Series.) pp. 17; 12 *plates.* *Madras*, 1897. 8°. **14171. b. 3.**

—— His Most Excellent Majesty King-Edward VII. A biographical sketch with an account of the great Coronation and a song for native schools and homes in the Tamil land. (*மாட்சிமைதங்கிய எ-ம் எட்வர்ட் சக்கரவர்த்தி சரித்திர ஸங்கிரகம்.) pp. 64; 4 *plates.* *Madras*, 1902. 8°. **14170. k. 51.**

—— பன்னிரு புலவர் சரித்திர ஸாரம். Brief Biographies of Twelve Standard Tamil Poets, together with an essay on முத்தமிழ் & நவரஸம், the three principal divisions of Tamil literature and poetical sentiments. pp. i. ii. xix. 195, i. *Madras*, 1906. 8°. **14171. e. 9.**

KṚUSHṆAM-ĀCHĀRYA SVĀMI, *Tirumalai Nallān Chakravartti.* See AṚAGIYA-MAṆAVĀḶA PERU-MĀḶ.

ஸ்ரீ . . . ஸ்ரீமதார்த்தி ப்ரபந்த ஞூ [Ārtti-prabandham. Edited by Kṛushṇam-āchārya Svāmi.] 1893. 8°. 14170. ee. 6.(1.)

KṚUSHṆA MIṢRA, *Dramatist.* ஸ்ரீ . . . பிரபோதசந்திரோதயம் என்னும மெய்ஞ்ஞானவிளக்கம். [Mey-ñāna-viḷakkam. Tiru-vēṅkaṭa-svāmi's poetical adaptation of Kṛushṇa's Prabōdha-chandrōdayam, a Sanskrit allegorical drama. Edited by Kōyilūr Ponn'-ambala Svāmi, Subba-rāya Svāmi, and Rāmānuja Mudaliyār.] pp. 7, iii. 273, xvii. சென்னை [*Madras*,] 1898. 8°. 14172. c. 27.

—— பிரபோதசந்திரோதயவசனம். [Prabōdha-chandrōdaya-vachanam. A prose rendering, by A. Muttu-tambi Piḷḷai, of Tiru-vēṅkaṭa-svāmi's Mey-ñāna-viḷakkam.] pp. i. 130. *Madras*, 1889. 12°. 14170. l. 21.

—— பிரபோதசந்திரோதய வசநம் அல்லது மெய்ஞ்ஞானவிளக்கம் [Prabōdha-chandrōdaya-vachanam. A simple prose version, by Rāma Yōgi of Conjevaram, of Tiru-vēṅkaṭa-svāmi's Mey-ñāna-viḷakkam.] pp. 2, ii. iii. 257. மதராஸ் [*Madras*,] 1902. 8°. 14170. l. 57.

KṚUSHṆANJĪ DAVE. *See* PURĀṆAS.—*Padma-purāṇam.* (†శ్రీమాఘమాహాత్మ్యసారము.) [Māgha-māhātmya-sāram. Compiled by Kṛushṇanjī.] 1897. 12°. 14016. b. 20.

KṚUSHṆA PAṆḌITAR, *son of Rāma Bhaṭṭar.* *See* SANDHYĀ-VANDANAM. யஜுர்வேத ஸந்த்யாவந்தநம் ஞூ [Sandhyā-vandanam, *etc.* With extracts, in a Tamil translation, from the commentaries of Kṛushṇa Paṇḍitar and others.] 1901. 8°. 14033. aa. 27.

KṚUSHṆA PIḶḶAI, *A., of Jaffna.* ००० சரமகவிகள். [Charama-kavigaḷ. Elegies on the death of certain of the author's relatives.] pp. 6. *Jaffna*, 1888. 8°. 14172. a. 30.(2.)

KṚUSHṆA-RĀJA OḌEYAR, *Maharaja of Mysore.* *See* NĀRĀYAṆA-SĀMI PIḶḶAI, *T. G.* Installation of his Highness Sri Krishnarajendra Wodayar Bahadur . . . and the Dasara Festivities. A poem, *etc.* 1903. 12°. 14172. bb. 8.

KṚUSHṆA-SĀMI AIYAR, *K.* *See* PERIODICAL PUBLICATIONS.—*Madras.* ஜனப்பிரியன் ஞூ [Janapriyan. Edited by Kṛushṇa-sāmi.] 1900-1901. 8°. 14172. i. 19.

KṚUSHṆA-SĀMI AIYAR, *N.* *See* MAHĀ-BHĀRATAM. Tamil translation [by Kṛushṇa-sāmi] of Mahabharata Niti Ratnavali, *etc.* 1888. 12°. 14003. c.

KṚUSHṆA-SĀMI MUDALIYĀR, *P., of Pachaiyappa's College, Madras.* *See* ACADEMIES, *etc.*—Madras.—*University of Madras.* Copious notes on the Tamil text-book for the Matriculation Examination, 1898, by . . . Krishnasawmy Mudaliyar. 1898. 8°. 14172. b. 16.(1.)

—— *See* ACADEMIES, *etc.*—Madras.—*University of Madras.* University of Madras. Matriculation Examination, 1900. Copious notes on the Tamil text-book. By . . . Krishnasawmy Mudaliar. 1900. 8°. 14172. bb. 6.(2.)

KṚUSHṆA-SĀMI MUDALIYĀR, *Ṣāttapākkam.* குசேலமுனிவர்சரித்திரம் [Kuchēla-munivar-charitram. The story of Kuchēla, as told in the Bhāgavata-purāṇam, bk. x., ch. 80-1.] *See* MAHĀ-BHAKTA-VIJAYAM. ००० ஸ்ரீமகாபக்தவிஜயம். [Mahā-bhakta-vijayam.] vol. i., pp. 310-338. 1893. 4°. 14170. f. 22.

—— —— vol. i., pp. 310-338. 1898-1905. 4°. 14170. f. 6.

KṚUSHṆA-SĀMI PIḶḶAI, *Tañjai, disciple of Ṣokkaliṅga Dēṣikar.* நளநாடகமென்னும் வழங்குகின்ற தமயந்திநாடகம். [Damayanti-nāṭakam, or Naḷa-nāṭakam. A drama on the epic story of Nala and Damayantī. Edited by Gōkulāpuram Ṣaravaṇa Paṇḍitar.] pp. 124. சுபானு [*Madras*, 1883.] 8°. 14170. l. 9.

KṚUSHṆA-SĀMI PIḶḶAI, *T. M., Librarian of the College, Madras.* *See* DICTIONARIES. A Polyglot Vocabulary in the English, Teloogoo, and Tamil Languages . . . arranged . . . and . . . translated . . . with the assistance of T. M. Kistnasawmy Pillay. 1851. 8°. 14172. h. 21.

KṚUSHṆA ṢĀSTRI, *Purāṇam Vēṅkaṭa-nārāyaṇa.* *See* ṢAṄKARĀCHĀRYAR. (†ఆత్మబోధప్రకాశిక) [Ātma-bōdham. With the Telugu interpretation and commentary Ātma-bōdha-prakāṣika of Kṛushṇa Ṣāstri, and a Tamil version of the same by Rāmānuja Kavi-rāyar.] [1840.] 12°. 14048. c. 44.

—— *See* ṢAṄKARĀCHĀRYAR. Ātma Bōd'a Prakāśika. Text, Übersetzung und Erklärung. [Ātma-bōdham, with extracts from Kṛushṇa Ṣāstri's

Telugu commentary, translated into German from Rāmānuja Kavi-rāyar's Tamil version.] 1854. 8°. [*Bibliotheca Tamulica.*] **14170. e. 42.(vol. i.)**

—— *See* ṢAṄKARĀCHĀRYAR. Ātma bōd'a prakāśika . . . text, translation, and commentary [from tho Telugu of Kṛushṇa Ṣāstri,] *etc.* 1867. 12°. **14048. b. 8.(1.)**

—— *See* ṢAṄKARĀCHĀRYAR. ००० ஆத்ம போதம். [Ātma-bōdham. With Rāmānuja Kavi-rāyar's Tamil version of Kṛushṇa Ṣāstri's Telugu commentary.] [1869.] 8°. **14048. c. 62.(2.)**

KṚUSHṆA ṢĀSTRI, *Viruṭṣiyūr, of Devakota.* *See* ĀRŪḌHA-ṢĀSTRAM. ००० ஞானப்ரதீபிகை ஸ்ரீ [Ārūḍha-ṣāstram. Edited by Kṛushṇa.] [1899.] 8°. **14053. ccc. 27.**

KṚUSHṆA SŪRI. *See* PERIYAV-ĀCHĀN PIḶḶAI.

KṚUSHṆA-SVĀMI. *See* KṚUSHṆA-SĀMI.

KŪḌALŪR-KIṞĀR, *Pula-tuṟai-muṭṭiya.* ००० ஐங்குறுநூறும், பழையவுரையும். [Aiṅ-guṟu-nūṟu. 50 poems on erotic themes by Ōram-bōgiyār, Ammūvanār, Kapilar, Ōdalāndai, and Pēyanār, forming the 3rd volume in the Eṭṭu-togai of the Kaḍai-saṅgham or last Academy of Madura, and compiled by Pula-tuṟai-muṭṭiya Kūḍalūr-kiṟār. With an ancient commentary. Edited with biographies, glossary, and indices by U. V. Sāminātha'-aiyar.] pp. i. ii. 17, 180. சென்னை [*Madras,*] 1903. 8°. **14172. c. 48.**

KUGA-DĀSAR. *See* GUHA-DĀSAR.

KULA-ṢĒKHARA PERU-MĀḶ. [For editions of the Tiru-moṟi of this devotee included in the editions of the whole or parts of the Nāl-āyira-prabandham:] *See* ĀṞVĀRGAḶ.—*Nāl-āyiram.*

KUMARA-GURU-DĀSA SVĀMI, *Pāmban Ṣ.* (APPĀVU PIḶḶAI). ஸ்ரீமத் குமரகுருதாசசுவாமிகள் பாடலும், திருவலங்கற்றிரட்டு முதலாங் (*இரண்டாங்) கண்டமும். [Pāḍal and Tiruv-alaṅgaṭ-ṭiraṭṭu. Two series of Ṣaiva poems.] 2 vols. சென்னை [*Madras,*] 1901-1902. 12°. **14170. d. 73.**

—— திவோதய சடாக்ஷரோபதேசம் என்னும் சிவஞானதேசிகம். [Divōdaya-shaḍākṣharōpadēṣam, or Ṣiva-ñāna-dēṣikam. A series of dialogues on Ṣaiva philosophy. First book, entitled Kaḍavuḷai kuṟitta vyāsam, on the nature of God.] pp. 45, i.; 3 *plates.* *Madras,* 1893. 8°. **14170. e. 47.(4.)**

—— ००० வேதத்தைக்குறித்த ௬-வது வியாசம். [Vēdattai kuṟitta vyāsam. Dialogue vi., on the Vēdam from the Ṣaiva standpoint.] pp. 4, 81. சென்னை [*Madras,*] 1903. 8°. **14170. eee. 1.**

—— இராம சேதுமான்மியம். [Rāma-sētu-mānmiyam. A dissertation, forming part of the 10th *vyāsam* of the Ṣiva-ñāna-dēṣikam, upon the legends of Rameswaram. Second edition.] pp. ii. 50. சென்னை [*Madras,*] 1897. 8°. **14170. ee. 38.**

—— ००० ஸ்ரீ சுப்பிரமணியமென்பதைக் குறித்த ௩௧-வது வியாசம் ஸ்ரீ [Subrahmaṇyam enbadai kuṟitta vyāsam, a dialogue between teacher and disciple on the metaphysical utterance of Subrahmaṇya in the Skanda-purāṇam (Ṣaṅkara-saṃhitā, Ṣiva-rahasyam); and Guru-ṣishya-sambhava-varalāṟu kuṟitta vyāsam, on the relation of master and pupil. Being the 31st and 32nd of the author's Vyāsas, and concluding the Divōdaya-shaḍākṣharōpadēṣam.] pp. iv. 116. சென்னை [*Madras,*] 1899. 8°. **14170. ee. 28.(4.)**

—— ००० நாலாயிரப்பிரபந்தவிசாரம். [Nāl-āyira-prabandha-vichāram. A criticism of the Nāl-āyiram or Vaishṇava scripture, from the Ṣaiva standpoint.] pp. x. 163. சென்னை [*Madras,*] 1905. 12°. **14170. dd. 7.**

—— திருப்பா. [Tiru-pā. A series of Ṣaiva devotional poems.] pp. ii. ii. 410. சென்னை [*Madras,*] 1899. 12°. **14170. d. 56.**

KUMARA-GURU-PARA TAMBIRĀN. ००० திருச்செந்தூர்க் கந்தர்கலிவெண்பா. [Kandar-kali-veṇ-bā. A hymn to the god Kandan or Skanda as worshipped at Tiruchendur.] pp. 25. சென்னபட்டணம் [*Madras,*] 1887. 16°. **14172. a. 7.(3.)**

The author was born early in the 17th century at Vaikuntham, near Tinnevelli; his home was Dharmapuram.

—— ००० மதுரை மீனாக்ஷியம்மை பிள்ளைத்தமிழ். [Madurai-mīnākshiy-ammai-piḷḷai-tamiṟ. A devotional poem to the goddess Mīnākshi of Madura. Edited by K. Kuppu-sāmi Mudaliyār.] pp. iv. 58. சென்னை [*Madras,*] 1903. 12°. **14172. a. 45.(4)**

Forms no. 1 *of the* Tamiṟ-kavi-mālai.

KUMARA-GURU-PARA TAMBIRĀN (*continued*). The நீதிநெறிவிளக்கம் [Nīti-neri-viḷakkam] of Cumara guru para Tambirān, containing a hundred and two stanzas on moral subjects, with an English translation, vocabulary, and notes . . . by H. Stokes. pp. xi. 15, 112, v. *Madras*, 1830. 8°. **14172. b. 1.**

—— நீதிநெறிவிளக்கம். Nidinerivilaccam. [Selections in Tamil and English.] *See* WALKER (J.). நீதிமொழித்திரட்டு. Nídimozhittirattu, *etc.* pp. 24-39. 1841. 8°. **14170. k. 35.**

—— ooo நீதிநெறி விளக்கம் உரைபாடம். [Nīti-neri-viḷakkam. With commentary.] pp. 48. *Madras*, 1865. 16°. **14172. a. 13.(1.)**

—— நீதிநெறிவிளக்கம். [Nīti-neri-viḷakkam.] *See* TAMIL MINOR POETS. Tamil Minor Poets, *etc.* pp. 32-46. 1864. 16°. **14172. a. 17.**

—— —— pp. 44-64. 1868. 16°. **14172. a. 18.**

—— நீதிநெறிவிளக்கம். [Nīti-neri-viḷakkam. With commentary.] *See* TAMIL MINOR POETS. Tamil Minor Poets, *etc.* pp. 109-156. 1865. 16°. **14172. a. 16.**

—— The Nithineri Vilakkam. [Translated into English.] *See* TAMIL MINOR POETS. Tamil Minor Poets, *etc.* pp. 36-51. 1872. 12°. **14172. c. 6.**

—— The Young Divine Teacher. [With a metrical translation of the Nīti-neri-viḷakkam.] *See* ROBINSON (E. J.). Tales and Poems of South India, *etc.* pp. 192-213. 1885. 8°. **14170. k. 63.**

—— *See* MRUGĒṢA MUDALIYĀR. நீதிமஞ்சரித்தருப்பணம். [Nīti-mañjari-darpaṇam. Interpretations of ethical works of Kumara-guru-paran and others.] 1881-1883. 16°. **14172. a. 8.**

KUMĀRA-SVĀMI (P.). A Half-hour with two ancient Tamil Poets († a translation . . . of two poems: one by Kapilar and the other by Muḍattámakkaṇṇiyár, both of which form part of the collection known as Pattupáṭṭu). By the Hon. P. Coomáraswámy. (Journal of the Ceylon Branch of the Royal Asiatic Society. Vol. xiii., no. 45, pp. 190-202.) *Colombo*, 1895. 8°. **Ac. 8830. (vol. 13, no. 45.)**

KUMĀRA-SVĀMI DĒṢIKAR, *Kāñchīpuram Ārumuga*. *See* ATIVĪRA-RĀMA PĀṆḌIYAN. நைடதம் மூ [Naiḍadam. With a commentary on cantos 6-28 by Kumāra-svāmi and others.] [1842.] 8°. **14172. b. 58.**

—— *See* ATIVĪRA-RĀMA PĀṆḌIYAN. ooo நைடதம் மூ [Naiḍadam. With commentaries of Kumāra-svāmi, *etc.*] 1881. 8°. **14172. b. 14.**

—— *See* KAḌAVUṈ MĀ-MUNI. மாணிக்கவாசகரென்னும் திருவாதவூரர்புராணம். [Tiru-vāda-vūrar-purāṇam. With paraphrase by Kumāra-svāmi.] 1896. 12°. **14171. a. 10.**

KUMĀRA-SĀMI MUDALIYĀR, *M.* மதனலீலாவதி. (Mathana Leelavathy [*i.e.* Madana-līlāvati]. A very excellent novel. By M. Coomoorasawmy [*sic*] Mudaliar.) pp. 128. *Madras*, 1901. 8°. **14170. k. 54.**

KUMĀRA-SĀMI MUDALIYĀR, *Sēlam*. ஜமீன்தாரியென்று வழங்குகிற ஸ்திதியைசார்ந்த சங்கிரக கிரந்தம். [Saṅgraha-grantham. A handbook on the law of tenancy applying to zamindari estates, and on the documents and legal instruments used thereunder.] pp. xxiv. 152. சென்னை [*Madras*,] 1897. 8°. **14170. g. 18.**

KUMĀRA-SĀMI MUDALIYĀR, *Uḍuppiṭṭi*. குமாரசாமிமுதலியார்கவித்திரட்டு. [Kumāra-sāmi-mudaliyār-kavi-tiraṭṭu. A collection of poems.] pp. vi. 33, 1, 4, i. வல்வை கஅஅள [*Valuvettiturai*, 1887.] 8°. **14172. b. 34.**

KUMĀRA-SĀMI PIḶḶAI, *Ṣunnāgam A.* *See* KĀLI-DĀSA. மேகதூதக்காரிகை. [Mēgha-dūta-kārikai. A metrical version by Kumāra-sāmi.] [1897.] 8°. **14170. l. 32.(4.)**

—— *See* KARAIṢAI. திருக்கரைசைப்புராணம் மூ [Tiru-karaiṣai-purāṇam. With interpretation by Kumāra-sāmi.] [1890.] 8°. **14170. e. 38.**

—— *See* VIṢVA-NĀTHA ṢĀSTRI, *A.N.* நகுலமலைக்குறவஞ்சிநாடகம். [Nakula-malai-kuravañji-nāṭakam. Edited by Kumāra-sāmi.] [1895.] 8°. **14170. l. 6.**

—— ஏகவிருத்தபாரதம் மூ [Ēka-vṛutta-bhāratam, Ēka-vṛutta-rāmāyaṇam, and Ēka-vṛutta-bhāgavatam. Epitomes, each in one verse, of the Mahā-bhāratam, Rāmāyaṇam, and Bhāgavata-purāṇam. Followed by a Ṣiva-tōttiram, or hymn to Ṣiva, and Vinōda-chitra-vināv-uttara-kavigaḷ, fanciful riddling verses. Translated by Kumāra-sāmi Piḷḷai.] pp. 12. கொக்குவில் துர்முகி [*Kokkuvil*, 1896.] 8°. **14172. b. 44.(9.)**

KUMĀRA-SĀMI UPĀDHYĀYAR, *Kalavai.* இரணியவிலாசம். [Hiraṇya-vilāsam. A drama on the puranic legend of the Daitya king Hiraṇya-kaṣipu. Edited by P. Nārāyaṇa-dāsar.] pp. 4, 7, 4, 332. சென்னை [*Madras,*] 1899. 8°. **14170. l. 50.**

KUMBAKONAM. *See* NĀRĀYAṆA-SĀMI AIYAR, *P.A.* ∘∘∘ மாணக்கராற்றுப்படை. [Māṇākkar-āṭṭu-paḍai. A poem in praise of the Kumbakonam Town High School.] 1900. 12°. **14172. a. 45.(3.)**

KUPPAN AIYAṄGĀR, *Taṇṇīrkuḷam.* [For works edited by Kuppan Aiyaṅgār, see under the following headings:]

AUVAIYĀR.—*Two or More Works.*
DIVĀKARAR.
EṆ-ṢUVAḌI.

KUPPU-SĀMI AIYAR, *Villavarambal.* *See* UPANISHADS. பஞ்சதசோபநிஷத: *etc.* [Pañcha-daṣōpanishadaḥ. Edited with Tamil introduction and translation by Kuppu-sāmi.] [1898.] 8°. **14010. cc. 12.**

—— *See* VĀSUDĒVA YATI. வாசுதேவமனனம் ஸ்ரீ [Vāsudēva-mananam. Translated by Kuppu-sāmi.] [1887.] 8°. **14170. e. 32.**

—— *See* VĀSUDĒVA YATI. வாஸுதேவமநநம். [Vāsudēva-mananam. With Tamil version by Kuppu-sāmi.] [1895.] 8°. **14048. dd. 19.**

—— The Aryamatasiddhanta Sangraha. By Villavarambal Cooppooswamy Aiyar. [A digest, in dialogue form, of the principles of the Dvaita, Advaita, Viṣishṭādvaita, and Ṣaiva philosophies. In Tamil, copiously illustrated from Sanskrit texts.] (*॥ आर्यमतसिद्धान्ताख्य ग्रन्थः ॥ ஆர்யமதஸித்தாந்தாக்ய க்ரந்த:... ஆரியமதஸித்தாந்தஸங்கிரகம்.) pp. 32, 566, 138. *Kumbakonam*, 1902. 8°. **14170. ee. 49.**

The Sanskrit extracts are printed in Nagari characters at the foot of the page, and reprinted in Grantham type in an appendix.

KUPPU-SĀMI MUDALIYĀR, *Kalkuḷam.* *See* AMIRTA KAVI-RĀYAR. ∘∘∘ நாணிக்கண்புதைத்தல் ஸ்ரீ [Oru-durai-kōvai. Edited by Kuppu-sāmi.] 1905. 12°. **14172. a. 55.**

—— *See* KUMARA-GURU-PARA TAMBIRĀN. ∘∘∘ மதுரை மீனாக்ஷியம்மை பிள்ளைத்தமிழ். [Madurai-mīnākshiy-ammai-piḷḷai-tamiṛ. Edited by Kuppu-sāmi.] 1903. 12°. **14172. a. 45.(4.)**

—— *See* NĀL-AḌIYĀR. The Nâladiyâr. With . . . English introduction and translation by K. Kuppuswami Mudaliyar. 1903. 8°. **14172. c. 45.**

—— *See* TĀYUMĀNAVAR. ஸ்ரீ . . . திருப்பாடற்றிரட்டு. [Tiru-pāḍaṭ-ṭiraṭṭu. With Sabhā-pati Mudaliyār's commentary on i. 1-3. The latter edited, with preface on Tāyumānavar's career, by Kuppu-sāmi.] 1905. 16°. **14170. dd. 6.**

—— *See* VĪRA-RĀGHAVA MUDALIYĀR. சேயூர்முருகன் பிள்ளைத்தமிழ் [Ṣēyūr-mrugan-piḷḷai-tamiṛ. Edited by Kuppu-sāmi.] 1902. 12°. **14172. a. 54.**

KUPPU-SĀMI MUDALIYĀR, *Tirupanaṅgāḍu.* *See* BESCHI (C. G. E.). ∘∘∘ சதுரகராதி. [Chatur-agarādi. Edited by Kuppu-sāmi.] [1880.] 8°. **14172. f. 8.**

KUPPU-SĀMI NĀYUḌU, *Madurai Tambu-sāmi.* [For works edited by Kuppu-sāmi Nāyuḍu, see under the following headings:]

MĀRIY-APPA KAVI-RĀYAR, *M.*, and ṢAṄKARA-MŪRTTI KŌNĀR, *A.*
PUGAṚENDI.
ṢAṄKARĀCHĀRYAR. [*Doubtful and Supposititious Works.*]

KUPPU-SVĀMI RĀJU, *V., of Tanjore.* *See* BĀLA-BŌDHAM. ஸ்ரீபாலபோதம். [Bāla-bōdham. Translated by Kuppu-svāmi.] 1902. 12°. **14170. d. 78.**

—— *See* BHĀSKARA. தருக்ககௌமுதி. [Tarka-kaumudi. Translated by Kuppu-svāmi.] [1898.] 12°. **14170. i. 57.**

—— *See* NIṢCHALA DĀSA. ஸ்ரீ ... ஸ்ரீவிசாரசாகரம். [Vichāra-sāgaram. Edited by Kuppu-svāmi.] 1904. 8°. **14170. ff. 12.**

—— *See* NIṢCHALA DĀSA. ∘∘∘ ஸ்ரீவிருத்திப்பிரபாகரம். [Vṛutti-prabhākaram. Translated and edited by Kuppu-svāmi.] 1901. 8°. **14170. ee. 41.**

—— *See* NIṢCHALA DĀSA. ஸ்ரீ விருத்திரத்நாவலி. [Vṛutti-ratnāvali. Translated by Kuppu-svāmi.] 1902. 12°. **14170. d. 77.**

—— *See* ṢAṄKARĀCHĀRYAR. ஸ்ரீ . . . அபரோக்ஷாநுபூதி. [Aparōkshānubhūti. With Tamil translation and notes by Kuppu-svāmi.] [1905.] 8°. **14049. b. 32.(1.)**

—— *See* SVĀTMĀRĀMA YŌGI. ஸ்ரீ . . . ஹட யோகப்பிரதீபிகை ஸூ [Haṭha-yōga-pradīpikā. Edited with Tamil translation and commentary styled Tattva-pradīpikai by Kuppu-svāmi.] [1897.] 8°. **14048. cc. 16.**

—— *See* TATTVA-BŌDHAM. ००० ஸ்ரீதத்துவபோதம். [Tattva-bōdham. Translated by Kuppu-svāmi.] 1898. 12°. **14170. d. 32.(4.)**

—— —— 1901. 12°. **14170. d. 81.**

—— *See* UTTARA-GĪTĀ. உத்தரகீதை. [Uttara-gītā. With Tamil paraphrase and notes by Kuppu-svāmi.] [1902.] 12°. **14048. a. 29.(3.)**

KUPPU-SVĀMI ŚĀSTRI, *T. S., of Tanjore.* A short History of the Tanjore Nayak Princes . . . தஞ்சாவூர் நாயக்கராஜவம்ச சரித்திரச்சுருக்கம். [Followed by a selection of Sanskrit verses.] pp. 28. *Tanjore,* 1903. 8°. **14171. a. 53.(3.)**

ḲUR'ĀN. *See* MUḤAMMAD ʻABD al-RAḤMĀN ibn ḲĀDIR MĪRĀN. تأييد الرحمن الخ [Ta'yīd al-raḥmān. A manual of the art of reciting from the Koran.] [1902.] 8°. **14173. b. 32.**

—— *See* SHĀH al-ḤAMĪD ibn ʻAIDARŪS. فوائد القران الخ [Fawā'id al-ḳur'ān. A treatise on the use of Koranic texts, *etc.*, for talismanic purposes.] [1905-1906.] 8°. **14173. c. 1.**

—— فتوحات الرحمانية في تفسير كلام الربانية [Ḳur'ān. The Arabic text, with an interlineary translation and marginal commentary in Tamil, together entitled al-Futūḥāt al-raḥmānīyat, by Ḥabib Muḥammad al-Ḳāhirī.] pp. vi. 626, *lith.* البمبئي ١٢٩٦-١٣٠٠ [*Bombay,* 1879-1884.] Fol. **14507. e. 4.**

—— رحمة المنان على المتعلمين من الولدان [Raḥmat al-mannān. Surah 78-114, with a translation into Tamil by Sulaimān ibn Muḥammad al-Sailānī.] pp. 112, *lith.* كولوفتي ١٣١٥ [*Kollupitiya, Colombo,* 1897.] 8°. **14507. b. 35.**

KURANDAI-VĒLU PILLAI, *Viṟupuram Kāṭṭa-perumāḷ.* *See* ACHALĀMBIKAI AMMĀḶ and KURANDAI-VĒLU PILLAI. மேலசேது ரென்றுவழங்கும் திருவிடையூர்த்தலப்புராணம். [Tiruviḍaiyūr-tala-purāṇam.] 1899. 8°. **14170. ee. 61.**

KŪRATT'-ĀṞVĀN (ŚRĪVATSĀṄKA MIŚRA), *disciple of Rāmānuja.* ஸ்ரீகூரத்தாழ்வானது ப்ரபாவம் என்கிற ஸ்ரீகூரேசவிஜயம். மூலமும் உரையும். [Kūrēṣa-vijayam, or Kūratt'-āṟvānadu prabhāvam. A poem on the distinction and successful propaganda of the Vaishṇava teacher Kūratt'-āṟvān, by a disciple of Addaṅgi Vēṅkaṭāchāryar, with an interpretation. Edited by Tiruvahīndrapuram Vīrarāghavāchāryar.] pp. 6, 381. கர [*Madras,* 1892.] 8°. **14170. e. 44.**

—— *See* SŌMA-SUNDARA NĀYAKAR. கூரேசவிஜயபங்கம். [Kūrēṣa-vijaya-bhaṅgam. A Śaiva polemical work against the Kūrēṣa-vijayam.] 1886. 8°. **14170. e. 27.**

KŪRĒṢAN. *See* KŪRATT'-ĀṞVĀN.

KURTZ (JOHANN HEINRICH). *See* BLOMSTRAND (A.). திருச்சபைசரித்திரம். [Tiru-sabhai-charitram. A history of the Church, based chiefly upon that of Kurtz.] 1867-1869. 8°. **14170. c. 13, 14.**

LAKSHMAṆA CHEṬṬI. *See* ṢINNAYA CHEṬṬI.

LAKSHMAṆA PILLAI, *P.A.* *See* VARĀHA-MIHIRA. புருஷ ஸாமுத்திரிகம். [Purusha-sāmudrikam and Strī-sāmudrikam. With English rendering by Lakshmaṇa Pillai.] 1892. 8°. [*Sāmudrika-lakshaṇa-śāstram.*] **14170. i. 26.**

LAKSHMAṆA PILLAI, *T., Sheristadar of Kottayam.* *See* SOPHOCLES. ००० வீலநாடகம். (Veelanatakam. A translation . . . of Sophocles' 'Philoctetes.') 1894. 8°. **14170. l. 32.(2.)**

LAWTON (RICHARD). தாராட்டு. [Tārāṭṭu. A song in honour of Albert, son of Thomas Rebairo.] pp. 8. யாழ்ப்பாணம் [*Jaffna,*] 1890. 12°. **14172. a. 5.**

LAZARUS (JOHN). *See* BIBLE.—New Testament.—*Epistles.* St. Paul's Epistle to the Ephesians, with introduction and notes . . . by . . . J. Lazarus. 1903. 12°. **14170. bbb. 2.**

—— *See* PAVAṆANDI. An English translation of the Nannul [bks. i.-ii.] . . . By a Tamil graduate of the Madras University [J. Lazarus]. 1878. 12°. **14172. e. 8.**

—— *See* TIRU-VALLUVAR. The Kural . . . To which is added an English translation . . . by . . . J. Lazarus. 1885. 8°. **14172. d. 15.**

LAZARUS (John) (*continued*). A Dictionary of Tamil Proverbs [in Tamil and English], with an introduction and hints in English on their meaning and application. pp. ii. xxv. 662. *Madras*, 1894. 8°. **14170. k. 76.**

LEO XIII., *Pope* [Vincenzo Gioacchino Pecci]. *See* Ṣubha-vākyam Piḷḷai. கடூ-ம் சிங்கராயர் ... கீர்த்தனைகள். [Kirttanaigaḷ. Songs for the Jubilee of Pope Leo XIII.] [1887.] 8°. **14170. b. 49.**

LESSONS. Third Book of Lessons, for the use of Schools, &c. Tamil Series. Second edition. மூன்றாம்பாடபுஸ்தகம் ௸. pp. x. 236. *Madras*, 1859. 16°. **14172. h. 28.**

LITURGIES.—England, *Church of*. [For separate editions of the Catechism :] *See* Catechism.

—— —— *See* Rhenius (C. T. E.). ஞானபோசன விளக்கம் ௸ [A Catechism on Baptism and the Lord's Supper.] 1825. 12°. **14170. bbb. 5.**

—— —— The Tamil Translation [by Christian David] of the Book of Common Prayer . . . with the Psalter, *etc.* (*பொதுவான செபப்பொஸதககம.) pp. 14, xviii. 378. *Mission Press: Serampore*, 1818. 8°. **14170. b. 51.**

—— —— இஙகிலிசுததேவாலயஙகளில வழககமாயிருககினற பொதுவானசெபஙகளும ஞானஸ்திரவியஙகளைபபரிமாறும ஒழுஙகும . . . தாவீதினுடைய சஙகீதஙகளுமடஙகியிருககினற புஸதகம. [The Book of Common Prayer, with the Occasional Services and Psalter. Translated into Tamil by J. P. Rottler.] pp. xvii. 491, 270. சென்னபட்டணததில ௲அ௱௰௯ [*Government Press : Madras*, 1819.] 4°. **14170. cc. 4.**

—— —— தேவாலயஙகளிலோதுமபடி குறிககபபட்ட தாவீதினுடைய சஙகீதஙகளும . . . காலையிலும அநதியிலுஞ செபிககவேணடிய செபததின ஒழுஙகும [The Book of Common Prayer, with Psalter. Translated by J. P. Rottler.] சென்னபட்டணதது ௲அ௱உ௰ [*S.P.C.K. Press: Madras*, 1820.] 8°. **14170. bb. 11.**

Pagination ceases after p. 115. The sheets are A—Uu.

—— —— The Book of Common Prayer . . . in Tamil. [Translated by J. P. Rottler.] (*பொதுவான செபங்கள் ௸.) pp. xix. 344, 176. *S.P.C.K. Press: Madras*, 1828. 8°. **3406. df. 20.**

LITURGIES. — England, *Church of* (*continued*). Prayers taken from the Liturgy of the United Church of England and Ireland; arranged for family worship. [Translated] from the original of the Prayer-book and Homily Society. செபங்கள் ௸. (†சமுசார செபங்கள்.) pp. 58. *S.P.C.K. Press: Madras*, [*n.d.*] 12°. **14170. b. 13.(1.)**

—— —— The Book of Common Prayer . . . together with the Psalms of David . . . in Tamil. By the Committee of Missionaries in Tinnevelly, appointed . . . for the revision of the Tamil Prayer Book. (பொதுவான செபபுத்தகம் ௸.) pp. 204, 216. *S.P.C.K. Press: Madras*, 1846. 8°. **1107. f. 24.**

—— —— Dureisâni-tamil-puttagam. The Lady's Tamil Book. Containing the Morning and Evening Services and other portions of the Book of Common Prayer in romanized Tamil accompanied by the English version . . . with an Anglo-Tamil grammar and vocabulary by Elijah Hoole. pp. 148. *London*, 1859. 8°. **3408. d. 23.**

—— —— கருத்தருடையசெபம் [Karttarudaiya-ṣebam. A sheet containing the Lord's Prayer, the Creed, and a summary of the Ten Commandments, with illustrations.] [*London, n.d.*] 8°. **14170. c. 27.**

—— Lutheran Churches. தாஙகனபாடித திருசசபையிலவழஙகும ஞானமுறமைகளின விளககம. Rituale Trangambaricum. pp. 141. தாஙகனபாடியிலெ ௲௭௱அ௰க [*Tranquebar*, 1781.] 8°. **3425. d. 20.**

Printed in a type apparently derived from the founts at that time in use in Ceylon.

—— —— Agenda என்னும் சுவிசேஷக லுத்தரன் திருச்சபையில் வழங்கும் ஞானமுறைமைகளின் புஸ்தகம். [The Book of Offices of the Evangelical Lutheran Communion.] pp. vi. 344. *Tranquebar*, 1878. 4°. **14170. cc. 3.**

Appended is a " Litaney " of 4 pp., dated 1881.

—— Netherlands, *Reformed Church of the*. திருததபபட்டதிருசசபைகளின வழிபாடு அலலது . . . முறைநூலகள [The liturgy of the Dutch Reformed Church. Translated by Philippus de Melho.] pp. 115, ii. கொழுமபில ௲௭௱௬௰ [*Colombo*, 1760.] 12°. **14170. a. 25.**

LITURGIES (*continued*).—ROME, *Church of.* [For editions of the Morning and Evening Prayers, *etc.*, prefixed to the Catechism:] *See* CATECHISM.

—— —— செபத்தியானக்குறள். [Ṣeba-dhyāna-kuṛal. Litanies and prayers for private use. Followed by the Order of Mass. Edited by T. M. Ñāna-prakāṣa-nātha Svāmi.] pp. 166. சென்னை [*Madras*,] 1878. 16°. 14170. a. 44.

—— —— நித்திய சீவனம். [Nitya-jīvanam. A collection of regular and occasional prayers and devotional readings, including the Lesser Catechism, Stations of the Cross, *etc.* Edited by Bhāgya-nātha Svāmi. Fifth edition.] pp. ii. 595; 1 *plate.* திருச்சிறுப்பள்ளி [*Trichinopoli*,] 1901. 32°. 14170. a. 55.

—— —— ... கொள்ளைநோய் காலங்களிற் தியானிக்கத்தக்கும் பிராச்சித்தத்தின் பிரார்த்தனை பாவப்பொறுத்தலுக்கான செபங்கள் செவஸ்தியார்பிரார்த்தனை. [Prayers to be used in times of pestilence, extracted from the Ṣebamālai-dhyānam, a Roman Catholic manual in use in Colombo.] pp. 24. யாழ்ப்பாணம் [*Jaffna*,] 1889. 12°. 14170. a. 35.(2.)

—— —— கொள்ளைநோய்ப்பிரார்த்தனை ஷ [A second edition of the preceding.] pp. 28. யாழ்ப்பாணம் [*Jaffna*,] 1892. 12°. 14170.a.35.(7.)

—— —— சேசுநாதருடைய திரு இருதய கீர்த்தன சங்கீதம் ... Officium Parvum Sacri Cordis Jesu. [In Tamil and Latin.] pp. 56. *Trichinopoly*, 1902. 16°. 14170. a. 57.(4.)

—— WESLEYAN METHODISTS. The Sunday Service: together with the order of administration of the Lord's Supper and Baptism; the forms of solemnization of matrimony and of the burial of the dead. As used by the Wesleyan Methodists. (*தெய்வாராதனைப்புத்தகம்.) pp. 126. *American Mission Press: Madras*, 1850. 8°. 14170. c. 3.(2.)

LOGANATHA MOODALIAR. *See* LŌKA-NĀTHA MUDALIYĀR.

LŌKAM-JĪYAR. *See* PILLAI LŌKĀCHĀRYAR.

LŌKA-NĀTHA MUDALIYĀR, *K.* *See* PERIODICAL PUBLICATIONS.—*Madras.* இகபரசுகசாதனி ஷ [Iha-para-sukha-sādhani.] ... Published by K. Loganatha Moodaliar. 1903-1904. 4°. 14172. k. 5.

LONGMANS, GREEN, and CO. Longmans' Anglo-Tamil Second Reader for Form ii. pp. viii. 153; 1 *plate.* *Bombay & Calcutta*, 1907. 12°. 14172.g.12.

LOUIS [GONZAGA], *Saint.* திருச்சிறுப்பள்ளி ... அர்ச். ஞானப்பிரகாசியார் சபையாரின் அமலோற்பவபொக்கிஷம் [Amalōrbhava-pokkisham. A manual for members of the Society of St. Louis founded in Trichinopoli, comprising rules, signed by A. Goris, and prayers. Second edition.] pp. 250, vi.; 1 *plate.* *Trichinopoly*, 1906. 32°. 14170. a. 45.

LOYOLA (IGNATIUS). *See* IGNATIUS [LOPEZ DE RECALDE, *de Loyola*].

LUTHER (MARTIN). [For editions of the Luttērin att'-iyalpu, attacking Luther and Lutheranism:] *See* BESCHI (C. G. E.).

—— *See* EVANGELICAL LUTHERAN CHURCH. Concordia ... VI. Articuli Smalcaldici. (*Pars Secunda. VII. Catechismus Minor. VIII. Catechismus Major, *etc.*) 1872-1880. 8°. 14170. c. 2.

—— மார்த்தின் லுத்தர் என்பவரின் ஞானோபதேசக் குறிப்பிடத்தை விஸ்தரிக்கும் வினாவிடைகள். [Martin Luther enbavarin ñānōpadēsa-kuripp'-idattai vistarikkum vinā-vidaigaḷ. A catechism of Protestant doctrine, based upon P. J. Spener's "Einfache Erklärung der Christlichen Lehre," embodying and amplifying Luther's Kleiner Catechismus. Translated into Tamil by B. Ziegenbalg. Revised by A. Blomstrand. Third edition.] pp. 160. *Tranquebar*, 1872. 12°. 14170. b. 20.

MACARTHUR (CHARLES CHAPMAN). *See* BIBLE.—*Complete Bibles.* A poetical version in Tamil of the Holy Scriptures ... Edited by ... C. C. Macarthur, *etc.* 1866. 8°. 3070. dd. 17.

MACDUFF (JOHN R.). The Faithful Promiser. சத்தியவாசகன். Second edition. pp. 71. *Jaffna*, 1859. 16°. 14170. a. 33.(5.)

—— The Footsteps of St. Paul ... A Tamil translation, with alterations and omissions, by the Rev. Frederic Baylis ... பவுல் அப்போஸ்தலன் நடைபடிவிளக்கம். pp. viii. 367. *Nagercoil*, 1863. 12°. 14170. b. 45.

MADANA-KĀMA-RĀJAN. மதனகாமராஜன்கதை ஷ [Madana-kāma-rājan-kathai, or the Twelve

Stories of the Prime Minister's son. Edited by Ṣēlai Ponn'-ambala Kavi-rāyar.] pp. 198. ஆனந்த [*Madras*, 1855.] 8°. **14170. k. 17.**

—— மதனகாமராஜன்கதை ஞூ [Madana-kāma-rājan-kathai. Edited by Ch. Karuṇānanda Svāmi.] pp. 179. கஅஅம் [*Madras*, 1880.] 8°. **14170. k. 22.**

—— மதனகாமராஜன்கதை ஞூ [Madana-kāma-rājan-kathai. Edited by T. Tyāga-rāya Svāmi.] pp. 179. சித்திரபானு [*Madras*, 1882.] 8°. **14170. k. 60.**

—— The Dravidian Nights Entertainments: being a translation [into English] of Madanakama-rajankadai. By Pandit S. M. Natesa Sastri. pp. xl. 289. *Madras*, 1886. 12°. **14170. k. 38.**

MĀDHAV'-AIYĀ, *Appāv-aiyā*. *See* SHAKSPERE (W.). ஷேக்ஸ்பியர் நாடகங்கள். க. ஒதெல்லோ ஞூ. (Shakespeare for Tamil Homes. I. Othello. [Translated] by A. Madhaviah.) 1902. 12°. **14171. i. 1.(1.)**

—— Padmavati Charitram. A story of the Tamil country ... by A. Madhaviah ... பத்மாவதிசரித்திரம் ஞூ. 2 vols. *Palghat*, 1898-1900. 12°. **14171. a. 21.**

MADHAVIAH. *See* MĀDHAV'-AIYĀ.

MADHURA-KAVI BHĀRATI (GAṆA-PATI SUBB'-AIYAR). மதுரகவிபதங்கள். [Madhura-kavi-padaṅgaḷ. Erotic verses.] *See* VIJAYA-RAṄGA MUDALIYĀR, *P.* ००० கவி ... பதங்கள். [Padaṅgaḷ.] pp. 37-88. 1886. 8°. **14172. c. 33.**

MADHURA-KAVIY-ĀṚVĀR. [For editions of the Kaṇṇi-nuṇ-ṣiṟu-tāmbu of this saint included in the editions of the whole or parts of the Nāl-āyira-prabandham:] *See* ĀṚVĀRGAḶ.—*Nāl-āyiram.*

MADHURA-MUTTU MUDALIYĀR, *Perambūr V.* Shabdarthachandrica. [A vocabulary] containing six languages [viz. Telugu, Kanarese, Tamil, English, Hindustani, and Marathi]. శబ్దార్థచంద్రిక. In Telugu [character]. Compiled by V. Mathuramuthu Mudaliar. pp. 96. *Madras*, 1896. 12°. **14174. m. 25.**

MADHU-SŪDANA SARASVATĪ, *disciple of Viṣvēṣvara*. *See* ṢAṄKARĀCHĀRYAR. ००० சித்தாந்தபிந்து. [Daṣa-ṣlōkī. With Madhu-sūdana's Siddhānta-bindu translated into Tamil.] 1906. 12°. **14049. aa. 1.**

MADHVĀCHĀRYAR. *See* ĀNANDA-TĪRTHA.

MADRAS, *City of*. Minute of the Madras Missionary Conference and other documents on the subject of Caste [in English and Tamil]. சாதியைக்குறித்து ... பத்திரிகைகள். pp. 39. [*Madras*,] 1850. 8°. **14170. c. 22.**

—— *Civil Engineering College.* Madras Engineering College Papers. No. I(-VI). *Madras*, 1860-1869. 8°. **14170. i. 7, 7.***

The Tamil works in the above series are catalogued under the heading Rāja-gōpāla Mudaliyār.

—— *Government Oriental MSS. Library.* Alphabetical Index of Manuscripts in the ... Library ... Sanskrit, Telugu, Tamil, *etc.* 10 pts. *Madras*, 1893. Fol. **14096. f. 9.**

—— *Public Reference Library.* Classified Catalogue of the Public Reference Library, consisting of books registered from 1867 to 1889 at the office of the Registrar of Books, Old College, Madras. pp. 466. *Madras*, 1894. 8°. **11899. dd. 19.**

—— *Viṣishṭādvaita-siddhānta-prabōdha-saṅgham.* கிறிஸ்துமதகண்டனம். [Kiṟistu-mata-khaṇḍanam. A tract against Christianity.] pp. 24. சென்னை [*Madras*,] 1887. 12°. **14170. i. 15.**

MADRAS, *Presidency of*. [A collection of Acts, extending over the years 1802-1814 and 1816-1820.] 3 vols. கூஅாஉ-கூஅாஉம் [*Madras*, 1802-1820.] Fol. **14170. h. 1**

—— உப்புசம்பந்தமாய் ... சட்டங்களும் ஆக்ட்டுகளும் ஞூ [Rules, Regulations and Revenue Board Circular Orders for the administration of the Salt Acts. Translated and edited by V. K. Rāghavāchāryar.] pp. 70. சென்னபட்டணம் கஅகள [*Madras*, 1867.] 8°. **14170. g. 5.(1.)**

—— சென்னை ரைவிந்யாசசபாஸ்தியமாநாது சாசநங்கள். என்னும் ரிவினியுபோர்ட்டாருடைய நிலையான உத்தரவுகள் ஞூ [The Standing Orders of the Madras Board of Revenue from 1820 to 1866. Compiled by R. A. Dalyell, and translated into Tamil by Ṣ. Jaya-rāma Cheṭṭiyār and Ș. Vijaya-rāghavulu Cheṭṭiyār.] சென்னப்பட்டணம் தூஅுசாஅு [*Madras*, 1868.] 8°. **14170. g. 6.**

Each Act has a separate pagination.

—— Supplementary Manual, showing the transliteration of Hindu names, Tamil and Telugu, peculiar to the Madras Presidency, *etc.* pp. 79. *Madras*, 1893. 8°. **14172. m. 2.**

—— Report on a Search for Sanskrit and Tamil Manuscripts for the year 1896-97 (*1893-94). By M. Seshagiri Sastri . . . Prepared under the orders of the Govt. of Madras. 2 vols. *Madras*, 1898-1899. 8°. **14096. ccc. 2.**

—— A collection of the inscriptions on copper-plates and stones in the Nellore district. Made by Alan Butterworth . . . and V. Venugopaul Chetty. 3 vols. pp. xi. i. 1520, i. i. i. i. *Madras*, 1905. 8°. **14058. c. 11.**

MADURA. *See* COLTON (J.). Description of Madura, *etc.* 1863. 12°. **14172. h. 66.**

—— *See* TAYLOR (W.). Oriental Historical Manuscripts . . . [chiefly bearing upon the history of the kingdom of Madura], *etc.* 1835. 4°. **14171. c. 5.**

—— [For the chief poems on the legends of the Șaiva sanctuary of Madura, see under the following headings :]

PARAÑ-JŌDI MUNIVAR.
PERUM-BAṬṬA-PULIY-ŪR-NAMBI.
VĪMA-NĀTHA PAṆḌITAR.

MADURAI PIḶḶAI, *P. Mārkaṇḍa-mūrtti.* *See* AṆṆĀ-MALAI MUDALIYĀR. மதுரை வெண்பாமாலை. (Madooray Venba Malei [a series of verses] . . . on P. M. Madooray Pillay, Esq., *etc.*) 1891. 8°. **14172. c. 21.**

MADURAI VĪRA-SVĀMI. *See* VĪRA-SVĀMI, *Madurai.*

MAHĀ-BHAKTA-VIJAYAM. ००० ஸ்ரீமகாபக்தவிஜயம். [Mahā-bhakta-vijayam. Lives of Vaishṇava saints, compiled and translated from Nābhājī's Bhakti-sāra, Mahī-pati's Bhakta-vijaya and Santa-vijaya, and Uddhava's Bhakta-mālā, *etc.* Vol. i. (two biographies), compiled and translated by Șiṭṭūr Aruḷ-vākku Vēṅkaṭa-dāsar. Edited by Ā. Tiru-vēṅkaṭa Piḷḷai.] pp. iv. 20, 56, 85. *Madras*, 1870. 4°. **14170. f. 5.**

MAHĀ-BHAKTA-VIJAYAM (*continued*). ००० ஸ்ரீமகாபக்தவிஜயம். [Mahā-bhakta-vijayam. Vol. i. (five biographies), by Vēṅkaṭa-dāsar, with a biography of Kuchēla by Șāṭṭapākkam Kṛushṇa-sāmi Mudaliyār. Edited by M. Nātha-muni Nāyuḍu.] vol. i. pp. iv. 338; 6 *plates*. [*Madras*,] 1893. 4°. **14170. f. 22.**

—— ००० ஸ்ரீமகாபக்தவிஜயம். [Mahā-bhakta-vijayam. Vol. i., compiled and translated by Vēṅkaṭa-dāsar and Kṛushṇa-sāmi, and edited by Puduvai Nārāyaṇa-dāsar. Vol. ii., translated by P. Nārāyaṇa-dāsar, and edited by P. Vēṅkaṭa-sāmi Nāyuḍu. Vol. iii., translated by Nārāyaṇa-dāsar.] 3 vols. சென்னை [*Madras*,] 1898-1905. 4°. **14170. f. 6.**

—— ००० ஸ்ரீமகா பக்தவிஜயம். [Mahā-bhakta-vijayam. A different hagiological collection. Vol. iii., iv., translated by Vēlūr Kaṇṇ'-aiya-dāsar. Edited by M. Nātha-muni Nāyuḍu.] pp. 36, 248. [*Madras*,] 1905. 4°. **14170. ff. 18.**

MAHĀ-BHĀRATAM. *See* AṆṆĀVIYĀR. ஸ்ரீ மகாபாரத அம்மானை [Mahā-bhārata-ammānai. A poetical paraphrase of the Mahā-bhāratam.] 1903. 8°. **14172. c. 49.**

—— [For editions of Perun-dēvanār's adaptation of the Sanskrit Mahā-bhāratam :] *See* PERUN-DĒVANĀR.

—— *See* RAṄGA-NĀTHA KAVI-RĀYAR. மகாபாரதம். [Mahā-bhāratam. An abbreviated adaptation.] [1903.] 8°. **14172. b. 9.**

—— *See* SUBBA-RĀYA MUDALIYĀR, *V.*, MUTTI-RĀMA KAVI-RĀYAR, *G.*, and KADIR-VĒL KAVI-RĀJA PAṆḌITAR. ஸ்ரீமஹாபாரதக்கீர்த்தனை ஆ [Mahā-bhārata-kīrttanai, or Mahā-bhārata-nāṭakam. An adaptation of the Mahā-bhāratam in lyric-dramatic form.] [1905.] 8°. **14172. bbb. 1.**

—— *See* VARADA-RĀJA DĪKSHITAR. The History of India . . . Sri Maha Bharata, *etc.* 1890. 8°. **14172. d. 9.**

—— [For editions of Villiputtūrar's adaptation of bks. 1-10 of the Sanskrit Mahā-bhāratam :] *See* VILLIPUTTŪRAR.

—— Tamil translation [by N. Kṛushṇa-sāmi Aiyar] of Mahabharata Niti Ratnavali : Moral

Gems from the Mahabharata. Edited by R. Sivasankara Pandiya. pp. 20. *Madras*, 1888. 12°. **14003. c.**

Forms no. ix. *of the* Hindu Excelsior Series.

—— ஸ்ரீ மகாபாரதம் ௸ [Mahā-bhāratam. Ādi to Bhīshma *parvam*. Translated into prose by Shaṇmukham Piḷḷai.] 2 vols. 1890-1894. *See* ITIHĀSA-MAÑJARI. Ithihasa Manjari Series. [1888]-1894. 8°. **14172. d. 11.**

—— அஸ்வமேதபர்வம். [Aṣva-mēdha-parvam. A prose abridgment. Edited by K. Aruṇāchala Mudaliyār from the recension of P. Rāja-gōpāla Piḷḷai.] pp. 217. யுவ [*Madras*, 1875.] 8°. **14172. c. 22.**

—— *See* TIRU-VĒṄKAṬA-NĀTHAR. கீதாசாரத்தாலாட்டு ௸ [Gītā-sāra-tālāṭṭu-prabandham. A poem on the philosophy of the Gītā.] 1887. 12°. [*Nānā-jīva-vāda-kaṭṭaḷai, etc.*] **14170. d. 26.**

—— *See* TIRU-VĒṄKAṬA-SĀMI MUDALIYĀR, *Ā. S.* பகவத் கீதை சாரசங்கிரகம். [Bhagavad-gītai-sāra-saṅgraham. A summary of the Bhagavad-gītā.] [1890.] 16°. **14170. d. 35.(1.)**

—— The Bhagavad-gita, a Sanskrit philosophical poem, in the form of dialogues between Krishná and Arjuná, translated into English and Tamil by the late Rev. H. Bower. (*பகவத்கீதை.) pp. lvi. 137. *Madras*, 1889. 8°. **14065. c. 44.**

—— ஸ்ரீபகவத்கீதை. [Bhagavad-gītā. Sanskrit text, with Tamil glosses and translations. Preceded by the Kṛushṇāshṭōttara-ṣata-nāma-stōtram, a short metrical prayer, the Bhagavad-gītā-māhātmyam, and *nyāsas*, in Sanskrit; and followed by Yāmunāchāryar's Gītārtha-saṅgraha, with Tamil version, and the Kṛushṇāshṭakam, also in Sanskrit. Edited and translated by A. Ṣrīnivāsa Tātāchāryar and K. Rāma-sāmi Nāyuḍu.] pp. 12, ii. 714, xxii.; 1 *plate*. சென்னை விகாரி [*Madras*, 1899.] 16°. **14065. b. 19.**

The Sanskrit text is printed in both the Grantham and the Tamil character.

—— பகவத்கீதா தாத்பரிய தீபிகை. [Bhagavad-gītā. Sanskrit text in the Tamil character, edited with a Tamil version styled Bhagavad-gītā-tātparya-dīpikai by Bāla-subrahmaṇya Brahma-svāmi.] pp. 494. சென்னை [*Madras*,] 1900. 32°. **14068. a. 10.**

—— ஸ்ரீமத் பகவத்கீதையும், ஸ்ரீ சங்கராசார்ய பாஷ்யமும் ௸ [Bhagavad-gītā. With Ṣaṅkara's commentary. The Sanskrit text of both, edited with Tamil translation of the whole by D. Sundara-rāja Ṣarmā.] *Madras*, 1906, *etc.* 8°. **14049. bb. 10.**

In progress.

—— பகவற்கீதை மூலமும்-உரையும். [Bhagavad-gītai. A free metrical translation from the Sanskrit, ascribed to Villiputtūrar. Edited by K. Vēda-giri Mudaliyār.] pp. ii. 231. பரிதாவி [*Madras*, 1852.] 8°. **14170. e. 19.**

—— பகவத்கீதை வெண்பா. (Bhagavad Gita Venba.) [A poetical rendering by Aṛagiya-maṇavāḷa Jīyar. Edited with notes by Ṣ. Sāmi-nātha Aiyar and P. R. Kṛushṇam-āchāryar.] (Pocket Tamil Classics.) 3 pts. *Srirangam*, 1906-1907. 16°. **14172. a. 59.**

—— மகாபாரதம். திரௌபதீசத்தியபாமாசம்வாதம். [Draupadī-satyabhāmā-saṃvādam. The dialogue of Draupadī and Satyabhāmā on wifely duty (Vana-parva, Mārkaṇḍēya-samasyā-parva, ch. ccxxxii.-iii.). In Sanskrit, with Tamil glosses and commentary.] *See* SUNDARA-RĀJA ṢARMĀ, *D.* வ்யாஸ வாத்ஸ்யாயந . . . பார்யாதருமம். (Vyasa and Vatsyayana's Bharyadharmam, *etc.*) pp. 96-178. 1901. 12°. **14085. b. 44.**

—— *See* VIṢVA-NĀTHA SŪRI, *K.* ००० மணிப்ரவாள விராடபர்வம். [Maṇi-pravāḷa-virāṭa-parvam. A metrical adaptation of the Virāṭa-parvam in mixed Tamil and Sanskrit.] 1905. 8°. **14172. bb. 16.**

—— ஸ்ரீமஹாபாரதம் தமிழ்வசனம் விராட-பர்வம். [Virāṭa-parvam. A prose version by Koṇḍaṅgi Kandāḍai Ṣrīnivāsa Rāghavāchāryar. With notes.] pp. vi. iv. 298. சென்னை [*Madras*,] 1905. 8°. **14172. d. 1.**

MAHĀ-LIṄG'-AIYAR, *Maṛavai.* *See* ELL'-APPA NĀVALAR. அருணாசலபுராணம் ௸ [Aruṇāchala-purāṇam. With commentary by Mahā-liṅg'-aiyar.] 1898. 12°. **14170. d. 52.**

—— —— 1903. 12°. **14170. d. 83.**

MAHĀ-LIṄG'-AIYAR, *Maṛavai (continued).* See Tol-kāppiyanār. தொல்காப்பியம் மூ [Tol-kāppiyam. Pt. i. Edited by Mahā-liṅg'-aiyar.] [1847.] 8°. **14172. f. 4.**

—— ◦ ◦ ◦ இலக்கணச்சுருக்கம். [Ilakkaṇa-churukkam. An abridged grammar.] pp. 96. சென்னை [*Madras,*] 1879. 16°. **14172. h. 41.**

—— ◦ ◦ ◦ இலக்கணச்சுருக்கம். [Ilakkaṇa-churukkam.] pp. 110. சென்னபட்டணம் [*Madras,*] 1882. 16°. **14172. h. 24.**

—— ◦ ◦ ◦ இலக்கணச் சுருக்கம். [Ilakkaṇa-churukkam. Revised by V. G. Sūrya-nārāyaṇa Ṣāstri.] pp. 100. சென்னை [*Madras,*] 1898. 12°. **14172. ee. 3.**

—— ◦ ◦ ◦ இலக்கணச்சுருக்கம் மூ [Ilakkaṇa-churukkam.] (A Manual of Tamil Grammar . . . Revised and improved.) pp. i. 140. *Madras,* 1893. 16°. **14172. ee. 6.**

MAHĪ-PATI. [For editions of the Mahā-bhakta-vijayam, partly derived from the Marathi Bhakta-vijaya and Santa-vijaya of Mahī-pati:] See Mahā-bhakta-vijayam.

—— ஸ்ரீ...வடதேசத்து பக்தசிரோமணிகளுடைய சரித்திரங்களடங்கிய பக்தமால வசனம். [Bhakta-māla-vachanam. A Tamil prose version by V. Bāla-kṛushṇa Mudaliyār of the Bhakta-māla, a Telugu *tōrā* poem by himself, paraphrasing the legends of the Northern Vaishṇava votaries narrated in Mahī-pati's Marathi poems, scil. the Bhakta-vijaya, Santa-vijaya, Santa-līlāmṛuta, and Bhakta-līlāmṛuta. Revised by V. Sundara Piḷḷai.] சென்னை [*Madras,*] 1907, *etc.* 8°. **14170. e. 17.**

In progress.

—— ◦ ◦ ◦ பிபாஜீராஜன் சரித்திரம். [Pipājī-rājan-charitram. The story of king Pipājī, a Vaishṇava devotee, in Telugu, taken from V. Bāla-kṛushṇa Mudaliyār's Bhakta-māla, with a Tamil transliteration, translation, and commentary by the same.] pp. 56; 1 *plate.* சென்னை [*Madras,*] 1900. 8°. **14170. ee. 35.(6.)**

—— ◦ ◦ ◦ ஸ்ரீமத்துக்காராம் ஸ்வாமிகள் சரித்திரம். ஸ்ரீஹரிநாமஸ்தோத்திரப்பா ஸங்கீர்த்தனம். [Tukārām-svāmigaḷ-charitram. The history of the Vaishṇava saint Tukārām, translated from Mahī-pati's Bhakta-vijaya by Jauḷi-kaṟār Muni-svāmi Mudaliyār, and edited by Rāma-svāmi Nāyuḍu. With a second part containing Hari-nāma-stōtra-pā and Hari-nāma-saṅkīrttanam, two series of hymns, translated by the same, and edited by Ṣ. G. Appu Mudaliyār.] pp. i. 292, 76; 18 *plates.* வேலூர் [*Vellore,*] 1887-1898. 8°. **14170. ee. 34**

Part i. *is in the second edition* (1898).

MAHOMED SULTAN MARICAR. See Muhammad Sulṭān ibn Aḥmad ʻUmar.

MAIKANDADEVA. See Mey-kaṇḍa Dēva.

MAILU PIḶḶAI. See Mayilu Piḷḷai.

MAKHDŪM MUḤAMMAD ibn MAKHDŪM PIḶḶAI, *Kaṇṇ'-Aḥmad.* [For works edited by Makhdūm Muḥammad, see under the following headings:]
Makhdūm Muḥammad ibn Pīr Muḥammad.
Muḥammad ibn Muḥammad, *al-Mu'izz.*
Muḥammad Ibrāhīm ibn ʻAbd al-Ghanī.
Muḥammad Mīrān Mastān ibn Luḳmān.
Periya Nūḥ Lebbai.
Shāh al-Ḥamīd ibn Mīrān Ṣāḥib.

—— இஃது தீனெறி விளக்கம் வசனகாவியம். [Dīn-neṟi-viḷakkam. An exposition of the Muhammadan religion.] pp. vii. 412. சென்னை தருமம் [*Madras,* 1892.] 8°. **14170. c. 42.**

MAKHDŪM MUḤAMMAD ibn PĪR MUḤAMMAD, *of Kayalpatnam.* மதுரவாக்யகீர்த்தனாரஞ்சிதம். [Madhura-vākya-kīrttanā-rañjitam. A series of Muhammadan lyrics. Edited by Kaṇṇ'-Aḥmad Makhdūm Muḥammad.] pp. xxvi. 186. தருஉம் [*Madras,* 1902.] 8°. **14173. b. 17.**

MALAIYA GAUṆḌAR, *C., of Municipal School, Coimbatore.* See Chidambara Kavi-rāyar. உசிதசூடாமணி நிகண்டு. († "Oositha Soodamani Nigandu," *etc.*) [Edited by Malaiya Gauṇḍar.] 1903. 12°. **14172. ee. 10.**

MALAIY-APPA PAṆḌITAR, *Vaidyam P.T., of Udamalpet, Coimbatore.* செங்குந்தமன்னர் குலதீபிகை. [Ṣeṅgunda-mannar-kula-dīpikai. An account of the Shengundar caste of weavers.] pp. iv. ii. 248, 171. ஈரோடு [*Erode,*] 1905. 8°. **14171. e. 7.**

MALL'-AYYAR, *Pālavāyal.* தாராசசாங்கவிஜயமென்னும் தாராசாங்க [*sic*] நாடகம். [Tārā-ṣaṣāṅka-vijayam, or Tārā-ṣaṣāṅka-nāṭakam. A mythological drama.] pp. 132. சென்னை [*Madras*,] 1905. 8°. **14170. l. 64.**

MALLIKAM MUDALIYĀR. The Dawn of Wisdom. [A Christian tract.] ... ஞானோதயம். Second edition. pp.16. *Jaffna*, 1841. 12°. **14170. b. 1.(27.)**

—— Evidence from Hinduism itself ... தற்சமயசாட்சி. Fourth edition. pp. 32. *Jaffna*, 1845. 12°. **14170. b. 1.(55.)**

MĀMBĀKKAM UPĀDHYĀYAR. *See* TIRU-CHITTAMBALA NĀVALAR.

MĀMBARA KAVI-ṢINGA NĀVALAR, *Paṟani.* *See* DĒVĀṄGAR. ००० தேவாங்கபுராணம். [Dēvāṅga-purāṇam. Versified by Māmbaṟar.] [1893.] 8°. **14170. e. 55.**

MANA-VĀCHAKAM KADANDAR, *Tiruvadigai, disciple of Mey-kaṇḍar.* உண்மைவிளக்கம். [Uṇmai-viḷakkam. A metrical tract on the Ṣaiva-Siddhāntam. With commentary.] *See* MEY-KAṆḌA-ṢĀTTIRAM. மெய்கண்டசாத்திரம் ௲ [Mey-kaṇḍa-ṣāttiram.] pp. 599-614. 1897. 8°. **14170. ff. 3.**

Said to have been written in Ṣaka 1177.

—— உண்மைவிளக்க ௲ [Uṇmai-viḷakkam.] pp. 8. *See* MEY-KAṆḌA-ṢĀTTIRAM. ००० சைவசித்தாந்தசாத்திரம் ௲ [Ṣaiva-siddhānta-ṣāttiram.] [1899.] 12°. **14170. d. 53.**

—— Light of Truth, or Unmai Vilakkam, *etc.* [Translated by J. M. Nalla-sāmi Piḷḷai.] 1902. *See* PERIODICAL PUBLICATIONS.—*Madras.* The Light of Truth, *etc.* vol. v., no. 11. 1897, *etc.* 4°. **14170. fff. 4.(vol. 5.)**

MAṆAVĀḶA MĀ-MUNI. *See* AṞAGIYA-MAṆAVĀḶA PERU-MĀḶ.

MAṆAVĀḶA MĀ-MUNI, *Viṣada-vāk-ṣirōmaṇi.* *See* [Addenda] AṞAGIYA-MAṆAVĀḶA PERU-MĀḶ. ००० ஆசாரியஹ்ருதயம் ௲ [Āchārya-hṛudayam. With commentary ascribed to Maṇavāḷa Mā-muni.] 1906. 8°. **14170. ff. 24.**

MAṆḌALA-PURUḌAR. *See* VĪRA-MAṆḌALAVAR.

MAṄGAḶĒSVARI. திருவுத்தரகோசமங்கை மங்களேசுவரி பிள்ளைத்தமிழ். [Uttara-kōṣa-maṅgai-maṅgaḷēṣvari-piḷḷai-tamiṟ. A hymn to the goddess Umā-Maṅgaḷēṣvari as worshipped at Uttara-kōṣa-maṅgai. Edited by V. G. Sūrya-nārāyaṇa Ṣāstri.] pp. ii. 62. சென்னை [*Madras*,] 1901. 12°. **14170. d. 89.**

MĀṄGUḌI MARUDANĀR. *See* MARUDANĀR.

MĀṆIKKAM PIḶḶAI, *Tirupattūr Rāma-sāmi.* *See* DĀṢARATHI CHETṬI, *T. K.*, and MĀṆIKKAM PIḶḶAI, *T. R.* Vithyabivirthi Sambashanam, *etc.* 1895. 8°. **14172. hh. 11.**

MĀṆIKKA SVĀMI, *Amarāpati M.* ஸ்ரீ ... ஸ்ரீமதாதிசங்கராசார்யசுவாமிகளது சரித்திரச்சுருக்கமும் . . . சாம்பிரதாயசிந்தனைவாக்யங்களும் . . . உபதேசவாக்கியமும். [Ādi-ṣaṅkarāchārya-charitra-churukkam, or Jagad-guru-paramparai. An account of Ṣaṅkara and the apostolic succession deriving through him. Followed by Sāmpradāya-chintanaigaḷ, a catechism of the doctrine of Ṣaṅkara's school by Kara-pātra Yōgīṣvara, and Upadēṣa-vākyam, a short tract by Dattātrēya Svāmi. Edited by A. M. Māṇikka Svāmi.] pp. 40, 283; 2 *plates.* சென்னை [*Madras*,] 1901. 12°. **14170. ee. 44.**

MĀṆIKKA-VĀCHAKA NĀḌĀR, *N. Ṣ.* *See* PERIYA-SUBBĀ REḌḌIYĀR, *P.* ००० மஹாராணி அம்மானை (The Maharani Ammanei ... with an introduction by N. S. Manikavasaka Nadar.) 1901. 8°. **14172. b. 7.**

MĀṆIKKA-VĀCHAKAR. [For editions of the Vādavūrar-purāṇam containing the legendary biography of this poet:] *See* KAḌAVUṈ MĀ-MUNI.

—— *See* TIRU-CHITTAMBALAM PIḶḶAI. மாணிக்கவாசகர். (Manickavachakar. [An essay], *etc.*) 1900. 12°. **14171. a. 33.(2.)**

—— *See* TIRUMALAI-KOṞUNDU PIḶḶAI. The Age of Manicka Vachakar, *etc.* 1899. 12°. **14171. a. 33.(1.)**

—— [For editions of this author's Tiru-vāchakam, which forms bk. 8 of the Tiru-muṟai:] *See* TIRU-MUṞAI.

—— திருப்பெருந்துறை ஆவுடையார் கோவில் விளக்கமென்னும் மாணிக்கவாசகர் அம்மானை. [Ammānai, or Tiru-perun-durai-āvuḍaiyār-kōvil-viḷakkam. A Ṣaiva devotional poem. Edited by Nāga-liṅgam Piḷḷai of Madura.] pp. 81. சென்னை [*Madras*,] 1904. 12°. **14170. d. 93.**

MĀṈIKKA-VĀCHAKAR (*continued*). ∘∘∘ திருச்சிற்றம்பலக் கோவையாருண்மை. [Tiru-chiṭṭam-bala-kōvaiyār-uṇmai. A Ṣaiva devotional poem in 400 stanzas. With a metrical commentary by Pēr-āṣiriyar, here ascribed to Nachinārkk'-iniyar. Edited by N. Ch. Tamb'-aiyā Piḷḷai.] pp. vi. 159, v. சென்னபட்டணம் ஜய [*Madras*, 1895.] 12°. **14172. a. 42.**

On the authorship of the commentary see the Madras Christian College Magazine, vol. xvii., *p.* 621 *f.*

—— ∘∘∘ திருக்கோவையார். [Tiru-kōvaiyār. With the commentary of Pēr-āṣiriyar, here attributed to Nachinārkk'-iniyar, and an interpretation and synopsis by Viṣākha Peru-māḷ Aiyar.] pp. ii. 434, 32, vii.; 1 *plate*. சென்னை துன்முகி [*Madras*, 1897.] 12°. **14172. a. 46.**

MANU. மநுதரும சாத்திரம். [Manu-dharma-ṣāstram. Edited with Tamil translation by C. T. Guru-sāmi Mudaliyār. Followed by the Vyavahāra-sāra-saṅgraham, a summary of law according to the school of Manu, in Tamil, edited by the same. Third edition.] pp. i. xiv. 559, xvi. lviii. 121, 6. *Madras*, 1896. 8°. **14039. b. 23.**

The text is printed in Telugu letters.

MANUEL. Manuel de la Conversation, ou Recueil de mots usuels et de phrases propres à faciliter l'étude du Français et du Tamoul. சம்பாஷணையநுசாரம் . . . சொல்வசனச்சேர்க்கை. pp. ii. 184. புதுவை தூஅச்சுகூடு [*Pondicherry*, 1865.] 12°. **14172. h. 15.**

Apparently by the R. P. Lap; *see* Histoire des Missions de l'Inde, iv., p. 584.

MARAI-ÑĀNA-SAMBANDHAR, *Tiruvāvaḍuduṟai.* அருணகிரிபுராணம். [Aruṇa-giri-purāṇam. The legends of the Ṣaiva sanctuary of Tiruvannamalai. Edited by Vāma-dēva Mṛuga-bhaṭṭārakar.] pp. i. 110. சென்னபட்டணம்விக்கிரம [*Madras*, 1880.] 16°. **14170. d. 15.**

—— Saiva-Samaya Neri. Or The Code of the Siva Religion, *etc.* [Translated by J. M. Nallasāmi Piḷḷai.] 1902. *See* PERIODICAL PUBLICATIONS.—*Madras.* The Light of Truth, *etc.* vol. vi., no. 2. 1897, *etc.* 4°. **14170. fff. 4.(vol. 6.)**

MARAṆA-GAṆḌI. மரணகண்டியென்னும் ஜோதிஷசாஸ்திரம். [Maraṇa-gaṇḍi. An astrological work on the fatal indications of the stars, *etc.* Edited by P. Mārga-liṅga Nāyanār.] pp. i. 92. யுவ [*Madras*, 1875.] 8°. **14172. b. 2.**

MĀṞAN PORAIYANĀR. ∘∘∘ ஐந்திணையைம்பது மூலமும் உரையும். [Ain-diṇaiy-aim-badu. A series of 50 quatrains on the five erotic themes, forming no. 10 of the 18 *kīṟ-kaṇakku* works of the third *Saṅgham* of Madura. With a paraphrastic commentary. Edited with preface, notes, and glossary by R. Rāghav'-aiyaṅgār.] pp. vi. iv. 19, iii. மதுரை [*Madura*,] 1903. 8°. **14172. bb. 3.(6.)**

Forms no. 1 of the Ṣen-damiṟ-prachuram.

—— [Another copy, without preface, &c.] *See* ACADEMIES, *etc.*—*Madura.* ["Ṣen-damiṟ" supplement.] no. 1. 1902, *etc.* 8°. **14172. i. 1.*(no. 1.)**

MARDEN (T.). The Third Reader. [An English reader for native students, with Tamil notes and explanations.] . . . Anglo-Tamil. Third edition. (*Madras Readers—English Series.) pp. iv. 234. *Madras*, 1882. 12°. **14172. h. 63.**

MĀRGA-LIṄGA NĀYANĀR, *Pichaipākkam.* *See* KAMALA MUNI. ∘∘∘ சாமுத்திரிகாலட்சணம் ஷ [Rēkhai-ṣāstram. Edited by Mārga-liṅga.] [1879.] 16°. **14172. a. 19.**

—— *See* KAUṢIKAR. The Kowseegasindamony . . . written [*i.e.* edited] . . . (by Margalinga, *etc.*). 1895. 8°. **14170. i. 35.**

—— *See* MARAṆA-GAṆḌI, மரணகண்டி ஷ [Maraṇa-gaṇḍi. Edited by Mārga-liṅga.] [1875.] 8°. **14172. b. 2.**

MARIADA RAMAN. *See* MARIYĀDAI-RĀMAN.

MĀRI-MUTTĀ PIḶḶAI, *Tillaiviḍaṅgan, son of Piḷḷai Peru-māḷ Aiyaṅgār.* மாரிமுத்தாப்பிள்ளை . . . கீர்த்தனம். [Kīrttanam. Ṣaiva hymns.] *See* MUTTU-TĀṆḌAVAR. சிதம்பரம் . . . கீர்த்தனம் ஷ [Kīrttanam.] pp. 45-61. [1870.] 8°. **14170. k. 20.**

—— ∘∘∘ புலியூர்வெண்பா. [Puliyūr-veṇ-bā. Quatrains in honour of Ṣiva, as worshipped in Chidambaram. With a commentary by T. K. Subbarāya Cheṭṭi. Second edition.] pp. vi. 82. சென்னை சர்வதாரி [*Madras*, 1888.] 12°. **14172. a. 31.**

MĀRI-MUTTU UPĀDHYĀYAR, *Māṉippāy K.* The Sixth Standard Arithmetic . . . by C. Marrimuttu

... அங்க கணிதம். pp. ii. 59. யாழ்ப்பாணம் [*Jaffna*,] 1890. 12°. **14172. h. 48.**

—— The Ceylon Governors ... இலங்கைத் தேசாதிபதிகள். [Laṅkai-dēṣādhipatigaḷ. A series of panegyrics on the British Governors in Tamil verse.] pp. v. 72. யாழ்ப்பாணம் [*Jaffna*,] 1889. 12°. **14170. k. 41.**

MARIYĀDAI - RĀMAN. மரியாதைராமன்கதை [Mariyādai-rāman-kathai. Tales of the ingenuity of the judge Mariyādai-rāman.] *See* KATHĀ-CHINTĀMAṆI. The Kathāchintāmani, *etc.* pp. 1-33. 1875. 8°. **14170. k. 27.**

—— மரியாதைராமன் கதை. [Mariyādai-rāman-kathai.] *See* PŪRṆA-LIṄGAM PIḶḶAI, *M. Ṣ.* Witty Stories, *etc.* pp. 1-32. 1897. 12°. **14171. a. 6.(2.)**

—— The Unerring Judge. [Tales of Mariyādai-rāman, translated into English.] *See* ROBINSON (E. J.). Tamil Wisdom, *etc.* pp. 101-148. 1873. 12°. **14170. k. 62.**

—— The Accomplished Judge. [A verse translation.] *See* ROBINSON (E. J.). Tales and Poems of South India, *etc.* pp. 265-308. 1885. 8°. **14170. k. 63.**

—— Tales of Mariada Raman. 21 amusing stories [translated] by P. Ramachandra Rao. pp. 8, 69. *Madras*, [1902.] 12°. **14171. aa. 14.**

MARIYA-DĀS PIḶḶAI. *See* PURĀṆAS.—*Bhāgavata-purāṇam.* Bagavadam, *etc.* [Translated into French by "Méridas Poullé," *i.e.* Mariya-dās Piḷḷai.] 1788. 8°. **279. d. 21.**

—— —— 1789. 8°. **14016. c. 1.**

MARIYA-DĀS PIḶḶAI, *K. T., of Tranquebar.* Tamil first book of lessons, for the use of pupils in "Our Lady of Lourdes" Anglo-Tamil School. முதற்பாட புத்தகம். Part i. pp. 31. *Singapore*, 1887. 16°. **14172. h. 51.(1.)**

MĀRIY-AMMAN. மாரியம்மன்தாலாட்டு. [Māriy-amman-tālāṭṭu. Songs in honour of the goddess Māriy-amman. Edited by T. Āṛu-muga Svāmi.] pp. 48. கஅஅஉ [*Madras*, 1882.] 16°. **14172. h. 35.(5.)**

MARIYA-NĀYAKAM PIḶḶAI, *Triṣirapuram Ṣavari-muttū.* மரண சாசனம். [Maraṇa-ṣāsanam. Advices and reflections of a dying man. A Roman Catholic work.] pp. ii. ii. i. ii. 240, i. ii. [*Trichinopoli*,] 1891. 8°. **14170. bb. 5.**

MĀRIY-APPA KAVI-RĀYAR, *M.*, and **ṢAṄKARA-MŪRTTI KŌNĀR,** *A.* ஸ்ரீமத் பாகவத அம்மானை. [Bhāgavata-ammānai. A metrical paraphrase of the Bhāgavata-purāṇam in *ammānai* style. Bk. i. by Māriy-appar, bk. ii. by Ṣaṅkara-mūrtti. Edited by T. Kuppu-sāmi Nāyuḍu.] 2 vols. சென்னை [*Madras*,] 1893. 8°. **14172. b. 54.**

MĀRIY-APPA MUDALIYĀR, *Sēlam.* *See* EPHEMERIDES. ஜந்திரி. [Jantri. Compiled by Māriy-appa.] 1893. 12°. **14172. i. 14.**

MĀRKAṆḌA MUNI-SĀMI PIḶḶAI. வீரகுமார நாடகம். [Vīra-kumāra-nāṭakam. A drama.] pp. 192. கஅசுஅ [*Madras*, 1868.] 8°. **14170. l. 13.**

MARRIMUTTU. *See* MĀRI-MUTTU.

MARSDEN (EDMUND). ° ° ° நான்காம் வாசக புஸ்தகத்தின் திறவுகோல். [Marsden's Fourth Reader, with a key by M. Mṛugēṣa Mudaliyār. Second edition.] pp. 163. *Madras*, 1899. 16°. **14172. g. 2.(2.)**

—— History of India for Middle Schools ... இந்துதேச சரித்திரம். (*Macmillan's Series of Text-books for Indian Schools.) pp. viii. 299. *Madras*, 1901. 12°. **14172. h. 18.**

MARSHMAN (JOHN CLARK). *See* NĀRĀYAṆA-SĀMI, *V. M.* Select Tamil Tales ... and a choice number of Dr. Marshman's dialogues, in English and Tamil, *etc.* 1839. 8°. **14170. k. 66.**

—— —— 1853. 8°. **14170. k. 75.**

MARTIN (J. S.), *of Jaffna.* *See* MAYILU PIḶḶAI.

MARUDANĀR, *Māṅguḍi.* மதுரைக்காஞ்சி. [Madurai-kāñji. A panegyric poem on king Neḍun-ṣeṛiyan and his capital Madura, being no. 6 of the Pattu-pāṭṭu. With commentary of Nachi-nārkk'-iniyar.] *See* PATTU-PĀṬṬU. பத்துப்பாட்டு [Pattu-pāṭṭu.] pp. 159-240. 1889. 8°. **14172. d. 10.**

MARY, *the Blessed Virgin.* ° ° ° அர்ச்.-தேவமாதாவின திருவிருதயச்சபை யநுசாரம். [Anusāram. A handbook of the Archconfraternity of the Sacred Heart of Mary.] pp. 342. புதுவை தூஅா௫௬ [*Pondicherry*, 1856.] 16°. **14170. a. 17.**

Ascribed to L. Saint-Cyr, S.J., by Backer, vol. vii., *col.* 412.

—— தேவமாதா அம்மானை. [Dēva-mātā-ammānai. A series of lyrics by a native Catholic on the history of the Virgin.] pp. i. 115. யாழ்ப்பாணம் [*Jaffna*,] 1893. 8°. **14170. bb. 3.**

—— சிந்தாகுலத்திரட்டு. [Chintākula-tiraṭṭu. Lyrics upon the lamentations of the Virgin Mary at the Cross.] 2 pts. pp. 32, 16. யாழ்ப்பாணம் [*Jaffna*,] 1893. 12°. **14170. a. 35.(8.)**

—— மருதமடு மரியம்மன் பேரிற் தோத்திர கிர்த்தனம். [Tōttira-kīrttanam. Hymns to the Virgin.] pp. 20. யாழ்ப்பாணம் [*Jaffna*,] 1891. 12°. **14170. a. 35.(5.)**

MĀ-ṢILĀMAṆI MUDALIYĀR, *Pārivākkam*. [For works edited by Mā-ṣilāmaṇi Mudaliyār, see under the headings :]

Appāvu Piḷḷai, *T. T.*
Tāṇḍava-rāya-mūrtti Svāmi.

MASTĀN ṢĀHIB ('Abd al-Ḳādir), *Kuṇaṅguḍi*. ∘∘∘ திருப்பாடற்றிரட்டு. [Tiru-pāḍaṭ-ṭiraṭṭu. A collection of Muhammadan religious poems.] pp. 182, i. [*Madras*,] 1889. 8°. **14173. b. 22.**

—— ∘∘∘ திருப்பாடற்றிரட்டு மூலமும் . . . பதவுரை முதலியவும் ஆ [Tiru-pāḍaṭ-ṭiraṭṭu. With commentary by Kāñchīpuram Rāma-sāmi Nāyuḍu. Edited by Neyinā Muḥammad Pāval.] pp. 2, i. i. 444, xiv. ; 1 *plate*. சென்னை [*Madras*,] 1905. 8°. **14173. b. 9.**

MATHURAMUTHU MUDALIAR. *See* Madhura-muttu Mudaliyār.

MATTEI (Cesare), *Conte*. *See* Muller (A.). ∘∘∘ மின்சாரச்சகுணகமருந்தின் கைத்துணை. (*A Guide to Count Cæsar Mattei's Electro-Homœopathic Medicines, *etc.*) 1892. 12°. **14170. i. 70.(3.)**

MĀṬṬIN. *See* Martin.

MAULT (Charles). The Catechist's Manual . . . போதகர் இலக்கணம். Second edition. pp. 24. *Jaffna*, 1844. 12°. **14170. b. 1.(20.)**

MAYAN. மனைநூலென்னும் சிற்பசாஸ்திரம் [Ṣirpa-ṣāstram, or Manai-nūl. A work on the rules and rituals for building, purporting to be from the Sanskrit book by the mythical Mayan. Second edition.] pp. v. 112. பவ [*Madras*, 1874.] 8°. **14172. b. 22.**

—— ∘∘∘ சிற்பநூலென்னும் மனையடிசாஸ்திரம் [Manaiy-aḍi-ṣāstram, or Ṣirpa-nūl. A similar work. Collected and enlarged by Rāma-kṛushṇa Siddhāntiyār and Aiyā-sāmi Piḷḷai.] pp. 92, iv. தூஅஅ௫ [*Madras*, 1885.] 8°. **14172. c. 30.**

—— ∘∘∘ விமேசுரர்சாத்திரப்படி விஸ்வகர்மாவாகிய மயனென்பவர் திருவாய்மலர்ந்தருளிய சிற்பசாஸ்திரமென்னும் சர்வார்த்த சிற்பசிந்தாமணி. [Sarvārtha-ṣirpa-chintāmaṇi, or Ṣirpa-ṣāstram. A similar work. Edited by V. Kann'-aiya Nāyuḍu.] pp. 4, 354. [*Madras*,] 1905. 8°. **14171. g. 5.**

The page on which the text begins is numbered 13.

MAYILU PIḶḶAI, *C.*, also known as Martin (J. S.). ஞானசவுந்தரி அம்மானை. [Ñāna-saundari-ammānai. A Catholic religious poem.] pp. 96. *Colombo*, 1890. 8°. **14170. c. 24.(2.)**

MEADOWS (Robert Rust). A Greek Grammar in Tamil. To assist Greek Testament Students. கிரேக்கு இலக்கணம். pp. i. 52. *Madras*, 1867. 8°. **14172. h. 80.**

MELHO (Philippus de). *See* Bible.—*New Testament*. Het Nieuw Testament, *etc.* [Translated by P. de Melho.] 1759. 4°. **1411. k. 16.**

—— *See* Liturgies. — Netherlands, *Reformed Church of the*. திருததபபடட திருசசபைகளின வழிபாடு ஆ [The Liturgy. Translated by P. de Melho.] [1760.] 12°. **14170. a. 25.**

—— *See* Vīra-maṇḍalavar. ∘∘∘ சூடாமணி நிகண்டு ஆ [Chūḍāmaṇi-nighaṇṭu. With additions on poetical metaphors by P. de Melho.] 1856. 12°. **14172. e. 9.**

—— Triumph der Waarheid, zynde eene . . . wederlegging van de voornaamste Dwaalingen der Roomsche Kerke, med Verdediginge van de daar tegen gestelde Catholyke Waarheid, die in de Gereformeerde Kerke geleerd word . . . in de Tamulsche Taale opgesteld . . . door Philippus de Melho. (*சததியததினசெயம.) pp. vii. vii. x. vi. ix. 150, iv. *Colombo*, 1753. 8°. **14170. b. 61.**

MÉRIDAS POULLÉ. *See* MARIYA-DĀS PIḶḶAI.

MEY-KAṆḌA DĒVA MUDALIYĀR, *Rāu Bahādur, of Bangalore.* *See* NĀRĀYAṆA-SĀMI PIḶḶAI, *T. G.* ம-ா-ா-ஸ்ரீ... மெய்கண்டதேவமுதலியார்... கீர்த்திமாலை. (Garland of Fame of ... Maikanda-deva Mudaliyar, *etc.*) 1901. 8°. **14172. bb. 3.(3.)**

MEY-KAṆḌA DĒVAR, *Tiruveṇṇey-nallūr, disciple of Parañ-jōdi.* *See* HOISINGTON (H. R.). Syllabus of the Siva-gnána-pótham, *etc.* 1851. 8°. [*American Oriental Society: Journal.*] **Ac. 8824.(vol. 2.)**

—— ◦◦◦ சிவஞானபோதமும் ... பொழிப்புரையும். [Ṣiva-ñāna-bōdham. A handbook of the philosophy of the Ṣaiva-siddhāntam, comprising 12 metrical aphorisms (*sūtram*) paraphrased from Sanskrit verses in the Pāṣa-vimōchana-paṭalam of the Rauravāgamam, with an interpretation or *vārttikam* and metrical examples (*udāraṇam*). Together with a commentary (*ṣiṯṯ'-urai*) by Ṣiva-ñāna Svāmi. Edited by Nallūr Āṟu-muga Nāvalar.] pp. iv. iii. 252, ii. i. சென்னபட்டணம் பார்த்திவ [*Madras*, 1885.] 12°. **14170. d. 1.**

This work was written in Ṣaka 1145.

—— Sivagnana Botham of Meikanda Deva. Translated with notes [based upon the smaller commentary of Ṣiva-ñānar, and with the Tamil version of the Sūtram and its Sanskrit original from the Rauravāgamam] and introduction by J. M. Nallasawmi Pillai. pp. xxxi. 126. *Madras*, 1895. 8°. **14170. e. 51.**

—— சிவஞானபோதம். [Ṣiva-ñāna-bōdham. With the smaller commentary by Ṣiva-ñānar.] *See* MEY-KAṆḌA-ṢĀTTIRAM. மெய்கண்டசாத்திரம் ஆ [Mey-kaṇḍa-ṣāttiram.] pp. 69-210. 1897. 8°. **14170. ff. 3.**

—— சிவஞானபோத ஆ [Ṣiva-ñāna-bōdham.] pp. 47. *See* MEY-KAṆḌA-ṢĀTTIRAM. ◦◦◦ சைவசித்தாந்தசாத்திரம் ஆ [Ṣaiva-siddhānta-ṣāttiram.] [1899.] 12°. **14170. d. 53.**

—— ◦◦◦ சிவஞானபோதமூலமும் ... சிவஞானபாஷ்யமும். [Ṣiva-ñāna-bōdham. With Ṣiva-ñānar's larger commentary, styled Drāviḍa-mahā-bāḍiyam (° bhāshyam) or Ṣiva-ñāna-bhāshyam, upon Sūtram I. i.-ii. & VI-XII, with some fragments, supplemented by his smaller commentary. Edited by M. Subrahmaṇya Piḷḷai. With English preface and biography of Ṣiva-ñānar by J. M. Nalla-sāmi Piḷḷai.] pp. xxix. 13, 406, 6. மதுரை [*Madura*,] 1906. 8°. **14170. eee. 15.**

—— ◦◦◦ சிவஞானபோதமும், வார்த்திகமென்னும் பொழிப்புரையும் ... சிவஞானபோதமாபாடியமும் சிற்றுரையும். [Ṣiva-ñāna-bōdham. With the Sanskrit original, Tamil commentary thereon, Ṣiva-ñānar's shorter commentary throughout and larger commentary on vi.-xii., and a gloss by Subrahmaṇya Dēṣikar on the shorter commentary. Edited by V. Sāmi-nātha Paṇḍitar.] pp. vii. vii. ii. x. iv. iii. 6, 9, 40, 342, xxviii.; 4 *plates.* சென்னபட்டணம் பராபவ [*Madras*, 1906.] 8°. **14170. ff. 20.**

—— சிவஞானபோதம். Siva-gnâna-pōtham, Instruction in the Knowledge of God. A metaphysical and theological treatise. Translated from the Tamiḷ, with an introduction and notes. By Rev. Henry R. Hoisington. 1854. (Journal of the American Oriental Society. Vol. iv., pp. 31-102.) *Boston*, 1854. 8°. **Ac. 8824. (vol. 4.)**

—— சிவஞானபோதம். மூலமும் உரையும் (Sivagnana Botham) with introduction and translation by ... J. M. Nallaswami Pillai. [With a commentary. Preceded by (1) the Sanskrit original; (2) the *sūtram* with notes (*adhikaraṇam*) and paraphrase (*poṟipp'-urai*), and (3) an extract from Aruṇandi's Ṣiva-ñāna-siddhiyār on *aḷavai* or the method of logic, with commentary and English translation. Compiled and edited by M. B. Rājā Hari-hara-putra Piḷḷai. Followed by a short account of the Santānam Gurus.] pp. vi. ii. viii. xiv. ii. 160. திரிசிரபுரம் [*Trichinopoli*,] 1906. 12°. **14170. d. 29.**

MEY-KAṆḌA-ṢĀTTIRAM. மெய்கண்டசாத்திரம் மூலமுமுரையும். [Mey-kaṇḍa-ṣāttiram. 15 works on the Ṣaiva-siddhāntam, viz. (1) Tiruviyalūr Uyya-vandar's Tiruv-undiyār, with Chidambara-tambirān's commentary; (2) Tirukaḍavūr Uyya-vandar's Tiru-kaḷiṯṯu-paḍiyār, with Ṣiva-prakā-ṣar's commentary; (3) Mey-kaṇḍa Dēvar's Ṣiva-ñāna-bōdham, with Ṣiva-ñānar's shorter commentary; (4) Aruṇandi's Ṣiva-ñāna-siddhiyār-para-pakkam, with Tattva-prakāṣar's commentary; Ṣiva-ñāna-siddhiyār-supakkam, by the same, with commentary by Subrahmaṇya Dēṣikar; and Iru-bāv-iru-badu, by the same, with Namaṣ-ṣivāyar's commentary; (5) Mana-vāchakam Kaḍanda Dēvar's Uṇmai-viḷakkam, with commentary; (6) 8 works of Umā-pati, with commentaries, viz. (i) Ṣiva-prakāṣam, with commentary of Chidambara-nāthar, (ii) Tiruv-aruṭ-payan, with Nirambav-aṟagiya Dēṣikar's commentary, (iii) Vinā-veṇ-bā, with Namaṣ-ṣivāyar's commentary, (iv) Pōṭṭi-pa'ṟoḍai, (v) Koḍi-kavi, (vi) Neñju-viḍu-dūdu, with commentary by Kalyāṇa-sundara Mudaliyār, (vii) Uṇmai-neṟi-viḷakkam, (viii) Saṅkarpa-nirā-karaṇam. Edited by Vaṇṇa-kalañjiyam Kāñchi Nāga-liṅga Mudaliyār.] pp. viii. 864. சென்னை [*Madras,*] 1897. 8°. **14170. ff. 3.**

—— ... சைவசித்தாந்தசாத்திரம் பதினான்கின் மூலம். [Ṣaiva-siddhānta-ṣāttiram. Comprising the same texts as in the preceding edition, without the commentaries, but with occasional notes, *etc.* Edited by A. Ṣiṅgāra-vēlu Mudaliyār.] 16 pts. சென்னை ௧௮௯௯ [*Madras,* 1899.] 12°. **14170. d. 53.**

MEY-ÑĀNAM. True Wisdom. மெஞ்ஞானம். [Meñ-ñānam. An old Christian tract against heathenism. Revised by J. M. V. Schwarz.] pp. 36. *Tranquebar,* 1880. 12°. **14170. b. 16.(4.)**

MILTON (JOHN). Paradise Lost. Books i & ii. Translated into Tamil [in *ammānai* metre] by Samuel V. Thomas ... பூங்காவனப்பிரளயம். [Pūṅgāvana-praḷayam.] pp. iii. xxiv. 79. *Trichinopoly,* 1887. 8°. **14172. b. 42.**

—— Paradise Lost, book i., in Tamil viruttam, by V. P. Subramania Mudaliar ... சுவர்க்க நீக்கம் முதற்காண்டம். pp. i. iii. viii. 194, 3. சென்னை [*Madras,*] 1895. 12°. **14170. a. 56.**

MĪNĀKSHI-SUNDARA KAVI-RĀYAR, *Mugavūr.* *See* APPAYA DĪKSHITAR. குவலயானந்தம். [Kuvalayānandam. Translated by Ṣaṅkara-nārāyaṇa and Mīnākshi-sundara.] 1895. 8°. **14170. i. 40.**

MĪNĀKSHI-SUNDARAM PIḶḶAI, *P.* The Student's Guide to Translation. With reference to grammatical exercises. For the use of Primary and Middle-school classes. pp. i. i. i. 109, vii. ii. *Madras,* 1890. 8°. **14172. h. 89.(1.)**

MĪNĀKSHI-SUNDARAM PIḶḶAI, *Triṣirapuram.* *See* VĪRAVANAM. வீரவனப்புராணம். [Vīravana-purāṇam. A poem translated into verse by Mīnākshi-sundaram from the Sanskrit.] 1903. 8°. **14170. ee. 63.**

—— மண்ணிப்படிக்கரைப்புராணம். [Maṇṇi-paḍikarai-purāṇam. A poem on the legends of the Ṣaiva sanctuary at Mannipadikarai, on the north bank of the Kaveri. Edited with glossary by U. V. Sāmināth'-aiyar.] pp. vi. 71. சென்னை [*Madras,*] 1907. 8°. **14170. eee. 23.**

—— கண்டதேவிப்புராணம். [Kaṇḍa-dēvi-purāṇam. A poem on the legends of Kaṇḍa Dēvi.] pp. 97. சென்னை யுவ [*Madras,* 1875.] 8°. **14172. c. 14.**

—— ... சீகாழிக்கோவையும் . . . அரும்பதவுரையும். [Ṣīgāḻi-kōvai. Lyrics on the cult of the Ṣaiva sanctuary of Ṣīgāḻi (Shiyali). With glosses. Edited by U. V. Sāmināth'-aiyar.] pp. i. vi. 104. சென்னபட்டணம் [*Madras,*] 1903. 8°. **14170. ee. 65.**

—— சூரைமாநகர்ப்புராணம். [Ṣūrai-mā-nagar-purāṇam. A poem on local Ṣaiva legends of Ṣūrai-kuḍi. Edited with notes by U. V. Sāmināth'-aiyar.] pp. iii. 88. சென்னை [*Madras,*] 1904. 8°. **14170. eee. 5.**

—— ... தனியூர்ப்புராணம். [Taniyūr-purāṇam. A poem upon the legends of Taniyūr (Pārijāta-vanam or Puṟugīṣam), a Ṣaiva sanctuary near Mayavaram. Edited with glossary by U. V. Sāmināth'-aiyar.] pp. ii. 30. சென்னை [*Madras,*] 1907. 8°. **14170. e. 29.**

—— திருவாரூர்த் தியாகராசலீலை. [Tiruvārūr-tyāgarāja-līlai, or Tiruvārūr-tiru-viḷaiy-āḍal. A poem on the sacred legends of the Ṣaiva sanctuary at Tiruvalur. Edited with glossary by V. Sāmināth'-aiyar.] pp. i. 3, 112. சென்னை [*Madras,*] 1905. 8°. **14172. bb. 20.**

MĪRĀN ṢĀHIB ĀṆḌAVAR. *See* SHĀH al-ḤAMĪD ibn ḤASAN ḲUDDŪS.

MLĒCHCHHA-MATA-KHAṆḌANA-SABHAI. *See* JAFFNA.

MLĒCHCHHA-MATĀNDHAKĀRA-BHĀSKARAN, *Pseud.* நிகாரநிகாரணம். [Nikāra-nikāraṇam. A tract against Christianity.] pp. 43. யாழ்ப்பாணம் கர [*Jaffna,* 1891.] 12°. **14170. a. 49.(1.)**

MŌKSHAM. மோக்ஷத்துக்கு[sic] போற வழியை வெளிப்படுத்துகிற ஞானஉபதேசம் [Mōkshattukku pōr-vaṟiyai veḷipaḍuttugiṟa ñāna-upadēṣam. A book of spiritual instruction, with prayers, by the early Lutheran missionaries.] pp. 48. தரங்கம்பாடியில் அச்சடிக்கப்பட்டது [Tranquebar, 1777.] 12°. **14170. a. 41.**

MOODOOKRISHNIA NAIDU. *See* MUTTU-KRUSHṆ'-AIYA NĀYUḌU.

MOOTHOOKRISHNA NAIKER. *See* MUTTU-KRUSHṆA NĀYAKAR.

MORE (HANNAH). Parley the Porter. காவலப்பன் கதை. [Translated into Tamil.] pp. 36. *Jaffna*, 1856. 16°. **14170. a. 33.(3.)**

No. 1 of the New Series of the Jaffna Religious Tract Society.

MORRIS (HENRY). The History of India, for the use of schools ... இந்துதேசசரித்திரம். Revised edition. pt. i., ii. *Madras*, 1880-1882. 12°. **14172. h. 60.**

Pt. i. bears date 1882, pt. ii. 1880.

—— A Key to Morris' History of India in English and Tamil ... Translated by T. Moothookrishna Naiker. (†மாரிஸ் இந்துதேச சரித்திரத்திற்கு ... உரை.) pp. 287. *Madras*, 1873. 12°. **14172. h. 54.**

MORRIS (JOHN CARNAC). Selections, with translation, by Mr. J. C. Morris ... to which are added a spelling and phraseology for the use of Tamil & English students, by T. Eterajooloo Naidoo, Moonshee. (*A Tamil and English Phrase Book.) pp. 44, 20. *Madras*, 1848. 8°. **14172. h. 20.**

MORTIMER (FAVELL LEE), *Mrs.* The Peep of Day. Translated into Tamil by John C. Aroolappen, Preacher. சட்டதிட்டம். [Third edition.] pp. vi. 228. *Madras*, 1852. 12°. **14170. b. 32.**

MORTON (WILLIAM). *See* AṢVA-GHŌSHA. Vajra Suchi ... English and Tamil versions [the former by W. Morton,] *etc.* 1851. 12°. **14028. c. 25.**

MṚUGA - BHAṬṬĀRAKAR, *Chidambaram Vāmadēva.* *See* MAṞAI-ÑĀNA-SAMBANDHAR. அருணகிரிபுராணம். [Aruṇa-giri-purāṇam. Edited by Mṛuga-bhaṭṭārakar.] [1880.] 16°. **14170. d. 15.**

MṚUGA-DĀSA SVĀMI, *of Tinnevelli.* *See* ACADEMIES, *etc.*—Madras.—*University of Madras.* University of Madras. F.A. Examination of 1903. Full notes on Pulavar Puranam, *etc.* 1903. 8°. **14172. hh. 19.**

—— ◦◦◦ புலவர்புராணம். [Pulavar-purāṇam.] ... Metrical Biographies of Tamil Poets, containing brief sketches of the leading Hindu classic poets of the Tamil country, by Murugadasa Swami. Published for the first time in three parts: with an introductory note [in English] by the editor [V. Krushṇam-āchāryar]. Part i. Prominent poets. (Part ii. Sivite Poets.) *Madras*, 1901, *etc.* 8°. **14172. c. 41.**

In progress.

—— University of Madras. F.A. Examination—1903. Pulawar Puranam. புலவர் புராணம். [Lives of Pugaṟēndi and Oṭṭa-kūttar, in verse, extracted from Mṛuga-dāsar's Pulavar-purāṇam.] ... Edited with notes by Dewan Bahadur V. Krishnama chariar. pp. ii. 20. *Madras*, 1901. 8°. **14172. bb. 3.(4.)**

MṚUG'-APPA CHEṬṬI, *Vāṇiyambāḍi Ṣaṅkara.* *See* AṄGA PIḶḶAI. முருகப்ப நவரச சிலேடை. [Mṛug'-appa-nava-rasa-ṣilēḍai. A poem, addressed to Mṛug'-appa Cheṭṭi.] 1894. 8°. **14172. b. 44.(4.)**

MṚUGĒṢA MUDALIYĀR, *Āraṇi C.* Mathar Neethy. [A reading-book of moral lessons and stories for girls and women.] With an appendix of Harichandra-puranam. By A. C. Murugasa Moodaliar ... மாதர் நீதி ஸ்ரீ. Third edition. pp. 8, 198. *Arni*, 1894. 8°. **14171. a. 1.**

MṚUGĒṢA MUDALIYĀR, *Kannigaipēr Sabhā-pati.* *See* TĒR AIYAR. ◦◦◦ மருத்துபாரதம் ஸ்ரீ [Maruttubhāratam. Edited by Mṛugēṣa.] 1907. 12°. **14172. a. 60.**

MṚUGĒṢA MUDALIYĀR, *Maiyūr Sōma-sundara.* *See* MARSDEN (E.). ◦◦◦ நான்காம் வாசக புஸ்தக ஸ்ரீ [Marsden's Fourth Reader, with a key by Mṛugēṣa.] 1899. 16°. **14172. g. 2.(2.)**

MṚUGĒṢA MUDALIYĀR, *Tirumayilai.* [For works edited by Mṛugēṣa Mudaliyār, see under the following headings:]

ATIVĪRA-RĀMA PĀṆḌIYAN. ṢIVA-PRAKĀṢA SVĀMI.
KANN'-UḌAIYA VAḶḶAL. TIRU-VAḶḶUVAR.

—— நீதிமஞ்சரித்தருப்பணம். [Nīti-mañjari-darpaṇam. Word-for-word interpretations of ancient ethical works, including those of Auvai-

yār, Ṣiva-prakāṣar, Kumara-guru-para Tambirān, Nallādanār (the Tri-kaṭukam), and others.] 2 pts. pp. 63, 144. சென்னை [*Madras*,] 1881-1883. 16°.
14172. a. 8.

MRUGĒṢA PIḶḶAI, *Ṣunnāgam P.* நீதிநூறு. [Nīti-nūṟu. One hundred quatrains on moral subjects.] pp. 17. கும்பகோணம் [*Kumbakonam*,] 1885. 8°.
14172. a. 29.(2.)

—— பதார்த்த தீபிகை. [Padārtha-dīpikai. A metrical description of the 7 Vaiṣēshika categories.] pp. 16. *Tirupattur*, 1897. 12°. **14170. d. 71.**

MRUGĒṢA UPĀDHYĀYAR, *Ṣaṇḍiruppāy K.* See Sāmi-nātha Mudaliyār, *M.A.* தருமபுத்திரநாடகம் [Dharma-putra-nāṭakam. Edited by Mrugēṣa.] 1890. 8°. **14170. l. 16.**

MRUTYUṂ-JAYA ṢĀSTRI, *Lakshmīnārāyaṇapuram.* See Ṣaṅkarāchārya. [*Doubtful and Supposititious Works.*] ஸ்ரீ . . . ஶிவாநந்தலஹரீ etc. [Ṣivānanda-laharī. With interpretations in Tamil. Edited by Mṛutyuṃ-jaya.] 1904. 12°.
14048. b. 48.

MUDALIY-ĀṆḌĀN-DĀSAR, *disciple of Bhaṭṭarbirān Rāmānuja-jīyar-svāmi.* வேதாந்தஸாரஸங்க்ரஹம். [Vēdānta-sāra-saṅgraham. A digest of Sanskrit texts supporting Viṣishṭādvaita philosophy, with Tamil introduction and translations, *etc.*] pp. xvi. 170. சென்னை ஸ்ரீபராங்குசர் திருவவதார ஸு 5000 [*Madras*, 1898.] 8°.
14048. cc. 17.

Each Sanskrit quotation is printed in both Grantham and Telugu script.

MUDATTĀMA-KAṆṆIYĀR. பொருநராற்றுப்படை. [Porunar-āṭṭu-paḍai. A poem in praise of the Chola king Karikāl and his country, being no. 2 of the Pattu-pāṭṭu. With Nachinārkk'-iniyar's commentary.] See Pattu-pāṭṭu. பத்துப்பாட்டு ஆ [Pattu-pāṭṭu.] pp. 41-66. 1889. 8°.
14172. d. 10.

—— Porunaráttupaḍai. [Translated into English.] See Kumāra-svāmi (P.). A Half-hour with two ancient Tamil Poets, *etc.* 1895. 8°.
Ac. 8830.(vol. 13, no. 45.)

MUDI-NĀKA-RĀYAR. Ode to a King. [In Tamil and English.] See Aruṇāchalam, *P.* Studies and translations, *etc.* pp. 1-5. 1898. 8°.
14170. ee. 12.(3.)

MUGAMMADU. See Muhammad.

MUGIYUTTĪN. See Muhyi al-Dīn.

MUHAMMAD, *Pīr.* திருமெஞ்ஞான சாரநூல். [Tiru-meñ-ñāna-sara-nūl. 30 verses on divination from the breath.] See [Addenda] Agastyar. பஞ்சபட்சிசாஸ்திரம் ஆ [Pañcha-pakshi-ṣāstram.] 1907. 8°. **14170. i. 3.**

MUHAMMAD, *Virasōṟam A., Shaikh.* See [Addenda] 'Abd al-Kādir Lebbai. பண்ணிரண்டுமாலை. [Pann'-irandu-mālai. Preceded by a Munājāt by the editor, Muhammad.] 1907. 8°. **14173. b. 44.**

MUHAMMAD ibn ABI BAKR ibn RASHĪD, *al-Baghdādī.* نفحات العطرية فى شرح الوترية [Al-Witrīyah. A poem in praise of the Prophet Muhammad, in 29 cantos, each rhyming in a different letter of the alphabet, with a "Takhmīs," or metrical amplification, by Ṣadakat Allāh al-Kāhirī. The Arabic text, with a Tamil translation and commentary, entitled al-Nafahāt al-'itrīyah, by Ṣadakat Allāh. With an appendix of other Arabic pieces, chiefly on religious themes.] pp. 688, 88, 2. بمبئى ١٣١٤ [*Bombay*, 1896.] 8°.
14576. cc. 1.

MUHAMMAD ibn AHMAD, *al-Kādirī.* فتح الديان فى فقه خير الاديان [Fath al-daiyān. A manual of Muhammadan religious instruction, in the Arabic character. Followed by a collection of religious pieces in prose and verse, by various authors, partly in Arabic, partly in Tamil.] 2 pts., *lith.* بمبئى ١٣١٢ [*Bombay*, 1898.] 8°. **14173. c. 9.**

MUHAMMAD ibn MUHAMMAD, *al-Fāsī.* [*Life.*] See Nūh ibn 'Abd al-Kādir, *al-Kāhirī.* [Minhat al-jawād.]

—— الياقوتية الخ [Al-Yākūtīyah. A prayer in Arabic, with a Tamil paraphrase.] See Nūh ibn 'Abd al-Kādir, *al-Kāhirī.* نفحات العنبر الخ [Nafahāt al-'anbar.] pp. 245-250. [1902.] 8°. **14173. c. 10.**

MUHAMMAD ibn MUHAMMAD, *al-Ghazzālī.* கீமியாயெ ஸஆதத்து. [Kīmiyā i sa'ādat. A treatise on Moslem religious philosophy, originally written by al-Ghazzālī in Persian. Translated into Tamil, from a Hindustani version, by Nelliguppam 'Abd al-Rahmān.] சென்னை [*Madras*,] 1906, *etc.* 8°.
14173. b. 10.

In progress.

MUḤAMMAD ibn MUḤAMMAD, *al-Mu'izz.* இஃது. பத்துகுல்மிசிர்-பஹனசா வசனகாவியம். [Futūḥ al-Miṣr wa'l-Bahnasā, or Ḳiṣṣat al-Bahnasā. A legendary history of the town of Bahnasā, in Upper Egypt. Translated from the Arabic by Muḥammad Labbai 'Ālim Ṣāḥib, and edited by Kaṇṇ'-Aḥmad Makhdūm Muḥammad.] pp. vi. ii. 432. சென்னை 1312 [*Madras*, 1894.] 8°. **14173. b. 31.**

MUḤAMMAD 'ABD ALLĀH, *Ḥakīm.* قاموس اروي An Arabic-Tamil Dictionary. Published with the approval of the Madras S. B. & L. Society. அறபு தமிழ் அகராதி. மதராஸ் [*Madras*,] 1905, *etc.* 8°. **14172. f. 26.**
In progress.

MUḤAMMAD 'ABD ALLĀH, *son of Bāburājapuram Bāwā Ṣāḥib.* See Tēr Aiyar. இராஜ வைத்திய மகுடம். [Rāja-vaidya-makuṭam. Edited with commentary by Muḥammad 'Abd Allāh.] 1899. 12°. **14170. i. 61.**

—— அநுபோகவைத்தியநவநீதம். [Anubhōga-vaidya-nava-nītam. A treatise on the pharmacopœia.] *Madras*, 1906, *etc.* 12°. **14171. g. 10.**
In progress.

—— பிரமேகநிவாரணபோதினி. [Pramēha-nivāraṇa-bōdhini. A Yūnānī treatise on the cure of gonorrhœa.] pp. xx. 232. சென்னை [*Madras*,] 1897. 12°. **14170. i. 71.**

—— யூநானி வைத்திய தாதுவிர்த்திபோதினி. [Yūnānī-vaidya-dhātu-vṛiddhi-bōdhini. An encyclopædia of Yūnānī medicine.] vol. ii. pp. xv. xxx. 636. மதராஸ் [*Madras*,] 1893. 12°. **14170. i. 41.**

MUḤAMMAD 'ABD al-ḲĀDIR, *Pulavar.* கீர்த்தனத்திரட்டு. [Kīrttana-tiraṭṭu. Lyrics addressed to Muḥammad and various Muhammadan saints.] pp. 58. சிங்கப்பூர் [*Singapore*,] 1896. 12°. **14173. a. 5.**

MUḤAMMAD 'ABD al-ḲĀDIR ibn ĀDAM, *Tēraḷandūrī*, called Ḳādir Ṣāḥib. سير السالكين الى حضرة رب العالمين (*معه نبذة الفوائد) [Sair al-sālikīn. A manual of religious discipline. Followed by a compendium of prayers and talismanic diagrams for religious purposes.] pp. xvi. 168, 72, *lith.* مدراس ۱۳۲۳-۲۴ [*Madras*, 1905-1906.] 8°. **14173. b. 2.**

—— شمس المعرفة [Shams al-ma'rifat. A manual of scholastic theology.] pp. x. 184, *lith.* مدراس ۱۳۲۲-۲۳ [*Madras*, 1904-1905.] 8°. **14173. b. 1.**

MUḤAMMAD 'ABD al-RAḤMĀN, *Nelliguppam.* See 'Abd al-Raḥmān.

MUḤAMMAD 'ABD al-RAḤMĀN ibn ḲĀDIR MĪRĀN. See [Addenda] Aḥmad ibn 'Abd Allāh. عباب الاخيار الخ [Lubāb al-akhbār. With a Tamil translation entitled 'Ubāb al-akhyār, by Muḥammad 'Abd al-Raḥmān.] [1904.] 8°. **14521. b. 31.**

—— تأييد الرحمن فى تجويد القران [Ta'yīd al-raḥmān. A manual of the art of reciting from the Koran.] pp. viii. 272, *lith.* بمدراس ۱۳۱۹ [*Madras*, 1902.] 8°. **14173. b. 32.**

MUḤAMMAD GHAUṢ, *al-Shāfi'ī al-Madrūsī.* نثر الجواهر فى مناقب السيد عبد القادر الجيلانى [Naṣr al-jawāhir. A life of 'Abd al-Ḳādir Jīlānī, originally composed in Arabic under the title Anhār al-mafākhir. Translated into Hindustani by the author's son Ḳāẓī Ṣibghat Allāh, and thence into Tamil by Muḥammad Madīnah Kōṭṭārī.] pp. xvi. 319; 1 *plate.* مدراس ۱۳۱۴ [*Madras*, 1896.] 8°. **14173. c. 7.**

MUḤAMMAD IBRĀHĪM ibn 'ABD al-GHANĪ, *Mēlvishāram, Kaḍaikkāra.* இஃது. நஸீஹத்துல் அனாம் பீ هي ஹிதாயத்தில் இஸ்லாம். [Nasīḥat al-anām fi hidāyat al-islām. A metrical work on the tenets of Islam, including texts in Arabic and Hindustani.] pp. 70. சென்னை தருடஉரு [*Madras*, 1906.] 8°. **14173. b. 11.**

—— இஃது தல்கீன்பீமுஹிம்மா துத்தீன். லி அவுலா துல் முஸ்லிமீன். [Talḳīn fi muhimmāt al-dīn li-aulād al-muslimīn. An elementary handbook of Moslem doctrine. Edited by Kaṇṇ'-Aḥmad Makhdūm Muḥammad.] pp. xxiv. 70. சென்னை தருடாமசு [*Madras*, 1901.] 8°. **14173. b. 7.**

MUḤAMMAD IMĀM GHAZZĀLĪ ibn MUḤAMMAD 'ALĪ, *Maraikkāyar, of Nagur.* கலறத்து மீரான்சாகிபு ஆண்டவரவர்கள் காரணசரித்திரம். [Ḥaẓrat Mīrān Ṣāḥib Āṇḍavar-avargaḷ kāraṇa-charitram. A biography of Mīrān Sulṭān Shāh al-Ḥamīd, a local Moslem saint of the 16th century, compiled from Persian, Hindustani, and other sources. Edited by Nāgūr Muḥammad Pulavar.] pp. 3, 165. காரைக்கால் தருஉாகூசு [*Karikal*, 1876.] 8°. **14173. b. 34.**

MUHAMMAD 'INĀYAT AHMAD. علم الفرايض ['Ilm al-farā'id. A manual of the Muhammadan law of inheritance. Translated from the Hindustani into Tamil by N. Muhammad 'Abd al-Rahmān.] pp. xvi. 176, viii., *lith.* مدراس ۱۳۲۴ [*Madras*, 1906.] 8°. **14173. b. 42.**

MUHAMMAD ISMĀ'ĪL ibn MUHAMMAD MADĪNAH. هداية السالكين فى تخليص الهالكين [Hidāyat al-sālikīn. Biographies of the principal teachers of the Shāzilī Order, followed by a manual of asceticism according to their precepts.] pp. xxxii. 478, *lith.* ١٨٩٨ بالمدراس [*Madras*, 1898.] 8°. **14173. b. 30.**

MUHAMMAD ḲĀDIRĪ. துத்திநாமா என்னும் கிளிக்கதை. [Tūtī-nāmah, in Tamil Kiḷi-kathai. The "Tales of a Parrot," translated from the Persian of Muh. Ḳādirī. Edited by G. Aruṇāchala Mudaliyār.] pp. ii. 112. *Madras*, 1883. 8°. **14170. k. 25.**

MUHAMMAD KAMĀL al-DĪN, *of Vellore.* *See* AHKĀM. இஃது அஹ்காமுஸ்ஸியாம். [Alikām al-ṣiyām. Edited by Muhammad.] 1905. 8°. **14173. b. 28.(6.)**

MUHAMMAD KANṆU, *Perumāḷ-durai Vaidyam A.* ஆஷுருக்காரணக்கும்மிச்சிந்து. ['Āshūrā-kāraṇa-kummi-chindu. A Muhammadan religious song for the 'Āshūrā festival.] pp. 18. கொழும்பு [*Colombo*,] 1893. 8°. **14173. b. 28.(2.)**

—— கம்ஸீனுபரீளாமாலை. [Khamsīnā-farīḍah-mālai. A metrical tract upon fifty essential observances of Islam.] pp. 14. கொழும்பு 1309 [*Colombo*, 1892.] 12°. **14173. a. 8.(2.)**

MUHAMMAD ḲĀSIM ibn ṢIDDĪK, *Labbai.* *See* PERIODICAL PUBLICATIONS.—*Kandy.* ஞானதீபம். [Ñāna-dīpam.] Edited . . . by M. C. Siddi Lebbe. 1892. 8°. **14173. b. 37.**

—— அஸ்றாறுல் ஆலம். [Asrār al-'ālam. A popular work on science.] pp. ii. 4, 200. *Colombo*, 1897. 8°. **14170. i. 54.**

—— هداية القاسمية فى تسهيل اللغة العربية [Al-Hidāyat al-kāsimīyat. A grammar of the Arabic language, in Tamil.] pp. xiii. 242, *lith.* الكنذ ۱۳۰۸ [*Kandy*, 1891.] 4°. **14173. b. 24.**

MUHAMMAD ḲĀSIM ibn ṢIDDĪK, *Labbai (continued).* [Kitāb al-hisāb. Elementary arithmetic in Tamil.] pp. 15, *lith.* كنذ ۱۳۰۹ [*Kandy*, 1891.] 16°. **14172. h. 74.**

—— தமிழ் முதற்புத்தகம். [Tamiẓ-mudaṟ-puttagam. A Tamil primer.] pp. 70. கொழும்பு [*Colombo*,] 1892. 12°. **14172. h. 51.(2.)**

—— طرفة النحو [Ṭurfat al-nahw. A shorter grammar of the Arabic language.] pp. 112, 1, *lith.* الكنذ ۱۳۰۹ [*Kandy*, 1891.] 4°. **14173. b. 29.**

—— كتاب اصول القراءة العربية للمبتدين [Uṣūl al-kirā'at al-'arabīyat. An elementary Arabic reading-book, with explanations in Tamil.] 2 pts., *lith.* كنذ ۱۳۰۸ [*Kandy*, 1891.] 16°. **14173. a. 2.**

MUHAMMAD LABBAI, *'Ālim Ṣāhib, of Kandy.* *See* MUHAMMAD ibn MUHAMMAD, *al-Mu'izz.* இஃது. பத்துகுல்மிசிர் ஷ [Futūh al-Miṣr. Translated by Muhammad Labbai.] [1894.] 8°. **14173. b. 31.**

MUHAMMAD MADĪNAH, *Kōṭṭāṟī.* *See* MUHAMMAD GHAUṢ. نثر الجواهر الخ [Naṣr al-jawāhir. Translated by Muh. Madīnah.] [1896.] 8°. **14173. c. 7.**

MUHAMMAD MASTĀN ibn MUHAMMAD TAMBI, *Maraikkayar, Ativiirapaṭṭinam.* *See* GHULĀM 'ALĪ ibn MUHAMMAD AMĪN al-DĪN. விவேகவிளக்கம். [Vivēka-viḷakkam. Compiled and translated into Hindi by Ghulām 'Alī, and thence rendered into Tamil by Muhammad.] [1870.] 8°. **14173. b. 39.**

MUHAMMAD MĪRĀN MASTĀN ibn LUḲMĀN, *Rauttar.* இஃது ஞானரத்திநாகரம். [Ñāna-ratnākaram. A series of Muhammadan religious poems. Edited by Kaṇṇ'-Ahmad Makhdūm Muhammad.] pp. xii. 59. சென்னை தஙுாக௲ [*Madras*, 1896.] 8°. **14173. b. 4.**

MUHAMMAD MĪR JAWĀD. *See* TURĀB MUHAMMAD HUSAIN ibn ISMĀ'ĪL. தொழுகைரஞ்சித அலங்காரம் ஷ [Toẓugai-rañjita-alaṅkāram. Edited by Muhammad Mīr Jawād.] 1897. 12°. **14173. a. 7.**

MUHAMMAD NIẒĀM MUHYI al-DĪN ibn MUHAMMAD, *Bāburājapuram.* குடும்பஸம்ரக்ஷணி. [Kuṭumba-samrakshaṇi. A treatise on social hygiene and morals. Edited by T. Vaḍi-vēlu Mudaliyār.] pp. xxiv. 410, vi. சென்னை [*Madras*,] 1896. 8°. **14170. i. 46.**

MUHAMMAD NIẒĀM MUḤYI al-DĪN ibn MUḤAMMAD, *Bāburājapuram* (*continued*). மஹா ஜால ரஹஸ்ய விளக்கம். [Mahā-jāla-rahasya-viḷakkam. A work upon the art of jugglery and optical illusion.] pp. 2, 105. சென்னை [*Madras*,] 1901. 8°. **14171. g. 2.**

—— மஹா விகட விநோதக் களஞ்சியம். [Mahā - vikaṭa - vinōda - kaḷañjiyam. Historical, medical, and literary miscellanea.] pp. 184. *Madras*, 1907. 8°. **14171. e. 19.**

—— நீதிசாரமஞ்சரி. [Nīti - sāra - mañjari. Moral stories.] pp. 67. சென்னை [*Madras*,] 1901. 12°. **14170. k. 48.(3.)**

—— நீதிவிநோதக் கதை. [Nīti-vinōda-kathai. Moral stories. Edited by 'Uthmān Lebbai.] pp. i. 38. கொழும்பு [*Colombo*,] 1893. 8°. **14173. b. 28.(3.)**

—— [Second edition.] pp. ii. 73. சென்னை [*Mudras*,] 1900. 12°. **14170. k. 48.(2.)**

MUḤAMMAD PĀVALAR, *M.A. Neyinā, of Chevval, Tinnevelli.* *See* MASTĀN ṠĀḤIB. ◦ ◦ ◦ திருப்பாடற்றிரட்டு ௲ [Tiru-pādaṭ-ṭiraṭṭu. Edited by Muḥammad.] 1905. 8°. **14173. b. 9.**

MUḤAMMAD ṠĀḤIB ibn ḤABĪB MUḤAMMAD. مفتاح الرحمن الخ [Miftāḥ al-raḥmān. A treatise on Muhammadan eschatology.] pp. 88, 31, *lith.* مدراس ١٣٠٨ [*Madras*, 1891.] 8°. **14173. b. 14.**

MUḤAMMAD SHARAF al-DĪN. عمدة النساء ['Umdat al-nisā. A compendium of the Muhammadan laws relating to women.] pp. 88, *lith.* بمدراس ١٣٢١ [*Madras*, 1903.] 8°. **14173. b. 43.**

MUḤAMMAD SULAIMĀN, *Lebbai, of Jaffna.* சருபந்தமேகபதார்த்தோவம தருக்கநிராகரணம். [Charu-bandham-ēka-padārthōvama-tarka-nirākaraṇam. Two controversial essays, (1) on the interpretation of a passage in the Futūḥ al-Shām, (2) on some verses published in the same connexion.] pp. 8. யாழ்ப்பாணம் [*Jaffna*,] 1895. 8°. **14173. b. 40.(2.)**

MUḤAMMAD SULṬĀN ibn AḤMAD 'UMAR, *Maraikkāyar.* ஆநந்தக்கீர்த்தனை. [Ānanda-kīrttanai. Muhammadan lyrics.] pp. 6, ii. 88. பினங்கில் [*Penang*,] 1901. 8°. **14173. b. 25.(1.)**

—— பதாநந்த மாலே. (The Padananda Mahlay. [Poems relating to Muhammadanism and Muhammadans.] By A. Mahomed Sultan Maricar.) pp. 51. *Penang*, 1890. 8°. **14173. b. 23.**

—— சீருச்சதகம். [Ṣīṟā-ṣatakam. A century of verses founded upon the Ṣīṟā of 'Umar. Followed by Tōttira-padigam, devotional verses.] pp. 16, 4. பினங்கு [*Penang*,] 1900. 8°. **14173. b. 25.(2.)**

MUḤAMMAD TAMBI ibn ZAIN al-DĪN, *Kāyaṟpaṭṭanam.* *See* ḤIKĀYĀT I LAṬĪF. மனோரஞ்சிதத்திரட்டு. [Manō-rañjita-tiraṭṭu. Translated by Muḥammad Tambi from the Hindustani version of the Ḥikāyāt i laṭīf.] 1901. 8°. **14173. b. 38.**

MUḤAMMAD TAMĪM ibn MUḤAMMAD. عمدة الصبيان فى بيان اركان الاسلام والايمان ['Umdat al-ṣibyān. A manual of Muhammadan religious instruction according to the Shāfi'ī school.] pp. viii. 288, 66, *lith.* مدراس ١٣٠٩ [*Madras*, 1891.] 8°. **14173. b. 15.**

MUḤAMMAD YŪSUF ibn ḲĀDIR AḤMAD, *Ammābaṭṭaṇam.* الدرر الحسان [Al-Durar al-ḥisān. A compendium of Muhammadan law, according to the Ḥanafī school.] vol. i. pp. xiv. 1011, 5, *lith.* مدراس ١٢٩٨ [*Madras*, 1880.] 12°. **14173. a. 9.**

—— ஷம்சுல் ஈமான். [Shams al-īmān. An elementary work on the Muhammadan faith.] pp. xii. 296, iv. சென்னை தருமாசு [*Madras*, 1888.] 16°. **14173. a. 1.**

MUḤYI al-DĪN ibn MUḤAMMAD, *Kōṭṭāṟī.* تحفة الاحباب [Tuḥfat al-aḥbāb. A manual of prayer for Muḥammad and of the religious exercises customary on the occasion of his nativity. Followed by two tracts in Arabic, viz.: (1) al-Maulid al-karīm al-nabawī, an account of the birth of Muḥammad, in prose and verse, by Ja'far al-Barzanjī; and (2) al-Khaṣā'iṣ al-nabawīyat, a similar account of Muḥammad's ascension, by Zain al-'Ābidīn al-Barzanjī.] pp. viii. 232, 55, *lith.* مدراس ١٣٢٣ [*Madras*, 1906.] 8°. **14173. b. 3.**

MUḤYI al-DĪN ibn MUḤAMMAD MUḤYI al-DĪN SULṬĀN PIḶḶAI, *of Tiruvangode.* *See* IRSHĀD AL-'IBĀD. இஃது . . . இருசாதுல் இபாத். [Irshād al-'ibād. Translated by Muḥyi al-Dīn.] 1901. 8°. **14173. b. 6.**

MUḤYI al-DĪN KAṞPUḌAIYĀR ibn ṢINNA IBRĀHĪM. ◦ ◦ ◦ நபியுல்லாபேரிற் பதிக்மும் . . . யானைக்காதலும். [Nabi-allāh-pēriṟ padigam. A lyric in praise of the prophet Muhammad. Followed by Yānai-kādal, verses in honour of a Muhammadan devotee.] pp. 20. யாழ்ப்பாணம் கஅகூக [Jaffna, 1891.] 8°. 14173. b. 40.(1.)

MUHYI al-DĪN MALUK MUDALIYĀR, *Kōṭṭāṟu, the Elder* (ÑĀNIYĀR ŚĀHIB VALI-ALLĀH). ००० மெய்ஞ்ஞானத் திருப்பாடற்றிரட்டு. [Mey-ñāna-tiru-pādaṭ-ṭiraṭṭu. A collection of Muhammadan poems by the Ñāniyār Śāhib. Followed by the Tiru-kōṭṭāṭṭu-kalambakam, Muhammadan poems by K. M. Karupp'-aiyā Pāvalar, *etc.* Edited by the latter and Ñāniyār Saiyid Ṭāhā Lebbai.] pp. ii. xvi. ii. 383, 36. சென்னை கஅ௲அ [Madras, 1898.] 8°. 14173. c. 2.(1.)

MUHYI al-DĪN MALUK MUDALIYĀR, *Kōṭṭāṟu, the Younger* (TAMBI ÑĀNIYĀR ŚĀHIB). ००० மெய்ஞ்ஞானவிளக்கம். [Mey-ñāna-viḷakkam. A poem on Muhammadan doctrine. With some verses by others. Edited by Ñāniyār Saiyid Ṭāhā Lebbai and K. M. Karupp'-aiyā Pāvalar.] pp. iii. 104. சென்னை கஅ௲அ [Madras, 1898.] 8°. 14173. c. 2.(2.)

MULLER (AUG.), *S.J.* ००० மின்சாரச்சகுணகமருந்தின் கைத்துணை. (*A Guide to Count Cæsar Mattei's Electro-homœopathic Medicines. Translated from the English edition of Revd. Father Aug. Muller's . . . Vade Mecum . . . by the Revd. S. Antony.) pp. 54. *Jaffna*, 1892. 12°. 14170. i. 70.(3.)

—— சகுணகமருந்தின் கைத்துணை. Homœopathic Guide. Translated . . . by Rev. S. Antony. pp. 18. *Jaffna*, 1892. 12°. 14170. i. 70.(2.)

MUNAI-PĀḌIYĀR. முனைப்பாடியார் இயற்றிய அறநெறிச்சாரம். (Aranericharam. [An ancient Jain poem in 225 stanzas] . . . [Edited by] T. Chelvakesavaroya Mudaliar.) pp. ii. iv. 42. *Madras*, 1905. 12°. 14172. a. 50.(5.)

MUNIAPPA. *See* MUNIY-APPA.

MUNI-SĀMI MUDALIYĀR, *Mōṣūr.* தொண்டைநாட்டுத்திருப்பதித் தோத்திரக்கோவை. [Toṇḍai-nāṭṭu-tiru-padi-tōttira-kōvai. A series of poems on the chief Ṣaiva sanctuaries in the Toṇḍai-nāḍu or country of which Conjevaram is the capital.] pp. xii. i. 200. சென்னை [Madras,] 1900. 12°. 14172. a. 51.

MUNI-SĀMI MUDALIYĀR, *Paramaṣivamaṅgalam Aṇṇā-sāmi.* *See* BHĪMA KAVI-RĀYAR. ००० ஸ்ரீராமர் அஸ்வமேதயாகம் ௵ [Ṣrī-rāmar-aṣva-mēdha-yāgam, *etc.* Edited by Muni-sāmi.] [1875.] 4°. 14172. dd. 1.

MUNI-SĀMI MUDALIYĀR, *Ṣiṟumaṇavūr.* Anuboga Vythia Bramah Rahasiam அனுபோகவைத்திய பிரம்மரகசியம். [A handbook of medical practice.] pts. i., ii. *Madras*, 1895-1896. 8°. 14170. i. 43.

—— —— [Another edition.] 8 pts. *Madras*, 1898-1900. 14170. i. 59.

Pts. 1-2 are re-issues of the publications of 1895-96.

—— இஃது சோதிட பிரமாண்டசேகரம் [Jōdiḍa-brahmāṇḍa-ṣēkharam. A metrical compendium of the astrological art, compiled by Muni-sāmi, as transmitted by Dēva-rāja Kavi-rāyar.] pt. i. pp. 94. சென்னை விளம்பி [Madras, 1898.] 8°. 14170. i. 66.

—— Mooligai Marmam. உயிரெழுத்து, மூலிகைமர்மம். [An alphabetical dictionary of medical remedies.] pp. 86. சென்னை [Madras,] 1899. 8°. 14170. i. 69.

—— Prapancha Vuthpathi. உலகரகசியமென்னும் பிரபஞ்சஉற்பத்தி. [Prapañcha-uṟpatti, or Ulaga-rahasyam. An encyclopædia of practical instruction in the Ṣaiva doctrines of the cosmogony, divinity, and religious and social observances. Edited by T. Mṛugēṣa Nāyakar.] pp. 28, 580. மதராஸ் [Madras,] 1900. 8°. 14170. i. 64.

—— Rajavamesa Paramparai. பூர்வ மஹா சக்கிரவர்த்திகளின் இராஜவம்சபரம்பரை [A history of various legendary kings and sages.] pp. 150. சென்னை [Madras,] 1901. 8°. 14171. a. 23.

—— மானிடரகசியமென்னும் சரீரசாஸ்திரம். (*Sarira Sastiram.) [A handbook of anatomy and physiology.] pp. 84. மதராஸ் [Madras,] 1900. 8°. 14170. i. 60.

—— சிறுத்தொண்டநாயனார்சரித்திரம். [Ṣiṟu-toṇḍa-nāyanār-charitram. A story from the Periya-purāṇam of Ṣēkkiṟār, told in easy verse by Muni-sāmi.] pp. 8. [Madras,] 1892. 8°. 14172. b. 44.(1.)

—— ००० திருவொற்றியூர் தியாகேசர்பதிகம். வடிவுடையம்மன் உயிர்வருக்கமாலை ௵ [Tiruvoṭṭiyūr-tyāgēṣar-padigam and Vaḍivuḍaiy-amman-uyir-varga-mālai. Two poems in honour of Ṣiva and his consort as worshipped at Tiruvottiyur near Madras.] pp. 8. [*Madras*,] 1892. 8°. **14170. e. 47.(3.)**

—— Whorvace Vythiachitka. *நாற்பத்தியெண்மர்களீண்டிய ஊர்வசி வயித்தியசிட்கா.* [Ūrvaṣi-vaidya-ṣiṭkā. A digest of medicine.] pt. i. pp. 8, 80. *Madras*, 1895. 8°. **14170. i. 37.**

MUNI-SĀMI MUDALIYĀR, *Vellūr Ṣeṅgalva-rāya, Jauḷi-kaṟār.* *See* MAHĪ-PATI. ∘ ∘ ∘ *ஸ்ரீமத்துக்காராம் . . . சரித்திரம்.* [Tukārām-svāmigaḷ-charitram. Translated by Muni-sāmi. With Hari-nāma-stōtra-pā and Hari-nāma-saṅkīrttanam, translated by the same.] 1887-1898. 8°. **14170. ee. 34.**

MUNI-SĀMI NĀYUḌU, *C. V.* A Catechism of Printing, in Tamil. Part i. A practical guide to the art of printing, *etc.* (*பதிப்பிலக்கண விருவிடை.) pp. viii. 88, i.; 2 *plates*. *Madras*, 1892. 8°. **14170. i. 27.**

MUNI-SĀMI PIḶḶAI, *Mārkaṇḍa.* *See* MUTTU-VĪRA KAVIÑAR. ∘ ∘ ∘ *வள்ளியம்மைநாடகம்.* [Vaḷḷiy-ammai-nāṭakam. Edited by Muni-sāmi.] [1871.] 8°. **14170. l. 7.**

MUNI-SVĀMI. *See* MUNI-SĀMI.

MUNIY-APPA MUDALIYĀR, *Pāripākkam.* *See* ASHTON (J. P.). An English Grammar ... Compiled by ... J. P. Ashton ... with the aid of ... Muniappa Muthaliar, *etc.* 1862. 16°. **14172. h. 45.**

—— *See* ÑĀNA-KŪTTA SVĀMI. *விருத்தாசல புராணம்.* [Vṛuttāchala-purāṇam. With commentary by Muniy-appa.] 1874. 8°. **14170. e. 4.**

—— *See* TĀṆḌAVA-RĀYA-MŪRTTI SVĀMI. *கைவல்யநவநீதம் ஆ* [Kaivalya-nava-nītam. Edited from the recension of Muniy-appa.] [1880.] 8°. **14170. e. 11.**

—— *See* VIVĒKA-SĀRAM. *வாசுதேவமனனம் ஆ* [Vivēka-sāram. An edition based on that of Muniy-appa.] 1896. 8°. **14170. e. 68.**

MUN-ṞURAIY-ARAIYAR. (†Pazhamozhi.) [A series of ethical stanzas, in English, with Tamil commentary and biography.] Chapter xi.(-xv.), *etc.* (†பழமொழி.) *See* ACADEMIES, *etc.*—Madras.—*University of Madras.* Notes on the Tamil text, *etc.* 1888. 12°. **14172. a. 41.**

MUNSHI (A. JOSEPH). The Dravidian Comparative Philology, or Decadence of Tamil Learning, solved with experimental illustrations ... based upon Dr. J. Murdoch's "Indian Teachers' Manual" ... *திராவிட இலக்கிய சித்தாந்தத் தீபிகை.* pp. xi. 168, i. *Madras*, 1902. 12°. **14172. e. 5.**

MURDOCH (JOHN). *See* MUNSHI (A. J.). The Dravidian Comparative Philology ... based upon Dr. J. Murdoch's "Indian Teacher's Manual," *etc.* 1902. 12°. **14172. e. 5.**

—— *See* TAMIL MINOR POETS. Tamil Minor Poets ... with an introduction [by J. Murdoch]. 1872. 12°. **14172. c. 6.**

—— Classified Catalogue of Tamil printed Books, with introductory notices. Compiled by John Murdoch. pp. ix. v. ci. 287. *Madras*, 1865. 12°. **11902. b. 15.**

MURUGADASA SWAMI. *See* MṚUGA-DĀSA SVĀMI.

MURUGASA MOODALIAR. *See* MṚUGĒṢA MUDALIYĀR.

MURUGESA. [For names beginning with this word:] *See* MṚUGĒṢA.

MUTHAIYA MUDALIYAR, *C.* *See* MUTT'-AIYA MUDALIYĀR, *Ṣ.*

MUTHIAH PILLAI. *See* MUTT'-AIYA PIḶḶAI.

MUTHUCUMARASWAMY, *V.* *See* MUTTU-KUMĀRA-SVĀMI MUDALIYĀR, *Vichūr.*

MUTHUSAMI. *See* MUTTU-SĀMI.

MUTT'-AIYA MUDALIYĀR, *Ṣeyyūr.* Rájarájésvari or The Triumph of Love. A new Tamil drama, by C. Muthaiya Mudaliyar. (*இராஜராஜேஸ்வரி அல்லது காதலின் வெற்றி.) pp. 12, ii. 146, 3; 1 *plate*. *Madras*, 1906. 12°. **14171. i. 2.**

MUTT'-AIYA PIḶḶAI, *E.* *கிறிஸ்தவர்களின் ஆசாரமும், குருமார் போதகமும்.* The Manners and Customs of Native Christians, and the Rules and Regulations of European Missionaries. By E. Muthiah Pillai. pp. 32. *Palamcottah*, 1894. 8°. **14170. c. 24.(10.)**

MUTT'-AIYĀ PULAVAR. வேதசாக்ஷியாகிய தேவசகாயம்பிள்ளை வாசகப்பா. [Dēva-sahāyam-pil-lai-vāchaka-pā. A lyrical drama on the martyrdom of Dēva-sahāyam Pillai, a native Catholic of Travancore.] pp. iv. 300. சென்னை [*Madras*,] 1894. 8°. **14170. l. 42.**

Pp. 289-296 *are missing.*

MUTT'-AIYA SVĀMI, *Vṛuttāchalam.* ∘∘∘ சின்மய தீபிகை. [Chin-maya-dīpikai. A poem on monistic psycho-theology. Edited with paraphrases, glosses, and notes by K. Rāmānanda Yōgi, on the basis of K. Rāma-linga Pillai's recension.] pp. 2, 171. சென்னை [*Madras*,] 1907. 12°. **14172. a. 58.**

MUT-TAMIṞ-KAVI-RĀYAR. ∘∘∘ சுசீந்திர ஸ்தல புராணம். [Ṣuchīndra-sthala-purāṇam. A poem on the local legend of the sanctuary of Ṣiva and Vishṇu near Cape Comorin where Indra was purified for his sin. Edited by Māvaḍi Chidambaram Pillai.] pp. iv. ii. 362, iii. திருநெல்வேலி [*Tinnevelli*,] 1894. 8°. **14170. e. 58.**

MUTTAN ĀCHĀRI, *V.* சத்தியவாக்கு அரிச்சந்திர நாடகம். [Satya-vāk-harișchandra-nāṭakam. A drama on the legend of the truthful Harișchandra.] pp. x. 528; 52 *plates.* சென்னை [*Madras*,] 1905. 8°. **14170. l. 63.**

MUTTA-TAMBI PULAVAR, *A. P.* யேசுக்கிறீஸ்துநாதருடைய திருப்பாடுகளின் மேல் ஒப்பாரி. [Yēṣu-kirīstu-nāthar-uḍaiya tiru-pādugalin mēl oppāri. Verses on the Passion and teaching of Christ.] pp. 16. யாழ்ப்பாணம் கஅகூஉ [*Jaffna*, 1892.] 12°. **14170. a. 35.(6.)**

MUTTAYYA. *See* MUTT'-AIYA.

MUTTI-CHIDAMBARAM PILLAI, *of St. Joseph's College, Trichinopoli.* யாப்பிலக்கணச்சுருக்கம். [Yāpp'-ilakkaṇa-churukkam. A primer of Tamil prosody.] pp. ii. 24. *Trichinopoly*, 1898. 8°. **14172. g. 3.**

MUTTI-RĀMA KAVI-RĀYAR, *G.* *See* SUBBA-RĀYA MUDALIYĀR, *V.*, MUTTI-RĀMA KAVI-RĀYAR, *G.*, and KADIR-VĒL KAVI-RĀJA PAṆḌITAR. ஸ்ரீமஹாபாரதக்கீர்த்தனை ஞூ [Mahā-bhārata-kīrttanai.] [1905.] 8°. **14172. bbb. 1.**

MUT-TOLL'-ĀYIRAM. முத்தொள்ளாயிரச்செய்யுட்கள். [105 verses from the Mut-toll'-āyiram, a collection of 2,700 *veṇ-bā* stanzas on moral, worldly, and erotic themes.] pp. 20. 1906. *See* ACADEMIES, *etc.*—*Madura.* ["Ṣen-damiṟ" supplement.] no. 18. 1902, *etc.* 8°. **14172. i. 1*.(no. 18.)**

MUTTU-KṚUSHṆA BRAHMAM. *See* ĀṞU-MUGA SVĀMI. ∘∘∘ நிஷ்டானுபூதி ஞூ [Nishṭhānubhūti. With commentary by Muttu-kṛushṇa.] [1852.] 8°. **14172. c. 23.**

MUTTU-KṚUSHṆ'-AIYA NĀYUḌU, *Simhādri.* The Anglo-Tamil Self Reader. சுயமாய் வாசிக்கத்தக்க புஸ்தகம் . . . for English and Tamil students . . . An easy method of acquiring the language . . . without the help of a teacher . . . by S. Moodookrishnia, *etc.* pt. i. pp. 17. *Penang*, 1889. 8°. **14172. hh. 4.**

—— The Anglo-Tamil Self-Reader. Part i. இங்கிலிஷு சுய வித்தியார்த்தம் . . . by Simhadry Moodookrishniah Naidu, *etc.* pt. i. pp. x. ii. 85, xxxix. *Madras*, 1892. 12°. **14172. h. 83.**

—— The Tamil and English Self-Reader. An easy method of acquiring Tamil in a short time . . . for the use of Europeans . . . Romanized. Family treasure. pp. ii. 104. *Madras*, 1894. 12°. **14172. h. 94.**

MUTTU-KṚUSHṆA NĀYAKAR, *T.* *See* MORRIS (H.). A Key to Morris' History of India ... Translated by T. Moothookrishna Naiker. 1873. 12°. **14172. h. 54.**

MUTTU-KṚUSHṆA NĀYUḌU, *Ṣ., of Triplicane.* [For volumes of the Iyaṟ-pā edited by Muttu-kṛushṇa:] *See* ĀṞVĀRGAL.—Nāl-āyiram.—*Iyaṟ-pā.*

—— *See* ṢAṬHAKŌPA-DĀSAR, *K.* ∘∘∘ அரிசமய தீபம் ஞூ [Hari-samaya-dīpam. With paraphrase by Muttu-kṛushṇa. Edited by the latter.] 1904. 8°. **14170. ee. 58.**

MUTTU-KUMĀRA KAVI-RĀJAR, *Ṣunnāgam.* ஞானக்கும்மி. [Ñāna-kummi. A song in 116 quatrains, against Christianity.] pp. 24. யாழ்ப்பாணம் கஅ [*Jaffna*, 1891.] 16°. **14170. a. 40.(2.)**

MUTTU-KUMĀRA PILLAI, *T.* நிராகரணதிமிரபானு. [Nirākaraṇa-timira-bhānu. A reply to Ṣ. Rāghavāchāryar's criticisms on Shaṇmukha Pillai's interpretation of the Bhārata-veṇ-bā.] pp. 46. கும்பகோணம் சர்வதாரி [*Kumbakonam*, 1888.] 16°. **14170. k. 2.(1.)**

MUTTU-KUMĀRA-SVĀMI, *Knight.* See HARIŚCHANDRA. Arichandra ... a ... drama, translated into English by Mutu Coomàra Swàmy, Mudeliàr. 1863. 12°. **14170. l. 33.**

MUTTU-KUMĀRA-SVĀMI, *Tumbainagar M.* See EPHEMERIDES. விளம்பிவர்ஷ . . . பஞ்சாங்கம். [Calendar for 1898-99. Calculated by Muttu-kumāra-svāmi.] 1897. 8°. **14172. i. 16.(2.)**

MUTTU-KUMĀRA-SVĀMI MUDALIYĀR, *Vichūr.* See PERIODICAL PUBLICATIONS.—*Madras.* யதார்த்த பாஸ்கரன் ஆ (*Yadhartha Bhaskaran ... Editor: V. M. Swamy.) 1902-1905. 8°. **14172. i. 7.**

—— Ratnamalikâ, or Helps to the Study of the Vedanta. By V. M. Swamy, B.A., with an [English] introduction by V. V. Ramanan. (*இரத்நமாலிகை.) pp. 16, 96; 1 *plate.* *Madras,* 1902. 8°. **14170. ee. 45.(1.)**

—— Samarasa Jnâna Chandrika. An unsectarian philosophical treatise from the standpoint of the Adwaita-wada by Vichur Muthucumaraswamy Mudr., B.A., the Adwaita Chanda Marudha. With an [English] introduction by Tandalam Balasundara Mudr. Avl. [Preceded by commendatory verses, and concluding with a short Sanskrit hymn.] (*ஸமரஸ ஞான சந்திரிகை.) pp. xx. 66. *Madras,* 1902. 8°. **14170. ee. 48.**

—— —— [Another copy.] **14170. ee. 45.(2.)**

MUTTU-KUṬṬI AYYĀ, *of Sivaganga* (TAMIṚ-CHAKRAVARTTI). ◦◦◦ வசனசம்பிரதாயக்கதை. [Vachana-sampradāya-kathai. A story in the form of an imaginary petition of peasants addressed to the god Kubēra.] pp. iv. 76. திருவாதி [*Tiruvadi,*] 1895. 16°. **14171. aa. 8.**

Said to have been composed 120 years ago, to amuse the local zamindar during the Śiva-rātri.

MUTTU-LIṄGA DĒŚIKAR, *Pālakkāḍu Kaṇṇapp'-aiyar.* கஜேந்த்ரமோக்ஷம் தோரா. [Gajēndra-mōksham. A series of poems in *tōrā* style on the legend of the rescue of the elephant by Vishṇu.] pp. 26. பாலக்காடு [*Palghat,*] 1898. 8°. **14170. ee. 35.(2.)**

MUTTU-SĀMI AIYAR, *C.S., of Kalyanasundaram High School.* Visvanatham. An historical drama in five acts († which narrates the noble thoughts and the commendable deeds of Visvanatha, the first of the Nayak Kings of Madura) ... விசுவநாதம் ஆ. [With English preface by T. Rājam Aiyaṅgār.] pp. xx. 131. *Tanjore,* 1906. 8°. **14171. k. 4.**

MUTTU-SĀMI BHĀRATIYĀR, *Tiruvaiyāṛu A.* See VIŚVA-BRAHMA-PURĀṆAM. விஸ்வபிரமபுராணம். [Viṣva-brahma-purāṇam. Metrically translated by Muttu-sāmi.] 1894. 8°. **14170. f. 16.**

MUTTU-SĀMI MUDALIYĀR, *Eṛumūr Nārāyaṇa.* See PAÑCHA-TANTRAM. பஞ்சதந்திரக்கதை. [Pañcha-tantra-kathai. Edited by Muttu-sāmi.] [1847.] 8°. **14170. k. 26.**

MUTTU-SĀMI MUDALIYĀR, *Tirumaṛiṣai Vaidyaliṅga.* See PURĀṆAS.—*Vināyaka-purāṇam.* பார்க்கவ புராணம் ஆ [Vināyaka-purāṇam. A prose paraphrase by Muttu-sāmi.] 1899. 8°. **14170. ee. 19.**

—— See VILLIPUTTŪRAR. ஐந்தாம்வேதமாகிய ஸ்ரீமகாபாரதம் ஆ [Mahā-bhāratam. Edited by Muttu-sāmi.] 1900. 4°. **14172. dd. 3.**

MUTTU-SĀMI PIḶḶAI, *Appu.* ஆத்தும-உத்தியானம். [Ātma-udyānam. A book for private devotional reading for Roman Catholics, compiled from various sources.] pp. xx. 512; 4 *plates.* சென்னமாநகரத்தில [*Madras,*] 1817. 12°. **14170. a. 13.**

MUTTU-SĀMI PIḶḶAI, *Triṣirapuram.* See APPĀVU PIḶḶAI.

MUTTU-SĀMI ŚĀSTRI, *T. Ṣ., of Madras Christian College.* See VEṄKAṬA-SUBBA RĀU, *R.* கதாரத்நாவளி. [Kathā-ratnāvaḷi. Translated by Muttu-sāmi.] 1893. 8°. **14171. b. 1.**

MUTTU-SVĀMI UPĀDHYĀYAR, *Diṇḍukkal Nellaiy-appa.* See NITYA-KARMA. விஸ்வப்ரம்ஹ ஆன்ஹிகதீபிகை. [Viṣva-brahma-āhnika-dīpikai. Translated by Muttu-svāmi.] 1907. 8°. **14033. aa. 46.**

MUTTU-SUBB'-AIYA, *Punalvēli Varada-rāj'-aiya.* ஜானகிபரிணயநாடகம். [Jānaki-pariṇayam. A drama in 7 acts upon the legend of Rāma's union with Sītā. Edited by P. Rāma-svāmi Bhārati, H. Hari-hara Bhārati, and T. Kavi-rāja Nellaiy'-appa Piḷḷai. Preceded by a prose epitome.] pp. 30, 2, 344. திருநெல்வேலி [*Tinnevelli,*] 1901. 8°. **14170. l. 15.**

MUTTU-TAMBI PILLAI, *Āvanna. See* VIVĒKĀNANDA, *Svāmi.* ○○○ பிரசங்கம். [Prasangam. Translated by Muttu-tambi Piḷḷai.] [1897.] 8°. **14170. ee. 28.(2.)**

MUTTU-TAMBI PIḶḶAI, *Mānippāy Ā. See* KṚUSHṆA MIṢRA, *Dramatist.* பிரபோதசந்திரோதயவசனம். [Prabōdha-chandrōdaya-vachanam. A prose rendering, by Muttu-tambi, of Tiru-vēṅkaṭa-svāmi's Mey-ñāna viḷakkam.] 1889. 12°. **14170. l. 21.**

—— The Tamil Classical Dictionary. அபிதான கோசம். pp. ii. 396, iii.; 3 *plates. Jaffna,* 1902. 8°. **14172. e. 38.**

MUTTU-TĀṆḌAVAR, *Ṣīrkāḻi.* சிதம்பரம் ஸ்ரீசபாநாதர்பேரில் . . . கீர்த்தனம்-பதம். [Kīrttanam. Eighty-four devotional poems (*padam*) in honour of Sabhā-nāthar, the name under which Ṣiva is worshipped at Chidambaram. Edited, with a life of the poet, by Karuṇānanda Svāmi. Followed by twenty-nine songs of the same kind by Māri-muttā Piḷḷai and others.] pp. vii. ii. 64. கஅாளஸ [*Madras,* 1870.] 8°. **14170. k. 20.**

MUTTU-VĪRA KAVIÑAR. ○○○ வள்ளியம்மைநாடகம். [Vaḷḷiy-ammai-nāṭakam. A drama founded upon the canto in the Skanda-purāṇam describing the marriage of Subrahmaṇya and Vaḷḷi. Edited by Mārkaṇḍa Muni-sāmi Piḷḷai.] pp. 116. கஅளக [*Madras,* 1871.] 8°. **14170. l. 7.**

MUTTU-VĪRA RĀMA. ஜாலத்திரட்டு. [Jāla-tiraṭṭu. 15 verses on magic, with commentary.] *See* PULI-PĀṆI. ஸ்ரீ . . . பலதிரட்டு ஜாலம் ஶ்ரீ [Puli-pāṇi-pala-tiraṭṭu-jālam.] pp. 1-5. 1906. 8°. **14171. g. 8.**

MUTU COOMÀRA SWÀMY, *Mudeliār. See* MUTTU-KUMĀRA-SVĀMI, *Knight.*

MUTUKISNA (HENRY FRANCIS). *See* JAFFNA. A new edition of the Thesawaleme . . . By H. F. Mutukisna. 1862. 8°. **14170. g. 3.**

—— *See* JAFFNA. The Tésawaḷamai . . . Reprinted from the edition . . . by . . . H. F. Mutukisna. 1891. 8°. **05319. k. 3.**

MYSORE, *Government of.* Epigraphia Carnataca. . . . Published for Government by B. Lewis Rice. *Bangalore,* 1886, *etc.* 4°. **14058 c. 8.**
In progress.

NĀBHĀJĪ. [For editions of the Mahā-bhakta-vijayam, partly based upon Nābhājī's Bhakti-sāra:] *See* MAHĀ-BHAKTA-VIJAYAM.

NACHEḶḶAIYĀR. ஆறும்பத்து. [Decade vi. Ten poems on the Chera king Ādu-gōṭ-pāṭṭu Chēral-ādan.] *See* PADIṬṬU-PATTU. ○○○ பதிற்றுப்பத்து ஶ்ரீ [Padiṭṭu-pattu.] pp. 80-99. 1904. 8°. **14172. bb. 14.**

NACHINĀRKK'-INIYAR, *Bhāradvāji, of Madura.* [For editions of the commentary upon the Tiru-kōvaiyār, sometimes ascribed to Nachinārkk'-iniyar:] *See* MĀṆIKKA-VĀCHAKAR.

—— *See* NALLANDUVANĀR. ○○○ கலித்தொகை [Kali-togai. With commentary by Nachinārkk'-iniyar.] 1887. 8°. **14172. b. 38.**

—— *See* PATTU-PĀṬṬU. பத்துப்பாட்டு ஶ்ரீ [Pattu-pāṭṭu. With commentary by Nachinārkk'-iniyar.] 1889. 8°. **14172. d. 10.**

—— *See* RUDRA-KAṆṆANĀR. University of Madras . . . Pattinappalai. With Nachchinarkkiniyar's commentary, *etc.* 1906. 8°. **14172. b. 37.(2.)**

—— *See* TIRU-TAKKA DĒVAR. ○○○ சீவகசிந்தாமணி ஶ்ரீ [Jīvaka-chintāmaṇi. With commentary of Nachinārkk'-iniyar.] 1887. 8°. **14172. d. 6.**

—— *See* TIRU-TAKKA DĒVAR. University of Madras . . . Jivakachintamani. Namagalilambakam. With Nachinarkkiniyar's commentary, *etc.* 1905. 8°. **14171. bb. 21.(2.)**

—— *See* TOL-KĀPPIYANĀR. தொல்காப்பியம் ஶ்ரீ [Tol-kāppiyam. With commentary by Nachinārkk'-iniyar.] 1885-[1892.] 8°. **14172. e. 13.**

—— *See* TOL-KĀPPIYANĀR. தொல்காப்பியம் ஶ்ரீ [Tol-kāppiyam. Pt. i., with commentary of Nachinārkk'-iniyar.] [1847.] 8°. **14172. f. 4.**

—— *See* TOL-KĀPPIYANĀR. (†தொல்காப்பியம் ஶ்ரீ.) [Ṣeyyuḷ-iyal. With Nachinārkk'-iniyar's commentary.] [1904, *etc.*] 8°. [*Ṣen-damiṟ Supplement.*] **14172. i. 1*.(no. 21.)**

NĀCHIYĀR. *See* ĀṆḌĀḶ.

NADAR (J. S. CORNELIUS). *See* CORNELIUS NĀḌĀR (J. S.).

NĀGA-LIṄGA MUDALIYĀR, *Vaṇṇa-kalañjiyam Kāñchi.* See MEY-KAṆḌA-ŚĀTTIRAM. மெய்கண்ட சாத்திரம் ௸ [Mey-kaṇḍa-śāttiram. Edited by Nāga-liṅga.] 1897. 8°. **14170. ff. 3.**

—— See TĀYUMĀNAVAR. தாயுமானசுவாமிகள் பாடல். [Tiru-pāḍaṭ-ṭiraṭṭu. Edited with glossary, *etc.*, by Nāga-liṅga.] 1906. 12°. **14170. eee. 25.**

NĀGA-RATNAM PILLAI, *J. M.* See PERIODICAL PUBLICATIONS.—*Madras.* The Light of Truth, *etc.* [Edited by Nāga-ratnam.] 1897, *etc.* 4°. **14170. fff. 4.**

NĀGA-RATNA NĀYAKAR, *P.* See CHID-GHANĀNANDA GIRI. ஸ்ரீ . . . நியாயப்பிரகாசம். [Nyāya-prakāśam. Translated by Nāga-ratna.] 1906, *etc.* 8°. **14170. ff. 21.**

NĀGA-SĀMI AIYAR, *Pūvāḷūr.* See SAPTARSHI. The Suptharishivakkiam 5500. Thoroughly examined by ... Nagasawmy, *etc.* [1899.] 8°. **14170. i. 63.**

NAKKĪRA DĒVAR, *Madurai Kaṇakkāyanār.* See IṞAIYANĀR. இறையனாரகப்பொருள் [Iṟaiyanār-aga-poruḷ. With commentary ascribed to Nakkīranār.] [1883.] 8°. **14172. e. 25.**

—— திருமுருகாற்றுப்படை (†நெடுநெல்வாடை). [Tiru-mṛug'-āṭṭu-paḍai and Neḍu-nal-vāḍai. Two poems, nos. 1 and 7 respectively of the Pattu-pāṭṭu, the former a devotional hymn on the god Mṛugan, the latter describing the winter campaign of the Pāṇḍiyan king Neḍuñ-śeṟiyan and the sorrow of his queen. With Nachinārkk'-iniyar's commentary.] See PATTU-PĀṬṬU. பத்துப்பாட்டு ௸ [Pattu-pāṭṭu.] pp. 1-40, 241-260. 1889. 8°. **14172. d. 10.**

Both the Tiru-mṛug'-āṭṭu-paḍai and Kayilai-bādi-kāḷatti-bādi-tiruv-antādi are included in the 11th Tiru-muṟai. The former is the only undoubtedly genuine work of Nakkīranār.

—— ००० கயிலைபாதிகாளத்திபாதிதிருவந்தாதி மூலமும் ... பதவுரையும். [Kayilai-bādi-kāḷatti-bādi-tiruv-antādi. 100 *antādi* Śaiva quatrains, alternately praising Kailāsa and Kālahasti. With interpretation by the editors of the Vidyā-vinōdini.] pp. 48. சென்னை [*Madras,*] 1892. 8°. **14172. c. 39.(4.)**

—— ००० திருமுருகாற்றுப்படை மூலபாடம். [Tiru-mṛug'-āṭṭu-paḍai. Followed by the Nēr-iśai-veṇ-bā.] pp. 19, 2. சென்னபட்டணம் [*Madras,*] 1887. 16°. **14172. a. 7.(4.)**

NAKKĪRA DĒVAR, *Madurai Kaṇakkāyanār (continued).* ००० திருமுருகாற்றுப்படை ௸ [Tiru-mṛug'-āṭṭu-paḍai.] pp. ii. 20. See SUNDARA MUDALIYĀR, *T.* ००० திருமுருகாற்றுப்படை ௸ [Tiru-mṛug'-āṭṭu-paḍai, *etc.*] pt. i. [1890.] 16°. **14172. a. 32.(1.)**

—— ००० திருமுருகாற்றுப்படை. [Tiru-mṛug'-āṭṭu-paḍai. Edited by P. Rāma-liṅga Piḷḷai.] pp. 21. சிதம்பரம் தன்முகி [*Chidambaram,* 1896.] 16°. **14170. d. 36.(4.)**

—— ००० விநாயகர் திருஅகவலும் . . . விநாயகர் அகவலும், வேழமுகமும் ௸ [Vināyakar-agaval. A hymn to Gaṇēśa, by Nakkīranār. Followed by Auvaiyār's Vināyakar-agaval and Vēṟa-mugam, Aruṇa-giri-nāthar's Mutti-vināyakar-agaval, and other hymns by divers authors.] pp. 24. *Madras,* 1903. 16°. **14170. d. 31.(3.)**

NĀL-AḌIYĀR. ००० நீதிநூலாகிய நாலடியார் மூலமும் உரையும். [Nāl-aḍiyār. Four hundred quatrains on ethical subjects. With commentary. Edited by Vēda-giri Mudaliyār.] pp. 170. இராக்கத [*Madras,* 1855.] 8°. **14172. c. 1.**

Forms the first of the class of poems styled Kīṟ-kaṇakku. *The compilation is ascribed to Padmanār.*

—— ००० நாலடியார் என்றுவழங்கும் நாலடி நானூறு மூலமும் . . . பதவுரையும். [Nāl-aḍiyār. With interpretation and commentary by Ū. Pushpa-ratha Cheṭṭi.] pp. ii. ii. 249, v. சென்னபட்டணம் [*Madras,*] 1885. 8°. **14172. b. 40.**

—— Naladyar. [Edited] with a clear Tamil commentary and an English translation of the text [by Ū. Pushpa-ratha Cheṭṭi]. (*நாலடியார்.) pp. 2, ii. 290, 5. *Madras,* 1892. 8°. **14172. b. 45.**

—— ००० நாலடியார். The Nālaḍiyār, or Four Hundred Quatrains, in Tamil, with introduction, translation, and notes . . . a concordance and lexicon . . . by the Rev. G. U. Pope. pp. 1. 440. *Oxford,* 1893. 8°. **14172. d. 12.**

—— The Nâladiyâr. With a Tamil commentary by the late Pandit C. Rajagopala Pillai, and an English introduction and translation by K. Kuppuswami Mudaliyar. (*நாலடியார் என்று வழங்கும் நாலடி நானூறுமூலமும் . . . உரையும்.) pp. 17, 5, ii. ii. 379, iv. *Madras,* 1903. 8°. **14172. c. 45.**

NĀL-ADIYĀR (*continued*). நாலடியார். Náladiyár. [Selections, in Tamil and English.] *See* WALKER (J.). நீதிமொழித்திரட்டு. Nidi mozhittirattu, *etc.* pp. 40-97. 1841. 8°. **14170. k. 35.**

—— University of Madras. F.A. Examination, 1900. Tamil poetry—the prescribed portions in Naladyar and Bharatam; and explanatory notes—grammatical and rhetorical annotations on these portions. By C. M. Swaminatha Iyer. 4 pts. *Madras,* 1899. 8°. **14172. b. 37.(1.)**

—— Trois chapitres du Naladiyar. *See* TIRU-VAḶḶUVAR. Le Livre de l'Amour, *etc.* pp. 101-118. 1889. 12°. **14172. a. 38.**

—— நாலடியார். (†Naladiyar. chap. vi.(-x.), *etc.*). [With commentary and English translation.] pp. 42, 5. *See* ACADEMIES, *etc.*—Madras.—*University of Madras.* University of Madras. F.A. Examination, *etc.* 1900. 8°. **14172. bb. 6.(5.)**

NALAN. The History of the Nella-rajah. A Hindoo romance. *See* KINDERSLEY (N. E.). Specimens of Hindoo Literature, *etc.* pp. 83-328. 1794. 8°. **980. k. 19.**

—— The History of Nala. நளச்சக்கிரவர்த்தியின் சரித்திரம். *See* POPE (G. U.). A Tamil Prose Reading-book, *etc.* bk. iii. 1859. 8°. **14172. h. 76.**

NALLĀDANĀR. *See* MRUGĒṢA MUDALIYĀR, *T.* நீதிமஞ்சரித்தருப்பணம். [Nīti-mañjari-darpaṇam. Interpretations of ethical works of Nallādanār (the Tri-kaṭukam) and others.] 1881-1883. 16°. **14172. a. 8.**

NALL'-AIYĀ PIḶḶAI, *Mayiliṭṭi.* *See* KOSTIN (D.). பூதத்தம்பி விலாசம். [Pūda-tambi-vilāsam. Edited by Nall'-aiyā.] 1888. 8°. **14170. l. 17.**

NALLANDUVANĀR. ∘∘∘ கலித்தொகை. [Kali-togai. An anthology of poems on erotic themes, in *kali* metre. With a commentary by Nachinārkk'-iniyar. Edited with an introduction by Ṣ. V. Dāmōdaram Piḷḷai.] pp. iv. xxxiv. iii. 487. *Madras,* 1887. 8°. **14172. b. 38.**

Forms no. 6 in the collection known as the Eṭṭu-togai.

NALLĀ PIḶḶAI, *Madalambēḍu.* *See* VILLIPUTTŪRAR. இதிகாசமாகிய ஸ்ரீமகாபாரத ஞு [Mahā-bhārata-vachanam. A prose paraphrase of Nallā Piḷḷai's amplified adaptation of Villiputtūrar's Bhāratam.] [1847-1854.] 4°. **14172. dd. 2.**

—— *See* VILLIPUTTŪRAR. இதிகாசமாகிய ... மஹாபாரதவசனம். [Draviḍa-mahā-bhārata-vachanam. The prose paraphrase of Nallā Piḷḷai's Bhāratam.] 1880. 4°. **14172. dd. 4.**

—— *See* VILLIPUTTŪRAR. ஐந்தாம்வேதமாகிய ஸ்ரீமகாபாரதம் ஞு [Mahā-bhāratam. The prose paraphrase of Nallā Piḷḷai's Bhāratam.] 1900. 4°. **14172. dd. 3.**

NALL'-APPĀ (*Tirukuḍaiyūr M.* ISRAEL). A Hand Book of Tamil Text and Grammar. செய்யுள், இலக்கண பரீக்ஷா தீபிகை. Intended for the use of I, II, and III Forms. (*Paritcha Theepeka.) pp. iv. 138. *Madras,* 1905. 12°. **14172. e. 23.(2.)**

NALLA-SĀMI PIḶḶAI, *J. M.* *See* ARUṆANDI DĒVA-NĀYANĀR. Sivagnana Siddhiyar, *etc.* [Translated by Nalla-sāmi.] 1897, *etc.* 4°. [*Siddhanta Deepika.*] **14170. fff. 4.(vol. 1, etc.)**

—— *See* MANA-VĀCHAKAM KAḌANDAR. Light of Truth, or Unmai Vilakkam, *etc.* [Translated by Nalla-sāmi.] 1902. 4°. [*Siddhanta Deepika.*] **14170. fff. 4.(vol. 5.)**

—— *See* MAṞAI-ÑĀNA-SAMBANDHAR. Saiva Samaya Neri, *etc.* [Translated by Nalla-sāmi.] 1902. 4°. [*Siddhanta Deepika.*] **14170. fff. 4.(vol. 6.)**

—— *See* MEY-KAṆḌA DĒVAR. Sivagnana Botham ... Translated with notes ... by J. M. Nallasawmi Pillai. 1895. 8°. **14170. e. 51.**

—— *See* MEY-KAṆḌA DĒVAR. ∘∘∘ சிவஞானபோத ஞு [Ṣiva-ñāna-bōdham. With Ṣiva-ñānar's larger commentary, *etc.* With English preface and biography of Ṣiva-ñānar by Nalla-sāmi.] 1906. 8°. **14170. eee. 15.**

—— *See* MEY-KAṆḌA DĒVAR. சிவஞானபோதம் ஞு (Sivagnana Botham) with introduction and translation by ... Nallaswami Pillai. 1906. 12°. **14170. d. 29.**

—— *See* UMĀ-PATI ṢIVĀCHĀRYAR. Light of Grace ... Translated with notes and introduction. By J. M. Nallaswami Pillai. 1896. 8°. **14170. ee. 12.(1.)**

NĀLU - MANTRI - KATHAI. Vier Geheimrath-Minister. [Nālu-mantri-kathai.] Eine indische Geschichte in Gleichnissen. Aus tamulischer Sprache übertragen von dem früheren Braminen Christian Rama Ayen. pp. vi. 94. *Hamburg*, 1855. 8°. **14171. a. 32.**

—— The King and his Four Ministers. An old Hindu romance, translated into English ... by Pandit S. M. Natesa Sastri ... With notes and introduction, by W. A. Clouston. Second edition. pp. xi. 58. *Madras*, 1888. 12°. **14170. k. 48.(1.)**

—— The King and his Four Ministers, [*i.e.* the Aḷakēṣa-kathai, or Nālu-mantri-k°., translated by Naṭēṣa Ṣāstri.] *See* CLOUSTON (W. A.). A group of Eastern Romances, *etc.* pp. 191-233. 1889. 8°. **14003. h. 21.**

NAMA-ṢIVĀYAM PIḶḶAI, *Māyūram.* ००० பட்டணத்துப்பிள்ளையார் சரித்திர சங்கிரகம். [Paṭṭa-ṇattu-piḷḷaiyār-charitra-saṅgraham. A prose biography of the Ṣaiva religious poet Paṭṭaṇattu Piḷḷai.] pp. 86. சென்னை எவினம்பி [*Madras*, 1898.] 12°. **14171. aa. 7.**

NAMAṢ-ṢIVĀYA CHEṬṬI, *Ṣ. R.* விவேகசுந்தரம் ... Vivekasundarum. A cheap pleasing Tamil pamphlet [on various social topics]. Third edition. (*Uthama Bhodha Ranjani Series, no. 1.) pp. 12. *Madras*, 1888. 8°. **14172. i. 6.**

NAMAṢ-ṢIVĀYA DĒVAR, *Kugai.* அருணகிரியந்தாதி (தனிவெண்பா). [Aruṇa-giriy-antādi and Tiruv-aruṇai-tani-veṇ-bā. Poems on the sanctuary of Tiruvannamalai.] *See* ELL'-APPA NĀVALAR. அருணாசலபுராணம் ஆ [Aruṇāchala-purāṇam.] pp. lxv.-lxxx. 1898. 12°. **14170. d. 52.**

—— —— pp. 69-90. 1902. 12°. **14170. d. 75.**

—— —— pp. 69-90. 1903. 12°. **14170. d. 83.**

NAMAṢ-ṢIVĀYA MUDALIYĀR, *K.* *See* PARAÑ-JŌDI MUNIVAR. திருவிளையாடற் புராணம் [Tiru-viḷaiy-āḍaṟ-purāṇam. A prose abstract by Namaṣ-ṣivāyar.] 1901-1902. 16°. **14170. dd. 8.**

NAMAṢ-ṢIVĀYA SVĀMI. சாரப்பிரபந்தம். [Sāra-prabandham. A Ṣaiva devotional poem.] *See* ELL'-APPA NĀVALAR. அருணாசலபுராணம் ஆ [Aruṇāchala-purāṇam.] pp. 423-428. 1898. 12°. **14170. d. 52.**

—— —— pp. 535-540. 1902. 12°. **14170. d. 75.**

—— —— pp. 535-540. 1903. 12°. **14170. d. 83.**

NAMAṢ-ṢIVĀYA SVĀMI, *Chidambaram, disciple of Kugai Namaṣ-ṣivāyar.* அண்ணாமலை வெண்பா. [Aṇṇāmalai-veṇ-bā. Verses on the sanctuary of Tiruvannamalai.] *See* ELL'-APPA NĀVALAR. அருணாசலபுராணம் ஆ [Aruṇāchala-purāṇam.] pp. xlix.—lxiv. 1898. 12°. **14170. d. 52.**

—— —— pp. 53-68. 1902. 12°. **14170. d. 75.**

—— —— pp. 53-68. 1903. 12°. **14170. d. 83.**

NAMAṢ-ṢIVĀYA TAMBIRĀN, *Tiruvāvaḍuduṟai.* *See* ARUṆANDI DĒVA-NĀYANĀR. சிவஞானசித்தியார் ஆ [Ṣiva-ñāna-siddhiyār-parapakkam, Ṣiva-ñāna-siddhiyār-supakkam, and Iru-bāv-iru-badu. With commentaries on the third by Namaṣ-ṣivāya Tambirān.] 1897. 8°. [*Mey-kaṇḍa-ṣāttiram.*] **14170. ff. 3.**

—— *See* UMĀ-PATI ṢIVĀCHĀRYAR. ००० சிவப்பிரகாசம் ஆ [Siddhāntāshṭakam. Comprising the Vinā-veṇ-bā, *etc.*, with commentaries founded upon those of Namaṣ-ṣivāyar and others.] [1895.] 12°. **14170. d. 37.**

—— *See* UMĀ-PATI ṢIVĀCHĀRYAR. சிவப்பிரகாசம். [Siddhāntāshṭakam, viz. Vinā-veṇ-bā, with commentary of Namaṣ-ṣivāyar, *etc.*] 1897. 8°. [*Mey-kaṇḍa-ṣāttiram.*] **14170. ff. 3.**

NAMBI, *Nāṟ-kavi-rāja.* *See* NĀṞ-KAVI-RĀJA NAMBI.

NAMBI NĀYUḌU, *A.* ००० பாசுரப்படி ராமாயணம் ... மோக்ஷசூக்ஷமமென்னும், ஸ்ரீவிஷ்ணுதோத்திரநாமாவளி ஆ [Pāṣura-paḍi-rāmāyaṇam of Periyav-āchān Piḷḷai; Rāghavalu Rāmānuja-dāsar's Mōksha-sūkshmam, or Vishṇu-tōttira-nāmāvaḷi; Charaṇa-saṅkīrttana-nāmāvaḷi; and Chaturviṃ-ṣati-nāma-saṅkīrttanam. Vaishṇava tracts and hymns, edited by Nambi Nāyuḍu.] pp. iv. 20. சென்னை [*Madras*,] 1903. 12°. **14170. d. 46.(4.)**

NAMBIY-ĀṆḌĀR NAMBI. [For the Tiru-muṟai codified by this devotee:] *See* TIRU-MUṞAI.

—— *See* UMĀ-PATI ṢIVĀCHĀRYAR. திருத்தொண்டர்-புராண வரலாறு [Tiru-toṇḍar-purāṇa-varal-āṟu, a poem on Şēkkiṟār; Tiru-muṟai-gaṇḍa-purāṇam, or Nambiy-āṇḍār-nambi-purāṇam, an account of the codifier of the Tiru-muṟai, *etc.*] 1880. 8°. [*Periya-purāṇam.*] **14170. f. 4.**

—— —— [1885]-1898. 8°. **14170. f. 1.**

—— கலித்துறைத் திருவந்தாதி. [Kali-tuṟai-tiruv-antādi. A devotional and hagiological poem.] *See* Şekkiṟār. ◦◦◦ பெரிய புராணம் ஷ [Periya-purāṇam.] [1880.] 8°. **14170. f. 4.**

—— —— vol. i. [1885]-1898. 8°. **14170. f. 1.**

NAMM'-ĀṞVĀR. [For editions of the Tiru-vāy-moṟi, Tiruv-āşiriyam, Tiru-vṛuttam, and Periya-tiruv-antādi of this saint included in the editions of the whole or parts of the Nāl-āyira-prabandham:] *See* Āṟvārgaḷ.—*Nāl-āyiram.*

—— ◦◦◦ நம்மாழ்வார்தாலாட்டு. [Namm'-āṟvār-tālāṭṭu. The story of the Vaishṇava saint Namm'-āṟvār, told in the form of a cradle-song. Edited by Pichuv-Ayyaṅgār.] pp. 25. திருநெல்வேலி [*Tinnevelli,*] 1900. 8°. **14170. ee. 35.(8.)**

ÑĀNA-KAṆṆĀḌI. ஞானக்கண்ணாடி. [Ñāna-kaṇ-ṇāḍi. A book of devotional readings for Roman Catholic teaching.] pp. 126, i. புதுவை தூஅாருஅ [*Pondicherry,* 1858.] 12°. **14170. b. 29.(2.)**

ÑĀNA-KUMMI. ஞானக்கும்மி. [Ñāna-kummi. A Şaiva poem.] pp. 24. *See* Siddhargaḷ. ◦◦◦ பெரிய ஞானக்கோவை [Periya-ñāna-kōvai.] 1899. 12°. **14170. ee. 33.**

—— —— pt. i., pp. 106-132. 1906. 12°. **14170. dd. 12.**

ÑĀNA-KŪTTA SVĀMI, *Şivanbākkam.* விருத்தாசலபுராணம். [Vṛuttāchala-purāṇam. The legends of the Şaiva sanctuary of Vṛuttāchalam, between the Kaveri and Trinomali, in 18 cantos and 435 stanzas. With commentary by Pāri-pākkam Muniy-appa Mudaliyār. Third edition.] pp. 142. [*Madras,*] 1874. 8°. **14170. e. 4.**

ÑĀNA-MAṆI NĀḌĀR, *C.* தமிழ் இலக்கண சிந்தாமணி. An explanatory Tamil Grammar, with notes, exercises and an appendix containing many useful facts. For use in the lower secondary classes. By C. Gnanamani. New edition. pp. ii. 120. *Madras,* 1893. 12°. **14172. e. 23.**

ÑĀNA-MUTTU NĀḌĀR, *Y.* Shanars are Kshatriyas, being a reply to the objectionable statements made by Chenthinatha Iyer regarding the Shanars, by Y. Gnanamuthoo Nadar . . . சாணார் க்ஷத்திரியர். [With a preface in English and Tamil, and an appendix of documents in both languages.] pp. xxvii. 140, 47. *Madras,* 1889. 12°. **14170. k. 47.**

ÑĀNĀNANDA SVĀMI, *Atyāşrama Bāla-sarasvati.* ◦◦◦ ஸ்ரீபஞ்சாக்ஷரரகசியம். [Pañchākshara-rahasyam, or Añj'-eṟutt'-uṇmai. A treatise on the mystic significance of the formula *namaş-şivāya.* Followed by a Sanskrit acrostic on the same words, entitled Şiva-pañchāksharī-stōtram.] pp. 43. சென்னை விகாரி [*Madras,* 1900.] 16°. **14170. d. 35.(7.)**

ÑĀNA-PRAKĀŞAM PIḶḶAI, *M. J.* நூதன அர்ச். இஸ்தாக்கியார் நாடகம். [Nūtana-archya-şishṭa-istākkiyār-nāṭakam. A drama upon the legend of St. Eustace. Edited by Ş. Madurai-muttu Piḷḷai.] pp. 7, 240. சென்னை [*Madras,*] 1896. 8°. **14170. l. 44.**

ÑĀNA-PRAKĀŞA MUDALIYĀR, *Puduvai.* A Sketch of Ancient History; with a version of the same in Tamil, by P. Gnanapragasa, Moodaliar (*ஆதிகாலச்சரித்திரச் சங்கிரகம்). pp. 39, 39. *Madras,* 1828. 8°. **14170. k. 11.**

—— A Summary of the History of Hindoost'han, from the Mahomedan invasion, [in English] with a Tamil translation, by P. Gnanapragasa, Moodeliar (இந்துஸ்தானிச்சரித்திரச் சங்கிரகம்). pp. 89, 89. *Vepery,* 1830. 8°. **14170. k. 12.**

ÑĀNA-PRAKĀŞA MUNIVAR, *Tiruvaṇṇāmalai.* *See* Aruṇandi Dēva-nāyanār. சிவஞானசித்தியார் ஷ [Şiva-ñāna-siddhiyār-supakkam. With commentary of Ñāna-prakāşar.] [1888.] 8°. **14170. ee. 10.**

ÑĀNA-PRAKĀŞA-NĀTHAR, *Ş.* *See* Jesus Christ. De Imitatione Christi, *etc.* [Translated by Ñāna-prakāşa-nāthar.] [1863.] 16°. **14170. a. 20.**

ÑĀNA-PRAKĀŞA-NĀTHA SVĀMI, *Rāyapuram T. M.* *See* Aṇḍa-piṇḍa-vyākhyānam. அண்டபிண்ட வியாக்கியானம். [Aṇḍa-piṇḍa-vyākhyā-nam. Edited by Ñāna-prakāşa-nātha.] 1874. 12°. **14170. i. 11.**

—— *See* Liturgies.—Rome, *Church of.* செபத்-

தியானக்குறள். [Şoba-dhyāna-kuraḷ. Edited by Ñāna-prakāṣa-nātha.] 1878. 16°. **14170. a. 44.**

ÑĀNA-PRAKĀṢA SVĀMI. *See* BERTOLDI (C. M.).

ÑĀNA-PRAKĀṢIYĀR, *Archya-ṣishṭa.* *See* LOUIS [GONZAGA], *Saint.*

ÑĀNA-SĀGARAM. ஞானசாகரவெண்பா. [Ñāna-sāgara-veṇ-bā. 100 Ṣaiva verses.] pp. 14. 1898. *See* VĒDĀCHALAM PIḶḶAI, *N.* சித்தாந்தஞான-போதம். [Siddhānta-ñāna-bōdham.] pt. i. 1898. 8°. **14170. ee. 39.**

ÑĀNA-SAMBANDHAR. [For the legends relating to Ñāna-sambandhar contained in the Periya-purāṇam :] *See* ṢEKKIṚĀR.

—— *See* ṢEKKIṚĀR. ∘∘∘ திருஞானசம்பந்த . . . புராணவசனம். [Tiru-ñāna-sambandha-mūrtti-nāyanār-purāṇa-vachanam. A history of Ñāna-sambandhar, abridged from the Periya-purāṇam.] 1900. 8°. **14170. e. 47.(10.)**

—— *See* SUNDARAM PIḶḶAI, *Ā. P.* Some Mile Stones in the History of Tamil Literature found in an enquiry into the age of Tiru Gnana Sambandha. 1895. 8°. **11825. c. 23.(9.)**

—— [For editions of the Dēvāram ascribed to Ñāna-sambandhar, Sundara-mūrtti, and Tiru-nāvukk'-araṣu :] *See* TIRU-MURAI.

ÑĀNA - SAMBANDHAR, *disciple of Nirambav-aṛagiya Dēṣikar.* *See* TIRUVARUR. திருவாரூர்ப்-புராணம். [Tiruvārūr-purāṇam. Translated into Tamil verse by Ñāna-sambandhar.] [1895.] 8°. **14170. e. 59.**

ÑĀNA-SAMBANDHA-SVĀMI PIḶḶAI. *See* TIRU-ÑĀNA-SAMBANDHA-SVĀMI PIḶḶAI.

ÑĀNA - SARA - NŪL. ஞானசரநூல் சாஸ்திரம். [Ñāna-sara-nūl-ṣāstram. A Ṣaiva tract on divination from the breath, *etc.*, with prose paraphrase.] pp. 48. *See* SIDDHARGAḶ. ∘∘∘ பெரிய ஞானக்கோவை [Periya-ñāna-kōvai.] pt. ii. 1899. 12°. **14170. ee. 33.**

—— —— pt. ii. 1906. 12°. **14170. dd. 12.**

—— —— *See* [Addenda] AGASTYAR. பஞ்சபட்-சிசாஸ்திரம் ௵ [Pañcha-pakshi-ṣāstram.] 1907. 8°. **14170. i. 3.**

ÑĀNA - SAUNDARI. ஞானசவுந்தரி அம்மானை. [Ñāna-saundari-ammānai. A series of Roman Catholic songs in honour of a female saint.] pp. 94. [*Jaffna,*] 1888. 12°. **14170. a. 35.(1.)**

—— —— [Second edition.] pp. 106. *Jaffna,* 1892. 8°. **14170. c. 39.**

ÑĀNA-SIDDHA SVĀMI, *Tirukurugūr.* திருமலைப்-பதிகம். [Tirumalai-padigam. Ṣaiva verses.] pp. 12. திருநெல்வேலி [*Tinnevelli,*] 1902. 12°. **14170. d. 88.**

—— ∘∘∘ சடாதாரவிளக்கமென்னும் திருமந்-திரம் இருநூறு. [Tiru-mantram, or Shaḍ-ādhāra-viḷakkam. Ṣaiva devotional lyrics, in 200 stanzas. With prefatory matter by divers authors, including a Sanskrit metrical life of the author. Second edition.] pp. i. xiii. 36. சென்னை விஜய [*Madras,* 1894.] 12°. **14170. d. 46.(1.)**

ÑĀNA-ṢIKHĀMAṆI PIḶḶAI, *of Tanjore.* The Identity of Popery and Heathenism. இருசமய-சம்பந்தம் ௵. pp. viii. 82. *Madras,* 1850. 16°. **14170. a. 33.(1.)**

ÑĀNA-UPADĒṢAM. *See* CATECHISM.

ÑĀNAV-UṆARTTUDAL. ஞானவுணர்த்துதல். [Ñānav-uṇarttudal. A Roman Catholic tract for purposes of propaganda, ascribed to Beschi.] pp. vi. 99. புதுவை ௲௮௱௪௰௨ [*Pondicherry,* 1842.] 12°. **14170. a. 21.(2.)**

NANDAN. நந்தமண்டலசதகம். மூலம் . . . உரை. [Nanda-maṇḍala-ṣatakam. A century of verses upon Nandan, a legendary king said to have issued leather coin. With commentary by Brahmapuri P. Tiru-vēṅkaṭam Piḷḷai.] pt. 1. pp. 32. சென்னை [*Madras,*] 1894. 8°. **14170. k. 37.**

Nandan is said to have been a cobbler, and reigned for three hours.

ÑĀNIYĀR ṢĀHIB VALI-ALLĀH. *See* MUHYI al-DĪN MALUK MUDALIYĀR, *Kōṭṭāṟu, the Elder.*

NAÑ-JĪYAR, *disciple of Parāṣara Bhaṭṭar.* *See* ĀṚVĀRGAḶ.—Nāl-āyiram.—*Periya-tiru-moṛi.* ∘∘∘ பெரிய திருமொழி ௵ [Periya-tiru-moṛi. With commentaries of Nañ-jīyar, *etc.*] 1881. 8°. **14170. f. 7.**

—— ∘∘∘ ఆత్మవివాహం, ముముక్షుకృత్యం, సామగ్రీ-పరంపరానాథం, అవస్థాత్రయం . . . పరందరహస్యము. [Ātma-vivāham, Mumukshu-kṛutyam, Sāmagrīparamparā-nādham, and Avasthā-trayam. Four Vaishṇava tracts of Nañ-jīyar. Followed by the Paranda-rahasyam of Periyav-āchān Piḷḷai. Edited by P. Tiru-vēṅkaṭāchāryar, K. P. Anantāchāryar, and T. Ṣēshādriy-āchāryar.] pp. 16, 29, 64. బళ్ళారి [Bellary,] 1893. 8°. **14170. ee. 40.**

NAPPŪDANĀR. முல்லைப்பாட்டு. [Mullai-pāṭṭu. A poem, no. 5 of the Pattu-pāṭṭu, describing the sorrow of a queen in the absence of her husband, and his return from the war. With Nachinārkk'-iniyar's commentary.] See PATTU-PĀṬṬU. பத்துப்பாட்டு ௸ [Pattu-pāṭṭu.] pp. 145-157. 1889. 8°. **14172. d. 10.**

NARA-SIṂHA BHĀRATI, *Tirunayam, of Anbil-alan-durai.* See PURĀṆAS.—*Ṣiva-purāṇam.* அன்பிலாலந்துறை . . . மான்மியம். [Prēmapuri-sthala-mānmiyam. In a Tamil paraphrase by Nara-siṃha and Kṛushṇa Bhārati.] [1895.] 12°. **14170. d. 42.**

NARA-SIMMA BHĀGAVATA-SVĀMI, *Tiruneytā-nam.* ஸத்குரு தியாகராஜஸ்வாமி சரித்திரம். (Thiyagarajaswamy Charithiram.) [Tyāga-rāja-svāmi-charitram. A biography of Tiruvaiyāṛu Rāma-brahmam Tyāga-rāja-svāmi, a devout Vaishṇava poet and musician.] pp. i. 16. கும்பகோணம் [Kumbakonam,] 1906. 12°. **14171. a. 48.(3.)**

NARA-SIMM'-ĀCHĀRI, *Ṣēṭlūr.* See SAURA BRAHMANS. அதர்வணவேத . . . ஹவ்யகவ்ய விதிகள். [Havya-kavya-vidhigaḷ. Edited by Nara-simm'-āchāri.] 1906. 8°. **14033. bbb. 36.**

NARA-SIMM'-AIYAR, *Maṇañjēri Mūrtti-rām'-aiyar.* அரிச்சந்திரோபாக்யான நாடகாலங்காரமென்னும் கீர்த்தனை. [Hariṣchandrōpākhyāna-nāṭakālaṅkāram, or °kīrttanai. A lyrical drama on the legend of the truthful Hariṣchandra. A new edition based on that of A. Vīrā-sāmi Nāyuḍu.] pp. 374. யுவ [Madras, 1875.] 8°. **14172. b. 13.**

NARA-SIMMALU NĀYUḌU, *Sēlam Pagaḍāla.* See SANDHYĀ-VANDANAM. ஆரியர் சந்தியாவந்தனம் ௸ [Āryar-sandhyā-vandanam. With Tamil version, etc., by Nara-simmalu.] 1898. 8°. **14170. e. 47.(8.)**

—— See UPANISHADS. இந்து பைபில் ௸ (The Hindu Holy Bible . . . Compiled by S. P. Nara-simmalu Nayudu.) 1898. 8°. **14170. ee. 15.**

—— —— 1906. 8°. **14007. b. 31.**

NARA-SIMMALU NĀYUḌU, *Sēlam Pagaḍāla (continued).* அத்துவைதாதுவைத விசிஷ்டாத்துவைதசித்தாந்த சாரசங்கிரஹ வினா விடை. [Advaita-dvaita-viṣishṭādvaita-siddhānta-sāra-saṅgraha-vinā-viḍai. Catechisms of the three philosophical systems, in Tamil and English.] pp. 64. கோயமுத்தூர் [Coimbatore,] 1897. 8°. **14170. ee. 13.**

—— ஆரியர் திவ்ய தேச யாத்திரை சரித்திரம். [Āryar-divya-dēsa-yātrai-charitram. An account of a journey through Northern India.] pp. 31, 320, 7. கோயமுத்தூர் [Coimbatore,] 1889. 8°. **14170. e. 34.**

—— ஆரியருடைய சங்கீத சாஸ்திரத்தின் சரித்திரம். [Āryar-uḍaiya saṅgīta-ṣāstrattin charitram.] (A Lecture on Ariyan Music, delivered on . . . the third anniversary of the Coimbatore Sūdasa Dharma Ratchini Sabha.) pp. ii. 24. *Coimbatore,* 1886. 8°. **14170. i. 19.(1.)**

—— பலிஜவாரு புராணம் ௸ [Balijavāru-purāṇam, or Vaṃṣa-prakāṣikai and Nāyaḍugāru-saṃsthāna-charitram.] (A brief Sketch of the Origin and History of the Balija Caste People or Nayudu Community.) pt. i. pp. 8, 8, lxviii. 51. *Coimbatore,* 1896. 8°. **14170. g. 20.**

—— ஸ்ரீ . . . பலிஜவாரு புராணம் அல்லது நாயடுகாரு சமஸ்தான சரித்திரம். [Balijavāru-purāṇam. Second edition.] pp. ii. 32, 16, 48, 128, 52, 226, 32, 72, 24, 8. கோயமுத்தூர் [Coimbatore,] 1905. 8°. **14171. e. 10.**

In the pagination, p. 194 b immediately succeeds p. 103 b, but the text is quite complete.

—— தக்ஷிண இந்தியாவின் சரித்திரசாரசங்கிரஹம் . . . A History on [sic] South India, etc. கோயமுத்தூர் சென்னை [Coimbatore, Madras,] 1905, etc. 8°. **14171. e. 6.**

In progress.

—— பிரஹ்ம சமய வினாவிடை அல்லது பூர்வ இந்துசமயம். (மதவிருக்ஷம்.) (Hinduism . . . or . . . The Great Religions of the World.) [Vol. i., Pūrva-hindu-samayam, or Brahma-samaya-vinā-viḍai, a theistic catechism; vol. ii., Mata-vṛuksham, an outline of the different Hindu sects.] 2 vols. *Coimbatore,* 1882-1883. 16°. **14170. d. 7.**

—— . . . ஸ்ரீகாஞ்சிபுரத்தின் மஹத்துவம். [Kāñchi-purattin mahattvam. A description of the sanctuary of Vishṇu at Conjevaram.] pp. 30. கோயமுத்தூர் [*Coimbatore*,] 1884. 8°. **14172. c. 12.(1.)**

—— பெண்களின் சரித்திரம். (The History and Philosophy of the Female Sex; or the gradual Progress of Women, towards Civilization . . . by S. P. Narasimhalu Naidoo.) pp. 25. *Coimbatore*, 1883. 16°. **14171. aa. 10.**

—— ◦◦◦ ஸ்ரீபெரும்பூதூரின் மஹத்துவம். [Perumbūdūrin mahattvam. A description of the sanctuary of Vishṇu at Perumbudur.] pp. 19. கோயமுத்தூர் [*Coimbatore*,] 1884. 8°. **14172. c. 12.(2.)**

—— ◦◦◦ ஸ்ரீரங்கக்ஷேத்ரமஹாத்வம் [*sic*]. [Śrīraṅga-kshētra-mahattvam. An account of the history, antiquities, calendar, *etc.*, of the Vaishṇava sanctuary at Srirangam.] pp. 98. கோயமுத்தூர் [*Coimbatore*,] 1898. 8°. **14170. ee. 35.(3.)**

—— ◦◦◦ திருப்பதி வேங்கடேசர் மஹத்துவம். [Tirupadi-vēṅkaṭēṣar-mahattvam. A panegyrical account of the sanctuary of Vishṇu at Tirupati.] pp. 42. கோயமுத்தூர் [*Coimbatore*,] 1884. 8°. **14172. c. 12.(3.)**

—— ஸ்ரீஉத்தர மதுரா கோகுலங் கோவர்த்தனம் பிருந்தாவன மஹாத்துவம் [*sic*]. [Uttara-mathurā-gōkulaṅ-gōvardhanam-bṛundāvana-mahattvam. An account of the Vaishṇava sacred places of Mathura, Gokul, Gobardhan, and Brindaban.] pp. ii. iv. 105. கோயமுத்தூர் [*Coimbatore*,] 1889. 8°. **14170. e. 35.**

—— (†வேதப்பொருள் சாரசங்கிரகம்.) [Vēda-poruḷ-sāra-saṅgraham. An epitome of the Vedas, Brāhmaṇas, Sūtras, and Upanishads, read before the Brāhma Samāj at Coimbatore, Oct. 15, 1896.] pp. 16. *Coimbatore*, [1896.] 8°. **14172. b. 44.(8.)**

Without title-page.

NĀRĀYAṆA, *son of Śrī ratnākara*. *See* UPANISHADS. ◦◦◦ நூற்றெட்டு உபநிஷத்துகள். [Nūṭṭ'-eṭṭu Upanishattugaḷ. With extracts from the commentaries of Nārāyaṇa, translated into Tamil.] 1887. 8°. **14010. dd. 2.**

NĀRĀYAṆA AIYAR. மனவுல்லாசகதை. [Manavullāsa-kathai. A series of stories.] pp. ii. 172. *Madras*, 1901. 8°. **14171. a. 43.**

NĀRĀYAṆA BHĀRATI. ◦◦◦ கோவிந்தசதகம். [Gōvinda-ṣatakam. A century of Vaishṇava verses.] pp. 22. 1906. *See* RĀMA-SĀMI NĀYUḌU, *K*. சதகத்திரட்டு. [Ṣataka-tiraṭṭu.] pt. 5. 1905-1906. 12°. **14170. dd. 10.**

NĀRĀYAṆA BHĀRATI, *Veṇmaṇi*. ◦◦◦ மணவாளநாராயணசதகம் என்னும் திருவேங்கடசதகம். [Tiru-vēṅkaṭa-ṣatakam, or Maṇavāḷa-nārāyaṇa-ṣ°. A century of panegyrical verses upon a certain Maṇavāḷa Nārāyaṇa.] pp. 62. 1905. *See* RĀMA-SĀMI NĀYUḌU, *K*. சதகத்திரட்டு. [Ṣataka-tiraṭṭu.] pt. 3. 1905-1906. 12°. **14170. dd. 10.**

NĀRĀYAṆA-DĀS, *Dēvēndrapuram*. *See* SAṄGĪTAM. Tamil Sungeatha Surabooshany, *etc.* [Translated by Nārāyaṇa-dās and Aruṇāchalam Piḷḷai.] 1900. 8°. **14170. i. 68.**

NĀRĀYAṆA-DĀSAR, *Puduvai, disciple of Tirukōvalūr Śrīnivāsāchāryar*. *See* KAMBAN. ஸ்ரீராமாயண ஷு [Rāmāyaṇa-vachanam. Edited by Nārāyaṇa-dāsar.] 1903. 8°. **14172. d. 27.**

—— *See* KUMĀRA-SĀMI UPĀDHYĀYAR, *K*. இரணியவிலாசம். [Hiraṇya-vilāsam. Edited by Nārāyaṇa-dāsar.] 1899. 8°. **14170. l. 50.**

—— *See* MAHĀ-BHAKTA-VIJAYAM. ◦◦◦ ஸ்ரீமகாபக்தவிஜயம். [Mahā-bhakta-vijayam. Vol. i., edited by Nārāyaṇa-dāsar. Vol. ii., iii., translated by the same.] 1898-1905. 4°. **14170. f. 6.**

—— *See* VĒMANA. மகா . . . வேமன்னபத்தியம் ஷு [Vēmanna-padyam. Edited with translation by Nārāyaṇa-dāsar.] 1903, *etc.* 8°. **14175. a. 12.**

—— A story of the victorious Sountharavally. ஜெயங்கொண்ட சௌந்தரவல்லிக்கதை. [Jayaṅ-goṇḍa-saundaravalli-kathai.] pp. 200; 1 *plate*. *Madras*, 1902. 8°. **14170. k. 74.**

NĀRĀYAṆA PIḶḶAI, *Vallipuram Chidambaranātha*. விட்டுணுதூஷணபரிகாரம். [Viṭṭuṇu-dūshaṇa-parihāram. A defence of the cult of Vishṇu against worshippers of Śiva.] pp. 47. சென்னை [*Madras*,] 1885. 16°. **14170. d. 9.**

NĀRĀYAṆA-SĀMI, *V. M.* Select Tamil Tales, with free translations in English and Teloogoo, to which are added a vocabulary . . . in English and Teloogoo, and a choice number of Dr. Marsh-

man's dialogues, in English and Tamil, by W. M. Narrainsawmy. pp. 190. *Madras*, 1839. 8°.
14170. k. 66.

—— Second edition. pp. 157. *Madras*, 1853. 8°.
14170. k. 75.

NĀRĀYAṆA-SĀMI AIYAR, *of Periya-tirukōṇam.* விநாயகப்பிரதிஷ்டை. [Vināyaka-pratishṭhai. Three religious poems, for the ritual of the god Vināyaka.] pp. 16. திருவாதி [*Tiruvadi*,] 1894. 16°.
14170. d. 35.(5.)

NĀRĀYAṆA-SĀMI AIYAR, *Neḍuvai Aṇṇā-sāmi.* சங்கிரக இராமாயணம். [Saṅgraha-rāmāyaṇam. A poem on the legend of the Rāmāyaṇam.] pp. viii. iv. 172, i. மதுரை [*Madura*,] 1905. 8°.
14172. bb. 19.

NĀRĀYAṆA-SĀMI AIYAR, *Pinnattūr A.* See Ādiy-appanār. ◦◦◦ திருக்களர்ப்புராணம். [Tiru-kaḷar-purāṇam. Edited by Nārāyaṇa-sāmi.] 1902. 12°.
14170. ee. 55.

—— ◦◦◦ மாணக்கராற்றுப்படை. [Māṇākkar-āṯṯu-paḍai. A poem in praise of the Kumbakonam Town High School.] pp. 13. கும்பகோணம் [*Kumbakonam*,] 1900. 12°.
14172. a. 45.(3.)

—— தில்லைவளாகம் ஸ்ரீ. வீரகோதண்டராமஸ்வாமி உலா. [Ulā, or elegies upon the cult of Tillai-vaḷāgam Vīra-kōdaṇḍa-Rāma-svāmi, a modern incarnation of Vishṇu, born in 1862.] pp. v. 84. கும்பகோணம் [*Kumbakonam*,] 1902. 12°.
14172. a. 53.

NĀRĀYAṆA-SĀMI AIYAR, *Ṣ., of Government College, Kumbakonam.* See Shakspere (W.). Shakespeare's Midsummer Night's Dream. Translated . . . by S. Narayanaswamy Aiyer. 1893. 8°.
14170. l. 32.(1.)

NĀRĀYAṆA-SĀMI NĀYAKAR, *L., disciple of Ñānānanda-nāthar.* குருவருட்பேறு. [Guruv-aruṭ-pēṟu. Devotional poems, forming the second Tiru-muṟai of the Anubhavānanda-dīpikai.] pp. ii. ii. 64. சென்னை [*Madras*,] 1896. 8°.
14170. ee. 23.

NĀRĀYAṆA-SĀMI NĀYUḌU, *Puduvai P.* சாரங்கதரன் சரித்திரப்பா. [Sāraṅgadharan-charitra-pā. A drama on the story of the chaste prince Sāraṅgadhara.] pp. ii. 146. சென்னை [*Madras*,] 1899. 8°.
14170. l. 51.

NĀRĀYAṆA-SĀMI PIḶḶAI, *Triṣirapuram Gōvinda, of Bangalore.* சித்திராங்காட்டிச்சத்தியம் நிறுத்தியகதை [Chitraṅgāṭṭi-satyam niṟuttiya kathai. A series of light stories.] pp. 88. பெங்களூர் [*Bangalore*,] 1879. 8°.
14170. k. 18.

—— ◦◦◦ மங்களவல்லிவிலாசம் [Maṅgaḷa-valli-vilāsam. A drama on womanly virtue.] pp. vi. 168. பெங்களூர் ௲அ௱அ௨ [*Bangalore*, 1882.] 8°.
14170. l. 14.

—— [Second edition.] pp. vi. 243. சென்னை [*Madras*,] 1893. 8°.
14170. l. 43.

—— ம-ா-ா-ஸ்ரீ . . . மெய்கண்டதேவமுதலியார் . . . கீர்த்திமாலை. (Garland of Fame of Rao Bahadur Maikandadeva Mudaliar . . . [A series of panegyric verses] by T. C. Narayanasawmy Pillay.) pp. 8. *Madras*, 1901. 8°.
14172. bb. 3.(3.)

—— Installation of his Highness Sri Krishna-rajendra Wodayar Bahadur, Maharaja of Mysore, and the Dasara Festivities. A poem in Tamil, with an English translation [by T. R. Veṅkaṭa-sāmi Nāyuḍu. Followed by Maisūr-prabhu-mālai, "The Garland of the Great Men of Mysore," a series of panegyric verses]. (மைசூர் சமஸ்தானம் மகாராஜா ஸ்ரீகிருஷ்ணராஜ வுடையார் பகதூரவர்கள் பட்டாபிஷேகம்.) pp. 4, iv. 52, 2, 13; 1 *plate*. *Madras*, 1903. 12°. **14172. bb. 8.**

NĀRĀYAṆA ṢĀSTRI, *T. Ṣ.* போஜசரித்திரம் ௵ [Bhōja-charitram. A drama on the life of king Bhoja of Dhara. With an English introduction.] (*Vidvan Mano Ranjani Series.) pp. ii. xvii. 2, ii. 355, 8. சென்னை [*Madras*,] 1900. 8°.
14170. l. 52.

NARĒNDRA-NĀTHA DATTA. *See* Vivēkānanda, *Svāmi.*

NĀṞ-KAVI-RĀJA NAMBI. [For the Tañjai-vāṇan-kōvai, illustrating the rules for expressing erotic sentiment given in this writer's Aga-poruḷ-viḷak-kam :] *See* Poyyā-moṟi Pulavar.

—— பொருளதிகாரம் அகப்பொருள்விளக்கம் [Aga-poruḷ-viḷakkam. Rules for erotic verse.] *See* Tāṇḍava-rāya Mudaliyār. இலக்கணப்பஞ்சக ௵ [Nan-nūl, *etc.*] pp. 34-59. [1835.] 8°.
14172. e. 3.

NĀṞ-KAVI-RĀJA NAMBI (*continued*). ∘∘∘ அகப்பொருள்விளக்கமூலமும் . . . உரையும். [Aga-poruḷ-viḷakkam. With a commentary by V. Ṣ. Vaidya-liṅga Piḷḷai.] pp. iv. ii. 148, ii. *Madras*, 1878. 8°. **14172. e. 34.**

—— Uebersetzung von Nampi's Akapporuḷ Viḷakkam. (†Von Dr. Graul.) 1857. *See* ACADEMIES, *etc.*—Germany.—*Deutsche Morgenlaendische Gesellschaft.* Zeitschrift, *etc.* Bd. xi. pp. 369-395. 1846, *etc.* 4°. **Ac. 8815/2.(Bd. 11.)**

NAṞKĪRAR. *See* NAKKĪRA DĒVAR.

NARRAINSAWMY. *See* NĀRĀYAṆA-SĀMI.

NAṬA-RĀJA AIYAR, *Iṇūvil.* *See* ARUṆANDI DĒVA-NĀYANĀR. சிவஞானசித்தியார் ஸூ [Ṣiva-ñāna-siddhiyār-supakkam. With commentary. Edited by Naṭa-rāja.] [1888.] 8°. **14170. ee. 10.**

NAṬA-RĀJA AIYAR, *Marudūr Veṅkaṭa-rāma.* தேவி சந்திரப்ரபா. (Devi Chandraprabah. A highly interesting novel in Tamil.) pp. i. 130. *Madras*, 1902. 8°. **14171. a. 50.(1.)**

—— ஞானபூஷணி. (Gnana Bhooshani, or The Lover of Wisdom.) [A novel.] pp. i. 192. *Madras*, 1896. 8°. **14171. a. 11.**

—— லோகோபகாரிப்பிரசுரங்கள் எனும் ஞானதரிசனி. (Guana-darisani. Selections of Vedanta religious teachings.) [Second edition.] pp. 112. *Madras*, 1900. 8°. **14170. ee. 28.(5.)**
The wrapper bears the date 1899.

—— லலிதாங்கி. (Lalithangi. An interesting Tamil novel.) pp. i. 102. *Madras*, 1902. 8°. **14170. k. 24.(2.)**

—— நிர்மலா. (Nirmala. An interesting Tamil novel.) pp. 96. *Madras*, 1903. 8°. **14171. e. 1.**

—— ∘∘∘ தத்துவதரிசனி. (Tatwa-darisani. Selections of Vedanta religious teachings.) pp. i. 95. *Madras*, 1899. 8°. **14170. e. 31.(2.)**

NAṬA-RĀJ'-AIYAR, *Nallūr Ṣ.* *See* BHŌJA-RĀJA PAṆḌITAR. சாரசோதிமாலை ஸூ [Chara-jōdi-mālai. Edited by Naṭa-rāj'-aiyar.] [1892.] 8°. **14170. i. 23.**

NAṬA-RĀJAR, *Kīranūr.* சாதகாலங்காரம். [Jātakālaṅkāram. A metrical work on astrology. Edited by K. V. Āṟu-muga Mudaliyār.] pp. ii. 171. [*Madras*, 1867?] 8°. **14170. i. 9.**

NAṬA-RĀJAR, *Kīranūr* (*continued*). Jathakalankaram . . . சாதகாலங்காரம் மூலமும் உரையும் [With a prose paraphrase by M. Vaḍi-vēlu Mudaliyār.] pp. 10, 349, 3. *Madras*, 1902. 8°. **14171. g. 4.**

NAṬA-RĀJA SVĀMI, *Tillai.* *See* PUGAḺĒNDI. ∘∘∘ அல்லியரசாணிமாலை. [Alliy-araṣāni-mālai. Edited by Naṭa-rāja.] [1884.] 8°. **14172. b. 30.**

NAṬĒSA AIYAR, *M.Ṣ.* *See* CHAUCER (G.). The Canterbury Tales. Chaucer's Life and the Clerk's Tale . . . Tamil translation. [By] M.S. Natesa Aiyar. 1904. 12°. **14171. d. 1.(2.)**

NATESAN, *M.* *See* NAṬĒṢA PIḶḶAI, *Maṅgāṇam.*

NAṬĒṢA PIḶḶAI, *Maṅgāṇam.* The Wonders of Science; being a manual of philosophical sports and pastimes, calculated to instruct and amuse the young. சாஸ்திர விசித்திரம். (The Sastra Vichitram; or, Wonders of Science, containing a series of most interesting and instructive experiments in every branch of science . . . to which is added a collection of the most curious and entertaining verbal puzzles and recreations in numbers. By M. Natesan. With illustrations. First series.) pp. 2, 80. *Madras*, 1898. 8°. **14170. i. 55.(1.)**

NAṬĒṢA PIḶḶAI, *Ṣ., of "Ārya-dharma-paripālana Sabhā," Palghat.* *See* CHIDAMBARA KAVI-RĀYAR. உசிதசூடாமணி நிகண்டு. (†"Oositha Soodamani Nigandu," *etc.*) [Edited by Naṭēṣa.] 1903. 12°. **14172. ee. 10.**

NAṬĒṢA ṢĀSTRI, *Ṣaṅgēndi Mahā-liṅgam.* *See* KĀLIDĀSA. இரகுவம்சம் ஸூ [Raghu-vaṃṣam. Translated into prose by Naṭēṣa.] 1901, *etc.* 8°. **14172. bb. 2.**

—— *See* KINGSCOTE (G.), *Mrs.*, and NAṬĒṢA ṢĀSTRI, *Ṣ. M.* Tales of the Sun, *etc.* 1890. 8°. **12431. c. 40.**

—— *See* MADANA-KĀMA-RĀJAN. The Dravidian Nights Entertainments . . . a translation . . . By . . . Natesa Sastri. 1886. 12°. **14170. k. 38.**

—— *See* NĀLU-MANTRI-KATHAI. The King and his Four Ministers . . . translated . . . by . . . Natesa Sastri, *etc.* 1888. 12°. **14170. k. 48.(1.)**

—— *See* NĀLU-MANTRI-KATHAI. The King and his Four Ministers [translated by Naṭēṣa.] 1889. 8°. [*A Group of Eastern Romances.*] **14003. h. 21.**

NATĒṢA ṢĀSTRI, *Ṣaṅgēndi Mahā-liṅgam (continued)*. *See* ṢŪDRAKA. Mrichhakati. [Translated] by ... Natesa, *etc.* 1887. 12°. **14170. k. 1.(2.)**

—— *See* TENNĀLU-RĀMAN. Tales of Tennalirama ... [Translated] by ... Natesa Sastri. 1900. 12°. **14171. a. 6.(4.)**

—— *See* VĀLMĪKI. வால்மீகிராமாயண ஞூ [Rāmāyaṇam. Translated into prose by Naṭēṣa.] 1901, *etc.* 8°. **14172. c. 42.**

—— Dinadayalu. A novel ... Second edition, revised and enlarged. (Pandit Natesa Sastri's Popular Novels. 1. ... தீனதயாளு.) pp. viii. 193. *Madras*, 1902. 12°. **14171. a. 42.(3.)**

—— Folklore in Southern India. [Compiled and translated into English by Naṭēṣa.] 4 pts. pp. 502, ix. vii. *Bombay*, 1884-1893. 12°. **14170. k. 59.**

—— Folklore in Southern India. In Tamil ... திராவிட பூர்வகாலக் கதைகள். pp. viii. 165. *Madras*, 1886. 12°. **14170. k. 1.(1.)**

—— —— [Another edition.] pp. vi. 170. *Madras*, 1897. 12°. **14171. a. 18.(1.)**

—— A Handbook of Sanitary Science ... சுக-சந்தர்சனதீபிகை. pp. 141. 1905. *See* ACADEMIES, *etc.*—*Madura.* ["Ṣen-damiẓ" supplement.] no. 17. 1902, *etc.* 8°. **14172. i. 1.*(no. 17.)**

—— Measure for Measure, a tale from Shakespeare, in Tamil ... தன்னுயிரைப்போல மன்னுயிரை நினை. pp. 15. *Madras*, 1893. 12°. **14171. a. 6.(1.)**

Reprinted from the Janavinodini.

—— Mediæval Tales of Southern India, in Tamil ... திராவிட மத்தியகாலக் கதைகள். pp. i. i. 134. *Madras*, 1886. 8°. **14170. k. 39.**

—— Mediæval Tales of Southern India ... திராவிட மத்தியகாலக் கதைகள். pp. v. 192. *Madras*, 1897. 12°. **14171. a. 18.(2.)**

An enlarged edition of the work published in 1886.

—— The Mother-in-law in Council. An 18th century Hindu life novel. (Pandit Natesa Sastri's Popular Novels. 5. ... ஸ்ரீமாமி கொலுவிருக்கை.) pp. vi. 148; 1 *plate.* *Madras*, 1903. 12°. **14171. a. 49.(3.)**

—— Mudrarakshasam: a tale in Tamil, founded on the Sanskrit drama by Visakhadatta, the sixth of a series of tales from the Sanskrit Dramatists ... முத்திரா ராக்ஷஸம். pp. vi. 95. *Madras*, 1885. 12°. **14170. k. 40.**

—— Le Porteur de Sachet. Traduction [from an English redaction by Naṭēṣa in the "Indian Antiquary," vol. xvi.,] de J.-H. Rosny. Illustrations de Gambard et Marold. pp. ii. 139; 8 *plates.* *Paris*, 1892. 16°. **14171. aa. 13.**

Forms part of the "Petite Collection Guillaume.—Littérature hindoue."

—— The Rejuvenation of Komalam. A (farcical) romance. (Pandit Natesa Sastri's Popular Novels. 2. ... கோமளம் குமரியானது.) pp. v. i. 166. *Madras*, 1902. 12°. **14171. a. 42.(4.)**

—— Twelfth Night, or What You Will. [A prose abstract of Shakspere's play] in Tamil ... வயோலா சரித்திரம். pp. 26. *Coimbatore*, 1892. 12°. **14170. l. 1.(2.)**

—— The Two Orphans. A pathetic and moral story. (Pandit Natesa Sastri's Popular Novels. 3. ... திக்கற்ற இருகுழந்தைகள்.) pp. 4, i. 412. *Madras*, 1902. 12°. **14171. a. 49.(1.)**

—— A Wife Condoned. (Pandit Natesa Sastri's Popular Novels. 4. ... மதிகெட்ட மனைவி.) pp. iv. 298; 1 *plate.* *Madras*, 1903. 12°. **14171. a. 49.(2.)**

NĀTHA-MUNIGAḶ-TUDAKKAMĀNĀR. *See* PINB'-AẒAGIYA PERU-MĀḶ JĪYAR.

NATIVE EVANGELICAL SOCIETY. *See* JAFFNA.

NATTATTANĀR, *Nallūr.* சிறுபாணாற்றுப்படை. [Ṣiru-bāṇ-āṭṭu-paḍai. A poetical panegyric on King Nalliya-kōḍan of Ēṟu-mā-nāḍu, being no. 3 of the Pattu-pāṭṭu. With commentary of Nachi-nārkk'-iniyar.] *See* PATTU-PĀṬṬU. பத்துப்பாட்டு ஞூ [Pattu-pāṭṭu.] pp. 67-94. 1889. 8°. **14172. d. 10.**

NĀYCHIYĀR. *See* ĀṆḌĀḶ.

NEELAMAGHACHARIAR. *See* NĪLA-MĒGHĀCHĀRYAR.

NEGRO. The Negro Servant, or The Conversation ... சம்பாஷணை. [Translated into Tamil by W. Adley. Second edition.] pp. 15. *Jaffna*, 1844. 12°. **14170. b. 1.(34.)**

NELLORE. *See* MADRAS, *Presidency of.* A collection of the inscriptions ... in the Nellore district, *etc.* 1905. 8°. **14058. c. 11.**

NICHOLAS (Innocent). A Vocabulary of English and Tamil Words; to which are added a collection of familiar dialogues, the English grammar, and a few letters, &c. Sixth edition. pp. iv. 192. *Madras*, 1851. 8°. **14172. h. 22.**

NICOL (Thomas). *See* Bible.—*Appendix.* [*Complete Bibles.*] The Bible and Ancient Monuments, etc. (†Based chiefly on "Recent Archæology and the Bible," by Professor Nicol.) 1901. 12°. **14171. a. 45.**

NIGAMĀNTA-MAHĀ-DĒṢIKAR. *See* Vēṅkaṭa-nātha Vēdāntāchāryar.

NIJA-GUṆA YŌGI. A Synopsis of Hindu Systems and Sects. [Abridged from the Kanarese work of Nija-guṇa.] (†Vivēkachintāmani.) Translated from the Tamil, by the Rev. Thomas Foulkes. pp. 40. *Madras*, 1860. 8°. **14170. e. 36.(3.)**

NĪLA-KAṆṬHA DĪKSHITAR, *son of Nārāyaṇa.* ஸ்ரீ ... 𑌕𑌲𑌿𑌵𑌿𑌡𑌂𑌬𑌨𑌕𑌂 [Kali-viḍambanam. A Sanskrit poem on the evils of the age, with a Tamil translation by Ṣ. Kalyāṇa-sundara Ṣāstri, assisted by Ī. Varadāchāryar.] pp. 48. *Madras*, 1904. 16°. **14070. a. 9.(1.)**

—— 𑌸𑍍𑌵𑌯𑌂𑌕𑍃𑌤 ... 𑌶𑌾𑌨𑍍𑌤𑌿𑌵𑌿𑌲𑌾𑌸𑌃 [Ṣānti-vilāsa. A Sanskrit poem in 51 stanzas on spiritual enlightenment and calm. Edited by P. N. Rāmanātha Ṣāstri, with a Tamil paraphrase.] pp. 37. ஜெஙு॥ [*Madras*,] 1907. 8°. **14070. dd. 42.(3.)**

NĪLA-KAṆṬHA ṢIVĀCHĀRYAR. *See* Ṣrīkaṇṭha Ṣivāchāryar.

NĪLA-MĒGHĀCHĀRYAR, *V.* Who is the Proprietor of the Soil? A lecture ... by V. Neelamaghachariar. (*பூமியின் பிராசுபாத்தியம் எவருக்கு?) pp. 22. *Tanjore*, 1891. 12°. **14170. g. 28.**

Published as supplement to the Tañjai-jana-mitran.

NILES (Daniel Poor). *See* Wesley (J.). A collection of Hymns ... Translated into Tamil [by D. P. Niles and others]. 1881. 12°. **14170. bbb. 10.**

—— சிலுவையின் உபதேசம். [Ṣiluvaiyin upadēṣam.] (*A sermon [upon 1 Cor. i. 18] preached ... at Wesley Chapel Vannarponne at the opening of a special mission on October 28th 1892.) pp. 8. *Wesleyan Mission Press: Jaffna*, 1893. 16°. **14170. a. 57.(2.)**

NIRAMBAV-AṚAGIYA DĒṢIKAR, *Sētu-maḍālam.* *See* Umā-pati Ṣivāchāryar. ००० சிவப்பிரகாசம் ஸ [Siddhāntāshṭakam, comprising the Tiruv-aruṭ-payan, *etc.*, with commentaries founded upon those of Nirambav-aṛagiyar and others.] [1895.] 12°. **14170. d. 37.**

—— *See* Umā-pati Ṣivāchāryar. சிவப்பிரகாசம். [Siddhāntāshṭakam, viz. Tiruv-aruṭ-payan, with commentary of Nirambav-aṛagiyar, *etc.*] 1897. 8°. [*Mey-kaṇḍa-ṣāttiram.*] **14170. ff. 3.**

—— திருப்பரங்கிரிப் புராணவசனம். (*திருப்பரங்கிரிப் பிள்ளைத்தமிழ்.) [Tiru-paraṅ-giri-purāṇa-vachanam. A prose version, by M. R. Aruṇāchala Kavi-rāyar, of Nirambav-aṛagiyar's poem on the legends of Tiru-paraṅ-giri, sacred to Kumāra; with a short life of the poet and two poems by Ñāna-sambandhar and Sundara-mūrtti. Followed by Tiru-paraṅ-giri-piḷḷai-tamiṛ, a devotional composition by Aruṇāchala on the childhood of the god Kumāra as worshipped there.] pp. x. 90, 43. சென்னை விகாரி [*Madras*, 1899.] 12°. **14170. d. 70.**

NIṢCHALA DĀSA, *disciple of Dādū.* விசாரசாகரம் எனனும் வேதாந்தசாரசங்கிரகம். [Vichāra-sāgaram. An exposition of orthodox Vedantic monism. Translated from the Hindi of Niṣchala Dāsa by A. Ṣiva Rāu of Kuttalam, with a Brahma-ñāna-churukkam or synopsis of the Vēdāntam appended.] pp. 3, 8, 42, 403, 3, 5, i. 82, 41, v. கும்பகோணம் [*Kumbakonam*,] 1893. 8°. **14170. e. 53.**

—— ஸ்ரீ... ஸ்ரீவிசாரசாகரம். [Vichāra-sāgaram. Translated by A. Ṣiva-rāu. Edited by V. Kuppu-svāmi Rāju.] pp. 3, 2, 8, xlii. vii. 480, 40. தஞ்சை [*Tanjore*,] 1904. 8°. **14170. ff. 12.**

—— ००० ஸ்ரீவிருத்திப்பிரபாகரம். [Vṛutti-prabhākaram. A commentary on Sāyaṇa's Pañchadaṣī. Translated and edited with preface, *etc.*, by V. Kuppu-svāmi Rāju.] pp. vii. xix. 580, iv. மதராஸ் [*Madras*,] 1901. 8°. **14170. ee. 41.**

—— ஸ்ரீ விருத்திரத்நாவலி. [Vṛutti-ratnāvali. A supercommentary upon the Pañchadaṣī, in the form of an epitome of Niṣchala Dāsa's Vṛutti-prabhākaram. Translated by V. Kuppu-svāmi Rāju.] pp. iv. xxi. ii. 160; 1 *plate.* சென்னை [*Madras*,] 1902. 12°. **14170. d. 77.**

NĪTI-ṢĀSTRAM. ஸ்ரீ ... நீதிஸாஸ்த்ர ... நீதி-சாஸ்திரம். [Nīti-ṣāstram. A collection of Sanskrit ethical verses from the Mahā-bhāratam, Manu, Bhartṛu-hari and other sources. With a Tamil commentary in *maṇi-pravāḷam* style.] pp. 76. வெஹுதான்ய விகுஜ [*Madras,* 1880.] 16°. **14085. a. 6.**

NITYA-KARMA. పంచకాలప్రకాశః [Pañcha-kāla-prakāṣa. A Sanskrit handbook of the daily rites of Ṣrī-vaishṇavas, with an appendix of Vaishṇava hymns and lections, partly Sanskrit and partly Tamil. Edited, under the direction of Ḍeṅkaṇī-koṭṭai Tirumalai Ṣrīnivāsāchāryar, by Kandāḍai Kāyṣina-vēndāchāryar and others.] pp. ii. iii. 154, i. 93. చెన్నపురి ౧౯౦౪ [*Madras,* 1904.] 8°. **14033. bbb. 26.**

—— விஸ்வப்ரம்ஹ ஆன்ஹிகதீபிகை. [Viṣva-brahma-āhnika-dīpikai. A treatise in catechetic form on the daily rituals of the Viṣva-brahma or goldsmith caste, with the Sanskrit formulæ and hymns in Tamil script. Translated from the Telugu by D. N. Muttu-svāmi Upādhyāyar. Revised by Ā. Muttu Āchāri and Ā. Ananta Perumāḷ Āchāri.] pp. 106. திண்டுக்கல் பாளையங்கோட்டை [*Dindigal, Palamcottah* printed,] 1907. 8°. **14033. aa. 46.**

NITYĀNANDA SVĀMI. *See* ṢANKARĀCHĀRYAR. [*Doubtful and Supposititious Works.*] ஸ்ரீ... இலக்ஷணவிரத்தி ஆ [A collection, comprising Dakshiṇā-mūrtti-ashṭakam, metrically translated by Nityānanda; Advaita-rasa-mañjari, translated by the same, *etc.*] [1888.] 16°. **14170. d. 28.**

NOBILI (ROBERTO DE'), called TATTVA-BŌDHAKA-SVĀMI. ஆத்தும நிருணயம். [Ātma-nirṇayam. A proof of the existence of the soul. Edited by the Jesuit College, with a preface by M. Ṣ. Iago Piḷḷai.] pp. viii. 306, iii. சென்னை [*Madras,*] 1889. 8°. **14170. c. 28.**

—— ஞானோபதேச மூன்றாங் காண்டம். [Ñā-nōpadēṣam. A manual of Catholic doctrine. Edited by M. Ṣ. Iago Piḷḷai. Second edition.] bk. iii. pp. ii. iii. 508, iii.; 1 *plate.* திருச்சிராப்பள்ளி [*Trichinopoli,*] 1907. 8°. **14170. bb. 9.**

NṚUSIMHA BHĀRATI, *Pontiff of Sringeri. Begin.* ஸ்ரீமச்சங்கர ஸ்ரீஜகத்குரு ... முத்ரா ஸ்ரீசங்கராசார்ய [Pastoral letters on the religious and legal relations of the brahmans holding the Shaṇṇavatī *agrahāram* to the Sringeri monastery, *etc.*, the first portion being a Sanskrit letter addressed to them in 1854 by Nṛusiṃha, and the remainder partly in Sanskrit and partly in Tamil.] pp. 20. ரக்தாக்ஷி [1865.] 16°. **14058. a. 5.(1.)**

NŪH ibn 'ABD al-ḲĀDIR, *al-Ḳāhirī.* هذا الكتاب المسمى بالدرر فى حكايات الغرر الملقب بقصص الاوليا [Al-Durar fī ḥikāyāt al-ghurar, also called Ḳiṣaṣ al-auliyā. A collection of anecdotes of Muhammadan saints.] pp. 331, *lith.* بمبئى ١٢٩٩ [*Bombay,* 1882.] 8°. **14173. b. 13.**

—— فتح الصمد فى اسماء اهل البدر والاحد بدرية واحدية [Fatḥ al-ṣamad. A treatise on the names of the Companions who fell at the battles of Badr and Uḥud, and their use for devotional purposes, in Tamil. Followed by a poem in Arabic on the same subject, by 'Alī al-Barzanjī.] pp. 90, *lith.* بمبئى ١٣٢٠ [*Bombay,* 1902.] 8°. **14173. b. 8.**

—— منحة الجواد فى مناقب الاجواد [Minḥat al-jawād. A life of Muḥammad ibn Muḥammad al-Fāsī.] *See* below: نفحات العنبر الخ [Nafaḥāt al-'anbar.] pp. 251-280. [1902.] 8°. **14173. c. 10.**

—— نفحات العنبر فى مناقب القطب الاكبر [Nafaḥāt al-'anbar. Life of the Ṣūfī saint Abū al-Ḥasan al-Shāẕilī, in Tamil. To which are added: 1.) al-Waẕīfat al-Shāẕilīyat, the prayer-book of al-Shāẕilī, the Arabic text with a Tamil paraphrase; 2.) al-Yāḳūtīyah, a prayer by Muḥammad ibn Muḥammad al-Fāsī, the Arabic text with Tamil paraphrase; 3.) Minḥat al-jawād, a life of Muḥammad ibn Muḥammad al-Fāsī, in Tamil, by Nūḥ ibn 'Abd al-Ḳādir; followed by several other pieces entirely in Arabic.] pp. vi. 398, *lith.* بمبئى ١٣٢٠ [*Bombay,* 1902.] 8°. **14173. c. 10.**

—— تحفة الكرام [Tuḥfat al-kirām. A treatise on Muhammadan ethics.] vols. 2, 3. *Lith.* بمبئى ١٣١٠ [*Bombay,* 1893.] 8°. **14173. c. 6.**

NŪH LEBBAI, *Periya.* *See* PERIYA NŪH LEBBAI.

ŌDALĀNDAI. பாலை. [Pālai. Erotic verses.] *See* KŪDALŪR-KIṚĀR. ௦௦௦ ஐங்குறுநூறு ஆ [Aiṅ-guṟu-nūṟu.] pp. 94-120. 1903. 8°. **14172. c. 48.**

ONDAATJE (Matthijs Jurgen). *See* Bronsveld (S. A.). Tamulsch Kinder-Catechismus . . . verbeetert en van veele fouten gezuyvert door M. I. Ondaatje. [1788.] 12°. **14170. a. 36.**

ŌRAM-BŌGIYĀR. மருதம். [Marudam. Erotic verses.] *See* Kūḍalūr-kiḻār. ००० ஐங்குறுநூறு. [Aiṅ-guṟu-nūṟu.] pp. 1-32. 1903. 8°. **14172. c. 48.**

ORDO SALUTIS. [For the catechetical Ordo Salutis :] *See* Catechism.

ORIENT READERS. A companion to the Orient Readers. No. i. Tamil. New edition. pp. 59. *Madras,* 1895. 12°. **14172. h. 97.(1.)**

OṬṬA-KŪTTAR. [*Life.*] *See* Mruga-dāsa Svāmi. University of Madras . . . Pulawar Puranam, *etc.* 1901. 8°. **14172. bb. 3.(4.)**

—— *See* Academies, *etc.*—Madras.—*University of Madras.* University of Madras. F.A. Examination of 1903. Full notes on . . . Bhoja Raja Charitram, *etc.* 1903. 8°. **14172. hh. 19.**

—— [For editions of the Kamba-rāmāyaṇam, of which the 7th canto (Uttara-kāṇḍam) is ascribed to Oṭṭa-kūttar :] *See* Kamban.

—— [Occasional verses, ascribed to Oṭṭa-kūttar and Pugaṟēndi, with interpretation.] *See* Tani-pāḍal. (†தனிப்பாடற்றிரட்டு) [Taní-pāḍaṭ-ṭiraṭṭu.] pp. 158-177. [1892, *etc.*] 8°. **14172. c. 39.(5.)**

OUVAIYAR. *See* Auvaiyār.

P. (Philip), *of Birmingham.* Renunciation of Evil Ways, or An account of Philip P. of Birmingham . . . துன்னெறிவிலக்கு. [Translated by J. Knight.] Third edition. pp. 16. *Jaffna,* 1844. 12°. **14170. b. 1.(31.)**

PACHECO (Francis). சந்தானாள் சமுக விலாசக்கும்மி. [Santānāḷ-samuga-vilāsa-kummi. Songs to be sung at the Feast of St. Anne.] pp. 24. யாழ்ப்பாணம் [*Jaffna,*] 1885. 12°. **14170. b. 34.(3.)**

PACHECO (Gabriel), *of the Oratory of San Filippo Neri.* தேவப்பிரசையின் திருக்கதை. [Dēva-prajaiyin tiru-kathai. A history of Israel and the Christian Church. Edited by Cyriacus a S. Eliseo.] 5 vols. மாஞ்ஞனம் கஅஅo-கஅஅசு [*Mannanam,* 1880-1886.] 8°. **14170. bb. 2.**

PAḌI-KĀṢU PULAVAR. ००० பழமொழிவிளக்கம் என்னும் தண்டலையார்சதகம். [Taṇḍalaiyār-ṣatakam, or Paṟa-moḻi-viḷakkam. 100 verses on the Ṣaiva cult at Taṇḍalai-nīṇeri, illustrating proverbial phrases. With biography.] pp. 29. 1905. *See* Rāma-sāmi Nāyuḍu, *K.* சதகத்திரட்டு. [Ṣataka-tiraṭṭu.] pt. 4. 1905-1906. 12°. **14170.dd.10.**

This author was born about 1650 at Tengalattur, or Ponvilainda-galattur.

PADIṮṮU-PATTU. ००० பதிற்றுப்பத்துமூலமும், பழையவுரையும். [Padiṭṭu-pattu. An anthology of 90 classical poems in praise of Chera kings, by Kaṇṇanār, Gautamanār, Kāppiyanar, Paraṇar, Nachellaiyār, Kapilar, Arisil-kiḻār, and Peruṅ-guṉṟūr-kiḻār, in 9 chapters, forming the 4th of the Eṭṭu-togai. With an ancient commentary. Edited with preface, biographical notices of the authors, and glossary by U. V. Sāminath'-aiyar.] pp. ii. 14, ii. 176. சென்னபட்டணம் [*Madras,*] 1904. 8°. **14172. bb. 14.**

This edition contains the text from bk. ii. *to bk.* ix., *or poems* 11-90.

PADMA-NĀBHA AIYAR, *Kōyamuttūr.* தேடச்சிறந்த தெரிசனம். [Tēḍa-chiṟanda deriṣanam. A Ṣaiva poem.] pp. 7. *Coimbatore,* 1894. 16°. **14170. d. 35.(4.)**

PADMĀSANI AMMĀḶ, *Kaṇṇanūr.* ராமாயண சரித்திரக் கும்மி. [Rāmāyaṇa-charitra-kummi. A ballad on the story of the Rāmāyaṇam.] pp. 66. *Madras,* 1905. 8°. **14172. a. 54.(3.)**

PAGAṚI-KŪTTAR. திருச்செந்தூர்ப்பிள்ளைத்தமிழ். [Tiruchendūr-piḷḷai-tamiḻ. A devotional poem on the childhood of the god Kumāra, as worshipped at Tiruchendur. Edited by M. R. Aruṇāchala Kavi-rāyar.] pp. 41, 1900. *See* Venṟi-mālai Kavi-rājar. திருச்செந்தூர்த்தலபுராண ஞ் [Tiruchendūr-tala-purāṇa-vachanam.] [1899-1900.] 12°. **14170. d. 59.**

PĀKKIYA-NĀTHA SUVĀMI. *See* Bhāgya-nātha Svāmi.

PALNI. *See* [Addenda] Bāla subrahmaṇya Kavi-rāyar. பழநித் தலபுராண ஞ் [Paṟani-tala-purāṇa-vachanam. A paraphrase of the sacred legend of Palni.] 1905. 12°. **14170. dd. 2.**

PĀMB'-ĀṬṬI SIDDHAR. பாம்பாட்டிசித்தர்பாடல். [Pāḍal. Ṣaiva verses.] pp. 20. *See* Siddhar-

GAḶ. ◦ ◦ ◦ பெரிய ஞானக்கோவை [Periya-ñāna-kōvai.] 1899. 12°. **14170. ee. 33.**

—— —— pt. i. pp. 36-55. 1906. 12°. **14170. dd. 12.**

PAÑCHĀKSHARAM. பஞ்சாக்கரமாலை. [Pañchākkhara-mālai. 61 verses on the mystic Ṣaiva formula *namaṣ-ṣivāya.*] pp. 9. 1898. *See* VĒDĀCHALAM PIḶḶAI, *N.* சித்தாந்தஞானபோதம். [Siddhānta-ñāna-bōdham.] pt. i. 1898. 8°. **14170. ee. 39.**

PAÑCHA-NADA ṢĀSTRI, *Karundaṭṭāṅguḍi.* பிரம்ஹவித்யாம்ருத ஸாகரம். [Brahma-vidyāmṛuta-sāgaram. A modern treatise on Vedantic philosophy, based on the Guru-jñāna-vāsishṭham, *etc.*, and illustrated from Sanskrit texts.] pp. iv. ii. x. 371, v. சென்னை விக்ருதி [*Madras,* 1890.] 16°. **14048. a. 13.**

PAÑCHA-PADAM. பஞ்சபதமகாவாக்கியம். [Pañcha-pada-mahā-vākyam. A catechism of Ṣaiva theology, purporting to be translated by Tauḍa Svāmi from the Sanskrit.] pp. 80. [*Madras?*] 1862. 8°. **14170. e. 13.**

Printed on yellow paper.

PAÑCHA-TANTRAM. இஃது . . . தாண்டவராய முதலியார் மொழிபெயர்த்த பஞ்சதந்திரக்கதை. [Pañcha-tantra-kathai. Translated from the Marathi and adapted by Tāṇḍava-rāya Mudaliyār.] pp. i. 100, i. சென்னை ௲அ௱உ௰௬ [*Madras,* 1826.] Fol. **14171. c. 4.**

—— [Another copy.] **14171. c. 3.**

—— பஞ்சதந்திரக்கதை. [Pañcha-tantra-kathai. Another reprint. Edited by E. N. Muttu-sāmi Mudaliyār.] pp. ii. 110. எழுமூர் பிலவங்க [*Egmore,* 1847.] 8°. **14170. k. 26.**

—— பஞ்சதந்திரக்கதை. [Pañcha-tantra-kathai. A reprint of the preceding. Edited by Ṣrīnivāsapuram Ṣrīnivās'-aiyaṅgār.] pp. 2, 84. *Madras,* 1852. 8°. **14170. k. 21.**

—— பஞ்சதந்திரக கதை. [Pañcha - tantra-kathai. Another reprint.] pp. vi. 143. புதுவை ௲அ௱௬௰ரு [*Pondicherry,* 1865.] 12°. **14170. k. 9.**

—— பஞ்சதந்திரக்கதை. [Pañcha-tantra-kathai. Another reprint. Edited by Tiruveṇgāḍu Āṟumuga Svāmi.] pp. 76. சென்னை ௲அஅக [*Madras,* 1881.] 8°. **14170. k. 15.**

—— Panchatantram. [Another reprint.] Part i.(–v.) with an English translation and a glossary, *etc.* 5 pts. *Madras,* 1891-1893. 8°. **14170. k. 57.**

—— The Panchatantra in Tamil [in the recension of Tāṇḍava-rāya Mudaliyār], with notes and translation. Being volume ii. of Arden Tamil Reader. pp. v. 224. 1893. *See* ARDEN (A. H.). A Progressive Grammar, *etc.* 1891-1893. 8°. **12907. c. 38.**

—— Pancha Tantra. Translated from the Tamil by the Rev. S. Winfred. pp. vi. i. 119. *Madras,* 1873. 12°. **14170. k. 61.**

—— Le Pantcha-Tantra, ou Les Cinq Ruses (†choix . . . extrait sur trois copies différentes, écrites l'une en tamoul, l'autre en telougou, et la troisième en cannada). *See* DUBOIS (J.-A.). Le Pantcha-Tantra, *etc.* pp. 1-228. 1826. 8°. **14170. k. 67.**

—— —— 1872. 8°. **14170. k. 68.**

—— சுஹிர்ல்லாப தந்திரம் . . . நட்புப்பேறு. [Suhṛil-lābha-tantram. Bk. ii. of the Pañchatantram.] *See* POPE (G. U.). A Tamil Prose Reading-book, *etc.* bk. ii. 1859. 8°. **14172. h. 76.**

—— பஞ்சதந்திரம். [Pañcha-tantram, bk. ii. (Suhṛil-lābham). In Tamil and English, with Tamil commentary, *etc.*] *See* ACADEMIES, *etc.*—Madras.—*University of Madras.* Copious notes, *etc.* 1898. 8°. **14172. b. 16.(1.)**

PĀṆḌI-TURAI DĒVAR, *of Palavanattam Zamindari, Ramnad.* பன்னூற்றிரட்டு. [Pan-nūṯ-ṯiraṭṭu. An anthology from various poems, arranged under the heads of virtue, wealth, and pleasure.] pp. v. vii. 235, xiii. i. *Ramnad,* 1898. 8°. **14172. d. 21.**

—— பன்னூற்றிரட்டு. அறத்துப்பால். [Pan-nūṯ-ṯiraṭṭu. 100 stanzas from the Aṟattu-pāl or section on virtue.] *See* ACADEMIES, *etc.*—Madras.—*University of Madras.* The Tamil text, *etc.* pp. 16-31. 1899. 8°. **14172. bb. 6.(7.)**

—— பன்னூற்றிரட்டு. [Pan-nūṯ-ṯiraṭṭu. The same stanzas, with notes and English translation.]

See ACADEMIES, *etc.*—Madras.—*University of Madras.* University of Madras. Matriculation Examination, 1900, *etc.* 1900. 8°. **14172. bb. 6.(2.)**

—— Pannulthirattu. Chapter i. (-ix.), *etc.* [In English, with Tamil notes.] *See* ACADEMIES, *etc.*—Madras.—*University of Madras.* Copious annotations, *etc.* 1900. 8°. **14172. bb. 6.(3.)**

—— Pannul thirattu. Or, Gleanings from many Wolls [*sic*] Virtue. Chapter i. (-ix.), *etc.* [In English, with Tamil aunotations.] *See* ACADEMIES, *etc.*—Madras.—*University of Madras.* University of Madras. Exhaustive notes, *etc.* 1900. 8°. **14172. bb. 6.(4.)**

PĀṆḌIYAN (THOMAS B.). The life of the Rev. Isaac Abraham, C.M.S., Panneivilei. *கனம் : ஈசாக்கு ஆபிரகம் ஐயரவர்களின் ஜீவிய விருத்தாந்தம்* . . . With a preface by . . . T. Walker. pp. ix. xvi. 169; 1 *plate.* *Palamcottah,* 1906. 12°. **14170. bbb. 11.**

PĀṆḌIYAR. Pàndion Chronicle. [Text and translation.] *See* TAYLOR (W.). Oriental Historical Manuscripts, *etc.* vol. i., pp. 3-44. 1835. 4°. **14171. c. 5.**

PANN'-IRU-BĀṬṬ'-IYAL. *பன்னிருபாட்டியல்* [Pann'-iru-bāṭṭ'-iyal. Rules for the art of poetry.] pp. 44. 1904. *See* ACADEMIES, *etc.*—*Madura.* ["Ṣen-damiḻ" supplement.] no. 10. 1902, *etc.* 8°. **14172. i. 1.* (no. 10.)**

PARA-HITAM. *சோதிசாத்திரம்.* [Jōdi-ṣāttiram.] The Oriental Astronomer [purporting to be a translation into Tamil by Uḷḷam-uḍaiyān of the Sanskrit work styled Para-hitam]: being a complete system of Hindu astronomy, accompanied with a translation [into English by H. R. Hoisington] and numerous explanatory notes. With an appendix. pp. i. 177, 2, 145, i. *Jaffna,* 1848. 8°. **14170. i. 8.**

PARAMĀNANDA. *பரமானந்ததீபம்.* [Paramānanda-dīpam. Ṣaiva verses.] *See* SIDDHARGAḶ. ∘∘∘ *பெரிய ஞானக்கோவை.* [Periya-ñāna-kōvai.] pt. ii. 1906. 12°. **14170. dd. 12.**

PARAMĒṢVARA AYYAR, *Subba-rāya.* Sangitha Sastram, or A treatise in Tamil on the art of Indian music . . . *சங்கீத சாஸ்திரம்.* (*Manasollasini Series.) pp. i. iv. 74. [*Madras,*] 1905. 8°. **14170. i. 19.(2.)**

PAṞA-MOḺI. (*†பழமொழித்திரட்டு.*) [Paṟa-moḻi-tiraṭṭu. A collection of proverbs.] pp. 82. [*Madras, n.d.*] 8°. **14170. k. 55.(1.)**

Without title-page.

PARAṆAR. *ஐந்தாம் பத்து.* [Decade v. Ten poems on the Chera king Ṣeṅ-guṭṭuvan.] *See* PADIṮṮU-PATTU. ∘∘∘ *பதிற்றுப்பத்து ௫* [Padiṯṯu-pattu.] pp. 60-79. 1904. 8°. **14172. bb. 14.**

PAṞANIY-APPA AIYĀ, *Ṣarnanādapuram.* ∘∘∘ *பாடற்றிரட்டு.* [Pāḍaṯ-ṯiraṭṭu. A series of religious poems addressed to Subrahmaṇya as worshipped on the Palni Hills.] pp. 146. *சென்னை* [*Madras,*] 1898. 8°. **14172. b. 6.**

PAṞAṆIY-APPA CHEṬṬI, *Dēvakoṭṭai M.P.* *See* POSTAL GUIDE. Postal Guide, *etc.* [Published by Paṟaṇiy-appa.] 1904. 8°. **14172. i. 23.**

PARAÑ-JŌDI MUNIVAR. *See* KṚUSHṆA BHĀRATI. *திருவிளையாடல் நாடகம்.* [Tiru-viḷaiy-āḍal-nāṭakam. A drama on the subject of the Tiru-viḷaiy-āḍaṟ-purāṇam.] 1899. 8°. **14170. l. 49.**

—— *See* SHAṆMUKHAM PIḶḶAI, *P. V.* *திருவிளையாடற் புராண சங்கிரகம்.* [Tiru-viḷaiy-āḍaṟ-purāṇa-saṅgraham. A metrical summary of the Tiru-viḷaiy-āḍaṟ-purāṇam.] 1901. 8°. **14170. ee. 5.(2.)**

—— *See* SUBRAHMAṆYA BHĀRATI, *M. S.* *திருவிளையாடற்கீர்த்தனை.* [Tiru-viḷaiy-āḍaṟ-kīrttanai. Lyrics on the legends of the Tiru-viḷaiy-āḍaṟ-purāṇam.] 1906. 8°. **14170. ff. 19.**

—— *திருவிளையாடற் புராணம்.* [Tiru-viḷaiy-āḍaṟ-purāṇam. A poem on the cult of Ṣiva at Madura, narrating his 64 sacred sports in 3363 quatrains and 72 chapters, and purporting to be translated from the Sanskrit Hālāsya-māhātmyam in the Īṣa-saṃhitā of the Skanda-purāṇam. Edited on the basis of the editions of Ṣara-vaṇa Peru-māḷ Aiyar and Nāgūr Tyāga-rāya Mudaliyār.] pp. ii. ii. 456. *சிந்தாத்திரைப்பெட்டை சாதாரண* [*Madras,* 1850.] 8°. **14170. ee. 1.**

Composed about **1650** *A.D.*

—— ∘∘∘ *திருவிளையாடற்புராணம் மதுரைக்காண்டம் (*கூடற்காண்டம், திருவாலவாய்க்காண்டம்).* [Tiru viḷaiy-āḍaṟ-purāṇam. An illustrated edition, with interpretation and commentary by T. K. Subba-rāya Cheṭṭi. Followed by the Tiruv-ālavāy-dēvāram, *etc.*] 2 vols. சென்னை சர்வசித்து [*Madras*, 1887.] 8°. **14170. f. 10.**

—— திருவிளையாடற் புராணம். [Tiru-viḷaiy-āḍar-purāṇam. Another reprint of the edition of Ṣara-vaṇa Peru-māḷ. Followed by the Tiruv-ālavāy-dēvāram.] pp. iii. i. 483. சென்னை விஷு [*Madras*, 1882.] 8°. **14170. ee. 2.**

—— மதுரைச்சோமசுந்தரக்கடவுள் திருவிளையாடற்புராணம் [Tiru-viḷaiy-āḍar-purāṇam. Preceded by the Tiruv-ālavāy-dēvāram and other poems. Edited by Chidambaram Īṣāniya-maṭham Rāma-liṅga Svāmi.] pp. xxvi. ii. ii. 476, ii. சென்னை [*Madras*,] 1896. 8°. **14170. ee. 3.**

—— [Third edition.] pp. xxxii. iv. ii. 494, ii. சென்னை [*Madras*,] 1906. 8°. **14170. eee. 24.**

—— மதுரைச் சோமசுந்தரக் கடவுளது திருவிளையாடற்புராணம். [Tiru-viḷaiy-āḍar-purāṇam. Edited with interpretation and commentary by Īkkāḍu Ratna-vēlu Mudaliyār.] சென்னை [*Madras*,] 1896, *etc.* 8°. **14170. ff. 1.**

Incomplete, extending only to p. 392 of the Tiruv-ālavāy-kāṇḍam. No more has been registered.

—— ... திருவிளையாடற்புராணம். வேதத்துக்குப்பொருளருளிச்செய்த படலமூலமும்... உரையும். [Vēdattukku poruḷ aruḷi cheyda paṭalam. The 16th canto of the Tiru-viḷaiy-āḍar-purāṇam. With paraphrase and commentary by M. Tillai-nātha Piḷḷai.] pp. 26. சென்னை ஜய [*Madras*, 1894.] 8°. **14170. e. 67.**

—— திருவிளையாடற் புராணம் [Tiru-viḷaiy-āḍar-purāṇam. A prose abstract by K. Namaṣ-ṣivāya Mudaliyār.] pts. 1-18. சென்னை [*Madras*,] 1901-1902. 16°. **14170. dd. 8.**

—— Madura Stalla Puràna. [An abstract in English.] *See* Taylor (W.). Oriental Historical Manuscripts, *etc.* vol. i., pp. 53-116. 1835. 4°. **14171. c. 5.**

—— ... வேதாரணியபுராணம். [Vēdāraṇya-purāṇam. The sacred legends of the Ṣaiva shrine of Vēdāraṇyam in Tanjore, in verse, ascribed to Parañ-jōdi. Edited by M. Sōmā-skanda Bhaṭṭārakar.] pp. iv. 206, i. சென்னை விளம்பி [*Madras*, 1899.] 12°. **14170. d. 54.**

PARĀṄKUṢA-DĀSAR. ஸ்ரீஹரிநாமசங்கீர்த்தனம். [Hari-nāma-saṅkīrttanam. Hymns on the names of Vishṇu.] pp. 75. பிரபவ [*Madras*, 1868.] 8°. **14172. b. 21.**

PARĀṢARA. பராசரஸ்ம்ருதி. [Parāṣara-smṛuti, or °saṃhitā. A code of sacred law. The Sanskrit text in both Grantham and Tamil characters. Edited with Tamil translation by Āḍūr Īchambāḍi Dēṣikāchāryar.] pp. 2, viii. 80, 68. சென்னை [*Madras*,] 1902. 8°. **14039. b. 30.**

—— ... பாராசரியம் ஸ்ரீ [Pārāṣaryam. An astrological work on the aspects and influences of the heavenly bodies, translated from the Sanskrit work ascribed to Parāṣara. Edited by Vaidi-liṅga Jōdishar.] pp. iv. 100. பவ [*Madras*, 1874.] 8°. **14170. i. 16.**

PARĀṢARA BHAṬṬAR, *son of Ṣrīvatsāṅka Kūratt'-āḻvān* (Raṅga-nātha). *See* Purāṇas.—*Varāha-purāṇam.* శ్రీ . . . శ్రీకైశికపురాణం. [Kaiṣika-purāṇam. With Tamil commentary by Parāṣara.] [1904.] 8°. **14028. c. 49.(2.)**

—— அஷ்டஶ்லோகீ [Ashṭa-ṣlōkī. A Vaishṇava religious poem in 8 Sanskrit stanzas. With Tamil version, analysis, and commentary.] *See* Varadāchāryar, *V. D.* ... ப்ரபன்னபாரிஜாதம் ஸ்ரீ [Prapanna-pārijātam.] pp. 128-147. [1895.] 8°. **14028. d. 55.**

PARAṢU-RĀMA PANTULU, *Liṅga-mūrtti Guru-mūrtti.* ... ஸ்ரீஸீதாராமாஞ்சநேய ஸம்வாதஸாரஸங்கிரகம் ஸ்ரீ [Sītā-rāmāñjanēya-saṃvāda-sāra-saṅgraham. A Telugu prose epitome, by Nārapa-rāju Rāma-chandra Pantulu, of the Sītā-rāmāñjanēya-saṃvādam, a Telugu poem expounding Yoga theories in a dialogue between Sītā, Rāma, and Hanumān. With Tamil translation and commentary and a concluding Tamil poem by S. Vijaya-rāghavalu Nāyuḍu.] pp. xviii. 164, 6, iii. ii. சென்னை ஏவிளம்பி [*Madras*, 1898.] 8°. **14170. ee. 27.**

PARIMĒL-AḺAGAR. *See* Tiru-vaḷḷuvar. The Cural . . . with the commentary of Parimelaragar, *etc.* 1840-1852. 8°. **14172. b. 48.**

PARIMĒL-AṞAGAR (*continued*). *See* TIRU-VAḶḶUVAR. ००० தமிழ்வேதமாகியதிருக்குறள் ௵ [Kuṟaḷ. With the commentary of Parimēl-aṟagar.] [1861.] 8°. **14172. d. 7.**

—— —— [1875.] 8°. **14172. d. 8.**

—— *See* TIRU-VAḶḶUVAR. ००० திருக்குறள் ௵ [Kuṟaḷ. With commentary of Parimēl-aṟagar.] [1875.] 8°. **14172. c. 10.**

—— *See* TIRU-VAḶḶUVAR. The Kural . . . with the commentary of Parimelazagar, *etc.* 1885. 8°. **14172. d. 15.**

—— *See* TIRU-VAḶḶUVAR. ००० தமிழ்வேதமாகிய திருக்குறள் ௵ [Kuṟaḷ. With commentary of Parimēl-aṟagar.] 1904. 8°. **14172. c. 46.**

—— [For editions of the Kuṟaḷ including commentaries based upon that of Parimēl-aṟagar :] *See* TIRU-VAḶḶUVAR.

PARNELL (THOMAS), *Archdeacon of Clogher.* Parnell's Hermit in Tamil prose. By C. Ramachandra Aiyar. (*மனங்குழம்பிய மாதவத்தோன்.) [Followed by the original.] pp. i. 25. *Tanjore,* 1904. 12°. **14172. a. 54.(2.)**

PĀRTHA-SĀRATHI AIYAṄGĀR. *See* PIḶḶAI LŌKĀCHĀRYAR. Tattva-traya . . . translated by Sri-Párthasárathy Aiyangár. 1900. 8°. **14170. ee. 17.**

PĀRTHA-SĀRATHI AIYAṄGĀR, *D. B.* *See* PERIODICAL PUBLICATIONS.—*Madras.* The "Gramathikari Gazette" . . . [Edited] by D. B. Parthasarathy Aiyangar. 1903. 8°. **14172. i. 3.(2.)**

PĀRTHA-SĀRATHI AIYANGĀR, *P.* *See* ŞĀNTALIṄGA SVĀMI. ००० வைராக்கிய சதகம் ௵ [Vairāgya-ṣatakam. Edited, with commentary, by Pārtha-sārathi.] 1906. 12°. **14170. dd. 11.(1.)**

PĀRTHA-SĀRATHI AIYAṄGĀR, *Tōḷṇāvūr.* ஸம்ஸ்க்ருதசப்தரத்நாகரமென்கிற அகராதி. [Saṃskṛuta-ṣabda-ratnākaram. A vocabulary of Sanskrit words explained in Tamil.] pp. xiv. 263, ii. சென்னை [*Madras,*] 1881. 8°. **14090. c. 35.**

PAṬṬAṆATTU PIḶḶAI (TIRUVEṆGĀḌAR). [*Life.*] *See* NAMA-ŞIVĀYAM PIḶḶAI, *M.* ००० பட்டணத்துப்பிள்ளையார் சரித்திர சங்கிரகம். [Paṭṭaṇattu-piḷḷaiyār-charitra-saṅgraham.] [1898.] 12°. **14171. aa. 7.**

—— திருவெண்காட்டடிகள்புராணம் என்னும் பட்டணத்துப்பிள்ளையார்புராணம் ௵ [Paṭṭaṇattu-piḷḷaiyār-purāṇam, or Tiruveṇgāṭṭ'-aḍigaḷ-purāṇam. A poem in 3 books, composed about five centuries ago by a *tambirān* of Chidambaram, on the legends connected with the life of the Ṣaiva poet and devotee Paṭṭaṇattu Piḷḷai. Edited with paraphrase and commentary by T. K. Vaḍi-vēlu Mudaliyār.] pp. ii. 246, ii. சென்னை [*Madras,*] 1901. 8°. **14170. k. 34**

—— ००० கோயினான்மணிமாலை முதலிய மூலமும் . . . கோயிற்றிருவகவல்முதலிய திருப்பாடற்றிரட்டுமூலமும் ௵ [A collection of Ṣaiva poems, comprising the Kōyin-nān-maṇi-mālai, Tirukaṟumala-mum-maṇi-kōvai, Tiruviḍaimarudūr-mum-maṇi-kōvai, Tiruv-ēkambam-uḍaiyār-tiruv-antādi, Tiruvoṭṭiyūr-togai, and Tiru-pāḍaṭ-ṭiraṭṭu, some being supposititious. With commentaries and a biography.] pp. 402. சென்னை [*Madras,*] 1892. 8°. **14172. c. 39.(vol. 2.)**

Forms part of the Vidyā-vinōdini Series.
In the pagination the nos. 137-146 *are dropped, but nothing is missing.*

—— ००० திருவெண்காட்டடிகள் சரித்திரம். அவரது பாடற்றிருமுறை ௵ [Pāḍaṭ-ṭiru-muṟai. The same poems of Paṭṭaṇattu Piḷḷai. With a biography and glossary, and also Ṣēndanār's Tiruv-iṣai-pā and Bhadra-giriyār's Pulambal. Reprinted from the edition of Toṟuvūr Vēl-āyudha Mudaliyār, and revised by his son T. V. Tiru-nāgēṣvara Mudaliyār. Second edition.] pp. 2, 2, iii. 133, iii. 155, xxiii. சென்னை [*Madras,*] 1906. 8°. **14170. ff. 16.**

—— ००० திருப்பாடற்றிரட்டு ௵ [Tiru-pāḍaṭ-ṭiraṭṭu, Pulambal, and Ñānam. With short life of the poet, and a few other Ṣaiva verses.] pp. 44, 36, 12. 1899. *See* SIDDHARGAḶ. ००० பெரிய ஞானக்கோவை [Periya-ñāna-kōvai.] 1899. 12°. **14170. ee. 33.**

—— —— 1906. 12°. **14170. dd. 12.**

—— பட்டணத்துப்பிள்ளையார் பாடல் ௵ (*பட்டணத்து பிள்ளையார் புலம்பல்.) [Pāḍal, *i.e.* the Tiru-pāḍaṭ-ṭiraṭṭu, and Pulambal, or Aruṭpulambal, plaints on the vanity of the world. Followed by the Pulambal of Bhadra-giriyār. With biographies of the poets and prose paraphrase of the verses by M. Vaḍi-vēlu Mudaliyār.] 3 pts. சென்னை [*Madras*,] 1899. 12°. **14170. d. 64.**

—— Pattanattar Padal. [63 stanzas on ethical and religious themes, in English, with Tamil commentary and biography.] *See* ACADEMIES, *etc.*—Madras.—*University of Madras.* Notes on the Tamil text, *etc.* 1888. 12°. **14172. a. 41.**

PAṬṬAR-PIRĀN. *See* PERIY-ĀṚVĀR.

PATTIRAGIRIYĀR. *See* BHADRA-GIRIYĀR.

PATTU-PĀṬṬU. பத்துப்பாட்டுமூலமும் ... நச்சினார்க்கினியருரையும். [Pattu-pāṭṭu. The "Ten Idylls," classical poems chiefly on amatory and romantic themes, comprising (1) Nakkīranār's Tirumṛug'-āṭṭu-paḍai, (2) Muḍattāma-kaṇṇiyār's Porunar-āṭṭu-paḍai, (3) Nattattanār's Ṣiru-bāṇ-āṭṭu-paḍai, (4) Rudra-kaṇṇanār's Perum-bāṇ-āṭṭu-paḍai, (5) Nappūdanār's Mullai-pāṭṭu, (6) Marudanār's Madurai-kāñji, (7) Nakkīranār's Neḍu-nal-vāḍai, (8) Kapilar's Kuriñji-pāṭṭu, (9) Rudra-kaṇṇanār's Paṭṭina-pālai, (10) Peruṅ-kauṣikanār's Malai-baḍu-gaḍām. With the commentary by Nachinārkk'-iniyar. Edited with glossary by U. V. Sāminath'-aiyar.] pp. i. viii. 420, i. சென்னை [*Madras*,] 1889. 8°. **14172. d. 10.**

—— [For separate editions of the poems collectively styled Pattu-pāṭṭu, see under the following headings:]

KAPILAR.
MUḌATTĀMA-KAṆṆIYĀR.
NAKKĪRA DĒVAR.

PAULINUS, *a Sancto Bartolomæo*, [JOHANN PHILIPP WERDIN]. Centum Adagia Malabarica, cum textu originali et versione latina. Nunc primum in lucem edita a Paulino a S. Bartholomæo. pp. 12. *Romae*, 1791. 4°. **14170. k. 77.**

The Tamil is printed in the Grantham character.

PAUL PHILIP. *See* PHILIP (C. PAUL).

PAVAṆANDI. நன்னூன்மூலம். [Nan-nūl. A classical grammar.] *See* TĀṆḌAVA-RĀYA MUDALIYĀR. இலக்கணப்பஞ்சக ஒ [Nan-nūl, *etc.*] pp. 1-33. [1835.] 8°. **14172. e. 3.**

PAVAṆANDI (*continued*). நன்னூல்விருத்தியுரை. [Nan-nūl. With commentary (*vruttiy-urai*) by Rāmānuja Kavi-rāyar.] pp. ii. 336, vii. பிலவங்க [*Madras*, 1847.] 8°. **14172. f. 1.**

—— Grammatica Tamuliensis, or An English version [with the Tamil text] of the celebrated Tamil Nunnool, with ... notes, vocabulary, appendices, and extracts from the ... commentary of Sunghara Nama Sivayur. By W. Joyes and S. Samuel Pillay. Revised and corrected by the Rev. T. Brotherton. 6 pts. *Madras*, 1848-1851. 8°. **14172. f. 10.**

Contains only ch. i. *No more was published.*

—— —— [Another copy, wanting p. 6.] **14172. f. 20.**

—— ... நன்னூன்மூலமும் ... விருத்தியுரையும் [Nan-nūl. With the commentary of Ṣaṅkara Namaṣ-ṣivāyar, as revised by Ṣiva-ñāna Svāmi of Tiruvāvaḍudurai. Edited by Nallūr Āṛu-muga Nāvalar.] pp. 312, vii. விரோதிகிருது [*Jaffna?* 1851.] 8°. **14172. f. 2.**

—— 1. Nannûl, *etc.*, 1858. *See* POPE (G. U.). A larger Grammar of the Tamil Language, *etc.* pp. 137-334. 1858-1859. 8°. **14172. h. 81.**

——Abridgment of the Nannûl; with the original text, explanations, examples, and notes, and an appendix ... by G. P. Savundranayagam Pillai. Third edition. (* நன்னூற் சுருக்கம்.) pp. 142. *Madras*, 1864. 12°. **14172. e. 7.**

—— நன்னூல் மூலமும் காண்டிகை உரையும். [Nan-nūl. With commentary (*kāṇḍikaiy-urai*) by Viṣākha Peru-māḷ Aiyar. Edited, on the basis of the revision made by the latter, by K. V. Āṛumuga Mudaliyār. With preface by Ṣēyūr Mutt'-aiya Mudaliyār.] pp. 224. யுவ [*Madras*, 1875.] 8°. **14172. f. 9.**

—— நன்னூல் மூலமும் காண்டிகை உரையும். [Nan-nūl. Another edition of the preceding. Edited by Tiruveṇgāḍu Āṛu-muga Svāmi. With a preface by Ṣēyūr Mutt'-aiya Mudaliyār.] pp. 200. கஅஅஉ [*Madras*, 1882.] 8°. **14172. e. 11.**

——நன்னூற் காண்டிகையுரை. [Nan-nūl. With a *kāṇḍikai* commentary. Edited and augmented by Nallūr Āṛu-muga Nāvalar.] pp. 400, ii. vii. சென்னபட்டணம் விக்கிரம [*Madras*, 1880.] 8°. **14172. e. 28.**

PAVAṆANDI (*continued*). நன்னூன் மூலமும் . . . விருத்தியுரையும். [Nan-nūl. With the commentary by Ṣaṅkara Namaṣ-ṣivāyar, as revised by Ṣiva-ñāna Svāmi. Edited by Āṟu-muga Nāvalar.] pp. 292, vi. சர்வசித்து [*Jaffna*, 1887.] 8°. **14172. e. 12.**

—— [Another edition.] pp. 328, vii. சென்னபட்டணம் சுபகிருது [*Madras*, 1903.] 8°. **14172. e. 39.**

—— The Nannul of Pavananthi. Part i.—Orthography, எழுத்ததிகாரம் (*Part ii.—Etymology, சொல்லதிகாரம்). With a clear commentary, revised and improved, with English headings to Sutrams, &c. (*நன்னூன்மூலமும் . . . காண்டிகையுரையும்.) 2 vols. *Madras*, 1889-1890. 12°. **14172. e. 14.**

Vol. i. is in the second edition.

—— Tamil grammar, with Nannûl sutrams and explanations, *etc.* Second edition. 1897. 12°. *See* SAUNDARA-RĀJA AIYAṄGĀR, *Ṣ.V.* **14172. ee. 1.**

—— Third edition. 1898. 12°. **14172. ee. 2.**

—— நன்னூற் காண்டிகையுரை. (Nannul kandikai. [Being the Nan-nūl with a commentary] by V. M. Satakoparamanujachariar, and S. Krishnamachariar. Revised and enlarged.) [Third edition.] pp. i. ii. ii. 256, i. சென்னை [*Madras*,] 1900. 8°. **14172. e. 32.**

—— [Fourth edition.] pp. i. ii. ii. 261. சென்னை [*Madras*,] 1903. 8°. **14172. e. 37.**

—— ◦◦◦ நன்னூல் மூலம். [Nan-nūl.] pp. 124. சென்னை [*Madras*,] 1903. 16°. **14172. ee. 11.**

—— Introduction to the Nannul: the Tamil text, and English translation, with appendices of notes and grammatical terms. By the Rev. H. Bower. pp. vi. 48. *Madras*, 1876. 16°. **14172. h. 37.**

—— An English translation of the Nannul [bks. i.-ii.] . . . By a Tamil graduate of the Madras University [J. Lazarus]. pp. 47. *Madras*, 1878. 12°. **14172. e. 8.**

PAVĀNI PULAVAR, *of Palghat* (SAIYID BUKHĀRĪ). இஃது அப்துறகுமானறபிச்சதகம். [ʻAbd al-Raḥmān ʻArabi ṣatakam. 100 stanzas in praise of ʻAbd al-Raḥmān, a Muhammadan saint buried at Vedasandur, Madura district.] pp. 58. சென்னை கஙடாகஉ [*Madras*, 1895.] 8°. **14173. b. 26.**

PEANIUS (CLEMENS). *See* AMADUZZI (G. C.). Alphabetum Grandonico-malabaricum, *etc.* [Compiled from materials supplied by Peanius.] 1772. 12°. **621. b. 5.(2.)**

PĒCHIY-APPA PIḶḶAI, *Ṣ. Vaḍivu-nāyakam.* *See* PURĀṆAS.—*Bhavishyōttara-purāṇam.* ◦◦◦ சங்கரநாராயண சுவாமிகோவில் மான்மியம். [Ṣaṅkara-nārāyaṇa-svāmi-kōvil-mānmiyam. Rendered into prose by Pēchiy-appa.] 1898. 12°. **14170. d. 45.(2.)**

PĒR-ĀṢIRIYAR. *See* MĀṆIKKA-VĀCHAKAR. ◦◦◦ திருச்சிற்றம்பலக் கோவையாருண்மை. [Tiru-chiṭṭambala-kōvaiyār-uṇmai. With metrical commentary by Pēr-āṣiriyar.] [1895.] 12°. **14172. a. 42.**

—— *See* MĀṆIKKA-VĀCHAKAR. ◦◦◦ திருக்கோவையார். [Tiru-kōvaiyār. With commentary of Pēr-āṣiriyar.] [1897.] 12°. **14172. a. 46.**

—— [For editions of the commentary upon the Ṣeyyuḷ-iyal of the Tol-kāppiyam ascribed usually to Nachinārkk'-iniyar and sometimes to Pēr-āṣiriyar:] *See* TOL-KĀPPIYANĀR.

PERCIVAL (PETER). *See* AṢVA-GHŌSHA. Vajra Suchi . . . English and Tamil versions [the latter by P. Percival,] *etc.* 1851. 12°. **14028. c. 25.**

—— *See* BIBLE.—*Complete Bibles.* The Holy Bible . . . revised [by P. Percival and others,] *etc.* 1850. 4°. **3070. d. 26.**

—— *See* TAMIL MINOR POETS. Tamil Minor Poets . . . [Compiled by P. Percival,] *etc.* 1872. 12°. **14172. c. 6.**

—— *See* VĪRĀ-SĀMI CHEṬṬIYĀR. Vinodarasamanjari . . . originally published by . . . P. Percival, *etc.* 1891. 8°. **14170. k. 56.**

—— Incarnate Grace . . . அருளவதாரம். Third edition. pp. 47. *Jaffna*, 1842. 12°. **14170. b. 1.(58.**

—— திருட்டாந்த சங்கிரகம். A Collection of Proverbs in Tamil, with their translation in English. pp. i. 266. *Jaffna*, 1843. 12°. **14170. k. 6.**

—— —— [Another copy, wanting title-page.] **14170. k. 8**

PERCIVAL (PETER) (*continued*). Tamil Proverbs with their English translation. Containing upwards of six thousand proverbs. Second edition. pp. xi. 573. *Madras*, 1874. 8°. **14170. k. 65.**

—— A Dictionary, English and Tamil . . . Authorised by the Director of Public Instruction. Revised edition. pp. 595. *Madras*, 1900. 8°. **14172. e. 33.**

PEREIRA (*Don* FRANCISCO). திருத்தலைவில்லின் வழிநடைப்பதம். [Tirutalaivillin vaṟi-naḍai-padam. Devotional songs for Catholic pilgrims to the sanctuary of Talavilla.] pp. 8. யாழ்ப்பாணம் [*Jaffna*,] 1893. 8°. **14170. c. 24.(7.)**

PERIODICAL PUBLICATIONS.

BOMBAY.

The Indian Antiquary. A journal of oriental research in archæology, history, literature, languages, philosophy, religion, folk-lore, *etc. Bombay*, 1872, *etc.* 4°. **14096. e.**

In progress.

CHIDAMBARAM.

ப்ரஹ்மவித்யா *etc.* [Brahma-vidyā. A monthly journal of literature, in Sanskrit and Tamil. Edited by K. R. Ṣrīnivāsa Dīkshitar.] சிதம்பரம் க௮௮௬ [*Chidambaram*, 1886, *etc.*] 4°. **14096. dd. 3.**

In progress?

JAFFNA.

The உதயதாரகை [Udaya-tārakai]. — Morning Star. Vol. v. (-xv.) . . . Devoted to education, literature, and religion, *etc.* [In Tamil and English.] *Jaffna*, 1845-1855. Fol. **14172. k. 4.**

KANDY.

ஞானதீபம். [Ñāna-dīpam. A monthly magazine for Muhammadans.] Edited . . . by M. C. Siddi Lebbe. vol. i., pts. 1, 5. *Colombo*, 1892. 8°. **14173. b. 37.**

MADRAS.

அபிநவ பத்திரிகை ஸ்ரீ [Abhinava-patrikai. A monthly literary magazine. Edited by K. R. Ṣrīnivāsa Aiyaṅgār and N. Rāmānujāchāryar.] vol. i., pts. 1-4. சென்னை [*Madras*,] 1902. 8°. **14172. i. 2.**

தேசாபிமானி. Désábhimáni. [A magazine of the Native Christian Improvement Society.] vol. x., no. 6. *Madras*, 1877. 8°. **14172. i. 3.(1.)**

தேசோபகாரி . . . Désópakári: an illustrated Tamil magazine. Published by the Madras Branch of the Christian Vernacular Education Society. [Edited by F. Baylis.] vols. i., iii., iv., x. 8, 10. *Nagercoil*, 1861-1870. 8°. **14172. i. 5.**

The "Gramathikari Gazette," a monthly journal in Tamil . . . a great boon bestowed upon the Village Officers. கிராமாதிகாரி கெஜட் . . . [Edited] by D. B. Parthasarathy Aiyangar. (*The Village Officers' Gazette.) vol. i., no. 1-7. *Madras*, 1903. 8°. **14172. i. 3.(2.)**

Apparently no more has been published.

இகபரசுகசாதனி ஸ்ரீ [Iha-para-sukha-sādhani. A monthly magazine for literature and philosophy.] . . . Published by K. Loganatha Moodaliar. vol. i. *Madras*, 1903-1904. 4°. **14172. k. 5.**

ஜனப்பிரியன் ஸ்ரீ [Jana-priyan. A monthly magazine for literature and science. Edited by K. Kṛushṇa-sāmi Aiyar.] vol. i., pt. 1—vol. ii., pt. 2. *Madras*, 1900-1901. 8°. **14172. i. 19.**

Apparently no more has been published.

ஞானபோதினி. ஒருமாதாந்தத்தமிழ்ப்பத்திரிகை. (*Jnâna Bodhini. A Tamil magazine and review devoted mainly to literature, science, philosophy & religion.) [Vol. 1-4, edited by M. Ṣ. Pūrṇa-liṅgam Piḷḷai; vol. 5, 6, edited by the same and V. G. Sūryā-nārāyaṇa Ṣāstri; vol. 7-8, edited by Pūrṇa-liṅgam Piḷḷai.] vols. i.-viii. 2. *Madras*, 1897-1905. 8°. **14172. i. 16.**

The Light of Truth, or Siddhanta Deepika. A monthly journal [chiefly in English,] devoted to religion, philosophy, literature, science, &c. [Edited by J. M. Nāga-ratnam Piḷḷai.] *Madras*, 1897, *etc.* 4°. **14170. fff. 4.**

In progress.

The Madras Christian College Magazine. New series. 1902, *etc.* 8°. **P.P. 910. da.**

In progress.

PERIODICAL PUBLICATIONS (*continued*).

MADRAS (*continued*).

மாதர் மித்திரி. (The Woman's Friend, in Tamil, "Mathar Mithiri.") vol. i., no. 1. pp. 12. *Madras*, 1887. 4°. **14172. i. 4.**

தர்மப்பள்ளிப்போதம். The Mission School Magazine. vols. i. and ii. (iii. and iv.). *Nagercoil* [printed,] 1859-1861. 16°. **14170. a. 10, 11.**

∘∘∘ ஞானசாகரம். [Ñāna-sāgaram. A monthly magazine of literature and philosophy. Edited by N. Vēdāchalam Piḷḷai.] சென்னை [*Madras*,] 1902, *etc.* 8°. **14172. i. 10.**

In progress.

உண்மை விளக்கம் அல்லது சித்தாந்ததீபிகை. [Siddhānta-dīpikai, or Uṇmai-viḷakkam. A monthly magazine of literature, chiefly of the Ṣaiva-siddhāntam. Edited by N. Vēdāchalam Piḷḷai.] vol. i. *Madras*, 1897. 4°. **14170. fff. 1.**

The Somaravi. An occasional (*A quarterly) publication on Hindu philosophy [in Tamil and English]. Edited . . . by C. E. Srinivasaragavacharriar . . . 'ஸோமரவி ஞூ. vol. i., pts. 1-5. *Madras*, 1895-1896. Fol. **14170. ccc. 1.**

The Viveka Chintamani. A monthly Tamil magazine & review, devoted to the diffusion of general knowledge ... விவேகசிந்தாமணி. . . Published by C. V. Swaminatha Iyer. vols. i.-ix. *Madras*, 1892-1901. 4°. **14172. i. 13.**

The Voice of Progress. A monthly journal [in English, Tamil, and Telugu,] conducted by a committee of the Madras Hindu Social Reform Association. vol. i., nos. 1-8. *Madras*, 1901-1902. 8°. **14172. i. 22.**

யதார்த்த பாஸ்கரன் ஞூ (*Yadhartha Bhaskaran, or The Sun of Truth. A Tamil magazine and review mainly devoted to religion, philosophy, sceince [*sic*] and literature. Editor: V. M. Swamy.) vols. i.-iii. *Madras*, 1902-1905. 8°. **14172. i. 7.**

No. 1 *of vol.* ii. *is wanting.*

MANAKUDI.

கிராமாதிகாரி ஞூ [Grāmādhikāri. A monthly magazine for matters of local government. Edited by Ṣ. Kōdaṇḍa-pāṇi Tañja-rāyar.] vol. i., pts. 1-2. *Manakudy, Negapatam* [printed], 1900-1901. 8°. **14172. i. 20.**

PENANG.

இந்து நேசன். "Hindu Nasen," *etc.* (Published bi-monthly.) vol. i., nos. 8-11. *Penang*, 1888. Fol. **14172. k. 7.(2.)**

The Penang News. (* பினாங்குவர்தமானி.) vol. i., nos. 1-3. *Penang*, 1897. Fol. **14172. l. 1.(3.)**

பினாங்கு விஜய கேதனன் [Pināṅgu-vijaya-kētanan]. (*The "Penang Standard," published monthly.) vol. ii., nos. 1-4, 6-7, vol. iii., nos. 1-8, vol. iv., nos. 1-4. *Penang*, 1888-1899. 4° & Fol. **14172. l. 1.(1.)**

உலகநேசன். The Olaga Naisan. [A Muhammadan journal.] Published every week. vol. i., nos. 1-28. *Penang*, 1887. Fol. **14172. k. 7.(1.)**

PERAK.

தேஜோபிமானி. Thajobimani. [Tējōbhimāni. A fortnightly magazine for political, social, and literary information. Edited by Ṣ. Ambala-vāṇa Piḷḷai.] vol. i., no. 1—vol. ii., no. i. *Perak*, ரு அகூகூ [1896]-1897. Fol. **14172. l. 1.(2.)**

SINGAPORE.

சிங்கைநேசன் . . . This Tamil Journal "Singai Nesan" is designed to commemorate the Jubilee of . . . the Queen-Empress Victoria. vols. i.-iii. *Singapore*, 1887-1890. Fol. **14172. l. 2.**

Wanting vol. ii., *nos.* 8-9, 51-2, *vol.* iii., *nos.* 6, 50-2.

SRIRANGAM.

ஸ்ரீ வாணீ விலாஸினீ (Sri Vani Vilasini.) [A monthly magazine of literature. Edited by T. K. Bāla-subrahmaṇya Aiyar.] *Srirangam*, 1905, *etc.* 8°. **14172. m. 1.**

In progress.

The Viṣishtâdvaitin. Edited by A. Govindacharya of Mysore. *Srirangam*, 1905, *etc.* 8°. **14170. eee. 11.**

In progress.

TANJORE.

தமிழகம். [Tamiẓ-agam. A monthly magazine of literature and science. Edited by T. Rājam

Aiyaṅgār.] vol. i. தஞ்சை [*Tanjore,*] 1905. 8°. **14172. i. 8.**

TIRUVADI.

சிவபக்திசந்திரிகை. [Şiva-bhakti-chandrikai. A monthly serial for the publication of Sanskrit and Tamil works bearing upon Şaiva theology and ritual, chiefly the Şiva-rahasya-khaṇḍam of the Skanda-purāṇam. Edited with translations of the Sanskrit by Ananta Vaidya-nātha Şivan.] திருவாதி [*Tiruvadi,*] 1890-1893. 8°. **14033. bb. 35.**

TRICHINOPOLI.

சுபோத பாரிஜாதம் ஒரு மாதாந்தரத் தமிழ்ச்சஞ்சிகை. [Subōdha-pārijātam. A monthly magazine of literature. Edited by V. B. Vēṅkaṭa-rāma Şāstri and T. S. Durai-sāmi Aiyar.] *Trichinopoly,* 1907, *etc.* 8°. *In progress.* **14172. i. 12.**

PERIYA-JĪYAR. *See* AṞAGIYA-MAṆAVĀḶA PERUMĀḶ.

PERIYA NŪH LEBBAI, *Kāyaṟpaṭṭaṇam.* வேதபுராணம். [Vēda-purāṇam. A poem on Muhammadan legends and teachings. Edited by Kaṇṇ'-Aḥmad Makhdūm Muḥammad.] pp. v. 138, i. சென்னை 1312 [*Madras,* 1894.] 8°. **14173. b. 16.**

PERIYA PARAKĀLA-SVĀMI, *disciple of Chandragiri Vēṅkaṭa-dēşikar.* *See* ĀṞVĀRGAḶ.—Nāl-āyiram. — *Entire Canon.* దివ్యప్రబన్ధవ్యాఖ్యాన రత్నావళి [Divya-prabandha-vyākhyāna-ratnāvaḷī. The Nāl-āyiram, with commentary by Periya Parakāla-svāmi,] *etc.* 1901, *etc.* 8°. **14170. ff. 9.**

—— *See* ĀṞVĀRGAḶ. — Nāl-āyiram. — *Tiru-vāy-moṟi.* ഭഗവദ്വിഷയം [Bhagavad-vishayam. Being the Tiru-vāy-moṟi with commentaries,—viz. Periya Parakāla-svāmi's Dramiḍa-şruti-tattvārtha-prakāşikai or Padin-eṇṇ'-āyira-paḍi, *etc.*] [1883-1904.] 4°. **14170. fff. 3.**

PERIY-ĀṞVĀR, also called PAṬṬAR-PIRĀN and VISHṆU-CHITTAN. [For editions of the Tiru-moṟi of this saint included in the editions of the whole or parts of the Nāl-āyira-prabandham:] *See* ĀṞVĀRGAḶ.—*Nāl-āyiram.*

PERIYA SAÑJĪVI-NĀTHA SVĀMI. *See* AṆḌA-PIṆḌA-VYĀKHYĀNAM. அண்டபிண்ட வியாக்கியானம். [Aṇḍa-piṇḍa-vyākhyānam. Translated into Tamil by "Periya Sañjīvi-nātha," an Italian Catholic missionary to Ceylon in the 18th century; followed by Ulaga-pramāṇa-şāstram, a tract by the same.] 1874. 12°. **14170. i. 11.**

PERIYA-SUBBĀ REḌḌIYĀR, *Pālvanam.* ००० மஹாராணி அம்மானை. (The Maharani Ammanei [, an account of the reign of Queen Victoria in *ammānai* metre] . . . with an [English and Tamil] introduction by N. S. Manikavasaka Nadar.) pp. iv. x. 132. *Madras,* 1901. 8°. **14172. b. 7.**

PERIYAV-ĀCHĀN PIḶḶAI (KṚUSHṆA SŪRI). *See* ĀṞVĀRGAḶ.—Nāl-āyiram.—*Iyaṟ-pā.* இயற்பா ஷ [Iyaṟ-pā. The Tiruv-āşiriyam, Periya-tiruv-antādi, and Tiruv-eṟuguṭṭ'-irukkai. With commentary of Periyav-āchān.] [1903-1904.] 8°. **14170. eee. 4.**

—— *See* ĀṞVĀRGAḶ. — Nāl-āyiram. — *Iyaṟ-pā.* ००० பெரிய திருமடல். [Periya-tiru-maḍal. With commentary of Periyav-āchān.] [1905.] 8°. **14170. ee. 6.(5.)**

—— *See* ĀṞVĀRGAḶ. — Nāl-āyiram. — *Iyaṟ-pā.* ००० சிறிய திருமடல். [Şiṟiya-tiru-maḍal. With commentary of Periyav-āchān.] [1905.] 8°. **14170. ee. 6.(4.)**

—— *See* ĀṞVĀRGAḶ.—Nāl-āyiram.—*Mudal-āyiram.* ००० முதலாயிரம் ஷ [Mudal-āyiram. With commentaries by Periyav-āchān and others.] 1880-1885. 8°. **14170. f. 9.**

—— —— ००० ముదలాయిర ము॥ [Mudal-āyiram. Another edition of the preceding, in Telugu characters.] 1881-[1886]. 8°. **14170. f. 8.**

—— *See* ĀṞVĀRGAḶ.—Nāl-āyiram.—*Mudal-āyiram.* ००० திருப்பல்லாண்டு ஷ [Tiru-pall'-āṇḍu. With commentary by Periyav-āchān.] [1870.] 8°. **14170. e. 15.**

—— *See* ĀṞVĀRGAḶ.—Nāl-āyiram.—*Periya-tiru-moṟi.* ००० பெரியதிருமொழி ஷ [Periya-tiru-moṟi. With commentaries of Periyav-āchān and others.] 1881. 8°. **14170. f. 7.**

—— *See* ĀṞVĀRGAḶ.—Nāl-āyiram.—*Periya-tiru-moṟi.* ००० திருக்குறுந்தாண்டகம் ஷ [Tiru-kuṟun-dāṇḍakam and Tiru-neḍun-dāṇḍakam. With commentaries by Periyav-āchān.] 1888. 8°. **14172. d. 4.**

PERIYAV-ĀCHĀN PIḶḶAI (KRUSHṆA SŪRI) (*continued*). *See* ĀḺVĀRGAḶ.—Nāl-āyiram.—*Tiru-vāy-moḻi.* ◦◦◦ తిరువాయ్మొఴి. [Tiru-vāy-moḻi. With commentaries in Telugu, based on the works of Periyav-āchān, *etc.*] 1902. 8°. **14170. ff. 10.**

—— *See* RĀMĀNUJA. శ్రీ . . . గద్యత్రయము ॥ [Gadya-trayam. With commentary by Periyav-āchān.] 1882. 8°. **14048. d. 47.**

—— *See* VĀLMĪKI. இந்த தனிஶ்லோகம். [Tani-ṣlōkam. Stanzas from the Rāmāyaṇam, with glosses and commentary by Periyav-āchān.] [1899, *etc.*] 8°. **14065. bbb. 6.**

—— *See* VĀLMĪKI. அபயப்ரதாநஸாரம். [Abhaya-pradāna-sāram. Being VI. xvii.—xix. 1-9 and 23, with exposition in Tamil by Periyav-āchān.] [1891.] 8°. **14060. c. 32.(1.)**

—— *See* YĀMUNĀCHĀRYAR. ◦ ◦ ◦ ஆளவந்தார் ஸ்தோத்ரம். [Āḷavandār-stōtram. With commentary by Periyav-āchān.] 1878. 8°. **14028. c. 46.**

—— —— 1879. 8°. **14028. b. 52.**

—— మాణిక్కమాల. [Māṇikka-mālai. A Vaishṇava theological tract.] *See* YĀMUNĀCHĀRYAR. శ్రీ . . . ప్రమేయరత్నం ॥ [Pramēya-ratnam.] pp. 43-61. [1904.] 8°. **14170. ee. 6.(3.)**

—— నిగమనపడి. [Nigamana-paḍi. A tract on two devotional formulæ and the "charama-ṣlōkam," *i.e.* Bhagavad-gītā xviii. 66.] *See* PIḶḶAI LŌKĀCHĀRYAR. శ్రీ . . . అష్టాదశరహస్యంగళ్ ॥ [Ashṭādaṣa rahasyaṅgaḷ.] [1905.] 8°. **14170. eee. 12.**

—— పరందరహస్యం ॥ [Paranda-rahasyam. A Srī-vaishṇava treatise.] pp. 29, 64. *See* NAÑJĪYAR. ◦◦◦ ఆత్మవివాహం ॥ [Ātma-vivāham, *etc.*] 1893. 8°. **14170. ee. 40.**

—— பாசுரப்படி ராமாயணம். [Pāṣura-paḍi-rāmāyaṇam. A religious tract based on the *pāṣurams* of the Nāl-āyira-prabandham.] pp. iv. *See* NAMBI NĀYUḌU. ◦◦◦ பாசுரப்படி ராமாயணம் மூல [Pāṣura-paḍi-rāmāyaṇam, *etc.*] 1903. 12°. **14170. d. 46.(4.)**

PERU-MĀḶ. *See* KULA-ṢĒKHARA PERU-MĀḶ.

PERUM-BATTA-PULIY-ŪR-NAMBI, *Ṣelli-nagar* (TILLAI-NAMBI). திருவாலவாயுடையார் திருவிளையாடற்புராணம். [Tiru-viḷaiy-āḍaṛ-purāṇam. A poem in 1753 stanzas on the legends of the Ṣaiva sanctuary of Madura, adapted from a Sanskrit Uttara-mahā-purāṇam. Edited with literary and critical prefaces, glossary, excerpts from other works, annotations, and index by U. V. Sāmināth'-aiyar.] pp. i. 67, 333, ii. சென்னை [*Madras*,] 1906. 8°. **14170. eee. 17.**

This work was written before Ṣaka 1150.

PERUN-DĒVANĀR. *See* BUDDHA-MITRAN. ◦◦◦ வீரசோழியம். [Vīra-ṣōḻiyam. With commentary by Perun-dēvanār.] [1881.] 8°. **14172. f. 12.**

—— —— 1895. 8°. **14172. e. 21.**

—— Bharata Venba. [An epic poem. Udyōga-parvam, in English, with Tamil commentary and biography.] (†பெருந்தேவனார் பாரதம்.) *See* ACADEMIES, *etc.* — Madras. — *University of Madras.* Notes on the Tamil text, *etc.* 1888. 12°. **14172. a. 41.**

—— பெருந்தேவனார் பாரதம். [Bhāratam, Udyōga-parvam, 256-346. In Tamil and English, with Tamil commentary, *etc.*] *See* ACADEMIES, *etc.*—Madras.—*University of Madras.* Copious notes, *etc.* 1898. 8°. **14172. b. 16.(1.)**

—— பெருந்தேவனார் பாரதம். [Bhāratam, Udyōga-parvam.] *See* ACADEMIES, *etc.*—Madras.—*University of Madras.* The Tamil text, *etc.* pp. 1-15. 1899. 8°. **14172. bb. 6.(7.)**

—— பெருந்தேவனார் பாரதம். [Bhāratam, Udyōga-parvam. With notes and English translation.] *See* ACADEMIES, *etc.*—Madras.—*University of Madras.* University of Madras. Matriculation Examination, 1900, *etc.* 1900. 8°. **14172. bb. 6.(2.)**

—— Perundevanar Bharatam. Udyoga Parvam. [In English, with Tamil notes.] *See* ACADEMIES, *etc.* — Madras. — *University of Madras.* Copious annotations, *etc.* 1900. 8°. **14172. bb. 6.(3.)**

—— Perunthevanar Bharatam. [Udyōga-parvam. In English, with Tamil notes.] *See* ACADEMIES, *etc.*—Madras.—*University of Madras.* University of Madras. Exhaustive notes, *etc.* 1900. 8°. **14172. bb. 6.(4.)**

PERUṄ-GUNṞŪR-KIṞĀR. ஒன்பதாம் பத்து. [Decade ix. Ten poems on the Chera king Ilañ-Chēral Irum-borai.] *See* PADIṬṬU-PATTU. ००० பதிற்றுப்பத்து ஆ [Padiṭṭu-pattu.] pp. 138-157. 1904. 8°. **14172. bb. 14.**

PERUṄ-KAUṢIKANĀR, *Peruṅ-gunṟūr.* மலைபடுகடாம். [Malai-badu-gaḍām, or Kūttar-āṭṭu-paḍai. A poem, forming no. 10 of the Pattu-pāṭṭu, in panegyric of a king Nannan and his country. With commentary of Nachinārkk'-iniyar.] *See* PATTU-PĀṬṬU. பத்துப்பாட்டு ஆ [Pattu-pāṭṭu.] pp. 317-372. 1889. 8°. **14172. d. 10.**

PERU-VĀYIN MULLIYĀR. ००० ஆசாரக்கோவை. [Āchāra-kōvai. An ancient ethical poem in 100 stanzas, forming the 13th of the class of *Kīr-kaṇakku* poems, with paraphrase. With preface by T. Ṣelva-kēṣava-rāya Mudaliyār.] pp. 6, 46. *Madras,* 1893. 8°. **14172. a. 29.(3.)**

PETER (ANNE). Life of Rev. V. Vethanayagam, by his daughter Anne Peter. கனம்: வீரவாகு வேதநாயகம் ஐயரின் ஜீவிய விருத்தாந்தம். [With preface by T. Kember.] pp. 135; 1 *plate.* *Madras,* 1899. 12°. **14171. a. 30.**

PETER (J. S.). இந்தியா, இலங்கை, பர்மா தேசங்களிலுள்ள பெரிய ஆலயங்கள். (The Great Temples of India, Ceylon, and Burma.) pp. 105; 1 *plate.* *London, Madras,* 1901. 4°. **14171. c. 6.**

PĒYANĀR. முல்லை. [Mullai. Erotic verses.] *See* KŪḌALŪR-KIṞĀR. ००० ஐங்குறுநூறு ஆ [Aiṅ-guṟu-nūṟu.] pp. 121-142. 1903. 8°. **14172. c. 48.**

PĒY-ĀṞVĀR. [For editions of the Tiruv-antādi of this saint included in the editions of the whole or parts of the Nāl-āyira-prabandham:] *See* ĀṞVĀRGAḶ.—*Nāl-āyiram.*

PHILALETHES, *A.M. Oxon.* *See* FELLOWES (R.).

PHILIP (C. PAUL). மஸ்கொல்லை அர்ச். ஆறுனீஸ்பரிபேரில் பதிகம். [A hymn of ten stanzas upon St. Anne of Maskollai.] pp. 8. யாழ்ப்பாணம் [*Jaffna,*] 1891. 32°. **14170. a. 58.(1.)**

PHILIP (J.). Resemblance between Paganism and Roman Catholicism. இந்துமத பாப்புமத சம்பந்தீபம். pp. 16. *Jaffna,* 1842. 12°. **14170. b. 1.(60.)**

PHILIPPI (FRIEDRICH ADOLPH). *See* WINKEL (E.). A brief Commentary ... on St. Paul's Epistle to the Galatians [chiefly based on the work of Philippi], *etc.* 1891. 8°. **14170. c. 36.**

PICHUV-AIYAṄGĀR. *See* NAMM'-ĀṞVĀR. ००० நம்மாழ்வார்தாலாட்டு. [Namm'-āṟvār-tālāṭṭu. Edited by Pichuv-Ayyaṅgār.] 1900. 8°. **14170. ee. 35.(8.)**

PICTET (BÉNÉDICT). *See* RHENIUS (C.T.E.). Summary of a Body of Divinity ... [abridged from the works of Pictet and Dwight], *etc.* 1838. 12°. **14170. b. 42.**

—— —— 1845. 12°. **14170. b. 43.**

PICTURE BOOK. Royal Coloured Picture Book. Containing views of remarkable places, etc., and accounts of remarkable people. வர்ணந்தீர்ந்த சிறந்த படப்புஸ்தகம். pp. 24; 12 *plates.* *Madras,* 1880. 4°. **14172. k. 3.**

PILLAI LŌKĀCHĀRYAR, *son of Vaḍakku Tiru-vīthi-Pillai, disciple of Nam-Billai.* ००० அஷ்டாதசரஹஸ்யங்கள். [Ashṭādaṣa rahasyaṅgaḷ. 18 treatises on Vaishṇava theology, viz. the Mumukshu-paḍi, Tattva-trayam, Artha-pañchakam, Vachana-bhūshaṇam, Archir-ādi, Pramēya-ṣēkharam, Prapanna-paritrāṇam, Sāra-saṅgraham, Saṃsāra-sām-rājyam, Nava-ratna-mālai, Nava-vidha-sambandham, Yādṛuchchhika-paḍi, Paranda-paḍi, Ṣriyaḥ-pati-paḍi, Tattva-ṣēkharam, Tani-dvayam, Tani-charamam, and Tani-praṇavam. Edited by A. K. Kṛushṇam-āchāryar and M. K. Ṣrīnivāsāchāryar. Second edition.] pp. 296. *Madras,* 1889. 8°. **14170. f. 12.**

——శ్రీ ... [Telugu text] ... [Telugu text]. [Ashṭādaṣa rahasyaṅgaḷ. Preceded by Periyav-āchān Pillai's Nigamana-paḍi. Edited by A. M. Ṣrīṣaila-nāthar.] pp. ii. 112, 220. [Telugu text] [*Madras,* 1905.] 8°. **14170. eee. 12.**

—— ००० முமுக்ஷுப்படி ஆ [Mumukshu-paḍi. A Ṣrī-vaishṇava theological work. With the commentary Tiru-mantrārtham by Periya-jīyar and a gloss by Embāv-ayyaṅgār. Edited by A. K. Kṛushṇam-āchāryar.] சென்னை [*Madras,*] 1889. 8°. **14170. f. 17.**

Incomplete, containing only pp. 1-32.

—— ००० முமுக்ஷுப்படியும் ... திருமந்த்ரார்த்தமென்னும்வ்யாக்யாநமும். [Mumukshu-paḍi. With the commentary styled Tiru-mantrārtham of Periya-jīyar (Aṟagiya-maṇavāḷa Peru-māḷ) and glosses by Ṣuddha-sattvam Doḍḍ'-ayyaṅgār and Ṣuddha-sattvam Embāv-ayyaṅgār. Edited by Ch. K. Tiru-vēnkaṭāchāryar.] pp. ii. 188. சென்னை [*Madras*,] 1890. 8°. **14170. f. 18.**

—— Mumukshuppaḍi or Rahasya-traya, or The way of the seeker of salvation. [With Periya-jīyar's commentary. Translated into English.] 1905, *etc.* *See* PERIODICAL PUBLICATIONS.—*Srirangam.* The Viṣishtâdvaitin, *etc.* vol. i., no. 2, *etc.* 1905, *etc.* 8°. **14170. eee. 11.(vol. 1, etc.)**
In progress.

—— ప్రపన్నజనాగ్రేసరరాన శ్రీపిళ్ళైలోకాచార్యర్ తిరువాయ్మలర్న్దరుళియ తత్త్వత్రయమ్, ఇతఱ్కు . . . శ్రీమణవాళమామునికళ్ అరుళిచ్చెయ్తవ్యాఖ్యానమ్. [Tattva-trayam. A treatise on the three categories of the Viṣishṭādvaita philosophy. With a commentary by Aṟagiya-maṇavāḷar. Edited by M. A. Āṟvār Tirumalai Ayyaṅgār, R. A. Dāmōdara Aṟagiya-ṣiṅgar Āchāryar, and A. K. Kṛushṇam-āchāryar.] pp. ii. x. 194; 2 *plates*. భావ [*Madras*, 1875.] 8°. **14170. f. 24.**

—— ప్రపన్నజనాగ్రేసరరాన శ్రీపిళ్ళైలోకాచార్యర్ తిరువాయ్ మలర్న్దరుళియ తత్త్వత్రయమ్. ఇతఱ్కు . . . శ్రీమణవాళమామునికళ్ అరుళిచ్చెయ్త వ్యాఖ్యానమ్. [Tattva-trayam. With the commentary of Aṟagiya-maṇavāḷar. Together with a Telugu translation of both text and commentary by Para-vastu Vēṅkaṭa-raṅga-nātha Svāmi.] pp. ii. 10, 232; 1 *plate*. చెన్నపురి ౧౯౦౪ [*Madras*, 1904.] 8°. **14170. ff. 11.**

—— Tattva-traya or Aphorisms on the Three Verities, Soul, Matter and God . . . translated [with annotations based chiefly on the commentary of Maṇavāḷa Mā-muni] by Sri-Párthasárathy Aiyangár. pp. viii. 237. *Madras*, 1900. 8°. **14170. ee. 17.**

—— ஸ்ரீ . . . ஸ்ரீவசநபூஷணமும் . . . வ்யாக்யாநமும்; [Vachana-bhūshaṇam. A treatise on the theology of the Tengalai Vaishṇava church. With a commentary by Aṟagiya-maṇavāḷar. Edited by A. K. Kṛushṇam-āchāryar and M. K. Ṣrīnivāsāchāryar.] pp. 317. *Madras*, 1879. 8°. **14172. b. 10.**

—— ∘∘∘ யதீந்த்ரப்ரவணப்ரபாவம். [Yatīndra-pravaṇa-prabhāvam. A panegyrical biography of Piḷḷai Lōkāchāryar and Aṟagiya-maṇavāḷa Mā-muni, ascribed to "Piḷḷai Lōkārya Jīyar." Edited by T. Ṣaṭhakōpa-rāmānujāchāryar.] pp. 124. சென்னை [*Madras*,] 1907. 8°. **14170. ff. 23.**

The work begins with the birth of Piḷḷai Lōkāchāryar and his younger brother Aṟagiya-maṇavāḷa Peru-māḷ I., and proceeds (p. 23) to the birth in Ṣaka 1292 of the famous "Yatīndra-pravaṇar" or "Saumya-jāmātā" Aṟagiya-maṇavāḷa Peru-māḷ II. (son of Tigaṟa-kiḍandān Tiru-nāvīr'-uḍaiya Birān Tātar Aṇṇar Aiyar, and grandson of Kōṭṭūr Aṟagiya-maṇavāḷa Peru-māḷ Piḷḷai or Kollikāvala-dāsar, the disciple of Piḷḷai Lōkāchāryar).

PIḶḶAI LŌKAM-JĪYAR. *See* AṞAGIYA-MAṆAVĀḶA PERU-MĀḶ. ∘∘∘ யதிராஜ விம்ஶதி. [Yati-rāja-viṃṣati. With commentary by Piḷḷai Lōkam-jīyar.] [1884.] 12°. **14028. b. 63.(1.)**

—— *See* AṞAGIYA-MAṆAVĀḶA PERU-MĀḶ. ∘∘∘ యతిరాజవింశతి. [Yati-rāja-viṃṣati. With commentary of Piḷḷai Lōkam-jīyar.] [1904.] 8°. **14028. c. 86.**

—— *See* ĀṞVĀRGAḶ.—Nāl-āyiram.—*Mudal-āyiram.* ∘∘∘ முதலாயிரம் ஞூ [Mudal-āyiram. With commentaries by Piḷḷai Lōkam-jīyar and others.] 1880-1885. 8°. **14170. f. 9.**

—— —— ∘∘∘ ముతలాయిర వ॥ [Mudal-āyiram. Another edition, in Telugu characters.] 1881-[1886.] 8°. **14170. f. 8.**

—— *See* ĀṞVĀRGAḶ.—Nāl-āyiram.—*Periya-tiru-moṟi.* ∘∘∘ பெரியதிருமொழி ஞூ [Periya-tiru-moṟi. With commentaries of Lōkam-jīyar and others.] 1881. 8°. **14170. f. 7.**

—— *See* ĀṞVĀRGAḶ.—Nāl-āyiram.—*Periya-tiru-moṟi.* ∘∘∘ திருக்குறுந்தாண்டகம் ஞூ [Tiru-kuṟun-dāṇḍakam and Tiru-neḍun-dāṇḍakam. With commentaries by Lōkam-jīyar.] 1888. 8°. **14172. d. 4.**

—— *See* VIḶĀÑ-JŌLAI PIḶḶAI. ∘∘∘ ஸப்தகாதை ஞூ [Sapta-gāthai. Together with a commentary by Piḷḷai Lōkam-jīyar.] [1882.] 16°. **14172. a. 9.**

—— ∘∘∘ இயல்சாத்து வ்யாக்யாநம். [Iyal-ṣāttu-vyākhyānam. An explanation of the concluding verses of the Nāl-āyiram.] *See* ĀṞVĀRGAḶ.—Nāl-āyiram.—*Iyaṟ-pā.* ∘∘∘ இராமாநுச நூற்றந்தாதி. [Rāmānuja-nūṭṭ'-antādi.] pp. 101-117. [1905.] 8°. **14170. ee. 6.(6.)**

—— ∘∘∘ ராமாநுஜார்யதிவ்யசரிதை. [Rāmā-nujārya-divya-charitai. A life of Rāmānuja.

Edited by Ch. K. Tiru-vēṅkaṭāchāryar.] pp. 301. திருவல்லிக்கேணி [*Triplicane,*] 1886. 8°.
14170. f. 11.

PIḶḶAI PERU-MĀḶ AIYAṄGĀR (Aḻagiya-maṇa-vāḷa-dāsar). [*Life.*] *See* Vēṅkaṭa-rāma Aiyaṅgār, *T.* வில்லிபுத்தூரர் . . . சரித்திரச் சுருக்கம். (Biographical Sketch of Villiputturer & Pillai Perumal, *etc.*) 1904. 12°. **14171. a. 48.(2.)**

—— அஷ்டப்பிரபந்தம். [Ashṭa-prabandham. Eight Vaishṇava devotional poems, viz. Tiruv-araṅga-kalambakam, Tiruv-araṅgattu mālai, Tiruv-araṅgatt' antādi, Ṣrīraṅga-nāyakar-ūṣal, Aḻagar-antādi, Tiru-vēṅkaṭa-mālai, Tiru-vēṅkaṭatt' antādi, and Nūṯṯ'-eṭṭu-tiru-padiy-antādi. Edited by K. Rāma-sāmi Nāyuḍu. With a preface by Kalkuḷam Kuppu-sāmi Mudaliyār.] 8 pts. சென்னை [*Madras,*] 1904. 12°. **14170. dd. 1.**

Each poem has a separate title-page, dated 1903. *The volume forms no.* 2 *of the* Tamiḻ-kavi-mālai.

—— திருமாலிருஞ்சோலைமலை அழகரந்தாதி ௸ [Aḻagar-antādi. Songs in honour of the Vaishṇava sanctuary of Sholingarh. Edited by Tiru-vēṅkaṭāchala Mudaliyār.] pp. 18. சென்னை பவ [*Madras,* 1874.] 16°. **14172. a. 20.(8.)**

—— நூற்றெட்டுத் திருப்பதியந்தாதி ௸ [Nūṯṯ'-eṭṭu-tiru-padiy-antādi. A religious poem on the 108 Vaishṇava sanctuaries. With a life of the author by T. Gōvinda Piḷḷai. Edited by Tiru-vēṅkaṭāchala Mudaliyār.] pp. iv. 24. சென்னை பவ [*Madras,* 1874.] 16°. **14172. a. 20.(1.)**

—— கோயிற்கலம்பகம் என்னும் திருவரங்கக்கலம்பகம் ௸ [Tiruv-araṅga-kalambakam, or Kōyiṟ-kalambakam. A series of poems in different metres on the Vaishṇava sanctuary at Srirangam. Edited by Tiru-vēṅkaṭāchala Mudaliyār.] pp. 39. சென்னை ஸ்ரீமுக [*Madras,* 1874.] 16°.
14172. a. 20.(6.)

—— கோயிற்கலம்பகம் - என்கின்ற திருவரங்கக்கலம்பகம் ௸ [Tiruv-araṅga-kalambakam. With a commentary. Edited by Taṇḍalam Subbarāya Mudaliyār.] pp. 72. வெகுதான்ய [*Madras,* 1879.] 8°. **14172. c. 9.**

—— கோயிலந்தாதி என்னும் திருவரங்கத்தந்தாதி ௸ [Tiruv-araṅgatt' antādi, or Kōyil-antādi. A religious poem on the Vaishṇava sanctuary of Srirangam. Edited by Tiru-vēṅkaṭāchala Mudaliyār.] pp. 20. சென்னை யுவ [*Madras,* 1875.] 16°.
14172. a. 20.(5.)

—— கோயின்மாலை என்னும் திருவரங்கத்துமாலை ௸ [Tiruv-araṅgattu mālai, or Kōyin-mālai. A religious poem in honour of the sanctuary of Srirangam. Edited by Tiru-vēṅkaṭāchala Mudaliyār.] pp. 20. சென்னை யுவ [*Madras,* 1876.] 16°. **14172. a. 20.(4.)**

—— திருவரங்கத்தூசற்றிருநாமம் ௸ [Tiruv-araṅgatt' ūsaṯ-ṯiru-nāmam, or Ṣīraṅga-nāyakar-ūṣal. A swinging-song for the service of Vishṇu at Srirangam. Followed by another swinging-song called Ṣīraṅga-nāyakiyār-ūṣal, for the service of Lakshmī, by Kōnēriy-appan Aiyaṅgār. Edited by Tiru-vēṅkaṭāchala Mudaliyār.] pp. 20. சென்னை யுவ [*Madras,* 1875.] 16°. **14172. a. 20.(7.)**

—— திருவேங்கடமாலை ௸ [Tiru-vēṅkaṭa-mālai. A century of verses on the Vaishṇava sanctuary at Tripati. Edited by Tiru-vēṅkaṭāchala Mudaliyār.] pp. 20. சென்னை ஸ்ரீமுக [*Madras,* 1874.] 16°. **14172. a. 20.(2.)**

—— o o o திருவேங்கடமாலை. [Tiru-vēṅkaṭa-mālai. With a commentary by P. N. Rāja-gōpāla Mudaliyār.] pp. ii. 40. பிரமாதி [*Madras,* 1879.] 8°. **14172. c. 25.**

—— ஸ்ரீ . . . திருவேங்கடமாலை மூலம். [Tiru-vēṅkaṭa-mālai. Edited by K. Rāma-sāmi Nāyuḍu.] pp. 16. சென்னை [*Madras,*] 1903. 12°.
14170. d. 4.(1.)

—— திருவேங்கடத்தந்தாதி. [Tiru-vēṅkaṭatt' antādi. A religious poem on the Vaishṇava sanctuary of Tripati. Edited by Tiru-vēṅkaṭāchala Mudaliyār.] pp. 18. சென்னை பவ [*Madras,* 1874.] 16°. **14172. a. 20.(3.)**

—— ஸ்ரீ . . . திருவேங்கடத்தந்தாதி மூலம். [Tiru-vēṅkaṭatt' antādi. Edited by K. Rāma-sāmi Nāyuḍu.] pp. 16. சென்னை [*Madras,*] 1903. 12°.
14170. d. 4.(2.)

PIḶḶAI TIRUMALAI NAMBI, *son of Periya Tirumalai* (Tiru-kurugai-pirāṉ Piḷḷāṉ). *See* Āḻvārgaḷ.—Nāl-āyiram.—*Tiru-vāy-moḻi.* பகவத்விஷயம் ॥ [Bhagavad-vishayam. Being the Tiru-vāy-moḻi with commentaries—viz. Piḷḷāṉ's Āṟ'-āyira-paḍi, *etc.*] [1883-1904.] 4°. **14170. fff. 3.**

PIḶḶĀN. *See* PIḶḶAI TIRUMALAI NAMBI.

PINB'-AṚAGIYA PERU-MĀḶ JĪYAR. ◦◦◦ குருபரம்பராப்ரபாவம். [Guru-paramparā-prabhāvam. A collection of legends bearing on the leaders of the southern Vaishṇava church. Edited by Chitrakūṭam Kandāḍai Tiru-vēṅkaṭāchāryar.] pp. 233. சென்னை [*Madras,*] 1892. 8°. **14170. i. 29.**

—— ◦◦◦ ஆறுயிரப்படி குருபரம்பராப்ரபாவம் ௸ [Guru-paramparā-prabhāvam. A new edition, with a commentary. Edited by Ṣ. Krushṇam-āchāryar, V. M. Gōpāla-krushṇam-āchāryar, and V. M. Ṣrīnivāsa Appaṅgār Svāmi.] pp. vii. 248, 9. சென்னை பராபவ [*Madras,* 1906.] 8°. **14170. ff. 22.**

—— ஸ்ரீ... வார்த்தாமாலை. [Vārttā-mālai. Precepts and homilies upon the beliefs and practices of the Tengalai Vaishṇavas. Edited by Ch. K. Tiru-vēṅkaṭāchāryar and A. K. Krushṇam-āchāryar.] pp. 192. சென்னைநகர் [*Madras,*] 1882. 8°. **14172. d. 3.**

PIṄGALAR, *son of Divākarar.* ◦◦◦ பிங்கலந்தையென்னும் பிங்கலநிகண்டு. [Piṅgala-nighaṇṭu, or Piṅgalandai. A lexicon in 10 sections, based upon that of Divākarar. With a commentary by Vīrākshimaṅgalam T. Ṣivan Piḷḷai. Edited by the latter and T. K. Subba-rāya Cheṭṭiyār.] pp. 4, 415, xxviii. ii. சென்னை [*Madras,*] 1890. 8°. **14172. f. 14.**

PINNOCK (WILLIAM HENRY). An Analysis of Ecclesiastical History. திருச்சபைச்சரித்திரவினாவிடை. [Abridged from the work of Pinnock, and containing the history of the first three centuries.] pp. 328. *Nagercoil,* 1856. 12°. **14170. b. 37.**

PIREIRA. *See* PEREIRA.

PĪR MUḤAMMAD. *See* MUḤAMMAD, *Pīr.*

PIUS IX., *Pope* [GIOVANNI MARIA GIOVANNI BATTISTA PIETRO PELLEGRINO ISIDORO MASTAI-FERRETTI]. *See* BRITO (C.). ஒன்பதாம் பத்திநாத ... சரித்திரம். [Life of Pius IX.] 1892. 8°. **14170. c. 44.**

PONN'-AMBALA-DĀSAR, *of Pādapūjai Ambalatt' āḍum Svāmi's Foundation, Chidambaram.* தில்லைச்சிவகாமசௌந்தரி திருவிரட்டைமணிமாலை திருநாமாவளி. [Tillai-ṣiva-kāma-saundari-tiruv-iraṭṭai-maṇi-mālai and °tiru-nāmāvaḷi. Hymns on the cult of Ṣiva and his consort at Chidambaram.] pp. ii. 8. சிதம்பரம் மன்மத [*Chidambaram,* 1895.] 12°. **14170. d. 32.(2.)**

PONN'-AMBALA GURU, *of Vṛuttāchalam. See* VĪRA PIḶḶAI. ◦◦◦ வன்னியர் புராணம் ௸ [Vanniyar-purāṇam. Edited by Ponn'-ambalar.] 1905. 8°. **14172. bb. 17.**

PONN'-AMBALA KAVI-RĀYAR, *Ṣēlai. See* MADANA-KĀMA-RĀJAN. மதனகாமராஜன்கதை ௸ [Madana-kāma-rājan-kathai. Edited by Ponn'-ambalar.] [1855.] 8°. **14170. k. 17.**

PONN'-AMBALA PIḶḶAI, *Nallūr Ṣ. See* KĀLIDĀSA. இரகுவம்மிசம். [Raghu-vamṣam. Edited by Ponn'-ambalar.] 1887. 8°. **14172. b. 33.**

—— *See* PURĀṆAS.—*Skanda-purāṇam.* திருக்கேதீச்சுரமகிமை. [Tiru-kētīṣvara-mahimai. Edited with translation, *etc.,* by Ponn'-ambalar.] [1891.] 8°. **14170. e. 41.(2.)**

—— *See* VĒDĀNTA-SUBRAHMAṆYA PIḶḶAI. மயூரகிரிபுராணம். [Mayūra-giri-purāṇam. With paraphrase by Ponn'-ambalar.] 1885. 8°. **14170. e. 66.**

—— *See* VILLIPUTTŪRAR. ◦◦◦ மகாபாரத ௸ [Mahā-bhāratam, Ādi-parvam. With interpretation by Ponn'-ambalar.] [1897.] 8°. **14172. d. 18.**

—— —— [1898.] 8°. **14172. d. 19.**

PONN'-AMBALA SVĀMI, *Kōvilūr. See* KRUSHṆA MIṢRA. ஸ்ரீ ... மெய்ஞ்ஞானவிளக்கம். [Meyñāna-viḷakkam. Edited by Ponn'-ambalar.] 1898. 8°. **14172. c. 27.**

—— *See* TĀṆḌAVA-RĀYA-MŪRTTI SVĀMI. ◦◦◦ கைவல்லிய நவநீதம் ௸ [Kaivalya-nava-nītam. With commentary styled Tattvārtha-dīpam by Ponn'-ambalar.] 1898. 8°. **14170. ee. 9.**

PONNAVAN. கனாநூல். [Kanā-nūl. An ancient poem in 30 quatrains on oneiromancy. Edited by R. Rāghav'-aiyaṅgār.] pp. 7. *See* PŪDAÑ-ṢENDAṆĀR. இனியது நாற்பது ௸ [Iniyadu nāṛ-padu, *etc.*] 1903. 8°. **14172. bb. 3.(7.)**

Forms no. 2 of the Ṣen-damiṛ-prachuram. *The name of the author is that given in the text, v. 30, which apparently describes him as son of Gaṇapura-dēvan.*

PONN'-ŌDUVĀR, *Tiruvāvaḍuduṛai Ṣ. See* ṢEKKIṚĀR. ◦◦◦ திருஞானசம்பந்த ... புராணவசனம். [Tiru-ñāna-sambandha-mūrtti-purāṇa-vachanam. Abridged by Ponn'-ōduvār.] 1900. 8°. **14170. e. 47.(10.)**

PONNU-SĀMI MUDALIYĀR, *Chidambaram.* See PUGAṚENDI. ◦◦◦ பவளக்கொடிமாலை. [Pavaḷa-koḍi-mālai. Edited by Ponnu-sāmi.] 1885. 8°. **14172. b. 28.**

PONNU-SĀMI NĀḌĀR, *A.K.* பாண்டியகுல விளக்கம். [Pāṇḍiya-kula-viḷakkam. An account of the race of the Pandiyan kings. Edited by Bāla-subrahmaṇya Nāṭṭār. Second edition.] pp. 44. சென்னை [*Madras,*] 1899. 12°. **14170. g. 17.(2.)**

The Shanars or Toddy-drawer caste, to which the writer belongs, claim descent from these kings.

PONNU-SĀMI PIḶḶAI, *Triṣirapuram M.* Kamalatchi. A novel . . . dedicated to the Tamilians, with an introduction in English and Tamil by . . . T. Balasundara Mudaliar Avergal. (*கமலாக்ஷி சரித்திரம்.) pp. 19, 327. *Madras,* 1903. 8°. **14171. a. 50.(2.)**

PONNU-SĀMI PIḶḶAI, *V.A.* See GŌVINDA-SĀMI UPĀDHYĀYAR and PONNU-SĀMI PIḶḶAI. ◦◦◦ சல்லாப லாவணி. Sallapa Lavany. [1893.] 8°. **14170. e. 47.(2.)**

POOR (DANIEL). The Notification, or Scripture Parables . . . வேதமொழி . . . அறிவித்தல். Third edition. pp. 12. *Jaffna,* 1844. 12°. **14170. b. 1.(47.)**

—— The Search after Truth . . . உண்மைநாட்டம். [A tract against Romanism.] Second edition. pp. 12. *Jaffna,* 1842. 12°. **14170. b. 1.(32.)**

POPE (GEORGE UGLOW). See AIYANĀR-IDANĀR. Extracts from the . . . "Purra-poruḷ Veṇbā-Mālai," and the "Purra-nānnūrru." By . . . G. U. Pope. 1899. 8°. **Ac. 8820/3 & 2110. e, f.**

—— *See* BIBLE.—New Testament.—*Gospels.* [*Matthew.*] Our Blessed Lord's Sermon on the Mount . . . in Tamil . . . with a vocabulary . . . grammatical praxis and . . . tables; by . . . G. U. Pope. 1860. 8°. **3068. cc. 11.**

—— *See* NĀL-AḌIYĀR. ◦◦◦ நாலடியார். The Nālaḍiyār .. with introduction, translation, and notes . . . a concordance and lexicon . . . by . . . G. U. Pope. 1893. 8°. **14172. d. 12.**

—— *See* SŪRYA-NĀRĀYAṆA ṢĀSTRI. Tani-paçura-togai . . . With English echoes by . . . G. U. Pope, *etc.* 1901. 12°. **14172. a. 28.**

POPE (GEORGE UGLOW) (*continued*). *See* TIRU-MURAI.—*Tiru-vāchakam.* A few hymns of Manikka Vachaka and Tayumanavar. Translated by . . . G. U. Pope. 1897. 8°. **14170. ee. 12.(2.)**

—— *See* TIRU-MURAI.—*Tiru-vāchakam.* The Tiruvāçagam . . . with English translation, introductions, and notes . . . a summary of the life and legends of the sage, with appendices illustrating . . . the Çaiva Siddhāntam . . . By . . . G. U. Pope. 1900. 8°. **14170. ff. 7.**

—— *See* TIRU-VAḶḶUVAR. திருவள்ளுவநாயனார் . . . திருக்குறள். The 'Sacred' Kurraḷ . . . With . . . translation, notes . . . and concordance. By . . . G. U. Pope. 1886. 8°. **14172. c. 40.**

—— Introductory Tamil Grammar. தமிழ் இலக்கணநூற்சுருக்கவினாவிடை. Second edition. pp. 39. *Madras,* 1846. 16°. **14172. h. 40.(1.)**

—— [Fifth edition.] pp. 34. *Madras,* 1855. 16°. **14172. h. 39.(1.)**

—— A larger Grammar of the Tamil language in both its dialects; to which are added the Nannûl, Yâpparungalam, and other native authorities; with commentary, copious exercises . . . and an analytical index, *etc.* Second edition. (*Pope's Third Tamil Grammar . . . இலக்கணநூல்.) 2 pts. *Madras,* 1858-1859. 8°. **14172. h. 81.**

—— A Tamil Prose Reading-book: or Companion to the Handbook, in five books, *etc.* *Madras,* 1859. 8°. **14172. h. 76.**

Contains only bks. i.-iii.

—— A first Catechism of Tamil Grammar . . . with an English translation by . . . D. S. Herrick and English notes by the author. (*தமிழ் இலக்கண வினாவிடை.) (*A Catechism of Tamil Grammar, no. ii.) 2 pts. *Oxford,* 1895-1905. 8°. **12906. m.**

—— Pope's Second Catechism of Tamil Grammar. தமிழ் இலக்கண வினாவிடை. Sixth edition. pp. 97. *Public Instruction Press: Madras,* 1858. 12°. **14172. h. 53.**

—— [Sixth edition.] pp. 88. *American Mission Press: Madras,* 1858. 16°. **14172. h. 39.(2.)**

—— A Handbook of the Ordinary Dialect of the Tamil Language. Seventh edition [of A

Tamil Handbook]. (*Part v. A Tamil Prose Reader adapted to the Handbook.) 5 pts. *Oxford*, 1904-1906. 8°. **2056. b.**

—— A Tamil Poetical Anthology, with grammatical notes and a vocabulary. தமிழ்ச்செய்யுட் கலம்பகம். [Second edition.] pp. xviii. 220. *Madras*, 1859. 8°. **14172. b. 46.**

POSTAL GUIDE. Postal Guide. தபால் ஸ்தலங்கள். [Published by Dēvakoṭṭai M. P. Paṛaṇiy-appa Cheṭṭi.] pp. 27. *Singapore*, 1904. 8°. **14172. i. 23.**

POULLÉ (MÉRIDAS). *See* MARIYA-DĀS PILLAI.

POYGAIYĀR. Kaḷavaḷi or The Battle-field. [A poem in praise of the Chola king Ṣeṅ-gaṇṇān, forming no. 4 of the Kīṟ-kaṇakku poems. Text with translation by V. Kanaka-sabhai Piḷḷai.] 1889. *See* PERIODICAL PUBLICATIONS. — *Bombay.* The Indian Antiquary, *etc.* vol. xviii., pp. 259-265. 1872, *etc.* 4°. **14096. e. (vol. 18.)**

POYGAIY-ĀṞVĀR. [For editions of the Tiruvantādi of this saint included in the editions of the whole or parts of the Nāl-āyira-prabandham :] *See* ĀṞVĀRGAḶ.—*Nāl-āyiram.*

POYYĀ-MOṞI PULAVAR. தஞ்சைவாணன் கோவைமூலம் நாற்கவிராசநம்பி அகப்பொருள்விளக்கத்திற்கிலக்கியமாகப் பொய்யாமொழிப்புலவர் இயற்றியது ... உரையுடன் [Tañjai-vāṇan-kōvai. A poem in 425 stanzas, illustrating the rules for expressing erotic sentiment given in Nāṟ-kavi-rāja Nambi's Aga-poruḷ-viḷakkam. With commentary by Kuṇṟattūr Ashṭāvadhāni Ṣokk'-appa Nāvalar. Edited by T. Teyva-ṣikhāmaṇi Mudaliyār and T. Shaṇmukham Piḷḷai.] pp. iii. ii. 275, iv. சென்னை [*Madras*,] 1893. 8°. **14172. b. 53.**

PRAṆATĀRTIHARA ṢIVANĀR, *P. A.* தமயந்தி. ஒரு புதிய தமிழ் நாடகம். (Damayanti. A new Tamil drama [on the epic legend].) pp. xvii. 168; 1 *plate*. சென்னை [*Madras*,] 1902. 12°. **14170. l. 55.**

Forms "Gem ii." in the series "The Anklet of Sarada" (Nā-magaḷ-ṣilambu).

PRICE (*Sir* JOHN FREDERICK). *See* ĀNANDA-RAṄGA PILLAI. The Private Diary of Ananda Ranga Pillai ... Translated ... and edited by Sir J. F. Price, *etc.* 1904, *etc.* 8°. **14171. e. 4.**

PŪDAÑ-ṢENDANĀR. இனியது நாற்பது மூலமும் உரையும், கனாநூலும். [Iniyadu nāṟ-padu. A series of 41 quatrains, forming the 5th of the *kīṟ-kaṇakku* poems of the last Madura *saṅgham*, with prose paraphrase. Followed by Kanā-nūl, an ancient poem on oneiromancy in 30 quatrains, ascribed to Ponnavan. Edited with a glossary to the former work by R. Rāghav'-aiyaṅgār.] 2 pts. மதுரை [*Madura*,] 1903. 8°. **14172. bb. 3.(7.)**

Form respectively nos. 5 and 2 of the Ṣen-damiṟ-prachuram.

—— [Another copy, without preface.] *See* ACADEMIES, *etc.*—*Madura.* ["Ṣen-damiṟ" supplement.] nos. 2, 5. 1902, *etc.* 8°. **14172. i. 1.*(nos. 2, 5.)**

PŪDATT'-ĀṞVĀR. [For editions of the Tiruvantādi of this saint included in the editions of the whole or parts of the Nāl-āyira-prabandham :] *See* ĀṞVĀRGAḶ.—*Nāl-āyiram.*

PUGAṞĒNDI. [*Life.*] *See* MRUGA-DĀSA SVĀMI. University of Madras ... Pulawar Puranam, *etc.* [Lives of Pugaṟēndi and Oṭṭa-kūttar.] 1901. 8°. **14172. bb. 3.(4.)**

—— The Nalavenba [by Pugaṟēndi] and Nanmanikadigai [by Viḷambiya-Nāganār], with grammatical and explanatory notes, &c., [and an English translation] for the use of Matriculation Examination, 1879. By C. Rajagopala Pillai ... Published by his pupil P. Vasudeva Mudaliar. pp. i. 147, 60, 30. *Madras*, 1879. 12°. **14172. a. 22.**

—— புகழேந்திப்புலவர் அருளிச்செய்த நளவெண்பா. [Naḷa-veṇ-bā. A poem on the epic legend of Nala and Damayantī. Edited with introduction by V. G. Sūrya-nārāyaṇa Ṣāstri.] (*கலை மயில் கலாபம்: கண்-உ.) pp. 39, 82. *Madras*, 1899. 12°. **14172. a. 50.(1.)**

—— நளவெண்பா. [Naḷa-veṇ-bā, Kali-doḍar-kāṇḍam. In Tamil and English, with Tamil commentary, *etc.*] *See* ACADEMIES, *etc.*—Madras.—*University of Madras.* Copious notes, *etc.* 1898. 8°. **14172. b. 16.(1.)**

—— ... அபிமன்னன் சுந்தரிமாலை. [Abimannan-sundari-mālai. A story in verse of Arjuna, Abhimanyu, and Sundari, attributed to Pugaṟēndi. Edited by T. Appāvu Piḷḷai.] pp. 156. [*Madras*,] 1884. 8°. **14172. b. 29.**

PUGAṞĒNDI (*continued*). ००० அல்லியரசாணிமாலை. [Alliy-araṣāni-mālai. A poem ascribed to Pugaṟēndi, on the legend of Arjuna's marriage with the princess Alli of Madura and his establishment of the Pāṇḍava kingdom in the South. Edited by T. Naṭa-rāja Svāmi.] pp. 135. கஅஅச [*Madras*, 1884.] 8°. **14172. b. 30.**

—— ००० நல்லதங்காள் கதை. [Nalla-daṅgāḷ-kathai. A popular poem on the misfortunes of a woman in the house of her married brother, ascribed to Pugaṟēndi. Edited by M. T. Kuppu-sāmi Nāyuḍu.] . . . Revised and enlarged. pp. 56. சென்னை [*Madras*,] 1904. 8°. **14172. cc. 1.**

—— ००० பஞ்சபாண்டவர் வனவாசம். [Pañcha-pāṇḍavar-vana-vāsam. An epic poem, ascribed to Pugaṟēndi, on the adventures of the Pāṇḍava princes as told in the Mahā-bhāratam, Vana-parvam. Edited by M. T. Kuppu-sāmi Nāyuḍu.] . . . Revised and enlarged. pp. 268; 12 *plates*. சென்னை [*Madras*,] 1904. 8°. **14172. bb. 11.**

—— ००० பவளக்கொடிமாலை. [Pavaḷa-koḍi-mālai. A metrical story, ascribed to Pugaṟēndi, about Arjuna's marriage to Pavaḷa-koḍi, a Southern princess. Edited by Chidambaram Karuṇānanda Svāmi.] pp. 96. கஅஅரு [*Madras*, 1885.] 8°. **14172. b. 27.**

—— ००० பவளக்கொடிமாலை. [Pavaḷa-koḍi-mālai. Edited by Ch. Ponnu-sāmi Mudaliyār.] pp. 96. [*Madras*,] 1885. 8°. **14172. b. 28.**

—— [Occasional verses, ascribed to Oṭṭa-kūttar and Pugaṟēndi. With interpretation.] *See* TANI-PĀḌAL. (†தனிப்பாடற்றிரட்டு) (Tani-pāḍaṭ-ṭiraṭṭu.] pp. 158-177. [1892, *etc.*] 8°. **14172. c. 39.(5.)**

PULI-PĀṆI, *Siddhar*. ००० புலிப்பாணி சோதிடம் (*Pulippani Jothidam [a metrical manual of astrology] . . . சோதிடம்முந்நூறு. Thoroughly examined and written by T. N. Rungasawmy Pillay.) 2 pts. *Madras*, 1894-1895. 8°. **14170. i. 38.**

—— ஸ்ரீ . . . பலதிரட்டு ஜாலம் ௲ [Puli-pāṇi-pala-tiraṭṭu-jālam. A handbook of sorcery. Preceded by another Jāla-tiraṭṭu, ascribed to Muttu-vīra Rāma, and followed by a Chidambara-pūjai or Ṣaiva ritual in 26 verses ascribed to Puli-pāṇi and a Vinōda-jāla-tiraṭṭu in 11 verses. Edited with commentary by M. Vaḍi-vēlu Mudaliyār.] pp. 118. *Madras*, 1906. 8°. **14171. g. 8.**

PUNARI MUDALIYĀR. *See* [Addenda] 'ABD al-MASĪḤ. Abdool Messee, or The Jewel of Mercy . . . a translation [by Punari Mudaliyār] of the life of Abdool Messee, as published in one of the quarterly papers of the Church Missionary Society. 1844. 12°. **14170. b. 1.(36.)**

PŪNDURUTTI NAMBI-GĀḌA NAMBI. [For the hymns of this author contained in the Tiruv-iṣai-pā :] *See* TIRU-MUṞAI.

PUṞA-NĀNŪṞU. ००० புறநானூறுமூலமும் உரையும். [Puṟa-nānūṟu. An ancient anthology forming the 8th of the Eṭṭu-togai, and comprising poems on the moral and social functions of royalty, *etc.* Edited with commentary, biographical and grammatical notes, glossary, and index by U. V. Sāmināth'-aiyar.] pp. 12, 3, 13, 18, 24, 310, 6, 83, 4, 3. சென்னை [*Madras*,] 1894. 8°. **14172. d. 16.**

PURĀṆAS. *See* CORNELIUS NĀḌĀR (J. S.). Amarar Puranam, being the antiquities of the gods of India, as described in the Sacred Writings of the Hindus, *etc.* 1901. 8°. **14170. k. 52.**

—— *See* SĀMI-NĀTHA AIYAR, *T. A.* Viveka-chandrika . . . moral stories culled mainly from Puranas, *etc.* 1904. 12°. **14171. aa. 16.**

—— *See* ṢRĪNIVĀSĀCHĀRYAR, *K. V.* புராணகதாஸாரம். [Purāṇa-kathā-sāram. Stories from Purāṇas.] 1895. 8°. **14170. ee. 7.**

—— *See* ṢRĪNIVĀSA RĀGHAVĀCHĀRYAR, *T. E.* அதிக கதாசங்கிரகம். (Adika Katha Sangraham, or Stories selected from the . . . Puranas, *etc.*) 1885. 12°. **14170. d. 23.**

—— திருமலைமஹாத்மியம். [Tirumalai-māhātmyam. A work in 108 chapters on the legends of the Vaishṇava sanctuary of Tirumalai on the Tirupati hills and the Vaishṇava faith generally, compiled from the Sanskrit Purāṇas by D. Appan Svāmi, under the instructions of M. Tirumalai-rāya Piḷḷai.] pp. 328, i. வெகுதான்ய [*Madras*, 1878.] 8°. **14170. e. 2.**

PURĀṆAS (*continued*).

AGNI-PURĀṆAM.

See BĀLA-SUBRAHMAṆYA PIḶḶAI, *T. N.* ००० ஆக்னேயபுராண சாரம் ஞூ [Vanniya-nāṭakam. A drama founded upon the Agni-purāṇam.] 1902. 8°. **14170. l. 58.**

BHĀGAVATA-PURĀṆAM.

See MĀRIY-APPA KAVI-RĀYAR, *M.*, and ṢAṄKARA-MŪRTTI KŌNĀR, *A.* ஸ்ரீமத் பாகவத அம்மானை. [Bhāgavata-ammānai. A metrical paraphrase of the Bhāgavata-purāṇam.] 1893. 8°. **14172. b. 54.**

Bagavadam, ou Doctrine Divine, ouvrage indien canonique, sur l'Être Suprême, les dieux, les géans, les hommes, les diverses parties de l'univers, *etc.* [An abstract of the Sanskrit text, translated into French from a Tamil version by "Méridas Poullé," *i.e.* Mariya-dās Piḷḷai, and edited by Foucher d'Obsonville.] pp. lxiv. 348. *Paris*, 1788. 8°. **279. d. 21.**

—— [Another edition.] *Paris*, 1789. 8°. **14016. c. 1.**

००० அவதூதசம்வாதமூலமும் . . . உரையும். [Avadhūta-saṃvādam. A philosophical-religious discourse from bk. xxiv. (corresponding to some extent with bk. xi. 7 ff. in the Sanskrit text). With paraphrastic commentary by Eḍuttukūṭṭi Aruṇāchala Nāyanār.] pp. 35. [*Madras*,] 1888. 12°. **14172. a. 35.(1.)**

BHAVISHYŌTTARA-PURĀṆAM.

ஶ்ரீ . . . ப்ரஸந்நவேங்கடேஶமாஹாத்ம்யம் . . . குணசீலமாஹாத்மியம் . . . பிரசன்னவெங்கடேசமாஹாத்மியம். [Prasanna-veṅkaṭēṣa-māhātmyam, or Guṇa-ṣila-māhātmyam. A legend of the Vaishṇava cult of Srirangam, in 10 chapters. Sanskrit text, edited with a Tamil translation by Īchambāḍi R. Kṛushṇam-āchāryar.] pp. 76. சென்னை [*Madras*,] 1906. 8°. **14016. dd. 18.**

००० சங்கரநாராயண சுவாமிகோவில் மான்மியம். [Ṣaṅkara-nārāyaṇa-svāmi-kōvil-mānmiyam. The legends attaching to the god Ṣaṅkara-Nārāyaṇa and his shrine called Pū-gailāyam or Bhū-kailāsam. Rendered into prose by M. R. Ṣrīnivāsa Aiyaṅgār and Ṣ. V. Pēchiy-appa Piḷḷai.] pp. 40; 2 *plates*. சென்னை [*Madras*,] 1898. 12°. **14170. d. 45.(2.)**

BRAHMA-KAIVARTTA-PURĀṆAM.

See SUBRAHMAṆYA AIYAR, *Tañjai Ṣatāvadhānam.* ००० காளையார்கோவிற்புராணம். [Kāḷaiyār-kōviṟ-purāṇam. Versified from the Brahma-kaivartta-purāṇam.] 1899. 8°. **14170. ee. 22.**

காளையார்கோவில் மான்மியவசனம். [Kāḷaiyār-kōvil-mānmiya-vachanam, or Tiru-kānapēr-purāṇa-v°. The legends of the Kāḷaiyār temple rendered into prose.] *See* SUBRAHMAṆYA AIYAR, *Tañjai Ṣatāvadhānam.* ००० காளையார்கோவிற் புராண ஞூ [Kāḷaiyār-kōviṟ-purāṇa-vachanam.] pp. 9-127. 1897. 12°. **14170. d. 61.**

BRAHMĀṆḌA-PURĀṆAM.

எயினனூர், சந்தானபுரியென்று வழங்கும் ஆதிபுரதலபுராணம். [Ādipura-tala-purāṇam. The sacred legends of the Ṣaiva sanctuary at Ādipuram (Sandanapuri), in the Chola-mandalam. Metrically adapted from the Uttara-bhāgam, Kshētra-vaibhava-kāṇḍam, ch. 68 ff., by Paṇṇuruṭṭi T. K. Subba-rāya Cheṭṭi, on the basis of the version of Vaḷavanūr Kachi Ṣāstri. Edited with a prose summary by Chidambaram A. Sāmi-nātha Piḷḷai.] pp. xx. 96. சென்னை தர்முகி [*Madras*, 1896.] 8°. **14170. ee. 8.**

BRAHMA-PURĀṆAM.

ஸகல . . . ஶ்ரீஹஸ்திகிரிமாஹாத்ம்யம் [Hasti-giri-māhātmyam. Eighteen *adhyāyas* from the Bhṛigu-nārada-saṃvāda, treating of the legends of the Vaishṇava shrine at Hastigiri or Anamalai. In Sanskrit, with a Tamil paraphrase in the *maṇi-pravāḷam* style.] pp. ii. ii. 255. காஞ்சீ [*Conjevaram*,] 1898. 8°. **14016. c. 51.**

KALKI-PURĀṆAM.

ஶ்ரீ . . . கலிக்காவதாரசரித்திரமாகிய கல்கிபுராணம். [Kalki-purāṇam. Translated from the Sanskrit by K. Dēṣikāchāryar.] pp. 4, 94. சென்னை [*Madras*, 1902.] 8°. **14170. ee. 50.**

KŪRMA-PURĀṆAM.

००० கூர்மபுராண மூலம் ஞூ [Kūrma-purāṇam. In the metrical version of Ativīra-rāma Pāṇḍiyan.

With commentary by N. Kadirai-vēr̤ Piḷḷai.] pts. i.-v. pp. 240. சென்னை [Madras,] 1898-1899. 8°. 14170. ff. 6.

கூர்மபுராணம். [Kūrma-purāṇam. Bk. 21-3 (Rāman avatarittav-adhyāyam, Rāman vanam bugundav-a°., and Rāvaṇa-vadhaiy-a°.). With commentary.] See ACADEMIES, etc. — Madras. — University of Madras. The University of Madras. The First in Arts Examination, etc. 1891. 8°. 14172. bb. 4.

MATSYA-PURĀṆAM.

∘∘∘ மச்சபுராணம். [Matsya-purāṇam (Machcha-p.°). A poetical version by Vaḍa-malaiy-appa Piḷḷai of the Sanskrit Matsya-purāṇam. Edited by T. Shaṇmukham Piḷḷai, with an introduction by S. Anavarata-vināyakam Piḷḷai, and commendatory verses by divers.] pp. i. xxviii. 620. சென்னை [Madras,] 1900. 8°. 14170. ee. 43.

PADMA-PURĀṆAM.

(† శ్రీమాఘమాహాత్మ్యసారము.) [Māgha-māhātmya-sāram. Comprising Māgha-snāna-phala-prabhāva, an excerpt in Sanskrit from the Māgha-māhātmyam of this Purāṇam (Uttara-khaṇḍam ccxxxix.) on the religious efficacy of bathing in the Mahā-māgham festival at Kumbakonam, with a Tamil and an abridged Telugu version, 10 Sanskrit stanzas on the holiness of Kumbakonam, etc. Compiled by Kṛushṇanjī Dave.] pp. 18. Madras, 1897. 12°. 14016. b. 20.

No title-page.

ஸ்ரீபாத்மோத்தரபுராணம். [Pādmōttara-purāṇam. A metrical adaptation from the Sanskrit by P. Rāmānuja Nāvalar.] pp. iv. xii. 532, iv. Madras, சுக்கில [1870.] 8°. 14170. f. 2.

ஸ்ரீசிவகீதை வசனம். [Ṣiva-gītā. A summary of the Ṣaiva-siddhāntam in the form of an episode in the adventures of Rāma, in 16 chapters, purporting to be taken from the Padma-purāṇam, Uttara-khaṇḍam. Rendered into Tamil prose by A. Rāma-sāmi Dīkshitar.] pp. iv. 124. தஞ்சை [Tanjore,] 1898. 16°. 14170. d. 35.(6.)

கீதாரத்தினமும் சகல சாஸ்திரஸாரமுமாகிய ஸ்ரீசிவகீதை ௸ [Ṣiva-gītā. Sanskrit text, with a Tamil interpretation by M. Gaṇēṣā Ṣāstri. Edited by P. Kalyāṇa-sundara Mudaliyār.] சென்னை [Madras,] 1906, etc. 8°. 14049. b. 40.

In progress.

ṢIVA-PURĀṆAM.

∘∘∘ ஸ்ரீசைவபுராணமென்னும் ஸ்ரீசிவமஹாபுராணம். [Ṣiva-mahā-purāṇam, or Ṣaiva-purāṇam. Translated into prose by Īkkāḍu Ratna-vēlu Mudaliyār. With illustrations.] 2 vols. pp. iv. iv. 500, 55, vii. 348. சென்னை [Madras,] 1900. 8°. 14170. ff. 2.

Wanting the illustrations and title-page of vol. 2.

அன்பிலாலந்துறையென்னும் பிரேமபுரிஸ்தல மான்மியம். [Prēmapuri-sthala-mānmiyam. The local legends of the Ṣaiva sanctuary at Anbil-ālan-durai or Prēmapuri, from the Rudra-saṃhitā. In a Tamil paraphrase by Nara-siṃha Bhārati and Kṛushṇa Bhārati.] pp. 8, 99. திருவாதி ஜெய [Tiruvadi, 1895.] 12°. 14170. d. 42.

SKANDA-PURĀṆAM.

[For the Tiru-viḷaiy-āḍar̤-purāṇam, based upon the Hālāsya-māhātmyam in the Īṣa-saṃhitā of this Purāṇam :] See PARAÑ-JŌDI MUNIVAR.

பிரமோத்தரகாண்டவசனம். [Brahmōttara-kāṇḍa-vachanam. A prose paraphrase, by V. T. Subrahmaṇya Piḷḷai, of Varatuṅga-rāma Pāṇḍiyan's Brahmōttara-kāṇḍam, a metrical adaptation in 22 cantos of the section bearing that name in the Skanda-purāṇam and treating the legends of certain Ṣaiva devotees.] pp. vi. i. 158, i. சென்னபட்டணம் [Madras,] 1878. 16°. 14170. d. 20.

Varatuṅga-rāma, according to tradition, was the younger brother of Ativīra-rāma Pāṇḍiyan, and author of a Karuvai-ven-bā-antādi, a Kali-tur̤aiy-antādi, a Padittu-patt'-antādi, etc.

கந்தபுராணத்தில் . . . கதை. [Kāḷaiyār-kōvil-mānmiya-vachanam. An excerpt from the Ṣaṅkara-saṃhitā, Kshētra-khaṇḍam, giving the legends of the Kāḷaiyār temple. Translated into prose]. See SUBRAHMAṆYA AIYAR, Tañjai Ṣatāvadhānam. ∘∘∘ காளையார்கோவிற் புராண ௸ [Kāḷaiyār-kōvir̤-purāṇa-vachanam.] pp. 128-146. 1897. 12°. 14170. d. 61.

காசிகாண்டம். [Kāṣi-khaṇḍam (here called °kāṇḍam). An adaptation in Tamil verse, attributed to King Ativīra-rāma Pāṇḍiyan, of the Sanskrit Kāṣīkhaṇḍam of the Skanda-purāṇam, containing the local legends of Benares, in 101 chapters and 2524 quatrains. Edited by Ṣūḷai Subba-rāya Nāyakar.] pp. 328. [*Madras,*] 1884. 8°. **14170. e. 24.**

ooo காசிகண்டம். [Kāṣi-khaṇḍam. Edited with interpretation by Ī. Ratna-vēlu Mudaliyār.] *சென்னை* [*Madras,*] 1892, *etc.* 8°. **14170. f. 20.**

Incomplete, containing only pp. 1-640.

ooo சேதுமாஹாத்மியம். [Sētu-māhātmyam. The legends of Adam's Bridge, forming 52 chapters in the Sanatkumāra-saṃhitā. Translated into Tamil prose by N. Sāmi-nātha Ṣāstri.] pp. v. 297. *சென்னை* [*Madras,*] 1901. 8°. **14170. ee. 42.**

ஸ்ரீ... ஸ்ரீஸ்காந்தே புராணாந்தர்கதாயாம் ஸ்ரீஶங்கர ஸம்ஹிதாயாம் ஶிவரஹஸ்யகண்ட:. [Ṣiva-rahasya-khaṇḍa. A section from the Ṣaṅkara-saṃhitā, in 91 *adhyāyas.* The Sanskrit text, with Tamil translation.] 1890. *See* PERIODICAL PUBLICATIONS.—*Tiruvadi.* சிவபக்திசந்திரிகை. [Ṣiva-bhakti-chandrikai.] 1890-1893. 8°. **14033. bb. 35.**

சிவதத்துவசுதாநிதி. [Ṣiva-tattva-sudhā-nidhi. 10 chapters from the Malayāchala-khaṇḍam of the Sanatkumāra-saṃhitā, on Ṣaiva theology. Sanskrit text, with a Tamil version of Ṣrīnivāsa Dīkshitar's commentary Chintāmaṇi.] pp. 191. *சிதம்பரம்* [*Chidambaram,*] 1898. 8°. **14016. d. 54.**

திருக்கேதீச்சுரமகிமை. [Tiru-kētīṣvara-mahimai. A short Sanskrit excerpt, purporting to be from ch. ii. of the Dakshiṇa-kailāsa-māhātmyam in this Purāṇam, on the origin and cult of the Ṣaiva sanctuary of Kētīṣvaram, on the Trikonachalam near Jaffna. Followed by 2 hymns from the Dēvāram. Edited with translation of the former and paraphrase of the latter by N. Ṣ. Ponn'-ambala Piḷḷai.] pp. ii. 2, 3, 9. *யாழ்ப்பாணம் கர* [*Jaffna,* 1891.] 8°. **14170. e. 41.(2.)**

ஜடூங்கிரு ஸ்ரீஃகஸ் ஸ்காந்தே புராணாந்தர்கதம் வடாரண்யமாஹாத்ம்யம் (*வடாரண்ய மான்மியம்.) [Vaṭaraṇya-māhātmyam. 11 *adhyāyas* from the Kshētra-vaibhava-vistāra, Uparibhāga, on the legends of the Vaṭāraṇya or Ālangāḍu. Followed by a Tamil version by S. Rāma-sāmi Aiyar of Enaṅguḍi.] pp. 112, 66. *நடுகாவேரி* [*Nadukkaveri,*] 1898. 16°. **14016. a. 27.**

See SAMBANDHA-ṢARAṆĀLAYA SVĀMI. ooo கந்தபுராணச் சுருக்கம். [Kanda-purāṇa-churukkam. A summary in verse of Kachiy-appar's Skanda-purāṇam.] [1848.] 8°. **14170. e. 5.**

See SAMBANDHA-ṢARAṆĀLAYA SVĀMI. கந்தபுராணச்சுருக்கம். [Kanda-purāṇa-churukkam.] [1906.] 8°. **14170. eee. 10.**

கந்தபுராணம். [Kanda-purāṇam. The Skanda-p°., adapted into Tamil verse by Kachiy-appar. Edited by Āṟu-muga Nāvalar.] pp. xviii. iii. 960. *சென்னபட்டணம் சுக்கில* [*Madras,* 1869.] 8°. **14170. f. 3.**

கந்தபுராணம். [Kanda-purāṇam. In the metrical version of Kachiy-appar. With commentary by Ṣ. Subba-rāya Nāyakar.] *சென்னை* [*Madras,*] 1896, *etc.* 8°. **14170. f. 23.**

Incomplete, breaking off at p. 360.

கந்தபுராணவசனம் ஸ்ரீ [Kanda-purāṇa-vachanam. The six cantos of Kachiy-appar's Kanda-purāṇam, done into prose by Shaṇmukham Piḷḷai, followed by K. Kōneriy-appa Mudaliyār's Upadēṣa-kāṇḍam.] 2 pts. 1890-1891. *See* ITIHĀSA-MAÑJARI. Ithihasa Manjari Series. [1888]-1894. 8°. **14172. d. 11.**

ஸ்ரீ கந்தபுராணச் சுருக்கம் வசனம். [Kanda-purāṇa-churukkam. A prose epitome of Kachiy-appar's Kanda-purāṇam, by V. Taṅga-vēlu-sāmi Dēvar.] pp. 8, 249. *சென்னை* [*Madras,*] 1907. 8°. **14170. e. 28.**

கந்தபுராணம். [Kanda-purāṇam, Tāraka-vadha-paṭalam. In the metrical version of Kachiy-appar. With life of the latter and commentary.] pp. 112. *See* ACADEMIES, *etc.*—Madras.—*University of Madras.* University of Madras. B.A. Examination, *etc.* 1900. 8°. **14172. bb. 6.(6.)**

ooo கந்தபுராணம் தெய்வயானையம்மைதிருமணப்படலம் ஸ்ரீ [Teyvayānaiy-ammai-tiru-maṇa-paṭalam. The legend of the bridal of Teyvayānai, from the Skanda-purāṇam as translated by Kachiy-appar. With a commentary by Valvai Ṣ. Vaidya-liṅga Piḷḷai.] pp. 116, i. *வல்வை* [*Valuvettiturai,* 1889.] 8°. **14170. e. 30**

ooo கந்தபுராணம் வள்ளியம்மைதிருமணப்படலம் ஸ்ரீ [Vaḷḷiy-ammai-tiru-maṇa-paṭalam. The legend of the marriage of Valli to the god Kanda-sāmi, from the Skanda-purāṇam as translated by Kachiy-appar. With a commentary by Valvai Ṣ. Vaidya-liṅga Pillai.] pp. 133. வல்வை [*Valu-vettiturai*, 1886.] 8°. **14170. e. 25.**

See Muttu-vīra Kaviñar. ◦◦◦ வள்ளியம்மைநாடகம். [Valliy-ammai-nāṭakam. A drama.] [1871.] 8°. **14170. l. 7.**

VARĀHA-PURĀṆAM.

◦◦◦ శ్రీ . . . వాక్షాక్షస్తసంతవ్ కాస శ్రీకైశికపురాణం. [Kaiṣika-purāṇam or Kaiṣikōpākhyānam. A Vaishṇava religious legend purporting to form ch. 66 in the dialogue of the Earth and the Boar, in Sanskrit. With Tamil commentary by Parā-ṣara Bhaṭṭar. Edited by V. Muḍumbai Ṣrīnivāsa Appaṅgār Svāmi.] pp. 30. [illegible] [*Madras*, 1904.] 8°. **14028. c. 49.(2.)**

Apparently not to be found in the printed texts.

VINĀYAKA-PURĀṆAM.

பார்க்கவபுராணமென்னும் விநாயகபுராணம். [Vināyaka-purāṇam, or Bhārgava-purāṇam. A metrical version by Tirutaṇigai Kachiy-appar. Edited with paraphrastic commentary by Īkkāḍu Ratna-vēlu Mudaliyār.] pts. 1—7. pp. 320. சென்னை [*Madras*,] 1899. 8°. **14170. f. 15.**

பார்க்கவ புராணமென்னும் விநாயக புராணம். [Vināyaka-purāṇam, or Bhārgava-purāṇam. A prose paraphrase, by T. V. Muttu-sāmi Mudaliyār, of the metrical version by Kachiy-appar. Fourth edition.] pp. ii. iii. 440, 378. சென்னை [*Madras*,] 1899. 8°. **14170. ee. 19.**

VISHṆU-PURĀṆAM.

புராணரத்தினமென்னும் ஸ்ரீவிஷ்ணுபுராணம். [Vishṇu-purāṇam. Metrically translated by Ṣ. Subba-rāya Aiyar.] pp. iv. xxii. 530, i. சென்னை [*Madras*,] 1904. 8°. **14170. ff. 13.**

PŪRṆA-LIṄGAM PILLAI, *M. Ṣ.* *See* Auvaiyār.—*Supposititious Works.* ஔவை குறள் ௸ [Auvai-kuraḷ. Edited by Pūrṇa-liṅgam.] 1899. 12°. **14172. a. 50.(2.)**

—— *See* Periodical Publications.—*Madras.* ஞானபோதினி ௸ (*Jnâna Bodhini, *etc.*) [Edited by Pūrṇa-liṅgam.] 1897-1905. 8°. **14172. i. 18.**

PŪRṆA-LIṄGAM PILLAI, *M. Ṣ.* (*continued*). A Primer of Tamil Literature. (The Madras Literary Bureau Series.) pp. v. 218. *Madras*, 1904. 12°. **14171. d. 3.**

—— Vâsaka Thirattu : a Tamil prose anthology. (†வாசகத்திரட்டு.) pp. i. i. 113, 2. *Madras*, 1896. 8°. **14171. a. 12.**

—— Witty Stories. I. மரியாதைராமன் கதை. II. இராயர் அப்பாஜி கதை. [Mariyādai-rāman-kathai and Rāyar-appāji-kathai.] Edited by M. S. Purnalingam Pillay. pp. i. 2, 56. *Madras*, 1897. 12°. **14171. a. 6.(2.)**

PURUḌŌTTAMA. *See* Purushōttama.

PURUSHŌTTAMA MUDALIYĀR, *Kūḍalūr.* *See* Kamban. ◦◦◦ ஸ்ரீமத்கம்பராமாயணக்கருப்பொருள். [Kamba-rāmāyaṇa-karu-poruḷ. Edited with interpretation *etc.* by Purushōttama.] 1882. 12°. **14172. a. 24.**

PURUSHŌTTAMA NAMBI. [For the hymns of this author contained in the Tiruv-iṣai-pā :] *See* Tiru-murai.

PUSHPA-RATHA CHETTI, *Ū.* *See* Nāl-aḍiyār. ◦◦◦ நாலடியார் ௸ [Nāl-aḍiyār. With interpretation *etc.* by Pushpa-ratha.] 1885. 8°. **14172. b. 40.**

—— *See* Nāl-aḍiyār. Naladyar. [Edited] with a . . . Tamil commentary and an English translation of the text [by Pushpa-ratha]. 1892. 8°. **14172. b. 45.**

PUVIMANNA-ṢIṄGA MUDALIYĀR JOSEPH. ஸ்நாபக சஞ்சுவாம் அம்மானை. [Snāpaka-sañjuvām-ammānai. A Catholic poem on St. John the Baptist.] pp. 34. யாழ்ப்பாணம் [*Jaffna*,] 1892. 8°. **14170. c. 24.(4.)**

RĀDHĀ-KṚUSHṆA AIYAR, *Ṣ.*, *Principal of Maharaja's College, Pudukottai.* *See* Sāmi-nātha Aiyar, *T.A.* Vivekachandrika . . . With an introduction by S. Rathakrishna Aiyar, *etc.* 1904. 12°. **14171. aa. 16.**

RĀGHAVĀCHĀRYAR, *Dāmal Āchāl.* ஸ்ரீ . . . ஸொருயண பரம்பரை தனியன்கள் ஸேவாக்ரம-த்தனியன் திருவரி *etc.* [Various Sanskrit and Tamil devotional lections of the Ṣuddha-sattvam order of Viṣishṭādvaita Vaishṇavas, by divers authors, giving metrical lists of the spiritual leaders of the sect, *etc.*] pp. 10, 19, 48, 4. பெருமாள் கோவில் ஸ்ரீஸூக்தம் [*Conjevaram*, 1903.] 12°. **14028. bb. 9.(2.)**

RĀGHAVĀCHĀRYAR, *Perumāḷ-kōyil Tirumalai Ichambāḍi.* See YĀMUNĀCHĀRYAR. ◦◦◦ ஆளவந்தார்ஸ்தோத்ரம். [Āḷavandār-stōtram. Edited by Rāghavāchāryar.] 1878. 8°. **14028. c. 46.**

—— —— 1879. 12°. **14028. b. 52.**

RĀGHAVĀCHĀRYAR, *Ṣikkināyakkambēṭṭai.* ◦◦◦ நியாயவாதாபாச நிராகரணம். [Nyāya-vādā-bhāsa-nirākaraṇam. Criticisms on Shaṇmukha Piḷḷai's interpretation of the Bhārata-veṇ-bā.] pp. 12. கும்பகோணம் [*Kumbakonam*,] [18]88. 16°. **14170. k. 2.(2.)**

RĀGHAVĀCHĀRYAR, *V. K.* See INDIA.—*Legislative Council.* சிவில் புரொசிடியூர்கோட் ௵ [The Civil Procedure Code. Edited by Rāghavāchāryar.] [1870.] 8°. **14170. g. 5.(2.)**

—— See MADRAS, *Presidency of.* உப்புசம்பந்தமாய் . . . சட்டங்கள் ௵ [Rules, *etc.*, for the administration of the Salt Acts. Translated by Rāghavāchāryar.] [1867.] 8°. **14170. g. 5.(1.)**

RĀGHAV'-AIYAṄGĀR, *R., of Ramnad.* See ACADEMIES, *etc.*—*Madura.* செந்தமிழ். [Ṣen-damiḻ. Edited by Rāghav'-aiyaṅgār.] 1902, *etc.* 8°. **14172. i. 1.**

RĀGHAVALU RĀMĀNUJA-DĀSAR, *P.* ஸ்ரீவிஷ்ணு நாமாவளி. [Vishṇu-nāmāvaḷi, or Mōksha-sūkshmam. A Vaishṇava hymn.] See NAMBI NĀYUḌU. ◦◦◦ பாசுரப்படி ராமாயணம் ௵ [Pāṣura-paḍi-rāmāyaṇam, *etc.*] pp. 1-8. 1903. 12°. **14170. d. 46.(4.)**

RĀGHAVA-MŪRTTI PIḶḶAI, *P.* பறையர் உற்பத்தி விளக்கம். [Paṟaiyar-uṟpatti-viḷakkam. A tract on the origin of the Paṟaiyar or "pariah" class.] pp. 12. சென்னை [*Madras*,] 1894. 12°. **14171. a. 7.(1.)**

RAGHU-NĀTH'-AIYAR, *Nallūr Chandra-ṣēkhar'-aiyar.* See BHŌJA-RĀJA PAṆḌITAR. சரசோதிமாலை ௵ [Chara-jōdi-mālai. Edited by Raghu-nāth'-aiyar.] [1892.] 8°. **14170. i. 23.**

—— See EPHEMERIDES. ◦◦◦ நந்தனவருஷ . . . பஞ்சாங்கம் . . . Tamil Calendar, *etc.* [Calculated for 1892-93 and 1893-94 by Raghu-nāth'-aiyar.] [1891-1896.] 8°. **14172. i. 11.**

RĀJA-GŌPĀLA AIYAṄGĀR, *M., of Kumbakonam.* A help to the thorough understanding of the Tamil இரண்டாம் ஸ்டாண்டர்டு புஸ்தகம் [Second Standard Book]. தெளி பொருள் விளக்கம். pp. 78. *Anaikara-Chattram*, [1898.] 12°. **14172. h. 97.(3.)**

Forms no. 7 of Gopal's Educational Series. Distinct from the readers of the Jaffna Catholic Mission which bear the same name.

RĀJA-GŌPĀLA BHŪPATI, *Tūṣi.* மதிமோச விளக்கம். (†The Mathimosa vilakkam.) [Mati-mōsha-viḷakkam. A description of varions kinds of imposture.] *Madras*, 1907, *etc.* 8°. **14171. a. 2.**

In progress.

RĀJA-GŌPĀLA MUDALIYĀR, *Puduvai Nayan-appa.* See PIḶḶAI PERU-MĀḶ AIYAṄGĀR. ◦◦◦ திருவேங்கடமாலை. [Tiru-vēṅkaṭa-mālai. With commentary by Rāja-gōpāla.] [1879.] 8°. **14172. c. 25.**

RĀJA-GŌPĀLA MUDALIYĀR, *P. Ṣ.* One thousand conversational sentences in Roman-Tamil. Specially adapted to the use of persons employed on public works, to which are added thirty selected stories from the Kadâ Manjari [with translation], *etc.* (* The Anglo-Tamil Primer: for the use of the students of the Civil Engineering College, *etc.*) 2 pts. 1860, 1862. See MADRAS, *City of.*—*Civil Engineering College.* Madras Engineering College Papers. nos. i., iv. 1860-1869. 8°. **14170. i. 7.(no. 1, 4.)**

—— A text-book containing fifteen hundred conversational sentences in Tamil with English translation . . . and forty selected stories of the Kadámañjari, with analysis and free translation. Second edition. pp. i. 131. 1869. See MADRAS, *City of.*—*Civil Engineering College.* Madras Engineering College Papers. no. 1 (B). 1860-1869. 8°. **14170. i. 7.***

—— Selection of Tamil words different in signification but similar in sound. [In Tamil and English.] pp. iv. 55. *Madras*, 1862. 12°. **12906. bb. 47.**

RĀJA-GŌPĀLA NĀYUḌU, *G.* தென்னை. [Tennai. A treatise on cocoanut-cultivation.] pp. i. i. 75. *Madras*, [1904.] 8°. **14171. g. 3.**

—— விவசாய விளக்கம். [Vyavasāya-viḷakkam. A manual of agriculture. Second edition.] pp. viii. 213. *Madras*, 1902. 8°. **14170. i. 4.**

RĀJA-GŌPĀLA PIḶḶAI, *A.* Anglo-Indian Vydya-chintamani. [A Kanarese Materia Medica, with names of drugs in English, Latin, Kanarese, Tamil, and Telugu.] ಇಂಗ್ಲಿಷ ಕರ್ನಾಟಕವೈದ್ಯಚಿಂತಾಮಣಿ. pp. 3, 3, i. 264, 26, i. 2, 29. *Bangalore,* 1899. 8°. **14176. c. 31.**

RĀJA-GŌPĀLA PIḶḶAI, *Kōmaḷapuram, of Presidency College, Madras.* See ACADEMIES, *etc.*—Madras.—*University of Madras.* The University of Madras. The First in Arts Examination—1892. The Tamil text . . . with . . . notes by . . . Rajagopaul Pillai . . . and . . . P. Vasudeva Mudelliar. 1891. 8°. **14172. bb. 4.**

—— See ĀṞVĀRGAḶ.—Nāl-āyiram.—*Tiru-vāy-moṟi.* ◦◦◦ திருவாய்மொழி ஆ [Tiru-vāy-moṟi. With commentary. Edited by Rāja-gōpāla.] [1859.] 8°. **14172. c. 18.**

—— See NĀL-AḌIYĀR. The Nâladiyâr. With a Tamil commentary by . . . Rajagopala, *etc.* 1903. 8°. **14172. c. 45.**

—— See PUGAṞĒNDI. The Nalavenba and Nanmanikadigai, with . . . notes . . . By C. Rajagopala Pillai, *etc.* 1879. 12°. **14172. a. 22.**

—— See TIRU-VĒṄKAṬĀCHALA PIḶḶAI. திருநீலகண்டநாயனார் விலாசம். [Tiru-nīlakaṇṭha-nāyanār-vilāsam. Edited by Rāja-gōpāla.] [1875.] 8°. **14170. l. 8.**

—— See VIRŪPĀKSHI LIṄG'-AIYAR. திரு. . .தென்திருப்பதிபுராணம் ஆ [Ten-tirupadi-purāṇam. Edited by Rāja-gōpāla.] [1890.] 8°. **14170. e. 49.**

RĀJA-GŌPĀLA PIḶḶAI, *P.* See MAHĀ-BHĀRATAM. அஸ்வமேதபர்வம். [Aṣva-mēdha-parvam. From the recension of Rāja-gōpāla.] [1875.] 8°. **14172. c. 22.**

RĀJA-GŌPĀLA ṢARMA, *K. P., of Dharapuram Board High School.* Principles of Translation. From Tamil into English. For use in Upper Primary and Lower Secondary Schools. pp. ii. 107. *Coimbatore,* 1898. 8°. **14172. h. 89.(2.)**

RAJAH (M. B.). See RĀJĀ HARI-HARA-PUTRA PIḶḶAI.

RĀJĀ HARI-HARA-PUTRAPIḶḶAI, *Muttu-kāmākshi B.* See MEY-KAṆḌA DĒVAR. சிவஞானபோதம் . . . (Sivagnana Botham), *etc.* [With commentary, *etc.* Compiled and edited by M. B. Rājā.] 1906. 12°. **14170. d. 29.**

RĀJAM AIYAṄGĀR, *T.* See PERIODICAL PUBLICATIONS.—*Tanjore.* தமிழகம். [Tamiṟ-agam. Edited by Rājam Aiyaṅgār.] 1905. 8°. **14172. i. 8.**

RĀJAM AIYAR, *B.R.* (ṢIVA-SUBRAHMAṆYA AIYAR). Kamalambal, or The Fatal Rumour . . . Revised and reprinted from the Viveka Chintamani. ஆபத்துக்கிடமான அபவாதம் அல்லது கமலாம்பாள் சரித்திரம். [Kamalāmbāḷ-charitram, or Āpattukk'iḍam āna apavādam. A novel.] pp. xiv. 414, ii. *Madras,* 1896. 12°. **14171. a. 8.**

Forms part of the "Viveka Chintamani Series."

RĀJĀ-RĀM GŌVINDA-RĀU, *Tañjai.* ஸ்ரீபக்தலீலாம்ருதவசநம். [Bhakta-līlāmṛuta-vachanam. A prose version, by K. Rāma-sāmi Nāyuḍu, of Rājā-rām's Bhakta-līlāmṛutam, or poetical histories of 82 Vaishṇava saints, from Puṇḍarīka to Tukā-rām, derived from Marathi sources.] pp. i. ii. 430. சென்னை விகாரி [*Madras,* 1899.] 8°. **14172. d. 24.**

RĀJA-RATNAM PIḶḶAI, *T.A., of Madras Christian College.* The Life of Rao Bahadur C. W. Thamotharam Pillai . . . by T. A. Rajaruthnam. (*T. A. R. Ruthnam's Biographical Series, no. 2.) pp. ii. 95, xxii.; 1 *plate.* *Madras,* 1902. 12°. **14170. k. 44.**

RAJARUTHNAM, *T. A.* See RĀJA-RATNAM PIḶḶAI, *T. A.*

RĀJA-ṢĒKHARA MUDALIYĀR, *Paṭṭūr.* [For Rāja-ṣēkhara's Rāmāyaṇa-ōr-aḍi-kīrttanai, or lyrics on the Rāmāyaṇam, as printed together with Aruṇāchala Kavi-rāyar's Rāma-nāṭakam :] See ARUṆĀCHALA KAVI-RĀYAR.

RĀJĒNDRAM PIḶḶAI, *B.A.A.* The Mysteries of the World. A hundred & one tales. By B. A. A. Rajaindrum Pillay. (*பூலோக விநோதக் கதைகள்.) 4 vols. pp. ii. ii. 518, iv. ii. iv. 933. *Madras,* 1897-1899. 8°. **14171. a. 19.**

RĀMA. ஸ்ரீராமகோடி. பஞ்சலக்ஷம் அடங்கியது. [Ṣrī-rāma-kōṭi. Being the sacred name *Ṣrī-rāma* repeated some 500,000 times, with a preface.] pp. 4, 1002. [*Madras,*] 1905. 8°. **14170. ff. 15.**

RĀMA AIYAN (CHRISTIAN). *See* NĀLU-MANTRI-KATHAI. Vier Geheimrath-Minister . . . übertragen von . . . Rama Ayen. 1855. 8°. **14171. a. 32.**

RĀMA-BHADRA DĪKSHITAR. ஜாநகீபரிணய நாடகம். [Jānakī-pariṇayam. A drama on the union of Rāma and Sītā. Translated from the Sanskrit of Rāma-bhadra by N. Sāmi-nātha Ṣāstri.] pp. 16, 331. சென்னை [*Madras*,] 1903. 12°. **14170. l. 24.(3.)**

RĀMA-BHADRAN. *See* DURAI-SĀMI MŪPPANĀR.

RĀMA-CHANDRA, *V. Ayōdhi-dāsar.* புரூரவச் சக்ரவர்த்திநாடகம். [Purūrvaṣ-chakravartti-nāṭakam. A drama on the legend of Purūravas.]. pp. 84. [*Madras*,] 1897. 8°. **14170. l. 32.(6.)**

RĀMA-CHANDRA AIYAR, *Kandāḍai.* *See* PARNELL (T.). Parnell's Hermit in Tamil prose. By C. Ramachandra Aiyar. 1904. 12°. **14172. a. 54.(2.)**

RĀMA-CHANDRA KAVI-RĀYAR, *Rājanallūr.* *See* BESCHI (C. G. E.). இ௦௦து . . . சதுரகராதி. [Chatur-agarādi. Edited by Rāma-chandra.] [1824.] 4°. **14172. f. 13.**

—— Çakuntalâ. Traduction [by G. Devèze] de la version tamoule [*i.e.* the Ṣakuntalā-vilāsam of Rāma-chandra]. (Revue de Linguistique et de Philologie Comparée. Tome xix., xx.) *Paris*, 1886-1887. 8°. **P.P. 4964. d. (tom. 19-20.)**

—— ஸ்ரீமகாபாரதவிலாசம் சூது-துகிலுரிதல். [Mahā-bhārata-vilāsam. A poetical play on the epic legend. Edited by T. Tyāga-rāya Svāmi.] pp. 88. பிரமோதூத [*Madras*, 1870.] 8°. **14170. l. 20.**

RĀMA-CHANDRA KAVI-RĀYAR, *Taṇḍalam.* *See* SŌMA-SUNDARA MUDALIYĀR. இரணியநாடகம். [Hiraṇya-nāṭakam. Edited by Rāma-chandra.] 1888. 8°. **14170. l. 27.**

RĀMA-CHANDRA PANTULU, *Imkollu Nārapa-rāju.* *See* PARAṢU-RĀMA PANTULU. ००० ஸ்ரீஸீதாராமாஞ்சநேய ஸம்வாதஸாரஸங்கிரகம் ஸ்ரீ [Sītā-rāmāñjanēya-saṃvāda-sāra-saṅgraham. An epitome, by Rāma-chandra, of the Sītārāmāñjanēya-saṃvādam. With Tamil translation, *etc.*] [1898.] 8°. **14170. ee. 27.**

RĀMA-CHANDRA RĀU, *P.* *See* MARIYĀDAI-RĀMAN. Tales of Mariada Raman . . . [translated] by P. Ramachandra Rao. [1902.] 12°. **14171. aa. 14.**

—— The Son-in-Law Abroad, and other Indian folk-tales of fun, folly, cleverness, and humour. pp. iv. ii. 105. *Madras*, 1904. 16°. **14171. aa. 17.**

RĀMA-CHANDRA ṢĀSTRI, *Kāñchīpuram.* *See* VEDAS. வேதார்த்ததீபிகா ஸ்ரீ [Vēdārtha-dīpikā. Being the Taittirīya-saṃhitā with Tamil commentary by Rāma-chandra.] [1889.] 8°. **14010. c. 46.**

RĀMA-CHANDRA ṢĀSTRI, *Mahārājapuram.* *See* VAIDYA-NĀTHA DĪKSHITAR. ००० ஸ்ருதிமுக்தாபலே ... [Smṛuti-muktā-phala. Vol. v., with Tamil translation by Rāma-chandra.] 1898, *etc.* 4°. **14039. c. 15. (vol. 5.)**

RĀMA-CHANDRA ṢĀSTRI, *Vishṇupuram Ṣ.* *See* ṢAṄKARĀCHĀRYAR. ००० சித்தாந்தபிந்து. [Daṣa-ṣlōkī. With Madhu-sūdana's Siddhānta-bindu translated into Tamil by Rāma-chandra.] 1906. 12°. **14049. aa. 1.**

RĀMA KAVI. அத்துவிதாநுபவம். [Advitānubhavam. A metrical Vedantic treatise.] *See* ṢAṄKARĀCHĀRYAR. [*Doubtful and Supposititious Works.*] ஸ்ரீ . . . இலக்ஷணவிர்த்தி ஸ்ரீ [A collection.] pp. 100-132. [1888.] 16°. **14170. d. 28.**

RĀMA KAVI-RĀYAR. ஸ்ரீராமகவிபதங்கள். [Rāma-kavi-padaṅgaḷ. Erotic verses.] *See* VIJAYA-RAṄGA MUDALIYĀR, *P.* ००० கவிகுஞ்சர பாரதி . . . பதங்கள். [Padaṅgaḷ.] pp. 89-96. 1886. 8°. **14172. c. 33.**

RĀMA-KṚUSHṆA BHAṬṬĀCHĀRYAR, *son of Gōpāla-kṛushṇa, of Karupur.* *See* VAIDYA-NĀTHA DĪKSHITAR. ஸ்ருதிமுக்தாபலே ... [Smṛuti-muktā-phala. Vol. ii., with Tamil translation by Rāma-kṛushṇa.] 1898, *etc.* 4°. **14039. c. 15. (vol. 2.)**

RĀMA-KṚUSHṆA SIDDHĀNTIYĀR. *See* MAYAN. ००० சிற்பநூலென்னும் மனையடிசாஸ்திரம் [Manaiy-aḍi-ṣāstram. Collected and enlarged by Rāma-kṛushṇa and Aiyā-sāmi.] [1885.] 8°. **14172. c. 30.**

RĀMA-LIṄGA BRAHMĀNANDA YATI, *of Madura.* *See* SĀYAṆĀCHĀRYAR. ஸ்ரீ . . ஸ்ரீவேதாந்தபஞ்சதசீ *etc.* [Pañchadaṣī. With interpretation and paraphrase in Tamil by Rāma-liṅga, preceded by a Sanskrit poem on the successes of Rāma-liṅga with Tamil translation.] 1905. 8°. **14049. bb. 7.**

RĀMA-LIṄGA DĒVAR, *Erumūr V.* தினக்கிரமாலங்காரச் சுருக்கம். [Dina-kramālaṅkāra-churukkam. A tract on medical diet and regimen.] *See* [Addenda] AGASTYAR. பஞ்சபட்சிசாஸ்திரம் ௵ [Pañcha-pakshi-ṣāstram.] 1907. 8°. **14170. i. 3.**

RĀMA-LIṄGA GURU. *Virudupaṭṭi Ponn'-ambala* (BĀL'-AYYĀ). *See* ATIVĪRA-RĀMA PĀṆḌIYAN. ∘∘∘ மாகபுராணம். [Māgha-purāṇam. Edited by Rāma-liṅga.] 1904. 8°. **14170. eee. 3.**

RĀMA-LIṄGAM PIḶḶAI, *Madurai N.* ஸ்ரீ . . . ஆரணியகாண்டம் ஸ்ரீராமர் வனவாசம். [Ṣrī-rāmar-vana-vāsam. A poem in *ammānai* metre upon the epic story of Rāma's exile in the forest, based upon the corresponding parts of the Ayōdhyā-kāṇḍam of Kamban's Rāmāyaṇam. Edited by Ṣ. P. Gaṇa-patiyā Piḷḷai.] pp. 6, 137. மதுரை [*Madura,*] 1907. 8°. **14172. bb. 24.**

RĀMA-LIṄGA MUDALIYĀR, *Upādhyāyar.* *See* SIDDHARGAḶ. ∘∘∘ பெரிய ஞானக்கோவை [Periya-ñāna-kōvai. Compiled by Rāma-liṅga.] 1899. 12°. **14170. ee. 33.**

RĀMA-LIṄGA MUDALIYĀR, *Tirumayilai.* *See* [Addenda] BAṄKIM-CHANDRA CHAṬṬŌPĀDHYĀYA. அந்தப்புரரகசியம் ௵ (Secrets of Zenana, or Anthappura Rahasyam. [A novel] by M. Rama-linga Mudalyar[, pt. i. being adapted from Baṅkim-chandra's Kapāla-kuṇḍalā, and pt. ii. from Dāmōdara Mukhōpādhyāya's Mṛiṇmayī.]) 1906. 8°. **14171. e. 20.**

—— ஜீவரத்நம். (Jeevarathnam. A Tamil novel.) pts. 1, 2. *Madras,* 1900-1901. 8°. **14170. k. 24.(1.)**

Pt. i. (1901) *is of the second edition, pt.* ii. (1900) *of the first.*

—— பழமொழிக்கதைகள். (Pallamollic Kathaigal. A novel of Tamil proverbs.) pp. 126. *Madras,* 1902. 8°. **14170. k. 33.**

—— ∘∘∘ பங்கஜவல்லிகதை. (Pangajavalli. A Tamil novel.) pp. 94. *Madras,* 1906. 8°. **14171. e. 16.**

RĀMA-LIṄGA PIḶḶAI, *Chidambaram Pēr-ambala, disciple of Āṟu-muga Nāvalar.* *See* NAKKĪRA DĒVAR. ∘∘∘ திருமுருகாற்றுப்படை. [Tiru-mṛug'-āṭṭu-paḍai. Edited by Rāma-liṅga.] [1896.] 16°. **14170. d. 36.(4.)**

RĀMA-LIṄGA PIḶḶAI, *Karuṅguṛi, of Chidambaram* (TIRUV-ARUṬ-PRAKĀṢA-VAḶḶALĀR). *See* BĀLA-SUNDARA NĀYAKAR. இராமலிங்க பிள்ளைபாடல் ஆபாசதர்ப்பணம் ௵ [Rāma-liṅga-piḷḷai-pāḍal-ābhāsa-darpaṇam, or Maruṭ-pā-maṟuppu. Critical essays on Rāma-liṅga's poems.] 1904. 12°. **14172. g. 6.**

—— *See* KAṆṆ'-UḌAIYA VAḶḶAL. ∘∘∘ ஒழிவிலொடுக்கம். [Oṛivil oḍukkam. With an exposition by Rāma-liṅga of the *ṣiṟappu-pāyiram.*] 1906. 16°. **14170. dd. 14.**

—— *See* MUTT'-AIYA SVĀMI. ∘∘∘ சின்மய தீபிகை. [Chin-maya-dīpikai. Edited on the basis of Rāma-liṅga's recension.] 1907. 12°. **14172. a. 58.**

—— ∘∘∘ திருவருட்பாத்திருமுறைத்திரட்டு. [Tiruv-aruṭ-pā-tiru-muṟai-tiraṭṭu. A collection of Ṣaiva devotional poems. With some appended matter in prose and verse. Compiled by P. Sundaram Piḷḷai, and revised by P. Kalyāṇa-sundara Mudaliyār.] pp. xxi. i. 919, xxxii. சென்னை [*Madras*], 1892. 8°. **14172. d. 14.**

—— ∘∘∘ திருவருட்பா திருமுறைகள் முழுதும். [Tiruv-aruṭ-pā-tiru-muṟaigaḷ. Edited with commentary by Kāñchīpuram Rāma-sāmi Nāyuḍu.] nos. 1-5. *Madras,* 1904-1905. 8°. **14170. ff. 17.**

Discontinued after publication of no. 6.

—— ∘∘∘ ஆறுதிருமுறையினின்றுந்திரட்டிய ஆநந்தத்திருவருட்பா. [Ānanda-tiruv-aruṭ-pā. Devotional Ṣaiva lyrics extracted from Rāma-liṅga's 6 Tiru-muṟai. Preceded by 3 Dēvāra-padigaṅgaḷ.] pp. xii. 135; 2 *plates.* சென்னை [*Madras,*] 1903. 12°. **14170. d. 92.**

—— ∘∘∘ திருவருட்பா இங்கிதமாலை. [Tiruv-aruṭ-pā-iṅgita-mālai. Ṣaiva devotional verses. Edited with a commentary by K. V. Tiru-vēṅkaṭa Nāyuḍu.] pp. iii. 104, ii. சென்னை [*Madras,*] 1904. 8°. **14170. eee. 7.**

—— ∘∘∘ திருவருட்பாத்திரட்டு. [Tiruv-aruṭ-pā-tiraṭṭu. Select hymns. With short life of the author, *etc.* Edited, with preface, by T. K. Vaḍi-vēlu Mudaliyār.] pp. viii. 120; 4 *plates.* சென்னை [*Madras,*] 1898. 12°. **14170. d. 50.**

—— ००० திருவருட்பாத்திரட்டு. [Tiruv-aruṭ-pā-tiraṭṭu. Edited by Paṛani Vēl-āyudha Mudaliyār.] pp. 8, 144; 4 *plates.* சென்னை [*Madras,*] 1903. 12°. **14170. d. 79.**

—— ००० திருவருட்பாத் திருமுறைத்திரட்டு மூலமும்-பொழிப்புரையும். [Tiruv-aruṭ-pā-tiru-muṛai-tiraṭṭu. Poems from the Tiruv-aruṭ-pā. Edited with commentary by M. Vaḍi-vēlu Mudaliyār.] pp. ii. 159; 1 *plate.* சென்னை [*Madras,*] 1901. 8°. **14172. c. 44.**

—— திருப்பாடற்றிரட்டு. [Tiru-pāḍaṟ-ṟiraṭṭu. Miscellaneous Ṣaiva poems. Followed by Ṣiva-nāmāvaḷi, a series of hymns.] pp. 38, 32. *See* SIDDHARGAḶ. ००० பெரிய ஞானக்கோவை [Periya-ñāna-kōvai.] 1899. 12°. **14170. ee. 33.**

—— சிவநாமாவளித்திரட்டு. [Ṣiva-nāmāvaḷi-tiraṭṭu.] *See* SIDDHARGAḶ. ००० பெரிய ஞானக்கோவை. [Periya-ñāna-kōvai.] pt. ii. 1906. 12°. **14170. dd. 12.**

RĀMA-LIṄGA SVĀMI, *Chidambaram Īṣāniya-maṭham.* *See* PARAÑ-JŌDI MUNIVAR. மதுரை . . . திருவிளையாடற்புராணம் [Tiru-viḷaiy-āḍaṟ-purāṇam. Edited by Rāma-liṅga.] 1896. 8°. **14170. ee. 3.**

—— —— 1906. 8°. **14170. eee. 24.**

—— *See* ṢIVA-PRAKĀṢA DĒṢIKAR. ००० நால்வர்நான்மணிமாலை. [Nālvar-nān-maṇi-mālai. With commentary by Rāma-liṅga.] 1896. 12°. **14170. d. 27.**

RĀMA-LIṄGA SVĀMI, *Chidambaram, priest of Bommapuram Ṣiva-ñāna-pālaiya Dēṣikar.* *See* ṢEKKIṚĀR. சேக்கிழார் . . . செய்த . . . பெரியபுராணம் ஆ [Periya-purāṇam. Edited with an interpretation by Āṟu-muga Tambirān, completed by Rāma-liṅga.] [1885]-1898. 8°. **14170. f. 1.**

RĀMA-LIṄGA SVĀMI, *Tiruv-aruṭ-prakāṣa-vaḷḷalār.* *See* RĀMA-LIṄGA PIḶḶAI, *K.*

RAMAN, *Mariada.* *See* MARIYĀDAI-RĀMAN.

RĀMĀNANDA SARASVATĪ. *See* BĀDARĀYAṆA. The Brahma Sutra Artha Deepika, or The Brahma Sutras . . . with . . . extracts from the glossaries of . . . Ramananda, *etc.* 1904, *etc.* 4°. **14170. fff. 5.**

RĀMĀNANDA SVĀMI, *Niṣchala, of Conjevaram.* ००० மோக்ஷசாதன விளக்கம். [Mōksha-sādhana-viḷakkam. An Advaita-vēdānti treatise on the methods for obtaining salvation. Edited by G. Vaḍi-vēlu Cheṭṭi.] pp. xxxix. ii. ii. 528, iv.; 1 *plate.* சென்னை [*Madras,*] 1906. 8°. **14170. eee. 16.**

RĀMĀNANDA YŌGI, *Kāñchīpuram.* *See* MUTT'-AIYA SVĀMI. ००० சின்மய தீபிகை. [Chin-maya-dīpikai. Edited with paraphrases, *etc.*, by Rāmānanda.] 1907. 12°. **14172. a. 58.**

RĀMA-NĀTHA AIYAR, *Tiruvārūr R.* *See* ACADEMIES, *etc.*—Madras.—*University of Madras.* University of Madras. Exhaustive notes on the Matriculation Tamil text for 1900 . . . With . . . translation by T. R. Ramanatha Aiyar. 1900. 8°. **14172. bb. 6.(4.)**

—— *See* VĀLMĪKI. Ramayana Niti Ratnavali, *etc.* [Translated into Tamil by Rāma-nātha.] 1886. 12°. **14003. c. (no. 6.)**

RĀMA-NĀTH'-AIYAR, *K., of Trichinopoli.* *See* EPHEMERIDES. ஜந்திரி. Jantri . . . Edited by K. Ramanathaiyar. 1899. 8°. **14172. i. 9.**

RĀMA-NĀTHA ṢĀSTRI, *Palāṣūr N.* *See* NĪLA-KAṆṬHA DĪKSHITAR. சுயம... ஶாந்திவிலாஸ: [Ṣānti-vilāsa. Edited by Rāma-nātha, with Tamil paraphrase.] 1907. 8°. **14070. dd. 42.(3.)**

RĀMAN CHEṬṬI, *Puduvūr Vīr'-appa.* திருவேங்கடமாலை. [Tiru-vēṅkata-mālai. Devotional lyrics on the sanctuary of Vishṇu at Tirupati.] pp. 11. யாழ்ப்பாணம் விய [*Jaffna,* 1886.] 16°. **14172. a. 6.(1.)**

RĀMĀNUJA (EM-BERUMĀNĀR). [*Life.*] *See* GŌVINDĀCHĀRYAR, *A.* The life of Râmânujâchârya, *etc.* 1906. 8°. **14170. eee. 26.**

—— —— *See* PIḶḶAI LŌKAM-JĪYAR. ००० ராமாநுஜார்யதிவ்யசரிதை. [Rāmānujārya-divya-charitai.] 1886. 8°. **14170. f. 11.**

—— —— *See* ṢRĪRAṄGĀCHĀRYAR, *T. K.* ஸ்ரீராமாநுஜசரிதம். (The Life of Sri Ramanuja, *etc.*) 1901. 12°. **14171. a. 48.(1.)**

RĀMĀNUJA (Em-berumānār) (*continued*). *See* Bādarāyaṇa. శ్రీ . . . శ్రీమద్భాష్యార్థసంగ్రహము. [Brahma-sūtram. With Ṣrīmad-bhāshyārtha-saṅgraham, an epitome of Rāmānuja's Ṣrī-bhāshyam, and ascribed to the latter, rendered into Tamil.] [1890.] 8°. **14048. c. 69.**

—— *See* Bādarāyaṇa. சங்கர . . . த்ராவிட-பாஷ்யம். [Brahma-sūtra-drāviḍa-bhāshyam. The Brahma-sūtram, with Tamil commentary based upon the works of Rāmānuja, *etc.*] 1905. 8°. **14049. bb. 8.**

—— *See* Upanishads. ◦ ◦ ◦ தசோபநிஷத்த்ரா-விடபாஷ்யம். [Daṣōpanishad-drāviḍa-bhāshyam. Ten Upanishads, with Tamil commentary comprising translations of the commentaries of Rāmānuja, *etc.*] [1897]-1898. 8°. **14010. dd. 14.**

—— శ్రీ . . . గద్యత్రయమున్ . . . వ్యాఖ్యానమున్. [Gadya-trayam. Three short Sanskrit treatises on Vaishṇava theology, viz. Ṣaraṇāgati-gadyam, Ṣrīraṅga-gadyam, and Vaikuṇṭha-gadyam, with a Tamil commentary by Periyav-āchān Piḷḷai. Edited by Tirumaṟiṣai Mahā-bhāshyam Ṣrīraṅgāchāryar.] pp. v. 112, i. *Madras*, 1882. 8°. **14048. d. 47.**

—— శ్రీ . . . భగవద్రామానుజనియమనపడి. [Rāmānuja-niyamana-paḍi. Rules of religious conduct, in verse, claiming the authority of Rāmānuja.] pp. 16. చన్నపుర్యామ్ తారణ [*Madras*, 1885.] 8°. **14172. a. 29.(1.)**

RĀMĀNUJĀCHĀRI, *Pandit*. *See* Āṟvārgaḷ.—Nāl-āyiram.—*Tiru-vāy-moṟi.* ◦ ◦ ◦ திருவாய்மொழி ௵ [Tiru-vāy-moṟi. With commentary. Edited by Rāmānujāchāri.] [1859.] 8°. **14172. c. 18.**

RĀMĀNUJĀCHĀRYAR, *N.* *See* Periodical Publications.—*Madras*. அபிநவ பத்திரிகை ௵ [Abhinava-patrikai. Edited by Rāmānujāchāryar.] 1902. 8°. **14172. i. 2.**

RĀMĀNUJĀCHĀRYAR, *Timmaguḍi Alluṇḍu.* *See* Vēṅkaṭa-nātha Vēdāntāchāryar. ஸர்வதந்த்ர-ஸ்வதந்த்ர ஸ்ரீமந்நிகமாந்த மஹாதேசிகன் . . . "பரமத-பங்கம்" ௵ [Para-mata-bhaṅgam. Edited by Rāmānujāchāryar.] 1893. 8°. **14170. e. 54.**

RĀMĀNUJĀCHĀRYAR, *Tirukuḍandai Komāṇḍūr Iḷaiyavalli.* *See* Vēṅkaṭa-nātha Vēdāntāchāryar. ◦ ◦ ◦ ஸ்ரீதேசிக ப்ரபந்தம். [Dēṣika-prabandham. With commentaries by Rāmānujāchāryar.] 1889-[1890.] 8°. **14170. f. 13.**

RĀMĀNUJĀCHĀRYAR, *Māḍabhūshi Tarka-tīrtha.* *See* Aḻagiya-maṇavāḷa Peru-māḷ. ◦ ◦ ◦ యతిరాజవింశతి. [Yati-rāja-viṃṣati. With commentary of Piḷḷai Lōkam-jīyar. Edited with Telugu interpretation by Rāmānujāchāryar.] [1904.] 8°. **14028. c. 86.**

—— *See* Āṟvārgaḷ.—Nāl-āyiram.—*Iyaṟ-pā.* இயற்பா ௵ [Iyaṟ-pā. With commentary of Periyav-āchān, together with paraphrases by Rāmānujāchāryar. Edited by the latter.] [1903-1904.] 8°. **14170. eee. 4.**

—— *See* Āṟvārgaḷ. — Nāl-āyiram. — *Iyaṟ-pa.* ◦ ◦ ◦ பெரிய திருமடல். [Periya-tiru-maḍal. Edited by Rāmānujāchāryar, with commentary.] [1905.] 8°. **14170. ee. 6.(5.)**

—— *See* Āṟvārgaḷ. — Nāl-āyiram. — *Iyaṟ-pā.* ◦ ◦ ◦ இராமாநுச நூற்றந்தாதி. [Rāmānuja-nūṭṭ'-antādi. Edited by Rāmānujāchāryar.] [1905.] 8°. **14170. ee. 6.(6.)**

—— *See* Āṟvārgaḷ. — Nāl-āyiram. — *Iyaṟ-pā.* ◦ ◦ ◦ சிறிய திருமடல். [Siṟiya-tiru-maḍal. Edited by Rāmānujāchāryar, with commentary.] [1905.] 8°. **14170. ee. 6.(4.)**

—— *See* Āṟvārgaḷ.—Nāl-āyiram.—*Tiru-vāy-moṟi.* ◦ ◦ ◦ తిరువాయ్మొழி. [Tiru-vāy-moṟi. With glosses and commentaries in Telugu by Rāmānujāchāryar.] 1902. 8°. **14170. ff. 10.**

—— *See* Bādarāyaṇa. சங்கர . . . த்ராவிடபா-ஷ்யம். [Brahma-sūtra-drāviḍa-bhāshyam. The Brahma-sūtram, with Tamil commentary. Compiled by Rāmānujāchāryar.] 1905. 8°. **14049. bb. 8.**

—— *See* Kaṇṇan Ayya. ◦ ◦ ◦ పరమవిలక్షణ తిరువారాధనక్రమసంగ్రహము. [Tiruv-ārādhana-krama-saṅgrahamu. Edited by Rāmānujāchāryar.] 1902. 12°. **14033. a. 46.**

—— *See* Vālmīki. ஸ்ரீ . . . சுந்தரகாண்டம். [Sundara-kāṇḍam. With Tamil paraphrase. Edited by Rāmānujāchāryar.] 1901. 12°. **14060. b. 18.**

RĀMĀNUJA-DĀSAR, *Kuravai.* ◦ ◦ ◦ நூற்றெட்டுத்-திருப்பதித் திருப்புகழ். [Nūṭṭ'-eṭṭu-tiru-padi-tiru-pugar. A series of religious poems, celebrating the 108 Vaishṇava sanctuaries. Edited by K. V. Tiru-vēṅkaṭa Nāyuḍu.] pp. vii. 135. சென்னை [*Madras*,] 1897. 12°. 14172. a. 48.

RĀMĀNUJA-DĀSAR, *Tiru-nagari*. *See* ĀṚVĀRGAḶ.—Nāl-āyiram.—*Mudal-āyiram*. ◦◦◦ తమిళ్వేద ప॥ [Mudal-āyiram. Edited by Rāmānuja-dāsar.] 1889. 8°. 14170. e. 33.

RĀMĀNUJA KAVI-RĀYAR. *See* PAVAṆANDI. நன்னூல் ஶ்ரீ [Nan-nūl. With commentary by Rāmānuja.] [1847.] 8°. 14172. f. 1.

—— *See* ṢAṄKARĀCHĀRYAR. (†ఆత్మబోధప్రకాశిక) [Ātma-bōdham. With the Telugu interpretation of Kṛushṇa Ṣāstri, and a Tamil version of the same by Rāmānuja.] [1840.] 12°. 14048. c. 44.

—— *See* ṢAṄKARĀCHĀRYAR. Ātma Bōd'a Prakāśika. Text, Übersetzung und Erklärung. [Ātma-bōdham, with extracts from Kṛushṇa Ṣāstri's commentary, translated into German from Rāmānuja's Tamil version.] 1854. 8°. [*Bibliotheca Tamulica.*] 14170. e. 42.(vol. 1.)

—— *See* ṢAṄKARĀCHĀRYAR. Ātma bōda prakāśika . . . text, translation [of the text] and [of the] commentary [of Rāmānuja,] *etc.* 1867. 12°. 14048. b. 8.(1.)

—— *See* ṢAṄKARĀCHĀRYAR. ◦◦◦ ஆத்ம போதம். [Ātma-bōdham. With Rāmānuja's version of Kṛushṇa Ṣāstri's Telugu commentary.] [1869.] 8°. 14048. c. 62.(2.)

—— *See* TIRU-VAḶḶUVAR. The Cural . . . with the commentary of Parimelaragar, an amplification . . . by Ramanuja Cavi-Rayar, *etc.* 1840-1852. 8°. 14172. b. 48.

RĀMĀNUJA MUDALIYĀR, *disciple of Ponn'-ambala Svāmi*. *See* TĀṆḌAVA-RĀYA-MŪRTTI SVĀMI. ◦◦◦ கைவல்லிய நவநீதம் ஶ்ரீ [Kaivalya-navanītam. Edited by Rāmānuja.] 1898. 8°. 14170. ee. 9.

RĀMĀNUJA NĀVALAR, *Puduvai*. *See* PURĀṆAS.—*Padma-purāṇam*. ஶ்ரீபாத்மோத்தரபுராணம். [Pādmōttara-purāṇam. A metrical adaptation by Rāmānuja.] [1870.] 8°. 14170. f. 2.

—— ஶ்ரீவைஷ்ணவதத்வம். [Ṣrī-vaishṇava-tattvam. An exposition of the doctrines of the Ṣrī-vaishṇava system.] pp. iv. 136. சென்னப்பட்டணம் கஅளூ [*Madras*, 1875.] 12°. 14170. e. 1.

RĀMA-RĀMA VASU. நிஸ்தார ரத்நாகரம் ஶ்ரீ [Nistāra-ratnākaram. A series of Christian lyrics with prose commentaries, directed against Hindu religious systems, originally written in Bengali by Rāma-rāma Vasu. Translated into Tamil, with additions, by H. M. Scudder.] pp. 124. *Madras*, 1851. 16°. 14170. a. 28.

RĀMA-SĀMI, *Vīra-kōdaṇḍa*. *See* VĪRA-KŌDAṆḌA-RĀMA-SVĀMI.

RĀMA-SĀMI AIYAṄGĀR, *Ṣarukkai*. லீலாவதி-சுலோசனையுரை. (F.A. Tamil Text, 1899. Full notes on [Sambandha Mudaliyār's] Lilavati-Sulochana, or The Two Sisters.) pp. iii. 26. *Madras*, 1898. 8°. 14172. bb. 6.(1.)

—— Suguna-Sukesar, or Friendship and Love. A Tamil drama [based upon Shakspere's "Two Gentlemen of Verona"] . . . With an [English] introduction by T. V. Vaidyanatha Aiyar. (†சுகுண சுகேசர் அல்லது நட்புங் காதலும்.) pp. viii. 8, ii. 100, i. *Madras*, 1899. 12°. 14170. l. 48.(2.)

RĀMA-SĀMI AIYAṄGĀR, *Ṣ. V.* Parallel Proverbs in Tamil and English. pp. 39. *Madras*, 1905. 12°. 14170. k. 58.(2.)

—— A Tamil grammatical primer. தமிழ் இலக்கண நூலாதாரம். pp. 72. *Madras*, 1905. 12°. 14172. e. 44.

RĀMA-SĀMI AIYAR, *Ṣ.* *See* COLLINS (M.). மார்க்க விளக்கம். [Mārga-viḷakkam.] . . . Translated by S. Ramaswamier. 1885. 16°. 14170. d. 6.

—— *See* TIRU-MURAI.—*Tiru-mantram*. Thirumantra, *etc.* [Text with translation by Rāmasāmi.] 1897, *etc.* 4°. [*Siddhanta Deepika.*] 14170. fff. 4.(vol. 1, etc.)

RĀMA-SĀMI AIYAR, *Ṣ., District Munsif of Parur.* Jewel Mania . . . நாகைப் பைத்தியம். [Nāgai-paittiyam. A study of the moral and economic results of the popular passion for wearing jewellery.] 2 pts. *Madras*, 1898-1899. 8°. 14171. a. 24.

RĀMA-SĀMI AIYAR, *Ṣ., of Enaṅguḍi.* *See* PURĀṆAS.—*Skanda-purāṇam*. ஹஉ௦ . . . வடாரண்யமாஹாத்ம்யம்

[Vaṭāraṇya-māhātmyam. Followed by a Tamil version by Rāma-sāmi.] 1898. 16°. **14016. a. 27.**

RĀMA-SĀMI AIYAR, *Vaiyai Pañchanad'-aiyar.* மஹாவைத்தியநாத விஜயஸங்கிரகம். [Mahā-vaidyanātha-vijaya-saṅgraham. A prose biography of the author's brother, Vaidyanāth'-aiyar, a distinguished musician, followed by an elegy on his death.] pp. 36. திருவாதி நந்தன [*Trivadi,* 1893.] 16°. **14171. aa. 9.**

RĀMA-SĀMI DĪKSHITAR, *Akhilāṇḍapuram.* See PURĀṆAS. — *Padma-purāṇam.* ஸ்ரீசிவகீதை ஷ [Śiva-gītā. Rendered into prose by Rāma-sāmi.] 1898. 16°. **14170. d. 35.(6.)**

RĀMA-SĀMI KAVI-RĀYAR, *Midulaipaṭṭi Aṟagiya-ṣiṭṭambalan, of Sivaganga.* ∘∘∘ கருப்பண்ணசுவாமி சதகம். [Karuppaṇṇa-svāmi-ṣatakam. A century of verses to Karuppaṇṇan, a manifestation of Śiva as worshipped at Sivaganga.] pp. 74. சென்னை [*Madras,*] 1897. 16°. **14170. d. 48.(2.)**

RĀMA-SĀMI NĀYUḌU, *Kāñchīpuram.* See AMBALA-VĀṆA KAVI-RĀYAR. ∘∘∘ சதுரகிரி அறப்பளீசுர-சதக ஷ [Aṟapaḷīṣura-ṣatakam. With paraphrase, *etc.*, by Rāma-sāmi.] 1905. 12°. **14172. a. 56.**

—— See AMIRTA KAVI-RĀYAR. ∘∘∘ நாணிக்-கண்புதைத்தல் ஷ [Oru-duṟai-kōvai. Edited by Rāma-sāmi.] 1905. 12°. **14172. a. 55.**

—— See ĀṞVĀRGAḶ. — Nāl-āyiram. — *Mudal-āyiram.* ∘∘∘ ஸ்ரீ . . . திருப்பாவை. [Tiru-pāvai. Edited, with commentary, by Rāma-sāmi.] 1902. 12°. **14170. d. 76.**

—— See ĀṞVĀRGAḶ.—Nāl-āyiram.—*Tiru-vāy-moṟi.* ∘∘∘ நம்மாழ்வாருடைய . . . திருவாய்-மொழி ஷ [Tiru-vāy-moṟi. With glossary by Rāma-sāmi.] [1899.] 8°. **14170. ff. 8.**

—— See DICTIONARIES. பேரகராதி. [Pēr-agarādi. With additions by Rāma-sāmi.] 1893. 8°. **14172. f. 15.**

—— See MAHĀ-BHĀRATAM. ஸ்ரீபகவத்கீதை. [Bhagavad-gītā. Edited and translated by Srīnivāsa and Rāma-sāmi.] [1899.] 16°. **14065. b. 19.**

RĀMA-SĀMI NĀYUḌU, *Kāñchīpuram (continued).* See MASTĀN ŚĀHIB. ∘∘∘ திருப்பாடற்றிரட்டு ஷ [Tiru-pāḍaṭ-ṭiraṭṭu. With commentary by Rāma-sāmi.] 1905. 8°. **14173. b. 9.**

—— See PIḶḶAI PERU-MĀḶ AIYAṄGĀR. அஷ்டப்ர-பந்தம். [Ashṭa-prabandham. Edited by Rāma-sāmi.] 1904. 12°. **14170. dd. 1.**

—— See PIḶḶAI PERU-MĀḶ AIYAṄGĀR. ஸ்ரீ . . . திரு-வேங்கடமாலை ஷ [Tiru-vēṅkaṭa-mālai. Edited by Rāma-sāmi.] 1903. 12°. **14170. d. 4.(1.)**

—— —— ஸ்ரீ . . . திருவேங்கடத்தந்தாதி ஷ [Tiru-vēṅkaṭatt' antādi. Edited by Rāma-sāmi.] 1903. 12°. **14170. d. 4.(2.)**

—— See RĀJĀ-RĀM GŌVINDA-RĀU. ஸ்ரீபக்தலீ-லாம்ருதவசநம். [Bhakta-līlāmṛuta-vachanam. A prose version, by Rāma-sāmi.] [1899.] 8°. **14172. d. 24.**

—— See RĀMA-LIṄGA PIḶḶAI, *K.* ∘∘∘ திருவ-ருட்பா ஷ [Tiruv-aruṭ-pā-tiru-muṟaigaḷ. Edited with commentary by Rāma-sāmi.] 1904-1905. 8°. **14170. ff. 17.**

—— See ṢAṬHAKŌPA-DĀSAR, *K.* ∘∘∘ அரிசமய-தீபம் ஷ [Hari-samaya-dīpam. Edited by Rāma-sāmi.] 1904. 8°. **14170. ee. 58.**

—— See ṢIVA-PRAKĀṢA DĒṢIKAR. பிரபுலிங்கலீலை வசனம். [Prabhu-liṅga-līlai-vachanam. A paraphrase by Rāma-sāmi.] 1903. 8°. **14170. ee. 62.**

—— See TĀYUMĀNAVAR. ஸ்ரீ . .·. திருப்பாடற்-றிரட்டு. [Tiru-pāḍaṭ-ṭiraṭṭu. With glosses by Rāma-sāmi.] 1905. 16°. **14170. dd. 6.**

—— See VIDYĀ-VINŌDINI. வித்தியாவிநோதினி. (Vidhya Vinodhini Series.) [Edited by Rāma-sāmi and others.] [1889]-1892. 8°. **14172. c. 39.**

—— சதகத்திரட்டு. [Ṣataka-tiraṭṭu. Seven centuries of verses, viz. Ambala-vāṇar's Aṟapaḷī-ṣura-ṣatakam, Guru-pāda-dāsar's Kumarēṣa-ṣ°., Veṇmaṇi Nārāyaṇa Bhārati's Tiru-vēṅkaṭa-ṣ°., Paḍi-kāṣu Pulavar's Taṇḍalaiyār-ṣ°., Nārāyaṇa Bhārati's Gōvinda-ṣ°., Gōpāla-kṛushṇa-dāsar's Embirān-ṣ°., and Vīrā-sāmi Upādhyāyar's Ṣiva-ṣaṅkara-ṣ°. Edited by Rāma-sāmi.] 7 pts. சென்னை [*Madras,*] 1905-1906. 12°. **14170. dd. 10.**

The general title-page is dated 1906, *but some of the parts are dated* 1905.

RĀMA-SĀMI NĀYUḌU, *Kāñchīpuram (continued).* *தனிப்பாடற்றிரட்டு* [Taṇi-pāḍaṭ-ṭiraṭṭu. An anthology from the works of various poets. With commentaries, *etc.*, by Rāma-sāmi.] 2 vols. *Madras*, 1902. 8°. **14172. c. 43.**

RĀMA-SĀMI PIḶḶAI, *Bhīmanagaram K., of Trichinopoli.* *சுகர்நாடி என்னும் ஜோதிடசிகாமணி.* [Jōdiḍa-ṣikhāmaṇi, or Ṣukar-nāḍi. A treatise on astrology, in verse. Edited with commentary, examples, and diagrams by V. Ārya-muttu Piḷḷai.] pp. 16, 20, xxii. 36, 354, 384, iii. *சென்னை* [*Madras*,] 1897. 8°. **14170. i. 52.**

RĀMA-SĀMI PIḶḶAI, *Karundiṭṭāṅguḍi Ashṭāvadhānam K.* *See* Aṇṇāviyār. *ஸ்ரீ மகாபாரத அம்மானை* [Mahā-bhārata-ammāṇai. Edited by Rāma-sāmi.] 1903. 8°. **14172. c. 49.**

RĀMA-SĀMI PIḶḶAI, *Koṭṭamaṅgalam, Librarian of Madras College.* Niti-sara-vakkiyam. Or A Glossary of Moral Sentences, [compiled] by C. Ramasami Pillei. (**நீதிசாரவாக்கியம்.*) pp. iv. ii. 90. *Madras*, 1844. 8°. **14170. k. 16.**

—— *நீதிசார வாக்கியங்களில் தெரியலானவை.* [Nīti-sāra-vākyaṅgaḷil teriyal-āṇavai. Selections from the Nīti-sāra-vākyam.] *See* Tāṇḍava-rāya Mudaliyār, *V.* *கதாமஞ்சரி ஸ்ரீ* [Kathā-mañjari.] pp. 114-176. [1864.] 16°. **14171. aa. 15.**

RĀMA-SĀMI PULAVAR, *Beṅgaḷūr Ṣ.* English translation of a Tamil poem [with the original] regarding the assumption of the title of "Empress of India" by . . . Queen Victoria. Composed by S. Ramasawmy Poolaver . . . Second edition. (*இந்தியா சக்கரவர்த்தினியுமாக எழுந்தருளியிராநின்ற தமது மாக்ஷிமைத்தங்கிய விக்ற்ரோரியாள் அவர்கள் பட்டாபிஷேகத்தைக்குறித்து.*) pp. 9. *Rangoon*, 1877. 8°. **14172. c. 28.(1.)**

—— The Phrase Book, or Idiomatical Exercises in English and Tamil . . . by P. Ramasawmy. Second edition. pp. vi. 315. *Bangalore*, 1865. 12°. **14172. h. 62.**

RĀMA-SĀMI ṢĀSTRI, *Brahmaṣrī.* *See* Vaidyanātha Dīkshitar. ∘∘∘ 𑌸𑍍𑌮𑍃𑌤𑌿𑌮𑍁𑌕𑍍𑌤𑌾𑌫𑌲𑍇 𑌪𑍍𑌰𑌥𑌮𑌃 . . . 𑌕𑌾𑌣𑍍𑌡𑌃 [Smṛuti-muktā-phala. Vol. i., with Tamil translation by Rāma-sāmi.] 1898, *etc.* 4°. **14039. c. 15.(vol. 1.)**

RĀMA-SĀMI ṢĀSTRI, *Ṣiṟugaḷattūr.* *See* Kāli-dāsa. 𑌰𑌘𑍁𑌵𑌂𑌶𑌮𑍍 ॥ [Raghu-vaṃṣam. Canto i., edited with interpretations in Tamil, styled Būla-sad-guru-bōdhikā, by Rāma-sāmi.] [1884.] 8°. **14070. c. 44.**

RĀMA-SĀMI SVĀMI, *Kōyilūr A., disciple of Chidambara Svāmi.* *See* Kaṇṇ'-uḍaiya Vaḷḷal. ∘∘∘ *ஒழிவிலொடுக்க ஸ்ரீ* [Oḻivil oḍukkam. Edited by Rāma-sāmi.] 1888. 12°. **14170. d. 29.**

—— *See* Ṣaṅkarāchāryar. [*Doubtful and Supposititious Works.*] *ஸ்ரீ . . . இலக்ஷணவிர்த்தி ஸ்ரீ* [A collection. Edited by Rāma-sāmi.] [1888.] 16°. **14170. d. 28.**

—— *See* Sāyaṇāchāryar. ∘∘∘ *ஜீவன்முக்திப்பிரகரணம்.* [Jīvan-mukti-prakaraṇam. Edited by Rāma-sāmi.] [1887.] 12°. **14170. d. 24.**

—— *நானாசீவவாதக்கட்டளை. கீதாசாரத்தாலாட்டு. சசிவர்ணன்சரித்திரம். சசிவர்ணபோதம். துவாதசநாமசங்கீர்த்தனம்.* [Nānā-jīva-vāda-kaṭṭaḷai, by Ṣēshādri Ṣivanār; Gītā-sāra-tālāṭṭu, by Tiru-vēṅkaṭa-nāthar; Ṣaṣi-varṇan-charitram, from the Vṛuttāchala-purāṇam; and Ṣaṣi-varṇa-bōdham and Dvādaṣa-nāma-saṅkīrttanam, by Tattva-rāya Svāmi. Tracts on the Ṣaiva Vēdāntam. Edited by Rāma-sāmi. Second edition.] pp. 64. *சென்னை சர்வசித்து* [*Madras*, 1887.] 12°. **14170. d. 26.**

RAMASAWMY POOLAVER. *See* Rāma-sāmi Pulavar.

RĀMA-SVĀMI. *See* Rāma-sāmi.

RAMASWAMIER. *See* Rāma-sāmi Aiyar.

RĀMĀYAṆAM. *இராமாயணம்.* [Four chapters of a prose Rāmāyaṇam—viz., Rāmar-koluv-irukkai, Araṣ'-iyaṭṭu-muṟaimai, Rāma-rāvaṇa-yuddham, and Hanuma-varal-āṟu.] *See* Academies, *etc.*—Madras.—*University of Madras.* The Tamil text, *etc.* pp. 32-48. 1899. 8°. **14172. bb. 6.(7.)**

—— Literal English translation . . . by V. Venkata Srinivasan . . . Ramayanam, *etc.* [The same 4 chapters.] *See* Academies, *etc.*—Madras.—*University of Madras.* University of Madras. Matriculation Examination, 1900, *etc.* 1900. 8°. **14172. bb. 6.(2.)**

RĀMĀYAṆAM (*continued*). Ramayana, *etc.* [The same 4 chapters, in English, with Tamil annotations.] *See* ACADEMIES, *etc.*—Madras.—*University of Madras.* Copious annotations, *etc.* 1900. 8°. **14172. bb. 6.(3.)**

—— Ramayanam, *etc.* [The same 4 chapters, in English, with Tamil annotations.] *See* ACADEMIES, *etc.*—Madras.—*University of Madras.* University of Madras. Exhaustive notes, *etc.* 1900. 8°. **14172. bb. 6.(4.)**

—— குசலவாக்கியம் என்று வழங்கும் இராமாயண உத்தரகாண்டம். [Kuṣa-lavākhyam, or Rāmāyaṇa-uttara-kāṇḍam. An old poem, sung by women, on the story of the Uttara-kāṇḍam. Edited by R. Ṣ. Subba-lakshmi Ammāḷ.] pp. 2, 50. *Madras,* 1906. 8°. **14172. bb. 22.(2.)**

—— இராமாயணக்கொம்மி. [Rāmāyaṇa-kommi. Songs in *kummi* style on the subject of the Rāmāyaṇam. Edited by T. Aṛagiya Ṣokka-nātha Piḷḷai.] pp. 32. திருநெல்வேலி சுக்கில [*Tinnevelli,* 1870.] 8°. **14172. a. 25.**

—— வால்மீகிராமாயணப் பாட்டும், ஞானராமாயணக் கப்பலும். [Vālmīki-rāmāyaṇa-pāṭṭu and Ñāna-rāmāyaṇa-kappal. Two old songs, sung by women, upon the legend and religious purport of the Rāmāyaṇam. Edited by R. Ṣ. Subba-lakshmi Ammāḷ.] pp. i. 40. *Madras,* 1906. 8°. **14172. bb. 22.(1.)**

RĀMA YŌGI, *of Conjevaram.* *See* KṚUSHṆA MIṢRA. பிரபோதசந்திரோதய ஞூ [Prabōdha-chandrōdaya-vachanam. A prose version, by Rāma Yōgi.] 1902. 8°. **14170. l. 57.**

RAṄGĀCHĀRYAR, *K.* *See* ĀNANDA-RAṄGA PIḶḶAI. The Private Diary of Ananda Ranga Pillai . . . Translated . . . and edited by Sir J. F. Price . . . assisted by K. Rangachari. 1904, *etc.* 8°. **14171. e. 4.**

RAṄGĀCHĀRYAR, *Kunṛattūr.* கல்யாணகீதம். [Kalyāṇa-gītam. Lyrics on the occasion of a marriage.] pp. 26. சென்னை [*Madras,*] 1906. 12°. **14172. a. 45.(5.)**

RAṄGĀCHĀRYAR, *Mahā-bhāshyam, Tirumaṛiṣai-kōyil Kandāḍai.* *See* YĀMUNĀCHĀRYAR. ∘∘∘ ஆளவந்தார்ஸ்தோத்ரம். [Āḷavandār-stōtram. Edited by Raṅgāchāryar.] 1878. 8°. **14028. c. 46.**

—— —— 1879. 12°. **14028. b. 52.**

RAṄGĀCHĀRYAR, *Muḷḷambūṇḍi Kastūri.* *See* VEṄKAṬA-NĀTHA VEDĀNTĀCHĀRYAR. ∘∘∘ ஸ்ரீதேசிகப்ரபந்தம். [Dēṣika-prabandham. With commentaries by Raṅgāchāryar, *etc.*] 1889-[1890.] 8°. **14170. f. 13.**

RAṄGĀCHĀRYAR, *Muṣuṛpākkam Kaḍāmbi.* *See* VĀLMĪKI. ஸ்ரீ . . . ஸுந்தரகாண்டம். [Sundara-kāṇḍam. Edited with Tamil translation by Raṅgāchāryar.] [1902.] 8°. **14065. bbb. 9.**

RAṄGĀCHĀRYAR, *Perumāḷ-kōyil Kiḍāmbi.* *See* BRAHMA-TANTRA-SVATANTRA SVĀMI. ∘∘∘ குருபரம்பராப்ரபாவம். [Guru-paramparā-prabhāvam. Edited by Raṅgāchāryar.] [1890.] 8°. **14170. e. 37.**

RAṄGĀCHĀRYAR, *Vyākaraṇam Ṣrīnivāsāchāryar.* விதவோத்வாககண்டனம். [Vidhavōdvāha-khaṇḍanam. An essay against the re-marriage of Hindu widows.] pp. 100. சென்னபட்டணம் [*Madras,*] 1875. 8°. **14170. g. 4.**

RAṄGA-NĀTHA KAVI-RĀYAR, *Ashṭāvadhānam.* மகாபாரதம். [Mahā-bhāratam. An abbreviated adaptation of the Sanskrit poem. Edited by Gōvinda Piḷḷai.] pp. vi. iv. ii. 295. சென்னை சுபகிருது [*Madras,* 1903.] 8°. **14172. b. 9.**

RAṄGA-NĀTHAN, *son-in-law of Periy-āṛvār.* *See* AṚAGIYA-MAṆAVĀḶA PERU-MĀḶ.

RAṄGA PIḶḶAI, *Palavaikāḍu.* *See* HARIṢCHANDRA. Arichandra . . . a . . . drama, translated . . . [partly from the Hariṣchandra-vilāsam or dramatic version ascribed to Raṅga Piḷḷai], *etc.* 1863. 12°. **14170. l. 33.**

RAṄGA-RĀMĀNUJA MAHĀ-DĒṢIKAR. *See* ĀṚVĀRGAḶ.–Nāl-āyiram.–*Tiru-vāy-moṛi.* பகவத்விஷயம்॥ [Bhagavad-vishayam. Being the Tiru-vāy-moṛi with commentaries—viz. Raṅga-rāmānuja's Dramiḍōpanishad-bhāshyam, or On-badin-āyira-paḍi (in Sanskrit), *etc.*] [1883-1904.] 4°. **14170. fff. 3.**

—— *See* SANDHYĀ-VANDANAM. யஜுர்வேத ஸந்த்யாவந்தநம் ஞூ [Sandhyā-vandanam, *etc.* With extracts, in a Tamil translation, from the commentaries of Raṅga-rāmānuja and others.] 1901. 8°. **14033. aa. 27.**

—— *See* UPANISHADS. ∘∘∘ நூற்றெட்டு உபநிஷத்துகள். [Nūṭṭ'-eṭṭu Upanishattugaḷ. With extracts from the commentaries of Raṅga-rāmānuja, translated into Tamil.] 1887. 8°. **14010.dd.2.**

RAṄGA-SĀMI-DĀSAN, *N. V.* ○○○ குதிரைப் பந்தய லாவணி. [Kudirai-pandaya-lāvaṇi. A song on horse-racing.] pp. 8. சிங்கப்பூர் [*Singapore,*] 1893. 8°. **14172. b. 44.(3.)**

RAṄGA-SĀMI PIḶḶAI, *Triṣirapuram Nārāyaṇa-sāmi.* See PULI-PĀṆI. ○○○ புலிப்பாணிசோதிடம் (*Pulippani Jothidam ... examined and written by T. N. Rangasawmy Pillay). 1894-1895. 8°. **14170. i. 38.**

—— சோதிடக்கடலகராதி. [Jōdiḍa-kaḍal-agarādi. An alphabetically arranged dictionary of astrological terms. Followed by Yōga-poruḷ-agarādi, a dictionary of the various *yōgas* known in astrology, and Jōdiḍa-kaḍal-bōdhini, an explanation of the calendar.] pp. 80. திண்டுக்கல் [*Dindigal,*] 1900. 8°. **14170. i. 65.**

RAṄGA-SVĀMI RĀU, *P. Ṣ.* The Linguist's Self-instructor [in Telugu, Kanarese, Malayalam, Marathi, Tamil, and English]. By P. S. Rungaswamy Row. pp. ii. 101. *Madras,* 1900. 8°. **14172. hh. 16.**

RATHAKRISHNA. See RĀDHĀ-KṚUSHṆA.

RATNA KAVI-RĀYAR, *Ṣiṟiya.* See ṢIṞIYA RATNA KAVI-RĀYAR.

RATNAM PIḶḶAI (T. JOHN). The Domestic's Manual, or A Tamil and English vocabulary for the use of employés under Europeans. With English and Tamil proverbs and a glossary, *etc.* pp. ix. 282. *Madras,* 1891. 8°. **14172. hh. 2.**

—— Second edition. Revised and enlarged. pp. x. 320. *Madras,* 1897. 8°. **14172. hh. 13.**

—— Third edition. pp. x. 357. *Madras,* 1905. 8°. **14172. hh. 20.**

RATNA-SABHĀ-PATI MUDALIYĀR, *Ālandūr Muttu-sāmi.* ம்ருகர் விசித்திர ஜாவளிகள் ௵ [Mṛugar-vichitra-jāvaḷigaḷ. Songs in honour of the god Skanda, in Tamil and English in the Tamil character. Arranged for music by T. Ṣiṅgar-āchāryar and T. Aṟagu-ṣiṅgar-āchāryar.] pp. ii. 34. *Madras,* 1888. 8°. **14170. ee. 5.(1.)**

RATNA-VĒLU MUDALIYĀR, *Ikkāḍu Raṅga-sāmi.* See PARAÑ-JŌDI MUNIVAR. மதுரை... திருவிளையாடற்புராணம். [Tiru-viḷaiy-āḍaṟ-purāṇam. With interpretation and commentary by Ratna-vēlu.] 1896, *etc.* 8°. **14170. ff. 1.**

—— See PURĀṆAS.—*Ṣiva-purāṇam.* ○○○ ஸ்ரீ ... சிவமஹாபுராணம். [Ṣiva-mahā-purāṇam. Translated into prose by Ratna-vēlu.] 1900. 8°. **14170. ff. 2.**

—— See PURĀṆAS.—*Skanda-purāṇam.* ○○○ காசிகண்டம். [Kāṣi-khaṇḍam. Edited with interpretation by Ratna-vēlu.] 1892, *etc.* 8°. **14170. f. 20.**

—— See PURĀṆAS.—*Vināyaka-purāṇam.* பார்க்கவபுராணம் ௵ [Vināyaka-purāṇam. Edited with commentary by Ratna-vēlu.] 1899. 8°. **14170. f. 15.**

—— பஸ்ம மஹாத்மியம். [Bhasma-māhātmyam. An anthology of passages bearing upon the ashes of burnt cow-dung with which Ṣaivas smear themselves. With Tamil translation.] pp. 42. சென்னை [*Madras,*] 1902. 8°. **14033. b. 55.(3.)**

RĀVAṆAN. சகஸ்திரமுகராவணன்கதையும், சதமுகராவணன்கதையும். [Sahasra-mukha-rāvaṇan-kathai and Ṣata-mukha-rāvaṇan-kathai. The stories of the thousand-faced and the hundred-faced Rāvaṇa, based on epic legends. Edited by K. V. Āṟu-muga Mudaliyār.] pp. 122. பவ [*Madras,* 1874.] 8°. **14172. b. 24.**

RĀY'-APPA SVĀMI, *Māṇikkam.* See BUTLER (J.). ஞானஉபதேசம் [Ñāna-upadēṣam. Translated by Rāy'-appa.] 1839. 16°. **14170. a. 6.**

RĀY'-APPA UPADĒṢIYĀR, *J., of Palamcottah.* மெய்ஞ்ஞான வேத ஒளி. [Mey-ñāna-vēda-oḷi. A controversial treatise, from the standpoint of Catholic orthodoxy, upon the worship of the Virgin Mary and other principles of Catholicism.] pp. ii. 3, 304, ii. *Madras,* 1904. 8°. **14170. bb. 15.**

RĀYAR-APPĀJI-KATHAI. See APPĀJĪ.

REGEL (J. A.). See BARTH (C. G.). A brief History of the Church of Christ . . . Translated [into Tamil by J. A. Regel], *etc.* 1845. 16°. **14170. a. 4.**

REṄGA-SĀMI PIḶḶAI. See RAṄGA-SĀMI PIḶḶAI.

RHENIUS (CARL GOTTLIEB EWALD). *See* RHENIUS (CHARLES THEOPHILUS EWALD).

RHENIUS (CHARLES THEOPHILUS EWALD). *See* BIBLE.—*Complete Bible.* The Old Testament . . . [Revised by C. T. E. Rhenius.] (*The New Testament [translated by C. Rhenius], *etc.*) 1827-1833. 8°. **3068. c. 21.**

—— —— [1840 ?] 8°. **1109. d. 6.**

—— —— 1844. 8°. **3070. i. 1.**

—— —— 1860. 4°. **3068. e. 10.**

—— *See* BIBLE.—Old Testament.—*Pentateuch.* The First Book of Moses, *etc.* [Ch. i.-ix., being a specimen of Rhenius' translation.] 1819. 16°. **T. 2070.(1.)**

—— *See* BIBLE.—*New Testament.* [New Testament, comprising Gospels and Acts in Rhenius' version, *etc.*] **1410. h. 3.**

—— *See* BIBLE.—*New Testament.* The New Testament . . . [Translated by Rhenius.] 1843. 8°. **1106. c. 13.**

—— *See* BIBLE.—*New Testament.* New Testament . . . [In Rhenius' version.] 1857. 12°. **3070. ee. 1.**

—— —— 1859. 8°. **3070. g. 6.**

—— *See* BIBLE. — New Testament. — *Gospels.* [*Mark.*] St. Mark's Gospel . . . [In Rhenius' version.] 1859. 16°. **3068. a. 35.**

—— ஞானபோசன விளக்கம். ஞானஸநானம நறகருணையெனபவைகளின மகிமையைச சொ-லலியது. [A Catechism on Baptism and the Lord's Supper.] pp. 63. *Church Mission Press : Madras,* 1825. 12°. **14170. bbb. 5.**

—— வேதவுதாரணத்திரட்டு. [Vēdav-udāraṇa-tiraṭṭu, or "Evidences of Christianity." A work partly based upon Horne's "Introduction to the critical Study of the Holy Scriptures."] pp. i. 314. *Madras,* 1835. 8°. **14170. c. 16.**

—— Rhenius's Evidences of Christianity. வே-தவுதாரணத் திரட்டு. [A revised edition of the preceding.] pp. 319. *Madras,* 1852. 12°. **14170. b. 41.**

RHENIUS (CHARLES THEOPHILUS EWALD) (*continued*). Summary of a Body of Divinity, in the Tamul language [chiefly abridged from the works of Pictet and Dwight] . . . வேதசாஸதிரச் சுருக்கம். pp. iv. 612, ix. 3. *Neyoor,* 1838. 12°. **14170. b. 42.**

—— [Third edition.] pp. xii. 588. *Madras,* 1845. 12°. **14170. b. 43.**

RICE (BENJAMIN LEWIS). *See* MYSORE. Epigraphia Carnataca . . . Published . . . by B. L. Rice. 1886, *etc.* 8°. **14058. c. 8.**

RIEMER (W. E. DE). Lyrics, Tamil. [Hymns and songs in use among Tamil Christians, with European musical notation.] pp. 23, *lith. Madras,* 1875. *obl.* 32°. **14170. a. 46.**

RIGG (EDMUND). *See* WESLEY (J.). A collection of Hymns . . . [Edited by E. Rigg and others]. 1881. 12°. **14170. bbb. 10.**

RITUALE TRANGAMBARICUM. *See* LITURGIES.—*Lutheran Churches.*

RIẒĀ ḢUSAIN KH̲ĀN, *of Tinnevelli.* *See* VIVĒKA-SĀGARAM. விவேகசாகரம். [Vivēka-sāgaram. Translated from the Persian by Riẓā Ḣusain.] [1858.] 8°. **14172. c. 11.**

ROBERTS (JOSEPH). *See* SAHĀDĒVAN. Extracts from the Sakaa Thevan Saasteram . . . Translated . . . by . . . J. Roberts. 1831. 8°. [*Oriental Translation Fund : Miscellaneous Translations.*] **14003. d. 5.**

ROBERTS (WILLIAM), *of Madras.* விககிறக பத-திககுந தெயவபததிககுஞ சமபாஷணை. [Vigraha-battikkun teyva-battikkuñ sambhāshanai. A dialogue on Hindu idolatry from a theistic standpoint.] pp. 116. செனனபடடணததில ௲அ௱உ௩ [*Madras,* 1823.] 8°. **14170. b. 48.**

ROBERTSON (ANDREW). A compilation of papers in the Tamil language. Including several on public business, to which is added a glossary in Tamil and English of many words used chiefly in the business of the courts and public cutcherries . . . ஒரு பத்திரத்திரட்டு ௸. pp. i. 209. *Madras,* 1839. 4°. **14171. c. 1.**

ROBERTSON (ANDREW) (*continued*). Papers in the Tamil language on matters of public business. With a glossary of technical terms in Tamil and English. pp. 29. *London*, 1890. 4°. **14171. c. 2.**

A reprint of the fourth section and glossary of the Madras edition.

ROBERTSON (WILLIAM ROWNTREE). *See* GREEN (H. W.). A Primer of Agriculture . . . Being an adaptation of the Agricultural Class book by W. R. Robertson, *etc.* 1885. 12°. **14172. h. 52.**

—— —— 1887. 12°. **14171. f. 5.**

ROBINSON (EDWARD JEWITT). Tales and Poems of South India (an improved and enlarged edition of *Tamil Wisdom*). From the Tamil. pp. x. 388. *London*, 1885. 8°. **14170. k. 63.**

—— Tamil Wisdom; traditions concerning Hindu sages, and selections from their writings . . . With an introduction by the late Rev. Elijah Hoole. pp. xi. 148. *London*, 1873. 12°. **14170. k. 62.**

ROBINSON (WILLIAM). *See* HYMNALS. சேலம் ஞானப்பாட்டுகளும், கீர்த்தனைகளும். The Salem Hymnal and Lyrics, arranged by W. Robinson. 1901. 8°. **14170. bbb. 3.**

ROMAN CATECHISM. *See* CATECHISM.

ROME, *Church of*. *See* EPHEMERIDES. நெடுநாட்பஞ்சாங்கம். [Neḍu-nāṭ-pañchāṅgam. A calendar of festivals.] [1844.] 16°. **14170. a. 34.(1.)**

—— *See* EPHEMERIDES. The Ceylon Catholic Almanac, *etc.* 1890-1893. 12°. **14170. a. 35.(4.)**

RŌRUMĒ, *Pseud.* *See* MEADOWS (R. R.).

ROSNY (JOSEPH-HENRY). *See* NAṬĒṢA ṢĀSTRI, *Ṣ. M.* Le Porteur de Sachet. Traduction de J.-H. Rosny, *etc.* 1892. 16°. **14171. aa. 13.**

ROTTLER (J. P.). *See* BIBLE.—*Complete Bibles.* The Old Testament . . . [Revised by C. Rhenius, with J. Rottler and others,] *etc.* 1827-1833. 8°. **3068. c. 21.**

—— *See* LITURGIES.—England, *Church of*. இங்கிலீசுசபைதேவாலயங்களில வழககமாயிருககினற பொதுவானசெப . . . புஸதகம். [The Book of Common Prayer. Translated by J. P. Rottler.] [1819.] 4°. **14170. cc. 4.**

ROTTLER (J. P.) (*continued*). *See* LITURGIES.—England, *Church of*. தேவாலயங்களிலோதும்படி . . . சங்கீதங்கள ஸ்ரீ [The Book of Common Prayer. Translated by J. P. Rottler.] [1820.] 8°. **14170. bb. 11.**

—— —— 1828. 8°. **3406. df. 20.**

RUDRA-KAṆṆANĀR, *Kaḍiyalūr*. *See* VĒDĀCHALAM PIḶḶAI, *N.* பட்டினப்பாலை ஆராய்ச்சி. (A critical commentary on Pattinappalai, *etc.*) 1906. 12°. **14171. d. 2.(2.)**

—— பெரும்பாணாற்றுப்படை (†பட்டினப்பாலை). [Perum-bāṇ-āṭṭu-paḍai and Paṭṭina-pālai. Two poems, being nos. 4 and 9 respectively of the Pattu-pāṭṭu, the former a panegyric on the king Toṇḍaimān Iḷandiraiyan of Kāñchi, the latter on the Chola king Karikāl and his capital. With commentary of Nachinārkk'-iniyar.] *See* PATTU-PĀṬṬU. பத்துப்பாட்டு ஸ்ரீ [Pattu-pāṭṭu.] pp. 95-144, 289-316. 1889. 8°. **14172. d. 10.**

—— University of Madras. B.A. Examination of 1906. Patthupattu. Pattinappalai. With Nachchinarkkiniyar's commentary and explanatory notes by V. Saminatha Aiyar. pp. 10, 42. *Madras*, 1906. 8°. **14172. b. 37.(2.)**

RUEDIGER (JOHANN CHRISTIAN CHRISTOPH). *See* AUVAIYĀR.—*Single Works.* Aweiar's Kalwiorhuckam . . . übersetzt . . . von J. C. C. Rüdiger. 1791. 12°. **14172. a. 40.**

RUNGASAWMY PILLAY. *See* RAṄGA-SĀMI PIḶḶAI.

RUNGASWAMY ROW. *See* RAṄGA-SĀMI RĀU.

RUTHNAM, *T. A. R.* *See* RĀJA-RATNAM PIḶḶAI, *T. A.*

SABAPATHY. *See* SABHĀ-PATI.

SABHĀ-PATI AIYAR, *Vaṇṇārpaṇṇai*. *See* EPHEMERIDES. ∘ ∘ ∘ நந்தன வருஷ . . . பஞ்சாங்கம். . . . Tamil Calendar, *etc.* [Calculated for 1895-97 by Sabhā-pati.] [1891-1896.] 8°. **14172. i. 11.**

SABHĀ-PATI MUDALIYĀR, *Kāñchipuram*. *See* AMURTA-LIṄGA TAMBIRĀN. திருமயிலைத்தலபுராணம். [Tiru-mayilai-tala-purāṇam. With commentary by Sabhā-pati.] [1893.] 8°. **14170. e. 60.**

—— *See* SAMBANDHA-ṢARAṆĀLAYA-SVĀMI. கந்தபுராணச்சுருக்கம் [Kanda-purāṇa-churukkam. With paraphrase by Sabhā-pati.] [1906.] 8°. **14170. eee. 10.**

SABHĀ-PATI MUDALIYĀR, *Kāñchīpuram (continued).* அருணசலசதகம். [Aruṇāchala-ṣatakam. A Ṣaiva devotional poem.] *See* Ellʼ-appa Nāvalar. அருணசலபுராணம் ௸ [Aruṇāchala-purāṇam.] pp. 673-688. 1903. 12°. **14170. d. 83.**

—— சைவசமயவிளக்க வினவிடை. [Ṣaiva-samaya-viḷakka-vinā-viḍai. A catechism of the Ṣaiva doctrines. Edited by Villiputtūr Ṣiva-ṣaṅkara Tambirān.] pp. 136. ௧௮௭௯ [*Madras*, 1879.] 16°. **14170. d. 14.**

—— A Catechism of the Shaiva Religion [being pts. i., ii., and a portion of pt. iii. of the Ṣaiva-samaya-viḷakka-vinā-viḍai] : by Sabhapati Mudaliyar . . . and Sadashiva Mudaliyar . . . Translated from the Tamil by the Rev. Thomas Foulkes. pp. 82. *London, Madras*, 1863. 8°. **14170. e. 36.(6.)**

SABHĀ-PATI MUDALIYĀR, *Puraṣai Ashṭāvadhānam.* *See* Tāyumānavar. ஸ்ரீ . . . திருப்பாடற்றிரட்டு. [Tiru-pāḍaṭ-ṭiraṭṭu. With Sabhā-pati's Tiruv-aruḷ-vilāsa-para-ṣiva-vaṇakkav-urai, a commentary on i. 1-3.] 1905. 16°. **14170. dd. 6.**

SABHĀ-PATI MUDALIYĀR, *P. V.* *See* Vīra-vanman. வீரவன்மன் வெற்றி. (Veeravanman Vetri . . . Translated into Tamil by . . . Sabapathy Moodaliar.) 1902. 8°. **14171. a. 54.**

SABHĀ-PATI MUDALIYĀR, *T.* Selected Tamil Proverbs, with appropriate English version . . . Edited by T. Sabapathy Moodeliar. pp. i. 204. *Madras*, 1898. 16°. **14171. aa. 3.**

SABHĀ-PATI NĀVALAR, *Tiruvāvaḍuduṛai.* *See* Ṣiva-ñāna Svāmi. ○○○ சித்தாந்தமரபுகண்டனகண்டனம் ௸ [Siddhānta - marabu - khaṇḍana-khaṇḍanam, *etc.* Edited by Sabhā-pati.] [1893.] 8°. **14170. e. 63.**

—— திராவிடப்பிரகாசிகை. [Drāviḍa-prakāṣikai. An account of Tamil literature and literary men.] pp. iv. 213, ii. கும்பகோணம் [*Kumbakonam*,] 1899. 8°. **14172. hh. 15.**

SABHĀ-PATI PIḶḶAI, *Kumbhaghōṇam R., of Coimbatore College.* *See* Dēvāṅgar. ○○○ தேவாங்கபுராணம். [Dēvāṅga-purāṇam. With commentary by Sabhā-pati.] [1893.] 8°. **14170. e. 55.**

—— *See* Vāsudēva Mudaliyār. ஸ்ரீ . . . அவிநாசிக் கருணாம்பிகை சதகம். [Avināṣi-karuṇāmbikai-ṣatakam. Edited by Sabhā-pati.] 1891. 8°. **14170. e. 47.(1.)**

SABHĀ-PATI SVĀMI. The Cosmic Psychological Spiritual Philosophy and Science of Communion with and Absorption in the Holy and Divine Infinite Spirit, or Vedhantha Siva Raja Yoga Samadhi Brumha Gnyana Anubuthi, by the Mahathma . . . Sabhapathy Svamy, *etc.* [In English, with numerous extracts in Sanskrit and Tamil.] (Edited by his . . . disciples.) pp. iv. 434, 8; 13 *plates.* *Madras*, 1884-1890. 8°. **759. b. 6.**

SABHĀ-PATI SVĀMI, *Tiruvaruṇai.* *See* Kaḍavuṇ Mā-muni. மாணிக்கவாசகர் . . . புராணம். [Tiru-vādavūrar-purāṇam. Edited by Sabhā-pati.] 1896. 12°. **14171. a. 10.**

SABHĀ-PATI YŌGI, *of Konnur.* ○○○ சகலாகமத்திரட்டு. [Sakalāgama-tiraṭṭu. A compendium of Ṣaiva Āgamik teaching.] pt. 1. *Madras*, 1894. 16°. **14170. d. 41.**

SACH-CHID-ĀNANDA SVĀMI, *Īṣūr, disciple of Aruṇāchala Svāmi.* *See* Tattva-rāya Svāmi. ○○○ சசிவன்னபோதம் ௸ [Ṣaṣi-varṇa-bōdham. Edited by Sach-chid-ānanda.] [1895.] 12°. **14170. d. 39.**

—— ஜீவகாருணியவிளக்கம், சுவானுபூதிவிளக்கம். [Jīva-kāruṇya-viḷakkam and Svānubhūti-viḷakkam. Two poems, in the spirit of Advaita philosophy, on the sorrows of bodily life, spiritual emancipation, *etc.*] pp. ii. ii. 55, 51. மதராஸ் சர்வதாரி [*Madras*, 1888.] 12°. **14170. d. 43.**

SADAGOPA CHARIAR. *See* Ṣaṭhakōpāchāryar.

ṠADAḲAT ALLĀH, *al Ḳāhirī.* *See* Muhammad ibn Abi Bakr ibn Rashīd. نفحات العطرية الخ [Al-Witrīyah. With a "Takhmīs," or metrical amplification, by Ṡadaḳat Allāh. The Arabic text, with a Tamil translation and commentary, entitled al-Nafaḥāt al-ʿiṭrīyah, by Ṡadaḳat Allāh.] [1896.] 8°. **14576. cc. 1.**

SADĀ-ṢIVA BRAHMĒNDRA. அத்துவிதரசமஞ்சரி. [Advita-rasa-mañjari. A Vedantic tract. Metrically translated from the Sanskrit by Nityānanda Svāmi.] *See* Ṣaṅkarāchāryar. [*Doubtful and Supposititious Works.*] ஸ்ரீ . . . இலக்ஷணவிர்த்தி ௸ [A collection.] pp. 88-99. [1888.] 16°. **14170. d. 28.**

SADĀ-ṢIVAM PIḶḶAI, *Aruṇāchalam.* *See* ARNOLD (J. R.).

SADĀ-ṢIVAM PIḶḶAI, *G., of Negapatam High School.* *See* AṞAGU-MUTTU PULAVAR. ○○○ ஸ்ரீ மெய்கண்ட வேலாயுத சதகம் ௸ [Mey-kaṇḍa-vēlāyudha-ṣatakam, *etc.* Edited by Sadā-ṣivam.] [1900.] 12°. **14170. d. 66.**

SADĀ-ṢIVA MUDALIYĀR, *Chaturaṅgapaṭṭaṇam.* *See* SABHĀ-PATI MUDALIYĀR, *Kāñchīpuram.* A Catechism of the Shaiva religion: by Sabhapati Mudaliyar . . . and Sadashiva Mudaliyar, *etc.* 1863. 8°. **14170. e. 36.(6.)**

SADĀ-ṢIVA MUDALIYĀR, *Koṟumbu Mayilu-piḷḷai.* ○○○ சரமகவிகள். [Charama-kavigaḷ. Elegies upon the death of Sadā-ṣiva.] pp. 8. [*Jaffna,*] 1887. 8°. **14172. a. 30.(1.)**

SADĀ-ṢIVA PAṆḌITAR, *Vaṇṇainagar Ṣ. N.* ○○○ வண்ணையந்தாதி வண்ணைநகரூஞ்சல் ௸ [Vaṇṇaiy-antādi, Vaṇṇai-nagar-ūñjal, and Ṣiṅgai-nagar-antādi. Hymns on the cult of Ṣiva in Vannainagar (Jaffna) and in Singapore. Followed by Chitra-kavigaḷ, or artificial verses.] pp. ii. 37; 4 *plates.* சிங்கப்பூர் [*Singapore,*] 1887. 8°. **14172. a. 26.**

SADĀ-ṢIVA PIḶḶAI, *Vaṭṭukōṭṭai V.* *See* JAFFNA. யாழ்ப்பாண வைபவம். [Yāṟpāṇa-vaibhavam, *etc.* Edited by Sadā-ṣiva.] 1884. 12°. **14171. d. 4.**

SADĀ-ṢIVA SVĀMI, *of Coimbatore.* *See* DĒVĀṄGAR. ○○○ தேவாங்கபுராணம். [Dēvāṅga-purāṇam. Versified from the version of Sadā-ṣiva and Doḍdaya.] [1893.] 8°. **14170. e. 55.**

SAHĀDĒVAN. ○○○ பாச்சிகைசாஸ்திரம் மூலமும்-உரையும் ௸ [Pāchikai-ṣāstram. A metrical tract on divination by throwing dice, attributed to the legendary Sahādēvan. Followed by Dēvadāsa-toḍu-guṟi, a similar tract on divination from deities' names. Edited and recast, with a prose paraphrase of the former, by Ṣ. Ēkāmbara Mudaliyār.] pp. 28. சென்னை [*Madras,*] 1905. 8°. **14171. g. 12.**

—— Extracts from the Sakaa Thevan Saasteram or Book of Fate. Translated . . . by the Rev. Joseph Roberts. pp. 68. *See* ACADEMIES, *etc.*—London.—*Oriental Translation Fund of Great Britain and Ireland.* Miscellaneous translations, *etc.* vol. i. 1831. 8°. **14003. d. 5.**

Differs from the preceding.

SAINT-CYR (LOUIS). கருணாகரக்கடல் ௸ [Karuṇākara-kaḍal. A Catholic book of devotions, addressed to "the divine heart of Jesus, and to the spotless heart of the Divine Mother."] pp. 800. புதுவை ௲௮௬௮ [*Pondicherry,* 1868.] 12°. **14170. a. 18.**

ṢAIVA-PARIPĀLANA-SABHAI. *See* JAFFNA.

ṢAIVA-PRAKĀṢA-SABHAI. *See* COLOMBO.

—— *See* JAFFNA.

ṢAIVA-PRAKĀṢA-SAMĀJAM. *See* TRINCOMALI.

SAIYAPPA MODELLIAR. *See* ṢEYY'-APPA MUDALIYĀR.

SAIYID BUKHĀRĪ. *See* PAVĀNI PULAVAR.

ṢALAṢA-LOCHANA CHEṬṬI. *See* SARASA-LŌCHANA CHEṬṬI.

SAMARA-PURI MUDALIYĀR, *Eṟumūr.* சுமதி-சதகம். [Sumati-ṣatakam. A century of Telugu ethical verses, in the Tamil character. With Tamil verbal interpretations, paraphrases, *etc.*] pp. 78. சென்னப்பட்டணம் [*Madras,*] 1904. 8°. **14175. a. 11.**

SAMBANDAM, *P.* *See* SAMBANDHA MUDALIYĀR, *P. V.*

SAMBANDHA MUDALIYĀR, *Pammal Vijaya-raṅga.* *See* RĀMA-SĀMI AIYAṄGĀR, *Ṣarukkai.* லீலாவதி-சுலோசனையுரை. (F. A. Tamil Text 1899. Full notes on [Sambandha Mudaliyār's] Lilavati-Sulochana or The Two Sisters.) 1898. 8°. **14172. bb. 6.(1.)**

—— லீலாவதி-சுலோசனை அல்லது இரண்டு சகோதரிகள். (†Lilavati Sulochana or The Two Sisters . . . a drama in Tamil . . . based on western principles.) [In five acts and in prose. With an introduction and analysis of the plot in English by V. V. Ṣrīnivāsa Aiyaṅgār.] pp. 2, 11, ix. 152. சென்னபட்டணம் [*Madras,*] 1895. 8°. **14170. l. 35.**

SAMBANDHA MUDALIYĀR, *Pammal Vijaya-raṅga (continued).* சாரங்கதரன். (Sarangadhara. A Tamil drama [in 3 acts on the legend of the chaste prince Sāraṅgadhara] by P. Sambandam.) pp. ii. 96. *Madras,* 1907. 8°. **14170. l. 46.(3.)**

—— இரண்டு நண்பர்கள். (The Two Friends. A new Tamil drama, by P. Sambandam.) pp. i. i. 139. *Madras,* 1906. 8°. **14170. l. 46.(1.)**

—— சத்ருஜித். (Blind Ambition, or Satrujit. A new Tamil drama by P. Sambandam.) pp. i. 131. *Madras,* 1907. 8°. **14170. l. 46.(2.)**

SAMBANDHAR. *See* Ñāṅa-sambandhar.

SAMBANDHA-ṢARAṆĀLAYA SVĀMI, *Dharmapuram.* ° ° ° கந்தபுராணச்சுருக்கம். [Kanda-purāṇa-churukkam. A summary in verse of Kachiy-appar's Kanda-purāṇam. Edited by Nalla-tambi Sōma-sundara Upādhyāyar.] pp. 163, i. பிலவங்க [*Madras,* 1848.] 8°. **14170. e. 5.**

—— கந்தபுராணச்சுருக்கம். [Kanda-purāṇa-churukkam. With paraphrase (*poripp'-urai*) by K. Sabhā-pati Mudaliyār, and a commentary (*vṛutti*). Edited by Ulaga-nātha Mudaliyār. Followed by Kāñchipuram Chidambara Munivar's Kshētra-kōvai-piḷḷai-tamiṟ.] pp. vii. 466, 27. சென்னப்பட்டணம் பராபவ [*Madras,* 1906.] 8°. **14170. eee. 10.**

SĀMBA-ṢIVA KAVI-RĀYAR. ° ° ° நுங்கம்பாக்கம், வரசித்திவிநாயகர், பஞ்சரத்தினம் ஆ [A series of hymns to the deities worshipped at the Ṣaiva temple of Nungambakam, Madras City, styled Vara-siddhi-vināyakar-pañcha-ratnam, °chanda-vṛuttam, °vaṇṇam, °kīrttanai, Agattīṣvarar-padigam, Akhilāṇḍēṣvariy-amman-padigam, (Ṣiva-) subrahmaṇya-pañcha-ratnam, °padigam, Tiru-taṇigai-malai-mṛugēṣar-pañcha-ratnam, Tiru-taṇigai-malai-taṇigēṣar-pañcha-ratnam, Teyvayānaiy-amman-p.°, Vaḷḷiy-amman-p.°, and Karukkāttaiy-amman-padigam. Followed by a hymn to Subrahmaṇya by K. Aruṇāchala Upādhyāyar.] pp. 47. நுங்கம்பாக்கம் [*Nungambakam,*] 1867. 12°. **14170. d. 25.(1.)**

SĀMI AIYAR, *Pudukoṭṭai.* *See* Collett (C.). A Manual of the Law of Torts . . . Translated . . . by . . . Samy Iyer. 1872. 8°. **14170. g. 10.**

SĀMI CHEṬṬIYĀR, *P. M.* விக்டோரியா மகாராணியவர்கள் ஞாபகச்சின்னம். [Victoria-mahā-rāṇiyavargaḷ-ñāpaka-chinnam. Observations and elegies on the reign of Queen Victoria.] (The Victoria Memorial . . . Compiled by P. M. Sawmi Chettiar.) pp. ii. 56, 46. *Madras,* 1901. 8°. **14171. a. 47.**

SĀMI-KUṬṬI AIYAR. *See* Subba-rāya Aiyar.

SĀMI-NĀTHA AIYAR, *C. V.* *See* Periodical Publications.—*Madras.* The Viveka Chintamani . . . Published by C. V. Swaminatha Iyer. 1892-1901. 4°. **14172. i. 13.**

SĀMI-NĀTHA AIYAR, *Palamārneṟi.* Familiar Indian Melodies and their characteristics. Tamil . . . இராகவிபோதினி. pp. 37. *Madras,* 1901. 8°. **14170. i. 24.**

SĀMI-NĀTHA AIYAR, *Ṣ.* *See* Mahā-bhāratam. பகவத்கீதை ஆ (Bhagavad Gita Venba.) [Edited by Sāmi-nātha.] 1906-1907. 16°. **14172. a. 59.**

SĀMI-NĀTHA AIYAR, *T. A., Editor of the "Arya."* The English and Tamil Standard Vocabulary, containing over 12,800 words . . . With an introduction by Rao Bahadur M. Rangacharya. pp. 6, i. 36, 232. *Madras,* 1904. 12°. **14172. e. 41.**

—— The English and Tamil Pocket Dictionary, *etc.* pp. 4, 604. *Madras,* 1905. 16°. **14172. ee. 13.**

—— Mahajana Mandali. மகாஜன மண்டலி . . . A series of character-sketches of illustrious personages . . . Edited by S. Anavaratavinayakam Pillai. *Madras,* 1904, *etc.* 12°. **14171. d. 5.**

In progress.

—— Vivekachandrika. விவேக சந்திரிகை. A collection of moral stories culled mainly from Puranas . . . With an introduction by S. Ratha-krishna Aiyar . . . Edited by M. S. Purnalingam Pillai. pp. 4, 8, 139. *Madras,* 1904. 12°. **14171. aa. 16.**

SĀMI-NĀTHA DĒṢIKAR, *Tiruvāvaḍuduṟai, disciple of Ambala-vāṇar.* திருச்செந்திற்கலம்பகம். [Tiru-chendiṟ-kalambakam. A century of Ṣaiva devotional verses. Edited by Ṣeṭṭūr Subrahmaṇya Kavi-rāyar.] pp. v. 21. 1905. *See* Academies, *etc.*—*Madura.* ["Ṣen-damiṟ" supplement.] no. 15. 1902, *etc.* 8°. **14172. i. 1.*(no. 15.)**

SĀMI-NĀTHA DĒṢIKAR, *Tiruvārūr Ṣ.* *See* TIRUVARUR. திருவாரூர்ப்புராணம். [Tiruvārūr-purāṇam. Edited by Sāmi-nātha.] [1895.] 8°. **14170. e. 59.**

SĀMINĀTH'-AIYAR, *Chidambaram M., of St. Joseph's College, Kudalur.* *See* CHIDAMBARA-NĀTHA MUNIVAR. ○○○ திருப்பாதிரிப் புலியூர்ப் புராணம். [Tirupādiri-puliyūr-purāṇam. With epitomes by Sāmināth'-aiyar.] 1896. 12°. **14170. d. 40.**

—— *See* GURU-ṢUKRA-NĀḌI. ○○○ கருணாநந்தசித்தர் சரித்திரம். [Karuṇānanda-siddhar-charitram. With prose rendering by Sāmināth'-aiyar.] 1906. 12°. **14171. d. 6.**

—— *See* NĀL-AḌIYĀR. University of Madras. F.A. Examination, 1900 . . . Naladyar and Bharatam; and . . . notes . . . By C. M. Swaminatha Iyer. 1899. 8°. **14172. b. 37.(1.)**

SĀMINĀTH'-AIYAR, *Uttamadānapuram V., of Madras Presidency College.* *See* AIYANĀR-IDANĀR. ○○○ புறப்பொருள்வெண்பாமாலை ஞூ [Puṟa-poruḷ-veṇ-bā-mālai. Edited by Sāmināth'-aiyar.] [1895.] 8°. **14172. f. 21.**

—— *See* AIYANĀR-IDANĀR. University of Madras . . . Purapporul Venbamalai . . . with . . . notes by V. Saminatha Aiyar. 1905. 8°. **14172. bb. 21.(1.)**

—— *See* ILAṄ-GŌV-AḌIGAḶ. ○○○ சிலப்பதிகார ஞூ [Ṣilapp'-adhikāram. Edited by Sāmināth'-aiyar.] 1892. 8°. **14172. d. 13.**

—— *See* KANDA-SĀMI PULAVAR, *Tirupūvaṇam.* ○○○ திருப்பூவணநாதருலா. [Tiru-pūvaṇa-nāthar-ulā. Edited by Sāmināth'-aiyar.] 1904. 8°. **14170. eee. 8.**

—— *See* KŪḌALŪR-KIṞĀR. ○○○ ஐங்குறுநூறு ஞூ [Aiṅ-guṟu-nūṟu. Edited by Sāmināth'-aiyar.] 1903. 8°. **14172. c. 48.**

—— *See* MĪNĀKSHI-SUNDARAM PIḶḶAI, *T.* மண்ணிப்படிக்கரைப்புராணம். [Maṇṇipaḍikarai-purāṇam. Edited by Sāmināth'-aiyar.] 1907. 8°. **14170. eee. 23.**

—— *See* MĪNĀKSHI-SUNDARAM PIḶḶAI, *T.* ○○○ சீகாழிக்கோவை ஞூ [Ṣīgāḻi-kōvai. Edited by Sāmināth'-aiyar.] 1903. 8°. **14170. ee. 65.**

SĀMINĀTH'-AIYAR, *Uttamadānapuram V., of Madras Presidency College (continued).* *See* MĪNĀKSHI-SUNDARAM PIḶḶAI, *T.* சூரைமாநகர்ப்புராணம். [Ṣūrai-mā-nagar-purāṇam. Edited by Sāmināth'-aiyar.] 1904. 8°. **14170. eee. 5.**

—— *See* MĪNĀKSHI-SUNDARAM PIḶḶAI, *T.* ○○○ தனியூர்ப்புராணம். [Taniyūr-purāṇam. Edited by Sāmināth'-aiyar.] 1907. 8°. **14170. e. 29.**

—— *See* MĪNĀKSHI-SUNDARAM PIḶḶAI, *T.* திருவாரூர்த் தியாகராசலீலை. [Tiruvārūr-tyāgarāja-līlai. Edited by Sāmināth'-aiyar.] 1905. 8°. **14172. bb. 20.**

—— *See* PADIṮṮU-PATTU. ○○○ பதிற்றுப்பத்து ஞூ [Padiṯṯu-pattu. Edited by Sāmināth'-aiyar.] 1904. 8°. **14172. bb. 14.**

—— *See* PERUM-SAṮṮA-PULIY-ŪR-NAMBI. திரு . . . விளையாடற்புராணம். [Tiru-viḷaiy-āḍaṟ-purāṇam. Edited by Sāmināth'-aiyar.] 1906. 8°. **14170. eee. 17.**

—— *See* PUṞA-NĀNŪṞU. ○○○ புறநானூறு ஞூ [Puṟa-nāṉūṟu. Edited with commentary by Sāmināth'-aiyar.] 1894. 8°. **14172. d. 16.**

—— *See* RUDRA-KAṆṆANĀR. University of Madras . . . Pattinappalai. With . . . notes by V. Saminatha Aiyar. 1906. 8°. **14172. b. 37.(2.)**

—— *See* ṢĀTTAN. ○○○ மணிமேகலை ஞூ [Maṇimēkhalai. Edited by Sāmināth'-aiyar.] 1898. 8°. **14172. d. 22.**

—— *See* ṢEṞAI KAVI-RĀJA PIḶḶAI. ○○○ திருக்காளத்திநாதருலா. [Tiru-kāḷatti-nāthar-ulā. Edited by Sāmināth'-aiyar.] 1904. 8°. **14170. eee. 6.**

—— *See* ṢOKKA-NĀTHA PIḶḶAI, *P.* (†தேவையுலா.) [Tēvaiy-ulā. Edited by Sāmināth'-aiyar.] 1907. 8°. ["*Ṣen-damiṟ*" *supplement.*] **14172. i. 1.*(no. 24.)**

—— *See* SUBRAHMAṆYA TAMBIRĀN, *Toṭṭikalai* ○○○ திருவாவடுதுறைக்கோவை. [Tiruvāvaḍu-duṟai-kōvai. Edited by Sāmināth'-aiyar.] 1903. 8°. **14170. ee. 54.**

—— *See* TIRU-TAKKA DĒVAR. ○○○ சீவகசிந்தாமணி ஞூ [Jīvaka-chintāmaṇi. Edited by Sāmināth'-aiyar.] 1887. 8°. **14172. d. 6.**

SĀMINĀTH'-AIYAR, *Uttamadānapuram V., of Madras Presidency College (continued).* See TIRU-TAKKA DĒVAR. University of Madras . . . Jivaka-chintamani. Namagalilambakam. With . . . notes by V. Saminatha Aiyar. 1905. 8°. **14171. bb. 21.(2.)**

—— See VĪRA-RĀGHAVA MUDALIYĀR. திருவாரூருலா. [Tiruvārūr-ulā. Edited by Sāminath'-aiyar.] 1905. 8°. [*"Ṣen-damiṛ" supplement.*] **14172. i. 1.*(no. 16.)**

—— See VĪRAVANAM. வீரவனப்புராணம். [Vīra-vana-purāṇam. Edited by Sāminath'-aiyar.] 1903. 8°. **14170. ee. 63.**

—— புத்தசரித்திரம். [Vocabulary to the Buddha-charitram and Bauddha-dharmam by Sāminath'-aiyar, which form an introduction to the latter's edition of Ṣāttan's Maṇi-mēkhalai.] pp. 34. See ACADEMIES, *etc.*—Madras.—*University of Madras.* University of Madras. B.A. Examination, *etc.* 1900. 8°. **14172. bb. 6.(6.)**

SĀMI-NĀTHA MUDALIYĀR, *Māṇippāy Aruṇāchala.* தருமபுத்திரநாடகம். [Dharma-putra-nāṭakam. A drama on the epic story of Yudhishṭhira. Edited by N. Ṣ. Vīra-ṣiṅga Uḍaiyār and Ṣ. K. Mṛugēṣa Upādhyāyar.] pp. 4,126. யாழ்ப்பாணம் [*Jaffna,*] 1890. 8°. **14170. l. 16.**

—— இராம நாடகம். [Rāma-nāṭakam. A drama on the epic legend of Rāma. Edited by Ṣ. K. Mṛugēṣa Upādhyāyar.] pp. 4, 98. யாழ்ப்பாணம் [*Jaffna,*] 1896. 8°. **14170. l. 37.(1.)**

SĀMI-NĀTHA PAṆḌITAR, *Vaṇṇainagar.* See MEY-KAṆḌA DĒVAR. ০০০ சிவஞானபோதம் மூலம் [Ṣiva-ñāna-bōdham. Edited by Sāmi-nātha.] [1906.] 8°. **14170. ff. 20.**

SĀMI-NĀTHA PIḶḶAI, *Chidambaram A.* See PURĀṆAS.—*Brahmāṇḍa-purāṇam.* எயினனூர் . . . ஆதிபுரதலபுராணம். [Ādipura-tala-purāṇam. Edited by Sāmi-nātha.] [1896.] 8°. **14170. ee. 8.**

—— வருகிற ஐயாயிரவருஷ அதிசயரகசியம். [Aiy-āyira-varsha-atiṣaya-rahasyam. A dialogue designed to check superstitious fears at the close of the century.] pp. 8. நடுக்காவேரி எவிளம்பி [*Nadukkaveri,* 1898.] 8°. **14170. i. 55.(2.)**

SĀMI-NĀTHA PIḶḶAI, *P. M., disciple of Rāma Brahma-svāmi.* சொரூப தரிசனம். [Sorūpa-darṣanam. Ṣaiva poems teaching monistic psychology.] pp. 83. மதுரை [*Madura,*] 1898. 16°. **14170. d. 62.**

SĀMI-NĀTHA ṢĀSTRI, *N., of Wesleyan Mission High School, Triplicane.* See PURĀṆAS.—*Skanda-purāṇam.* ০০০ சேதுமாஹாத்மியம். [Sētu-māhātmyam. Translated into prose by Sāmi-nātha.] 1901. 8°. **14170. ee. 42.**

—— See RĀMA-BHADRA DĪKSHITAR. ஜாநகீபரிணய மூலம் [Jānakī-pariṇayam. Translated by Sāmi-nātha.] 1903. 12°. **14170. l. 24.(3.)**

SĀM NAYINĀ. See SĀM SHIHĀB al-DĪN.

SĀM SHIHĀB al-DĪN ibn SULAIMĀN, *of Kayal-patnam.* மலுகறுல் அஹ்காம் . . . தொழுகைமாலை மூலம் [Maẕhar al-aḥkām. A series of poems summarising various heads of Moslem doctrine, the first being entitled Toḷugai-mālai.] pt. i. pp. ii. 78. சென்னை [*Madras,*] 1901. 12°. **14173. a. 4.**

—— مظهر الاحکام [Maẕhar al-aḥkām. Another collection. Edited by Saiyid Aḥmad ibn Muḥammad ibn Shaikh Tīkā.] pp. viii. 160, *lith.* مدراس ١٩٠١ [*Madras,* 1901.] 8°. **14173. b. 27.(3.)**

—— ০০০ சலாத்துல் அறுக்கான்மாலை மூலம் [Ṣalāt al-arkān mālai. A book of Muhammadan devotions.] pp. 138. கூஉகூக [*Madras,* 1879.] 12°. **14173. a. 10.**

SĀMUDRIKAM. ০০০ புருஷசாமுத்திரிகாலக்ஷணம். [Purusha-sāmudrikā-lakshaṇam. A tract, ascribed to Agastyar, on the physiognomy of men. Edited by Ṣinna-sāmi Piḷḷai.] pp. 38. சென்னை [*Madras,*] 1879. 16°. **14170. d. 21.**

—— புருஷ (†ஸ்திரீ) ஸாமுத்திரிகம். [Purusha-sāmudrikam and Strī-sāmudrikam. A work on divination from the bodily characteristics of both sexes.] pp. 80. See GURU-SĀMI MUDALIYĀR. சாமுத்திரிக லக்ஷண மூலம் [Sāmudrika-lakshaṇa-ṣāstram.] pt. 2. 1892. 8°. **14170. i. 26.**

SAMUEL AIYAR, *N.* History of the Tranquebar Mission, A.D. 1706-1906. தரங்கை மிசியோன் சரித்திரம். pp. iv. 179. *Tranquebar,* 1906. 12°. **14170. bbb. 8.**

SAMUEL PIḶḶAI, *S.* See PAVAṆANDI. Grammatica Tamuliensis, or An English version of the

. . . Nunnool . . . By W. Joyes and S. Samuel Pillay, *etc.* 1848-1851. 8°. **14172. f. 10.**

—— [Another copy.] **14172. f. 20.**

SAMY IYER. *See* Sāmi Aiyar.

SANDHYĀ-VANDANAM. ஆரியர் சந்தியாவந்தநம் ஶ்ரீ [Āryar-sandhyā-vandanam. The Sanskrit text of the *sandhyā* prayers in Tamil characters, with Tamil version and notes by S. P. Nara-simmalu Nāyuḍu.] pp. 8. *Coimbatore,* 1898. 8°. **14170. e. 47.(8.)**

Printed on pink paper.

—— யஜுர்வேத ஸந்த்யாவந்தநம் ஸாமவேத ஸந்த்யாவந்தநம் புருஷ . . . ஶ்ரீ . . . பூ . . . நீளா . . . நாராயணஸூக்தம் ஶ்ரீ [Sandhyā-vandanam, according to the Yajur-vēdi and Sāma-vēdi schools. Followed by the Purusha-sūktam, Ṣrī-sūktam, Bhū-sūktam, Nīlā-sūktam, and Nārāyaṇa-sūktam. With extracts, in a Tamil translation, from the commentaries of Raṅga-rāmānuja, Sāyaṇa, Ānanda-tīrtha, Vaidya-nātha Dīkshitar, Bhaṭṭa Bhāskara, Kṛushṇa Paṇḍitar, and others. Edited and translated by Ṣyāma-dēṣika Ṣrīṣaila Tātāchāryar.] pp. 104, 38. சென்னை [*Madras,*] 1901. 8°. **14033. aa. 27.**

SAṄGĪTAM. Tamil Sungeatha Surabooshany . . . சங்கீதஸ்வரபூஷணி [Saṅgīta-svara-bhūshaṇi. A manual of Hindu music. Translated into Tamil by D. Nārāyaṇa-dās and P. Aruṇāchalam Piḷḷai.] pt. i. pp. 88. சென்னை [*Madras,*] 1900. 8°. **14170. i. 68.**

SAÑJĪVI-NĀTHA SVĀMI, *Periya.* *See* Periya Sañjīvi-nātha Svāmi.

ṢAṄKARĀCHĀRYAR. [*Life.*] *See* Māṇikka Svāmi, *A. M.* ஶ்ரீ . . . ஶ்ரீமதாதிசங்கராசார்ய . . . சரித்திரச்சுருக்கம் ஶ்ரீ [Ādi-ṣaṅkarāchārya-charitra-churukkam, *etc.*] 1901. 12°. **14170. ee. 44.**

—— —— *See* Sāyaṇāchāryar. Life of Sankaracharyar, commonly called Sankaravijayam, *etc.* 1879. 8°. **14170. k. 19.**

—— —— ஶ்ரீ சங்கராசாரியாரது அவதாரமகிமை. [Ṣaṅkarāchāriyāradu avatāra-mahimai. A controversial tract by "A Hindu," vindicating the divine birth of Ṣaṅkara.] pp. 56. சென்னை [*Madras,*] 1893. 8°. **14170. e. 47.(5.)**

ṢAṄKARĀCHĀRYAR (*continued*). *See* Bādarāyaṇa. The Brahma Sutra Artha Deopika, or The Brahma Sutras . . . with the commentaries of Sri Sankaracharya, *etc.* 1904, *etc.* 4°. **14170. fff. 5.**

—— *See* Bādarāyaṇa. சங்கர . . . த்ராவிடபாஷ்யம். [Brahma-sūtra-drāviḍa-bhāshyam. The Brahma-sūtram, with Tamil commentary based upon the works of Ṣaṅkara, *etc.*] 1905. 8°. **14049. bb. 8.**

—— *See* Mahā-bhāratam. ஶ்ரீமத் பகவத்கீதை ஶ்ரீ [Bhagavad-gītā. With Ṣaṅkara's commentary. With Tamil translation.] 1907. 8°. **14049. bb. 10.**

—— *See* Upanishads. ° ° ° நூற்றெட்டு உபநிஷத்துகள். [Nūṭṭ'-eṭṭu Upanishattugaḷ. With extracts from the commentaries of Ṣaṅkara, *etc.*, translated into Tamil.] 1887. 8°. **14010. dd. 2.**

—— *See* Upanishads. ° ° ° தசோபநிஷத்த்ராவிடபாஷ்யம். [Daṣōpanishad-drāviḍa-bhāshyam. Ten Upanishads in Sanskrit, and a Tamil commentary comprising translations of the commentary of Ṣaṅkara, *etc.*, with the Kārikās of Gauḍapāda and Ṣaṅkara's commentary thereupon in Tamil.] [1897]-1898. 8°. **14010. dd. 14.**

—— ஶ்ரீ . . . அபரோக்ஷானுபூதி. [Aparōkshānubhūti. An Advaita tract. With Tamil translation and notes by V. Kuppu-svāmi Rāju.] pp. ii. 50. *Tanjore,* விசுவாச [1905.] 8°. **14049. b. 32.(1.)**

Forms vol. 1 *of the* Ṣaṅkara-granthāvali.

—— (ఆత్మబోధప్రకాశిక) [Ātma-bōdham. A Sanskrit metrical tract on the Vedantic philosophy. With the Telugu interpretation and commentary Ātma-bōdha-prakāṣika of Purāṇam Vēṅkaṭa-nārāyaṇa Kṛushṇa Ṣāstri, and a Tamil version of the same by Rāmānuja Kavi-rāyar.] pp. v. 167. சென்னபட்டணத்து தூஅாசமி [*Madras,* 1840.] 12°. **14048. c. 44.**

No title-page.

—— Ātma Bōdȧ Prakāṣika. Text, Übersetzung und Erklärung. [Ātma-bōdham, in Sanskrit and German, with extracts from Kṛushṇa Ṣāstri's Telugu commentary, translated into German from Rāmānuja Kavi-rāyar's Tamil version.] 1854. *See*

GRAUL (K. F. L.). Bibliotheca Tamulica, *etc.* vol. 1, pp. 173-203. 1854-1865. 8°.
14170. e. 42.(vol. 1.)

——— Ātma bōdʻa prakāśika. A Vedanta standard treatise, [Sanskrit] text, [English] translation [of the text] and [of the Tamil] commentary [of Rāmānuja Kavi-rāyar, from the Telugu of Krushṇa Ṣāstri,] . . . By Rev. J. F. Kearns. pp. 40, iii. *Madras,* 1867. 12°. **14048. b. 8.(1.)**

——— ००० ஆத்ம போதம். [Ātma-bōdham. The Sanskrit text in Tamil character with Rāmānuja Kavi-rāyar's Tamil version of Krushṇa Ṣāstri's Telugu commentary. Edited by Ṣ. G. Subbarāya Mudaliyār.] pp. iii. 48. சென்னை கஅசுக [*Madras,* 1869.] 8°. **14048. c. 62.(2.)**

Printed on light-coloured greenish-blue paper.

——— ००० சித்தாந்தபிந்து. [Daṣa-ṣlōkī. An Advaita tract. The Sanskrit text in Tamil script, together with Madhu-sūdana Sarasvatī's commentary Siddhānta-bindu translated into Tamil by V. S. Rāma-chandra Ṣāstri and re-written in higher style and edited with notes by G. Vaḍi-vēlu Cheṭṭi and M. Shaṇmukha Mudaliyār. Followed by the Daṣakam in Ulaga-nāthar's version.] pp. 5, xii. 2, 149, 2. சென்னை [*Madras,*] 1906. 12°. **14049. aa. 1.**

——— [*Doubtful and Supposititious Works.*] ஸ்ரீ . . . இலக்ஷணவிருத்தி ஆ [A collection of Vedantic tracts, comprising Lakshaṇā-vrutti, metrically translated from the Sanskrit by Kōyilūr Chidambara Svāmi; Daṣakam, Vivēka-shaṭkam, Sorūpānusandhāna-dudi, Manīshā-pañchakam, and Sōpāna-pañchakam, Vedantic tracts metrically rendered by Ulaga-nātha Svāmi; Dakshiṇā-mūrtti-ashṭakam, metrically translated by Nityānanda Svāmi; Sadā-ṣiva Brahmēndra's Advaita-rasa-mañjari, translated by the same; and Rāma Kavi's Advitānubhavam. Edited by A. Rāma-sāmi Svāmi.] pp. vi. ii. 132, i. சென்னை சர்வதாரி [*Madras,* 1888.] 16°. **14170. d. 28.**

——— ——— உலோககுரு ஆதிசங்கராச்சாரிய சுவாமிகள் திருவாய்மலர்ந்தருளிய சோதிட சங்கராச்சாரியம், மூஉதூல் ஆயுட்பாவகம். [Āyuṭbhāvakam. An astrological work in 1000 stanzas, professing to be an excerpt from a Jōdiḍa-ṣaṅkarāchāryam in 12,000 stanzas, ascribed to Ṣaṅkara. Edited by M. Subrahmaṇya Piḷḷai and T. Kuppu-sāmi Nāyuḍu.] pp. 4, 200. சென்னை [*Madras,*] 1895. 8°. **14170. i. 39.**

——— ——— ஸௌந்தர்யலஹரீ . . . லக்ஷ்மீதரா-வ்யாக்யயா . . . ஸஹிதா . . . ஸௌந்தர்யலஹரீ. [Saundarya-laharī. A Sanskrit poem on the mystic Ṣaiva cult of the Ṣakti. With Lakshmīdhara's commentary, and a Tamil interpretation styled Paramārtha-chandrikā by T. S. Ṣrīnivāsa Ṣāstri. Edited by M. Ṣaṅkara-nārāyaṇa Ṣāstri.] pp. 6, 248. *Madras,* 1907. 8°. **14049. b. 48.**

——— ——— ஸ்ரீ... ஶிவானந்தலஹரீ. உரைவ்யாக்யா ஸஹிதா *etc.* [Sivānanda-laharī. A century of Ṣaiva verses, in Sanskrit, with word-for-word interpretations and paraphrases in Tamil. Edited by Lakshmīnārāyaṇapuram Mrutyum-jaya Ṣāstri and Veṅkaṭa-svāmi Aiyar of Mysore.] pp. i. 122, iv. *Madras,* 1904. 12°. **14048. b. 48.**

——— ——— உ.ஸ்ரீஸுப்ரஹ்மண்யபுஜங்கஸ்தோத்ரம் [Subrahmaṇya-bhujaṅga-stōtram. A Sanskrit hymn of 33 stanzas in the *bhujaṅga-prayāta* metre. Edited with grammatical notes and with Tamil interpretation and commentary by Mēlmaṅgalam N. Subrahmaṇya Ṣāstri.] pp. viii. 105. நடுக்காவேரி [*Nadukkaveri,*] 1902. 16°.
14028. a. 30.

The wrapper bears a corresponding title in Tamil.

——— [For the Tattva-bōdham, usually ascribed to Ṣaṅkara:] *See* TATTVA-BŌDHAM.

——— [For the Praṣnōttara-ratna-mālikā sometimes ascribed to Ṣaṅkara:] *See* VIMALA-CHANDRA SŪRI.

ṢAṄKARA-LIṄGAM PIḶḶAI, *Muttūr Appāvu.* ००० திருவல்லிக்கேணிக்கலம்பகம். [Tirnvallikkēṇi-kalambakam. A series of poems in various metres upon Vishṇu as worshipped at Triplicane or Vrundāvanam.] pp. 8, 33. சென்னை [*Madras,*] 1898. 8°. **14170. ee. 35.(1.)**

ṢAṄKARA-MŪRTTI KŌNĀR, *A.* *See* MĀRIY-APPA KAVI-RĀYAR, *M.,* and ṢAṄKARA-MŪRTTI KŌNĀR, *A.* ஸ்ரீமத் பாகவத அம்மானை. [Bhāgavata-ammānai.] 1893. 8°. **14172. b. 54.**

ṢAṄKARA NAMAṢ-ṢIVĀYAR, *Tirunelvēli.* See PAVAṆANDI. Grammatica Tamuliensis, or An English version of the . . . Nunnool, with . . . extracts from the . . . commentary of Sunghara Nama Sivayur, *etc.* 1848-1851. 8°. **14172. f. 10.**

—— —— [Another copy.] **14172. f. 20.**

—— *See* PAVAṆANDI. ∘∘∘ நன்னூல் மூ [Nannūl. With commentary of Ṣaṅkara.] [1851.] 8°. **14172. f. 2.**

—— *See* PAVAṆANDI. நன்னூல் மூ [Nan-nūl. With commentary by Ṣaṅkara.] [1887.] 8°. **14172. e. 12.**

—— —— [1903.] 8°. **14172. e. 39.**

ṢAṄKARA-NĀRĀYAṆA ṢĀSTRI, *of Ettayapuram. See* APPAYA DĪKSHITAR. குவலயானந்தம். [Kuvalayānandam. Translated by Ṣaṅkara-nārāyaṇa and Mīnākshi-sundara.] 1895. 8°. **14170. i. 40.**

SANTA-CRUZ, *Pulavar.* அர்ச். அலசம்மானை, விருத்தம். [Archya-ṣishṭa-alaṣ'-ammānai and °vṛuttam. The legend of St. Alexis, in both *ammānai* and *vruttam* metres, the latter by Santa-Cruz.] 1893. 12°. *See* [Addenda] ALEXIS, *St.* **14170. b. 59.**

ṢĀNTA-LIṄGA SVĀMI. *See* [Addenda] AGASTYAR. பஞ்சபட்சிசாஸ்திரம் மூ [Pañcha-pakshi-ṣāstram. With paraphrase, *etc.*, by Ṣānta-liṅga.] 1907. 8°. **14170. i. 3.**

ṢĀNTA-LIṄGA SVĀMI, *Tiruturaiyūr.* Eclectic Vedantism. A philosophical poem in frequent use amongst Hindu women, translated from the Tamil, by the Rev. Thomas Foulkes. (†Avirōtavuntiyār, or The Non-Controversialists' Dance. By Sāntalingasuvāmi of Tiruttureiyur.) pp. 20. *Madras,* 1860. 8°. **14170. e. 36.(2.)**

—— ∘∘∘ வைராக்கிய சதகம் மூ [Vairāgya-ṣatakam. 50 verses on spiritual calm. Edited, with a commentary, by P. Pārtha-sārathi Aiyaṅgār.] pp. 73. *Madras,* 1906. 12°. **14170. dd. 11.(1.)**

SANTIAGO, *Puttūr Ṣavari-nāyakar.* The Violin Tutor of Hindu Music . . . கீதபோதகம். pp. 4, 14. *Trichinopoly,* 1892. 4°. **14171. h. 1.**

SANTIAGO PIḶḶAI, *Puttuḷam A.* பிரலாபசாகரம் மூ [Pralāpa-sāgaram. Lyrics upon the Passion of Christ.] pp. 32. யாழ்ப்பாணம் [*Jaffna,*] 1889. 8°. **14170. c. 24.(1.)**

SANTIAGO PIḶḶAI, *Puttaḷam A. (continued).* ∘∘∘ யாத்திரைக்கீர்த்தனை. [Yātrai-kīrttanai. Lyrics on a journey from Colombo to the sanctuary of St. Anne at Talavilla.] pp. 10. கொழும்பு [*Colombo,*] 1893. 8°. **14170. bb. 8.(1.)**

SANTIAGO-PIḶḶAI CHANDRA-VARṆAM, *A. See* KATHĀ-CHINTĀMAṆI. The Katháchintámani . . . Edited . . . by . . . Santiagopulle, *etc.* 1875. 8°. **14170. k. 27.**

SAPTARSHI. The Suptharishivakkiam 5500. [Saptarshi-vākyam. A metrical work on astrology in 12 chapters.] Thoroughly examined by Poovaloor Nagasawmy Aiyar ... and by Arasarkoolam Venkatasubramaniya Aiyar. (*சப்தரிஷிவாக்கியம் ருருoo.) pp. iii. 792. *Madras, Vicari* [1899.] 8°. **14170. i. 63.**

SARAH. Old Sarah, or The Walk of Purity . . . தூய்ய நடை. A translation [by L. Spaulding] of the Parent Society's Tract—Poor Sarah, no. 583. Second edition. pp. 12. *Jaffna,* 1842. 12°. **14170. b. 1.(24.)**

SARASA-LŌCHANA CHEṬṬI, *Tiruvevvulūr Rāmasāmi.* Sarasangi. A Tamil drama by T. R. Sarasalochanam [adapted from Shakspere's "Cymbeline." With English introduction by M. S. Daṇḍāyudha-pāṇi Aiyar]. (*சாசாங்கி நாடகம்.) pp. i. xii. viii. 4, iv. 138, i. i. *Madras,* 1897. 8°. **14170. l. 45.**

—— சாவித்திரி சரிதை. [Sāvitri-charitai. The story of Sāvitri, based on the legend of the Mahā-bhāratam, Vana-parvam. Followed by two cradle-songs by T. Rāma-sāmi Cheṭṭi.] pp. 56, 8. சென்னை [*Madras,*] 1897. 16°. **14171. aa. 2.**

SARASALOCHANAM. *See* SARASA-LŌCHANA CHEṬṬI.

ṢARA-VAṆA-MUTTU PIḶḶAI, *Tirukōṇamalai T.* மோகனாங்கி. ஒருகதை. [Mōhanāṅgi. A novel.] pp. 384. சென்னை [*Madras,*] 1895. 12°. **14171. a. 4.**

—— The Parrot Messenger. [A poem in 33 stanzas.] (*தத்தைவிடுதூது.) pp. 8. *Madras,* 1892. 8°. **14172. bb. 15.**

—— தமிழ்ப்பாஷை (The Study of Tamil Literature. An essay in Tamil.) pp. 34. *Madras,* 1892. 16°. **14171. aa. 11.**

ṢARA-VAṆA PAṆḌITAR, *Gōkulāpuram.* See KṚUSHṆA-SĀMI PIḶḶAI, *Tañjai.* நளநாடகம் ஶ்ரீ [Damayanti-nāṭakam. Edited by Ṣara-vaṇa.] [1883.] 8°. **14170. l. 9.**

ṢARA-VAṆA PERU-MĀḶ AIYAR, *Tirutaṇigai Kandapp'-aiyar.* See ATIVĪRA-RĀMA PĀṆḌIYAN. நைடதம் ஶ்ரீ [Naiḍadam. With commentary on cantos 1-5 by Ṣara-vaṇa Peru-māḷ.] [1842.] 8°. **14172. b. 58.**

—— See ATIVĪRA-RĀMA PĀṆḌIYAN. ००० நைடதம் ஶ்ரீ [Naiḍadam. With commentaries by Ṣara-vaṇa Peru-māḷ, *etc.*] [1875.] 8°. **14172. b. 59.**

—— See ATIVĪRA-RĀMA PĀṆḌIYAN. ००० நைடதம் ஶ்ரீ [Naiḍadam. With commentaries of Ṣara-vaṇa Peru-māḷ, *etc.*] 1881. 8°. **14172. b. 14.**

—— See AUVAIYĀR.—*Two or More Works.* வாக்குண்டாம் ஶ்ரீ [Vākk'-uṇḍām and Nal-vaṟi, *etc.* With commentaries by Ṣara-vaṇa Peru-māḷ.] [1841.] 16°. **14172. a. 1.**

—— —— [1859.] 16°. **14172. a. 12.**

—— —— 1882. 16°. **14172. a. 11.(1.)**

—— See PARAÑ-JŌDI MUNIVAR. திருவிளையாடற் புராணம். [Tiru-viḷaiy-āḍaṟ-purāṇam. Edited on the basis of the editions of Ṣara-vaṇa Peru-māḷ and Tyāga-rāya Mudaliyār.] [1850.] 8°. **14170. ee. 1.**

—— [For editions of the Tiru-viḷaiy-āḍaṟ-purāṇam reprinted from that of Ṣara-vaṇa Peru-māḷ :] See PARAÑ-JŌDI MUNIVAR.

—— Sec ṢIVA-PRAKĀṢA DĒṢIKAR. பழமலையந்தாதி ஶ்ரீ [Paṟa-malaiy-antādi, *etc.* Edited by Ṣara-vaṇa Peru-māḷ.] [1832.] 8°. **14172. b. 23.(1.)**

—— See TĀYUMĀNAVAR. ००० திருப்பாடற்றிரட்டு. [Tiru-pāḍaṭ-ṭiraṭṭu. In the recension of Ṣara-vaṇa Peru-māḷ.] [1851.] 8°. **14172. c. 24.**

—— See TĀYUMĀNAVAR. தாயுமான . . . பாடற்றிரட்டு. [Tiru-pāḍaṭ-ṭiraṭṭu. From the recension of Ṣara-vaṇa Peru-māḷ.] 1885. 8°. **14172. b. 32.**

—— See TIRU-MUṞAI.—*Tiru-vāchakam.* திருவாசகம். [Tiru-vāchakam. Edited by Ṣara-vaṇa Peru-māḷ.] [1857.] 8°. **14172. b. 15.**

ṢARA-VAṆA PERU-MĀḶ AIYAR, *Tirutaṇigai Kandapp'-aiyar (continued).* See TIRU-VAḶḶUVAR. ००० திருக்குறள் ஶ்ரீ [Kuṟaḷ. With interpretations and prolegomena by Ṣara-vaṇa Peru-māḷ.] [1875.] 8°. **14172. c. 10.**

—— யாப்பிலக்கணம். [Yāpp'-ilakkaṇam.] (A treatise on Tamil Prosody.) pp. 32. சென்னை [*Madras,*] 1900. 8°. **14172. hh. 17.**

SARGENT (EDWARD), *Assistant Bishop in the Diocese of Madras.* பூர்விகசரித்திரம் ஶ்ரீ [Pūrvika-charitram. A manual of ancient history for mission schools.] pp. 121; 1 *plate.* *Palamcottah,* 1850. 8°. **14170. c. 17.**

—— Tamil Reading Book . . . தமிழ் வாசகபுத்தகம். [Tamiṟ-vāchaka-puttagam. Second edition.] pp. 72. *Madras,* 1848. 12°. **14172. h. 58.(2.)**

SĀRVABHAUMA AIYAṄGĀR. See VILLIPUTTŪRAR.

SARVĀTMA-ṢAMBHU ṢIVĀCHĀRYAR. ००० சித்தாந்தப்பிரகாசிகை. [Siddhānta-prakāṣikai. An exposition of Ṣaiva psycho-metaphysics. Translated from the Sanskrit by Ṣiva-ñāna Svāmi.] pp. 24. சென்னை [*Madras,*] 1897. 12°. **14170. d. 32.(3.)**

SASHIENGAR. See ṢĒSH'-AIYAṄGĀR.

SATAKOPARAMANUJACHARIAR. See ṢAṬHAKŌPA-RĀMĀNUJĀCHĀRYAR.

ṢATA-MAṆI. சதமணிக்கோவை. [Ṣata-maṇi-kōvai. 105 stanzas on the esoteric Ṣaiva creed.] pp. 25. 1898. See VĒDĀCHALAM PIḶḶAI. சித்தாந்தஞானபோதம். [Siddhānta-ñāna-bōdham.] pt. i. 1898. 8°. **14170. ee. 39.**

ṢAṬHAKŌPĀCHĀRYAR, *Iyyuṇṇi Jagannāthāchāryar.* See VĔṄKAṬĀCHĀRYAR, *son of Gōvindāchāryar.* ००० చాత్తాద . . . శ్రీవైష్ణవ. [Chāttāda-ṣrī-vaishṇava-dvija-shōḍaṣa-karmāṇi. Edited by Ṣatha-kōpāchāryar.] [1902.] 8°. **14170. ee. 47.**

ṢAṬHAKŌPĀCHĀRYAR, *M. C.* See HARSHA-DĒVA. நாகானந்தம். (Naganauda. A Tamil version by M. C. Sadagopa Chariar, *etc.*). 1900. 8°. **14170. l. 24.(1.)**

ṢAṬHAKŌPA-DĀSAR, *Kiṟaiyūr.* ००० அரிசமயதீபம் என்னும் குருபரம்பரை. [Hari-samaya-dīpam, or Guru-paramparai. A poem on the history and teachings of the Vaishṇava Viṣishṭādvaita school and its leaders. With a paraphrase by Ṣ. Muttu-kṛushṇa Nāyuḍu. Edited by the latter and K. Rāma-sāmi Nāyuḍu.] pp. 6, ii. 436, ii. *Madras*, 1904. 8°. **14170. ee. 58.**

This author is said to have been known by the name of Ṣaṭhakōpa-rāmānuja Mudaliyār, and to have flourished some 250 years ago.

ṢAṬHAKŌPA-RĀMĀNUJĀCHĀRYAR, *Tiruvaruṇdūr*. See PIḶḶAI LŌKĀCHĀRYAR. ◦◦◦ யதீந்த்ர-ப்ரவணப்ரபாவம். [Yatīndra-pravaṇa-prabhāvam. Edited by Ṣaṭhakōpa-rāmānujāchāryar.] 1907. 8°. **14170. ff. 23.**

ṢAṬHAKŌPA-RĀMĀNUJĀCHĀRYAR, *Vaittamānidhi Muḍumbai*. See ACADEMIES, *etc.*—Madras.—*University of Madras*. Copious annotations on the Matriculation Tamil text for 1900 by V. M. Satakoparamanujachariar, *etc.* 1900. 8°. **14172. bb. 6.(3.)**

—— —— University of Madras. F.A. Examination of 1901. Tamil poetry ... with ... notes ... by V. M. Satakoparamanujachariar, *etc.* 1900. 8°. **14172. bb. 6.(5.)**

—— —— University of Madras. B.A. Examination of 1901 ... A Tamil text-book ... with ... annotations ... by V. M. Satakoparamanujachariar, *etc.* 1900. 8°. **14172. bb. 6.(6.)**

—— —— University of Madras. F.A. Examination of 1903. Full notes ... by V. M. Satakoparamanujachariar, *etc.* 1903. 8°. **14172. hh. 19.**

—— See ĀṚVĀRGAḶ.—Nāl-āyiram.—*Iyaṟ-pā*. ◦◦◦ திருவிருத்தம். [Tiru-vṛuttam. Edited with commentary by Ṣaṭhakōpa-rāmānujāchāryar.] [1899.] 8°. **14170. ee. 35.(5.)**

—— See PAVAṆANDI. நன்னூற் காண்டிகையுரை. (Nannul kandikai. [Being the Nan-nūl with a commentary] by V. M. Satakoparamanujachariar, and S. Krishnamachariar, *etc.*) [Third edition.] 1900. 8°. **14172. e. 32.**

—— —— [Fourth edition.] 1903. 8°. **14172. e. 37.**

—— ஆழ்வார்கள் சரித்திரம். [Āṛvārgaḷ-charitram. A prose history of the Āṛvārs or Vaishṇava saints.] pp. ii. 76. சென்னை ஏவிளம்பி [*Madras*, 1898.] 8°. **14170. ee. 35.(7.)**

—— ஆழ்வார்கள்சரித்திரத்தி லுள்ள செய்யுள்களின் உரை. [Notes on the Āṛvārgaḷ-charitram of Ṣaṭhakōpa-rāmānujāchāryar.] pp. 31. See ACADEMIES, *etc.*—Madras.—*University of Madras*. University of Madras. F.A. Examination, *etc.* 1900. 8°. **14172. bb. 6.(5.)**

SATHIANADEN. See SATYA-NĀTHAN.

ṢĀTTAN, *Kūlavāṇigan*. மணிமேகலை. [Maṇi-mēkhalai. A romance in verse, forming one of the 5 classical poems. Edited by T. Shaṇmukham Piḷḷai.] pp. iv. 134, 3, 2. சென்னை [*Madras*,] 1894. 8°. **14172. b. 50.**

—— ◦◦◦ மணிமேகலை மூலமும் ... அரும்பதவுரையும். [Maṇi-mēkhalai. Edited with prefaces, life of Ṣāttan, Buddha-charitram or history of Buddha, Bauddha-dharmam or an essay on Buddhism, Bauddha-saṅgham or an account of the Buddhist Church, glossaries, notes, and indexes by U. V. Sāmināth'-aiyar.] pp. i. x. ii. cvi. lvi. xvi. i. 453. சென்னை [*Madras*,] 1898. 8°. **14172. d. 22.**

—— Le Manimêgalei. [A French epitome.] See VINSON (E. H. J.). Légendes Bouddhistes et Djainas, *etc.* vol. i., pp. 177-227, vol. ii., pp. 1-100. 1900. 12°. **14171. aa. 4.**

SATTHIANADHAN (S.), *Mrs.* See KṚUPAI SATYA-NĀTHAN.

SATTIANADEN. See SATYA-NĀTHAN.

SATYA-NĀTHAN, *R., of Tanjore.* See JAENICKE (D.). The life of Rev. R. Sathianaden, *etc.* 1893. 8°. **14170. bb. 4.**

—— Translation [by J. C. Kohlhoff] of a sermon [on Ezek. xxxiii. 11] in the Malabar or Tamulian language; composed and preached by Sattianaden, on the 26th day of December, 1790, *etc.* pp. viii. 14. *London*, 1792. 4°. **115. h. 9.**

SAUNDARA-NĀYAKAM PIḶḶAI (GABRIEL P.). See PAVAṆANDI. Abridgment of the Nannûl ... by G. P. Savundranayagam Pillai. 1864. 12°. **14172. e. 7.**

SAUNDARA-RĀJA AIYAṄGĀR, *Ṣ. Vēṅkaṭa-rāma.* Tamil Grammar, with Nannûl sutrams and explanations. Specially adapted for High and Middle Schools. By V. Soundararaja Aiyengar. Second edition. pp. i. 208, v. *Kumbhakonam*, 1897. 12°. **14172. ee. 1.**

—— Third edition. pp. 233, v. *Kumbakonam*, 1898. 12°. **14172. ee. 2.**

SAUNDARA-RĀJA UḌAIYĀR, *Ṣanbagakollai Vēṅkaṭāchala.* *See* TIRUKOVALUR. தெய்வீகபுராணம் ஆ [Tirukōvalūr-purāṇam. Edited by Saundara-rāja.] 1901. 8°. **14170. ee. 57.**

SAURA BRAHMANS. அதர்வணவேத ஸௌர்யசாகை சௌரமான ஸூத்ர விதிப்படி சௌரப்ராம்ஹணர்களாகிய கருணீகர்களின் ஹவ்யகவ்ய விதிகள். [Havya-kavya-vidhigaḷ. A ritual for the *havya* and *kavya* offerings of the Saura Brahmans, a class of accountants claiming descent from the Sun, and following the rules of a *sūrya-ṣākhā* purporting to belong to the Atharva-vēda. Sanskrit text of the *mantras* in Telugu and Tamil script, with rubrics, hymns, and other matter in Tamil. Edited by Ṣ. Narasimm'-āchāri and Ṣ. Sundara Guru.] pp. viii. iii. 256. சென்னை [*Madras*,] 1906. 8°. **14033. bbb. 36.**

SAURĀSHṬRAS. A short history of the Sourashtras [a silk-weaver caste] of Southern India. தென் இந்தியா சௌராஷ்டிரஜாதியாரின் சரித்திரசாரசங்கிரகம். pp. 36. *Kumbakonam*, 1903. 12°. **14171. a. 7.(2.)**

ṢAVARI-RĀYAN, *D.* *See* [Addenda] ACADEMIES, *etc.* —*Trichinopoli.* The Tamilian Antiquary. [Edited by Ṣavari-rāyan.] 1907, *etc.* 8°. **14172. m. 3.**

ṢAVARI-RĀYA PIḶḶAI (JOHN DĒVA-SAHĀYAM). *See* ṢAVARI-RĀYA PIḶḶAI, *M.* சவரிராய பிள்ளை யவர்கள் சர்னலும் காகிதங்களும் ஆ (*The Journal and Letters of Savariraya Pillai, *etc.*) [Edited by J. D. Ṣavari-rāya Piḷḷai.] 1898-1902. 8°. **14171. a. 27.**

—— சவரிராய பிள்ளை வம்சவரலாறு. The Ancestors of Savariraya Pillai, a catechist of the Church Missionary Society, Tinnevelly, South India. Compiled by his son [J. D. Ṣavari-rāya Piḷḷai]. (* சவரிராய பிள்ளை சரித்திரம் . . . The Life of Savariraya Pillai.) 2 vols. *Palamcottah*, 1899-1900. 8°. **14171. a. 27.***

ṢAVARI-RĀYA PIḶḶAI, *Madurēndram.* *See* ṢAVARI-RĀYA PIḶḶAI (J. D.). சவரிராய பிள்ளை வம்சவரலாறு. The Ancestors of Savariraya Pillai, *etc.* (* சவரிராய பிள்ளை சரித்திரம் . . . The Life of Savariraya Pillai.) 1899-1900. 8°. **14171. a. 27.***

—— சவரிராய பிள்ளை யவர்கள் சர்னலும் காகிதங்களும் ஆ (*The Journal and Letters of Savariraya Pillai, a catechist of the Church Missionary Society, Tinnevelly District, South India. 1836-1874.) [Edited by J. D. Ṣavari-rāya Piḷḷai.] 3 vols. *Palamcottah*, 1898-1902. 8°. **14171. a. 27.**

ṢAVĒRI-MUTTU PIḶḶAI, *Mayilai.* இலக்கணச்சுருக்கம். [Ilakkaṇa-churukkam. An abridged Tamil grammar.] pp. 180. புதுவை நூஅாகூம் [*Pondicherry*, 1860.] 12°. **14172. h. 6.**

SĀVITRI. സാവിത്രിനാടകം. [Sāvitri-nāṭakam. A drama on the epic legend of Sāvitrī, printed in the Malayalam character.] pp. 60. പാലക്കാട ഫ്യൽം [*Palghat*, 1890.] 8°. **14170. l. 30.(2.)**

SAVUNDRANAYAGAM PILLAI. *See* SAUNDARA-NĀYAKAM PIḶḶAI.

SAWMI CHETTIAR. *See* SĀMI CHEṬṬIYĀR.

SĀYAṆĀCHĀRYAR. *See* NIṢCHALA DĀSA. ००० ஸ்ரீவிருத்திப்பிரபாகரம். [Vṛutti-prabhākaram. A commentary on Sāyaṇa's Pañchadaṣī.] 1901. 8°. **14170. ee. 41.**

—— *See* NIṢCHALA DĀSA. ஸ்ரீ விருத்திரத்நாவளி. [Vṛutti-ratnāvali. An epitome of Vṛutti-prabhākaram.] 1902. 12°. **14170. d. 77.**

—— *See* SANDHYĀ-VANDANAM. யஜுர்வேத ஸந்த்யாவந்தநம் ஆ [Sandhyā-vandanam, *etc.* With extracts, in a Tamil translation, from the commentaries of Sāyaṇa, *etc.*] 1901. 8°. **14033. aa. 27.**

—— ००० ஜீவன்முக்திப்பிரகரணம். [Jīvan-mukti-prakaraṇam. A manual of Advaita-Vēdāntam. Translated from the Sanskrit of Sāyaṇa by Ulaga-nātha Svāmi. Edited, with notes and additions, by A. Rāma-sāmi Svāmi.] pp. viii. iv. 149, iii. சென்னை சர்வசித்து [*Madras*, 1887.] 12°. **14170. d. 24.**

—— ஸ்ரீ... ஸ்ரீவெ உ ாஜங்ப ஜு உ மீ *etc.* [Pañchadaṣī, or Vēdānta-pañchadaṣī. A metrical treatise on Vēdāntam. With a word-for-word interpretation and paraphrase in Tamil by Rāma-liṅga Brahmā-nanda Yati of Madura, preceded by an epitome in Tamil and a Sanskrit poem called Rāma-liṅga-vaibhava on the successes of Rāma-liṅga with a Tamil translation, all three by his son Sundara-rāma Ṣāstri of Madura.] pp. xvi. vi. 688, iv.; 1 *plate*. *Madras*, 1905. 8°. **14049. bb. 7.**

The text is printed in both Nagari and Grantham type.

—— ∘∘∘ பஞ்சதசப்பிரகரணம். [Pañchadaṣa-prakaraṇam. An anonymous adaptation of Sāyaṇa's Pañchadaṣī, in dialogue form.] pp. i. 148. சென்னை சார்வரி [*Madras*, 1901.] 12°. **14170. ee. 46.**

—— Pańćadaśa prakaraṇa. Übersetzung. *See* GRAUL (K. F. L.). Bibliotheca Tamulica, *etc.* vol. 1, pp. 91-172. 1854-1865. 8°. **14170. e. 42.(vol. 1.)**

—— Life of Sankaracharyar, commonly called Sankaravijayam. Translated from Sanscrit [*i.e.* from the Saṅkshēpa-ṣaṅkara-vijayam ascribed to Mādhava or Sāyaṇa] into Tamil [prose] with the assistence [*sic*] of Bangalore Siddhanthi Sree Subramanya Sastryar . . . by Tholuvoor Valayudha Moodeliar. (*சங்கரவிஜயம் என்றுவழங்கும் சங்கராசாரியார்சரித்திரம்.) pp. ii. ii. 102, i. *Madras*, 1879. 8°. **14170. k. 19.**

This biography is said to have been compiled from the Saṅkara-vijaya-vilāsam of Chid-vilāsa and Vijñāna-kanda, the Vyāsalīyam (?), Padma-pāda's biography, and the Skanda-purāṇam (Ṣiva-rahasya-khaṇḍam), etc.

SCHAFFTER (PAUL PACIFIQUE). கானான்தேசவிலாசம். [Kānān-dēṣa-vilāsam. The geography of the land of Canaan.] pp. i. 264; 5 *plates*. *Palamcottah*, 1849. 8°. **14170. c. 11.**

SCHANZ (HUGO). *See* HYMNALS. Spiritual Songs, *etc.* [Hymns selected by H. Schanz.] 1867. *obl.* 16°. **14170. a. 9.**

SCHULTZE (BENJAMIN). *See* ARNDT (J.). Joannis Arndtii . . . Libellus Precum . . . dictus Hortulus Paradisiacus . . . in tamulicum convertit B. Schulzius. 1749-1750. 12°. **14170. bbb. 7.**

—— *See* ARNDT (J.). Joannis Arndtii . . . de Vero Christianismo liber primus . . . in tamulicum convertit B. Schulzius. 1751. 8°. **G. 19,737.**

—— *See* BIBLE.—*Complete Bibles.* Biblia Damulica, *etc.* (*Pars secunda . . . tertia . . . Libri apocryphi . . . studio & opera B. Ziegenbalgii & B. Schultzii . . . versi.) [1714]-1728. 4°. **3068. g. 6.**

—— *See* BIBLE.—*Old Testament.* Librorum Sacrorum Veteris Testamenti . . . editio secunda, *etc.* [From the version of Ziegenbalg and Schultze.] 1777-1796. 4°. **3068. g. 10.**

—— *See* BIBLE.—Old Testament.—*Psalms.* Liber Psalmorum . . . in linguam damulicam versus opera & studio B. Schultze. 1724. 12°. **3090. ccc. 6.**

—— [For editions of the translation of the Bible as revised by Fabricius and subsequent translators on the basis of Ziegenbalg and Schultze's version:] *See* BIBLE.

—— *See* HYMNALS. Hymnologia Damulica . . . exhibita a B. Schultze. 1723. 12°. **14170. b. 17.**

—— [For later editions of the Tranquebar Hymnal:] *See* HYMNALS.

—— Historia Passionis Jesu Christi Filii Dei et Mariae Virginis damulicè ex quatuor Evangelistis conscripta (*எசுகிறிஷததுநாதாானவா . . . பாடுபடடாரொனறு . . . வெளிபபடுததுகிற கதைப பொஷததகம). pp. 77. *Tranquebariae*, 1723. 16°. **14170. a. 24.**

SCHULZIUS (BENJAMIN). *See* SCHULTZE (B.).

SCHWARZ (JOHANN MICHEL NIKOLAUS). *See* BOGATZKY (C. H. VON). Golden Treasury . . . [Revised by J. Schwarz] *etc.* 1876-1878. 8°. **14170. c. 1.**

—— *See* MEY-ÑĀNAM. True Wisdom, *etc.* [Revised by J. Schwarz.] 1880. 12°. **14170. b. 16.(4.)**

SCOTT (T. M.). *See* TIRU-VAḶḶUVAR. ∘∘∘ குறள் ஶ்ரீ [Kuṟaḷ. With commentary by "Sugāttiyar," *i.e.* T. M. Scott.] 1889. 8°. **14172. c. 35.**

—— ∘∘∘ முப்பொருட்போதம். [Mup-poruṭ-bōdham. 276 Christian quatrains on moral and religious subjects.] pp. 48. *Madras*, 1889. 12°. **14172. a. 34.**

SCOTT (*Sir* WALTER). *See* SUBB'-AIYĀ AIYAR, *K. V.* Kanthimati: a novel . . . After Scott's Talisman, *etc.* 1902. 12°. **14171. aa. 12.**

SCUDDER (HENRY MARTYN). *See* RĀMA-RĀMA VASU. நிஸ்தார ரத்நாகரம் ஷ [Nistāra-ratnākaram. Translated into Tamil, with additions, by H. M. Scudder.] 1857. 16°. **14170. a. 28.**

—— The Bazaar Book, or Vernacular Preacher's Companion. கிரணமாலிகை. [Kiraṇa-mālikai.] pp. vi. 413. *Madras*, 1865. 8°. **14170. c. 7.**

SCUDDER (JOHN). *See* WINSLOW (M.) and SCUDDER (J.). Attributes of the Hindu Triad, *etc.* 1844. 12°. **14170. b. 1.(22.)**

—— Address to Roman Catholics . . . உரோமைமார்க்கத்தார் கொடுக்கிற எதிர்மொழிக்கு மறுமொழி. Third edition. pp. 28. *Jaffna*, 1843. 12°. **14170. b. 1.(6.*)**

—— Exposition of the Second Commandment ... இரண்டாங்கற்பனை விளக்கம். Second edition. pp. 16. *Jaffna*, 1843. 12°. **14170. b. 1.(10.)**

—— Friendly Epistle. Pointing out some of the chief errors taught by the Roman Catholic Church ... நேசநிருபம். Fourth edition. pp. 20. *Jaffna*, 1843. 12°. **14170. b. 1.(5.)**

—— Mantras, or Incantations . . . மந்திரம். Sixth edition. pp. 4. *Jaffna*, 1844. 12°. **14170. b. 1.(14.)**

—— On the Marriage of Priests ... குருவிவாகவிளக்கம். [A tract against the celibacy of the Catholic clergy.] Second edition. pp. 20. *Jaffna*, 1844. 12°. **14170. b. 1.(11.)**

—— On withholding the Cup from the Laity. A tract . . . for Roman Catholics . . . நற்கருணைக் குறைபாடு. Second edition. pp. 16. *Jaffna*, 1844. 12°. **14170. b. 1.(18.)**

—— The Ten Commandments . . . contrasted with the Decalogue of the Roman Church . . . எதிர்மொழிக்கு மறுமொழி. Third edition. pp. 4. *Jaffna*, 1843. 12°. **14170. b. 1.(6.)**

ṢEDI-RĀYAR. *See* CHEDI-RĀYAR.

ṢEKKIṞĀR. *See* ĀṞU-MUGA UPĀDHYĀYAR. சிறுத்தொண்டநாயனார்புராணம். [Ṣiṟu-toṇḍa-nāyanār-purāṇam. A legend based upon the Periya-purāṇam.] [1894.] 8°. **14170. ee. 4.(1.)**

ṢEKKIṞĀR (*continued*). *See* GŌPĀLA-KṚUSHṆA AIYAR, *Ā. Bh.* பெரியபுராணம் ஷ [Nandanār-charitra-kīrttanai. Lyrics upon Nandanār, a Ṣaiva devotee celebrated in the Periya-purāṇam, and based upon the latter.] [1882.] 8°. **14170. e. 9.**

—— —— ° ° ° நந்தனார்சரித்திரகீர்த்தனை ஷ [Nandanār-charitra-kīrttanai.] 1899. 8°. **14170. ee. 25.**

—— *See* MUNI-SĀMI MUDALIYĀR, *Ṣ.* சிறுத்தொண்டநாயனார்சரித்திரம். [Ṣiṟu-toṇḍa-nāyanār-charitram. A story from the Periya-purāṇam.] 1892. 8°. **14172. b. 44.(1.)**

—— *See* SUNDARA ĀCHĀRYAR, *C. K.* ° ° ° அப்பூதியடிகள் . . . கீர்த்தனை. [Appūdiy-aḍigaḷ-nāyanār-charitra-kīrttanai. Lyrics on the legend of Appūdiy-aḍigaḷ, based upon the Periya-purāṇam.] 1895. 8°. **14170. ee. 4.(2.)**

—— ° ° ° பெரிய புராணம் ஷ [Periya-purāṇam, or Tiru-toṇḍar-purāṇam. A Ṣaiva poetical hagiology in 4316 verses. Prefaced by devotional and hagiological matter from the works of Umā-pati, Nambiy-āṇḍār Nambi, and others.] pp. iii. lxxxiv. iv. 911. சென்னை பிரமாதி [*Madras*, 1880.] 8°. **14170. f. 4.**

Composed at the request of king Anapāya Chōṟan (Rāja-kēsari-varma Kulōttuṅga), and later than the Jīvaka-chintāmaṇi.

—— சேக்கிழார்சுவாமிகளருளிச்செய்த திருத்தொண்டர்புராணமென்னும் பெரியபுராணம் ... மூலமும் . . . பதவுரையும். [Periya-purāṇam. Edited with an interpretation by Āṟu-muga Tambirān Svāmi, completed by C. Rāma-liṅga Svāmi.] 4 vols. சென்னை பார்திப [*Madras*, 1885]-1898. 8°. **14170. f. 1.**

Illustrated with numerous woodcut plates. The volumes bear the following dates—vol. i., 1888; vol. ii., 1890; vol. iii., 1885; vol. iv., 1898.

—— [Another copy of vol. 3.] **14170. f. 1.***

—— ° ° ° திருத்தொண்டர்புராணம் என்னும் பெரியபுராணம் ஷ [Periya-purāṇam. With a paraphrase and commentary by Ṣ. Subba-rāya Nāyakar.] vols. i. 1.—ii. 8. சென்னை [*Madras*,] 1891-1895. 8°. **14170. f. 21**

—— பெரியபுராணம் என்றுவழங்குகின்ற திருத்தொண்டர்புராணம். [Periya-purāṇam. A prose summary by Āṟu-muga Nāvalar.] pp. 6, 8, 235, 3. பரிதாபி [Jaffna, 1852.] 8°. 14170. e. 10.

—— திருத்தொண்டர் பெரியபுராண வசனச்சுருக்கம். [Tiru-toṇḍar-periya-purāṇa-vachana-churukkam. A prose epitome.] pp. xii. ix. 156, vi.; 79 plates. சென்னை [Madras,] 1900. 16°. 14170. d. 72.

—— ... திருஞானசம்பந்தமூர்த்தி நாயனார் புராணவசனம். [Tiru-ñāna-sambandha-mūrtti-nāyanār-purāṇa-vachanam. A prose history of the Ṣaiva saint Ñāna-sambandhar, abridged from pt. ii. of the Periya-purāṇam, by Ṣ. Ponn'-ōduvār.] pp. 44. அணிக்காரன் சத்திரம் [Anaikkaran Chatram,] 1900. 8°. 14170. e. 47.(10.)

ṢELL'-AIYĀ PIḶḶAI, *Māṇippāy Tambā* (T. C. Ladd). ஈழமண்டலத்துத் திருவேரக முருகர் பதிகம். [Tiruvēraga-mṛugar-padigam. A hymn of 10 verses for a Sinhalese local cult of the god Mṛugan.] pp. 14, i. கொழும்பு [Colombo,] 1907. 12°. 14170. dd. 16.

ṢELL'-AIYĀ PIḶḶAI, *Ṣ., of Colombo.* ... கொட்டாஞ்சேனை முத்துமாரியம்மன் நவரத்தினம். [Muttu-māriy-amman-nava-ratnam. Nine hymns to Māri, the goddess of small-pox.] pp. 8. யாழ்ப்பாணத்தில் [Jaffna,] 1893. 16°. 14170. d. 36.(5.)

ṢELLI-NAGAR PERUM-BAṮṮA-PULIY-ŪR-NAMBI. *See* Perum-baṯṯa-puliy-ūr-nambi.

ṢELVA-KĒṢAVA-RĀYA MUDALIYĀR, *Tirumaṇam, of Pachaiyappa's College.* *See* Munai-pāḍiyār. முனைப்பாடியார் ... அறநெறிச்சாரம். (Aranericharam ... [Edited by] T. Chelvakesavaroya Mudaliar.) 1905. 12°. 14172. a. 50.(5.)

—— *See* Peru-vāyin Muḷḷiyār. ... ஆசாரக்கோவை. [Āchāra-kōvai. With preface by Ṣelva-kēṣava-rāyar.] 1893. 8°. 14172. a. 29.(3.)

—— Kambar. [A literary-historical study.] pp. 38. *Madras*, 1902. 8°. 14171. a. 53.(2.)

—— Parallel Proverbs. Tamil and English, and English and Tamil. pp. 8, 123. *Madras*, 1900. 8°. 14171. a. 38.(1.)

—— —— Revised and enlarged. Second edition. pp. i. 234. *Madras*, 1903. 8°. 14171. a. 55.

ṢELVA-KĒṢAVA-RĀYA MUDALIYĀR, *Tirumaṇam, of Pachaiyappa's College (continued).* Tamil. An essay. (தமிழ்.) pp. i. 128. *Madras*, 1904. 12°. 14172. g. 5.(2.)

—— [Another edition.] pp. 116; 1 *plate*. *Madras*, 1906. 12°. 14172. g. 9.

—— Notes. Essay on Tamil. (†தமிழ் அரும்பதவுரை.) pp. 53. *Madras*, 1906. 12°. 14172. h. 2.

—— University of Madras. F. A., 1908. Notes. Tamil Essays. (†தமிழ் வியாசங்கள் அரும்பதவுரை.) [In Tamil and English.] pp. 47. *Madras*, 1907. 12°. 14172. g. 11.

—— Tiruvalluvar. An essay. (University of Madras. First Examination in Arts—1905. Tamil prose. Essay on Tiruvalluvar. With notes.) pp. i. 100; 1 *plate*. *Madras*, 1904. 12°. 14171. d. 2.

ṢELVA-NĀYAKAM PIḶḶAI (Joseph). இது ... யோசேப்பு செல்வநாயகம்பிள்ளை தேகவியோகமானதின்பேரிற் சொல்லிய காதல். [An elegy upon the death of J. Ṣelva-nāyakam Piḷḷai.] pp. 16. யாழ்ப்பாணம் [Jaffna,] 1892. 32°. 14170. a. 58.(2.)

SĒNĀDHIPATI PIḶḶAI, *Meyya.* பதார்த்தகுணக்கொத்து. [Padārtha-guṇa-kottu. A metrical account of the medicinal qualities of various drugs, foods, *etc.*] pp. vi. 52. கூடலூர் [Cuddalore,] 1895. 8°. 14170. i. 14.

SĒNĀV-ARAIYAR. *See* Tol-kāppiyanār. தொல்காப்பியம் ஆ [Tol-kāppiyam. With commentary by Sēnāv-araiyar.] [1868.] 8°. 14172. e. 6.

ṢĒNDANĀR. [For editions of the Divākaram, commonly ascribed to Ṣēndanār:] *See* Divākarar.

ṢĒNDANĀR, *Tirunāṅgūr.* [For the hymns of Ṣēndanār contained in the Tiruv-iṣai-pā:] *See* Tiru-muṟai.

—— [For editions of Ṣēndanār's Tiru-pall'-āṇḍu appended to the Tiruv-iṣai-pā:] *See* Tiru-muṟai.

ṢENDINĀTHA AIYAR. *See* Ñāna-muttu Nāḍār. Shanars are Kshatriyas, being a reply ... to the objectionable statements made by Chenthinatha Iyer regarding the Shanars, *etc.* 1889. 12.° 14170. k. 47.

ṢENDINĀTH'-AIYAR, *Kāṣi-vāsi.* *See* [Addenda] BĀDARĀYAṆA. ஸ்ரீ ... சைவபாடியம். [Brahma-sūtram. With Tamil version of Ṣrī-kaṇṭha's Ṣivādvita-bhāshyam, translated by Ṣendināth'-aiyar.] [1907.] 8°. **14049. bb. 22.**

—— A Table of all the Tatwas according to the Suddhâdvaita Saiva-siddhânta System. Graphically and luminously presented by ... Sêntinâtha Aiyer ... உ சுத்தாத்துவித சைவ சித்தாந்த தத்துவப்படம். [*Madras,* 1899.] *s. s.* **14170. ee. 18.**

ṢENDU-LĀLĀ, *Sēlam.* ◦ ◦ ◦ பாஷிய ஒக்கபிலேரி. (Tamil, Telugu, English and Hindustani Vocabulary.) Second edition. pp. 91. *Madras,* 1883. 16°. **14172. h. 32.**

—— Third edition. pp. 91. *Madras,* 1884. 16°. **14172. h. 33.**

ṢEṄGALVA-RĀYA MUDALIYĀR, *Karuvūr C. S.* *See* TIRU-VAḶḶUVAR. ◦ ◦ ◦ நவரத்தின வைத்திய-சிந்தாமணி ௸ [Nava-ratna-vaidya-chintāmaṇi, *etc.* Edited by Ṣeṅgalva-rāyar.] 1889. 8°. **14170. i. 21.**

ṢEṄGALVA-RĀYA PIḶḶAI, *V. Ṣ.* History of the Tamil Prose Literature. pp. 54, i. ii. *Madras,* 1904. 8°. **14172. hh. 20.**

ṢENNAI-ṢEN-DAMIṞ-URAI-SAṄGHAM. *See* ACADEMIES, *etc.—Madras.*

ṢENNA-VĪRAPPA CHEṬṬIYĀR, *Sēlam Ṣ.* கனகவல்லி. [Kanaka-valli. A romance, partly dramatic in form.] pp. i. 160; 1 *plate.* *Madras,* 1906. 8°. **14171. e. 11.**

SÊNTINÂTHA AIYER. *See* ṢENDINĀTH'-AIYAR.

ṢĒṞAI KAVI-RĀJA PIḶḶAI. ◦◦◦ திருக்காளத்திநாதருலா. [Tiru-kāḷatti-nāthar-ulā. A series of 578 Ṣaiva devotional stanzas on the cult of Kalahasti. Edited with notes by U. V. Sāmināth'-aiyar.] pp. ii. 10, 50. சென்னபட்டணம் [*Madras,*] 1904. 8°. **14170. eee. 6.**

ṢĒSHA AIYAR, *K. R.* *See* APPĀJĪ. The Tales of Royar Appaji ... [Translated] by K. R. Sesha Iyer. 1903. 12°. **14171. d. 1.(1.)**

ṢĒSHĀCHALAM NĀYUḌU, *Pōkala Rāma-gōpāla.* ◦◦◦ ஜடபரதோபாக்கியானம் ௸ [Jaḍa-bharatōpākhyānam. A prose romance, supposed to be narrated by Ṣuka to Parīkshit, telling of the enlightenment of Jaḍa-bharata and his adventures in various births, and so conveying principles of the Vaishṇava Vēdāntam. Translated from the Telugu by K. Varada-rājulu Nāyuḍu.] pp. i. 126. சென்னை [*Madras,*] 1898. 12°. **14170. ee. 26.**

—— ◦◦◦ ஸ்ரீகிருஷ்ணபோதாம்ருதமெனும் பன்னிரண்டு இராஜர்கள் கதை. [Pann'-iraṇḍu-rājargaḷ-kathai, or Ṣrī-kṛushṇa-bōdhāmṛutam. Romances of legendary kings, illustrating popular conceptions of the Vaishṇava system of Vedantic philosophy. Translated from the Telugu by Vīramuttu Mudaliyār.] pp. 2, 194. சென்னை [*Madras,*] 1897. 8°. **14171. a. 13.**

—— ◦ ◦ ◦ ஸ்ரீராமஹ்ருதயமென்னும் ஷட்சக்கரவர்த்திகளின் இந்திரஜாலக்கதைகள். [Shaṭ-chakravarttigaḷin indra-jāla-kathaigaḷ, or Ṣrī-rāma-hṛudayam. Tales of the magical adventures of legendary kings, illustrating popular conceptions of Vedantic philosophy, translated from the Telugu by K. Varada-rājulu Nāyuḍu.] pp. ii. 124. சென்னை [*Madras,*] 1898. 8°. **14171. a. 36.**

—— ◦ ◦ ◦ சுத்தநிராலம்பமார்க்கம். [Ṣuddha-nirālamba-mārgam, or Kṛushṇa-nṛugu-mahā-rāja-saṃvādam. A discourse on the Vaishṇava-Vedantic metaphysics. Translated from the Telugu by K. Varada-rājulu Nāyuḍu.] pp. 48. *Madras,* 1898. 12°. **14170. d. 63.**

ṢĒSHĀDRI ṢIVANĀR. நானாசீவவாதக்கட்டளை. [Nānā-jīva-vāda-kaṭṭaḷai, or Tattva-kaṭṭaḷai. A treatise upon the psychology and physiology of the Advaita-vēdāntam.] *See* RĀMA-SĀMI SVĀMI, *K. A.* நானாசீவவாதக்கட்டளை ௸ [Nānā-jīva-vāda-kaṭṭaḷai, *etc.*] pp. 1-25. [1887.] 12°. **14170. d. 26.**

—— ◦◦◦ நானாசீவவாதக்கட்டளை மூலமும் ... வியாக்கியானமும். [Nānā-jīva-vāda-kaṭṭaḷai. With copious catechetical commentary by Madurai Ṣivānanda Svāmi.] pp. 50, i. 664. தஞ்சை [*Tanjore,*] 1905. 12°. **14170. dd. 5.**

—— தத்துவக்கட்டளை. Tattuva-kaṭṭaḷei, Law of the Tattuvam. A synopsis of the mystical philosophy of the Hindûs, translated from the Tamiḷ, with notes. By Rev. Henry R. Hoisington. (Journal of the American Oriental Society. Vol. iv., pp. 1-30.) *Boston,* 1854. 8°. **Ac. 8824.(vol. 4.)**

ṢĒSHĀDRI ṢIVANĀR (*continued*). The Elements of the Vedantic Philosophy, translated from the Tamil, by Thomas Foulkes. (†Nānāsīvavāthakkattalei: or The Elements of the Controversy respecting the Plurality of Souls, by Sēshāttrisivatēsikar.) pp. 33. *Madras*, 1860. 8°. 14170. e. 36.(1.)

—— Loi de la Fin des différents Êtres, Nânâdjîvavâdakaṭṭaḷei. [Translated by J. Vinson.] (Revue de Linguistique et de Philologie Comparée. Tome xxxv., pp. 163-180.) *Paris*, 1902. 8°. PP. 4964. d. (vol. 35.)

ṢĒSHĀDRIY-ĀCHĀRYAR, *Tiruvindaḷūr Para-vastu.* See NAÑ-JĪYAR. ००० ఆత్మవివాహం &c. [Ātma-vivāham, *etc.* Edited by Ṣēshādriy-āchāryar.] 1893. 8°. 14170. ee. 40.

ṢĒSHA-GIRI ṢĀSTRI, *Miṭṭādār.* Essay on Tamil Literature... Number i. pp. v. 60. *Madras*, 1897. 8°. 14172. hh. 14.

—— Tamil Literature. தமிழ்க்கவி சரிதம். pp. 72. *Madras*, 1904. 12°. 14172. g. 5.(1.)

—— Report on a Search for Sanskrit and Tamil Manuscripts for the year 1896-97 (*1893-94). By M. Seshagiri Sastri . . . Prepared under the orders of the Govt. of Madras. 2 vols. *Madras*, 1898-1899. 8°. *See* MADRAS, *Government of.* 14096. ccc. 2.

—— த்ரவிடசப்ததத்த்வம். பாகம்—க. வினையியல். (Tamil Philology. Part i. Verbs.) pp. 5, i. 146. *Madras*, 1899. 8°. 14172. e. 31.

ṢĒSH'-AIYAṄGĀR, *D.V.* Athiyuravadhani, or The Self-made Man. An original Tamil Novel [in verse], delineating pictures of modern Hindu life. By Professor Sashiengar. (*ஆதியூர் அவதானி சரிதம்.) pp. i. i. i. 100, i. *Madras*, 1875. 8°. 14170. k. 30.

ṢĒSH'-AMMĀḶ, *Kumbhaghōṇam.* த்ருவசரித்திரகீர்த்தனை. [Dhruva-charitra-kīrttanai. Religious lyrics founded upon the story of Dhruva.] pp. 39. கும்பகோணம் துர்முகி [*Kumbakonam*, 1897.] 8°. 14172. b. 44.(6.)

ṢEYAṄGOṆḌĀN. *See* JAYAṄ-GOṆḌĀN.

SEYMER (JOHN GUNNING). தமிழும் இங்கிலிசுமாகிய முதலாவது வாசிப்பு பொஸ்தகம் . . . First Tamil and English Reading Book. pp. ii. iv. 90. *Madras*, 1850. 8°. 14172. h. 93.

ṢEYY'-APPA MUDALIYĀR, *P.T.* தமிழ் வித்தியார்த்தி விளக்கம். [Tamiẓ-vidyārthi-viḷakkam.] (General Tamil. Ever indispensable to students of all classes, both in High Schools and Colleges. By P. T. Saiyappa Modelliar.) pt. i. pp. vi. 94. *Madras*, 1894. 8°. 14172. hh. 9.

SHĀH al-ḤAMĪD ibn 'AIDARŪS. فوائد القران للمهمات منافع الاسماء والطلسمات [Fawā'id al-ḳur'ān. A treatise on the use of Koranic texts, prayers, pious formulæ, and mystic diagrams, for talismanic purposes.] pp. 544, *lith.* مدراس ۱۳۲۳-۲۴ [*Madras*, 1905-1906.] 8°. 14173. c. 1.

—— مفتاح الصلاح فى ايضاح النكاح [Miftāh al-ṣalāh. A treatise on marriage and sexual intercourse.] pp. viii. 240, *lith.* بمدراس ۱۳۲۰ [*Madras*, 1902.] 8°. 14173. b. 45.

—— Mifthahussalah fee eilahinnikkah. மிபுத்தாஹுஸ்ஸலாஹ் பீ, யீலாஹின்னிக்காஹ். [Another edition in the Tamil character.] pp. iv. 200. திருவல்லிக்கேணி [*Triplicane*,] 1905. 8°. 14170. g. 26.

SHĀH al-ḤAMĪD ibn ḤASAN ḲUDDŪS, *Mīrān Sulṭān* (MĪRĀN ṢĀḤIB ĀṆḌAVAR), *of Nagur.* [*Life.*] *See* MUḤAMMAD IMĀM GHAZZĀLĪ ibn MUḤAMMAD 'ALĪ. கலறத்து மீருன்சாகிபு ஆண்டவரவர்கள் காரணசரித்திரம். [Ḥaẓrat Mīrān Sāḥib Āṇḍavar-avargaḷ kāraṇa-charitram.] [1876.] 8°. 14173. b. 34.

SHĀH al-ḤAMĪD ibn MĪRĀN ṢĀḤIB, *Mēlapāḷaiyam Attiyaditteru.* இ○○து . . . கந்தூரி அலங்காரச்சிந்து. [Muḥyi-al-dīn-āṇḍavargaḷ-kandūri-alaṅkāra-ṛayil-vaẓi-naḍai-chindu. Verses on a railway journey to Kanduri and on Muḥyi al-Dīn, a local Moslem devotee.] pp. 12. திருநெல்வேலி [*Tinnevelli*,] 1907. 12°. 14172. a. 52.(2.)

—— இ○○து சங்கீத சிந்தாமணி. [Saṅgīta-chintāmaṇi. A collection of Muhammadan devotional lyrics by Shāh al-Ḥamīd, Ḥasan 'Alī Pulavar, *etc.* Edited by Kaṇṇ'-Aḥmad Makhdūm Muḥammad.] pp. iv. i. 176. சென்னை தருடாமடு [*Madras*, 1897.] 8°. 14173. b. 12.

SHAIKH MUḤYI al-DĪN, *K. M.* *See* [Addenda] MUḤYI al-DĪN ibn ḤAMĪD MUḤYI al-DĪN.

SHAIKH TAMBI PĀVALAR, *Kōṭṭāṟu Fakīr Mīrān.* *See* BADR al-DĪN, *Pulavar.* முகியித்தீன்புராணம். [Muhyi-al-dīn-purāṇam. Edited by Shaikh Tambi.] 1901-1903. 8°. **14172. bb. 1.**

—— *See* 'UMAR, *Poet.* சீறாப்புராணம் [Ṣīrā-purāṇam. With paraphrase by Shaikh Tambi.] 1902, *etc.* 8°. **14173. b. 18.**

—— எட்டுக் கிரிமினல் கேஸ். (Eight Criminal Cases. [Travesties of 8 myths, in the form of law-court reports.] By K. P. Shaikuthambi Pavalar.) pp. viii. 263. *Madras,* 1907. 8°. **14171. e. 17.**

SHAKSPERE (WILLIAM). *See* KANDA-SĀMI PILLAI, *Madurai Ā.* விகடசுந்தரி ௲ (Vigata Sundari.) [A romance based on Shakspere's "Taming of the Shrew."] 1906. 8°. **14171. e. 8.**

—— *See* NAṬĒSA ṢĀSTRI, *Ṣ. M.* Measure for Measure, a tale from Shakespeare, *etc.* 1893. 12°. **14171. a. 6.(1.)**

—— *See* NAṬĒSA ṢĀSTRI, *Ṣ. M.* Twelfth Night . . . [A prose abstract] in Tamil, *etc.* 1892. 12°. **14170. l. 1.(2.)**

—— *See* RĀMA-SĀMI AIYAṄGĀR, *Ṣ.* Suguna-Sukesar . . . A Tamil drama [based upon Shakspere's "Two Gentlemen of Verona"], *etc.* 1899. 12°. **14170. l. 48.(2.)**

—— *See.* SARASA-LŌCHANA CHEṬṬI, *T. R.* Sarasangi. A Tamil drama . . . [adapted from "Cymbeline"]. 1897. 8°. **14170. l. 45.**

—— விப்ரம விஹாஸம். (Vibhrama Vihasam. Shakespeare's Comedy of Errors.) [Translated by Anbil Vēṅkaṭāchāryar.] 1905-1906. *See* PERIODICAL PUBLICATIONS.—*Srirangam.* ஸ்ரீ வாணி விலாஸினி (Sri Vani Vilasini.) vol. i.-ii. 1905, *etc.* 8°. **14172. m. 1.(vol. 1-2.)**

—— வெனிஸ் வர்த்தகன் (Shakespeare's Merchant of Venice, in Tamil, by S. V. Kallapiran Pillai.) pp. xxv. 169, 14. *Madras,* 1904. 12°. **14171. i. 1.(2.)**

Forms no. 1 *of the* Dravidian Research Institute Series.

—— Shakespeare's Midsummer Night's Dream. Translated into Tamil [prose] by S. Narayanaswamy Aiyer. (*நடுவேனிற்கனவு.) pp. 78, i. *Tanjore,* 1893. 8°. **14170. l. 32.(1.)**

—— ஷேக்ஸ்பியர் நாடகங்கள். க. ஒதெல்லோ என்ற வெநிஸ் மோரியன். (Shakespeare for Tamil Homes. I. Othello. [Translated into Tamil prose, with life of the poet and notes,] by A. Madhaviah.) pp. xii. 192; 1 *plate. Madras,* 1902. 12°. **14171. i. 1.(1.)**

SHAṆMUKHA GRĀMAṆI, *Kaḍalūr.* பள்ளிகள் வாயாப்பு. [Paḷḷigaḷ-vāyāppu. A tract, in dialogue form, maintaining the claims of the Shanar caste to Kshatriya origin, as against the Palli caste.] pp. iii. 54. சென்னை [*Madras,*] 1892. 12°. **14170. g. 17.(1.)**

—— சான்றோராகிய சூரியசந்திரவம்ஸபரம்பரை சரித்திரம். [Sūrya-chandra-vaṃṣa-param-parai-charitram. Traditions of the solar and lunar races, and the claims of the Shanar caste to Kshatriya origins on these grounds.] pp. vi. 90. சென்னை [*Madras,*] 1889. 12°. **14170. k. 46.**

SHAṆMUKHA KAVI-RĀJAR, *Taraṅgāpuram.* *See* VILLIPUTTŪRAR. இதிகாசமாகிய ஸ்ரீமகாபாரத ௲ [Mahā-bhārata-vachanam. A prose paraphrase by Shaṇmukha of Nallā Piḷḷai's adaptation of Villiputtūrar's Bhāratam.] [1847-1854.] 4°. **14172. dd. 2.**

—— *See* VILLIPUTTŪRAR. இதிகாசமாகிய . . . மஹாபாரத ௲ [Draviḍa-mahā-bhārata-vachanam. The paraphrase by Shaṇmukha of Nallā Piḷḷai's Bhāratam.] 1880. 4°. **14172. dd. 4.**

—— *See* VILLIPUTTŪRAR. ஐந்தாம்வேதமாகிய ஸ்ரீமகாபாரதம். [Mahā-bhāratam. The paraphrase by Shaṇmukha of Nallā Piḷḷai's Bhāratam.] 1900. 4°. **14172. dd. 3.**

SHAṆMUKHAM PIḶḶAI, *Ṣōṟavandān A.* ००० மாலைமாற்றுமாலை மூலமும் . . . உரையும். [Mālai-māṭṭu-mālai. A series of artificial verses. Edited with commentary by M. R. Kanda-sāmi Kavirāyar.] pp. 32. மதுரை [*Madura,*] 1903. 8°. **14172. bb. 3.(5.)**

SHAṆMUKHAM PIḶḶAI, *K. P.* The Life of Empress Victoria, *etc.* (†விக்டோரியா சக்கிரவர்த்தினியார் சரித்திரம்.) pp. xii. i. 228; 6 *plates. Madras,* 1902. 12°. **14171. a. 44.**

SHAṆMUKHAM PIḶḶAI, *Pāḷaiyaṅkōṭṭai Veṅkaṭāchalam.* திருவிளையாடற்புராண சங்கிரகம். [Tiru-viḷaiy-āḍaṟ-purāṇa-saṅgraham. A metrical summary of the Tiru-viḷaiy-āḍaṟ-purāṇam of Parañ-jōdi. With preface by Vaḷḷi-nāyaka Svāmi.] pp. xi. 68, ii. vii. பாளையங்கோட்டை [*Palamcotta*,] 1901. 8°. **14170. ee. 5.(2.)**

SHAṆMUKHAM PIḶḶAI, *Tirumayilai*. *See* ITIHĀSA-MAÑJARI. Ithihasa Manjari Series. [A collection of works in prose versions by Shaṇmukham.] [1888]-1894. 8°. **14172. d. 11.**

—— *See* KAMBAN. ஸ்ரீ . . . ராமாயணம் ஆ [Kamba-rāmāyaṇam, Ayōdhyā-kāṇḍam. With paraphrase, *etc.*, by Shaṇmukham.] 1896. 8°. **14172. d. 17.**

—— *See* KAṆṆ'-UḌAIYA VAḶḶAL. மாயாப்பிரலாபம். [Māyā-pralāpam. Edited by Shaṇmukham.] [1869.] 16°. **14170. d. 8.(1.)**

—— *See* POYYĀ-MOḺI PULAVAR. தஞ்சைவாணன்கோவை ஆ [Tañjai-vāṇan-kōvai. Edited by Shaṇmukham.] 1893. 8°. **14172. b. 53.**

—— *See* PURĀṆAS.—*Matsya-purāṇam*. ∘∘∘ மச்சபுராணம். [Matsya-purāṇam. Edited by Shaṇmukham.] 1900. 8°. **14170. ee. 43.**

—— *See* ṢĀTTAN. மணிமேகலை. [Maṇi-mēkhalai. Edited by Shaṇmukham.] 1894. 8°. **14172. b. 50.**

—— *See* ṢIVA-VĀKYAR. சிவவாக்கியர் பாடல். [Siva-vākyar-pāḍal. Edited by Shaṇmukham.] 1891. 8°. **14172. b. 43.**

—— *See* VIDYĀ-VINŌDINI. வித்தியாவிநோதினி. (Vidhya Vinodhini Series.) [Edited by Shaṇmukham and others.] [1889]-1892. 8°. **14172. c. 39.**

SHAṆMUKHAM PIḶḶAI, *T.*, *disciple of Rājagōpāla Piḷḷai*. *See* VIRŪPĀKSHI LIṄG'-AIYAR. திரு . . . தென்திருபதிபுராணம் ஆ [Ten-tirupadi-purāṇam. Edited by Shaṇmukham.] [1890.] 8°. **14170. e. 49.**

SHAṆMUKHA MUDALIYĀR, *Maṅgalam*. *See* SIVA-RAHASYAM. ரிபுகீதை ஆ [Ṛibhu-gītai-tiraṭṭu. Edited with notes by Vaḍi-vēlu and Shaṇmukha.] 1906. 16°. **14170. dd. 15.**

SHAṆMUKHA MUDALIYĀR, *R.*. *See* TĀYUMĀNAVAR. Thayumanavar's Poems. [With translation by Shaṇmukha.] 1897, *etc.* 4°. [*Siddhanta Deepika.*] **14170. fff. 4.(vol. 1, etc.)**

—— *See* TĀYUMĀNAVAR. The Philosophical Poem of . . . Tháyumánavar . . . Translated . . . by R. Shanmuga Mudaliar. 1897. 12°. **14170. d. 47.**

SHAṆMUKHA ÑĀNIYĀR, *Tirupādiripuliyūr*. முருகர்அந்தாதி. [Mṛugar-antādi. A hymn to Skanda.] pp. 13. *See* SUNDARA MUDALIYĀR, *T.* ∘∘∘ திருமுருகாற்றுப்படை ஆ [Tiru-mṛug'-āṭṭu-paḍai, *etc.*] pt. iii. [1890.] 16°. **14172. a. 32.(3.)**

SHAṆMUKHA-NĀTHA KAVI-RĀYAR. Life of Shanmuganadha Kavirayar [a native Christian]. சண்முகநாத கவிராயர் ஜீவிய விருத்தாந்தம். pp. 55. *Madras*, 1902. 12°. **14171. a. 46.**

SHAṆMUKHA-SUNDARA MUDALIYĀR, *K.* *See* ĀGAMAS. ஸ்ரீமத் ஸகலாகமஸார ஸங்க்ரஹம். [Sakalāgama-sāra-saṅgraham. With introduction by Shaṇmukha-sundara.] [1900.] 8°. **14033. aa. 11.**

—— *See* ĀGAMAS. ஸ்ரீமத் . . . காரணாகமம் ஆ [Kāraṇāgamam. Edited with introduction, *etc.*, by Shaṇmukha-sundara.] [1900-1902.] 8°. **14033. aa. 8.**

—— *See* ĀGAMAS. ∘∘∘ பௌஷ்கராகமம் ஆ [Paushkarāgamam. With interpretation and commentary by Shaṇmukha-sundara.] [1890.] 12°. **14028. b. 65.**

—— *See* UMĀ-PATI ṢIVĀCHĀRYAR. ∘∘∘ சிவப்பிரகாசம் ஆ [Ṣiva-prakāṣam, *etc.* Edited by Shaṇmukha-sundara, with commentaries.] [1895.] 12°. **14170. d. 37.**

—— *See* UYYA-VANDA DĒVA-NĀYANĀR, *Tiruviyalūr*. திருவுந்தியார் ஆ [Tiruv-undiyār, *etc.* Edited by Shaṇmukha-sundara.] [1896.] 12°. **14170. d. 65.**

SHAṆṆAVATĪ. *See* NṚUSIṂHA BHĀRATĪ. *Begin.* ஸ்ரீ೦ ஜௌ ஸ்ரீஜ ம ஸ ... ஜாதிய உவாள் etc. [Pastoral letters on the relations of the brahmans holding the Shaṇṇavatī *agrahāram* to the Sringeri monastery.] [1865.] 16°. **14058. a. 5.(1.)**

SHARJĪ. *See* AḤMAD ibn AḤMAD.

SHĀẔILĪ. *See* 'ALĪ ibn 'ABD ALLĀH (ABU al-ḤASAN).

SHIHĀB al-DĪN AḤMAD, *al-Sharjī al-Yamanī*. *See* AḤMAD ibn AḤMAD, *al-Sharjī al-Zabīdī*.

SICÉ (F. EUGÈNE). *See* KANDA-SĀMI PULAVAR, *Madurai*. Vyavahara-sara-sangraha, *etc.* (*Législation Hindoue . . . Traduite du Tamil par F.-E. Sicé.) 1857. 8°. **14170. g. 14.**

SIDDHARGAL. ◦◦◦ ஆத்மரக்ஷாமிர்தமென்னும் வயித்தியசாரசங்கிரகம் [Ātma-rakshāmirtam, or Vaidya-sāra-saṅgraham. A treatise on medicine, ascribed to the legendary eighteen Siddhars. Edited by K. V. Kanda-sāmi Mudaliyār. Second edition.] pp. 546, ii. xxiii. ௧௮௭௪ [*Madras*, 1874.] 8°. **14170. i. 42.**

—— ◦◦◦ பெரிய ஞானக்கோவை [Periya-ñāna-kōvai. A collection of religious poems by the 18 Ṣaiva Siddhars and others, the most important being—Ṣiva-vākyar's Pādal; Paṭṭaṇattu Pillai's Pādal, Pulambal, and Ñānam; Bhadra-giriyār's Pulambal; Pāmb'-āṭṭi Siddhar, Iḍai-kāṭṭu Siddhar, and Agappey Siddhar's Pādal; Koṅgana Nāyanār's Vālai-kummi; the Karuvūrār-pūjā-vidhi; the Ñāna-sara-nūl, with prose exposition; the Ṣivānanda-bōdham, Neñj'-aṟi-viḷakkam, Ñāna-kummi; K. Rāma-liṅga Pillai's Pādal and Ṣiva-nāmāvaḷi-tiraṭṭu, *etc.* Compiled by Rāma-liṅga Mudaliyār.] 2 vols. சென்னை [*Madras*,] 1899. 12°. **14170. ee. 33.**

A collection of pamphlets, each with its own pagination.

—— ◦◦◦ பெரிய ஞானக்கோவை. [Periya-ñāna-kōvai. Another publication, containing the same works with a few additions and omissions.] 2 pts. சென்னை [*Madras*,] 1906. 12°. **14170. dd. 12.**

The pagination of pt. 2 *is* 1–216, 289–336, 264–300.

—— ◦◦◦ வாதக்கோவை மூலமும்-பொழிப்புரையும். [Vāta-kōvai. Verses on medicine and chemistry, ascribed to the 18 legendary Siddhars. Compiled with paraphrase by M. Vaḍi-vēlu Mudaliyār.] pp. 120. சென்னை [*Madras*,] 1901. 8°. **14170. ee. 60.**

—— பதினெண்சித்தர்கள் திருவாய்மலர்ந்தருளிய வயித்தியத்திரவுகோல். [Vaidya-tiravu-kōl. A handbook of medicine in verse and prose, ascribed to the 18 Siddhars. With some additions by Vīrōjī Rāu and others.] 12 pts. சென்னை [*Madras*,] 1896. 8°. **14170. i. 47.**

—— ◦◦◦ வைத்தியஅனுபோகசாரசங்கிரகம் [Vaidya-anubhōga-sāra-saṅgraham. A treatise on medicine, based on the works ascribed to the legendary 18 Siddhars.] 1893. 8°. *See* Tiru-veṅ-gidāchāri, *T. K.* **14170. i. 34.**

SIDDI LEBBE (M. C.). *See* Muhammad Kāsim ibn Siddīk.

SINDHU-RĀYALU, *T.*, **and JONAS,** *T. C. R.* Baradha Sungeeta Swayabodini. பரத சங்கீத சுய போதினி. Or Violin Self-Instructor. For the use of beginners. Containing directions for tuning & playing, illustrations, exercises &c., with a selection of popular tunes. By T. Chindurayeloo and T. C. R. Johannas. pt. i. pp. iv. 60. *Madras*, 1895. 12°. **14170. i. 45.**

ṢIṄGĀRA-BALAVĒNDRAM PILLAI, *P.* A Tamil Vade-mecum, or Guide to ungrammatical expressions used in ordinary conversation . . . for the use of foreigners. Compiled and published by P. Singarapelavanderam Pillay. Sections i.-v. pp. 4, 320. *Madras*, 1859. 8°. **14172. h. 85.**

The Prospectus of the work announced ten sections.

ṢIṄGĀRA-VĒLU MUDALIYĀR, *A., of Pachaiyappa's College. See* Mey-kaṇḍa-ṣāttiram. ◦◦◦ சைவசித்தாந்தசாத்திரம் ௵ [Mey-kaṇḍa-ṣāttiram. Edited by Ṣiṅgāra-vēlu.] [1899.] 12°. **14170. d. 53.**

ṢINNA GAUṆḌAR. உண்ணாமுலையம்மன் சதகம். [Uṇṇā-mulaiy-amman-ṣatakam. A Ṣaiva devotional poem.] *See* Ell'-appa Nāvalar. அருணாசலபுராணம் ௵ [Aruṇāchala-purāṇam.] pp. 625-661. 1903. 12°. **14170. d. 83.**

ṢINN'-AIYĀ MUDALIYĀR, *Hariharabāḍi.* சாதிசமயாசாரவிளக்கம். [Jāti-samayāchāra-viḷakkam. A tract expounding and advocating the observances of caste.] pt. i. pp. 20. சென்னை [*Madras*,] 1896. 16°. **14170. g. 21.**

ṢINNA-SVĀMI MUDALIYĀR, *A. M.* Oriental Music, in European notation. A monthly periodical by A. M. Chinnaswami Mudaliyar, M.A. With words [chiefly Telugu] in English, Telugu and Tamil characters. nos. 1-6. *Madras*, 1892. Fol. **14053. g. 13.**

—— nos. 1-10. *Madras*, 1895. Fol. **14053. g. 14.**

ṢINNA-TAMBI PILLAI, *C.* *See* Jeremiah (S. S.).

ṢINNA-TAMBI PILLAI, *Valvai.* கோணேசர்கல்வெட்டு [Kōṇēṣar-kal-veṭṭu. Verses upon the Ṣaiva cult at Trincomali.] pp. 38. வல்வை சர்வதாரி [*Valuvettiturai*, 1888.] 8°. **14170. e. 48.(2.)**

ṢINNA-TAMBI PULAVAR, *Nallūr.* ◦◦◦ கல்வளையந்தாதி ௵ [Kal-vaḷaiy-antādi. Songs in honour of the god of Kalvalai. With commentary by Valvai Ṣ. Vaidya-liṅga Piḷḷai.] pp. 83. வல்வை சர்வசித்து [Valuvettiturai, 1887.] 16°. 14172. a. 3.

—— கல்வளையந்தாதி. [Kal-vaḷaiy-antādi.] pp. 15. சென்னபட்டணம் ஜய [Madras, 1894.] 12°. 14172. a. 45.(2.)

—— ००० மறைசையந்தாதி மூலமும் . . . உரையும். [Maṟai-ṣaiy-antādi. 100 devotional verses on the cult of Ṣiva at Vēdāraṇyam. With a commentary by U. A. Ṣiva-ṣambhu Pulavar.] pp. 42. யாழ்ப்பாணம் [Jaffna,] 1893. 8°. 14170. e. 45

ṢINNAVĀPPU MARAIKKĀYAR, *Taḷavāy M.* *See* HURMUZ. ஹுர்முஜ்கதை.[Hurmuz-kathai. Translated by Ṣinnavāppu.] 1904. 8°. 14173. b. 41.

—— *See* [Addenda] JURJĪ ZAIDĀN. ‘கஸ்ஸான் கன்னிகை ௸ [Ghassān - kannigai - charitram. Translated from Zaidān's "Fatāt Ghassān" by Aḥmad Ghanī, and recast into literary style by Ṣinnavāppu.] 1908. 8°. 14170. k. 3.

—— அற்புத வல்லிக் கதை. [Aṟpuda-valli-kathai. A romance.] சிங்கப்பூர் [Singapore,] 1908, *etc.* 12°. 14171. d. 1.(3.)

In progress.

ṢINNA-VĪRAPPA CHEṬṬI, *Agaram Muttu-māri.* ஆண்டாகுப்பம் பாலசுப்பிரமணியர்பேரில் பாமாலைவிருத்தம் ௸ [Bāla-subrahmaṇyar pēril pāmālai-vṛuttam, Paṟaniy-āṇḍavar-kīrttanai, Ānanda-kaḷippu, Ṣennai-ēga-valliy-amman-kīrttanai, and Peṇ-buddhi-mālai. Ṣaiva religious and ethical lyrics.] pp. 13. சென்னை ஜய [Madras, 1894.] 8°. 14170. e. 47.(6.)

ṢINNAYA CHEṬṬI, *Dēvikoṭṭai Lakshmaṇa* (LAKSHMAṆA CHEṬṬI). திருவெற்றியூர்ப்புராணம். [Tiru-veṭṭiyūr-purāṇam. The sacred legends of Tiruvettiyur, South Madras, in verse. With preface by A. S. Subrahmaṇya Cheṭṭi.] pp. i. i. iii. 122. சென்னபட்டணம் பிலவ [Madras, 1901.] 8°. 14170. ee. 52.

ṢIṞIYA RATNA KAVI-RĀYAR, *son of Tirumēni Ratna Kavi-rāyar.* ००० புலவராற்றுப்படை. [Pulavar-āṭṭu-paḍai. A panegyric poem upon Iraṣai Vaḍa-malaiy-appa Piḷḷai.] pp. 21. 1903. *See* ACADEMIES, *etc.*—*Madura.* ["Ṣen-damiṟ" supplement.] no. 3. 1902, *etc.* 8°. 14172. i. 1.*(no. 3.)

ṢIṞU-PIḶḶAIGAḶ. சிறுபிள்ளைகள் வாசிக்கப் பழகிறதற்காகச் செய்த புத்தகம் [A Tamil first reading-book.] 2 pts. pp. 48, 64. *Manepy*, 1835. 16°. 14172. h. 1.(1.)

—— சிறுபிள்ளைகளுக்கு . . . முதற்புத்தகம். Tamil Series. No. i. [A Tamil primer.] pp. 72. *Madras*, 1841. 16°. 14172. h. 35.(1.)

ṢIṞUVAR. சிறுவரெண்சுவடி. [Ṣiṟuvar-eṇ-ṣuvaḍi. An arithmetic for children.] pp. 36. புதுவை துஅாசுரு [Pondicherry, 1863.] 12°. 14172. h. 4.

—— சிறுவர்கல்விப்புதையல். [Ṣiṟuvar-kalvi-pudaiyal. A collection of verses from standard Tamil poets, for use in elementary schools.] pp. 169. புதுவை துஅசுச [Pondicherry, 1864.] 12°. 14172. h. 19.

—— சிறுவர்சுவடி. [Ṣiṟuvar-ṣuvaḍi. A Tamil spelling-book, with easy reading lessons from Auvaiyār and others.] pp. 48. புதுவை துஅாசுரு [Pondicherry, 1863.] 12°. . 14172. h. 14.

ṢISHṬA-DĒṢIKAR. குருஸ்தோத்திரகதம்பம் சிஷ்டதேசிகத்துவய பத்ததி. [Ṣishṭa-dēṣika-dvaya-paddhati. Ṣaiva rituals. Preceded by Guru-stōtra-kadambam, a series of hymns in Tamil and Sanskrit. Edited by P. V. Bāla-dēṣika Nāyanār.] pp. 4, 11, 15, iv. 202. சென்னை [Madras,] 1903. 12°. 14170. d. 86.

ṢIṢIRA-KUMĀRA GHŌSHA. ஸ்ரீக்ருஷ்ண சைதன்ய ஸ்வாமிகள் சரித்திரம் ௸ (Sri Krishna Chaitanya: His Life and Teachings. Salvation for all. [Translated chiefly from the "Lord Gauranga" of Ṣ. Ghōsha] by T. Bhaktavatsalam . . . V. Venkata Srinivasan. With an introduction in English by N. Balasubramanya Mudaliar.) pp. xxxii. 329, i.; 1 *plate.* *Madras*, 1902. 8°. 14170. ee. 51.

Forms no. 1 of the Sri Krishna Sahaya Series.

SĪTĀ-PATI NĀYAKAR, *Tiruvallikkēṇi.* *See* TIRU-VEṄKAṬĀCHALA KAVI-RĀYAR. ००० வல்லாளமகாராசன்கதை [Vallāḷa-mahā-rājau-kathai. Edited by Sītā-pati.] [1879.] 8°. 14170. k. 13.

SĪTĀ-RĀMA ṢĀSTRI, *Kuṟalmaṇam Lakshmī-nārāyaṇa.* സ്കന്ദാനന്ദനർത്തനഗീതം [Skandānanda-narttana-gītam. Devotional lyrics to the god Skanda.] pp. 122, ii. പാലക്കാട [Palghat, 1902.] 12°. 14170. d. 74.

SĪTĀ-RĀM-PRASĀD, *of Hindu Religious School, Purasawakam.* See VĒMANA. தெய்வீகத்தன்மைபொருந்திய வேமன்ன . . . பத்தியங்கள்-ா. [Padyangaḷ. Edited, with Tamil paraphrase, by Sītā-rām-prasād.] 1892. 8°. **14174. k. 48.(1.)**

ṢITTAMBALA-NĀḌIGAḶ, *Ṣīgāṛi.* துகளறுபோதம். (†சிற்றம்பலநாடிவெண்பா.) [Tugaḷ-aṛu-bōdham and Ṣiṭṭambala-nāḍi-veṇ-bā. Poems upon the Ṣaiva creed.] pp. 2, 38, 3, 9. 1898. See VĒDĀCHALAM PIḶḶAI. சித்தாந்தஞானபோதம். [Siddhānta-ñāna-bōdham.] pt. i. 1898. 8°. **14170. ee. 39.**

ṢIṬṬAMBALA-TAMBIRĀN SVĀMI, *Tiruvāvaḍuduṛai.* See UYYA-VANDA DĒVA-NĀYANĀR, *Tiruviyalūr.* திருவுந்தியார் ஷ [Tiruv-undiyār. With commentary by Ṣiṭṭambala-tambirān.] [1896.] 12°. **14170. d. 65.**

—— See UYYA-VANDA DĒVA-NĀYANĀR, *Tiruviyalūr.* திருவுந்தியார். [Tiruv-undiyār. With commentary by Ṣiṭṭambala-tambirān.] 1897. 8°. [*Mey-kaṇḍa-ṣāttiram.*] **14170. ff. 3.**

ṢIVA. Siva-prakasha Kaṭṭaḷai: or The Elements of the Saiva Philosophy. Translated from the Tamil, by the Rev. Thomas Foulkes. pp. 25. *London, Madras,* 1863. 8°. **14170. e. 36.(5.)**

—— சிவபூசைதிரட்டு . . . பஞ்சபூதத்தலத்தேவாரப்பதிகங்கள். [Ṣiva-pūjai-tiraṭṭu. A ritual of Ṣaiva worship; to which is added Pañcha-bhūta-tala-dēvāra-padigangaḷ, a series of hymns belonging to the Dēvāram. Edited by K. S. Bālasubrahmaṇya Mudaliyār.] pp. ii. 116; 7 *plates.* யுவ [*Madras,* 1875.] 12°. **14170. d. 11.**

ṢIVA-CHIDAMBARA AIYAR, *Kārainagar.* காளிகதிரேசரடைக்கலப்பத்து. [Kāli-kadirēṣar-aḍaikkala-pattu. Ten stanzas in honour of Ṣiva.] pp. 8. *Colombo,* 1887. 16°. **14170. d. 5.(2.)**

—— முனீசுரர் நவமணி மாலை. [Munīṣurar-nava-maṇi-mālai. Songs in honour of Ṣaiva devotees.] pp. 10. *Colombo,* 1887. 12°. **14172. a. 6.(2.)**

ṢIVA-CHIDAMBARA MUDALIYĀR, *Tirupādiri-puliyūr K.* See ARUṆA-GIRI-NĀTHA SVĀMI. ∘∘∘ திருப்புகழ். [Tiru-pugaṛ. Edited by Ṣiva-chidambara.] 1894-1901. 8°. **14172. b. 51.**

—— See BĀLA-SUBRAHMAṆYA PIḶḶAI, *T.N.* ∘∘∘ ஆக்னேயபுராண சார ஷ [Vanniya-nāṭakam. Edited by Ṣiva-chidambara.] 1902. 8°. **14170. l. 58.**

ṢIVA-KOṚUNDU DĒṢIKAR, *Koṭṭaiyūr.* See TIRU-MUṚAI.—*Tiru-vāchakam.* திருவாசகம். [Tiru-vāchakam. Edited by Siva-koṛundu.] [1857.] 8°. **14172. b. 15.**

ṢIVA-LINGAM PIḶḶAI, *R., of Bhavani.* See KAPILAR. The Song of Kapila: being a translation in blank verse of the . . . Kapilar Agaval, by R. Sivalingam Pillay. 1901. 8°. **14172. bb. 3.(1.)**

ṢIVA-LINGAM PIḶḶAI, *Rāmānujapuram Tāṇḍavarāya.* See TIRUVAIGAVUR. திருவைகாவூர்ப்புராணம். [Tiruvaigāvūr-purāṇam. Edited by Ṣivalingam.] [1894.] 8°. **14170. e. 56.**

ṢIVA-LINGA NĀYANĀR, *Ṣāṅgu-siddha Raṅg'-aiyar.* பூரணாநந்தோதயம். [Pūraṇānandōdayam. A series of poems on the Ṣaiva theosophy and the worship of Ṣiva as the only real being. Edited by Vairakkaṇ Vēlāyudha Pulavar.] pp. xiii. 110, ii. i. சென்னை [*Madras,*] 1879. 8°. **14172. b. 11.**

ṢIVA-ÑĀNA SVĀMI, *Tiruvāvaḍuduṛai.* See MEY-KAṆḌA DĒVAR. ∘∘∘ சிவஞானபோதம் ஷ [Ṣiva-ñāna-bōdham. With the smaller commentary by Ṣiva-ñānar.] [1885.] 12°. **14170. d. 1.**

—— See MEY-KAṆḌA DĒVAR. Sivagnana Botham . . . with notes [based upon the commentary of Ṣiva-ñanar,] *etc.* 1895. 8°. **14170. e. 51.**

—— See MEY-KAṆḌA DĒVAR. சிவஞானபோதம். [Ṣiva-ñāna-bōdham. With the smaller commentary by Ṣiva-ñānar.] 1897. 8°. [*Mey-kaṇḍa-ṣāttiram.*] **14170. ff. 3.**

—— See MEY-KAṆḌA DĒVAR. ∘∘∘ சிவஞானபோதம் ஷ [Ṣiva-ñāna-bōdham. With Ṣiva-ñānar's larger commentary, styled Drāviḍa-mahā-bāḍiyam (°bhāshyam) or Ṣiva-ñāna-bhāshyam, supplemented by his smaller commentary. With English preface and biography of Ṣiva-ñānar.] 1906. 8°. **14170. eee. 15.**

—— See MEY-KAṆḌA DĒVAR. ∘∘∘ சிவஞானபோதம் ஷ [Ṣiva-ñāna-bōdham. With Ṣiva-ñānar's shorter commentary throughout, and larger commentary on vi.-xii.] [1906.] 8°. **14170. ff. 20.**

—— See PAVAṆANDI. ∘∘∘ நன்னூல் ஷ [Nannūl. With commentary of Ṣaṅkara Namaṣ-ṣivāyar, as revised by Ṣiva-ñānar.] [1851.] 8°. **14172. f. 2.**

ṢIVA-ÑĀNA SVĀMI, *Tiruvāvaḍuduṟai (continued).* *See* PAVAṆANDI. நன்னூல் மூலம் [Nan-nūl. With the commentary by Ṣaṅkara Namaṣ-sivāyar, as revised by Ṣiva-ñānar.] [1887.] 8°. **14172. e. 12.**

—— —— [1903.] 8°. **14172. e. 39.**

—— *See* SARVĀTMA-ṢAMBHU ṢIVĀCHĀRYAR. ◦◦◦ சித்தாந்தப்பிரகாசிகை. [Siddhānta-prakāṣikai. Translated by Ṣiva-ñānar.] 1897. 12°. **14170. d. 32.(3.)**

—— ◦◦◦ காஞ்சிப்புராணம். [Kāñchi-purāṇam. The local Ṣaiva legends of Conjevaram. The first part by Ṣiva-ñānar, and the second part by his disciple Kachiy-appar. Edited with commentary by T. K. Subba-rāya Cheṭṭi.] சென்னை விருத்தி [*Madras*, 1891, *etc.*] 4°. **14172. f. 14.**
Incomplete, extending only to p. 680.

—— ◦◦◦ சித்தாந்தமரபுகண்டனகண்டனம், சிவசமவாதவுரைமறுப்பு... வைரக்குப்பாயம்... சிவசமவாதவுரைமறுப்பு. [Siddhānta-marabu-khaṇḍana-khaṇḍanam; Ṣiva-samavādav-urai-maṟuppu and another work of the same name, also called Ṣiva-samavāda-khaṇḍanam; and Vaira-kuppāyam. Four polemical tracts on behalf of the Ṣaiva creed. Edited by Sabhā-pati Nāvalar.] pp. vi. 77. சிதம்பரம் விஜய [*Chidambaram*, 1893.] 8°. **14170. e. 63.**

ṢIVA-ÑĀNA YŌGI, *Virudai, of Virudubaṭṭi.* *See* TYĀGA-RĀJA DĪKSHITAR. விபூதிருத்திராக்ஷதாரண மூலம் [Vibhūti-rudrāksha-dhāraṇa-nirūpaṇam. With notes by Ṣiva-ñānar.] 1901. 12°. **14170. d. 85.(1.)**

—— பூதிருத்திராக்கதூஷண கண்டனம். [Bhūti-rudrākka-dūshaṇa-khaṇḍanam. A defence of the Ṣaiva practice of smearing the body with burnt cow-dung and wearing rosaries of *elæocarpus* berries, in answer to objections raised against Tyāga-rāja Dīkshitar's work on the subject.] pp. 68. சென்னை [*Madras*,] 1901. 12°. **14170. d. 85.(2.)**

—— ◦◦◦ ஆ. கருத்தமுத்துப்பிள்ளை . . . சரித்திரம். [Karutta-muttu-piḷḷai-charitram. A biography of Karutta-muttu Piḷḷai, of Ettayapuram, followed by short elegies by various authors.] pp. 15. திருநெல்வேலி [*Tinnevelli*,] 1897. 12°. **14171. aa. 5.**

ṢIVĀNANDA-BŌDHAM. சிவானந்தபோதம் [Ṣivānanda-bōdham. A poem on Ṣaiva metaphysics.] pp. 46. *See* SIDDHARGAḶ. ◦◦◦ பெரிய ஞானக்கோவை [Periya-ñāna-kōvai.] 1899. 12°. **14170. ee. 33.**

—— —— pt. ii. 1906. 12°. **14170. dd. 12.**

ṢIVĀNANDA-SĀGARA YŌGĪṢVARAR, *Tiruṣirapuram.* *See* UPANISHADS. கைவல்யபாஷ்யம். [Kaivalya-bhāshyam. Translated by Ṣivānanda-sāgara.] 1898. 8°. **14170. ee. 31.**

—— *See* VĒDAS. ◦◦◦ புருடசூக்தபாஷ்யம். [Purusha-sūkta-bhāshyam. Translated by Ṣivānanda-sāgara.] 1894. 8°. **14170. ee. 30.**

ṢIVĀNANDA SVĀMI, *Madurai, of Dakshiṇāmūrti-svāmi-maṭham, Tiruvalur.* *See* ṢĒSHĀDRI ṢIVANĀR. ◦◦◦ நானாஜீவவாதக்கட்டளை மூலம் [Nānā-jīva-vāda-kaṭṭaḷai. With commentary by Ṣivānanda.] 1905. 12°. **14170. dd. 5.**

ṢIVAN PIḶḶAI, *Vīrākshi-maṅgalam T.* *See* GĀṄGĒYAR. ◦◦◦ உரிச்சொல்நிகண்டு. [Uri-chol-nighaṇṭu. Edited by Ṣivan Piḷḷai.] [1890.] 12°. **14172. e. 15.**

—— *See* PIṄGALAR. ◦◦◦ பிங்கலந்தை மூலம் [Piṅgala-nighaṇṭu. With commentary by Ṣivan Piḷḷai. Edited by the latter.] 1890. 8°. **14172. f. 14.**

ṢIVA-PRAKĀṢA DĒṢIKAR, *Tuṟaimaṅgalam.* ◦◦◦ பழமலையந்தாதி. திருச்செந்திநிரோட்டகயமகவந்தாதிமூலபாடம். [Paṟa-malaiy-antādi and Tiruchendin-nirōṭṭaga-yamakav-antādi. Lyrics on two Ṣaiva sanctuaries, the latter being composed without any labial sounds. Edited by Ṣara-vaṇa Peru-māḷ Aiyar.] pp. 19. நந்தன [*Madras*, 1832.] 8°. **14172. b. 23.(1.)**

—— ◦◦◦ நால்வர்நான்மணிமாலை. [Nālvar-nān-maṇi-mālai. Panegyrical verses on four Ṣaiva saints. With copious commentary by Chidambaram Rāma-liṅga Svāmi.] pp. 137. சென்னை நன்முறி [*Madras*, 1896.] 12°. **14170. d. 27.**

—— [For texts of the Nan-neṟi with Ṣara-vaṇa Peru-māḷ's commentary printed together with Auvaiyār's Vākk'-uṇḍām and Nal-vaṟi:] *See* AUVAIYĀR.—*Two or More Works.*

ṢIVA-PRAKĀṢA DĒṢIKAR, *Turaimaṅgalam* (*continued*). நன்னெறி. [Nan-neri. An ethical poem.] *See* TAMIL MINOR POETS. Tamil Minor Poets, *etc.* pp. 26-31. 1864. 16°. **14172. a. 17.**

—— —— pp. 35-43. 1868. 16°. **14172. a. 18.**

—— நன்னெறி. [Nan-neri. With commentary.] *See* TAMIL MINOR POETS. Tamil Minor Poets, *etc.* pp. 89-108. 1865. 16°. **14172. a. 16.**

—— Nanneri, *etc.* [In English.] *See* TAMIL MINOR POETS. Tamil Minor Poets, *etc.* pp. 30-35. 1872. 12°. **14172. c. 6.**

—— *See* MṚUGĒṢA MUDALIYĀR, *T.* நீதிமஞ்சரித்தருப்பணம். [Nīti-mañjari-darpaṇam. Interpretations of ethical works of Ṣiva-prakāṣar and others.] 1881-1883. 16°. **14172. a. 8.**

—— பிரபுலிங்கலீலை வசனம். [Prabhu-liṅga-līlai-vachanam. A prose paraphrase by K. Rāmasāmi Nāyuḍu of the Prabhu-liṅga-līlai, a poem on a myth of Ṣaiva theosophy, adapted from Chāmarasa's Kanarese poem of the same name. With a life of Ṣiva-prakāṣar.] pp. 3, 179. மதராஸ் [*Madras*,] 1903. 8°. **14170. ee. 62.**

The original Sanskrit Prabhu-liṅga-līlā, of which Chāmarasa's work is a version, is ascribed to the Bhavishya-purāṇam.

—— சோணசைலமாலை. [Sōṇa-ṣaila-mālai. A hymn on Saiva legends and doctrine, composed on a visit to the sanctuary of Tiruvanamalai.] *See* ELL'-APPA NĀVALAR. அருணாசலபுராணம் ௸ [Aruṇāchala-purāṇam.] pp. 403-422. 1898. 12°. **14170. d. 52.**

—— —— pp. 515-534. 1902. 12°. **14170. d. 75.**

—— —— pp. 515-534. 1903. 12°. **14170. d. 83.**

—— ... சோணசைலமாலை. சிவநாமமகிமை. [Sōṇa-ṣaila-mālai. Followed by Ṣiva-nāma-mahimai, another Ṣaiva hymn. Edited with interpretation and commentary by K. V. Tiru-vēṅkaṭa Nāyuḍu.] pp. ii. 118, vi. i. சென்னை விகாரி [*Madras*, 1899.] 12°. **14170. d. 60.**

—— வேதாந்தசூளாமணி ௸ [Vēdānta-chūḷāmaṇi. A Ṣaiva theological treatise, adapted from the Brahma-sūtram. With a commentary by Piṟaiṣai Aruṇāchala Svāmi.] pp. xii. ii. 300, iii. [*Madras*,] 1861. 8°. **14170. e. 14.**

—— [16 occasional verses, with interpretation.] *See* TANI-PĀḌAL. (†தனிப்பாடற்றிரட்டு) [Tani-pāḍaṯ-tiraṭṭu.] pp. 189-199. [1892, *etc.*] 8°. **14172. c. 39.(5.)**

ṢIVA-PRAKĀṢA PAṆḌITAR, *Nīrvēli Ṣ.* *See* VENṞIMĀLAI KAVI-RĀJAR. ... திருச்செந்தூர்ப்புராணம். [Tiruchendūr-purāṇam. Edited with commentary by Ṣiva-prakāṣar.] 1907. 8°. **14172. bb. 26.**

—— Tamil Second (*Third) Book. By S. Sivapirakasa Panditbar ... பாலபாடம் ௸. 2 pts. கொக்குவில் யாழ்ப்பாணம் [*Kokkuvil, Jaffna*, 1886-1893.] 12°. **14172. h. 69.**

Bk. ii. (Kokkuvil, 1893) appears to be a first edition; bk. iii. (Jaffna, 1886) is a third edition.

—— [Third book. Third edition.] pp. 126. யாழ்ப்பாணம் [*Jaffna*,] 1890. 12°. **14172. h. 96.**

ṢIVA-PRAKĀṢA SVĀMI, *Nan-nūl.* *See* ṢIVA-PRAKĀṢA SVĀMI, *Turaiyūr.* அத்துவிதவெண்பா ௸ [Advita-veṇ-bā. With commentary by Nan-nūl Ṣiva-prakāṣa.] [1885.] 8°. **14172. c. 32.**

ṢIVA-PRAKĀṢA SVĀMI, *Turaiyūr, disciple of Namaṣ-ṣivāya-mūrtti, and son of Vēḷān Cheṭṭi.* அத்துவிதவெண்பா மூலம். [Advita-veṇ-bā. 407 *veṇ-bā* quatrains on the Advaita system. With a commentary by Nan-nūl Ṣiva-prakāṣa Svāmi, the sixth guru in succession from him, and a life of the poet compiled from a work of Tiruvāvaḍuduṟai Ambala-vāṇa Dēṣikar. Edited by Tuṟaiyūr Ṣokka-liṅga Ṣiva-prakāṣa Svāmi and M. Mṛugēṣa Mudaliyār.] pp. xviii. 167. சென்னபட்டணம்தாரண [*Madras*, 1885.] 8°. **14172. c. 32.**

According to the biography, the author was fourth in spiritual succession from the great Umā-pati (14th century), whom he visited.

ṢIVA-PRAKĀṢA-TAMBIRĀN SVĀMI, *Tiruvāvaḍuduṟai.* *See* UYYA-VANDA DĒVA-NĀYANĀR, *Tiruviyalūr.* திருவுந்தியார் ௸ [Tiruv-undiyār. Followed by the Tiru-kaḷiṭṭu-paḍiyār of Tirukaḍavūr Uyya-vandar. With commentary on the latter by Ṣiva-prakāṣa-tambirān.] [1896.] 12°. **14170. d. 65.**

ṢIVA-PRAKĀṢA-TAMBIRĀN SVĀMI, *Tiruvāvaḍu-durai (continued).* *See* UYYA-VANDA DĒVA-NĀYANĀR, *Tirukaḍavūr.* திருக்களிற்றுப்படியார். [Tiru-kaḷiṭṭu-paḍiyār. With commentary by Ṣiva-prakāṣa-tambirān.] 1897. 8°. [*Mey-kaṇḍa-ṣāttiram.*] **14170. ff. 3.**

ṢIVA-RAHASYAM. ரிபுகீதைத் திரட்டு குறிப்-புரையுடன். [Ribhu-gītai-tiraṭṭu. 874 stanzas from Ulaga-nātha Svāmi's metrical version in 1924 *vruttam* stanzas of the Ribhu-gītā, a poetical exposition of monistic philosophy, purporting to belong to pt. 6 of the *itihāsa* styled Ṣiva-raha-syam. Edited with notes by G. Vaḍi-vēlu Cheṭṭi and M. Shaṇmukha Mudaliyār.] pp. vi. i. 477. *Madras,* 1906. 16°. **14170. dd. 15.**

ṢIVA-RĀMA-LIṄG'-AIYAR, *Nallūr Raghu-nāth'-aiyar.* *See* EPHEMERIDES. ○○○ நந்தனவருஷ . . . பஞ்சாங்கம் . . . Tamil Calendar, *etc.* [Calculated for 1897-98 by Ṣiva-rāma-liṅg'-aiyar.] [1891-1896.] 8°. **14172. i. 11.**

ṢIVA-RĀMA MUDALIYĀR, *Ṣ. Ṣ.* *See* KANDA-SĀMI PULAVAR, *M.* வியவகாரசாரசங்கிரகம். [Vyavahāra-sāra-saṅgraham. Edited by Ṣiva-rāma.] 1894. 8°. **14170. g. 16.**

ṢIVA-RĀU, *A., of Kuttalam.* *See* BĀDARĀYAṆA. The Brahma Sutra Artha Deepika . . . Published by:—A. Siva Row, *etc.* 1904, *etc.* 4°. **14170. fff. 5.**

—— *See* NIṢCHALA DĀSA. விசாரசாகரம் ஆ [Vichāra-sāgaram. Translated by Ṣiva-rāu, with a Brahma-ñāna-churukkam or synopsis of the Vē-dāntam appended.] 1893. 8°. **14170. e. 53.**

—— —— 1904. 8°. **14170. ff. 12.**

SIVA ROW. *See* ṢIVA-RĀU.

ṢIVA-ṢAMBHU PULAVAR, *Uḍuppiṭṭi A.* *See* ṢINNA-TAMBI PULAVAR, *N.* ○○○ மறைசையந்தாதி ஆ [Maṟai-ṣaiy-antādi. With commentary by Ṣiva-ṣambhu.] 1893. 8°. **14170. e. 45.**

—— புலோலி நால்வர்நான்மணிமாலை . . . ஊஞ்-சல் ஆ [Nālvar-nān-maṇi-mālai, Ūñjal, *etc.* Hymns to the gods worshipped at Puloli.] pp. 35. வல்-வை சர்வசித்து [*Valuvettiturai,* 1888.] 16°. **14170. d. 5.(3.)**

ṢIVA-ṢAMBHU PULAVAR, *Uḍuppiṭṭi A. (continued).* குகமயம் திருச்செந்திலயமகவந்தாதி [Tiru-chendil-yamakav-antādi. A poem of 100 stanzas in honour of the god Skanda.] pp. 20. வல்வை சர்வசித்து [*Valuvettiturai,* 1888.] 16°. **14172. a. 4.(1.)**

—— குகமயம் திருச்செந்திற்றிருக்கந்தாதி [Ti-ruchendiṟ-ṟirukk' antādi. A Ṣaiva hymn.] pp. 20. வல்வை சர்வதாரி [*Valuvettiturai,* 1888.] 16°. **14170. d. 5.(4.)**

ṢIVA-ṢAṄKARA-MŪRTTI PIḶḶAI, *Paṟaṅgipeṭṭai A.* பழநிப்பாமாலை. [Paṟani-pā-mālai. A series of devotional poems on the Ṣaiva cult of Palni.] pp. ix. i. 128. சென்னை கஅஉ௫ [*Madras,* 1904.] 12°. **14170. d. 91.**

ṢIVA-ṢAṄKARA PAṆḌYĀJĪ, *R.* *See* MAHĀ-BHĀRATAM. Tamil translation of Mahabharata Niti Ratnavali . . . Edited by R. Sivasankara Pandiya. 1888. 12°. **14003. c. (no. 9.)**

—— *See* VĀLMĪKI. Ramayana Niti Ratnavali . . . Edited by R. Sivasankara Pandiah. 1886. 12°. **14003. e. (no. 6.)**

—— *See* VIMALA-CHANDRA SŪRI. The Aryan Catechism . . . Edited by R. Sivasankara Pandiah. 1887. 12°. **14003. c. (no. 7.)**

—— Arya Niti Mata Bodhini: First Book of Aryan Morality and Religion . . . containing excel-lent stanzas from ancient Sanskrit works with Tamil and English translations and explanations, &c. Edited by R. Sivasankara Pandiyaji. pp. 70. *Madras,* 1891. 12°. **14003. c. (no. 1.)**

Forms no. 1 *of the* Hindu Excelsior Series. *The Sanskrit is in the Tamil character.*

ṢIVA-ṢAṄKARA PAṆḌYĀJĪ, *R.,* **and VARAD'-AYYA,** *C.* திராவிட பால நீதி போதினி. Dravida Bala Niti Bodhini: the Tamil Juvenile Moral Instructor: containing excellent moral maxims in Tamil, with English translations and useful information about Hinduism, &c. pp. 48. *Ma-dras,* 1889. 12°. **14003. c. (no. 11.)**

Forms no. 11 *of the* Hindu Excelsior Series.

ṢIVA-ṢAṄKARA TAMBIRĀN, *Villiputtūr.* *See* SABHĀ-PATI MUDALIYĀR, *K.* சைவசமயவிளக்க ஆ [Ṣaiva-samaya-viḷakka-vinā-viḍai. Edited by Ṣiva-ṣaṅkara.] [1879.] 16°. **14170. d. 14.**

ṢIVA-SHAṆMUKHA MEY-ÑĀNA ṢIVĀCHĀRYA SVĀMI. *See* CHIDAMBARA-NĀTHA MUNIVAR. ○○○ திருப்பாதிரிப் புலியூர்ப் புராணம். [Tirupādiri-puliyūr-purāṇam. Edited by Ṣiva-shaṇmukha.] 1896. 12°. **14170. d. 40.**

ṢIVA-SHAṆMUKHAM PIḶḶAI, *Ēgai.* ○○○ கண்டி-ராஜா நாடகம். [Kaṇḍi-rājā-nāṭakam, or Kīrtti-ṣiṅga-mahā-rājan-charitram. A drama on the history of King Kīrtti-siṃha of Kandy.] pp. 4, 126. சென்னை [*Madras,*] 1906. 8°. **14171. k. 3.**

ṢIVA-SUBRAHMAṆYA AIYAR, *B.R.* *See* RĀJAM AIYAR.

ṢIVA-VĀKYAR. சிவவாக்கியர் பாடல். [Pāḍal. 330 stanzas, expounding theism and attacking popular superstitions. Edited by T. Shaṇmukham Piḷḷai.] pp. 38, i. சென்னை [*Madras,*] 1891. 8°. **14172. b. 43.**

—— சிவவாககியர்பாடல. [Pāḍal. 518 stanzas. Edited by M. Vaḍi-vēlu Mudaliyār. Revised edition.] pp. 83. 1900. *See* SIDDHARGAḶ. ○○○ பெரிய ஞானக்கோவை [Periya-ñāna-kōvai.] 1899. 12°. **14170. ee. 33.**

—— —— 1906. 12°. **14170. dd. 12.**

—— பெரிய சிவவாக்கியர்பாடல் மூலமும்—உரையும். [Periya-ṣiva-vākyar-pāḍal. 518 stanzas. With commentary by M. Vaḍi-vēlu Mudaliyār.] pp. 4, 380. [*Madras,*] 1904. 12°. **14170. dd. 3.**

SKETCHES. Brief and familiar Sketches of the different Countries of the World. Book i.–Europe. Book ii.—Asia. (*பலதேசசரித்திரச்சுருக்கம்.) 2 pts. *Madras,* 1857. 12°. **14172. h. 56.**

SNAKES. Snakes, Crocodiles, and other Reptiles. பாம்பு, முதலே முதலிய ஊர்வன. (The Anna Library.) pp. 53. *Madras,* 1898. 12°. **14170. i. 10.**

ṢOKKA-LIṄGA CHEṬṬI, *Kāraikuḍi Rāma-nātha.* திருவுசாத்தானமாகிய சூதவனபுராணம் ஆ [Sūta-vana-purāṇam. The legends of the Ṣaiva sanctuary at "Sūta-vanam" or Tiruvuṣātānam (Kōyil-ūr, near Muttupet, Tiruturaipundi *taluk,* Tanjore *zillah*), metrically rendered, with a prose paraphrase. With a preface by Ā. R. Ch. Chidambara Cheṭṭi.] pp. 23, 206, 52, 2. மதுரை [*Madura,*] 1905. 8°. **14170. eee. 13.**

ṢOKKA-LIṄGA CHEṬṬI, *Kāraikuḍi Rāma-nātha* (*continued*). திருப்புத்தூர்ப்புராணம். [Tiruputtūr-purāṇam. A poem on the legends of the Ṣaiva sanctuary at Tiruputur. Preceded by extracts from the Dēvāram, *etc.*] pp. xiv. ii. iv. 169. சென்னை விளம்பி [*Madras,* 1898.] 8°. **14170. ee. 24.**

ṢOKKA-LIṄGA ṢIVA-PRAKĀṢA SVĀMI, *Tuṟaiyūr.* *See* ṢIVA-PRAKĀṢA SVĀMI, *Tuṟaiyūr.* அத்துவித-வெண்பா ஆ [Advita-veṇ-bā. Edited by Ṣokka-liṅga.] [1885.] 8°. **14172. c. 32.**

ṢOKKA-NĀTHA PIḶḶAI, *Palabaṭṭaḍai.* (†தேவையுலா) [Tēvaiy-ulā. Ṣaiva devotional verses on the cult of Ramnad. Edited with notes by U. V. Sāmināth'-aiyar.] 1907. *See* ACADEMIES, *etc.*—*Madura.* ["Ṣen-damiḻ" supplement.] no. 24. 1902, *etc.* 8°. **14172. i. 1.*(no. 24.)**

ṢOKKA-NĀTHA PULAVAR. [40 occasional verses, with interpretation.] *See* TANI-PĀḌAL. (†தனிப்பாடற்றிரட்டு) [Tani-pāḍaṭ-ṯiraṭṭu.] pp. 216-234.] [1892, *etc.*] 8°. **14172. c. 39.(5.)**

ṢOKK'-APPA NĀVALAR, *Kunṟattūr Ashṭāvadhāni.* *See* POYYĀ-MOḺI PULAVAR. தஞ்சைவாணன் கோவை ஆ [Tañjai-vāṇan-kōvai. With commentary by Ṣokk'-appa.] 1893. 8°. **14172. b. 53.**

ṢŌLAI-MUTTU PIḶḶAI, *Karandaiyambadi Ṣiva-rāma.* *See* TIRUVADI. ஸ்ரீ . . . திருவையாற்றுப்புராணம். [Tiruv-aiy-āṭṭu-purāṇam. Stylistically recast by Ṣōlai-muttu Piḷḷai.] 1907. 8°. **14170. eee. 22.**

SŌMA-DĒVA, *son of Rāma.* கதாசரித் சாகரம் (Kathasarithsagaram . . . in Tamil. [Translated from Sōma-dēva's Sanskrit tales] by V. B. Venkata-rama Sastry.) *Madras,* 1905, *etc.* 8°. **14171. e. 5.**

In progress. Forms no. 1 *of the* Subōdha-pārijātam Series.

SŌMĀ-SKANDA BHAṬṬĀRAKAR, *M., of Vedaraṇyam,* *See* PARAÑ-JŌDI MUNIVAR. ○○○ வேதாரணியபுராணம். [Vēdāraṇya-purāṇam. Edited by Sōmā-skanda.] [1899.] 12°. **14170. d. 54.**

SŌMA-SUNDARA MUDALIYĀR, *of Saram, Pondicherry.* இரணிய நாடகம். [Hiraṇya-nāṭakam. A drama founded on the legend of the impious Daitya king Hiraṇya-kaṣipu, his pious son Prahlāda, and

the salvation of the latter by Vishṇu incarnated as the Man-lion. Edited by T. Rāma-chandra Kavi-rāyar.] pp. 360. *Madras*, 1888. 8°.
14170. l. 27.

SŌMA-SUNDARA NĀYAKAR, *Ṣūlai*. சித்தாந்தரத்நாகரம். [Siddhānta-ratnākaram. A collection of Ṣaiva theological works, viz. Ṣuklāmbaradhara-ṣlōka-vichāram, Āchārya-prabhāvam, Brahma-vidyā-vikarpa-nirasanam, Ṣiva-tattva-chintāmaṇi, Ābhāsa-ñāna-nirōdham, Ṣiva-pāramya-pradarṣini, Sama-rasa-ñāna-dīpam, Ṣrī-ṣekkiṛār-tiru-vākk'-uṇmai, Siddhānta-ṣēkharam, Ṣivādhikya-ratnāvali, *etc.* Second edition, edited by P. Appāvu Cheṭṭi.] சென்னை [*Madras*,] 1906, *etc.* 8°.
14170. eee. 14.
In progress.

—— கூரேசவிஜயபங்கம். [Kūrēsa-vijaya-bhaṅgam. A Ṣaiva polemical work against the Vaishṇava legends and doctrine contained in the Kūrēṣa-vijayam. Followed by some verses of Kāḷa-mēgha Pulavar.] pp. 128, 2, 2. *Madras*, 1886. 8°.
14170. e. 27.

—— பாஞ்சராத்திரமதசபேடிகை என்னும் சைவசூளாமணி. [Ṣaiva-chūḷāmaṇi. A controversial work defending the Ṣaiva Sakti system against the Pāñcharātra doctrines.] pp. 172. *Madras*, 1883. 8°.
14170. e. 20.

SŌMA-SUNDARA PILḶAI, *Ṣ., of Mailapur*. அளவியல் என்னும் தருக்க விளக்கம். [Tarka-viḷakkam, or Aḷav'-iyal. A treatise upon the logic of the Vaiṣēshika school.] pp. viii. vi. x. 127. *Madras*, 1907. 12°.
14170. d. 34.
No. 1 of the Mati-vanappu-chĕy Series.

SŌMA-SUNDARA UPĀDHYĀYAR, *Nalla-tambi*. *See* SAMBANDHA-ṢARAṆĀLAYA SVĀMI. ००० கந்தபுராண ஸ் [Kanda-purāṇa-churukkam. Edited by Sōma-sundara.] [1848.] 8°.
14170. e. 5.

SOOBBOROYA MOODELIAR (C. RAJAH). *See* SUBBA-RĀYA MUDALIYĀR.

SOOBROYA MODELLIAR. *See* SUBBA-RĀYA MUDALIYĀR.

SOPHOCLES. ००० வீலநாடகம். (Veelanatakam. A translation into Tamil blank verse of Sophocles' 'Philoctetes' by T. Lakshmana Pillay.) pp. v. i. 52. *Madras*, 1894. 8°.
14170. l. 32.(2.)

ṢORNA-ṢĀSTRI, *K., of Devakota*. *See* ĀRŪḌHA-ṢĀSTRAM. ००० ஞானப்ரதீபிகை ஸ் [Ārūḍha-ṣāstram. With Tamil commentary by Sorna-ṣāstri and Ṣrīnivāsāchāryar, entitled Bhāva-prakāṣikai.] [1899.] 8°.
14053. ccc. 27.

SOUNDARARAJA. *See* SAUNDARA-RĀJA.

SPAULDING (LEVI). *See* BIBLE.—*Complete Bibles.* The Holy Bible . . . revised [by L. Spaulding and others], *etc.* 1850. 4°.
3070. d. 26.

—— *See* BUNYAN (J.). The Pilgrim's Progress, *etc.* [Translated by L. Spaulding.] [1853.] 12°.
14170. b. 19.

—— [A collection of Christian tracts, composed or translated into Tamil by L. Spaulding.] 31 pts. *Jaffna*, 1842-1845. 12°.
14170. b. 1.
Nos. 1, 3, 7, 9, 12, 13, 16, 17, 19, 24, 27*, 28–30, 35, 37, 39, 42–45, 48–54, 56, 56*, 57 *in order of binding.*

SPENER (PHILIPP JACOB). *See* LUTHER (M.). மார்த்தின் லுத்தர் என்பவரின் ஞானோபதேச ஸ் [Martin Luther enbavarin ñānōpadēṣa-kuripp'-idattai vistarikkum vinā-viḍaigaḷ. A catechism based upon Spener's "Einfache Erklärung der Christlichen Lehre."] 1872. 12°.
14170. b. 20.

SREENIVASA. *See* ṢRĪNIVĀSA.

SREERANGACHARIAR. *See* ṢRĪRAṄGĀCHĀRYAR.

ṢRĪDHARA NĀYUDU, *Kēṣava* (ṢRĪDHARA SVĀMI). [*Life.*] *See* TIRU-VEṄKAṬA-SVĀMI MUDALIYĀR, *S.* ஸ்ரீ . . . The Life of . . . Sridhara Svami. 1907. 12°.
14171. d. 9.

ṢRI-HARSHA. [For editions of the Naiḍadam, founded on the Naishadha-charita of Ṣrī-harsha:] *See* ATIVĪRA-RĀMA PĀṆḌIYAN.

ṢRĪ-KAṆṬHA PAṆḌITAR. ஜீவரக்ஷாமிர்தம். [Jīva-rakshāmirtam. A work on medicine, compiled from Sanskrit sources. Translated into Tamil by T. M. Subrahmanya Paṇḍitar.] pp. viii. viii. 367, xxx. i. ரக்தாட்சி [*Madras*, 1864.] 8°.
14170. i. 17.

ṢRĪ-KAṆṬHA ṢIVĀCHĀRYAR (NĪLA-KAṆṬHA), *disciple of Ṣvētāchāryar*. *See* [Addenda] BĀDA-RĀYAṆA. ஸ்ரீ . . . பிரமசூத்திர சிவாத்துவித சை-

வ்யாடியம். [Brahma-sūtram. With Tamil version of Srī-kantha's Sivādvita-bhāshyam or monistic Saiva exposition.] [1907.] 8°. 14049. bb. 22.

—— See BĀDARĀYAṆA. சங்கர . . . த்ராவிட-பாஷ்யம். [Brahma-sūtra-drāviḍa-bhāshyam. The Brahma-sūtram, with Tamil commentary based upon the works of Nīla-kaṇṭha, etc.] 1905. 8°. 14049. bb. 8.

ṢRĪNIVĀSA AIYAṄGĀR, *K. R.* See PERIODICAL PUBLICATIONS.—*Madras.* அபிநவ பத்திரிகை ௵ [Abhinava-patrikai. Edited by Srīnivāsa.] 1902. 8°. 14172. i. 2.

—— நன்றியறியாமகன். ஒரு தமிழ்க் கதை. (The Ungrateful Son. A Tamil novel.) pp. 140, i. *Madras*, 1901. 12°. 14171. a. 42.(2.)

Forms the 5*th* malar *of the* Inba-valli *Series.*

—— ப்ரிதுலை: ஓர் உழவன்மகள். ஒருசரித்திர விநோதகதை. (Prithula: the Farmer's Daughter. A historical romance in Tamil [with English introduction.]) pp. 4, 117. *Madras*, 1901. 12°. 14171. a. 42.(1.)

Forms the 19*th* malar *in the* Inba-valli *Series.*

—— வித்யாரண்யநகரம். (The City of Vidyaranya. A historical romance [upon the story of the foundation of Vizianagram,] in Tamil, by C. R. Sreenivasa Aiyangar.) pp. 2, 120. சென்னை [*Madras*,] 1901. 12°. 14171. a. 6.(5.)

ṢRĪNIVĀSA AIYAṄGĀR, *Maṇḍayam B.* See ĀṚVĀRGAḶ.—Nāl-āyiram.—*Selections.* The Nityânusandhânam Series . . . with word-for-word meaning . . . paraphrase . . . and English translation . . . Edited by M. B. Srinivasa Aiyangar. 1898, *etc.* 8°. 14170. ff. 4.

—— —— நித்தியாநுஸந்தானம். [Another edition, in Tamil only.] 1898, *etc.* 8°. 14170. ff. 5.

—— —— The Nityânusandhânam Series . . . With word-for-word meaning . . . paraphrase . . . and English translation. Kanarese language. Edited by M. B. Srinivasa Aiyangar. 1898, *etc.* 8°. 14176. b. 49.

—— —— ನಿತ್ಯಾನುಸನ್ಧಾನವು ॥ [Nityānusandhānam. Edited with Kanarese glossaries, paraphrases, *etc.*, by Srīnivāsa Aiyaṅgār.] 1898, *etc.* 8°. 14176. b. 48.

—— —— The Nityânusandhânam Series . . . with word-for-word meaning . . . paraphrase . . . and English translation. Telugu language. Edited by M. B. Srinivasa Aiyangar. 1898, *etc.* 8°. 14174. b. 51.

ṢRĪNIVĀSA AIYAṄGĀR, *M. Rāyilu.* See PURĀṆAS. —*Bhavishyōttara-purāṇam.* ००० சங்கரநாராயண-சுவாமிகோவில் மான்மியம். [Saṅkara-nārāyaṇa-svāmi-kōvil-mânmiyam. Rendered into prose by Srīnivāsa.] 1898. 12°. 14170. d. 45.(2.)

ṢRĪNIVĀSA AIYAṄGĀR, *Tiruneydānam Raṅgasāmi.* See VĒṄKAṬA-NĀTHA VĒDĀNTĀCHĀRYAR. ந்யாஸதசக ௵ [Nyāsa-daṣaka-veṇ-bā. A version, by Srīnivāsa, of Vēṅkaṭa-nātha's Nyāsa-daṣaka.] 1907. 16°. 14170. d. 33.(4.)

ṢRĪNIVĀSA AIYAṄGĀR, *V. V.* See SAMBANDHA MUDALIYĀR. லீலாவதி-சுலோசனை ௵ (†Lilavati Sulochana, *etc.*) [With introduction *etc.* by Srīnivāsa.] 1895. 8°. 14170. l. 35.

ṢRĪNIVĀSA APPAṄGĀR SVĀMI, *Vaittamānidhi Muḍumbai.* See PINB'-AṚAGIYA PERU-MĀḶ JĪYAR. ००० குருபரம்பராப்ரபாவம் ௵ [Guru-paramparā-prabhāvam. Edited by Srīnivāsa.] [1906.] 8°. 14170. ff. 22.

—— See PURĀṆAS.—*Varāha-purāṇam.* శ్రీ . . . కైశికపురాణం. [Kaiṣika-purāṇam. With Tamil commentary. Edited by Srīnivāsa.] [1904.] 8°. 14028. c. 49.(2.)

—— See VĀLMĪKI. அபயப்ரதாநஸாரம். [Abhaya-pradāna-sāram. Edited by Srīnivāsa.] [1891.] 8°. 14060. c. 32.(1.)

—— See YĀMUNĀCHĀRYAR. శ్రీ . . . ప్రమేయరత్నం ౹౹ [Pramēya-ratnam, *etc.* Edited by Srīnivāsa.] [1904.] 8°. 14170. ee. 6.(3.)

ṢRĪNIVĀSĀCHĀRYAR, *Kōṛiyālam V.* மைசூர் அரசு. (Mysore Arasu. A history in Tamil verse of the kings of Mysore.) 2 pts. சென்னை பிலவ-சுபகிருத் [*Madras*, 1901-1904.] 8°. 14170. k. 7.

ṢRĪNIVĀSĀCHĀRYAR, *Kōriyālam V.* (*continued*). புராணகதாஸாரம். [Purāṇa-kathā-sāram. A series of stories from the Purāṇas.] pt. i. pp. ii. 98. சென்னை [*Madras*,] 1895. 8°. **14170. ee. 7.**

ṢRĪNIVĀSĀCHĀRYAR, *Maṇḍayam Krushṇ'-ayyan.* *See* PIḶḶAI LŌKĀCHĀRYAR. ◦◦◦ அஷ்டாதஸரஹஸ்யங்கள். [Ashṭādaṣa rahasyangaḷ. Edited by Ṣrīnivāsāchāryar.] 1889. 8°. **14170. f. 12.**

—— *See* PIḶḶAI LŌKĀCHĀRYAR. ஸ்ரீ . . . ஸ்ரீவசநபூஷணம் ஷூ [Vachana-bhūshaṇam. Edited by Ṣrīnivāsāchāryar.] 1879. 8°. **14172. b. 10.**

ṢRĪNIVĀSĀCHĀRYAR, *Neḍumaram V. R.* *See* ĀRŪḌHA-ṢĀSTRAM. ◦◦◦ ஞானப்ரதீபிகை ஷூ [Ārūḍha-ṣāstram. With commentary by Ṣrīnivāsāchāryar and Ṣorna-ṣāstri, entitled Bhāva-prakāṣikai.] [1899.] 8°. **14053. ccc. 27.**

ṢRĪNIVĀSĀCHĀRYAR, *Pagaltīvaṭṭi, of Conjeevaram.* தத்துவவிளக்கம். [Tattva-viḷakkam. A tract on moral philosophy, in the form of a dialogue.] (Conjeeveram Oriental Litrary [*sic*] Series.) pt. i. pp. 69. *Conjeeveram*, 1902. 16°. **14171. f. 4.**

ṢRĪNIVĀSA DĒṢIKAR, *Ṣrīṣaila.* *See* VĒṄKAṬANĀTHA VĒDĀNTĀCHĀRYAR. த்ரமிடோபநிஷத்தாத்பர்யரத்நாவளி: [Dramiḍōpanishat-tātparya-ratnāvaḷi and Dramiḍōpanishat-sāra. With the Tamil commentaries respectively of Vēṅkaṭēṣāchāryar and Ṣrīnivāsa.] [1883-1904.] 4°. [*Bhagavad-vishayam.*] **14170. fff. 3.**

ṢRĪNIVĀSA DĪKSHITAR, *Kumbhaghōṇam Rāmasvāmi.* *See* KAMALĀKARA BHAṬṬAR. ஶூத்ரகமலாகரம் ‖ [Ṣūdra-kamalākara. Edited with commentary and Tamil translation by Ṣrīnivāsa.] 1901, *etc.* 4°. [*Brahma-vidyā.*] **14096. dd. 3.** (vol. 15, etc.)

—— *See* PERIODICAL PUBLICATIONS. — *Chidambaram.* ப்ரஹ்மவித்யா *etc.* [Brahma-vidyā. Edited by Ṣrīnivāsa.] [1886, *etc.*] 4°. **14096. dd. 3.**

—— *See* PURĀṆAS.—*Skanda-purāṇam.* சிவதத்துவசுதாநிதி. [Ṣiva-tattva-sudhā-nidhi. With Tamil version of Ṣrīnivāsa's commentary.] 1898. 8°. **14016. d. 54.**

ṢRĪNIVĀSA DĪKSHITAR, *Kumbhaghōṇam Rāmasvāmi* (*continued*). *See* UPANISHADS. உபநிஷத்வித்யா *etc.* [Upanishad-vidyā. Compiled and edited by Ṣrīnivāsa.] 1898-[1901.] 8°. **14010. cc. 13.**

—— *See* UPANISHADS. ◦◦◦ ஜாபாலோபநிஷத் ஷூ [Jābālōpanishad. With commentary of Ṣrīnivāsa.] 1900. 8°. **14007. b. 12.(2.)**

—— *See* UPANISHADS. கைவல்யபாஷ்யம். [Kaivalya-bhāshyam. Comprising the Kaivalya-upanishad with the commentary of Ṣrīnivāsa, translated from the Sanskrit.] 1898. 8°. **14170. ee. 31.**

—— *See* VĒDAS. ◦◦◦ புருஷசூக்தபாஷ்யம். [Purusha-sūktam. With commentary by Ṣrīnivāsa, translated into Tamil.] 1894. 8°. **14170. ee. 30.**

—— Transmigaration [*sic*] of Souls. An important doctrine of Hinduism . . . Translated from Tamil. pp. 28. *Chidambaram*, 1891. 8°. **4503. c. 24.(13.)**

ṢRĪNIVĀS'-AIYAṄGĀR, *Ṣrīnivāsapuram.* *See* PAÑCHA-TANTRAM. பஞ்சதந்திரக்கதை. [Pañcha-tantra-kathai. Edited by Ṣrīnivās'-aiyaṅgār.] 1852. 8°. **14170. k. 21.**

ṢRĪNIVĀSA MUDALIYĀR, *Kuvalai.* *See* ĀṞVĀRGAḶ.—Nāl-āyiram.—*Entire Canon.* திராவிடவேதம் ஷூ [Nāl-āyira-divya-prabandham. Edited by Ṣrīnivāsa.] [1861.] 8°. **14172. c. 16.**

ṢRĪNIVĀSA MUDALIYĀR, *Rāyapēṭṭai.* An Abridgment of Tamil Grammar. Simplified, with questions and exercises. (தமிழ் இலக்கணச்சுருக்கம்.) 2 pts. *Madras*, 1892-1893. 12°. **14172. e. 22.**

ṢRĪNIVĀSA RĀGHAVĀCHĀRYAR, *K.*, *of C. H. Orphanage, Vepery.* *See* ACADEMIES, *etc.*—Madras.—*University of Madras.* Notes on the Tamil text for the Matriculation Examination of 1888 . . . Pazhamozhi, &c. [annotated] by K. Srinivasaraghavacharyar. 1888. 12°. **14172. a. 41.**

ṢRĪNIVĀSA RĀGHAVĀCHĀRYAR, *K. I.* *See* PERIODICAL PUBLICATIONS.—*Madras.* The Somaravi . . . Edited . . . by C. E. Srinivasaragavacharriar, *etc.* 1895-1896. Fol. **14170. ccc. 1.**

ṢRĪNIVĀSA RĀGHAVĀCHĀRYAR, *Koṇḍaṅgi Kaṇḍāḍai.* See MAHĀ-BHĀRATAM. ஸ்ரீமஹாபாரதம் ௸ [Virāṭa-parvam. A prose version by Ṣrīnivāsa.] 1905. 8°. **14172. d. 1.**

—— See VĀLMĪKI. ஸ்ரீமத் வால்மீகி ராமாயண ௸ [Vālmīki-rāmāyaṇa-vachanam. Translated by Tāta-dēṣika and Ṣrīnivāsa.] 1902-1903. 8°. **14172. d. 26.**

ṢRĪNIVĀSA RĀGHAVĀCHĀRYAR, *Parandaṇḍalam Aṛagar-tirumalai Māḍabhūshi.* See VĀLMĪKI. ஸ்ரீ... ராமாயணம் ௸ [Rāmāyaṇam. Edited with introductions, glosses, and paraphrases in Tamil by Ṣrīnivāsa.] 1897, *etc.* 4°. **14068. c. 14.**

ṢRĪNIVĀSA RĀGHAVĀCHĀRYAR, *Piḷḷapākkam Vēlāmūr, of Ahōbila-maṭham.* See UPANISHADS. ००० நூற்றெட்டு உபநிஷத்துகள். [Nūṭṭ'-eṭṭu Upanishattugaḷ. Edited with commentaries by Ṣrīnivāsa.] 1887. 8°. **14010. dd. 2.**

ṢRĪNIVĀSA RĀGHAVĀCHĀRYAR, *T. E., of Presidency College, Madras.* See ACADEMIES, *etc.*—Madras.—*University of Madras.* Notes on the Tamil text for the Matriculation Examination of 1888. Bharata Venba [annotated] by . . . Srinivasa Raghavacharyar, *etc.* 1888. 12°. **14172. a. 41.**

—— அதிக கதாசங்கிரகம். (Adika Katha Sangraham, or Stories selected from the Indian Puranas. By the late T. E. Streenevasa Raghava Charriar.) pp. i. ii. 145. *Madras,* 1885. 12°. **14170. d. 23.**

ṢRĪNIVĀSA RĀGHAVĀCHĀRYAR, *Tirumalai Ī-chambāḍi, of Triplicane.* See AṚAGIYA-MAṆAVĀḶA PERU-MĀḶ. ஸ்ரீ . . . உபதேசரத்தினமாலை ௸ [Upadēṣa-ratna-mālai, *etc.* Edited by Ṣrīnivāsa.] [1836.] 8°. **14172. b. 3.**

ṢRĪNIVĀSA RĀGHAVĀCHĀRYAR, *Tirunīrmalai Aṛagar-tirumalai Māḍabhūshi.* See [Addenda] AṚAGIYA-MAṆAVĀḶA PERU-MĀḶ. ००० ஆசாரிய-ஹ்ருதயம் ௸ [Āchārya-hṛudayam. Edited by Ṣrīnivāsa.] 1906. 8°. **14170. ff. 24.**

ṢRĪNIVĀSA RĀGHAVĀCHĀRYAR, *U., of Rayapetta Wesleyan Mission College.* See BESCHI (C. G. E.). ஐந்திலக்கணத் தொன்னூல்விளக்கம் ௸ [Tonnūl-viḷakkam. Edited by Ṣrīnivāsa.] [1891.] 8°. **14172. f. 16.**

ṢRĪNIVĀSA RĀMĀNUJA-DĀSAR, *Rāyapēṭa Laksh-m'-ayya.* See ĀṚVĀRGAḶ.—Nāl-āyiram.—*Selections.* ००० నిత్యానుసంధానము ౖ॥ [Nityānusandhānam. With Telugu interpretation, *etc.*, by Ṣrīnivāsa.] 1906. 8°. **14170. eee. 21.**

ṢRĪNIVĀSA RĀU, *T.* See EPHEMERIDES. Universal Encyclopedic Calendar . . . by T. Streeneevasa Row. 1892. 8°. **759. h. 8.**

ṢRĪNIVĀSA ṢĀSTRI, *Kumbhaghōṇam Rāma-svāmi.* See ṢRĪNIVĀSA DĪKSHITAR, *K. R.*

ṢRĪNIVĀSA ṢĀSTRI, *T. S.* See ṢAṄKARĀCHĀRYAR. [*Doubtful and Supposititious Works.*] ஸௌந்தர்ய-லஹரீ *etc.* [Saundarya-laharī. With a Tamil interpretation styled Paramārtha-chandrikā by Ṣrīnivāsa.] 1907. 8°. **14049. b. 48.**

ṢRĪNIVĀSA SVĀMI, *Īchambāḍi.* See BĀDARĀYAṆA. శ్రీ...శ్రీమద్భాష్యార్థసంగ్రహం. [Brahma-sūtram. With Srīmad-bhāshyārtha-saṅgraham. Edited by Ṣrīnivāsa.] [1890.] 8°. **14048. c. 69.**

ṢRĪNIVĀSA TĀTĀCHĀRYAR, *T., disciple of Kṛushṇa Tātayāryar.* See VEṄKAṬA-NĀTHA VĒDĀNTĀCHĀRYAR. ஸ்ரீ . . . ஸ்ரீரஹஸ்யத்ரயஸாரः [Rahasya-traya-sāra. Edited by Ṣrīnivāsa.] 1889. 8°. **14048. c. 68.**

ṢRĪNIVĀSA TĀTĀCHĀRYA SVĀMI, *Addaṅgi-tirumalai Lakshmī-nṛusiṃha.* See ĀṚVĀRGAḶ.—Nāl-āyiram.—*Mudal-āyiram.* ००० ஸ்ரீ... திருப்பாவை. [Tiru-pāvai. Edited by Ṣrīnivāsa.] 1902. 12°. **14170. d. 76.**

—— See ĀṚVĀRGAḶ.—Nāl-āyiram.—*Tiru-vāy-moṛi.* ००० நம்மாழ்வாருடைய . . . திருவாய்மொழி ௸ [Tiru-vāy-moṛi. Edited by Ṣrīnivāsa.] [1899.] 8°. **14170. ff. 8.**

—— See MAHĀ-BHĀRATAM. ஸ்ரீபகவத்கீதை. [Bhagavad-gītā. Edited and translated by Ṣrīnivāsa and Rāma-sāmi.] [1899.] 16°. **14065. b. 19.**

—— See UPANISHADS. ००० தசோபநிஷத்த்ராவிடபாஷ்யம். [Daṣōpanishad-drāviḍa-bhāshyam. Compiled and edited by Ṣrīnivāsa.] [1897]-1898. 8°. **14010. dd. 14.**

ṢRĪNIVĀSA VARADĀCHĀRI, *T., of Kumbakonam.* The illustrated conversation and reading lessons with poetry. For the use of the Third Standard. Anglo Tamil & Telugu. Book i. Fifth edition. (T. Sreenivasavarada Chari & Co. Primary School Series.) pp. 64. *Kumbhakonam, Madras* [printed], 1902. 12°. **14172. g. 4.(1.)**

—— The illustrated conversation and reading lessons with poetry for the Fourth Standard. Anglo Tamil and Telugu. Book ii. (T. Sreenivasavarada Chari & Co. Primary School Series.) pp. 64. *Kumbakonam, Madras* [printed], 1902. 12°. **14172. g. 4.(2.)**

ṢRĪRAṄGĀCHĀRYAR, *T. K., of Church of Scotland Mission College, Madras.* ஸ்ரீராமாநுஜசரிதம். [Rāmānuja-charitam.] (The Life of Sri Ramanuja, in Tamil prose, by T. K. Sreerangachariar.) pp. viii. 96, ii. *Madras,* 1901. 12°. **14171. a. 48.(1.)**

ṢRĪRAṄGĀCHĀRYAR, *Tirumaṛiṣai Mahā-bhāshyam.* See Rāmānuja. శ్రీ . . . గద్యత్రయము ॥ [Gadya-trayam. Edited by Ṣrīraṅgāchāryar.] 1882. 8°. **14048. d. 47.**

SRIRANGAM. *See* Tiru-vēṅkaṭāchāri, *M. S.* A collection of the papers relating to Sri Runganathaswami Temple, *etc.* 1887. Fol. **14170. h. 2.**

ṢRĪRAṄGA-NĀCHIYĀR AMMĀḶ, *Paḷḷigoṇḍai.* கோலப்புத்தகம். [Kōla-puttagam. A book of designs for floor decoration.] pp. ii. 54, *lith.* சென்னை [*Madras,*] 1899. 8°. **14170. i. 67.**

ṢRĪṢAILA-NĀTHAR, *A. Maṇavāḷa-māmunigaḷ* (Tiruvāy-moṛi Piḷḷai). *See* Piḷḷai Lōkāchāryar. శ్రీ . . . అష్టాదశరహస్యములు. [Ashṭādaṣa rahasyaṅgaḷ, *etc.* Edited by Ṣrīṣaila-nāthar.] [1905.] 8°. **14170. eee. 12.**

ṢRĪṢAILA TĀTĀCHĀRYAR. *See* Āṛvārgaḷ.—Nālāyiram.—*Entire Canon.* దివ్యప్రబంధ ॥ [Divyaprabandha-vyākhyāna-ratnāvaḷī.] Edited by Srisailatatacharya. 1901, *etc.* 8°. **14170. ff. 9.**

ṢRĪṢAILA TĀTĀCHĀRYAR, *Kāñchīpuram Ṣyāmadēṣikar.* *See* Sandhyā-vandanam. யஜுர்வேத ஸந்த்யாவந்தநம் ஆ [Sandhyā-vandanam, *etc.* With extracts from commentaries. Edited and translated by Ṣrīṣaila Tātāchāryar.] 1901. 8°. **14033. aa. 27.**

ṢRĪVATSĀṄKA MIṢRA. *See* Kūratt'-āṛvān.

STAPLEY (L. A.). Part i. of a series of graduated Translation Exercises, English-Tamil, Tamil-English, *etc.* pp. ii. 29. *Madras,* 1875. 8°. **14172. hh. 5.**

STATIONS OF THE CROSS. [For editions of this work included in devotional collections:] *See* Liturgies.—Rome, *Church of.*

—— சிலுவைப்பாதை. [Ṣiluvai-pādai. A Tamil version of the "Stations of the Cross," a Catholic devotional work. With appended prayers, *etc.*] pp. ix. 380. புதுவை நகராருகோ [*Pondicherry,* 1856.] 16°. **14170. a. 19.**

STICKNEY (D.). போதகாபிஷேகபிரசங்கம். A sermon at the ordination of Rev. S. Elyatamby, pastor of the church at Pandateruppu. pp. 22. *Jaffna,* 1888. 16°. **14170. a. 39.(1.)**

STOKES (Hudleston). *See* Kumara-guru-para Tambirān. The நீதிநெறிவிளக்கம் of Cumara guru para Tambirān . . . with . . . translation . . . and notes . . . by H. Stokes. 1830. 8°. **14172. b. 1.**

STRANGE (Thomas Lumisden). ஹிந்துதர்மசாஸ்திரம். [Hindu-dharma-ṣāstram. A Tamil translation of Strange's 'Manual of Hindoo Law,' by Ṣ. Vīra-sāmi Piḷḷai.] pp. v. 99. சென்னபட்டணம் [*Madras,*] 1857. 8°. **14170. g. 11.**

STREENEVASA RAGAVA CHARRIAR. *See* Ṣrīnivāsa Rāghavāchāryar.

STREENEEVASA ROW. *See* Ṣrīnivāsa Rāu.

SUBB'-AIYĀ AIYAR, *K. V.* Kanthimati: a novel in Tamil. After Scott's Talisman . . . காந்திமதி. (The Viveka Chintamani Series.) pp. viii. 229. *Madras,* 1902. 12°. **14171. aa. 12.**

SUBB'-AIYĀ CHEṬṬI, *P. T.* *See* Subrahmaṇya Paṇḍitar, *T. O.* மோகனாங்கி விலாசம். [Mōhanāṅgi-vilāsam. With musical notation by Subb'-aiyā.] 1899. 8°. **14170. l. 53.**

SUBB'-AIYA DĒṢIKAR, *Periya-maṇakuḷam.* இது . . . சையதுதாமின் ஞானியார் அவர்கள்பேரில் . . . இயற்றப்பட்டு ஆ [Panegyrical verses upon the author's teacher, Saiyid Ẓāmin Ñāniyār. Followed by verses by Ṣ. G. Gaṇa-pati Piḷḷai.] pp. 39. [*Madras,*] 1900. 16°. **14172. a. 63.**

SUBB'-AIYAR, *K.* சிவநாமவிளக்கம். [Ṣiva-nāma-viḷakkam. An explanation of the names of the god Ṣiva.] pp. 32. யாழ்ப்பாணம் சர்வதாரி [*Jaffna*, 1888.] 8°. **14170. e. 48.(3.)**

SUBBA-LAKSHMI AMMĀḶ, *R. Ṣ.* *See* RĀMĀYAṆAM. குசலவாக்கியம் ஷ [Kuṣa-lavākhyam. Edited by Subba-lakshmi Ammāḷ.] 1906. 8°. **14172. bb. 22.(2.)**

—— *See* RĀMĀYAṆAM. வால்மீகிராமாயணப் பாட்டு ஷ [Vālmīki-rāmāyaṇa-pāṭṭu, *etc.* Edited by Subba-lakshmi Ammāḷ.] 1906. 8°. **14172. bb. 22.(1.)**

SUBBA-RĀYA ĀCHĀRYAR, *Taṇḍarai.* அகம்புற ஆராய்ச்சி விளக்கம். [Agam-buṟa-ārāychi-viḷakkam. A Ṣaiva psycho-metaphysical treatise. Edited by T. K. Vaḍi-vēlu Mudaliyār.] pp. 12, 330. சென்னை சார்வரி [*Madras*, 1900.] 12°. **14170. d. 69.**

SUBBA-RĀYA AIYAR, *Ṣ., of Sirukudalpatti, Tirupattur* (SĀMI-KUṬṬI AIYAR). *See* PURĀṆAS.—*Vishṇu-purāṇam.* புராணரத்தினம் ஷ [Vishṇu-purāṇam. Metrically translated by Subba-rāya.] 1904. 8°. **14170. ff. 13.**

SUBBA-RĀYA CHEṬṬI, *Paṇṇuruṭṭi T. K., Shōḍa-ṣāvadhānam.* *See* CHIDAMBARA SVĀMI, *Tirupōrūr.* ஸ்ரீ ... திருப்போரூர்ச் சந்நிதிமுறை ஷ [Tirupōrūr-sannidhi-muṟai. With commentary by Subba-rāya.] [1892.] 8°. **14170. f. 19.**

—— *See* GĀṄGĒYAR. ... உரிச்சொல்நிகண்டு. [Uri-chol-nighaṇṭu. Edited by Subba-rāya.] [1890.] 12°. **14172. e. 15.**

—— *See* KAMBAN. ஸ்ரீ . . . ராமாயணம் ஷ [Kamba-rāmāyaṇam, Ayōdhyā-kāṇḍam. With commentary by Subba-rāya.] 1904. 8°. **14172. bb. 12.**

—— *See* MĀRI-MUTTĀ PIḶḶAI. புலியூர்வெண்பா. [Puliyūr-veṇ-bā. With commentary by Subba-rāya.] [1888.] 12°. **14172. a. 31.**

—— *See* PARAÑ-JŌDI MUNIVAR. ... திருவிளையாடற்புராணம் ஷ [Tiru-viḷaiy-āḍaṟ-purāṇam. With commentary by Subba-rāya.] [1887.] 8°. **14170. f. 10.**

—— *See* PURĀṆAS.—*Brahmāṇḍa-purāṇam.* வயிடனூர் . . . ஆதிபுரதலபுராணம். [Ādipura-tala-purāṇam. Metrically adapted by Subba-rāya.] [1896.] 8°. **14170. ee. 8.**

SUBBA-RĀYA CHEṬṬI, *Paṇṇuruṭṭi T. K., Shōḍa-ṣāvadhānam (continued).* *See* ṢIVA-ÑĀNA SVĀMI, *Tiruvāvaḍuduṟai.* ... காஞ்சிப்புராணம். [Kāñchi-purāṇam. Edited with commentary by Subba-rāya.] [1891, *etc.*] 4°. **14170. f. 14.**

SUBBA-RĀYA MUDALIYĀR, *Kūva-mānagaram Rāja.* *See* AESOP. Aesop's Fables . . . revised by C. Rajah Soobboroya Moodeliar. 1853. 8°. **14170. k. 32.**

SUBBA-RĀYA MUDALIYĀR, *Ṣ. K.* *See* ṢAṄKARĀCHĀRYAR. ... ஆத்மபோதம். [Ātma-bōdham. Edited by Subba-rāya.] [1869.] 8°. **14048. c. 62.(2.)**

—— *See* YŌGA-VĀSISHṬHA-RĀMĀYAṆAM. சீதாவிஜய ஷ [Sītā-vijaya-vachanam. Edited by Subba-rāya.] [1869.] 16°. **14170. d. 18.(1.)**

SUBBA-RĀYA MUDALIYĀR, *Taṇḍalam.* *See* ATI-VĪRA-RĀMA PĀṆḌIYAṆ. ... நைடதம் ஷ [Naiḍadam. Edited by Subba-rāya.] [1875.] 8°. **14172. b. 59.**

—— *See* DHANVANTARI. ... பாலவாகடம் ஷ [Ṣimiṭṭu-ratna-ṣurukkam. Edited by Subba-rāya.] [1874.] 8°. **14172. c. 19.**

—— *See* PIḶḶAI PERU-MĀḶ AIYAṄGĀR. கோயிற்கலம்பகம் ஷ [Tiruv-araṅga-kalambakam. Edited by Subba-rāya.] [1879.] 8°. **14172. c. 9.**

—— *See* VAIYĀPURI PIḶḶAI. நல்லதங்காள் நாடகம் [Nalladaṅgāḷ-nāṭakam. A musical adaptation by Subba-rāya.] [1875.] 8°. **14172. c. 13.**

SUBBA-RĀYA MUDALIYĀR, *Tiruvēṟkāḍu.* ... தமிழ்விளக்கம். A Tamel Expositor, containing a brief account of its idiom, by way of question and answer: composed and translated into English, by Teroovercaudoo Soobroya Modelliar. pp. ix. 97; 5 *plates.* *Madras*, 1811. 4°. **14172. f. 6.**

—— [Second edition.] pp. xii. 97; 5 *plates.* *Madras*, 1817. 4°. **14172. f. 7.**

SUBBA-RĀYA MUDALIYĀR, *Vēlūr*, **MUTTI-RĀMA KAVI-RĀYAR,** *G.*, and **KADIR-VĒL KAVI-RĀJA PAṆḌITAR.** ஸ்ரீமஹாபாரதக்கீர்த்தனை என்று வழங்காநின்ற ஸ்ரீமஹாபாரதநாடகம். [Mahā-bhārata-kīrttanai, or Mahā-bhārata-nāṭakam. An adaptation of the Mahā-bhāratam in lyric-dramatic form. Second edition.] pp. 752. சென்னப்பட்டணம் விசுவாவசு [*Madras*, 1905.] 8°. **14172. bbb. 1.**

SUBBA-RĀYA NĀYAKAR, *Ṣūḷai, of Madras Christian College.* See PURĀṆAS.—*Skanda-purāṇam.* கந்தபுராணம். [Kanda-purāṇam. With commentary by Subba-rāya.] 1896, *etc.* 8°. **14170. f. 23.**

—— See PURĀṆAS. — *Skanda-purāṇam.* காசிகாண்டம். [Kāṣi-khaṇḍam. Edited by Subba-rāya.] 1884. 8°. **14170. e. 24.**

—— See ṢEKKIṞĀR. ००० திருத்தொண்டர்புராணம் ஶ்ரீ [Periya-purāṇam. With commentary by Subba-rāya.] 1891-1895. 8°. **14170. f. 21.**

SUBBA-RĀYA SVĀMI, *disciple of Ponn'-ambala Svāmi.* See TĀṆḌAVA-RĀYA-MŪRTTI SVĀMI. ००० கைவல்லிய நவநீதம் ஶ்ரீ [Kaivalya-nava-nītam. Edited by Subba-rāya.] 1898. 8°. **14170. ee. 9.**

ṢUBHA-VĀKYAM PIḶḶAI, *P., of St. Patrick's College, Jaffna.* See [Addenda] ANTONY, *St.* St. Anthony of Padua. [Translated] by F. J. Subhavakyampillay, *etc.* 1907. 12°. **14170. bbb. 14.**

—— கர்த்தரின் ஜெனனகீர்த்தனை. [Karttarin jenana-kīrttanai. Roman Catholic hymns for Christmas.] pp. 18. யாழ்ப்பாணம் [*Jaffna*,] 1886. 16°. **14170. a. 38.(1.)**

—— கரு-ம் சிங்கராயர் என்னும் அர்ச். பாப்பானவர் குருப்பட்டாபிஷேகம் பெற்ற ஐம்பதாம்வருட மகோற்சவத்தைப்பற்றிய கீர்த்தனைகள். [Kīrttanaigaḷ. Songs for the Jubilee of Pope Leo XIII.] pp. 7. யாழ்ப்பாணம் கஅஅஎ [*Jaffna*, 1887.] 8°. **14170. b. 49.**

SUBRAHMAṆYA AIYAR, *Dēvaiyambadi Guru.* திருவிரிஞ்சைப்புராணவசனம். [Tiru-viriñchai-purāṇa-vachanam. A prose epitome of Ell'-appa Nāvalar's Tiru-viriñchai-purāṇam, on the Ṣaiva religious legends of Virinchipuram, near Vellore. Edited by V. L. Ṣinnaya Cheṭṭi.] pp. 6, 48. சென்னை ஏவிளம்பி [*Madras*, 1897.] 12°. **14170. d. 51.**

SUBRAHMAṆYA AIYAR, *Gaṇa-pati, Editor of "Svadēṣa-mitran."* [*Life.*] See SUNDARAM PIḶḶAI, *G.* ஸ்ரீ ஜி. சுப்பிரமணிய ஐயர் சரித்திரம். (Sri G. Subramania Iyer, *etc.*) 1907. 12°. **14171. d. 10.**

—— ஆரியஜன ஐக்கியம் ஶ்ரீ [Āriya-jana-aikyam, or Kāṅres-jana-sabhai. An account of the Indian National Congress.] pp. 45, 4. சென்னை [*Madras*,] 1888. 8°. **14170. k. 45.(1.)**

SUBRAHMAṆYA AIYAR, *P. Ṣ., Pleader, of Madura.* Savitri, a new drama in Tamil [on the legend of Sāvitrī, the ideal of wifely devotion]. (பதிவிரதாபாரம்மியம் என்ற சாவித்திரி நாடகம்.) pp. 3, 99, 3. *Tinnevelly*, 1901. 8°. **14170. l. 54.**

SUBRAHMAṆYA AIYAR, *R.* Mahommedan Law. மகமதியன் லா. [Compiled and translated from English works. New edition.] (Vivaharabodini Series.) pp. 2, 118. *Madras*, 1903. 8°. **14170. g. 25.**

SUBRAHMAṆYA AIYAR, *Tañjai Ṣatāvadhānam.* ००० காளையார்கோவிற் புராணவசனம். [Kāḷaiyār-kōviṟ-purāṇa-vachanam, or Kānapēr-purāṇa-v°. Being the legends of the Ṣaiva Kāḷaiyār temple, and comprising two *māhātmyas*, or Kāḷaiyār-kōvil-mānmiya-vachanam, translated into prose from the Brahma-kaivartta-purāṇam and the Skanda-purāṇam, preceded by extracts from the Dēvāram.] pp. 146. சென்னை [*Madras*,] 1897. 12°. **14170. d. 61.**

—— ००० காளையார்கோயிற்புராணம். [Kāḷaiyār-kōviṟ-purāṇam. The legends of the Kāḷaiyār sanctuary, versified by Subrahmaṇya Aiyar from the Brahma-kaivartta-purāṇam, and preceded by hymns from the Dēvāram.] pp. vi. 162, i. சென்னை [*Madras*,] 1899. 8°. **14170. ee. 22.**

—— சிருங்கபுரமென்னும்,கோட்டூர்ப்புராணம். [Kōṭṭūr-purāṇam. The legends of the Ṣaiva sanctuary of Kottur or Ṣṛuṅgapuram, rendered into verse.] pp. viii. 82, i. சென்னை விளம்பி [*Madras*, 1898.] 8°. **14170. ee. 37.**

—— The Indian Seasons, Paruva Varunanai Kalambakam, and what the old-time poets of the Tamil land say about them. Poems selected by Tanjore Satávathánam Subramania Iyer, from standard works, with due regard to the accuracy of the passages selected and purity of sentiment combined with old-world flavour, *etc.* (* பருவ வருணனைக்கலம்பகம்.) pp. 3, 46. *Deva Kottai*, 1904. 8°. **14172. bb. 13.**

SUBRAHMAṆYA BHĀRATI, *C.* Vande Mataram. National Songs . . . ஸ்வதேச கீதங்கள். pp. ii. 32. *Madras*, 1908. 12°. **14172. a. 64.**

SUBRAHMAṆYA BHĀRATI, *Maṟavāpuri Sundaram-aiyar.* திருவிளையாடற்கீர்த்தனை. [Tiru-viḷaiy-āḍar-kīrttanai. Lyrics on the Ṣaiva legends of the Tiru-viḷaiy-āḍar-purāṇam. Third edition.] pp. ii. x. 515, iii. i.; 1 *plate.* திருவாதி [*Tiru-vadi,*] 1906. 8°. **14170. ff. 19.**

SUBRAHMAṆYĀCHĀRYAR, *Ṣiṭṭūr.* ஔவையார் சரித்திரம் [Auvaiyār-charitram. A biography of the poetess Auvaiyār.] pp. 44. *Madras,* 1902. 8°. **14171. a. 53.(1.)**

Forms the 11*th* kalai *of the* Kalā-nidhi *Series.*

SUBRAHMAṆYA CHEṬṬI, *A. S., disciple of Ṣin-naya.* *See* ṢINNAYA CHEṬṬI. திருவெற்றியூர்ப்புராணம். [Tiruveṯṯiyūr-purāṇam. With preface by Subrahmaṇya.] [1901.] 8°. **14170. ee. 52.**

SUBRAHMAṆYA DĒṢIKAR. *See* ARUṆANDI DĒVA-NĀYANĀR. சிவஞானசித்தியார்பரபக்கம். [Ṣiva-ñāna-siddhiyār-parapakkam, °supakkam, *etc.* With commentaries on the second by Subrah-maṇya.] 1897. 8°. [*Mey-kaṇḍa-ṣāttiram.*] **14170. ff. 3.**

SUBRAHMAṆYA DĪKSHITAR, *Kurugūr.* ००० பிரயோக விவேகம் மூலமுமுரையும். [Prayōga-vivēkam. A work in verse, with a prose commen-tary, on Tamil grammar. Edited by Āṟu-muga Nāvalar.] pp. 72. சென்னபட்டணம் விஷு [*Madras,* 1882.] 8°. **14172. f. 27.**

SUBRAHMAṆY'-AIYAR, *Vaiyai R.* திருவருட்கோவை. [Tiruv-aruṭ-kōvai. A century of verses on attainment of divine grace.] pp. 32, ii. தஞ்சை [*Tanjore,*] 1906. 12°. **14170. dd. 11.(2.)**

SUBRAHMAṆYA KAVI-RĀYAR, *Ṣēṯṯūr, of Tiru-vavadudurai.* *See* SĀMI-NĀTHA DĒṢIKAR. திருச்செந்திற்கலம்பகம். [Tiruchendiṟ-kalambakam. Edited by Subrahmaṇya.] 1905. 8°. [*Ṣen-damiẓ supplement.*] **14172. i. 1.*(no. 15.)**

—— *See* VILLIPUTTŪRAR. வில்லிபுத்தூராழ்வார் ... மகாபாரதம். [Mahā-bhāratam. Edited with notes, glossary, *etc.*, by Subrahmaṇya.] 1907. 8°. **14172. bbb. 2.**

—— *See* YŌGA. அட்டாங்க யோக கு [Aṭṭāṅga-yōga-kuṟaḷ, *etc.* Edited by Subrahmaṇya.] 1905. 8°. [*Ṣen-damiẓ supplement.*] **14172. i. 1.* (no. 10.)**

SUBRAHMAṆYA MUDALIYĀR, *V. P.* *See* MILTON (J.). Paradise Lost, book i., in Tamil viruttam, by V. P. Subramania Mudaliar, *etc.* 1895. 12°. **14170. a. 56.**

SUBRAHMAṆYA MUNIVAR, *Toṭṭikalai.* *See* SUBRAHMAṆYA TAMBIRĀN.

SUBRAHMAṆYA PAṆḌITAR, *Taḷavariṣai Mutt'-aiya-Ñāniyār.* *See* ṢRĪ-KAṆṬHA PAṆḌITAR. ஜீவரக்ஷாமிர்தம். [Jīva-rakshāmirtam. Translated by Subrahmaṇya.] [1864.] 8°. **14170. i. 17.**

—— ००० பதார்த்தகுணசிந்தாமணி. [Padārtha-guṇa-chintāmaṇi. A work on Materia Medica in 1598 verses, with a commentary founded on the works of Tēr Aiyar. Second edition.] pp. viii. 368, ii. xxvi. i. சென்னபட்டணம் அக்ஷய [*Madras,* 1867.] 8°. **14170. i. 62.**

SUBRAHMAṆYA PAṆḌITAR, *Tiruchendūr Oli-muttu, disciple of Rāma-sāmi.* மோகனாங்கி விலாசம். [Mōhanāṅgi-vilāsam. A drama of love and conjugal loyalty. Edited by M. I. Ṣaṅkara-subbu-dāsar and A. Vīra-sāmi Nāyuḍu, with musical notation by P. T. Subb'-aiyā Cheṭṭi.] pp. 18, 418. சென்னை [*Madras,*] 1899. 8°. **14170. l. 53.**

—— சிவ சுப்பிறமணிய சுவாமிபேரில திருச்செந்தூர் வழிநடைப்பதம். [Ṣiva-subrahmaṇya-svāmi pēril Tiruchendūr-vaṟi-naḍai-padam. A ritual of hymns for the worship of Subrahmaṇya in Tiruchendur.] pp. 22. கொழும்பு தூஅஅள [*Colombo,* 1887.] 8°. **14170. e. 48.(1.)**

SUBRAHMAṆYA PIḶḶAI, *G. V. A., of Manippay.* பதார்த்தவிஞ்ஞானம். [Padārtha-viññānam. A dictionary of Materia Medica.] pp. ii. 70. [*Jaffna,*] 1887. 12°. **14170. i. 18.**

—— பாலவைத்தியம். [Bāla-vaidyam. A work on the medical treatment of children.] pp. iii. 90, vi. [*Jaffna,*] 1889. 12°. **14171. f. 3.**

—— பிரசவவைத்தியம். Midwifery. pp. ii. 86. யாழ்ப்பாணம் [*Jaffna,*] 1892. 12°. **14170. i. 70.(1.)**

SUBRAHMAṆYA PIḶḶAI, *Madurai.* *See* MEY-KAṆḌA DĒVAR. ००० சிவஞானபோத கு [Ṣiva-ñāna-bōdham. With Ṣiva-ñānar's commentary. Edited by Subrahmaṇya.] 1906. 8°. **14170. eee. 15.**

SUBRAHMAṆYA PIḶḶAI, *Naḍuvapaṭṭi Muttu-kumāru.* *See* ṢAṄKARĀCHĀRYAR. [*Doubtful and Supposititious Works.*] உலோககுரு ... ஆயுட்பாவகம். [Āyuṭ-bhāvakam. Edited by Subrah-maṇya.] 1895. 8°. **14170. i. 39.**

SUBRAHMANYA PILLAI, *V.T., of Cuddalore.* See PURĀṆAS.—*Skanda-purāṇam.* பிரமோத்தரகாண்டவசனம். [Brahmōttara-kāṇḍa-vachanam. A paraphrase, by Subrahmaṇya.] 1878. 16°. **14170. d. 20.**

SUBRAHMANYA ŞĀSTRI, *Mēlmaṅgalam N.* See ŞAṄKARĀCHĀRYAR. [*Doubtful and Supposititious Works.*] ஐ உ ஒ ஶ்ரீ ஸு ப்ரஹ்மண்ய புஜங்க ஸ்தோத்ரம் [Subrahmaṇya-bhujaṅga-stōtram. Edited with grammatical notes and with Tamil interpretation, *etc.*, by Subrahmaṇya.] 1902. 16°. **14028. a. 30.**

SUBRAHMANYA ŞĀSTRI, *Nellapalli.* ○ ○ ○ ശ്രീമീനാക്ഷിനാടകം. [Mīnākshi-nāṭakam. A drama on the legend of the goddess Pārvatī, in the Malayalam character.] pp. 54. പാലക്കാട വികൃതി [*Palghat,* 1890.] 8°. **14170. l. 30.(1.)**

SUBRAHMANYA ŞĀSTRI, *Şennimalai.* See VAIDYANĀTHA DĪKSHITAR. ○ ○ ○ ஸ்மிருதிமுக்தாபலே ... காண்டா: [Smṛuti-muktā-phala. Vol. iii., iv., with translation by Subrahmaṇya.] 1898, *etc.* 4°. **14039. c. 15. (vol. 3, 4.)**

SUBRAHMANYA ŞĀSTRI, *Tumbainagar Ş.* See EPHEMERIDES. விளம்பிவருஷ ... பஞ்சாங்கம். [Calendar for 1898-99. Calculated by Subrahmaṇya.] 1897. 8°. **14172. i. 16.(2.)**

SUBRAHMANYA SVĀMI, *Mayilam.* [For works edited by Subrahmaṇya Svāmi, see under the following headings :]

VAṆṆA-KALAÑJIYA PULAVAR.
VĪRA-BHADRA AIYAR.

SUBRAHMANYA TAMBIRĀN, *Toṭṭikalai, of Tiruvavadudurai.* ○○○ திருத்தணிகைவிருத்தம். [Tirutaṇigai-vṛuttam. Hymns in honour of Şiva as worshipped at Tirutani, near Madras.] pp. 8. சென்னை [*Madras,*] 1892. 16°. **14170. d. 36.(1.)**

—— ○ ○ ○ திருவாவடுதுறைக்கோவை. [Tiruvāvaḍuduṛai-kōvai. Religious verses on the Şaiva cult of Tiruvavadudurai. Edited with introduction, *etc.*, by V. Sāmināth'-aiyar.] pp. i. xxii. 82. சென்னபட்டணம் [*Madras,*] 1903. 8°. **14170. ee. 54.**

ŞŪḌI KOḌUTTA NĀCHIYĀR. See ĀṆḌĀḶ.

ŞŪDRAKA. Mrichhakati in Tamil. [Translated from the Sanskrit drama of Şūdraka] by Pandit S. M. Natesa Sastri. மிருச்சகடி நாடகம். pp. 90. *Madras,* 1887. 12°. **14170. k. 1.(2.)**

SUGĀTTIYAR. See SCOTT (T. M.).

ŞUKA. Sugarnadi Sothidam. ... சுகர்நாடிசோதிடம். [Şukar-nāḍi-jōdiḍam. A metrical work on astrology, fabled to have been taught by the sage Şuka to king Parīkshit. Edited by Aṅgamuttu Mudaliyār.] pt. 1. pp. ii. 208. *Madras,* 1895. 8°. **14170. i. 36.**

SULAIMĀN ibn MUḤAMMAD, *al-Sailānī.* See ḲUR'ĀN. رحمة المنان [Raḥmat al-mannān. Surah 78-114, with a translation into Tamil by Sulaimān.] [1897.] 8°. **14507. b. 35.**

SULṬĀN MUḤYI al-DĪN, *Tiruvāngōḍu M. K.* பவனியலங்காரம். [Pavaniy-alaṅkāram. Muhammadan songs for religious processions.] pp. 8. கொழும்பு 1310 [*Colombo,* 1893.] 8°. **14173. b. 28.(1.)**

SUNDARA ĀCHĀRYAR, *Chintādripeṭṭai Kṛushṇ'-appa.* ○ ○ ○ அப்பூதியடிகள் நாயனார் சரித்திரக்கீர்த்தனை. [Appūdiy-aḍigaḷ-nāyanār-charitra-kīrttanai. Lyrics on the legend of Appūdiy-aḍigaḷ, one of the 63 *nāyanārs* or Şaiva saints, based upon the Periya-purāṇam.] pp. 38. சென்னை [*Madras,*] 1895. 8°. **14170. ee. 4.(2.)**

SUNDARĀCHĀRYAR, *Tirukōṭṭiyūr.* See YŌGA-VĀSISHṬHA-RĀMĀYAṆAM. சீதாவிஜய ஸ்ரீ [Sītā-vijaya-vachanam. Translated by Sundarāchāryar.] [1869.] 16°. **14170. d. 18.(1.)**

SUNDARA GURU, *Şālabākkam.* See SAURA BRAHMANS. அதர்வணவேத ... ஹவ்யகவ்ய விதிகள். [Havya-kavya-vidhigaḷ. Edited by Sundara Guru.] 1906. 8°. **14033. bbb. 36.**

SUNDARAM PILLAI, *Ālappuṛai Peru-māḷ.* மனோன்மணீயம். (Manônmanîyam. A play in Tamil verse, after the Shakespearean model) [based on "The Secret Way," one of Lord Lytton's "Lost Tales of Miletus"]. pp. 29, 177, 14. *Madras,* 1891. 8°. **14170. l. 31.**

—— Some Mile Stones in the History of Tamil Literature found in an enquiry into the age of Tiru Gnana Sambandha. pp. 4, 61. *Madras,* 1895. 8°. **11825. o. 23.(9.)**

—— Some early Sovereigns of Travancore, for the first time brought to notice with their dates determined by inscriptions. pp. viii. 74. *Madras,* 1894. 8°. **14170. e. 23.**

SUNDARAM PIḶḶAI, *Gurumalai.* Pottodi. A Tamil novel ... பொற்றொடி ஆ. (Reform Series.) pp. 166. *Tinnevelly,* 1906. 8°. **14171. e. 15.**

—— ஸ்ரீ ஜி. சுப்பிரமணிய ஐயர் சரித்திரம். (Sri G. Subramania Iyer. By G. M. Sundram Pillai.) pp. ii. 130. சென்னை [*Madras,*] 1907. 12°. **14171. d. 10.**

SUNDARAM PIḶḶAI, *Purāṇikar P.* *See* RĀMA-LIṄGA PIḶḶAI, *K.* ∘ ∘ ∘ திருவருட்பாத்திருமுறைத்திரட்டு. [Tiruv-aruṭ-pā-tiru-muṟai-tiraṭṭu. Compiled by Sundaram.] 1892. 8°. **14172. d. 14.**

SUNDARA MUDALIYĀR, *Tirumayilai V.* *See* GŌPĀLA-KṚUSHṆA AIYAR, *Ā. Bh.* ∘ ∘ ∘ நந்தனார்-சரித்திரக்கீர்த்தனை ஆ [Nandanār-charitra-kīrtanai, *etc.* Edited by Sundara.] 1899. 8°. **14170. ee. 25.**

—— ∘ ∘ ∘ திருமுருகாற்றுப்படை ஆ (*வேல்-விருத்தம் *etc.*) [Tiru-mṛug'-āṯṯu-paḍai of Nakkīrar, Aruṇa-giri-nāthar's Vēl-vṛuttam and Mayil-vṛuttam, Shaṇmukha Ñāniyār's Mṛugar-antādi, and Chidambara Svāmi's Vēda-giriy-īṣvara-padigam. Edited by Sundara Mudaliyār.] 4 pts. சென்னை கஅகூo [*Madras,* 1890.] 16°. **14172. a. 32.(1-4.)**

SUNDARA MUDALIYĀR, *Vyāsarbāḍi Appā-sāmi.* சிவநாம சங்கீர்த்தநம். [Ṣiva-nāma-saṅkīrttanam. Hymns on the names of Ṣiva.] pp. 56. சென்னை பிரபவ [*Madras,* 1867.] 8°. **14172. c. 8.**

SUNDARA-MŪRTTI NĀYANĀR. [For editions of the Dēvāram composed by Ñāna-sambandhar, Sundara-mūrtti, and Tiru-nāvukk'-araṣu :] *See* TIRU-MUṞAI.

—— ஞானம். [Ñānam. Ṣaiva verses ascribed to Sundara-mūrtti.] *See* SIDDHARGAḶ. ∘ ∘ ∘ பெரிய ஞானக்கோவை. [Periya-ñāna-kōvai.] pt. i., pp. 11-24. 1906. 12°. **14170. dd. 12.**

SUNDARA RĀGHAV'-AYYAṄGĀR, *Rām'-ayyaṅgār.* விநோத கதாசங்கிரகம் [Vinōda-kathā-saṅgraham. A collection of 15 amusing stories. Edited by C. S. Raṅgāchāryar.] pp. 53. கும்பகோணம் [*Kumbakonam,*] 1892. 12°. **14170. k. 53.**

SUNDARA-RĀJA ṢARMĀ, *D.* *See* MAHĀ-BHĀRATAM. ஸ்ரீமத் பகவத்கீதை ஆ [Bhagavad-gītā. With Ṣaṅkara's commentary. Edited with Tamil translation by Sundara-rāja.] 1907. 8°. **14049.·bb. 10.**

—— வ்யாஸ வாத்ஸ்யாயந மகர்ஷிகள் அருளிச்-செய்த பார்யாதருமம். (Vyasa and Vatsyayana's Bharyadharmam. [Comprising 37 aphorisms of Vātsyāyana's Kāma-sūtram on wifely duty and tho dialogue of Satyabhāmā and Draupadī from the Vana-parvam of the Mahā-bhāratam. Edited in Sanskrit] with a Tamil commentary [and glosses], and a Tamil version of [portions of] Kalidasa's Abhijnanasakuntala . . . by D. Sundararaja Sarma, with an [English] introduction by K. Sundara-rama Aiyer . . . New edition.) pp. i. i. ii. xviii. 197, i. சென்னை [*Madras,*] 1901. 12°. **14085. b. 44.**

SUNDARA-RĀMA ṢĀSTRI, *Madurai Rāma-liṅga.* *See* SĀYAṆĀCHĀRYAR. ஸ்ரீ . . . ஸ்ரீவெஉடாஜ-ப்ஜஉடரீ *etc.* [Pañchadaṣī. With interpretation and paraphrase in Tamil by Rāma-liṅga, preceded by an epitome in Tamil and a Sanskrit poem called Rāma-liṅga-vaibhava on the successes of Rāma-liṅga with Tamil translation, all three by Sundara-rāma.] 1905. 8°. **14049. bb. 7.**

SUNDARĀRYAR, *Goshṭhīpuram Eli.* *See* VEṄKAṬA-NĀTHA VĒDĀNTACHĀRYAR. ∘ ∘ ∘ சில்லரை ரஹச்-யங்கள்-கள. [Ṣillarai-rahasyaṅgaḷ. With notes by Sundarāryar.] [1900.] 8°. **14170. ee. 36.**

SUNDARA SVĀMI, *of Tinnevelli.* ∘ ∘ ∘ நிஜாநந்த-விலாசம். [Nijānanda-vilāsam. An account of various systems of religion and philosophy. Edited by Māvaḍi Chidambaram Piḷḷai. Second edition.] pp. 213, 19. திருநெல்வேலி [*Tinnevelli,*] 1904. 8°. **14170. eee. 9.**

SUNDIRAM PIḶḶAI. ∘∘∘ மதுரை மீனாட்சியம்மை நாடகம். [Madurai-mīnākshiy-ammai-nāṭakam. A drama on the legend of the goddess Mīnākshi and her incarnation as child of king Malaya-dhvaja Pāṇḍiyan of Madura. Edited by T. Tyāga-rāja Piḷḷai.] pp. 112. [*Madras,*] 1889. 8°. **14170. l. 26.**

SUNGHARA NAMA SIVAYUR. *See* ṢAṄKARA NAMAṢ-ṢIVĀYAR.

SŪRYA-NĀRĀYAṆA ṢĀSTRI, *V. G.* *See* JAYAṄ-GOṆḌĀN. சயங்கொண்டான் . . . கலிங்கத்துப்-பரணி. [Kaliṅgattu paraṇi. Edited by Sūrya-nārāyaṇa.] 1898. 12°. **14172. a. 49.**

SŪRYA-NĀRĀYAṆA ṢĀSTRI, *V.G.* (*continued*). *See* MAHĀ-LIṄG'-AIYAR. ◦ ◦ ◦ இலக்கணச்சுருக்கம். [Ilakkaṇa-churukkam. Revised by Sūrya-nārāyaṇa.] 1898. 12°. **14172. ee. 3.**

—— *See* MAṄGALĒṢVARI. திரு . . . மங்கலேசுவரி பிள்ளைத்தமிழ். [Uttara-kōsa-maṅgai-maṅgaḷē-ṣvari-piḷḷai-tamiṟ. Edited by Sūrya-nārāyaṇa.] 1901. 12°. **14170. d. 89.**

—— *See* PERIODICAL PUBLICATIONS.—*Madras.* ஞானபோதினி ஃ (Jnâna Bodhini, *etc.*) [Vol. 5, 6, edited by Sūrya-nārāyaṇa.] 1897-1905. 8°. **14172. i. 18.**

—— *See* PUGAṞĒNDI. புகழேந்தி . . . நளவெண்பா. [Naḷa-veṇ-bā. Edited by Sūrya-nārāyana.] 1899. 12°. **14172. a. 50.(1.)**

—— Kalâvati. An original Tamil drama . . . With an [English] introduction by T. Ramakrishna Pillai. (*கலாவதி. ஒருபுதியதமிழ்நாடகம்.) pp. iii. ii. xx. 256, i. *Madras,* 1898. 12°. **14170. l. 48.(1.)**

—— Mana Vijayam. A drama in one act. 1902. *See* PERIODICAL PUBLICATIONS.—*Madras.* The Madras Christian College Magazine. New Series. vol. i., nos. 8-12. 1902, *etc.* 8°. **P.P. 910. da.(new ser., vol. 1.)**

—— மதிவாணன் புதுவது புனைந்தேோர் செந்தமிழ்க் கதை. (Mativâṇan. A classical . . . novel.) pp. 113. *Madras,* 1902. 12°. **14171. a. 42.(5.)**

Forms "Flower" 2 of the series "The Pleasure-creeper" (Inba-valli).

—— நாடகவியல். (Nâtaka Viyal.) [A work on the principles of dramaturgy, in verse.] pp. 23. *Madras,* 1897. 12°. **14172. a. 47.**

—— பாவலர் விருந்து. முதல் நாள். (The Poets' Feast. A collection of Tamil poems. First Day.) pp. i. i. i. 92. *Madras,* 1901. 12°. **14172. a. 50.(3.)**

Forms "Pendant" 3 of "The Girdle of the Tamil Muse."

—— Rûpâvathi, or The Missing Daughter. [An historical drama in prose. With an English introduction by M. Ṣ. Pūrṇa-liṅgam Piḷḷai.] pp. 9, 2, x. 5, i. 111, i. *Madras,* 1895. 8°. **14170. l. 41.**

—— ரூபாவதி அல்லது காணமற்போனமகள் ஃ [Rūpāvati. Second edition.] pp. 12, 168. சென்னை [*Madras,*] 1902. 12°. **14170. l. 56.**

Forms no. 1 in the author's series Nā-magaḷ-ṣilambu (*"The Anklet of Sarada"*).

SŪRYA-NĀRĀYAṆA ṢĀSTRI, *V.G.* (*continued*). History of the Tamil Language . . . With an English introduction by the Rev. F. W. Kellett. (*தமிழ்மொழியின் வரலாறு.) pp. 12, xvi. 155. *Madras,* 1903. 12°. **14171. a. 52.**

Forms Kalai 14 *of the* Kalā-nidhi.

—— Tani-paçura-togai. A book of sonnets in Tamil . . . With English echoes by the Rev. G. U. Pope . . . First Course. (*தனிப்பாசுரத்தொகை.) pp. xxviii. 88. *Madras,* 1901. 12°. **14172. a. 28.**

Forms "Pendant" 2 in the series "The Girdle of the Tamil Muse."

SUTĒṢAMITTIRAN. *See* SVADĒṢA-MITRAN.

SVADĒṢA-MITRAN, *Pseud.* ஸ்தானீக சுய ஆட்சி வினாவிடை. [Sthānīka-suya-ātṣi-vinā-viḍai. A catechism on local self-government.] pp.45. சென்னபட்டணம் [*Madras,*] 1884. 8°. **14170. g. 12.**

According to the Official Catalogue of Books Registered, 1884, i., *p.* 6, *the author is G. Subrahmaṇya Aiyar.*

SVĀMI-NĀTHA. [For names beginning with this word :] *See* SĀMI-NĀTHA.

SVĀNUBHAVA YŌGĪNDRAR. *See* VEṄKAṬA-RĀYA YŌGĪNDRAR.

SVĀTMĀRĀMA YŌGI, *disciple of Gōraksha-nāthar.* ஸ்ரீ . . . ஹடயோகப்பிரதீபிகை ஃ [Haṭha-yōga-pradīpikā. A Sanskrit work on the mystic practices of the Haṭha-yōga. Edited with a Tamil translation and commentary styled Tattva-pradīpikai by V. Kuppu-svāmi Rāju.] pp. vi. iv. ii. 272. திருவையாறு துர்முகி [*Trivadi,* 1897.] 8°. **14048. cc. 16.**

ṢVĒTĀRAṆYA ṢĀSTRI, *Ṣ.* "ஸத்யமேஜயம்." [Satyamē jayam] . . . A Tamil play in two acts illustrative of the maxim, "Truth is great & it will prevail." pp. 3, 45. *Madras,* 1907. 12°. **14171. i. 2.(2.)**

SWAMINATHA. [For names beginning with this word :] *See* SĀMI-NĀTHA.

SWAMY (V. M.). *See* MUTTU-KUMĀRA-SVĀMI MUDALIYĀR, *Vichūr.*

SWINTON (ROBERT BLAIR). *See* TĀṆḌAVA-RĀYA MUDALIYĀR, *V.* 'An Indian Tale or Two' . . . with an introduction by R. B. Swinton. [1899.] 12°. **14171. a. 20.**

ṢYĀMA-DĒṢIKA ṢRĪṢAILA TĀTĀCHĀRYAR. *See* ṢRĪṢAILA TĀTĀCHĀRYAR.

SYMBOLA ŒCUMENICA. *See* EVANGELICAL LUTHERAN CHURCH.

ṬĀHĀ LEBBAI, *Saiyid, Ñāniyār.* *See* MUḤYI al-DĪN MALUK MUDALIYĀR, *Kōṭṭāru, the Elder.* ∘∘∘ மெய்ஞ்ஞானத் திருப்பாடற்றிரட்டு. [Mey-ñāna-tiru-pāḍaṯ-ṯiraṭṭu. Edited by Ṭāhā.] [1898.] 8°. **14173. c. 2.(1.)**

—— *See* MUḤYI al-DĪN MALUK MUDALIYĀR, *Kōṭṭāṟu, the Younger.* ∘ ∘ ∘ மெய்ஞ்ஞானவிளக்கம். [Mey-ñāna-viḷakkam. Edited by Ṭāhā.] [1898.] 8°. **14173. c. 2.(2.)**

TALES. Pleasing Tales, or Stories, designed to improve the understanding and direct the conduct of young persons; with a Tamil translation. (†இனிமையானகதைகள்.) pp. 42. *Madras,* 1847. 12°. **14171. aa. 14.(1.)**

TAMB'-AIYĀ PILḶAI, *Nallūr C., disciple of Ponn'-ambala Piḷḷai.* [For works edited by Tamb'-aiyā Piḷḷai, see under the following headings:]

KAḌAVUṈ MĀ-MUNI.
MĀṆIKKA-VĀCHAKAR.

TAMB'-AIYĀ PIḶḶAI, *Ṣ.* திருமரியாயி பேரிற் தோத்திரப் பதிகம். [Tiru-mariyāyi pēriṟ tōttira-padigam. A hymn to the Virgin Mary.] pp. 6. யாழ்ப்பாணம் [*Jaffna,*] 1888. 12°. **14170. a. 38.(2.)**

TAMB'-AIYĀ UPĀDHYĀYAR, *J. P.* ∘∘∘ பிரலாபகவிதை. [Pralāpa-kavitai. Elegiac verses on the death of Monsignor J. Vistarini.] pp. 6. *Colombo,* 1896. 8°. **14170. c. 24.(11.)**

TAMBA PIḶḶAI (GEORGE C.). Arithmetical Exercises. For Standards iii. iv. & v. . . . கணித அப்பியாசங்கள். Compiled by G. C. Thampapillai. pp. i. 132; 1 *plate.* *Jaffna,* 1891. 16°. **14172. h. 86.**

—— A School Arithmetic. Parts i. & ii. Notation, numeration addition & subtraction, *etc.* (Part iii. Multiplication & division. Part v. Reduction, compound rules. Part vi. Simple and compound proportion.) 4 pts. *Jaffna,* 1892-1893. 12°. **14172. h. 68.(6.)**

—— இலங்கைப் பூமிசாத்திரம். [Laṅkai-bhūmi-ṣāttiram.] Geography of Ceylon, by G. C. Thampapillai. pp. ii. 69. *Jaffna,* 1891. 8°. **14172. h. 64.**

TAMBA PIḶḶAI (GEORGE C.) (*continued*). இலங்கை ஃ [Laṅkai-bhūmi-ṣāttiram.] Second edition. pp. 72. *Jaffna,* 1892. 12°. **14172. h. 68.(3.)**

TAMBI-MUTTU PIḶḶAI, *Achuvēli Ṣ.* எஸ்தாக்கியார்நாடகம். [Estākkiyār-nāṭakam. A Christian drama on the history of the martyr Saint Eustathius.] pp. 7, 110, i. யாழ்ப்பாணம் [*Jaffna,*] 1890. 8°. **14170. l. 22.**

—— பாலியக்கும்மி. [Bālya-kummi. 20 moral quatrains.] pp. 8. யாழ்ப்பணம் [*Jaffna,*] 1886. 32°. **14172. a. 2.**

—— சம்சோன்கதை. [Samsōn-kathai.] Story of Samson [in verse]. pp. i. 24. *Jaffna,* 1892. 8°. **14170. c. 24.(3.)**

TAMBI ÑĀNIYĀR ṢĀHIB. *See* MUḤYI al-DĪN MALUK MUDALIYĀR, *Kōṭṭāṟu, the Younger.*

TAMBI PĀVALAR, *Shaikh.* *See* SHAIKH TAMBI PĀVALAR.

TAMBIY-APPAN, *J.* A Glossary of select [commercial] Forms and English Words in Indian use with their pronunciation and meanings in Tamil. அரும்பொருளகராதி. By J. Thumbiappen. Third edition. pp. 96. *Bangalore,* 1894. 8°. **14172. hh. 3.**

TAMBU CHEṬṬIYĀR, *Triṣirapuram Rāyalu Ārōgya-sāmi.* [*Life.*] *See* VEṄKAṬA-SUBBU PIḶḶAI, *A.* The Thumboo Sindhamani, *etc.* 1905. 8°. **14171. b. 4.**

TAMIL. *See* ENGLISH. First Lessons in English and Tamul, *etc.* 1835-1836. 16°. **14172. h. 1.(5.)**

—— Tamil Primer . . . முதலாம்புத்தகம். [Second edition.] pp. 26. *Madras,* 1848. 12°. **14172. h. 58.(1.)**

—— Tamil First Book. ஆதிமூலபுஸ்தகம். Twelfth edition. pp. 48. *Tranquebar,* 1881. 16°. **14172. h. 36.**

—— Tamil First Book, or First Standard Reader. தமிழ் முதலாம் புத்தகம் ஃ. Sixth edition. pp. 36. *Batticaloa,* 1893. 16°. **14172. g. 1.**

—— *See* RĀJA-GŌPĀLA AIYAṄGĀR, *M.* A help to the thorough understanding of the Tamil இரண்டாம் ஸ்டண்டர்டு புஸ்தகம், *etc.* [1898.] 12°. **14172. h. 97.(3.)**

TAMIL (*continued*). Second Book of Reading for the use of native children in the Madras Presidency. Tamil. pp. 61. [*Madras*,] 1853. 16°. **14172. h. 29.**

—— Tamil Second Book. இரண்டாம் புத்தகம். [A reading book issued by the Roman Catholic Mission at Jaffna.] Second edition. pp. 74. யாழ்ப்பாணம் [*Jaffna*,] 1885. 12°. **14172. h. 68.(1.)**

—— [Fifth edition, considerably altered and revised.] pp. 69. யாழ்ப்பாணம் [*Jaffna*,] 1892. 12°. **14172. h. 68.(4.)**

—— Tamil Second Book, or Second Standard Reader. தமிழ் இரண்டாம் புத்தகம் ஞூ. Fourth edition. pp. 104. *Batticaloa*, 1891. 16°. **14172. g. 2.(1.)**

—— Tamil Third Book, or Third Standard Reader. தமிழ் மூன்றாம் புத்தகம் ஞூ. Second edition. pp. 128. *Batticaloa*, 1890. 12°. **14172. h. 99.**

—— Tamil Third Book. மூன்றாம் புத்தகம். [A reader for Roman Catholic schools.] pp. ii. 86. யாழ்ப்பாணம் [*Jaffna*,] 1893. 12°. **14172. h. 68.(5.)**

—— Tamil Fourth-book. நான்காம் புத்தகம். [For the use of Roman Catholic schools.] pp. v. 148. யாழ்ப்பாணம் [*Jaffna*,] 1889. 12°. **14172. h. 49.**

—— [Another set of readings.] pp. ii. 120. யாழ்ப்பாணம். [*Jaffna*,] 1892. 12°. **14172. h. 98.**

—— Tamil Fifth Book. ஐந்தாம் புத்தகம். [A reader for use in Catholic schools.] pp. iv. 156. யாழ்ப்பாணம் [*Jaffna*,] 1893. 12°. **14172. h. 91.**

TAMIL AUTHORS. ००० இலக்கிய சங்கிரகம். The Classical Reader, or Selections from standard Tamil Authors (prepared primarily and chiefly for the use of the Batticotta Seminary). pp. ii. 261. *Jaffna*, 1847. 8°. **14172. h. 79.**

TAMIL GRAMMAR. *See* GRAMMAR.

TAMIL HOUSEHOLD WORDS. *See* HOUSEHOLD WORDS.

TAMIL IDIOMS. An Aid to Translation. Containing Tamil idioms with their appropriate English equivalents. For the use of the Lower Secondary & the High School students. pp. 27. *Madras*, 1900. 12°. **14172. h. 97.(2.)**

The editor is, according to the Register of books printed, A. Rāma-sāmi Dikshitar.

TAMIL MINOR POETS. Tamil Minor Poets. நீதிநூற்றிரட்டு. [Nīti-nūṭ-ṭiraṭṭu. Containing the Ātti-ṣūḍi, Konṟai-vēndan, Mūd'-urai, Nal-vaṟi of Auvaiyār; the Veṭṭi-vēṟ-kai of Ativīra-rāman; the Nan-neṟi of Ṣiva-prakāṣar; and the Nīti-neṟi-viḷakkam of Kumara-guru-parar.] pp. 46. *Madras*, 1864. 16°. **14172. a. 17.**

—— Fifth edition. pp. 64. *Madras*, 1868. 16°. **14172. a. 18.**

—— Tamil Minor Poets. நீதிநூற்றிரட்டு உரைபாடம். [Another edition, with commentary.] pp. 156. *Madras*, 1865. 16°. **14172. a. 16.**

—— Tamil Minor Poets. First Book. நீதிநூற்றிரட்டு ஞூ. [Containing the Ātti-ṣūḍi, Konṟai-vēndan, and Veṭṭi-vēṟ-kai.] pp. 55. *Madras*, 1865. 16°. **14172. h. 35.(2.)**

Reprinted with a different wrapper-title from the complete edition of 1865.

—— Tamil Minor Poets: containing, Attisudi, Konreiventhan, Vettiverkei, Muthurei, Nalvali, Nanneri, and Nithinerivilakkam. [Compiled by P. Percival, and] translated into English, [with notes,] by the Rev. S. Winfred; with an introduction [by J. Murdoch]. pp. viii. 51. *Madras*, 1872. 12°. **14172. c. 6.**

TAMIL PROVERBS. Tamil Proverbs with their English equivalents . . . prepared for the use of Lower Secondary students by an experienced teacher. pp. 12. *Madras*, 1893. 12°. **14170. k. 58.**

TAMĪM ibn SULṬĀN. تحفة الاحباب فى بيان ضرور المسلمين [Tuḥfat al-aḥbāb. A manual of elementary religious instruction for Muhammadans.] pp. 64, *lith.* مدراس ۱۳۰۸-۱۳۰۹ [*Madras*, 1892.] 8°. **14173. a. 6.**

TĀṆḌAVA-RĀYA MUDALIYĀR, *Villipākkam*. *See* BESCHI (C. G. E.). இ௸ . . . சதுரகராதி. [Chatur-agarādi. Edited by Tāṇḍava-rāya.] [1824.] 4°. **14172. f. 13.**

TĀṆḌAVA-RĀYA MUDALIYĀR, *Villipākkam (continued)*. *See* DIVĀKARAR. சேந்தன்திவாகரம் ஷ [Divākaram. Edited by Tāṇḍava-rāya.] 1877. 12°. **14172. e. 4.**

—— *See* VĪRA-MAṆḌALAVAR. ○ ○ ○ சூடாமணி நிகண்டு ஷ [Chūḍāmaṇi-nighaṇṭu. From the recension of Tāṇḍava-rāya.] 1856. 12°. **14172. e. 9.**

—— இலக்கணப்பஞ்சகங்களில் நன்னூன்மூலமும் அகப்பொருண்மூலமும் புறப்பொருட்கிலக்கியத்தோடு வெண்பாமாலைமூலமும் [Nannūl of Pavaṇandi, Nāṟ-kavi-rājar's Aga-porul-vilakkam; and Aiyanār-idanār's Veṇ-bā-mālai. Three texts on grammar and rhetoric, edited by Tāṇḍava-rāya.] pp. i. 119. ௲௮௱௩௫ [*Madras*, 1835.] 8°. **14172. e. 3.**

Pp. 1–89 are printed on light blue paper.

—— இஃது ... இலக்கணவினாவிடை. [Ilakkaṇa-vinā-viḍai. A catechism of Tamil grammar.] pp. i. 330, iv. iv. சென்னை ௲௮௱௨௰ [*Madras*, 1820.] 8°. **14172. f. 3.**

—— கதாமஞ்சரி [Kathā-mañjari. A collection of tales. Compiled by Tāṇḍava-rāya.] pp. i. 84, i. சென்னை ௲௮௱௨௰௬ [*Madras*, 1826.] 8°. **14170. k. 23.**

—— [Second edition.] pp. 80, i. ௲௮௱௪௰௬ [*Madras*, 1846.] 8°. **14170. k. 69.**

—— The Katha Manjari, or Bouquet of Stories. In Tamil and English, *etc.* pp. i. 82. *Bangalore*, 1850. 8°. **14170. k. 28.**

—— Thirty selected stories from the Kadâ Manjari [with translation] ... Arranged by P. S. Râjagôpâla Mudaliyâr. 1860. *See* MADRAS, *City of.—Civil Engineering College.* Madras Engineering College Papers. No. 1. pp. 51–85. 1860–1869. **14170. i. 7.(no. 1.)**

—— கதாமஞ்சரியும் நீதிசாரவாக்கிய ஷ [Kathā-mañjari. Followed by selections from Rāma-sāmi Piḷḷai's Nīti-sāra-vākyam.] pp. 176. புதுவை ௲௮௱௬௰௪ [*Pondicherry*, 1864.] 16°. **14171. aa. 15.**

—— Forty selected Stories of the Kadámañjari, with analysis and free translation by P. S. Râjagópâla Mudaliyâr. 1869. *See* MADRAS, *City of.—Civil Engineering College.* Madras Engineering College Papers. No. 1 (B). 1860–1869. 8°. **14170. i. 7.***

—— 'An Indian Tale or Two' [mostly selected from the Kathā-mañjari]. Reprinted from the 'Blackheath Local Guide.' With an introduction by R. B. Swinton. pp. xix. 28. *Blackheath*, [1899.] 12°. **14171. a. 20.**

—— [For editions of the Pañcha-tantram in Tāṇḍava-rāya's recension:] *See* PAÑCHA-TANTRAM.

TĀṆḌAVA-RĀYA-MŪRTTI SVĀMI. Kaivaljanavanīta. Übersetzung und Erklärung [in German]. (*Kaivaljanavanīta. A Vedanta poem. The Tamil text with a translation, a glossary, and grammatical notes, to which is added an outline of Tamil grammar [in English].) 1854–1855. *See* GRAUL (K. F. L.). Bibliotheca Tamulica, *etc.* vols. 1, 2. 1854–1865. 8°. **14170. e. 42.**

—— கைவல்யநவநீதம் ஷ [Kaivalya-nava-nītam. With commentary by Piṟaiyāṟu Aruṇāchala Svāmi. Based on the recension of Muniyappa Mudaliyār.] pp. ii. 160. திரிசிரபுரம் இரக்தாக்ஷி [*Trichinopoli*, 1864.] 8°. **14172. c. 17.**

—— கைவல்யநவநீதம் ஷ [Kaivalya-nava-nītam. With Aruṇāchala Svāmi's commentary. Edited from the recension of P. Muniy-appa Mudaliyār by T. Āṟu-muga Svāmi.] pp. iv. 154. ௲௮௱௮௰ [*Madras*, 1880.] 8°. **14170. e. 11.**

—— ○ ○ ○ கைவல்லிய நவநீதம் மூலமும் ... தத்துவார்த்ததீபமென்னும் உரையும். [Kaivalya-nava-nītam. With a commentary styled Tattvārtha-dīpam by Kōvilūr Poun'-ambala Svāmi. Edited by Subba-rāya Svāmi, Rāmānuja Mudaliyār, and Pārivākkam Mā-ṣilāmaṇi Mudaliyār. Second edition.] pp. xviii. 423. சென்னை [*Madras*,] 1898. 8°. **14170. ee. 9.**

TAṄGA-VĒLU-SĀMI DĒVAR, *V., of Ramnad.* *See* PURĀṆAS.—*Skanda-purāṇam.* ஸ்ரீ கந்தபுராண ஷ [Kanda-purāṇa-churukkam. A prose epitome of Kachiy-appar's Kanda-purāṇam, by Taṅga-vēlu-sāmi.] 1907. 8°. **14170. e. 28.**

TANI-PĀḌAL. (†தனிப்பாடற்றிரட்டு) [Tani-pāḍaṯ-ṯiraṭṭu. A collection of occasional verses ascribed to Kāḷa-mēgham, Auvaiyār, Tiru-vaḷḷuvar,

Kamban, Oṭṭa-kūttar, Pugaṛēndi, Andhaka-kavi Vīra-rāghava Mudaliyār, Ṣiva-prakāṣar, Iraṭṭaiyar, Ṣokka-nāthar, and others. With interpretations by the editors of the Vidyā-vinōdini.] சென்னை கஅகூஉ [*Madras*, 1892, *etc.*] 8°. **14172. c. 39.(5.)**

Forms part of the Vidyā-vinōdini *Series. Not completed.*

TARKA-KUṬHĀRA TĀLUDĀRI, *of Kumbakonam.* ஆன்மவிசாரம் : [Ānma-vichāram. An essay on Ṣaiva psychology.] pp. 8. சென்னை [*Madras*,] 1893. 16°. **14170. d. 33.(3.)**

TĀTĀCHĀRYAR, *Kāñchipuram Ṣyāma-dēṣika Ṣrī-ṣaila.* *See* ṢRĪṢAILA TĀTĀCHĀRYAR.

TĀTA-DĒṢIKA TĀTĀCHĀRYAR, *Eḍūrimmaḍi Tirumalai Lakshmī-kumāra Kōṭi-kannikādānam Mēl-pākkam.* *See* VĀLMĪKI. ஸ்ரீமத் வால்மீகிராமாயண ௸ [Vālmīki-rāmāyaṇa-vachanam. Translated by Tāta-dēṣika and Ṣrīnivāsa.] 1902-1903. 8°. **14172. d. 26.**

—— *See* VEṄKATA-NĀTHA VĒDĀNTĀCHĀRYAR. ○○○ ஸ்ரீதேசிகப்ரபந்தம். [Dēṣika-prabandham. With commentaries. Edited by Tāta-dēṣika.] 1889-[1890.] 8°. **14170. f. 13.**

TATTVA-BŌDHAKA SVĀMI. *See* NOBILI (R. DE').

TATTVA-BŌDHAM. ○○○ஸ்ரீதத்துவபோதம். [Tattva-bōdham. A catechism of monist Vedantic philosophy, by a disciple of Vāsudēvēndra, but here ascribed to Ṣaṅkara. Translated from the Sanskrit by V. Kuppu-svāmi Rāju.] pp. 14. சென்னை [*Madras*,] 1898. 12°. **14170. d. 32.(4.)**

—— [Second edition.] pp. 14. சென்னை [*Madras*,] 1901. 12°. **14170. d. 81.**

TATTVA-PRAKĀṢA SVĀMI, *Ṣīgāṛi, disciple of Ṣiṯṯambala-nāḍinār.* ○○○ தத்துவப்பிரகாசம் மூலமும் உரையும். [Tattva-prakāṣam. A treatise in 337 stanzas, with prose commentary, upon both the speculative and the practical themes of the Ṣaiva-siddhāntam theology. Edited by Vēlaṇai Kanda Piḷḷai.] pp. ii. iv. 258, i. கொக்குவில் நந்தன [*Kokkuvil*, 1893.] 8°. **14170. e. 46.**

TATTVA-PRAKĀṢA-TAMBIRĀN SVĀMI, *Tiruvoṯṯiyūr.* *See* ARUṆANDI DĒVA-NĀYANĀR. சிவஞானசித்தியார் ௸ [Ṣiva-ñāna-siddhiyār-parapakkam, *etc.* With commentaries on the first by Tattva-prakāṣa-tambirān.] 1897. 8°. [*Mey-kaṇḍa-ṣāttiram.*] **14170. ff. 3.**

TATTVA-RĀYA SVĀMI. சசிவர்ணபோதம். [Ṣasi-varṇa-bōdham, a poem in 110 stanzas on Ṣuddhādvaita philosophy, and Dvādaṣa-nāma-saṅkīrttanam, a Ṣaiva hymn.] *See* RĀMA-SĀMI SVĀMI. நானாஜீவவாதக்கட்டளை ௸ [Nānā-jīva-vāda-kaṭṭaḷai, *etc.*] pp. 44-64. [1887.] 12°. **14170. d. 26.**

—— ○○○ சசிவன்னபோதம் மூலமும் . . . உரையும். [Ṣaṣi-varṇa-bōdham. With Aruṇāchala Svāmi's commentary. Edited by Īṣūr Sach-chid-ānanda Svāmi. Second edition.] pp. ii. 84. மதராஸ் மன்மத [*Madras*, 1895.] 12°. **14170. d. 39.**

—— Sasivarna Potham: or The Doctrine of Sasivarna. A Vedantic poem . . . Translated from the Tamil by the Rev. Thomas Foulkes. pp. 19. *London, Madras*, 1862. 8°. **14170. e. 36.(4.)**

—— [Another copy.] **14170. e. 50.**

TATTVA-VĀDI, *Pseud.* (†ஜீவான்மாவின் பரிமாணம்.) [Jīvānmāvin parimāṇam. A tract on the constitution of the soul.] pp. 8. மதராசு [*Madras*,] 1897. 8°. **14170. ee. 28.(1.)**

No title-page.

TAUḌA SVĀMI, *Chidambaram, disciple of Ṣiva-yōga-ñāna Dharma-rāyar.* *See* PAÑCHA-PADAM. பஞ்சபதமகாவாக்கியம். [Pañcha-pada-mahā-vākyam. Purporting to be translated by Tauḍa Svāmi.] 1862. 8°. **14170. e. 13.**

TAYLOR (WILLIAM). *See* KOṄGU-DĒṢAM. Translation of the Kongu-desa-rajakal. By . . . W. Taylor. 1848. 8°. **Ac. 8829. (vol. 14.)**

—— Oriental Historical Manuscripts, in the Tamil language [chiefly bearing upon the history of the kingdom of Madura]: translated; with annotations. 2 vols. *Madras*, 1835. 4°. **14171. c. 5.**

—— Examination and Analysis of the Mackenzie Manuscripts deposited in the Madras College Library. pp. 144. *Calcutta*, 1838. 8°. **620. f. 28.**

—— A Catalogue Raisonnée [*sic*] of Oriental Manuscripts in the library of the late College,

Fort Saint George, *etc.* 3 vols. *Madras,* 1857-1862. 8°. **011900. ee. 54.**

—— A Tamil Primer for the use of beginners. pp. 46. *Madras,* 1861. 8°. **14172. h. 82.**

TĀYUMĀNAVAR. ○○○ திருப்பாடற்றிரட்டு. [Tiru-pāḍaṭ-ṭiraṭṭu. Ṣaiva devotional lyrics, in the recension of Ṣara-vaṇa Peru-māḷ Aiyar. Edited by Karuṇānanda Svāmi.] pp. iii. iv. 181. சாதாரண [*Madras,* 1851.] 8°. **14172. c. 24.**

—— ○ ○ ○ திருப்பாடற்றிரட்டு. [Tiru-pāḍaṭ-ṭiraṭṭu.] pp. vi. ii. 314, xxviii.; 3 *plates.* சென்னை [*Madras,*] 1885. 16°. **14170. d. 30.**

—— தாயுமான சுவாமிகள் . . . திருப்பாடற்றிரட்டு. [Tiru-pāḍaṭ-ṭiraṭṭu. From the recension of Ṣara-vaṇa Peru-māḷ Aiyar. Re-edited by T. Ādi-mūla Mudaliyār.] pp. 164. திரிசிரபுரம் [*Trichinopoli,*] 1885. 8°. **14172. b. 32.**

—— தாயுமானசுவாமிகள்பாடல். [Tiru-pāḍaṭ-ṭiraṭṭu. With commentary and life of the author by T. Sambandha Mudaliyār.] pp. iii. xiii. 4, 596; 1 *plate.* சென்னை [*Madras,*] 1891. 8°. **14172. c. 39.(vol. 1.)**

Forms part of the Vidyā-vinōdini Series.

—— ஸ்ரீ . . . திருப்பாடற்றிரட்டு. [Tiru-pāḍaṭ-ṭiraṭṭu. With glosses by K. Rāma-sāmi Nāyuḍu, and P. Sabhā-pati Mudaliyār's Tiruv-aruḷ-vilāsa-para-ṣiva-vaṇakkav-urai, a commentary on hymn i. 1-3. The latter edited, with a preface on Tāyu-mānavar's career, by K. Kuppu-sāmi Mudaliyār.] pp. ii. 27, 452, 29; 1 *plate.* மதராஸ் [*Madras,*] 1905. 16°. **14170. dd. 6.**

—— தாயுமானசுவாமிகள்பாடல். (†திருப்பாடற்றிரட்டு.) [Tiru-pāḍaṭ-ṭiraṭṭu. Edited with glossary, preface, *etc.*, by K. Nāga-liṅga Mudaliyār.] pp. xxiv. xii. ii. 260, xiv. i. சென்னை [*Madras,*] 1906. 12°. **14170. eee. 25.**

—— Thayumanavar's Poems. [With translation by R. Shaṇmukha Mudaliyār.] 1897, *etc.* *See* Periodical Publications.—*Madras.* The Light of Truth, *etc.* vol. i., no. 1, *etc.* 1897, *etc.* 4°. **14170. fff. 4.(vol. 1, etc.)**

In progress?

—— The Philosophical Poem [no. 1] of the saint Tháyumánavar, a great Tamil Vedanta Siddhanti. Translated [into English] with [Tamil text and] annotation &c., by R. Shanmuga Mudaliar. (†திருவருள்விலாசப்பரசிவவணக்கம்.) pp. 14. *Salem,* 1897. 12°. **14170. d. 47.**

—— Tayumanavar. A Revel in Bliss. *See* Tiru-murai.—*Tiru-vāchakam.* A few hymns of Manikka Vachaka and Tayumanavar, *etc.* pp. 33-46. 1897. 8°. **14170. ee. 12.(2.)**

—— A Revel in Bliss. (†A Supplication, God and the World, Ode to Sakti.) [In Tamil and English.] *See* Aruṇāchalam, *P.* Studies and translations, *etc.* pp. 28-62. 1898. 8°. **14170. ee. 12.(3.)**

TENNĀLU-RĀMAN. தென்னாலு இராமன்கதை. [Tennālu-rāman-kathai.] *See* Kathā-chintāmaṇi. The Katháchintámani, *etc.* pp. 61-85. 1875. 8°. **14170. k. 27.**

—— Tennālu-rāman. [Selected tales, in English.] *See* Robinson (E. J.). Tales and Poems of South India, *etc.* pp. 342-356. 1885. 8°. **14170. k. 63.**

—— Tales of Tennalirama, the famous court jester of Southern India. [Translated] by Pandit S. M. Natesa Sastri. pp. i. vi. 46. *Madras,* 1900. 12°. **14171. a. 6.(4.)**

TĒNUVARAI PERU-MĀḶ. *See* Bhōja-rāja Paṇḍitar.

TĒR AIYAR. *See* Subrahmaṇya Paṇḍitar, *T. M.* ○○○ பதார்த்தகுணசிந்தாமணி. [Padārtha-guṇa-chintāmaṇi. With commentary founded on works of Tēr Aiyar.] [1867.] 8°. **14170. i. 62.**

—— ○ ○ ○ மருத்துபாரதம் மூலம். [Maruttu-bhāratam. A poem on the theme of the Mahā-bhāratam and containing a number of medical prescriptions, ascribed to the legendary Tēr Aiyar. Edited by K. S. Mṛugēṣa Mudaliyār.] (V. M. Medical Series. No. 1.) pp. 108. சென்னை [*Madras,*] 1907. 12°. **14172. a. 60.**

—— இராஜவைத்தியமகுடம். [Rāja-vaidya-makuṭam. A treatise on medicine, comprising excerpts from the Edugai-yamaka-veṇ-bā of Tēr Aiyar, edited with a commentary by B. Muhammad 'Abd Allāh.] vol. i. pp. 12, 20, 358, 5. சென்னை [*Madras,*] 1899. 12°. **14170. i. 61.**

TĒRAN. *See* TĒR AIYAR.

TEROOVERCAUDOO SOOBROYA MODELLIAR. *See* SUBBA-RĀYA MUDALIYĀR, *Tiruvēṟkāḍu.*

TEYVAM. தெய்வப்பரிட்சை. [Teyva-parīkshai. A criticism of the cults and histories of Hindu divinities, by Roman Catholic missionaries.] pp. 97, i. புதுவை ௲அ௱சமசு [*Pondicherry,* 1816.] 12°. **14170. b. 23.**

TEYVA-NĀYAKA MUDALIYĀR, *Valli P.* *See* TIRU-VAḶḶUVAR. ◦◦◦ தமிழ்வேதமாகிய திருக்குறள் ௸ [Kuṟaḷ. Edited by Teyva-nāyakar.] 1904. 8°. **14172. c. 46.**

TEYVA-ṢIKHĀMAṆI AYYAR, *Ṣivagengai.* *See* VEṆṆI-MALAI PIḶḶAI. நைடதம் ௸ [Nala-chakra-vartti-ammānai. Edited by Teyva-ṣikhāmaṇi.] 1904. 8°. **14172. cc. 2.**

TEYVA-ṢIKHĀMAṆI MUDALIYĀR, *P.* *See* ĀḶAVANDĀR. ◦◦◦ ஞானவாசிட்ட ௸ [Yōga-vāṣiṭṭav-amala-rāmāyaṇam. Edited by Teyva-ṣikhāmaṇi.] 1902. 8°. **14170. ee. 53.**

TEYVA-ṢIKHĀMAṆI MUDALIYĀR, *Tirumayilai.* *See* POYYĀ-MOḺI PULAVAR. தஞ்சைவாணன்கோவை ௸ [Tañjai-vāṇan-kōvai. Edited by Teyva-ṣikhāmaṇi.] 1893. 8°. **14172. b. 53.**

THAMOTHERAM. *See* DĀMŌDARAM.

THAMPAPILLAI. *See* TAMBA PIḶḶAI.

THAVARAJA PUNDIT. *See* DĒVA-RĀJA KAVI-RĀYAR.

THEOLOGY. Outlines of systematic Theology. கிறிஸ்துமார்க்கத்தின் போதசாரம். [Edited and revised by J. P. Jones.] pp. lii. 379. *Madras,* 1901. 8°. **14170. bbb. 1.**

THEROOVENGADA. *See* TIRU-VĒṄKAṬA.

THIRUVENKATA CHARI. *See* TIRU-VĒṄKAṬĀCHĀRI.

THOMAS (SAMUEL VĒDA-NĀYAKAM). *See* MILTON (J.). Paradise Lost. Books i. & ii. Translated into Tamil by S. V. Thomas, *etc.* 1887. 8°. **14172. b. 42.**

THOMAS (VĒDA-MUTTU FRANCIS). *See* DIALOGUE. A Dialogue between a Protestant Christian and a Càsi Pandáram . . . Edited . . . by V. F. Thomas. 1857. 8°. **14170. c. 20.**

THUMBIAPPEN. *See* TAMBIY-APPAN.

THUMBOO CHETTIAR. *See* TAMBU CHEṬṬIYĀR.

TILLAI-NAMBI. *See* PERUM-BAṮṮA-PULIY-ŪR-NAMBI.

TILLAI-NĀTHA PIḶḶAI, *Pulōli M.* *See* PARAÑ-JŌDI MUNIVAR. ◦◦◦ திருவிளையாடற்புராணம் ௸ [Vēdattukku poruḷ aruḷi cheyda paṭalam. With paraphrase and commentary by Tillai-nātha Piḷḷai.] [1894.] 8°. **14170. e. 67.**

TINNEVELLI.—*Hindu-dēvālaya-rakshaṇa-sabhai.* திருநெல்வேலி ஜில்லா ஹிந்து தேவாலயரக்ஷண சபையின் விதானங்கள். [Rules of the Society for the Preservation of Hindu Temples in the *zillah* of Tinnevelli.] pp. 7. *Tinnevelly,* ௲அ௱௯௩ [1893.] 16°. **14170. a. 61.**

TIRAṆA-DŪMĀKKINI. *See* TOL-KĀPPIYANĀR.

TĪRTHA PIḶḶAI, *Kōyil-Kandāḍai Lakshmaṇā-chāryar.* திருமுடி அடைவு. [Tiru-muḍiy-aḍaivu. A list of eminent Vaishṇava devotees and their works, *etc.*] *See* VĒṄKAṬA-NĀTHA VĒDĀNTĀCHĀRYAR. ஸ்ரீ . . . வைபவஸாரஸங்கிரகம் ௸ [Nigamānta-mahā-dēṣikan-vaibhava-sāra-saṅgraham.] pp. 17-36. [1894.] 12°. **14170. d. 46.(2.)**

TIRU-CHELVA-RĀYAN. *See* ARUḶ-APPA NĀVALAR. திருச்செல்வர்காவியம். [Tiru-chelvar-kāvyam. A poem on the life of Tiru-chelva-rāyan, a Catholic devotee.] 1896. 8°. **14170. bb. 6.**

TIRU-CHIṮṮAMBALA DĒṢIKAN. *See* VĀLMĪKI. ◦◦◦ ராமாயண ௸ [Uttara-kāṇḍa-kathai. A prose version, by Tiru-chiṭṭambala Dēṣikan.] [1815.] 8°. **14172. b. 4.**

TIRU-CHIṮṮAMBALAM PIḶḶAI, *Ṣ., of Coimbàtore.* மாணிக்கவாசகர். (Manickavachakar. [An essay] by . . . C. Thiruchittambalam Pillay.) pp. i. 90. *Madras,* 1900. 12°. **14171. a. 33.(2.)**

TIRU-CHIṮṮAMBALA NĀVALAR, *Māmbākkam Upādhyāyar.* அண்ணாமலைச்சதகம். [Aṇṇāmalai-ṣatakam. A poem on the Ṣaiva sanctuary of Tiru-vannamalai.] *See* ELL'-APPA NĀVALAR. அருணசல புராணம் ௸ [Aruṇāchala-purāṇam.] pp. 541-576. 1902. 12°. **14170. d. 75.**

—— pp. 541-576. 1903. 12°. **14170. d. 83.**

TIRUKADAVUR. திருக்கடவூர் புராணம். [Tiru-kaḍavūr-purāṇam. The legends of the Ṣaiva sanctuary at Tirukadavur, summarised by Ṣ. Bāla-kṛushṇa Dīkshitar.] pp. i. i. 198. சென்னை [*Madras*,] 1905. 12°. **14170. dd. 4.**

TIRUKOVALUR. தெய்வீகபுராணம் என்னும் திருக்கோவலூர்ப்புராணம். [Tirukōvalūr-purāṇam, or Teyvīga-purāṇam. The legends of the Ṣaiva cult at Tirukovalur, in verse. Edited with introduction by Ṣ. V. Saundara-raja Uḍaiyār.] pp. xxxviii. 319. கும்பகோணம் [*Kumbakonam*,] 1901. 8°. **14170. ee. 57.**

TIRU-KURUGAI-PIRĀN PILḶĀN. *See* PILḶAI TIRUMALAI NAMBI.

TIRUMALĀCHĀRYAR, *Kandāḍai.* *See* TIRU-MUḌIY-AḌAIVU. శ్రీ . . . పెరియ తిరుముడి యడవు. [Periya-tiru-muḍiy-aḍaivu. Edited by Tirumalāchāryar.] 1898. 12°. **14170. d. 49.**

TIRUMALĀCHĀRYAR, *M. K.* *See* ĀṞVĀRGAḶ.—Nāl-āyiram.—*Mudal-āyiram.* ००० తమిళ్వేదమ్ వ॥ [Mudal-āyiram. Edited by Tirumalāchāryar.] 1889. 8°. **14170. e. 33.**

TIRUMALĀCHĀRYAR, *Yadu-giri Jīyar-sannidhi.* *See* AṞAGIYA-MAṆAVĀḶA PERU-MĀḶ. ००० யதிராஜவிம்ஶதி. [Yati-rāja-viṃṣati. Edited by Tirumalāchāryar.] [1884.] 12°. **14028. b. 63.(1.)**

—— *See* ĀṞVĀRGAḶ.—Nāl-āyiram.—*Selections.* ००० நித்யானுஸந்தாநம் ஷ [Nityānusandhānam, *etc.* Edited by Tirumalāchāryar.] 1886. 8°. **14170. ee. 14.**

TIRUMALAI-KOṞUNDU PILḶAI, *Ṣ. A.* The Age of Manicka Vachakar. With an account of the Third Academy at Madura. pp. i. i. iii. 117, i. *Madras*, 1899. 12°. **14171. a. 33.(1.)**

TIRUMALAI NĀYAKAR, *Raja of Madura.* The Accounts of Tirumali-Naicker, and of his Buildings. (†The Arrangement of the Palace of Tirumali-Naicker, *etc.*) [Tamil text with English translation.] *See* TAYLOR (W.). Oriental Historical Manuscripts, *etc.* vol. ii., pp. 147-168. 1835. 4°. **14171. c. 5.**

TIRU-MĀḶIKAI DĒVAR. [For the hymns of this author contained in the Tiruv-iṣai-pā :] *See* TIRU-MUṞAI.

TIRU-MAṄGAIY-ĀṞVĀR. [For editions of the Periya-tiru-moṛi, Tiruv-eṛugūṭṭ'-irukkai, Periya-tiru-maḍal, and Ṣiṛiya-tiru-maḍal of this saint included in the editions of the whole or parts of the Nāl-āyira-prabandham :] *See* ĀṞVĀRGAḶ.—*Nāl-āyiram.*

TIRU-MAṞIṢAI PIRĀN. [For editions of the Tiru-chanda-vṛuttam and Tiruv-antādi of this saint included in the editions of the whole or parts of the Nāl-āyira-prabandham :] *See* ĀṞVĀRGAḶ.—*Nāl-āyiram.*

TIRU-MUḌIY-AḌAIVU. திருமுடியடைவு. [Tiru-muḍiy-aḍaivu. A short chronicle of the Church Fathers of the Rāmānujīya Vaishṇavas.] *See* AṞAGIYA-MAṆAVĀḶA PERU-MĀḶ. ஸ்ரீ . . . உபதேசரத்தினமாலை ஷ [Upadēṣa-ratna-mālai, *etc.*] [1836.] 8°. **14172. b. 3.**

—— శ్రీ . . . ఆచార్య పరమ్పరావైభవ సంగ్రహమైన పెరియ తిరుముడి యడవు. [Periya-tiru-muḍiy-aḍaivu. A fuller chronicle with interspersed verses. Edited by Kandāḍai Tirumalāchāryar.] pp. 110. [*Madras*,] 1898. 12°. **14170. d. 49.**

TIRU-MUṞAI. [For poems of Nambiy-āṇḍār Nambi, the compiler of this collection, other than those included in the latter :] *See* NAMBIY-ĀṆḌĀR NAMBI.

TWO OR MORE SECTIONS.

००० தேவாரத்திரட்டு. (திருவாசகம், திருவிசைப்பா, *etc.*) [Dēvāram, by Ñāna-sambandhar, Sundara-mūrtti, and Tiru-nāvukk'-araṣu (Appar), forming bks. 1-7 of the Tiru-muṛai, in a recension ascribed to Agastyar; Māṇikka-vāchakar's Tiru-vāchakam, forming bk. 8; Tiruv-iṣai-pā, by various authors, forming bk. 9; Ṣēndanār's Tiru-pall'-āṇḍu; and extracts from the Periya-purāṇam. Ṣaiva devotional lyrics. Edited (pts. 1-2) by Nallūr Āṟū-muga Nāvalar.] 3 pts. சென்னப்பட்டணம் விக்கிரம [*Madras*, 1880.] 8°. **14172. b. 8.**

Pt. 1 is a third edition.
The traditional authors of the Tiruv-iṣai-pā *are* Tiru-māḷikai Dēvar, Ṣēndanār, Karuvūr Dēvar, Pūndurutti Nambi-gāḍa Nambi, Kaṇḍar-āditttar, Vēṇāṭṭ'-aḍigaḷ, Tiruv-āliy-amudanār, Puruḍōttama Nambi, *and* Chēdi-rāyar.

००० தேவாரத்திரட்டு. (*திருவாசகம், *etc.*) [Dēvāram, Tiru-vāchakam, Tiruv-iṣai-pā, Tiru-pall'-āṇḍu, and Periya-purāṇam. Another issue of the preceding collection. Fourth edition.] 3 pts. சென்னப்பட்டணம் பார்த்திவ [*Madras*, 1885.] 8°. **14172. b. 35.**

DĒVĀRAM.

∘∘∘ தேவாரத்திரட்டு மூலமும் . . . உரையும். [Dēvāra-tiraṭṭu. The hymns of the Dēvāram in the recension ascribed to Agastyar. Edited, with biographies of their traditional authors Ñāna-sambandhar, Appar, and Sundara-mūrtti, by K. Rāma-sāmi Nāyuḍu.] pp. iv. xliv. 163. சென்னை [*Madras*,] 1906. 8°. **14170. eee. 30.**

கோயில் (†திருக்காளத்தி, திருஅண்ணமலை, திருவானைக்கா, திருவாரூர்) தேவாரப்பதிகங்கள். [Pañcha-bhūta-tala-dēvāra-padigaṅgaḷ. A series of hymns by Ñāna-sambandhar, Sundara-mūrtti, and Appar, for the rituals of the sanctuaries of Chidambaram, Kalahasti, Tiruvanna-malai, Tiruvanaika, and Tiruvalur.] pp. 116. *See* Ṣiva. சிவபூசைத்திரட்டு ஸூ [Ṣiva-pūjai-tiraṭṭu.] [1875.] 12°. **14170. d. 11.**

தேவாரம். [Dēvāram. Another collection by the same authors.] pp. 20, i. i. *See* Aghōra Dēvar. ∘∘∘ வேதாரணிய புராணம் ஸூ [Vēdā-raṇya-purāṇam.] 1898. 8°. **14170. e. 65.**

தேவாரப்பதிகங்கள். [Dēvāra-padigaṅgaḷ. Hymns on the Kāḷaiyār or Kānapēr sanctuary.] *See* Subrahmaṇya Aiyar, *T. Ṣ.* ∘∘∘ காளையார்கோவிற்புராண ஸூ [Kāḷaiyār-kōvir-purāṇa-vachanam.] pp. 1-8. 1897. 12°. **14170. d. 61.**

—— [The same.] *See* Subrahmaṇya Aiyar, *T. Ṣ.* ∘∘∘ காளையார்கோவிற்புராணம். [Kāḷaiyār-kōvir-purāṇam.] pp. 1-4. 1899. 8°. **14170. ee. 22.**

தேவாரத்திருப்பதிகம். [Two hymns, on the sanctuary of Kētīṣvaram. With paraphrase.] pp. 9. *See* Purāṇas.—*Skanda-purāṇam.* திருக்கேதீச்சரமகிமை. [Tiru-kētīṣvara-mahimai.] [1891.] 8°. **14170. e. 41.(2.)**

∘∘∘ திருஏகம்பத்தேவாரப்பதிகங்கள். [Tiru-ēkamba-dēvāra-padigaṅgaḷ. 12 hymns on the cult of Ṣiva as Ēkāmbara-nāthar and Dēvi as Kāmākshi-ammai. Edited by K. S. Bāla-subrahmaṇya Mudaliyār.] pp. 22; 1 *plate.* யுவ [*Madras*, 1875.] 16°. **14170. d. 12.**

[The Dēvāram of Tirupunkur.] pp. 6. *See* [Addenda] Kanaka-sabhai Kavi-rāyar. திருப்புன்கூர்ப்புராணம். [Tirupunkūr-purāṇam.] 1907. 8°. **14170. eee. 27.**

திருவாலவாய்த்தேவாரம். [Tiruv-ālavāy-dēvāram. Eleven hymns on the Ṣaiva cult of Ālavāy or Madura.] *See* Parañ-jōdi Munivar. திருவிளையாடற் புராணம். [Tiru-viḷaiy-āḍar-purāṇam.] pp. 464-483. [1882.] 8°. **14170. ee. 2.**

—— [The same.] *See* Parañ-jōdi Munivar. ∘∘∘ திருவிளையாடற்புராணம் ஸூ [Tiru-viḷaiy-āḍar-purāṇam.] vol. ii., pp. 919-934. [1887.] 8°. **14170. f. 10.**

—— [The same.] *See* Parañ-jōdi Munivar. மதுரை . . . திருவிளையாடற்புராணம் [Tiru-viḷaiy-āḍar-purāṇam.] pp. i.-xix. 1896. 8°. **14170. ee. 3.**

—— —— 1906. 8°. **14170. eee. 24.**

தேவாரம். [Hymns on the sanctuary of Tiru-vadi.] pp. 27. *See* Tiruvadi. ஸ்ரீ . . . திருவையாற்றுப்புராணம். [Tiruv-aiy-āṭṭu-purāṇam.] 1907. 8°. **14170. eee. 22.**

தேவாரப்பதிகம். [Dēvāra-padigam. Five hymns on the sanctuary of Tiruvannamalai.] *See* Ell'-appa Nāvalar. அருணசலபுராணம் ஸூ [Aruṇā-chala-purāṇam.] pp. 1-10. 1898. 12°. **14170. d. 52.**

—— —— pp. 1-14. 1902. 12°. **14170. d. 75.**

—— —— pp. 1-14. 1903. 12°. **14170. d. 83.**

—— —— pp. xvii.-xxvi. 1903. 12°. **14170. d. 84.**

TIRU-MANTRAM.

Thirumantra by Thirumoolar. [Text with translation by Ṣ. Rāma-sāmi Aiyar.] 1897, *etc.* *See* Periodical Publications.—*Madras.* The Light of Truth, *etc.* vol. i., no. 1, *etc.* 1897, *etc.* 4°. **14170. fff. 4.(vol. 1, etc.)**

In progress.

TIRU-VĀCHAKAM.

திருவாசகம். [Tiru-vāchakam. Edited by Ṣiva-koḻundu Dēṣikar and Ṣara-vaṇa Peru-māḷ Aiyar. With life of the poet.] pp. iii. 122. பிங்கள [*Madras?* 1857.] 8°. **14172. b. 15.**

∘∘∘ திருவாசகம் மூலமும் உரையும் ஸூ [Tiru-vāchakam. With a life of the poet, commendatory verses, glossary of Sanskrit terms, indices, and glosses on the text.] pp. ii. iv. iv. ii. ii. i. 508, vi.; 1 *plate*. [*Madras*,] 1897. 8°. **14172. b. 56.**

∘∘∘ திருவாசகமும் . . . உரையும் ஆ [Tiru-vāchakam. With commentary, glossaries, indices, *etc*. Preceded by a prose version of Kaḍavuṇ Māmuni's Tiruvādavūrar-purāṇam, by the same. Edited by P. Vāsudēva Mudaliyār.] pp. iii. 102, 516, vii. ii. viii.; 3 *plates*. சென்னை [*Madras*,] 1897. 8°. **14172. b. 57.**

The Tiruvāçagam, or 'Sacred Utterances' of . . . Māṇikka-Vāçagar . . . with English translation, introductions, and notes. To which is prefixed a summary of the life and legends of the sage, with appendices illustrating the great South-Indian system of philosophy and religion called the Çaiva Siddhāntam. With Tamil lexicon and concordance. By . . . G. U. Pope. (*திருவாசகம்.) pp. xcvii. 354, 84. *Oxford*, 1900. 8°. **14170. ff. 7.**

திருவெம்பாவை. (†திருவம்மானை.) [Tiruv-embāvai and Tiruv-ammānai, being nos. 7 and 8 of the Tiru-vāchakam.] *See* ELL'-APPA NĀVALAR. அருணசலபுராணம் ஆ [Aruṇāchala-purāṇam.] pp. xi.-xxii. 1898. 12°. **14170. d. 52.**

—— —— pp. 15-26. 1902. 12°. **14170. d. 75.**

—— —— pp. 15-26. 1903. 12°. **14170. d. 83.**

—— —— pp. xxvii.-xxxviii. 1903. 12°. **14170. d. 84.**

A few hymns of Manikka Vachaka [viz. nos. 22, 4, and 20] and Tayumanavar. Translated by P. A[ruṇāchalam] and G. U. Pope. (The "Siddhanta Deepika" Series:—No. 1.) pp. 46. *Madras*, 1897. 8°. **14170. ee. 12.(2.)**

The House of God. (†The Pilgrim's Progress.) [Hymns xxii. and iv. of the Tiru-vāchakam, in Tamil and English.] *See* ARUṆĀCHALAM, *P*. Studies and translations, *etc*. pp. 7-27. 1898. 8°. **14170. ee. 12.(3.)**

திருவெம்பாவை. [Tiruv-em-bāvai.] pp. 4. *See* KAḌAVUṆ MĀ-MUNI. ∘∘∘ திருவாதவூரடிகள்புராணம் ஆ [Tiruvādavūr-aḍigaḷ-purāṇam.] [1897.] 8°. **14171. a. 16.**

—— *See* TIRU-CHIṮṮAMBALAM PIḶḶAI. மாணிக்கவாசகர். (Manickavachakar, *etc*.) 1900. 12°. **14171. a. 33.(2.)**

—— *See* TIRUMALAI-KOṞUNDU PIḶḶAI. The Age of Manicka Vachakar, *etc*. 1899. 12°. **14171. a. 33.(1.)**

TIRUV-IṢAI-PĀ.

திருவிசைப்பா. [Tiruv-iṣai-pā of Tirunāṅgūr Ṣēndanār. Ṣaiva hymns.] *See* PAṬṬAṆATTU PIḶḶAI. ∘∘∘ திரு . . . பாடற்றிருமுறை ஆ [Pāḍaṯ-ṯiru-muṟai.] pp. 135-141. 1906. 8°. **14170. ff. 16.**

TIRU-NĀGĒṢVARA MUDALIYĀR, *Toṟuvūr Vēlāyudha*. *See* PAṬṬAṆATTU PIḶḶAI. ∘∘∘ திரு . . . பாடற்றிருமுறை. [Pāḍaṯ-ṯiru-muṟai, *etc*. Revised by Tiru-nāgēṣvara.] 1906. 8°. **14170. ff. 16.**

TIRU-ÑĀNA-SAMBANDHAR, *Ṣaiva Apostle*. *See* ÑĀNA-SAMBANDHAR.

TIRU-ÑĀNA-SAMBANDHA-SVĀMI PIḶḶAI, *Triṣirapuram Kumāra-svāmi*. சித்தாந்தசைவவினாவிடை [Siddhānta-ṣaiva-vinā-viḍai. A catechism of the Ṣaiva Siddhāntam.] pp. 7, 232. சென்னை விகாரி [*Madras*, 1899.] 16°. **14170. d. 55.**

TIRU-NĀRĀYAṆA-DĀSAR, *Tiruppattūr R. K., disciple of Tirumalai-Bhaṭṭāryar*. *See* YĀDAVA-GIRI. ∘∘∘ சதுர்வேதி சரித்திர சங்கீர்த்தனை. [Chaturvēdi-charitra-saṅkīrttanai. Translated by Tiru-nārāyaṇa-dāsar.] 1900. 8°. **14170. ee. 35.(4.)**

TIRU-NĀVUKK'-ARAṢU (APPAR). [For editions of the Dēvāram composed by Ñāna-sambandhar, Sundara-mūrtti, and Tiru-nāvukk'-araṣu :] *See* TIRU-MUṞAI.

TIRU-PADI. நூற்றெட்டுத்திருப்பதி ப்ரபாவம். [Nūṯṯ'-eṭṭu-tiru-padi-prabhāvam. A condensed account of the 108 Vaishṇava shrines.] pp. 78. சென்னை [*Madras*,] 1898. 16°. **14170. d. 67.**

TIRU-PĀṈ ĀṞVĀR. [For editions of the Amalanādi-birān of this saint included in the editions of the whole or parts of the Nāl-āyira-prabandham :] *See* ĀṞVĀRGAḶ.—*Nāl-āyiram*.

TIRU-TAKKA DĒVAR. ∘∘∘ சீவகசிந்தாமணி-மூலமும் . . . நச்சினார்க்கினியருரையும். [Jīvaka-chintāmaṇi. One of the classical epics, on a romantic Jain legend. With the commentary of Nachinārkk'-iniyar. Edited with preface, indices, *etc.*, by U. V. Sāminātli'-aiyar.] pp. iv. i. v. xvi. iii. i. 875, ii. iv. iii. xxiv. iv. சென்னை [*Madras,*] 1887. 8°. **14172. d. 6.**

This author is later than Guṇa-bhadra (c. 900 A.D.), *and earlier than Ṣēkkiṟār.*

—— ◦◦◦ சீவகசிந்தாமணி ஞூ [Jīvaka-chintāmaṇi. With Nachinārkk'-iniyar's commentary. Edited by U. V. Sāmināth'-aiyar. Second edition.] pp. ii. 28, cxi. 1048. சென்னை [*Madras,*] 1907. 8°. **14172. bb. 28.**

—— ◦◦◦ சீவக சிந்தாமணி வசனகாவியம். (Jeevaga Chinthamani. One of the five Kaviams.) [A prose paraphrase by Ā. K. Kumāra-svāmi Mudaliyār.] pp. 8, 144. *Tirupatur*, 1907. 8°. **14171. e. 23.(1.)**

—— Le Sindamani. [A French epitome.] *See* Vinson (É. H. J.). Légendes Bouddhistes et Djainas, *etc.* vol. i., pp. 1-109. 1900. 12°. **14171. aa. 4.**

—— Un épisode du poème épique Sindâmaṇi. [Edited and translated by J. Vinson.] *See* Academies, *etc.*—Paris.—*École Spéciale des Langues Orientales Vivantes.* Mélanges Orientaux, *etc.* pp. 547-577. 1883. 8°. **14003. i. 16.**

—— University of Madras. B.A. Examination of 1906. Jivakachintamani. Namagalilambakam. With Nachinarkkiniyar's commentary and explanatory notes by V. Saminatha Aiyar. pp. 40, 215. *Madras*, 1905. 8°. **14172. bb. 21.(2.)**

—— ◦◦◦ நரிவிருத்தம் [Nari-vṛuttam. A fable in 51 stanzas, similar in theme to Hitōpadēṣa I., fab. 7. Edited with notes and glosses by M. Rāghav'-aiyaṅgār.] pp. 20. 1907. *See* Academies, *etc.*—*Madura.* ["Ṣen-damiṛ" supplement.] no. 20. 1902, *etc.* 8°. **14172. i. 1.*(no. 20.)**

TIRUVĀDAVŪRAR. *See* Māṇikka-vāchakar.

TIRUVADI. ஸ்ரீபஞ்சநதமான்மியம் என்னும் திருவையாற்றுப்புராணம். [Tiruv-aiy-āṯṯu-purāṇam, or Pañcha-nada-mānmiyam. The legends of the Ṣaiva sanctuary at Tiruvadi, Tanjore District. Done into prose by K. Veṅkaṭa-rāma Ṣāstri, and stylistically recast by K. Ṣ. Ṣōlai-muttu Piḷḷai. Followed by the local Dēvāram.] pp. iv. 88, 27. தஞ்சை [*Tanjore,*] 1907. 8°. **14170. eee. 22.**

TIRUVAIGAVUR. திருவைகாவூர்ப்புராணம். [Tiruvaigāvūr-purāṇam. A metrical account of the legends of the Ṣaiva sanctuary at Tiruvaigavur. Translated from the Sanskrit by Kavitalam C. Vēlai Dēṣikar. Edited by Rāmānujapuram Ṣivaliṅgam Piḷḷai.] pp. x. ii. 71. கும்பகோணம் கஅகூச [*Kumbakonam*, 1894.] 8°. **14170. e. 56.**

TIRUV-ĀLIY-AMUDANĀR. [For the hymns of this author contained in the Tiruv-iṣai-pā :] *See* Tiru-muṟai.

TIRU-VAḶḶUVAR. *See* Dvita-mata-tiraskāri, *Pseud.* (†முதற்குறள்வாதம்.) [Mudaṟ-kuṟaḷ-vādam. A tract on the first verse of the Kuṟaḷ.] 1897. 8°. **14170. ee. 32.(1.)**

—— *See* Dvita-mata-tiraskāri, *Pseud.* ◦◦◦ முதற்குறளுண்மை . . . The Truth of the First Kural, *etc.* 1900. 8°. **14170. ee. 29.**

—— *See* Ṣelva-kēṣava-rāya Mudaliyār. Tiruvalluvar. An essay. 1904. 12°. **14171. d. 2.**

—— *See* Vēdāchalam Piḷḷai. முதற்குறள்வாதநிராகரணம். [Mudaṟ-kuṟaḷ-vāda-nirākaraṇam. A reply to the Mudaṟ-kuṟaḷ-vādam.] 1898. 8°. **14170. ee. 32.(2.)**

—— (†அறப்பால On Virtue.) [Kuṟaḷ. Three series of verses on ethical and erotic themes. Edited by F. W. Ellis, with translation and commentary in English.] pp. 304. [*Madras*, 1816?] 4°. **14172. c. 5.**

Published without title-page or date, the work having been left unfinished on the editor's death.

The Kuṟaḷ forms the 11th of the Kiṟ-kaṇakku *poems.*

—— The Cural of Tiruvalluvar . . . with the commentary of Parimelaragar, an amplification of that commentary by Ramanuja Cavi-Rayar, and an English translation of the text, by the Rev. W. H. Drew. 2 pts. *Madras*, 1840-1852. 8°. **14172. b. 48.**

This edition extends to v. 630, or 63 chapters out of 133.

—— ◦◦◦ திருக்குறள் மூலம் ஞூ [Kuṟaḷ. With a commentary based on that of Parimēl-aṟagar and other works, compiled by Vēda-giri Mudaliyār. Followed by the Tiru-vaḷḷuva-mālai, 53 stanzas by various authors in praise of Tiruvalluvar, with commentary by Ṣara-vaṇa Peru-māḷ.] pp. iv. xvi. iii. 488, 32, xix. இலக [*Madras*, 1849.] 8°. **14172. c. 2.**

—— Der Kural des Tiruvalluver. Ein gnomisches Gedicht über die drei Strebeziele des Menschen. Übersetzung und Erklärung von Karl Graul. (*Kural of Tiruvalluver. High-Tamil text with translation into common Tamil and Latin, notes and glossary. By Charles Graul . . . Published after the author's death by William Germann.) (*Tiruvalluveri Kural versione latina adnotationibus glossarioque illustratus.) 2 pts. 1856-1865. *See* GRAUL (K. F. L.). Bibliotheca Tamulica, *etc.* vols. 3-4. 1854-1865. 8°. **14170. e. 42.**

—— ◦◦◦ தமிழ்வேதமாகிய திருக்குறண் மூலமும் பரிமேலழகருரையும். [Kuṟaḷ. With the commentary of Parimēl-aṟagar. Followed by the Tiru-vaḷḷuva-mālai with Ṣara-vaṇa Peru-māḷ's commentary. Edited by Āṟu-muga Nāvalar.] pp. viii. ii. 384, 28, xi. சென்னபட்டணம் துன்மதி [*Madras*, 1861.] 8°. **14172. d. 7.**

—— —— [Second edition.] pp. viii. ii. 365, 26, x. சென்னபட்டணம் யுவ [*Madras*, 1875.] 8°. **14172. d. 8.**

—— ◦◦◦ திருக்குறள் மூலமும் உரையும் ௵ [Kuṟaḷ. With commentary based chiefly upon that of Parimēl-aṟagar, together with interpretations and prolegomena purporting to be those of Ṣara-vaṇa Peru-māḷ Aiyar. Edited by M. Vīrāsāmi Piḷḷai. Followed by the Tiru-vaḷḷuva-mālai with Ṣara-vaṇa Peru-māḷ's commentary.] pp. 434, 24, ii. x. ii. யுவ [*Madras*, 1875.] 8°. **14172. c. 10.**

A reprint of the edition of 1849.

—— ◦◦◦ திருக்குறண்மூலம். [Kuṟaḷ.] pp. 133. சென்னபட்டணம் [*Madras*,] 1881. 16°. **14172. h. 35.(4.)**

—— The Kural of Tiruvalluvar, with the commentary of Parimelazagar and a simple and clear padavuray. [Edited by Mṛugēṣa Mudaliyār.] To which is added an English translation of the text by the Rev. J. Lazarus. [Followed by the Tiru-vaḷḷuva-mālai.] (*தமிழ்வேதமாகிய திருக்குறள் மூலமும் . . . இலக்கணவுரையும்.) pp. 4, 4, 623, 29, x.; 1 *plate*. *Madras*, 1885. 8°. **14172. d. 15.**

—— திருவள்ளுவநாயனார் அருளிச்செய்த திருக்குறள். The 'Sacred' Kurraḷ of Tiruvaḷḷuva-Nâyanâr. With introduction, grammar, translation, notes, in which are reprinted Fr. C. J. Beschi's and F. W. Ellis's versions, lexicon, and concordance. By the Rev. G. U. Pope. pp. vi. ii. xxviii. i. 328, 80. *London*, 1886. 8°. **14172. c. 40.**

—— ◦◦◦ குறள் மூலமும் சுகாத்தியர் இயற்றிய கருத்துரையட்டவணையும் பொழிப்புரையும் ௵ [Kuṟaḷ. Edited with a commentary by "Sugāttiyar," *i.e.* Ṭ. M. Scott of Madura.] pp. 275. [*Madras*,] 1889. 8°. **14172. c. 35.**

This edition is peculiar in writing அய் *for* ஐ *throughout, a double consonant for a single consonant preceded by the "muppuḷḷi," and other innovations. The text has apparently been emended with great freedom, and differs considerably from that of the current editions.*

—— ◦◦◦ தமிழ்வேதமாகிய திருக்குறள்மூலமும், பரிமேலழகருரையும். [Kuṟaḷ. With commentary of Parimēl-aṟagar, and with paraphrases, notes, and biography by G. Vaḍi-vēlu Cheṭṭi. Followed by the Tiru-vaḷḷuva-mālai with Ṣara-vaṇa Peru-māḷ's commentary. Edited by Vaḍi-vēlu and V. P. Teyva-nāyaka Mudaliyār.] pp. iii. vi. ii. 1208, 30, 28, xi. ii.; 1 *plate*. சென்னை [*Madras*,] 1904. 8°. **14172. c. 46.**

—— Der tamulische Gnomen-Dichter Tiruvalluver, als Spiegel des tamulischen Volksgeistes. [The Kuṟaḷ, translated into German by K. Graul.] *See* GRAUL (K. F. L.). Indische Sinnpflanzen und Blumen, *etc.* pp. 33-174. 1865. 16°. **14172. a. 39.**

—— Extracts from the Teeroo-vaulaver-kuddul, or the Ocean of Wisdom [*sic*]. *See* KINDERSLEY (N. E.). Specimens of Hindoo Literature, *etc.* pp. 51-82. 1794. 8°. **980. k. 19.**

—— Kuṟaḷ de Tiruvaḷḷuvar, fragments traduits du tamoul [by E. Ariel]. (Journal Asiatique. Quatrième série, tome xii., pp. 423-433, xix., pp. 381-435.) *Paris*, 1848, 1852. 8°. **Ac. 8808. (4e série, tom. 12, 19.)**

—— Maximes traduites des Courals de Tirouvallouvar, ou la Morale des Pariahs, d'après des extraits de poésies tamoules . . . par P. G. de Dumast. (Extrait des Mémoires de l'Académie de Stanislas.) pp. 25. *Nancy*, 1854. 8°. **14172. b. 47.**

—— [Another edition.] *See* INDIA. Fleurs de l'Inde, *etc.* pp. 151-172. 1857. 8°. **14085. d. 4.**

TIRU - VAḶḶUVAR (*continued*). Odes from the Cural [in English verse, preceded by a life of the poet]. *See* GOVER (C. E.). The Folk-songs of Southern India, *etc.* pp. 200-245. 1872. 8°. **14170. k. 71.**

—— Le Livre des Devoirs de Tirouvallouva le divin Pariah. [Comprising portions of the Aṟattu pāl and Poruṭ-pāl.] *See* JACOLLIOT (L.). Le Pariah dans l'Humanité. pp. 77-220. 1876. 8°. **10058. cc. 1.**

—— The Divine Pariah. [The legends connected with the life of Tiru-vaḷḷuvar, with a metrical translation of pts. i. and ii. of his Kuṟaḷ.] *See* ROBINSON (E. J.). Tales and Poems of South India, *etc.* pp. 49-149. 1885. 8°. **14170. k. 63.**

—— ००० குறட்சங்கிரகம் ஞூ [Kuṟaṭ-saṅgraham. An abridgment of the Aṟattu pāl of the Kuṟaḷ, with commentary, for the use of Catholic schools.] pp. 50. புதுவை ௲௮௱௬௰ [*Pondicherry*, 1860.] 12°. **14172. a. 21.**

—— குறள் . . . அறத்துப்பால். [Kuṟaḷ. Part i., or Aṟattu pāl, treating of virtue, in 380 stanzas. With commentary.] pp. 77, i. *Tranquebar*, 1872. 12°. **14172. a. 15.**

—— Cural. [A metrical translation of the first 240 couplets. Preceded by a life of Tiru-vaḷḷuvar.] *See* ROBINSON (E. J.). Tamil Wisdom, *etc.* pp. 14-52. 1873. 12°. **14170. k. 62.**

—— Le Livre de l'Amour de Tirouvallouva [i.e. the Kāmattu pāl of the Kuṟaḷ] traduit du tamoul par G. de Barrigue de Fontainieu. [With an introduction by J. Vinson.] (†Appendice. Trois Chapitres du Naladiyar.) pp. xix. 124. *Paris*, 1889. 12°. **14172. a. 38.**

—— திருக்குறள். [Kuṟaḷ, bk. ii., stanzas 701-800. With a commentary based on that of Parimēlaṟagar, life of the latter and of Tiru-vaḷḷuvar, *etc.*] pp. 114, 6. *See* ACADEMIES, *etc.*—Madras.—*University of Madras.* University of Madras. B.A. Examination, *etc.* 1900. 8°. **14172. bb. 6.(6.)**

—— [Extracts from the Kuṟaḷ, bk. i., ch. 1-13, with commentary, F. W. Ellis' English explanation, and a life of Tiru-vaḷḷuvar.] *See* KṚUSHṆAMĀCHĀRYAR, *V.* பன்னிரு புலவர் சரித்திர ஸாரம். Brief Biographies, *etc.* pp. i.-xix., 15-72. 1906. 8°. **14171. e. 9.**

—— ००० ஞானவெட்டி-௲௫௱. [Ñāna-veṭṭi. A recent work in 1899 stanzas on the Ṣaiva theosophy and physiology, falsely attributed to Tiru-vaḷḷuvar. Edited by T. Vaidi-liṅga Dēṣikar.] pp. 240. சென்னை [*Madras*,] 1884. 8°. **14172. b. 19.**

—— ००० நவரத்தின வைத்திய சிந்தாமணி ௮௱-ம் கெவுனமணி வயது ௱-ம் ஞூ [Nava-ratna-vaidya-chintāmaṇi and Kevuna-maṇi (*i.e.* Gauṇa-maṇi). Two works in verse upon medical and physical pseudo-science, the former professing to be a summary of the Ñāna-veṭṭi and the latter ascribed directly to Tiru-vaḷḷuvar. Edited by Karuvūr C. S. Seṅgalva-rāya Mudaliyār.] pp. viii. xxxv. 192, i. [*Madras*,] 1889. 8°. **14170. i. 21.**

TIRUV-ARAṄGATT'-AMUDANĀR. [For editions of the Rāmānuja-nūṯṯ'-antādi included in the editions of the whole or parts of the Nāl-āyira-prabandham:] *See* ĀṞVĀRGAḶ.—*Nāl-āyiram.*

TIRUVARUR. திருவாரூர்ப்புராணம். [Tiruvārūr-purāṇam. The legends of the Ṣaiva sanctuary at Tiruvarur. Translated from the Sanskrit into Tamil verse by Ñāna-sambandha Muni. Edited by T. Ṣ. Sāmi-nātha Dēṣikar.] pp. ii. iv. 410, ii. சென்னை ஜய [*Madras*, 1895.] 8°. **14170. e. 59.**

Said to have been composed on the occasion of a visit in 1513 Ṣaka.

TIRUV-ARUṬ-PRAKĀṢA-VAḶḶALĀR. *See* RĀMALIṄGA PIḶḶAI, *K.*

TIRUVEṆGĀḌAR. *See* PAṬṬAṆATTU PIḶḶAI.

TIRU - VEṄGIḌĀCHĀRI, *Tiruvaḷḷūr Kṛushṇamāchāri.* ००० வைத்தியஅனுபோகசாரசங்கிரகம் [Vaidya-anubhōga-sāra-saṅgraham. A treatise on medicine, based on the works ascribed to the legendary 18 Siddhars. Second edition.] pp. 231. *Palghat*, 1893. 8°. **14170. i. 34.**

TIRU-VĒṄKAṬĀCHALA KAVI-RĀYAR, *Tiruvaṇṇāmalai, disciple of Ell'-appar.* ००० வல்லாளமகாராசன்கதை [Vallāḷa-mahā-rājan-kathai. A story of the sorrows of King Vallāḷan previous to the birth of a son to him, illustrative of Ell'-appar's Aruṇāchala-purāṇam, chapter vii. Edited by T. Sītā-pati Nāyakar.] pp. 64. சென்னை பிரமாதி [*Madras*, 1879.] 8°. **14170. k. 13.**

TIRU-VĒṄKAṬĀCHALA PIḶḶAI. திருநீலகண்ட நாயனார் விலாசம். [Tiru-nīla-kaṇṭha-nāyanār-vilāsam. A drama founded on the legend of a devotee of Ṣiva. Edited by K. Rāja-gōpāla Piḷḷai.] pp. 70. சென்னை புவ [Madras, 1875.] 8°. 14170. l. 8.

TIRU-VĒṄKAṬĀCHĀRI, *M. S.* A collection of the papers relating to Sri Runganathaswami Temple, its management & the rights and privileges of the Tengalais in the same, and consisting of Decisions of Civil Courts, Orders & Sunnads of Collectors, Proceedings of the Board of Revenue etc., compiled by M. S. Thiruvenkata Chari. pp. vii. 186, 4, iii. 59. *Trichinopoly,* 1887. Fol. 14170. h. 2.

TIRU-VĒṄKAṬĀCHĀRI, *Sarasvati.* See VARĀHA-MIHIRA. மங்களேஸ்வர்யம் ஶ்ரீ [Maṅgaḷēṣvaryam. Being a Tamil version of the Bṛuhaj-jātakam and its Telugu prose paraphrase by Tiru-vēṅkaṭāchāri.] 1905. 8°. 14171. g. 6.

TIRU-VĒṄKAṬĀCHĀRYAR, *Chitrakūṭam Kandāḍai.* [For works edited by Tiru-vēṅkaṭāchāryar, see under the following headings :]

ĀṞVĀRGAḶ.—Nāl-āyiram.—*Entire Canon.*
„ „ *Mudal-āyiram.*
„ „ *Periya-tiru-moḻi.*
PIḶḶAI LŌKĀCHĀRYAR.
PIḶḶAI LŌKAM-JĪYAR.
PINB'-AṞAGIYA PERU-MĀḶ JĪYAR.

TIRU-VĒṄKAṬĀCHĀRYAR, *Perumāḷ-kōvil Paravastu.* See NAÑ-JĪYAR. ००० ఆత్మవివాహం [Ātma-vivāham, *etc.* Edited by Tiru-vēṅkaṭāchāryar.] 1893. 8°. 14170. ee. 40.

TIRU-VĒṄKAṬAM PIḶḶAI, *Brahmapuri P.* See NANDAN. நந்தமண்டலசதகம் ஶ்ரீ [Nanda-maṇḍala-ṣatakam. With commentary by Tiru-vēṅkaṭam.] 1894. 8°. 14170. k. 37.

TIRU-VĒṄKAṬA-NĀTHAR. கீதாசாரத்தாலாட்டுப்பிரபந்தம். [Gītā-sāra-tālāṭṭu-prabandham. A poem on the philosophy of the Gītā, in the form of a cradle-song.] See RĀMA-SĀMI SVĀMI. நானாசீவவாதக்கட்டளை ஶ்ரீ [Nānā-jīva-vāda-kaṭṭaḷai, *etc.*] pp. 26-39. [1887.] 12°. 14170. d. 26.

TIRU-VĒṄKAṬA NĀYUḌU, *K. V., of Pachaiyappa's College.* See RĀMA-LIṄGA PIḶḶAI, *K.* ००० திருவருட்பா இங்கிதமாலை. [Tiruv-aruṭ-pā-iṅgita-mālai. Edited with commentary by Tiru-vēṅkaṭa.] 1904. 8°. 14170. eee. 7.

—— [For other works edited by Tiru-vēṅkaṭa, see under the following headings :]
RĀMĀNUJA-DĀSAR, *K.*
ṢIVA-PRAKĀṢA DĒṢIKAR.

—— ००० சிவபுராணாதிதோத்திரமஞ்சரி. [Ṣiva-purāṇādi-tōttira-mañjari. A collection of Ṣaiva hymns, chiefly from the local Purāṇas.] pp. xiii. 344, 8, ii. சென்னை விளம்பி [*Madras,* 1899.] 12°. 14170. d. 58.

TIRU-VĒṄKAṬA PIḶḶAI, *A.* See AESOP. Aesop's Fables . . . translated into Tamil by A. Theroovengada Pillay, *etc.* 1853. 8°. 14170. k. 32.

TIRU-VĒṄKAṬA-SVĀMI, *Mādai* (VĒṄKAṬĒṢA PAṆḌITAR). See KṚUSHṆA MIṢRA. ஶ்ரீ . . . மெய்ஞ்ஞானவிளக்கம். [Mey-ñāna-viḷakkam. Tiru-vēṅkaṭa-svāmi's poetical adaptation of Prabōdha-chandrōdayam.] 1898. 8°. 14172. c. 27.

—— See KṚUSHṆA MIṢRA. பிரபோதசந்திரோதய ஶ்ரீ [Prabōdha-chandrōdaya-vachanam. A prose rendering of Tiru-vēṅkaṭa-svāmi's Mey-ñāna-viḷakkam.] 1889. 12°. 14170. l. 21.

—— See KṚUSHṆA MIṢRA. பிரபோதசந்திரோதய ஶ்ரீ [Prabōdha-chandrōdaya-vachanam. A prose version of Tiru-vēṅkaṭa-svāmi's Mey-ñāna-viḷakkam.] 1902. 8°. 14170. l. 57.

TIRU-VĒṄKAṬA-SĀMI MUDALIYĀR, *Ā. Sāminātha.* பகவத்கீதை சார சங்கிரகம். [Bhagavad-gītai-sāra-saṅgraham. A prose summary of the Bhagavad-gītā.] pp. 33. பெங்களூர் க அுகூ0 [*Bangalore,* 1890.] 16°. 14170. d. 35.(1.)

—— ஸ்ரீதரஸ்வாமிகளுடைய சரித்திரம். The Life of Sreemath Sridhara Swami [a modern theistic reformer. Reprinted from the "Hindu Nēsan"]. pp. 23. சென்னப்பட்டணம் [*Madras,*] 1907. 12°. 14171. d. 9.

TIRUVĒṞKĀḌU. திருவேற்காட்டுப்புராணம். [Tiruvēṟkāṭṭu-purāṇam, or Vaḍa-vēdāraṇya-purāṇam. A poetical account of the legends of the Ṣaiva sanctuary of Tiruverkadu or Vada-vedaranyam. Edited by Pūvai Kalyāṇa-sundara Mudaliyār.] pp. 4, 141. சென்னை [*Madras,*] 1903. 8°. 14170. ff. 14.

TIRUV-IṢAI-PĀ. [For editions of this collection, which forms bk. 9 of the Tiru-muṟai :] *See* TIRU-MUṞAI.

TŌLĀ-MOṞI DĒVAR. ◦◦◦ சூளாமணி. [Chūḷāmaṇi. One of the five minor epic poems. Edited by Ṣ. V. Dāmōdaram Piḷḷai.] pp. xvii. iv. xix. 308. சென்னபட்டணம் [*Madras,*] 1889. 8°. **14172. b. 39.**

—— ◦◦◦ திவிட்டகுமாரன்கதை அல்லது வசன-சூளாமணி. [Vachana-chūḷāmaṇi, or Tiviṭṭa-kumāran-kathai. The story of the Chūḷāmaṇi rendered into prose by Ṣ. V. Dāmōdaram Piḷḷai.] pp. 2, 162, i. சென்னபட்டணம் [*Madras,*] 1898. 12°. **14171. a. 31.**

TOL-KĀPPIYA DĒVAR. ◦◦◦ திருப்பாதிரிப்புலியூர்க்கலம்பகம். [Tirupādiri-puliyūr-kalambakam. A series of devotional verses, in various metres, on the Ṣaiva cult of Tirupapuliyur. Edited by U. V. Sāminàth'-aiyar.] pp. iv. 31. சென்னபட்டணம் [*Madras,*] 1908. 8°. **14170. ee. 5.(3.)**

TOL-KĀPPIYANĀR. தொல்காப்பியம் மூ [Tol-kāppiyam. An ancient Tamil grammar, in three books, styled Eṟutt'-adhikāram, Ṣoll'-adhikāram, and Poruḷ-adhikāram. With the commentary by Nachinārkk'-iniyar. Edited by Ṣ. V. Dāmōdaram Piḷḷai.] 3 vols. சென்னபட்டணம் [*Madras,*] 1885-நந்தந [1892.] 8°. **14172. e. 13.**

Vol. 1 *appeared in* 1891, *vol.* 2 *in* 1892, *and vol.* 3 *in* 1885. *The name Tol-kāppiyanār simply means 'author of the ancient poem'* (tol-kāppiyam). *The writer is also known by the title Tiraṇa-dūmākkini* (*Skt.* Triṇa-dhūmāgni).
There is some evidence that the commentary upon the Ṣeyyuḷ-iyal of the Tol-kāppiyam, here ascribed to Nachinārkk'-iniyar, is really by Pēr-āṣiriyar (*Iṟaiyanār?*). *See Ṣeṅgalva-rāya Piḷḷai's* History of Tamil Prose Literature, *p.* 10, *and Ṣēsha-giri Ṣāstri's* Report, *no.* 2, *p.* 115.

—— தொல்காப்பியம் . . . எழுத்ததிகாரம். [Tol-kāppiyam. Pt. i., or Eṟutt'-adhikāram, with the commentary of Nachinārkk'-iniyar. Edited by Maṟavai Mahā-liṅg'-aiyar.] pp. ii. iv. 228. பிலவங்க [*Madras,* 1847.] 8°. **14172. f. 4.**

—— தொல்காப்பியம். சொல்லதிகாரம். [Tol-kāppiyam. Bk. ii. (Ṣoll'-adhikāram.) With commentary by Sēnāv-araiyar. Edited by Āṟu-muga Nāvalar.] pp. i. 305, viii. சென்னபட்டணம் விபவ [*Madras,* 1868.] 8°. **14172. e. 6.**

—— தொல்காப்பியச் சண்முகவிருத்தியின் . . . பாயிரவிருத்தி. [Tol-kāppiyam. With a commentary styled Shaṇmukha-vṛutti by Ṣōṟavandā-nūr Araṣan-Shaṇmukhanār.] தஞ்சை [*Tanjore,*] 1905, *etc.* 8°. **14172. e. 43.**

In progress?

—— († தொல்காப்பியம் பொருளதிகாரம் அ. செய்யுளியல் நச்சினார்க்கினியருரை.) [Ṣeyyuḷ-iyal. The chapter on the art of versification in the Poruḷ-adhikāram of the Tol-kāppiyam. With Nachinārkk'-iniyar's commentary.] [1904, *etc.*] *See* ACADEMIES, *etc.*—*Madura.* ["Ṣen-damiṟ" supplement.] no. 21. 1902, *etc.* 8°. **14172. i. 1.*(no. 21.)**

Apparently discontinued after verse 104.

TOṆḌAR-AḌI-PODIY-ĀṞVĀR. [For editions of the Tiru-mālai and Tiru-paḷḷiy-eṟuchi of this saint, included in the editions of the whole or parts of the Nāl-āyira-prabandham :] *See* ĀṞVĀRGAḶ.—*Nāl-āyiram.*

TOṬṬAYA. *See* DOḌḌAYA.

TOṬṬAYYAṄGĀR. *See* DOḌḌ'-AYYAṄGĀR.

TŌTTIRA-GĪTAM. தோத்திர கீதம். [Tōttira-gītam. A Roman Catholic collection of hymns to St. Michael and other saints.] pp. 10. யாழ்ப்பாணம் [*Jaffna,*] 1890. 12°. **14170. a. 35.(3.)**

TRIKŪṬA-RĀJ'-APPAR, *Mēlagaranagar.* இது திருக்குற்றாலத்தலபுராணவசனம். [Tiru-kuṭṭāla-tala-purāṇa-vachanam. A poem by Trikūṭa-rāj'-appar on the legends and cult of the Ṣaiva sanctuary of Kuttalam (Courtallum), from a Sanskrit *māhātmyam* based on the Sanatkumāra-saṃhitā in the Ṣaṅkara-saṃhitā of the Skanda-purāṇam, rendered in prose by M. R. Aruṇāchala Kavirāyar.] pp. 6, 339, i. 2. மதுரை [*Madura,*] 1906. 12°. **14170. dd. 13.**

TRIMMER (GEORGE J.). "Stewards of the Mysteries of God." Translation of an ordination charge delivered at the ordination of the Rev. D. V. Thamotheram, at Christ Church, Point Pedro, January 27th 1892. pp. 29. *Batticaloa,* 1892. 16°. **14170. a. 57.(1.)**

TRINCAL (JEAN-BAPTISTE), *S. J.* *See* BIBLE.—*New Testament.* The New Testament . . . Translated . . . from the Latin Vulgate with annotations by . . . J. B. Trincal, *etc.* 1906. 8°. **14170. cc. 10.**

TRINCOMALI. — *Hindu - mata - khaṇḍana - sabhai.* இந்துமதகண்டனம். நிகார நிகாரண நிக்கிரகம்.

(*காகலகோஷதோஷம்.) [Hindu-mata-khaṇḍanam. A series of tracts against popular Hinduism, by a society of Theistic reformers.] 2 pts. *Jaffna*, 1891. 8°. **14170. c. 29.(1.)**

—— *Ṣaiva-prakāṣa-samājam.* ○○○ சைவப்பிரகாசசமாசாவேதனம். [Ṣaiva-prakāṣa-samājāvēdanam. Report of the Society at Trincomali for the first year, 1890-91.] pp. 16. *Jaffna*, விகிர்தி [1891.] 8°. **14170. e. 41.(1.)**

TRUṆA-DHŪMĀGNI. *See* Tol-kāppiyanār.

TULASIṄGA MUDALIYĀR, *Pūvirundavalli Ṣ.* கைமுறை பாக்கெட்வயித்தியம். [Kai-murai pocket-vaidyam. A compilation on medical practice.] pp. 32, 352. மதராஸ் [*Madras*,] 1905. 16°. **14171. f. 6.**

TURĀB MUḤAMMAD ḤUSAIN ibn ISMĀʿĪL. தொழுகைரஞ்சித அலங்காரம் ஆ [Toṛugai-rañjita-alaṅkāram, or Sharīʿatin tulakkam bidʿatin viḷakkam. Devotional lyrics for Moslems. Edited by Muḥammad Mīr Jawād.] 2 pts. திண்டுக்கல் [*Dindigal*,] 1897. 12°. **14173. a. 7.**

TURAI-SĀMI. *See* Durai-sāmi.

TYĀGA-RĀJA DĒṢIKAR, *son of Vaidya-nātha.* பாட்டியல். [Pāṭṭ'-iyal. A chapter on Ars Poetica, ascribed to Tyāga-rāja, and forming the 5th section of Vaidya-nātha's Ilakkaṇa-viḷakkam.] *See* Vaidya-nātha Dēṣikar, *Tiruvārūr.* ○○○ இலக்கணவிளக்கம் ஆ [Ilakkaṇa-viḷakkam.] pp. 784-851. [1889.] 8°. **14172. e. 24.**

TYĀGA-RĀJA DĪKSHITAR, *Mahā-mahōpādhyāyar, of Mannarguḍi.* விபூதிருத்திராக்ஷதாரண நிரூபணம். [Vibhūti-rudrāksha-dhāraṇa-nirūpaṇam. A treatise on the Ṣaiva practice of smearing the body with burnt cow-dung and wearing rosaries of *elæocarpus* berries. Translated from Tyāga-rāja's Sanskrit work called Durjanōkti-nirāsa into Tamil by Eṭṭayapuram Vēṅkaṭāchala Dīkshitar, with the quotations in the original Sanskrit. With notes by Virudai Ṣiva-ñāna Yōgi.] pp. vi. 130, iii. சென்னை [*Madras*,] 1901. 12°. **14170. d. 85.(1.)**

—— *See* Ṣiva-ñāna Yōgi. பூதிருத்திராக்கதூஷண கண்டனம். [Bhūti-rudrākka-dūshaṇa-khaṇḍanam. A defence of Tyāga-rāja's work.] 1901. 12°. **14170. d. 85.(2.)**

TYĀGA-RĀJA MUDALIYĀR, *P., disciple of Ṣinna-svāmi Piḷḷai.* *See* Vidyānanda Svāmi. சகலகலாபூஷணம். [Sakala-kalā-bhūshaṇam. Edited by Tyāga-rāja.] 1899. 8°. **14171. a. 37.**

TYĀGA-RĀJA PIḶḶAI, *Nallūr.* *See* Aruḷ-appa Nāvalar. திருச்செல்வர்காவியம். [Tiru-chelvar-kāvyam. Edited with explanations *etc.* by Tyāga-rāja.] 1896. 8°. **14170. bb. 6.**

TYĀGA-RĀJA PIḶḶAI, *Triṣirapuram.* ○○○ செண்பகவல்லியென்னும் பவளக்கொடிநாடகம் [Pavaḷakoḍi-nāṭakam. A drama on the legend of Arjuna's marriage with Pavaḷakoḍi. Edited by Vīra-sāmi Nāyuḍu.] pp. 180. சென்னை விஜய [*Madras*, 1893.] 8°. **14170. l. 40.**

—— பொன்னரர் சங்கரர் நாடகம். [Ponnarar-ṣaṅkarar-nāṭakam. A drama.] pp. 134. திரிசிரபுரம் பிலவ [*Trichinopoli*, 1902.] 8°. **14170. l. 28.**

TYĀGA-RĀJA-SVĀMI, *Tiruvaiyāṟu Rāma-brahmam.* [*Life.*] *See* Nara-simma Bhāgavata-svāmi. ஸத்குரு தியாகராஜஸ்வாமி சரித்திரம். [Tyāga-rāja-svāmi-charitram.] 1906. 12°. **14171. a. 48.(3.)**

TYĀGA-RĀYA MUDALIYĀR, *Nāgūr.* *See* Parañ-jōdi Munivar. திருவிளையாடற் புராணம். [Tiru-viḷaiy-āḍaṟ-purāṇam. Edited on the basis of the editions of Ṣara-vaṇa Peru-māḷ and Tyāga-rāya.] [1850.] 8°. **14170. ee. 1.**

TYĀGA-RĀYA SVĀMI, *Tiruvālūr.* [For works edited by Tyāga-rāya Svāmī, see under the following headings :]

Aruṇāchala Kavi-rāyar.
Madana-kāma-rājan.
Rāma-chandra Kavi-rāyar.

UḌAL. உடலறிவிளக்கம். [Uḍal-aṟi-viḷakkam. Ṣaiva verses on physiology.] *See* Siddhargaḷ. ○○○ பெரிய ஞானக்கோவை. [Periya-ñāna-kōvai.] pt. ii. 1906. 12°. **14170. dd. 12.**

UDDHAVA CHID-GHANA. *See* Mahā-bhakta-vijayam. ○○○ ஸ்ரீமகாபக்தவிஜயம். [Mahā-bhakta-vijayam. Compiled and translated from Uddhava's Bhakta-mālā, *etc.*] 1870. 4°. **14170. f. 5.**

—— —— 1893. 4°. **14170. f. 22.**

—— —— 1898-1905. 4°. **14170. f. 6.**

ULAGA-NĀTHA MUDALIYĀR. *See* Sambandha-ṣaraṇālaya Svāmi. கந்தபுராண ஆ [Kanda-purāṇa-churukkam. Edited by Ulaga-nātha.] [1906.] 8°. **14170. eee. 10.**

ULAGA-NĀTHA-SVĀMI, *Tiruviḍai-marudūr* (BHIKSHU ṢĀSTRI). *See* ṢAṄKARĀCHĀRYAR. [*Doubtful and Supposititious Works.*] இலகுஷ்ணுவிர்த்தி ஸ்ரீ [A collection, comprising Daṣakam, Vivēka-shaṭkam, Sorūpānusandhāna-dudi, Manīshā-pañchakam, and Sōpāna-pañchakam, metrically rendered by Ulaga-nātha, *etc.*] [1888.] 16°. **14170. d. 28.**

—— *See* SĀYAṆĀCHĀRYAR. ∘∘∘ ஜீவன்முக்தி ஸ்ரீ [Jīvan-mukti-prakaraṇam. Translated by Ulaga-nātha.] [1887.] 12°. **14170. d. 24.**

—— *See* ṢIVA-RAHASYAM. ரிபுகீதை ஸ்ரீ [Ṛibhu-gītai-tiraṭṭu. 874 stanzas from Ulaga-nātha's metrical version of the Ṛibhu-gītā.] 1906. 16°. **14170. dd. 15.**

UḶḶAM-UDAIYĀN. *See* PARA-HITAM. சோதிசாத்திரம். The Oriental Astronomer [purporting to be a translation into Tamil by Uḷḷam-uḍaiyān of the Para-hitam], *etc.* 1848. 8°. **14170. i. 8.**

UMĀ-PATI ṢIVĀCHĀRYAR, *Koṭṭavanguḍi, disciple of Maṟai-ñāna-sambandhar.* ∘∘∘ சிவப்பிரகாசம் திருவருட்பயன் வினாவெண்பா ஸ்ரீ [Siddhāntāshṭakam. Eight works on the Ṣaiva-siddhāntam, comprising (1) the Ṣiva-prakāṣam, (2) the Tiruv-aruṭ-payan, (3) the Vinā-veṇ-bā, (4) the Pōṭṭi-paʻroḍai, (5) the Koḍi-kavi, (6) the Neñju-viḍu-dūdu, (7) the Uṇmai-neṟi-viḷakkam, and (8) the Saṅkarpa-nirākaraṇam. Edited by K. Shaṇmukha-sundara Mudaliyār, with commentaries founded upon those of Chidambara-nāthar upon (1), of Nirambav-aṟagiyar upon (2), of Namaṣ-ṣivāya Tambirān upon (3), and others. Second edition.] pp. xxvii. 550, viii. 93, xi. iii. 9, iii. 24, ii. 10, iv. 51, ii. 8, 24, 139. சென்னை ஜய [*Madras*, 1895.] 12°. **14170. d. 37.**

These 8 works are said to have been written, in their present order, in Ṣaka 1228-1235.

—— சிவப்பிரகாசம். (திருவருட்பயன், வினாவெண்பா, *etc.*) [Siddhāntāshṭakam, with commentaries, viz. (i) Ṣiva-prakāṣam, with commentary of Chidambara-nāthar, (ii) Tiruv-aruṭ-payan, with commentary of Nirambav-aṟagiyar, (iii) Vinā-veṇ-bā, with commentary of Namaṣ-ṣivāya Tambirān, (iv) Pōṭṭi-paʻroḍai, (v) Koḍi-kavi, (vi) Neñju-viḍu-dūdu, with commentary of Kalyāṇa-sundara Mudaliyār, (vii) Uṇmai-neṟi-viḷakkam, (viii) Saṅkarpa-nirākaraṇam.] *See* MEY-KAṆḌA-ṢĀTTIRAM. மெய்கண்டசாத்திரம் ஸ்ரீ [Mey-kaṇḍa-ṣāttiram.] pp. 615-856. 1897. 8°. **14170. ff. 3.**

—— ∘∘∘ சித்தாந்தாஷ்டகம் ஸ்ரீ [Siddhāntāshṭakam. Comprising the same 8 works as in the two preceding editions, without commentaries.] 7 pts. *See* MEY-KAṆḌA-ṢĀTTIRAM. ∘∘∘ சைவசித்தாந்தசாத்திரம் ஸ்ரீ [Ṣaiva-siddhānta-ṣāttiram.] [1899.] 12°. **14170. d. 53.**

—— திருத்தொண்டர்புராண வரலாறு (திருமுறைகண்டபுராணம், திருத்தொண்டர்புராண சாரம்.) [Tiru-toṇḍar-purāṇa-varalāṟu, or Ṣēkkiṟār-nāyanār-purāṇam, a poem on the legends of the religious poet Ṣēkkiṟār; Tiru-muṟai-gaṇḍa-purāṇam, or Nambiy-āṇḍār-nambi-purāṇam, an account of the codifier of the Tiru-muṟai; and Tiru-toṇḍar-purāṇa-sāram, an abstract of the Periya-purāṇam.] *See* ṢEKKIṞĀR. ∘∘∘ பெரிய புராணம் ஸ்ரீ [Periya-purāṇam.] [1880.] 8°. **14170. f. 4.**

—— [The same works.] *See* ṢEKKIṞĀR. சேக்கிழார் ... பெரியபுராணம் ஸ்ரீ [Periya-purāṇam.] vol. i. [1885]-1898. 8°. **14170. f. 1.**

—— கோயிற் புராணம். [Kōyiṟ-purāṇam. A Ṣaiva poem on the cult and legends of the temple at Chidambaram. With commentary by Āṟumuga Nāvalar.] pp. iv. v. 275. சென்னபட்டணம் பிரபவ [*Madras*, 1868.] 12°. **14170. d. 13.**

—— சிவபிரகாசம். Siva-pirakâsam, Light of Sivan. A metaphysical and theological treatise, translated from the Tamiḷ, with notes. By Rev. Henry R. Hoisington. (Journal of the American Oriental Society. Vol. iv., pp. 125-244.) *Boston*, 1854. 8°. **Ac. 8824.(vol. 4.)**

—— Light of Grace, or Thiruvarutpayan, of Umapathi Siva Charya. Translated with notes and introduction. By J. M. Nallaswami Pillai. [With the Tamil text appended.] pp. iv. i. 32, ix. *Trichinopoly, Madras* [printed], 1896. 8°. **14170. ee. 12.(1.)**

—— The Mystic Formula of the Five Letters, *etc.* (†The Form of Grace, The Nature of Grace, *etc.*). [Chapters ix., v., iv., vi.-viii., x., of the Tiruv-aruṭ-payan, translated into English, with notes.] *See* TIRU-MURAI.—*Tiru-vāchakam.* The Tiruvāçagam, *etc.* pp. xxxix.-lx. 1900. 8°. **14170. ff. 7.**

'UMAR, *Poet.* *See* MUHAMMAD SULTĀN ibn AHMAD 'UMAR. சீருச்சதகம். [Ṣīrā-ṣatakam. Verses founded on the Ṣīrā.] 1900. 8°. **14173. b. 25.(2.)**

—— சீருவெண்கின்றபுராணம். [Ṣīrā-purāṇam (*i.e.* Arab. Sīrah). A poem on the legends relating to Muhammad. Edited, from a copy corrected by Shaikh 'Abd al-Kādir of Kayalpatnam, by Allāh-bīchai Pulavar.] pp. viii. 536. தநாஉ [*Madras*, 1885.] 8°. **14173. b. 20.**

—— சீருப்புராணம் [Ṣīrā-purāṇam. With prose paraphrase by Shaikh Tambi Pāvalar.] சென்னை [*Madras*,] 1902, *etc.* 8°. **14173. b. 18.**

In progress.

UPANISHADS. ◦◦◦ நூற்றெட்டு உபநிஷத்துகள். [Nūṯṯ'-eṭṭu Upanishattngaḷ. The Sanskrit text in Telugu characters. Edited with a Tamil translation and extracts from the commentaries of Ṣaṅkara, Nārāyaṇa, Raṅga-rāmānuja, and Ānanda-tīrtha, also translated into Tamil, and Tamil notes, by P. V. Ṣrīnivāsa Rāghavāchāryar.] pt. 1. pp. 32. சென்னபட்டணம் [*Madras*,] 1887. 8°. **14010. dd. 2.**

—— ◦ ◦ ◦ தசோபநிஷத்த்ராவிடபாஷ்யம். [Daṣōpanishad-drāviḍa-bhāshyam. Ten Upanishads in Sanskrit,—viz. the Īṣāvāsya, Kēna, Kaṭha, Praṣna, Muṇḍaka, Māṇḍūkya, Aitarēya, Bṛuhad-āraṇyaka, Chhāndōgya, and Taittirīya—and a Tamil commentary comprising word-for-word interpretations of the text and translations of the commentaries of Ṣaṅkara and Rāmānuja, together with the Kārikās of Gauḍa-pāda in Sanskrit and Ṣaṅkara's commentary thereupon in Tamil. Compiled and edited by A. Ṣrīnivāsa Tātāchārya Svāmi.] 6 pts. சென்னை கஅகூஎ [*Madras*, 1897]-1898. 8°. **14010. dd. 14.**

The text of each verse is printed in both Grantham and Telugu character.

—— பஂசதஶோபநிஷத: ... பஞ்சதசோபநிஷத் ஸ்ரீ [Pañchadaṣōpanishadaḥ. Fifteen Upanishads, *scil.* the Kaivalya, Nārāyaṇa, Amṛuta-bindu (Brahma-bindu), Maitrāyaṇi, Maitrēyi, Sarva-sāra, Nirālamba, Ātma-bōdha, Nārada-pari-vrājaka, Skanda, Paiṅgala, Ṣārīraka, Varāha, Kali-santāraṇa, and Muktikā. Edited with Tamil introduction, notes, and translation by Villa-varambal Kuppu-sāmi Aiyar.] pp. ii. x. iv. ii. 449, ix. சென்னபட்டணம் ஹேவிளம்பி [*Madras*, 1898.] 8°. **14010. cc. 12.**

—— உபநிஷத்வித்யா. உப்நிஷத்வித்யா. [Upanishad-vidyā. A collection of Upanishads in Sanskrit with Tamil translations, commentaries, *etc.* Compiled and edited by K. R. Ṣrīnivāsa Dīkshitar.] vol. i., pt. 1—vol. iii., pt. 8. நடுக்காவேரி [*Nadukkaveri*,] 1898-சார்வரி [1901.] 8°. **14010. cc. 13.**

No more published.

—— இந்து பைபில் என்னும் ஆரியர் சத்திய வேதம் ஸ்ரீ (The Hindu Holy Bible, containing the Old Testament: or [selections from the] Upanishaths [printed in Tamil characters, with English translation and Tamil introductions, translation, commentary, *etc.*]. Compiled by S. P. Narasimmalu Nayudu.) vol. i. pp. viii. vi. 24, ii. 272. *Coimbatore*, 1898. 8°. **14170. ee. 15.**

—— Second edition. pp. ii. 22, ii. xxxviii. xxi. 302, 109; 1 *plate.* *Madras*, 1906. 8°. **14007. b. 31.**

—— ஈசாவாஸ்யோபநிஷத்டீகா ஸ்ரீ (Isavasyopanishad [in Telugu and Tamil characters]. With [Tamil glosses and] commentaries [by] Sreemat Paramahamsa Bala Subrahmania Brahma Swamy.) pp. i. 106. சென்னை [*Madras*, 1899.] 8°. **14010. b. 21.**

Forms no. 1 of the Bala Brahmam Series.

—— ◦◦◦ ஜாபாலோபநிடதத்தின் பொழிப்புரையும்விசேடவுரையும் [Jābālōpanishad. The Sanskrit text, with the Tamil commentary of Ṣrīnivāsa Dīkshitar. Edited by Ṣivānanda-sāgara Yōgīṣvarar. Second edition.] pp. 88, vii. நடுக்காவேரி [*Nadukkaveri*,] 1900. 8°. **14007. b. 12.(2.)**

—— கைவல்யபாஷ்யம். [Kaivalya-bhāshyam. Comprising the Sanskrit text of the Kaivalya-upanishad with the commentary of K. Ṣrīnivāsa Dīkshitar, translated from the Sanskrit by T. Ṣivānanda-sāgara Yōgīṣvarar.] pp. 52. சிதம்பரம் [*Chidambaram*,] 1898. 8°. **14170. ee. 31.**

—— கேநோபநிஷத்தீபிகை ஸ்ரீ [Kēnōpanishad. Sanskrit text, with the commentary Kēnōpanishad-dīpikai of Bāla-subrahmaṇya Brahma-svāmi, in Tamil.] pp. 207. சென்னை [*Madras,*] 1900. 12°. **14007. b. 13.(1.)**

The Sanskrit verses are printed in the Grantham character, with transliteration into Tamil letters.

'UTHMĀN ibn MUḤAMMAD, *Maulavī Saiyid.* See AḤMAD ibn AḤMAD, *al-Sharjī al-Zabīdī.* هذا كتاب الفوائد والصلاة والعوائد الخ [Al-Fawā'id fi al-ṣalāt wa'l-'awā'id. Translated by 'Uthmān.] [1880.] 8°. **14173. c. 3.**

UTTARA-GĪTĀ. உத்தரகீதை. [Uttara-gītā. A Sanskrit philosophical poem, forming a supplement to the Bhagavad-gītā. With a Tamil paraphrase and notes, based upon the commentary of Gauḍa-pāda, by V. Kuppu-svāmi Rāju.] pp. ii. 61. தஞ்சை சோபகிருது [*Tanjore,* 1902.] 12°. **14048. a. 29.(3.)**

Forms no. 1 of the series Gītai-kottu.

UYYA-VANDA DĒVA-NĀYANĀR, *Tirukaḍavūr.* திருவுந்தியாரும் திருக்களிற்றுப்படியாரும். [Tiruv-undiyār, a poem in 45 stanzas on the Ṣaiva Siddhāntam, by Tiruviyalūr Uyya-vandar. Followed by the Tiru-kaḷiṭṭu-paḍiyār of Tirukaḍavūr Uyya-vandar, a like work in 100 stanzas. With commentary on the former by Ṣiṭṭambala-tambirān Svāmi and on the latter by Ṣiva-prakāṣa-tambirān Svāmi. Edited by K. Shaṇmukha-sundara Mudaliyār. Second edition.] [1896.] 12°. See UYYA-VANDA DĒVA-NĀYANĀR, *Tiruviyalūr.* **14170. d. 65.**

—— திருக்களிற்றுப்படியார். [Tiru-kaḷiṭṭu-paḍiyār. With commentary by Ṣiva-prakāṣa-tambirān Svāmi.] See MEY-KAṆḌA-ṢĀTTIRAM. மெய்கண்டசாத்திரம் ஃ [Mey-kaṇḍa-ṣāttiram.] pp. 23-68. 1897. 8°. **14170. ff. 3.**

Said to have been written in Ṣaka 1100.

—— திருக்களிற்றுப்படியார். [Tiru-kaḷiṭṭu-paḍiyār.] pp. 16. See MEY-KAṆḌA-ṢĀTTIRAM. ००० சைவசித்தாந்தசாத்திரம் ஃ [Ṣaiva-siddhānta-ṣāttiram.] [1899.] 12°. **14170. d. 53.**

UYYA-VANDA DĒVA-NĀYANĀR, *Tiruviyalūr.* திருவுந்தியாரும் திருக்களிற்றுப்படியாரும். [Tiruv-undiyār, a poem in 45 stanzas on the Ṣaiva Siddhāntam, by Tiruviyalūr Uyya-vandar. Followed by the Tiru-kaḷiṭṭu-paḍiyār of Tirukaḍavūr Uyya-vandar, a like work in 100 stanzas. With commentary on the former by Ṣiṭṭambala-tambirān Svāmi and on the latter by Ṣiva-prakāṣa-tambirān Svāmi. Edited by K. Shaṇmukha-sundara Mudaliyār. Second edition.] pp. viii. 39, xxiv. 95. சிந்தாதிரிப்பேட்டை தர்முசி [*Chintadripet,* 1896.] 12°. **14170. d. 65.**

The Tiruv-undiyār is said to have been written about Ṣaka 1070.
The editor ascribes both the commentaries to Ṣiva-prakāṣar, whom he identifies with Ṣiṭṭambala-tambirān; see however the Mey-kaṇḍa-ṣāttiram (1897), *preface, p. v.*

—— திருவுந்தியார். [Tiruv-undiyār. With commentary by Ṣiṭṭambala-tambirān Svāmi.] See MEY-KAṆḌA-ṢĀTTIRAM. மெய்கண்டசாத்திரம் ஃ [Mey-kaṇḍa-ṣāttiram.] pp. 3-22. 1897. 8°. **14170. ff. 3.**

—— திருவுந்தியார் ஃ [Tiruv-undiyār.] pp. 4. See MEY-KAṆḌA-ṢĀTTIRAM. ००० சைவசித்தாந்தசாத்திரம் ஃ [Ṣaiva-siddhānta-ṣāttiram.] [1899.] 12°. **14170. d. 53.**

VAḌA-MALAIY-APPA PIḶḶAI, *Irasai.* See PURĀṆAS.—*Matsya-purāṇam.* ०००மச்சபுராணம். [Matsya-purāṇam. A poetical version by Vaḍa-malaiy-appa.] 1900. 8°. **14170. ee. 43.**

—— See ṢIRIYA RATNA KAVI-RĀYAR. ००० புலவராற்றுப்படை. [Pulavar-āṭṭu-paḍai. A panegyric upon Vaḍa-malaiy-appa Piḷḷai.] 1903. 8°. ["*Ṣen-damiẓ*" *supplement.*] **14172. i. 1.*(no. 3.)**

VADARĪṢAR. வதரீசர் பிரபந்தத் திரட்டு. [Vadarīṣar-prabandha-tiraṭṭu. Hymns for the cult of Vināyakar and Sabhā-nāyakar at the Ṣaiva sanctuary of Vadarinagar or Ilandainagar.] pp. 17. சென்னை [*Madras,*] 1902. 12°. **14170. d. 32.(5.)**

VADE MECUM. See ANGLO-TAMIL READER.

VAḌI-VĒLU CHEṬṬI, *G.* See APPĀ-SVĀMI PIḶḶAI. நவநீதசாரம். [Nava-nīta-sāram. Edited by Vaḍi-vēlu.] 1903. 12°. **14170. d. 87.**

—— See [Addenda] DHARMA-RĀJA DĪKSHITAR. ००० வேதாந்தபரிபாஷை. [Vēdānta-paribhāshai. Revised by Vaḍi-vēlu.] 1907. 16°. **14170. dd. 18.**

—— See ṢAṄKARĀCHĀRYAR. ०००சித்தாந்தபிந்து. [Daṣa-ṣlōkī. With Madhu-sūdana's Siddhānta-bindu translated into Tamil by Rāma-chandra Ṣāstri and re-written and edited by Vaḍi-vēlu.] 1906. 12°. **14049. aa. 1.**

—— See ṢIVA-RAHASYAM. ரிபுகீதை ஃ [Ṛibhu-gītai-tiraṭṭu. Edited with notes by Vaḍi-vēlu and Shaṇmukha.] 1906. 16°. **14170. dd. 15.**

VAḌI-VĒLU CHEṬṬI, *G.* (*continued*). *See* TIRU-VALLUVAR. ००० தமிழ்வேதம் ஸ்ரீ [Kuṛal. With commentary of Parimēl-aṛagar, and with paraphrases, *etc.*, by Vaḍi-vēlu. Edited by Vaḍi-vēlu.] 1904. 8°. **14172. c. 46.**

VAḌI-VĒLU MUDALIYĀR, *Māṅgāḍu, disciple of Appan Chetti*. *See* [Addenda] ARUṆA-GIRI-NĀTHA SVĀMI. ஸ்ரீ . . . திருப்புகழ் ஸ்ரீ [Tiru-pugaṛ. Edited with paraphrase by Vaḍi-vēlu.] 1906, *etc.* 12°. **14172. a. 61.**

—— *See* [Addenda] AUVAIYĀR.—*Supposititious Works*. ஔவையார் . . . குறள் ஸ்ரீ [Kuṛal. Edited with glosses, paraphrases, *etc.*, by Vaḍi-vēlu.] 1906. 12°. **14172. a. 57.**

—— *See* [Addenda] GAṆA-PATI-DĀSAR. நெஞ்சறிவிளக்கம் ஸ்ரீ [Neñj'-aṛi-viḷakkam. Edited with interpretation *etc.* by Vaḍi-vēlu.] 1906. 8°. **14170. eee. 28.**

—— *See* [Addenda] MASTĀN ŚĀHIB. ००० மஸ்தான்சாகிபு . . . பாடல் [Pāḍal. With paraphrase *etc.* by Vaḍi-vēlu.] 1908. 8°. **14172. bb. 27.**

—— *See* NAṬA-RĀJAR, *Kīranūr*. Jathakalankaram, *etc.* [With paraphrase by Vaḍi-vēlu.] 1902. 8°. **14171. g. 4.**

—— *See* PAṬṬAṆATTU PIḶḶAI. பட்டணத்துப்பிள்ளையார் பாடல் ஸ்ரீ [Pāḍal, *etc.* With biographies and paraphrase by Vaḍi-vēlu.] 1899. 12°. **14170. d. 64.**

—— *See* PULI-PĀṆI. ஸ்ரீ . . . பலதிரட்டு ஜாலம் ஸ்ரீ [Puli-pāṇi-pala-tiraṭṭu-jālam. Edited with commentary by Vaḍi-vēlu.] 1906. 8°. **14171. g. 8.**

—— *See* RĀMA-LIṄGA PIḶḶAI, *K.* ००० திருவருட்பா ஸ்ரீ [Tiruv-aruṭ-pā-tiru-muṛai-tiraṭṭu. Edited with commentary by Vaḍi-vēlu.] 1901. 8°. **14172. c. 44.**

—— *See* SIDDHARGAḶ. ००० வாதக்கோவை ஸ்ரீ [Vāta-kōvai. Compiled with paraphrase by Vaḍi-vēlu.] 1901. 8°. **14170. ee. 60.**

—— *See* ṢIVA-VĀKYAR. சிவவாக்கியர்பாடல். [Pāḍal. Edited by Vaḍi-vēlu.] 1900. 12°. [*Periya-ñāna-kōvai.*] **14170. ee. 33.**

—— —— 1906. 12°. **14170. dd. 12.**

VAḌI-VĒLU MUDALIYĀR, *Māṅgāḍu, disciple of Appan Chetti* (*continued.*) *See* ṢIVA-VĀKYAR. பெரிய சிவவாக்கியர்பாடல் ஸ்ரீ [Periya-ṣiva-vākyar-pāḍal. With commentary by Vaḍi-vēlu.] 1904. 12°. **14170. dd. 3.**

—— தற்கால வயித்தியபோதினி. [Vaidya-bōdhini. A modern guide to medicine.] pp. 79. சென்னை [*Madras*,] 1901. 8°. **14170. i. 53.**

VAḌI-VĒLU MUDALIYĀR, *Tirukaṛukunṛam Ambala-vāṇa*. சூரபத்ம நாடகம். [Ṣūra-padma-nāṭakam. A mythological drama.] pp. i. 204, ii. சென்னை [*Madras*,] 1905. 8°. **14171. k. 2.**

VAḌI-VĒLU MUDALIYĀR, *Tirumaṛiṣai Kandasāmi, disciple of Rāma-liṅga Tambirān*. *See* PAṬṬAṆATTU PIḶḶAI. [*Life.*] திருவெண்காட்டடிகள்புராணம் ஸ்ரீ [Paṭṭaṇattu-piḷḷaiyār-purāṇam. Edited with paraphrase and commentary by Vaḍi-vēlu.] 1901. 8°. **14170. k. 34.**

—— [For other works edited by Vaḍi-vēlu Mudaliyār, see under the following headings :]

RĀMA-LIṄGA PIḶḶAI, *K.*
SUBBA-RĀYA ĀCHĀRYAR, *Taṇḍaṛai*.

VĀG-BHAṬA, *son of Siṃha-gupta*. அஷ்டாங்கஹ்ருதயம் சாரீரஸ்தானம். [Ashṭāṅga-hṛudayam. The Ṣārīra-sthānam, *i.e.* bk. ii., an analysis of the human body, translated from the Sanskrit by Pāṇḍēṣuram Vēṅkaṭa-sāmi Gaṅgādhara Dēvar.] pp. xii. 70. சென்னை [*Madras*,] 1898. 8°. **14170. i. 56.**

VAIDI-LIṄGA DĒṢIKAR, *Tirumayilai*. *See* TIRU-VALLUVAR. ००० ஞானவெட்டி ஸ்ரீ [Ñāna-veṭṭi. Edited by Vaidi-liṅgar.] 1884. 8°. **14172. b. 19.**

VAIDI-LIṄGA JŌDISHAR, *Uttaramallūr*. [For works edited by Vaidi-liṅgar, see under the following headings :]

JAIMINI. PARĀṢARA.

VAIDYA-LIṄGA PATTAR, *Tirumalairāyan-baṭṭanam Raṅga-sāmi*. *See* VARĀHA-MIHIRA. மிருஹஜ்ஜாதகம் ஸ்ரீ [Maṅgaḷēṣvaryam. Being a Tamil version by Vaidya-liṅga of the Bṛuhaj-jātakam and its Telugu prose paraphrase by Tiru-vēṅkaṭāchāri.] 1905. 8°. **14171. g. 6.**

VAIDYA-LIṄGA PIḶḶAI, *Valvai Ṣ.* *See* NAṚ-KAVI-RĀJA NAMBI. ००० அகப்பொருள்விளக்க ஸ்ரீ

[Aga-poruḷ-viḷakkam. With commentary by Vaidya-liṅga.] 1878. 8°. **14172. e. 34.**

—— *See* PURĀṆAS.—*Skanda-purāṇam.* ∘∘∘ கந்தபுராணம் ஷ [Teyvayānaiy-ammai-tiru-maṇa-paṭalam. With commentary by Vaidya-liṅga.] [1889.] 8°. **14170. e. 30.**

—— *See* PURĀṆAS.—*Skanda-purāṇam.* கந்தபுராணம் ஷ [Vaḷḷiy-ammai-tiru-maṇa-paṭalam. With commentary by Vaidya-liṅga.] [1886.] 8°. **14170. e. 25.**

—— *See* ṢINNA-TAMBI PULAVAR. ∘∘∘ கல்வளையந்தாதி ஷ [Kal-vaḷaiy-antādi. With commentary by Vaidya-liṅga.] [1887.] 16°. **14172. a. 3.**

—— *See* VARADA-RĀJA PAṆḌITAR, *K. R.* ∘∘∘ சிவராத்திரிபுராணம். [Ṣiva-rātri-purāṇam. Edited by Vaidya-liṅga.] [1881.] 8°. **14170. e. 7.**

—— *See* VĪRA-MAṆḌALAVAR. சூடாமணிநிகண்டு. [Chūḍāmaṇi-nighaṇṭu. Edited by Vaidya-liṅga.] [1875.] 8°. **14172. e. 30.**

—— ∘∘∘ சித்திவிக்கினேசுரர் ஊஞ்சல். [Siddhi-vighnēṣvara-ūñjal. Hymns for the ceremony of swinging the image of Gaṇēṣa.] pp. 14. யாழ்ப்பாணம் விஜய [*Jaffna*, 1893.] 16°. **14170. d. 36.(3.)**

VAIDYA-LIṄGA PIḶḶAI, *Vaṇṇainagar K.* நல்லைவடிவேலர் ஆசிரியவிருத்தம். [Nallai-vaḍi-vēlar-āṣiriya-vṛuttam. Devotional verses to Skanda.] pp. 24. யாழ்ப்பாணம் நந்தன [*Jaffna*, 1892.] 16°. **14170. d. 35.(3.)**

VAIDYA-NĀTHA CHEṬṬI, *Uṟaiyūr.* சிவத்துரோக கண்டன நிராகரணம். [Ṣiva-drōha-khaṇḍana-nirākaraṇam. A Ṣaiva controversial tract.] pp. 6. சென்னை [*Madras*,] 1896. 8°. **14170. e. 47.(7.)**

VAIDYA-NĀTHA DĒṢIKAR, *Tiruvārūr.* ∘∘∘ இலக்கணவிளக்கம் மூலமும் உரையும். [Ilakkaṇa-viḷakkam. A treatise on grammar and Ars Poetica, with commentary by the author. To which is appended as ch. 5 of its Poruḷ-adhikāram, or bk. 3, a Pāṭṭ'-iyal ascribed to Vaidya-nātha's son Tyāga-rāja Dēṣikar. Edited with introduction, indices, *etc.*, by Ṣ. V. Dāmōdaram Piḷḷai.] pp. xx. 851, ii. xiv. iii. சென்னப்பட்டணம் விரோதி [*Madras*, 1889.] 8°. **14172. e. 24.**

—— இலக்கணவிளக்கப்பதிப்புரைமறுப்பு. [Ilakkaṇa-viḷakka-padipp'-urai-maṟuppu. A criticism of Ṣ. V. Dāmōdaram Piḷḷai's introductory commentary on the Ilakkaṇa-viḷakkam, by a disciple of Sabhā-pati Nāvalar.] pp. 16. சிதம்பரம் [*Chidambaram*,] 1894. 8°. **14172. f. 22.**

The official "Catalogue of Books printed in Madras Presidency," 1894, ii., *p.* 30, *gives the name of the author as M. Kārttikēya Mudali.*

—— ∘∘∘ இலக்கணவிளக்கம். செய்யுளியல். [Ṣeyyuḷ-iyal. Being ch. 4 of the Poruḷ-adhikāram of the Ilakkaṇa-viḷakkam, and treating of poetic composition. Edited with introduction *etc.* by Ṣ. V. Dāmōdaram Piḷḷai.] pp. xii. 72. சென்னை [*Madras*,] 1900. 8°. **14172. e. 35.**

VAIDYA-NĀTHA DĪKSHITAR, *Kandaramāṇikkam.* *See* SANDHYĀ-VANDANAM. யஜுர்வேத ஸந்த்யாவந்தநம் ஷ [Sandhyā-vandanam, *etc.* With extracts, in Tamil, from the commentaries of Vaidya-nātha, *etc.*] 1901. 8°. **14033. aa. 27.**

—— ∘∘∘ [Grantha script title] *etc.* ([Grantha script]) [Smruti-muktā-phala. A Sanskrit digest of ceremonial law and tradition. With the commentary Prabhā of Ṣrīnivāsa Dīkshitar. Vol. i., or Varṇāṣrama-dharma-kāṇḍam, on the forms of caste-life, with Tamil translation by Rāma-sāmi Ṣāstri. Vol. ii., or Āhnika-kāṇḍam, on the encyclic rituals, with Tamil translation by Rāma-krushṇa Bhaṭṭāchāryar. Vol. iii., or Āṣaucha-kāṇḍam, on formal uncleanness, and vol. iv., or part i. of the Ṣrāddha-kāṇḍam, on *ṣrāddha* rites, with Tamil translation by Ṣ. Subrahmaṇya Ṣāstri. Vol. v., or Tithi-nirṇaya-kāṇḍam, on determination of the calendar, with Tamil translation by M. Rāma-chandra Ṣāstri.] [Grantha script] [*Chidambaram, Nadukkaveri*,] 1898, *etc.* 4°. **14039. c. 15.**

In progress!

VAIDYANĀTH'-AIYAR, *Vaiyai Pañchanad'-aiyar.* [*Life.*] *See* RĀMA-SĀMI AIYAR, *V. P.* மஹாவைத்தியநாத விஜயஸங்கிரகம். [Mahā-vaidyanātha-vijaya-saṅgraham.] [1893.] 16°. **14171. aa. 9.**

VAIDYA-NĀTHA MUDALIYĀR, *T.* The Looking-glass for the Mind; or, Intellectual Mirror; being an elegant collection of ... stories ... chiefly translated from ... L'Aim [*sic*] des Enfans. With analysis and close translation in Tamil, serving to show the nature and construction of sentences, by T. Vytheanatha Moodeliar. pp. i. 157. *Madras*, 1838. 8°. **14170. k. 36.**

VAIYĀPURI MUDALIYĀR, *Tirutoṭṭikaḷai.* See ARUṆĀCHALA KAVI-RĀYAR: இராமநாடகம். [Rāma-nāṭakam. Edited by Vaiyāpuri Mudaliyār.] [1867.] 8°. **14170. l. 3.**

VAIYĀPURI PIḶḶAI, *T. Aiyā-gaṇṇu.* நல்லதங்காள் நாடகம் [Nalla-daṅgāḷ-nāṭakam. A drama on the story of Nalla-daṅgāḷ and her ill-treatment in her brother's house. A musical adaptation by T. Subba-rāya Mudaliyār, edited by K. Aruṇāchala Mudaliyār.] pp. 132. யுவ [*Madras*, 1875.] 8°. **14172. c. 13.**

VĀKYA-GURU. ००० వాక్యగురుపరంపర ॥ [Vākya-guru-paramparai. Notes upon the tenets and teachers of the Rāmānujīya Vaishṇava church.] pp. 24. [*Madras*,] 1884. 12°. **14170. d. 8.(2.)**

VĀLAI-BĀVA ŜĀHIB, *Āmūr.* தொழுகை அகீகத்துவிளக்கம். [Toṟugai-ḥakīkat-viḷakkam. An adaptation of the Ḥakīkat al-ṣalāt of Maulavī ʿAbd Allāh, a Hindustani manual of Islam.] pp. 44. துந்துபி [*Madras*, 1862.] 8°. **14173. b. 33.**

VĀLĀMBĀḶ, *V. S., of Egmore, Madras.* வேதாந்தப்பாட்டுகள். [Vēdānta-pāṭṭugaḷ. 7 poems, conveying principles of monistic Vaishṇava theology in the form of hymns on spiritual ceremonies of worship, *etc.* Compiled and edited by Vālāmbāḷ Ammāḷ.] pp. ii. 28. *Madras*, 1907. 8°. **14170. eee. 29.(1.)**

—— ஜீவநாடகம் முதலிய அத்வைதப் பாட்டுகளும். பஞ்சீகரண மகாவாக்கியமும். [Jīva-nāṭakam. A short lyrical play allegorically describing the soul's enlightenment according to monistic theology. With Pañchīkaraṇa-mahā-vākyam, a tract on the monistic theory of the cosmogony, and four hymns of the same theological school. Compiled and edited by Vālāmbāḷ Ammāḷ.] pp. 40, 22; 1 *plate.* *Madras*, 1908. 8°. **14170. eee. 29.(2.)**

VĀLAR. வாலர்கணிதம். [Vālar-gaṇitam. An elementary arithmetic.] pp. 196. புதுவை தூஅா்மேரு [*Pondicherry*, 1853.] 12°. **14172. h. 13.**

VALAYUDHA MOODELIAR. See VĒLĀYUDHA MUDALIYĀR.

VALENTINE. ஊசோன் பாலந்தை கதை. [Ūsōn-bālandai-kathai. The story of Valentine and Orson.] pp. 95. யாழ்ப்பாணம் [*Jaffna*,] 1891. 8°. **14170. k. 50.**

VALLABHA-DĒVAR. See ATIVĪRA-RĀMA PĀṆḌIYAN.

VAḶḶIY-AMMAN. ००० முத்தையன்விலாசமென்னும் வள்ளியம்மன்விலாசம். [Vaḷḷiy-amman-vilāsam, or Mutt'-aiyan-vilāsam. A drama on the loves of the god Mutt'-aiyan or Subrahmaṇya and Vaḷḷi. Edited by K. Aruṇāchala Mudaliyār.] pp. 87. சென்னை [*Madras*,] 1895. 8°. **14170. l. 38.**

VĀLMĪKI. [For editions of Bhīmā Kavi-rāyar's prose version of the Rāmar-aṣva-mēdham:] See BHĪMA KAVI-RĀYAR.

—— [For editions of Kamban's Rāmāyaṇam imitated and adapted from the Sanskrit of Vālmiki:] See KAMBAN.

—— [For anonymous poems and prose narratives on the subject of the Rāmāyaṇam:] See RĀMĀYAṆAM.

—— See VEṄKAṬA-RĀM'-AIYAR, *K. K.* இராமாயணக்கும்மி ஸ்ரீ [Rāmāyaṇa-kummi. A poem on the Rāmāyaṇam.] 1901. 16°. **14172. a. 32.(5.)**

—— See VĒṄKAṬA-RĀMA AIYAṄGĀR, *T.* வால்மீகி ராமாயண ஸ்ரீ (Episodes from the Valmiki-ramayana in ... prose, *etc.*) 1906, *etc.* 12°. **14171. d. 7.**

—— ஸ்ரீ ... ஸ்ரீராமாயணம்-வாலகாண்டம் (ஸுந்தரகாண்டம் *etc.*). [Rāmāyaṇam. Edited with introductions, glosses, and paraphrases in Tamil by P. A. M. Ṣrīnivāsa Rāghavāchāryar.] சென்னை [*Madras*,] 1897-1901. 4°. **14068. c. 14.**

The volume containing the Sundara-kāṇḍam is in the second edition, and differs from the other volumes by being of smaller size and containing no transcription of the text in Telugu characters. Only the Bāla-k.°, Sundara-k.°, and Yuddha-k.° (no. 1-5) have been published.

—— Sri Valmiki Ramayana, slokas in Grantha characters, with Tamil translation and Sanskrit notes by Pandit S. G. Ananthacharya ... Part ii. Ayodhyakanda. (ஹரவல்லாஞீகீவுணிதே ஸ்ரீராமாயணே ... அயோத்யாகாண்ட: ... ஸ்ரீவால்மீகிரா-

மாயணம் ஞ.) pp. xvi. 296, 296. *Madras*, 1907. 8°. **14065. bbb. 15.**

In progress?

—— வால்மீகிராமாயணவசனம். [Rāmāyaṇam. Translated into Tamil prose by S. M. Naṭēsa Śāstri. Edited by V. M. Śaṭhakōpa-rāmānujāchāryar (bks. i.-ii.), U. V. Sāmināth'-aiyar (bk. i.), *etc.*] சென்னை [*Madras*,] 1901, *etc.* 8°. **14172. c. 42.**

In progress.

—— ஸ்ரீமத் வாலமீகிராமாயணவசனம் அயோத்தியா (*யுத்த, உத்தர) காண்டம். [Vālmīki rāmāyaṇa-vachanam. The Ayōdhyā-kāṇḍam, Yuddha-k°., and Uttara-k°., translated into Tamil prose by M. Tāta-dēśika Tātāchāryar and K. K. Śrīnivāsa Rāghavāchāryar.] 3 vols. *Madras*, 1902-1903. 8°. **14172. d. 26.**

The Ayōdhyā-kāṇḍam is of the second edition (1903).

—— Ramayana Niti Ratnavali: Moral Gems from the Ramayana . . . Containing excellent moral stanzas from Valmeeki Ramayana, with Telugu, Tamil, and English translations and explanations. . . . Edited by R. Sivasankara Pandiah. [Translated into Tamil by T. Rāma-nātha Aiyar.] pp. 24, 120. *Madras*, 1886. 12°. **14003. c. (no. 6.)**

Forms no. 6 of the "Hindu Excelsior Series."

—— அபயப்ரதாநஸாரஸஹிதமான தனிஶ்லோகம். [Tani-ślōkam. Select Sanskrit stanzas from the Rāmāyaṇam, with Tamil glosses and *maṇipravāḷam* commentary by Periyav-āchān Piḷḷai expounding Viśishṭādvaita doctrine. With notes by M. T. Rāmānujāchāryar. Edited by the latter and S. Muttu-krushṇa Nāyuḍu.] pp. iv. 2, 410. சென்னப்பட்டணம் கஒகக [*Madras*, 1901.] 8°. **14065. bbb. 6.**

—— [Another edition of the preceding, in Telugu characters, with the glosses and notes in Telugu. Edited by M. T. Rāmānujāchāryar, T. Śrīrangāchāryulu, and S. Muttu-krushṇa Nāyuḍu.] pp. iv. ii. 408. చెన్నపట్టణము ౧౯౦౧ [*Madras*, 1901.] 8°. **14065. bbb. 7.**

—— அபயப்ரதாநஸாரம். [Abhaya-pradāna-sāram. Being VI. (Yuddha-kāṇḍam) xvi.-xix. 1-9 and 23, in Sanskrit, with an exposition in Tamil by Periyav-āchān Piḷḷai according to the Tengalai Vaishṇava school. Edited by V. M. Śrīnivāsa Appaṅgār Svāmi.] pp. 78. சென்னைப்பட்டணம் கா [*Madras*, 1891.] 8°. **14060. c. 32.(1.)**

The text is given in Telugu and Tamil characters.

—— ஸ்ரீவால்மீகி ராமாயணம். சுந்தரகாண்டம். [Sundara-kāṇḍam. Sanskrit text, with Tamil paraphrase by Tenmaḍam Vēṅkaṭa-narasiṃhāchāryar. Edited by Māḍabhūshi Tarka-tīrtha Rāmānujāchāryar.] pp. xiv. 770; 8 *plates*. சென்னை [*Madras*,] 1901. 12°. **14060. b. 18.**

—— ஸ்ரீவால்மீகிராமாயண ஸுந்தரகாண்டம். [Sundara-kāṇḍam. Sanskrit text, edited with Tamil translation by Muśuṟpākkam Kaḍāmbi Raṅgāchāryar.] pp. ix. 182, 233. சென்னை பலவ [*Madras*, 1902.] 8°. **14065. bbb. 9.**

—— . . . ராமாயணத்துத்தரகாண்டக்கதை [Uttara-kāṇḍa-kathai. A Tamil prose version of the last book of the Sanskrit Rāmāyaṇam, by Tiru-chiṯṯambala Dēśikan.] pp. ii. 132. சென்னபட்டணத்து தஅ௱௰௫ [*Madras*, 1815.] 8°. **14172. b. 4.**

VALOOPPILLAI. *See* VELU PIḶḶAI.

VĀMA-DĒVA MṚUGA-BHAṬṬĀRAKAR. *See* MṚUGA-BHAṬṬĀRAKAR.

VĀNA-MĀ-MALAI RĀMĀNUJA-JĪYAR (AṞAGIYA-VARADA MUNI). శ్రీవానమామల రామానుజ జీయర్ స్వామలవారి మఠగురుపరంపర తనియన్లు మొదలైనవి [Devotional verses in Sanskrit addressed to various heads of the Rāmānujīya church; Tiru-nakshatra-taniyanlu and Vāṟi-tiru-nāmamulu, Sanskrit verses on the nativities and Tamil hymns in praise of Maṇavāḷa Mā-muni, of Vāna-mā-malai Rāmānuja-jīyar, a teacher of the Mā-muni's doctrines, and of the abbots of the Vāna-mā-malamaṭham; and Vānāchala-yōgi-vijaya-daṇḍaka and Vānāchala-svāmi-suprabhātam, Sanskrit religious poems.] pp. iv. 68. చెన్నపురి [*Madras*,] 1906. 12°. **14048. b. 45.(3.)**

VAṆṆA-KAḶAÑJIYA PULAVAR, *Madurai.* சாருதேசத்தரசராகிய அலிபாதுஷாநாடகம். ['Alī-pādshā-nāṭakam. A drama on the adventures of 'Alī Pādshāh, a legendary Muhammadan king, and his son. Edited by M. Subrahmaṇya Svāmi.] pp. 160. வண்ணாரப்பேட்டை [*Washermanpet*,] 1887. 8°. **14173. b. 21.**

VANNA-KALAÑJIYA PULAVAR, *Madurai (continued).* [Another edition.] pp. 160. வண்ணாரப்பேட்டை [*Washermanpet,*] 1889. 8°. **14170. 1. 25.**

VANNIYAR. வன்னியகுல கல்யாண கொத்து. [Vanniya-kula-kalyāṇa-kottu. Wedding-ballads of the Vanniyar tribe.] pp. 8. சேலம் ஜெய [*Salem,* 1894.] 16°. **14172. a. 27.**

VARADĀCHĀRYAR, *Īgai.* *See* VARĀHA-MIHIRA. புருஷ ஸாமுத்திரிகம். [Purusha-sāmudrikam and Strī-s°. With Tamil version by Varadāchāryar.] 1892. 8°. [*Sāmudrika-lakshaṇa-ṣāstram.*] **14170. i. 26.**

VARADĀCHĀRYAR, *Ṣarukkai.* ஜோதிமாலை இது நாடிகை ஙூ (Jyotimalai. A Tamil drama.) pp. 8, 98, i. *Madras,* 1902. 12°. **14170. 1. 24.(2.)**

Forms " Gem 17 " in the series " The Anklet of Sárada " (Nā-magaḷ-ṣilambu).

VARADĀCHĀRYAR, *Vātsya Dēva-rāja* (NADĀDŪR AMMĀḶ). ◦ ◦ ◦ ப்ரபன்னபாரிஜாதம் ஙூ [Prapanna-pārijātam. A Sanskrit poem on the religious system of Viṣishṭādvaita Vaishṇavas, in 10 *paddhatis.* Followed by Paratvādi-pañchaka-stuti and Paramārtha-stuti, short poems of like nature, also by Varadāchāryar; Parāṣara Bhaṭṭar's Ashṭa-ṣlōkī; Yāmunāchāryar's Chatuḥ-ṣlōkī; and a life of Varadāchāryar, in Tamil prose. Edited with Tamil interpretations and commentary, *etc.,* by Ahōbilāchāryar.] pp. ii. 160, v. சென்னை மங்மத [*Madras,* 1895.] 8°. **14028. d. 55.**

The Sanskrit stanzas are printed in both Grantham and Telugu character.

VARADA-RĀJA DĪKSHITAR. The History of India from the earliest ages. ஹிந்துதேசசரித்திரம். ஆதிகாலந்தொடங்கி. ஸ்ரீமஹாபாரதம். Sri Maha Bharata. [A treatise in Tamil prose.] From a comparative study of all current records on the subject. pts. i.-xii. pp. viii. 88. சென்னை [*Madras,*] 1890. 8°. **14172. d. 9.**

VARADA-RĀJA PANDITAR, *Kāṣi Ranga-nātha.* ஏகாதசிபுராணம். [Ēkādaṣi-purāṇam. A treatise on the legends and ritual of the Ēkādaṣi festival. Followed by 108 names of Nārāyaṇa. Edited and annotated by N. Kadirai-vēr̤ Piḷḷai.] pp. 71. சென்னை [*Madras,*] 1898. 12°. **14170. ee. 21.**

—— ◦ ◦ ◦ சிவராத்திரிபுராணம். [Ṣiva-rātri-purāṇam. A metrical treatise upon the Ṣiva-rātri festival. Edited by V. Ṣ. Vaidya-linga Piḷḷai.] pp. 100, ii. சென்னபட்டணம் விசு [*Madras,* 1881.] 8°. **14170. e. 7.**

—— ◦ ◦ ◦ சிவராத்திரி புராண மூலமும் . . . விருத்தி உரையும். [Ṣiva-rātri-purāṇam. Edited with a commentary by N. Kadirai-vēr̤ Piḷḷai.] pts. i.-ii. pp. 120. சென்னை [*Madras,*] 1902. 8°. **14170. ee. 59.**

Discontinued after pt. 3.

VARADA-RĀJULU NĀYUDU, *Kendam.* *See* ṢĒSHĀCHALAM NĀYUDU. ◦ ◦ ◦ ஜடபரதோபாக்கியானம் ஙூ [Jaḍa-bharatōpākhyānam. Translated by Varada-rājulu.] 1898. 12°. **14170. ee. 26.**

—— *See* ṢĒSHĀCHALAM NĀYUDU. ◦ ◦ ◦ ஸ்ரீராமஷ்ருதயம் ஙூ [Shaṭ-chakravarttigaḷin indra-jāla-kathaigaḷ. Translated by Varada-rājulu.] 1898. 8°. **14171. a. 36.**

—— *See* ṢĒSHĀCHALAM NĀYUDU. ◦ ◦ ◦ சுத்தநிராலம்பமார்க்கம். [Ṣuddha-nirālamba-mārgam. Translated by Varada-rājulu.] 1898. 12°. **14170. d. 63.**

VARADA-VĒDĀNTĀCHĀRYAR, *Kavi-kuñjaram Ṣatāvadhānam.* *See* ĀR̤VĀRGAḶ.—Nāl-āyiram.—*Tiru-vāy-mor̤i.* [Grantha] [Bhagavad-vishayam. Edited by Varada-vēdāntāchāryar.] [1883-1904.] 4°. **14170. fff. 3.**

—— ஸ்ரீ [Grantha] [Ṣaṭhakōpādy-āchārya-ṣrī-sūkti-sudhāsvādinī. A collection of works in Sanskrit and sanskritised Tamil on the principles of Viṣishṭādvaita philosophy and religion.] [Grantha] [*Kumbakonam,* 1903, *etc.*] 8°. **14049. bb. 6.**

In progress.

VARAD'-AYYA, *C.* *See* ṢIVA-ṢANKARA PANDYĀJĪ, *R.,* and VARAD'-AYYA, *C.* திரவிட பால நீதி . . . Dravida Bala Niti Bodhini, *etc.* 1889. 12°. **14003. c. (no. 11.)**

VARĀHA-MIHIRA. பிருஹஜ்ஜாதகமென்னும் மங்களேஸ்வரியம் மூலமும்-உரையும். [Mangaḷēṣvaryam, or Bṛuhaj-jātakam. Being a Tamil version by Vaidya-linga Pattar of the Sanskrit Bṛuhaj-jātakam of Varāha-mihira and its Telugu prose paraphrase by Sarasvati Tiru-vēnkaṭāchāri.]

pp. iv. 443; 1 *plate.* சென்னை [*Madras,*] 1905. 8°. **14171. g. 6.**

—— புருஷ (†ஸ்த்ரீ) ஸாமுத்திரிகம். [Purusha-sāmudrikam and Strī-sāmudrikam. Being ch. 68-70 of the Bṛuhat-saṃhitā, on the art of reading characters and fortunes from bodily features. Sanskrit text in Telugu and Tamil characters, with Tamil version by Īgai Varadāchāryar and English rendering by P. A. Lakshmaṇa Piḷḷai.] pp. 178. *See* GURU-SĀMI MUDALIYĀR. சாமுத்திரிக ழூ [Sāmudrika-lakshaṇa-ṣāstram.] pt. 1. 1892. 8°. **14170. i. 26.**

VARAIY-AṞUTTA-BĀṬṬ'-IYAL. வரையறுத்த-பாட்டியல். [Varaiy-aṟutta-bāṭṭ'-iyal. A tract on metrical composition, with prose commentary.] *See* GUṆA-VĪRA PAṆḌITAR. வச்சணந்திமாலை ழூ [Veṇ-bā-pāṭṭ'-iyal, *etc.*] pp. 46-51. 1900. 12°. **14172. ee. 7.**

VARATUṄGA-RĀMA PĀṆḌIYAN. *See* PURĀṆAS.—*Skanda-purāṇam.* பிரமோத்தரகாண்டவசனம். [Brahmōttara-kāṇḍa-vachanam. A prose paraphrase of Varatuṅga-rāma's Brahmōttara-kāṇḍam, a metrical adaptation of the section bearing that name in the Skanda-purāṇam.] 1878. 16°. **14170. d. 20.**

VARA-VARA-MUNI, or **VARA-YŌGI.** *See* AḺAGIYA-MAṆAVĀḶA PERU-MĀḶ.

VARṆA-KULĀDITTAN. *See* KĀTTĀN.

VĀSUDĒVA MUDALIYĀR, *of Chettipalayam, Coimbatore.* ஸ்ரீ ... அவிநாசிக் கருணாம்பிகை சதகம். [Avināṣi-karuṇāmbikai-ṣatakam. 100 stanzas to the goddess Karuṇāmbikai (Pārvati) as worshipped in Avināṣi or Ten-kasi. Edited by K. R. Sabhā-pati Piḷḷai.] pp. 8, 43. கோயமுத்தூர் [*Coimbatore,*] 1891. 8°. **14170. e. 47.(1.)**

VĀSUDĒVA MUDALIYĀR, *Paṭṭālam.* *See* ACADEMIES, *etc.*—Madras.—*University of Madras.* The University of Madras. The First in Arts Examination—1892. The Tamil text ... with ... notes by ... Rajagopaul Pillai ... and ... Vasudeva Mudelliar. 1891. 8°. **14172. bb. 4.**

—— *See* TIRU-MUṞAI.—*Tiru-vāchakam.* ००० திருவாசகம் ழூ [Tiru-vāchakam. With commentary, *etc.* Edited by Vāsudēva.] 1897. 8°. **14172. b. 57.**

VĀSUDĒVA MUDALIYĀR, *Paṭṭālam* (*continued*). *See* VIDYĀ-VINŌDINI. வித்தியாவிநோதினி. (Vidhya Vinodhini Series.) [Edited by Vāsudēva.] [1889]-1892. 8°. **14172. c. 39.**

VĀSUDĒVA NĀYUḌU, *Tañjai Gōvinda-sāmi.* The Practitioner's Materia Medica and Therapeutics, in English and Tamil. Being an account of the drugs comprised in the new British pharmacopœia and the pharmacopœia of India. (*ஆயுர்வேதபாராவாரம்.) pp. ii. ii. 949, lii. *Madras,* 1901. 8°. **14170. i. 74.**

VĀSUDĒVA YATI. வாசுதேவமனனம் ழூ [Vāsudēva-mananam. An Advaita-Vedantic treatise, translated from the Sanskrit into Tamil by V. Kuppu-sāmi Aiyar.] pp. ii. 82, i. சென்னைபுரி ஸர்வஜித் [*Madras,* 1887.] 8°. **14170. e. 32.**

—— வாஸுதேவமநநாக்யஃ த்ராவிடபாஷாஸஹிதஃ ... வாசுதேவமனனமென்கிற கிரந்தம் ழூ [Vāsudēva-mananam. Sanskrit text, with a Tamil version by V. Kuppu-sāmi Aiyar.] pp. i. i. 195, i. சென்னை ஜய [*Madras,* 1895.] 8°. **14048. dd. 19.**

VĀTSYĀYANA (MALLA-NĀGA). வாத்ஸ்யாயநசூத்திரம். [Vātsyāyana-sūtram. 37 Sanskrit aphorisms on wifely duty, consisting chiefly of the Kāma-sūtram IV. i. With Tamil glosses and commentary.] *See* SUNDARA-RĀJA ṢARMĀ. வ்யாஸ வாத்ஸ்யாயந ... பார்யாதருமம். (Vyasa and Vatsyayana's Bharyadharmam, *etc.*) pp. 1-95. 1901. 12°. **14085. b. 44.**

VAYITTIYA-LIṄGA. *See* VAIDYA-LIṄGA.

VAYITTIYA-NĀTHA. *See* VAIDYA-NĀTHA.

VĒDĀCHALAM PIḶḶAI, *Nāgapaṭṭinam* (R. S. VĒDĀCHALAM PIḶḶAI). *See* PERIODICAL PUBLICATIONS.—*Madras.* ००० ஞானசாகரம். [Ñāna-sāgaram. Edited by Vēdāchalam.] 1902, *etc.* 8°. **14172. i. 10.**

—— *See* PERIODICAL PUBLICATIONS.—*Madras.* உண்மை விளக்கம் ழூ [Siddhānta-dīpikai. Edited by Vēdāchalam.] 1897. 4°. **14170. fff. 1.**

—— முதற்குறள்வாதநிராகரணம். [Mudaṟ-kuṟaḷ-vāda-nirākaraṇam. A reply to the pamphlet entitled Mudaṟ-kuṟaḷ-vādam.] pp. 50. *Madras,* 1898. 8°. **14170. ee. 32.(2.)**

VĒDĀCHALAM PIḶḶAI, *Nāgapaṭṭinam* (R. S. VĒDĀCHALAM PIḶḶAI) (*continued*). பட்டினப்பாலை ஆராய்ச்சி. (A critical commentary on [Rudrakaṇṇanār's poem] Pattinappalai.) pp. 8, 80. *Madras*, 1906. 12°. 14171. d. 2.(2.)

—— சித்தாந்தஞானபோதம். [Siddhānta-ñānabōdham. A collection of poems on the esoteric Saiva creed. Edited with commentary and notes by Vēdāchalam Piḷḷai.] pt. i. *Madras*, 1898. 8°. 14170. ee. 39.

The works contained in part i., which apparently is all that has been published, are to be found under the headings:—

Ñāna-sāgaram. Sata-maṇi.
Pañchāksharam. Siṭṭambala-nāḍigaḷ.

—— திருவொற்றி முருகர் மும்மணிக்கோவை. [Tiruvoṭṭi-mrugar-mum-maṇi-kōvai.] (A String-of-Three Gems, an oblation to Muruga, the War-God. A panegyric Tamil poem.) pp. 49. *Madras*, 1900. 8°. 14172. bb. 3.(2.)

VĒDĀCHALAM PIḶḶAI, *R. S.* *See* VĒDĀCHALAM PIḶḶAI, *N.*

VĒDA-GIRI MUDALIYĀR, *Kaḷattūr*. *See* AMIRTA-SĀGARAN. ∘∘∘ காரிகை ஷ [Kārikai. Edited by Vēda-giri.] [1851.] 8°. 14172. e. 36.

—— *See* ATIVĪRA-RĀMA PĀṆḌIYAN. நைடதம் ஷ [Naiḍadam. Edited with interpretation and paraphrase by Vēda-giri.] [1859.] 8°. 14172. c. 3.

—— —— [1875.] 8°. 14172. b. 59.

—— *See* MAHĀ-BHĀRATAM. பகவற்கீதை ஷ [Bhagavad-gītai. Edited by Vēda-giri.] [1852.] 8°. 14170. e. 19.

—— *See* NĀL-AḌIYĀR. ∘∘∘ நீதிநூல் ஷ [Nālaḍiyār. Edited by Vēda-giri.] [1855.] 8°. 14172. c. 1.

—— *See* TIRU-VAḶḶUVAR. ∘∘∘ திருக்குறள் ஷ [Kuṟaḷ. With commentary compiled by Vēda-giri.] [1849.] 8°. 14172. c. 2.

—— *See* VĪRA-MAṆḌALAVAR. Nogandu: part xi., *etc.* [With supplements by Vēda-giri.] 1843. 8°. 14172. f. 23.

VĒDA-NĀYAKAM, *Vīravāgu*. [*Life.*] *See* PETER (A.). Life of . . . Vethanayagam, *etc.* 1899. 12°. 14171. a. 30.

VĒDA-NĀYAKAM PIḶḶAI (SAMUEL), *of Mayaveram*. *See* DURAI-SĀMI MUDALIYĀR, *T. S.* வேதபுரியந்தாதி. [Vēda-puriy-antādi. Edited by Vēda-nāyakam.] [1868.] 8°. 14170. c. 32.

—— Suguna Sunthari, a Tamil novel, by S. Vedanayagum Pillay (†to illustrate different principles of morality) . . . சுகுணசுந்தரிசரித்திரம். pp. ii. v. 76, 49. *Madras*, 1887. 16°. 14170. k. 49.

VĒDA-NĀYAKA ṢĀSTRI, *Tirunelvēli Dēva-sahāyam, of Tanjore*. Jepamalei, or Rosary of Songs and Prayers (*செபமாலை) to be sung in the morning and evening, *etc.* pp. xii. 244. *Tanjore*, 1907. 12°. 14170. bbb. 4.

—— தேவாலயத்திலும் குடும்பத்திலும் பாடத்தக்க ஞானகீர்த்தனைகள். [Ñāna-kīrttanaigaḷ. Christian hymns.] pp. 216. சென்னபட்டணம் ௲அ௱௫௰௩ [*Madras*, 1853.] 8°. 14170. c. 12.

—— ஞானத்தச்சன் நாடகம். [Ñāna-tachan-nāṭakam. A Christian dramatic poem on the Creation and cognate scriptural topics.] pp. ii. 68. யாழ்ப்பாணம் [*Jaffna*,] 1897. 8°. 14170. l. 32.(5.)

—— GnanathatchaNatagam. Or A Drama of the spiritual Carpenter, *etc.* (ஞானத்தச்சனுடகம்.) pp. 108. *Tanjore*, 1908. 12°. 14170. l. 21.(2.)

—— சாஸ்திரக்கும்மி. Sastherukkoomme, a satirical poem on the superstitions of the Hindoos. pp. iv. 125. *Madras*, 1850. 12°. 14170. a. 48.

—— [Another copy.] 14170. a. 47.

—— [Another edition.] pp. vi. 135. *Madras*, 1861. 16°. 14170. a. 42.

VĒDA-NĀYAKA ṢĀSTRI, *T. Dēva-sahāyam*, and **WINSLOW** (MIRON). Blind Way. Part. i.-iv. [A Christian controversial tract in which the futility of the four Ṣaiva modes of worship is illustrated by verses from Tamil poets. To which are added] Incantations and True Way. இதில் குருட்டுவழி ஷ. pp. 142. *Jaffna*, 1852. 32°. 14170. a. 3.

—— The Blind Way . . . குருட்டுவழி ஷ. pp. 128. *Madras*, 1861. 16°. 14170. a. 37.

VĒDĀNTA-DĒṢIKAR. *See* VĒṄKAṬA-NĀTHA VĒDĀNTĀCHĀRYAR.

VĒDĀNTA-RĀMĀNUJA MAHĀ-DĒṢIKAR, *disciple of Raṅga-nātha.* See Āṟvārgaḷ.—Nāl-āyiram.—*Tiru-vāy-moṟi.* ஸ்ரீபகவத்விஷயம் ॥ [Bhagavad-vishayam. Being the Tiru-vāy-moṟi with commentaries—viz. Vēdānta-rāmānuja's Iru-batti-nāl-āyira-paḍi, *etc.*] [1883-1904.] 4°. **14170. fff. 3.**

—— ந்யாஸவித்யாதர்பணம் ॥ [Nyāsa-vidyā-darpaṇam. A treatise in Sanskritised Tamil upon the Vaishṇava doctrines of Rāmānuja's school.] pp. 60. [1905.] See Varada-vēdāntachāryar, *K. Ṣ.* ஸ்ரீ . . . ஸ்ரீஸூக்திஸுதாஸ்வாதிநீ *etc.* [Ṣaṭha-kōpādy-āchārya-ṣrī-sūkti-sudhāsvādinī.] no. 5. [1903, *etc.*] 8°. **14049. bb. 6.(5.)**

VĒDĀNTA-SUBRAHMAṆYA PIḶḶAI, *Ṣivagaṅgai.* மயூரகிரிபுராணம். [Mayūra-giri-purāṇam. A poem upon the cult of the sanctuary of Subrahmaṇya at Mayūra-giri or Kunṟa-kuḍi, near Tiru-puttur. With a prose paraphrase by N. Ṣ. Ponn'-ambala Piḷḷai.] pp. ii. ii. 163. யாழ்ப்பாணம் [*Jaffna,*] 1885. 8°. **14170. e. 66.**

VĒDAS. [For the Vedic texts comprised in the Sandhyā-vandanam :] See Sandhyā-vandanam.

—— வேதார்த்ததீபிகா ஆ [Vēdārtha-dīpikā. Being the Sanskrit text of the Taittirīya-saṃhitā with Tamil commentary and paraphrase by Kāñchīpuram Rāma-chandra Ṣāstri.] pt. 1. pp. 60. சென்னைபுரி விரோதி [*Madras,* 1889.] 8°. **14010. c. 46.**

—— புருஷஸூக்தம் (†ஸ்ரீஸூக்தம்). [Purusha-sūktam (Ṛig-vēda x. 90) and Ṣrī-sūktam (a *khila* to Ṛig-vēda v. 87). With Tamil interpretation and extracts, in a Tamil translation, from the commentaries of Sāyaṇa, Ānanda-tīrtha, and the Viṣishṭādvaita school.] See Sandhyā-vandanam. யஜுர்வேத ஸந்த்யாவந்தநம் ஆ [Sandhyā-vandanam.] 1901. 8°. **14033. aa. 27.**

—— ∘∘∘ புருடசூக்தபாஷ்யம். [Purusha-sūktam. With a commentary by K. Ṣrīnivāsa Dīkshitar giving a Ṣaiva interpretation of the text, translated into Tamil by T. Ṣivānanda-sāgara Yōgīṣvarar.] pp. iii. 46, iii. சிதம்பரம் [*Chidambaram,*] 1894. 8°. **14170. ee. 30.**

VEERASAWMY CHETTIAR. See Vīrā-sāmi Cheṭṭiyār.

VĒLAI DĒṢIKAR, *Kavitalam C.* See Tiruvaigāvūr. திருவைகாவூர்ப்புராணம். [Tiruvaigāvūr-purāṇam. Translated by Vēlai Dēṣikar.] [1894.] 8°. **14170. e. 56.**

VĒL-ĀYUDHA MUDALIYĀR, *Paṟani.* See Rāmaliṅga Piḷḷai, *K.* ∘∘∘ திருவருட்பா ஆ [Tiruv-aruṭ-pā-tiraṭṭu. Edited by Vēl-āyudha.] 1903. 12°. **14170. d. 79.**

VĒL-ĀYUDHA MUDALIYĀR, *Toṟuvūr.* See Paṭṭaṇattu-piḷḷai. ∘∘∘ திரு . . . பாடற்றிருமுறை ஆ [Pāḍaṭ-ṭiru-muṟai. With a biography. Reprinted from the edition of Vēl-āyudha.] 1906. 8°. **14170. ff. 16.**

—— See Sāyaṇāchāryar. Life of Sankaracharyar . . . Translated . . . into Tamil . . . by Tholuvoor Valayudha Moodeliar. 1879. 8°. **14170. k. 19.**

VĒL-ĀYUDHA PAṆḌITAR, *Karuppa, of Vīmarāyar-agrahāram.* தாராபுரதலப்புராணம். [Dhārāpura-tala-purāṇam. The legends of the Ṣaiva sanctuary at Dharapuram, Coimbatore, in verse. Edited by T. A. Ṣ. Rāma-liṅgam Piḷḷai.] pp. x. 95. சென்னை [*Madras,*] 1906. 8°. **14170. eee. 18.**

VĒLU DĒṢIKAR, *Pālūr.* See Kamban. இதிஹாச சிரேஷ்டமாகிய . . . கம்பராமாயண ஆ [Kamba-rāmāyaṇa-vachanam. Revised by Vēlu Dēṣikar.] 1903. 8°. **14172. d. 2.**

VĒLU PIḶḶAI, *D.K., of Tellipali.* See Euclid. க்ஷேத்திரகணிதம். (The Elements of Euclid in Tamil . . . By D. C. Valoopillai.) 1888. 8°. **14170. i. 20.**

VĒLU PIḶḶAI, *Kōppāy V.* See Jaffna.—*Ṣaiva-prakāṣa-sabhai.* பாலபாடம். [Bāla-pāṭham. Pts. iii. and v., readers by Vēlu Piḷḷai.] [1893-1894.] 12° & 8°. **14172. h. 92.(pt. 3, 5.)**

VĒLU PIḶḶAI, *Trikōṇamalai M.* திரான்ஸ்வால் யுத்தக்கும்மி. [Transvaal-yuddha-kummi. A popular poem on the Boer War.] pp. 19. கொழும்பு [*Colombo,*] 1902. 12°. **14172. a. 52.**

VĒLU PIḶḶAI, *Vaḍagōvai Vināyaka-tambi.* திருத்தில்லை நிரோட்டக யமக அந்தாதி. [Tiru-tillai-nirōṭṭaga-yamaka-antādi. 100 quatrains in honour of Ṣiva as worshipped in Chidambaram, composed without labial sounds.] pp. 15. யாழ்ப்பாணம் கா [*Jaffna,* 1891.] 12°. **14170. d. 32.(1.)**

VĒLU PIḶḶAI, *Vayāvilān K., of Jaffna.* சிங்கை முருகேசர் பேரில் பதிகம். [Ṣiṅgai-mrugēṣar-padigam. Hymns in praise of Mṛugan, or Skanda, as worshipped in Singapore.] pp. ii. 12. சிங்கப்பூர் [*Singapore,*] 1893. 12°. **14170. d. 36.(2.)**

VĒMANA. தெய்வீகத்தன்மைபொருந்திய வேமன்னயோகீஸ்வரர் . . . திருவாய்மலர்ந்தருளிய தெலுங்குபத்தியங்கள்-ா. [Padyaṅgaḷ. 100 Telugu stanzas of Vēmana on religious, moral, and philosophic themes. Edited in Tamil characters, with Tamil paraphrase, by Sītā-rām-prasād.] pp. 8, 40. [*Madras,*] 1892. 8°. **14174. k. 48.(1.)**

——— மகாமகத்துவம்பொருந்திய வேமன்னபத்தியம் ஆயிரம்பாடல் ஆ [Vēmanna-padyam. The religious and philosophical verses of Vēmana. The Telugu text in Tamil letters, edited on the basis of C. P. Brown's edition, with Tamil translation by Puduvai Nārāyaṇa-dāsar.] pp. 276. சென்னை [*Madras,*] 1903. 8°. **14175. a. 12.**

VĒMBU AMMĀḶ, *daughter of Chakra-pāṇi Aiyaṅgār.* வச்சலா கல்யாணம். [Vachalā-(Vatsalā-)kalyāṇam. A series of songs on the legendary wedding of Abhimanyu and Vatsalā, daughter of Bala-rāma. Edited by Vaikuṇṭham Tirumalāchāryar.] pp. 48. [*Kumbakonam,*] 1906. 8°. **14172. bb. 10.**

VĒṆĀTT'-AḌIGAḶ. [For the hymns of this author contained in the Tiruv-iṣai-pā :] *See* TIRU-MUṞAI.

VENCATARAMA IYENGAR. *See* VĒṄKAṬA-RĀMA AIYAṄGĀR.

VENCAT ROW. *See* VĒṄKAṬA-RĀU.

VEṄGIḌA VĪRA-RĀGHAVĀCHĀRYAR, *Vakulābharaṇam Sōma-yāji Vēlāmūr.* த்ரிம்சத்ப்ரச்நோத்தரகண்டனம். தொன்னடைத்துலக்கம். [Trimṣat-praṣnōttara-khaṇḍanam and Ton-naḍai-tulakkam. Two controversial tracts, in sanskritised Tamil, supporting the theological doctrines of Vēṅkaṭa-nātha Vēdāntāchāryar. Preceded by an epitome of the 30 points attacked in the former, by Kandāḍai Aṇṇāv-aiyaṅgār.] pp. iv. 70, 52. விளம்பி [*Chidambaram,* 1899.] 8°. **14170. ee. 16.**

VEṄGIṬṬA RĀYAR, *Eṭṭayapuram.* *See* GAṆA-PATI NĀYUḌU. எட்டயபுரம் . . . படுகளச்சிந்து [Veṅgiṭṭa-rāyar-avargaḷ-paḍugaḷa-chindu. A series of elegies upon a riot which caused the death of Veṅgiṭṭa Rāyar.] 1895. 8°. **14172. b. 52.**

VĒṄKAṬĀCHALA DĪKSHITAR, *Eṭṭayapuram.* *See* TYĀGA-RĀJA DĪKSHITAR. விபூதிருத்திராக்ஷதாரண நிருபணம். [Vibhūti-rudrāksha-dhāraṇa-nirūpaṇam. Translated by Vēṇkaṭāchala.] 1901. 12°. **14170. d. 85.(1.)**

VĒṄKAṬĀCHALA MUDALIYĀR, *Tiruvaṇṇāmalai.* [For works edited by Vēṅkaṭāchala Mudaliyār, see under the following headings :]

DHANVANTARI.
VĒṄKAṬ-RĀMA UPĀDHYĀYAR, and others.
VĪRA KAVI-RĀYAR.

VĒṄKAṬĀCHĀRYA-DĀSAN, *Tūppul.* *See* VĒṄKAṬA-NĀTHA VĒDĀNTĀCHĀRYAR. శ్రీ . . . పరమతభఙ్గమ్. [Para-mata-bhaṅgam. Edited by Vēṅkaṭāchārya-dāsan.] [1890.] 8°. **14170. e. 43.**

VĒṄKAṬĀCHĀRYAR, *Anbil.* *See* SHAKSPERE (W.). விப்ரம விஹாஸம். (Vibhrama Vihasam. Shakespeare's Comedy of Errors.) [Translated by Vēṅkaṭāchāryar.] 1905-1906. [*Vāṇī-vilāsinī.*] **14172. m. 1.(vol. 1-2.)**

VĒṄKAṬĀCHĀRYAR, *son of Gōvindāchāryar, son of Naināchāryar.* ○○○ చాత్తాదశ్రీవైష్ణవద్విజషోడశకర్మాణి. [Chāttāda-ṣrī-vaishṇāva-dvija-shōḍaṣa-karmāṇi. The liturgies for the 16 chief domestic rites of Chāttāda-Ṣrīvaishṇava Brahmans, in Sanskrit, Tamil, and Telugu. Edited by Iyyūṇṇi Ṣaṭhakōpāchāryar.] pp. xiv. 192. చన్నపురి ౧౯౦౨ [*Madras,* 1902.] 8°. **14170. ee. 47.**

VĒṄKAṬĀCHĀRYAR, *T. E., of Hindu High School, Triplicane.* *See* ACADEMIES, *etc.*—Madras.—*University of Madras.* Copious annotations on the Matriculation Tamil text for 1900 . . . With . . . English translation by T. E. Venkatachariar. 1900. 8°. **14172. bb. 6.(3.)**

VĒṄKAṬA-DĀSAR, *Ṣiṭṭūr Aruḷ-vākku, disciple of Māri-muttu.* *See* MAHĀ-BHAKTA-VIJAYAM. ○○○ ஸ்ரீமகாபக்தவிஜயம். [Mahā-bhakta-vijayam. Vol. i., compiled and translated by Vēṅkaṭa-dāsar.] 1870. 4°. **14170. f. 5.**

——— ——— 1893. 4°. **14170. f. 22.**

——— ——— 1898-1905. 4°. **14170. f. 6.**

VĒṄKAṬA-DĒṢIKAR, *Chandra-giri.* ராமாநுஜ-தயாபாத்ரவ்யாக்யாநம். [Rāmānuja-dayā-pātra-vyākhyānam. A dissertation, in Tamil, upon a Sanskrit stanza of salutation to Vēṅkaṭa-nātha Vēdāntāchāryar.] pp. 28. காஞ்சீ சுபாநு [*Conjevaram,* 1883.] 8°. **14028. d. 59.(1.)**

VEṄKAṬĀDRI SVĀMI, *Allūru, Parama-haṃsa.* ஸ்ரீ . . . ஸ்ரீஹரிநாமசங்கீர்த்தனைகள். [Hari-nāma-saṅkīrttanaigal. 166 Vaishṇava hymns. Translated by Puduvai Nārāyaṇa-dāsar from the Telugu of Veṅkaṭādri.] pp. 87; 1 *plate.* சென்னை [*Madras,*] 1907. 12°. **14170. dd. 17.**

VĒṄKAṬA-NARASIṂHĀCHĀRYAR, *Tenmaḍam.* *See* VĀLMĪKI. ஸ்ரீ . . . சுந்தரகாண்டம். [Sundara-kāṇḍam. With Tamil paraphrase by Vēṅkaṭa-narasiṃhāchāryar.] 1901. 12°. **14060. b. 18.**

VĒṄKAṬA-NĀTHA VĒDĀNTĀCHĀRYAR (VĒDĀNTA-DĒṢIKAR, KAVI-TĀRKIKA-SIṂHA). *See* ANANTA BHĀRATI. ஸ்ரீமத் வேதாந்ததேசிக . . . கீர்த்தனை. [Vēdānta-dēṣika-vaibhava-prakāṣikai-kīrttanai. Songs in honour of Vēṅkaṭa-nātha.] [1890.] 8°. **14172. c. 37.**

—— *See* VEṄGIḌA VĪRA-RĀGHAVĀCHĀRYAR, *V.* த்ரிம்சத்ப்ரச்நோத்தரகண்டனம் ஞ [Triṃṣat-praṣnōttara-khaṇḍanam and Ton-naḍai-tulakkam. Tracts supporting the doctrines of Vēṅkaṭa-nātha.] [1899.] 8°. **14170. ee. 16.**

—— ००० ஸ்ரீதேசிகப்ரபந்தம். [Dēṣika-prabandham. A religious poem of the Rāmānuja school. With commentaries by T. K. I. Rāmānujāchāryar and M. Kastūri Raṅgāchāryar. Edited by Tāta-dēṣika Tātāchāryar.] pts. 1-7. சென்னபட்டணம் [*Madras,*] 1889—கஅகூ௦ [1890.] 8°. **14170. f. 13.**

—— த்ரமிடோபநிஷத்தாத்பர்யரத்நாவலி: (த்ரமிடோபநிஷத்ஸார:) [Dramiḍōpanishat-tātparya-ratnāvaḷi and Dramiḍōpanishat-sāra. A paraphrase and a compendium, in Sanskrit, of the Dramiḍōpanishad or Tiru-vāy-mori. With the Tamil commentaries respectively of Vēṅkaṭēṣāchāryar and Ṣrīnivāsa Dēṣikar.] *See* ĀRVĀRGAḶ.—Nāl-āyiram.—*Tiru-vāy-mori.* ஸமவத்விஷயர் [Bhagavad-vishayam.] [1883-1904.] 4°. **14170. fff. 3.**

—— ஸ்ரீநிகமாந்தமஹாதேசிகன் வைபவஸாரஸங்கிரகம் . . . திருமுடியடைவு. [Nigamānta-mahā-dēṣikan-vaibhava-sāra-saṅgraham. An account, in *maṇi-pravāḷam* style, of Vēṅkaṭa-nātha. Followed by K. L. Tīrtha Piḷḷai's Tiru-muḍiy-aḍaivu, a list of eminent Vaishṇava devotees and their works, *etc.* Edited by Tirukuḍandai Taṭṭai Kṛushṇam-āchāryar and others.] pp. 36. சென்னை கூஉ௫ [*Madras,* 1894.] 12°. **14170. d. 46.(2.)**

—— ந்யாஸதசகவெண்பா. [Nyāsa-daṣaka-veṇ-bā. A version in *veṇ-bā* metre, by T. R. Ṣrīnivāsa Aiyaṅgār, of Vēṅkaṭa-nātha's Nyāsa-daṣaka, 10 Sanskrit stanzas on the Vaishṇava doctrine of *nyāsa,* or devotion by surrender of the soul. With a table of the divisions of Vaishṇava theology, by the former.] pp. 7; 1 *plate.* தஞ்சை [*Tanjore,*] 1907. 16°. **14170. d. 33.(4.)**

—— శ్రీ . . . పరమతభంగము. [Para-mata-bhaṅgam. A polemical treatise in defence of the Vadagalai Vaishṇava theology. Edited by Tūppul Vēṅka-ṭāchārya-dāsan.] pp. 188. బెంగుళూరు ౧౮౯౦ [*Bangalore,* 1890.] 8°. **14170. e. 43.**

—— ஸவைதம்துல்லுதம்து ஸ்ரீமந்நிகமாந்தமஹாதேசிகன் அருளிச்செய்த ஆதிரமஉறுஸஞ்ஞங்களில் நடவதான "பரமதஸம்பம்" ஞ [Para-mata-bhaṅgam. Edited by Timmaguḍi Alluṇḍu Rāmānujāchāryar.] pp. 168; 1 *plate.* கூ௦ஸவொள ॥ [*Kumbakonam,*] 1893. 8°. **14170. e. 54.**

—— ஸ்ரீ . . . ஸ்ரீரஹஸ்யத்ரயஸார: [Rahasya-traya-sāra. A Sanskrit work on the three fundamental formulæ of the Viṣishṭādvaita Vaishṇavas. With Tamil verse-rendering and commentary. Edited by T. Gōpāla Tātāchāryar and T. Ṣrīnivāsa Tātāchāryar.] pp. 320. காஞ்சீ [*Conjevaram,*] 1889. 8°. **14048. c. 68.**

—— ००० சில்லரை ரஹஸ்யங்கள் - கள. [Ṣillarai-rahasyaṅgaḷ. Tracts, in *maṇi-pravāḷam* style, on topics of Viṣishṭādvaita doctrine—scil. Sampradāya-pariṣuddhi, Tattva-padavī, T°.-nava-nītam, T°.-mātṛukā, T°.-sandēṣam, T°.-ratnāvali, T°.-ratnāvali-pratipādya-saṅgraha, T°.-traya-chuḷakam, Rahasya-padavī, R°.-nava-nītam, R°.-mātṛukā, R°.-sandēṣam, R°.-sandēṣa-vivaraṇam, R°.-ratnāvali, R°.-ratnāvali-hṛudayam, and R°.-traya-chuḷakam. With notes by E. Sundarāryar. Edited by Bhāshyam Kṛushṇam-āchāryar.] pp. i. 186, ix. சென்னை சார்வரி [*Madras,* 1900.] 8°. **14170. ee. 36.**

VĒṄKAṬA-PRAPANNA SVĀMI, *Rāja-yōgānanda.* ப்ரஹ்மோத்ஸவ தத்வதீபிகை. [Brahmōtsava-tattva-dīpikai. A Tamil treatise on the cult of Vishṇu, with quotations from Sanskrit authorities. Part i., or Kshētra-kāṇḍam, on the sacred places.] (Part ii. Utsavakanda, containing illustrations of the various vahanas in vogue in temple festivities.) 2 pts. திரிசிரபுரம் [*Trichinopoli,*] 1903-1904. 8°. **14170. ee. 66.**

VĒṄKAṬA-RĀGHAVĀCHĀRYAR, *Kārakuruchi.* See Bādarāyaṇa. శ్రీ...శ్రీమద్భాష్యార్థసంగ్రహం. [Brahma-sūtram. With Ṣrīmad-bhāshyārtha-saṅgraham, rendered into Tamil by Vēṅkaṭa-rāghavāchāryar.] [1890.] 8°. **14048. c. 69.**

VĒṄKAṬA-RĀMA AIYAṄGĀR, *Tillaiyambūr.* See Yaṣōdharan. Yasódhara-kāvyam ... With argument in prose, &c., by T. Venkatarama Iyengar, *etc.* 1908. 12°. **14172. a. 66.**

—— வால்மீகி ராமாயணக் கிளைக் கதைகள். (Episodes from the Valmiki-ramayana in Tamil prose, by ... T. Vencatarama Iyengar ... With an English introduction by Arthur Davies.) *Madras,* 1906, *etc.* 12°. **14171. d. 7.**

In progress.

—— வில்லிபுத்தூரார் பிள்ளைப்பெருமாள் ஐயங்கார். இவ்விருவர்களின் சரித்திரச் சுருக்கம். (Biographical Sketch of Villiputturer & Pillai Perumal ... with an English introduction by T. Ramakrishna Pillai.) pp. 4, 67, iii. *Madras,* 1904. 12°. **14171. a. 48.(2.)**

Forms part of the series "Tamil Men of Letters" (Tamiṛ-kalaivāṇargaḷ-vagai).

VEṄKAṬA-RĀMA AIYAR, *Kallūri.* A manual of translation from Tamil into English, based on the analysis of sentences, with numerous exercises. Compiled by K. Venkatarama Aiyar. pp. ii. 112. *Kumbakonam,* 1900. 12°. **14172. h. 97.(4.)**

VĒṄKAṬA-RĀM'-AIYĀ, *Ṣ. N.* The First Book of Tamil. pp. i. i. 92. *Madras,* 1903. 8°. **14172. hh. 18.**

VĒṄKAṬA-RĀM'-AIYAR, *Kuruṅgaḷāvanam Kṛushn'-aiyar.* இராமாயணக்கும்மி ஃ [Rāmāyaṇa-kummi. A ballad on the Āraṇya-kāṇḍam, Kishkindhā-k°., and Sundara-k°. of the Rāmāyaṇam.] pp. ii. 62. திருநெல்வேலி [*Tinnevelli,*] 1901. 16°. **14172. a. 32.(5.)**

VEṄKAṬA-RAMAṆA AIYAR, *Ṣ. Subba-rāya.* See India.—*Legislative Council.* நீதிவிவாதமஞ்சரி ஃ [Nīti-vivāda-mañjari. Various acts, edited with commentaries *etc.* by Veṅkaṭa-ramaṇa.] 1901, *etc.* 8°. **14170. g. 23.**

VEṄKAṬA-RĀMA ṢĀSTRI, *Karandaiyambadi.* See Tiruvadi. ஸ்ரீ ... திருவையாற்றுப்புராணம். [Tiruv-aiy-āṭṭu-purāṇam. Done into prose by Veṅkaṭa-rāma.] 1907. 8°. **14170. eee. 22.**

VĒṄKAṬA-RĀMA ṢĀSTRI, *V. B., of Native High School, Chingleput.* See Periodical Publications.—*Trichinopoli.* சுபோத பாரிஜாதம் ஃ [Subōdha-pārijātam. Edited by Vēṅkaṭa-rāma.] 1907, *etc.* 8°. **14172. i. 12.**

—— See Sōma-dēva. கதாசரித் சாகரம் (Katha-sarithsagaram ... in Tamil. [Translated] by V. B. Venkatarama Sastry.) 1905, *etc.* 8°. **14171. e. 5.**

—— சஞ்சீவிகிரி. அல்லது செஞ்சி (Sañjīvi-giri. A historical prose work [*i.e.* romance] in Tamil.) *Madras,* 1903, *etc.* 12°. **14171. a. 51.**

In progress? Forms no. 6 *of the* Vidvan Mano Ranjani Series.

VEṄKAṬA-RĀMA-SVĀMI, *Kāvali.* Moolika Sankalitum; or Mingling of Herbs: a work on medicine traslated [*sic*] from Teloogoo into English, having the names of the various medicines in Tamul, by Cavelly Venkata Ramasawmy Brahbin [*sic*]. [Professedly founded on a Sanskrit work of Dhanvantari.] pp. ii. 90. *Madras,* 1835. 8°. **14170. i. 31.**

VĒṄKAṬA-RAṄGA-NĀTHA SVĀMI, *Para-vastu.* See Piḷḷai Lōkāchāryar. ప్రపన్నజనాగ్రేసర రామానుజాచార్యుల్ ... తత్త్వత్రయము ॥ [Tattva trayam. With commentary of Aṛagiya-maṇavāḷa Peru-māḷ. Together with a Telugu translation by Vēṅkaṭa raṅga-nātha.] [1904.] 8°. **14170. ff. 11.**

VĒṄKAṬA-RAṄGA RĀMĀNUJA-DĀSAR, *Kōyambēḍu Kāḷiṅga-rāya Piḷḷai.* ஸ்ரீமந்மணவாளமாமுநிகள்திருவந்தாதி. [Maṇavāḷa-mā-munigaḷ-tiruv-antādi. A poem on the Tengalai teacher Aṛagiya-maṇavāḷar.] pp. 17. சென்னைமாநகரம் கக்ல [*Madras,* 1869.] 8°. **14172. b. 23.(2.)**

VEṄKAṬA-RĀU, *Rubugunḍai, Rāya.* See Koviladi. History of the Kovilady Charities . . . Founded . . . by . . . R. Vencat Row, Dewan of Travancore and the Native Assistant to the Commissioner of Mysore. 1899. 12°. **14171. a. 35.**

VEṄKAṬA-RĀYALU NĀYUḌU, *Ṣettūr.* See Kamban. ஸ்ரீ . . . ராமாயணம் ௸ [Kamba-rāmāyaṇam, Āraṇya-kāṇḍam. With commentary by Kanda-sāmi and Veṅkata-rāyalu.] 1900. 8°. **14172. d. 25.**

VĒṄKAṬA-RĀYA YŌGĪNDRAR, *Kanakambākkam Tummal* (Svānubhava Yōgīndrar). யோகஞா-னுபவதீபிகை. [Yōga-ñānānubhava-dīpikai. A treatise on Yoga doctrine and practice. Edited by T. Vaḍi-vēlu Mudaliyār.] pp. xi. 246, ii. vi.; 3 *plates.* சென்னை ஜய [*Madras,* 1895.] 12°. **14170. d. 38.**

VĒṄKAṬĀRYA YAJVA, *Araṣāṇipālai Raghu-nātha.* உலககுணக்கண்ணுடியென்னுந்தெய்வகுணவெ-ளிச்சம். [Teyva-guṇa-veḷicham, or Ulaga-guṇa-kaṇṇāḍi. A free prose rendering, by B. A. Aiyā-sāmi Mudaliyār, of Vēṅkaṭārya's Viṣva-guṇādarṣa-champū, a Sanskrit dialogue describing various places and characters of India.] pp. 184. சென்னை [*Madras,*] 1906. 8°. **14171. e. 13.**

VĒṄKAṬA-SĀMI AIYAR, *Mōṣūr.* A Novel Exercise Book on Tamil Grammar. pp. 36. *Madras,* 1892. 8°. **14172. hh. 1.**

—— A Manual of Tamil Grammar, specially adapted for the first three Forms, with many clear examples and exercises making the subject easy and interesting. இளைஞர் பயில் இலக்கணம். pp. vii. iv. 208. *Madras,* 1894. 12°. **14172. e. 20.**

—— Five hundred instructive Tamil Proverbs with their English equivalents . . . ஆராய்ந்தெ-டுத்த ஐந்நூறு பழமொழி ௸. pp. 49. *Madras,* 1907. 12°. **14170. k. 58.(3.)**

VĒṄKAṬA-SĀMI NĀYUḌU, *C.* See Antōni Piḷḷai. The English, Tamil, Telugu and Hindustani Son-malai . . . revised by C. Venkataswamy Naidoo, *etc.* 1880. 8°. **14172. e. 10.**

VEṄKAṬA-SĀMI NĀYUḌU, *T. R.* See Nārāyaṇa-sāmi Piḷḷai, *T. G.* Installation of . . . Sri Krishna-rajendra Wodayar Bahadur, Maharaja of Mysore, and the Dasara Festivities . . . with . . . translation [by Veṅkaṭa-sāmi]. 1903. 12°. **14172. bb. 8.**

VEṄKAṬA-ṢRĪNIVĀSAN, *V.* See Academies, *etc.*—Madras.—*University of Madras.* University of Madras. Matriculation Examination, 1900. Copious notes on the Tamil text-book, *etc.* [With English translations by Veṅkaṭa-ṣrīnivāsan.] 1900. 8°. **14172. bb. 6.(2.)**

—— See Ṣiṣira-kumāra Ghōsha. ஸ்ரீக்ருஷ்ண சைதன்ய . . . சரித்திரம் ௸ (Sri Krishna Chaitanya . . . [Translated] by . . . Venkata Srinivasan, *etc.*) 1902. 8°. **14170. ee. 51.**

VEṄKAṬA-SUBBĀ RĀU, *Renṭāla.* ஆனந்த தீபி-கை. [Ānanda-dīpikai. Instructive and entertaining miscellanies, translated from the Telugu.] pp. i. 160. *Mylapore,* 1901. 8°. **14171. a. 25.**

—— கதாரத்நாவளி. [Kathā-ratnāvaḷi. A collection of stories from the Arabian Nights and other works. Translated from the Telugu of Veṅkaṭa-subbā Rāu by T. S. Muttu-sāmi Ṣāstri.] pp. 8, 464. *Madras,* 1893. 8°. **14171. b. 1.**

—— மர்மசாஸ்திரம் . . . Marma Sastra, or The Secrets of Life. [A study of physical and moral conditions of life, with a view to reform. From the Telugu original] by R. Venkata Subba Rau. pp. 200. *Madras,* 1894. 8°. **14170. i. 32.**

VĒṄKAṬA-SUBBU PIḶḶAI, *A., of St. Joseph's College, Bangalore.* The Thumboo Sindhamani. Being a poetical sketch of the life of Raja Dharma Pravina, T. R. A. Thumboo Chettiar, C.I.E. [in verse, with prose paraphrase] . . . with an introduction in English by S. Krishnaswami Aiyangar. (*தம்புசிந்தாமணி.) pp. viii. xx. 276, ii.; 3 *plates. Madras,* 1905. 8°. **14171. b. 4.**

VEṄKAṬA-SUBRAHMAṆYA AIYAR, *Araṣarkuḷam.* See Saptarshi. The Suptharishivakkiam 5500. Thoroughly examined by . . . Nagasawmy Aiyar . . . and by . . . Venkatasubramaniya Aiyar. [1899.] 8°. **14170. i. 63.**

VEṄKAṬA-SVĀMI AIYAR, *of Mysore.* See Ṣaṅkarā-chāryar. [*Doubtful and Supposititious Works.*] ஸ்ரீ . . . ஶிவாநந்தலஹரீ *etc.* [Ṣivānanda-laharī. With interpretations in Tamil. Edited by Veṅkaṭa-svāmi.] 1904. 12°. **14048. b. 48.**

VĒṄKAṬĒSĀCHĀRYAR (VĒṄKAṬĀCHĀRYAR). *See* VĒṄKAṬA-NĀTHA VĒDĀNTĀCHĀRYAR. த்ரமிடோபநி-ஷத்தாத்பர்யரத்நாவளி: [Dramiḍōpanishat-tātparya-ratnāvaḷi and Dramiḍōpanishat-sāra. With the Tamil commentaries respectively of Vēṅkaṭēṣā-chāryar and Ṣrīnivāsa Dēṣikar.] [1883-1904.] 4°. [*Bhagavad-vishayam.*] **14170. fff. 3.**

VĒṄKAṬĒṢA PAṆḌITAR, *Mūdai.* *See* TIRU-VĒṄKAṬA-SVĀMI.

VĒṄKAṬĒṢA PIḶḶAI, *Paval.* ஸ்ரீ ... பவல்-வேங்கடேசப்பிள்ளை மரபினர் இயற்றிய யதுவம்சஸ்தர்களின் குலகாயம். [Yaduvaṃṣasthargaḷin kula-kāyam. Rules framed by the members of the family of Vēṅkaṭēṣa Piḷḷai for guidance in their social and religious relations.] pp. 43. சென்னப்பட்டணம் [*Madras,*] 1889. 8°. **14170. k. 43.**

VĒṄKAṬ-RĀMA UPĀDHYĀYAR, and others. மார்க்கண்டேயர் விலாசம். [Mārkaṇḍēyar-vilāsam. A drama upon a Ṣaiva legend. Edited by T. Vēṅkaṭāchala Mudaliyār.] pp. viii. 136. சுக்ல [*Madras,* 1869.] 8°. **14170. l. 12.**

VEṄKAṬ-RĀYA ṢĀSTRI, *Sadar Adalat Court Pandit* *See* KANDA-SĀMI PULAVAR, *M.* தருமநூல் ஷு [Vyavahāra-sāra-saṅgraham. Edited by Veṅkaṭ-rāya.] 1826. Fol. **14170. g. 15.**

VEṆṆI-MALAI PIḶḶAI, *Ṣivngeṅgai Sundaram, Jauḷi-vyāpāram.* நைடதமென்னும் நளச்சக்கரவர்த்தி அம்மானை. [Naḷa-chakravartti-ammānai, or Naiḍadam. A poem on the legend of Nala and Damayantī. Edited by Teyva-ṣikhāmaṇi Ayyar and others.] pp. 10, 3, 2, ii. 186. மதுரை [*Madura,*] 1904. 8°. **14172. cc. 2.**

VENṞI-MĀLAI KAVI-RĀJAR. ∘ ∘ ∘ திருச்செந்தூர்ப்புராணம். [Tiruchendūr-purāṇam. A poem in 18 cantos on the legends of the Ṣaiva sanctuary at Tiruchendur, Tinnevelli District. Edited with a commentary by Nīrvēli Ṣ. Ṣiva-prakāṣa Paṇḍitar.] pp. 280, ii. யாழ்ப்பாணம் [*Jaffna,*] 1907. 8°. **14172. bb. 26.**

—— திருச்செந்தூர்த்தலபுராணவசனம். (*திருச்செந்தூர்ப்பிள்ளைத்தமிழ்.) [Tiruchendūr-tala-purāṇa-vachanam. A prose version of Venṟi-mālai Kavi-rājar's poem on the legends of the Ṣaiva sanctuary of Kumāra at Tiruchendur, with a biography of the author, by M. R. Aruṇāchala Kavi-rāyar. Followed by Pagaṟi-kūttar's Tiruchendūr-piḷḷai-tamiṟ, a devotional poem on the god's child-hood, edited by the same.] pp. 142, 41. சென்னை விகாரி [*Madras,* 1899-1900.] 12°. **14170. d. 59.**

VĒṆU-GŌPĀLA CHEṬṬI, *V.* *See* MADRAS, *Presidency of.* A collection of the inscriptions . . . in the Nellore district. Made by A. Butterworth . . . and V. Venugopaul Chetty. 1905. 8°. **14058. c. 11.**

VĒṞ PIḶḶAI, *Maṭṭuvil K.* [For works edited by Vēṟ Piḷḷai, see under the headings :]
AGHŌRA DĒVAR. KAḌAVUṈ MĀ-MUNI.

VĒṞ PIḶḶAI, *Tumbalai P.* *See* EPHEMERIDES. ∘∘∘ ஏவிளம்பிவருஷ ... பஞ்சாங்கம் . . . Tamil Calendar for 1897-98. [Calculated by Vēṟ Piḷḷai.] [1897.] 8°. **14172. i. 16.(1.)**

VĒTĀLA-PAÑCHA-VIṂṢATI. The Vedàla Cadai, being the Tamul version of a collection of ancient tales in the Sanscrit language; popularly known throughout India, and entitled the Vetàla Pancha-vinsati. Translated by B. G. Babington. pp. 90. *See* ACADEMIES, *etc.*—London.—*Oriental Translation Fund of Great Britain and Ireland.* Miscellaneous translations, *etc.* vol. i. 1831. 8°. **14003. d. 5.**

VETHANAYAGAM. *See* VĒDA-NĀYAKAM.

VEṬṬI-VĒṞ PIḶḶAI. *See* JAFFNA.—*Ṣaiva-pari-pālana-sabhai.* சிவத்துரோக கண்டன திக்கார தண்டனம். [Ṣiva-drōha-khaṇḍana-dhikkāra-daṇḍanam. An answer to the tract entitled Ṣiva-drōha-khaṇḍanam by Veṭṭi-vēṟ Piḷḷai.] [1896.] 16°. **14170. d. 57.**

VICTORIA, *Queen of Great Britain and Ireland.* *See* JEREMIAH (S. S.). Jubilee Songs . . . for the . . . celebration of . . . the Queen Empress Victoria's accession, *etc.* 1887. 8°. **14172. c. 28.(2.)**

—— *See* PERIYA-SUBBĀ REḌḌIYĀR. ∘ ∘ ∘ மஹாராணி அம்மானை. (The Maharani Ammanei[, an account of the reign of Queen Victoria in *ammānai* metre], *etc.*) 1901. 8°. **14172. b. 7.**

—— *See* RĀMA-SĀMI PULAVAR, *B. Ṣ.* English translation of a . . . poem regarding the assumption of the title of "Empress of India" by . . . Queen Victoria, *etc.* 1877. 8°. **14172. c. 28.(1.)**

VICTORIA, *Queen of Great Britain and Ireland (continued).* See Sāmi Cheṭṭiyār, *P. M.* விக்டோரியா ...ஞாபகச்சின்னம். [Victoria-mahārāṇiyavargaḷ-ñāpaka-chinnam. Observations and elegies on the reign of Queen Victoria.] 1901. 8°. **14171. a. 47.**

—— *See* Shaṇmukham Piḷḷai, *K. P.* The Life of Empress Victoria, *etc.* 1902. 12°. **14171. a. 44.**

VIDYĀNANDA SVĀMI, *Ñānānanda-svarūpar, of Benares.* சகலகலா பூஷணம். [Sakala-kalā-bhūshaṇam. A series of stories chiefly on religious legends. Edited by P. Tyāga-rāja Mudaliyār.] pp. 7, 394. *Madras,* 1899. 8°. **14171. a. 37.**

VIDYĀ-VINŌDINI. வித்தியாவிநோதினி. (Vidhya Vinodhini Series.) [A collection of religious poems, with prose commentaries, edited by K. Rāma-sāmi Nāyuḍu, T. Shaṇmukham Piḷḷai, and P. Vāsudēva Mudaliyār.] no. 1-42. சென்னை கஅஅசு [*Madras,* 1889]-1892. 8°. **14172. c. 39.**

Works published in this series are catalogued separately under the headings:—

Aruṇa-giri-nātha Svāmi.
Nakkīra-dēvar.
Paṭṭaṇattu Piḷḷai.
Tani-pāḍal.
Tāyumānavar.

VIJAYA-RĀGHAVĀCHĀRYAR, *Araṣāṇipālai Kandāḍai.* See Aḻagiya-maṇavāḷa Peru-māḷ. ○○○ யதிராஜவிம்ஶதி. [Yati-rāja-vimṣati. Edited by Vijaya-rāghavāchāryar.] [1884.] 12°. **14028. b. 63.(1.)**

VIJAYA-RĀGHAVALU NĀYUḌU, *Sēlam.* See Parasu-rāma Pantulu. ○○○ ஸ்ரீஸீதாராமாஞ்சநேய ஸம்வாத ஞு [Sītā-rāmāñjanēya-saṃvāda-sāra-saṅgraham. With Tamil translation and commentary *etc.* by Vijaya-rāghavalu.] [1898.] 8°. **14170. ee. 27.**

VIJAYA-RĀGHAVULU CHEṬṬIYĀR, *Ṣ.* See Madras, *Presidency of.* சென்னை ரைவிந்யாசசபாஸ்திய்யமாநாது சாசநங்கள் ஞு [The Standing Orders of the Madras Board of Revenue. Translated by Vijaya-rāghavulu.] [1868.] 8°. **14170. g. 6.**

VIJAYA-RAṄGA MUDALIYĀR, *Pammal.* ○○○ கவிகுஞ்சர பாரதி மதுரகவிபாரதி ... ஸ்ரீராமகவிராயர் அவர்களும் பாடிய பதங்கள். [Padaṅgaḷ. Erotic poems by Kavi-kuñjara Bhārati, Madhura-kavi Bhārati, and Rāma Kavi-rāyar. Edited by P. Vijaya-raṅga Mudaliyār.] pp. ii. iv. 96. சென்னபட்டணம் [*Madras,*] 1886. 8°. **14172. c. 33.**

VIKRAMA-CHŌṞAN. The Vikrama-cholan-ula. [Text and translation by V. Kanaka sabhai Piḷḷai of a poem panegyrising apparently Vikrama-chōṟan, who reigned 1112-27.] 1893. *See* Periodical Publications.—*Bombay.* The Indian Antiquary, *etc.* vol. xxii., pp. 141-150. 1872, *etc.* 4°. **14096. e. (vol. 22.)**

VIKRAMĀRKA-CHARITAM. முப்பத்திரண்டுபதுமைகதை. [Muppatt'-iraṇḍu padumai-kathai. The Tales of the Thirty-two Images. Edited by G. Aruṇāchala Mudaliyār.] pp. 207. [*Madras,*] 1882. 8°. **14170. k. 14.**

VIḶAMBIYA-KĀGANĀR. *See* Viḷambiya-Nāganār.

VIḶAMBIYA-NĀGANĀR. நான்மணிக்கடிகை ஞு [Nān-maṇi-ghaṭikai. A series of ethical stanzas. With commentary.] pp. 31. 1904. *See* Academies, *etc.*—*Madura.* [" Ṣen-damiḻ " supplement.] no. 14. 1902, *etc.* 8°. **14172. i. 1.*(no. 14.)**

Forms no. 2 of the 18 Kiḻ-kaṇakku *poems.*

—— நான்மணிக்கடிகை. († Nanmanikkadigai.) [Verses 50-108, with commentary and English translation.] *See* Pugaḻēndi. The Nalavenba, *etc.* 1879. 12°. **14172. a. 22.**

VIḶĀÑ-JŌLAI PIḶḶAI, *disciple of Piḷḷai Lōkāchāryar.* ○○○ ஸப்தகாதை ஞு [Sapta-gāthai. A Vaishṇava religious tract, in 7 verses, with interpretation. Together with a copious commentary by Piḷḷai Lōkam-jīyar. Edited by A. K. Kṛushṇam-āchāryar.] pp. 78. திருவல்லிக்கேணி கஅஅ௨ [*Triplicane,* 1882.] 16°. **14172. a. 9.**

—— ஸப்தகாதை. [Sapta-gāthai.] *See* Āḻvārgaḷ.—Nāl-āyiram.—*Selections.* ○○○ நித்யாநுஸந்தாநம் ஞு [Nityānusandhānam.] pp. 120-121. 1886. 8°. **14170. ee. 14.**

—— సప్తగాథ. [Sapta-gāthai. With Telugu interpretation, paraphrase, *etc.*] *See* Āḻvārgaḷ.—Nāl-āyiram.—*Selections.* ○○○ నిత్యానుసంధానము ॥ [Nityānusandhānam.] pp. 648-654. 1906. 8°. **14170. eee. 21.**

VILLIPUTTŪRAR (Sārva-bhauma Aiyaṅgār). [*Life.*] *See* Veṅkaṭa-rāma Aiyaṅgār, *T.* வில்லிபுத்தூரார் ... சரித்திரச் சுருக்கம். (Biographical Sketch of Villiputturer & Pillai Perumal, *etc.*) 1904. 12°. **14171. a. 48.(2.)**

VILLIPUTTŪRAR (SĀRVA-BHAUMA AIYAṄGĀR) (*continued*). வில்லிபுத்தூராழ்வார் ... மகாபாரதம். [Mahā-bhāratam. A poetical adaptation of bks. i.—x. of the Sanskrit epic. Edited with notes, glossary, and index by Ṣeṭṭūr Subrahmaṇya Kavi-rāyar.] pp. vii. 503, 117, ix. i. iv. xxxii. *Madura*, 1907. 8°. **14172. bbb. 2.**

A metrical preface (ṣirappu-pāyiram) *by Villiputtūrar's son Varandaruvār is prefixed to this and the other editions of the poem.*

—— ००० மகாபாரதமூலமும் ... புத்துரையும். [Mahā-bhāratam, Ādi-parvam. With interpretation and notes by N. Ṣ. Ponn'-ambala Piḷḷai.] pt. ii. pp. 41-80. யாழ்ப்பாணம் ஏவிளம்பி [*Jaffna*, 1897.] 8°. **14172. d. 18.**

—— ००० மகாபாரதம் ஆதிபருவம் மூலமும் ... புத்துரையும். [Mahā-bhāratam, Ādi-parvam. With interpretation and notes by Nallūr Ṣ. Ponn'-ambala Piḷḷai.] pp. 400, viii. மதராஸ் விளம்பி [*Madras*, 1898.] 8°. **14172. d. 19.**

—— மகாபாரதம். [Mahā-bhāratam, Ṣalya-parvam. With commentary.] *See* ACADEMIES, *etc.*—Madras.—*University of Madras*. The University of Madras. The First in Arts Examination, *etc.* 1891. 8°. **14172. bb. 4.**

—— மகாபாரதம். [Mahā-bhāratam, Drōṇa-parvam xi.-xiii. With notes.] pp. 43, 208. *See* NĀL-AḌIYĀR. University of Madras. F. A. Examination 1900 . . . Naladyar and Bharatam, *etc.* 1899. 8°. **14172. b. 37.**

—— மகாபாரதம். (†துரோணபருவம், கன்னபருவம்.) [Mahā-bhāratam, Drōṇa-parvam xiv.-xv. and Karṇa-parvam xi. With commentary.] pp. 212, 52. *See* ACADEMIES, *etc.* — Madras. — *University of Madras*. University of Madras. F. A. Examination, *etc.* 1900. 8°. **14172. bb. 6.(5.)**

—— இதிகாசமாகிய ஸ்ரீமகாபாரதவசநம். [Mahā-bhārata-vachanam. A prose paraphrase by Taraṅgāpuram Shaṇmukha Kavi-rājar of Nallā Piḷḷai's amplified adaptation of Villiputtūrar's Bhāratam. Published by A. Umā-pati Mudaliyār and A. Ṣiṭṭambala Mudaliyār. Pts. i.-vii., from Ādi-parvam to Drōṇa-parvam.] 7 pts. சென்னை ௧௮௪௭-௧௮௫௪ [*Madras*, 1847-1854.] 4°. **14172. dd. 2.**

—— இதிகாசமாகிய ஸ்ரீமத்திராவிடமஹாபாரதவசனம். [Draviḍa-mahā-bhārata-vachanam. The prose paraphrase by Shaṇmukha Kavi-rājar of Nallā Piḷḷai's adaptation of Villiputtūrar's Bhāratam. With occasional verses (*vṛuttam*) and other additions by T. Vīra-bhadra Aiyar. A new and revised edition.] 4 vols. [*Madras*,] 1880. 4°. **14172. dd. 4.**

—— ஐந்தாம்வேதமாகிய ஸ்ரீமகாபாரதம்வசனகாவியம். [Mahā-bhāratam. The prose paraphrase by Shaṇmukha Kavi-rājar of Nallā Piḷḷai's adaptation of Villiputtūrar's Bhāratam. Edited by T. V. Muttu-sāmi Mudaliyār. Second edition.] 4 vols. *Madras*, 1900. 4°. **14172. dd. 3.**

VIMALA-CHANDRA SŪRI. The Aryan Catechism [*i.e.* the Praṣnōttara-ratna-mālikā or Ārya-praṣnōttara-ratnāvalī, here ascribed to Ṣaṅkarāchāryar]: in Sanskrit ... English, Telugu, and Tamil. Edited by R. Sivasankara Pandiah. pp. 11, 72. *Madras*, 1887. 12°. **14003. c. (no. 7.)**

Forms no. 7 of the Hindu Excelsior Series.

VĪMA-NĀTHA PAṆḌITAR, *Ilamburi*. கடம்பவனபுராணம் . . . இலீலாசங்கிரகவத்தியாயம். [Kaḍamba-vana-purāṇam. A poem on the legends of the Ṣaiva sanctuary of Madura, adapted from a Sanskrit Kaḍamba-vana-purāṇam or Nīpāranya-māhātmyam. Canto x., or Līlā-saṅgrahav-adhyāyam.] *See* PERUM-BAṬṬA-PULIY-ŪR-NAMBI. திரு-... விளையாடற்புராணம். [Tiru-viḷaiy-āḍaṟ-purāṇam.] pp. 259-269. 1906. 8°. **14170. eee. 17.**

VINĀYAKA-MŪRTTI CHEṬṬI, *Nallūr C.* கதிரையாத்திரைவிளக்கம். [Kadirai-yātrai-viḷakkam. Songs for the pilgrimage to Kadirai-tīrtham. With introductory poem by N. K. Paramānanda Pulavar.] pp. 49. பார்த்திப [*Jaffna*, 1886.] 16°. **14172. a. 11.(2.)**

VINCENT [DE PAUL], *Saint*. Rules of the Society of St. Vincent de Paul. சென் வின்செண்டீ போல் சபைச் சட்டங்கள். pp. 47. *Jaffna*, 1907. 12°. **14170. bbb. 15.**

VINŌDAM. விநோதவிடிகதை. [Vinōda-viḍi-kathai. Riddles and facetious stories in verse.] pt. i. pp. 8. [*Madras*,] 1892. 8°. **14170. k. 55.(2.)**

VINSON (ÉLIE HONORÉ JULIEN). *See* ACADEMIES, *etc.*—Paris.—*Bibliothèque Nationale*. Manuscrits tamouls. [Catalogue compiled by J. Vinson.] [1880 ?] Fol. **14172. k. 1.**

VINSON (Élie Honoré Julien) (*continued*). See Academies, *etc.*—Paris.—*École Spéciale des Langues Orientales Vivantes.* Ānanda-raṅga Piḷḷai. Les Français dans l'Inde . . . Extraits du journal d'Anandarangappoullé . . . Traduits . . . par J. Vinson. 1894. 8°. **14003. i. 32.**

—— *See* Ānanda-raṅga Piḷḷai. Les Français dans l'Inde. Le Journal d'Ânandarangappoullé, 1736-1761. (Par J. Vinson.) 1889. 8°. [*École Spéciale des Langues Orientales Vivantes : Recueil de Textes et de Traductions.*] **14003. i. 23.**

—— *See* Ēla-pāṭṭu. Yêlappâṭṭu, *etc.* [Translated by J. Vinson.] 1902. 8°. **P.P. 4964. d. (vol. 35.)**

—— *See* Ṣeshādri Ṣivanār. Loi de la Fin des différents Êtres, *etc.* [Translated by J. Vinson.] 1902. 8°. **P.P. 4964. d. (vol. 35.)**

—— *See* Tiru-takka Dēvar. Un épisode du poème épique Sindâmaṇi. [Edited and translated by J. Vinson.] 1883. 8°. [*École Spéciale des Langues Orientales Vivantes : Mélanges Orientaux.*] **14003. i. 16.**

—— *See* Tiru-vaḷḷuvar. Le Livre de l'Amour, *etc.* [With an introduction by J. Vinson.] 1889. 12°. **14172. a. 38.**

—— Littérature Tamoule Ancienne. Poésie Épique. Le Ramayana de Kamban'. கம்ப ராமாயணம், Kamba Râmâyanam, *etc.* [An essay on the poem of Kamban, with a translation of three short extracts from the text.] pp. 23. *Pondichéry,* 1861. 8°. **14172. b. 26.**

—— Spécimen de Paléographie Tamoule. *See* Academies, *etc.*—Paris.—*École Spéciale des Langues Orientales Vivantes.* Nouveaux Mélanges Orientaux, *etc.* pp. 431-469. 1886. 8°. **14003. i. 18.**

—— Légendes Bouddhistes et Djainas. Traduites du tamoul par Julien Vinson. [Comprising summaries of the Chintāmaṇi, Ṣilapp'-adhikāram, Maṇi-mēkhalai, essays, and tales.] (Conteurs et Poètes de tous Pays, tome v^e, vi^e.) 2 vols. *Paris, Vannes* [printed], 1900. 12°. **14171. aa. 4.**

—— Manuel de la Langue Tamoule. Grammaire, textes, vocabulaire. (Bibliothèque de l'École des Langues Orientales Vivantes.) pp. xlvi. 240. *Paris,* 1903. 8°. **14172. e. 40.**

VIPRA-NĀRĀYAṆA. *See* Toṇḍar-aḍi-poḍiy-āṛvār.

VĪRA-BHADRA AIYAR, *Tiruvaṇṇāmalai.* *See* Villiputtūrar. இதிகாசமாகிய . . . மஹாபாரதம் [Dravida-mahā-bhārata-vachanam. With occasional verses and other additions by Vīra-bhadra.] 1880. 4°. **14172. dd. 4.**

—— தேசிங்குராஜன் நாடகம். [Dēṣiṅgu-rājan-nāṭakam. A romantic comedy on the story of Dēṣiṅgu Rāja, of the Fort of Ginji or Ṣeñji. Edited by M. Subrahmaṇya Svāmi.] pp. 104. விஷு [*Madras,* 1881.] 8°. **14170. l. 4.**

VĪRA-BRAHMĒNDRIYA SVĀMI, *Pōdalūr Ṣaṅkara-nārāyaṇa Virāṭ.* Arputha Kalakgiyana Manchari Vachanakaviam . . . அற்புத காலக்ஞியான மஞ்சரி வசனகாவியம். [A series of prophetical utterances anent the present era, chiefly in prose, and including Gaṇēṣa-pūjā or ritual of Gaṇēṣa, Ñāna-kāṇḍam, and Sannyāsa-yōga-kāṇḍam. Edited by Ṣ. Ēkāmbara Mudaliyār.] pt. i. pp. 56. *Madras,* 1897. 8°. **14170. i. 73.**

The author is believed to be the 11th avatar of Vishṇu.

VĪRA KAVI-RĀYAR, *Nellūr.* அரிச்சந்திரபுராணம் மூலமும்-உரையும். [Hariṣchandra-purāṇam. The legend of the truthful king Hariṣchandra, in verse. With interpretation. Edited by T. Vēṅkaṭāchala Mudaliyār.] pp. 128, 134, 18, 94. சுக்கில [*Madras,* 1869.] 8°. **14170. e. 6.**

—— அரிச்சந்திரபுராணம் ஷ [Hariṣchandra-purāṇam. With commentary. Edited by G. Aruṇāchala Mudaliyār.] pp. 314. யுவ [*Madras,* 1875.] 8°. **14172. c. 15.**

—— Harichandra Purana Vachanam. [A prose abstract.] *See* Mrugēṣa Mudaliyār, *A. C.* Mathar Neethy, *etc.* pp. 127-198. 1894. 8°. **14171. a. 1.**

VĪRA-KŌDAṆḌA RĀMA-SVĀMI, *Tillai-vaḷāgam.* *See* Nārāyaṇa-sāmi Aiyar, *P. A.* தில்லைவளாகம் ஸ்ரீ. வீரகோதண்டராமஸ்வாமி உலா. [Ulā, or elegies upon the cult of Vīra-kōdaṇḍa-Rāma-svāmi.] 1902. 12°. **14172. a. 53.**

VĪRA MĀ-MUNIVAR. *See* Beschi (C. G. E.).

VĪRA-MAṆḌALAVAR (MAṆḌALA-PURUḌAR). ∘∘∘ சூடாமணி நிகண்டு, மூலமும் உரையும். [Chūḍāmaṇi-nighaṇṭu. Bks. i.—x. of twelve metrical vocabularies. With an anonymous commentary. Edited from the recension of Tāṇḍava-rāya Mudaliyār and others, with additions on poetical metaphors by Philippus de Melho.] pp. 191. *Jaffna*, 1856. 12°. **14172. e. 9.**

Vīra-maṇḍalavar was a disciple of Guṇa-bhadra, probably the famous Jain writer of that name whose Sanskrit Uttara-purāṇam was finished in A.D. 897.

—— சூடாமணிநிகண்டு ௸ [Chūḍāmaṇi-nighaṇṭu. Another edition, edited by N. Āṛu-muga Nāvalar.] pp. 196, xx. சென்னபட்டணம் பிரபவ [*Madras*, 1867.] 8°. **14172. f. 11.**

—— —— [Third edition.] pp. i. 196, 20. சென்னபட்டணம் விக்கிரம [*Madras*, 1880.] 8°. **14172. e. 29.**

—— சூடாமணிநிகண்டு ௸ [Chūḍāmaṇi-nighaṇṭu. Another issue, edited by Āṛu-muga Nāvalar. Second edition.] pp. 196. கொக்குவில் ஜய [*Kokkuvil*, 1894.] 8°. **14172. e. 17.**

—— சூடாமணிநிகண்டு ௸ [Chūḍāmaṇi-nighaṇṭu. Bks. i.-x., text only. Edited by Valvai Ṣ. Vaidya-liṅga Piḷḷai.] pp. 101. சென்னை யுவ [*Madras*, 1875.] 8°. **14172. e. 30.**

—— (†பதினொராவது.) [Chūḍāmaṇi-nighaṇṭu. Ch. xi., on homonyms.] pp. 84. *Manepy*, 1835. 16°. **14172. h. 1.(4.)**

No title-page.

—— Negandu : part xi. நிகண்டு. ஒருசொற் பலபொருட்டொகுதி, மூலமும் உரையும். [Re-arranged, with supplements, by Vēda-giri Mudaliyār, and glosses.] pp. i. 171. *Jaffna*, 1843. 8°. **14172. f. 23.**

—— இரண்டாவது மூன்றாவது சூடாமணி நிகண்டு. [Chūḍāmaṇi-nighaṇṭu. Pts. ii., iii.] pp. 37. சென்னை [*Madras*,] 1897. 12°. **14172. ee. 4.**

VĪRA-MUTTAṆṆĀ NĀṬṬĀR, *of Nadukkaveri.* ∘∘∘ தோத்திரப்பாமாலை [Tōttira-pā-mālai, or Hari-brahmēṣvara-t°. Religious lyrics upon the local Ṣaiva cult.] pp. ii. 42. நடுக்காவேரி ஏவிளம்பி [*Nadukkaveri*, 1898.] 8°. **14170. e. 47.(9.)**

VĪRA-MUTTU MUDALIYĀR, *Chaturaṅgapaṭṭaṇam.* *See* ṢESHĀCHALAM NĀYUḌU. ∘∘∘ ஸ்ரீ... பன்னிரண்டு இராஜர்கள் கதை. [Pann'-iraṇḍu-rājargaḷ-kathai. Translated by Vīra-muttu.] 1897. 8°. **14171. a. 13.**

VĪRAṆA PULAVAR, *Kāñchi.* அருணாசலகீர்த்தனை. [Aruṇāchala-kīrttanai. Hymns on the cult of Ṣiva at Arunachalam. With a life of the poet. Edited by E. Vīrā-sāmi Upādhyāyar.] pp. ii. 260. நள [*Madras*, 1856.] 8°. **14172. b. 12.**

VĪRA PIḶḶAI, *Ṣaiva K.* ∘∘∘ வன்னியர் புராணம் மூலமும்-உரையும் [Vanniyar-purāṇam. A poem, with commentary by the author, on the legends of the Vanniyar tribe. Edited by Ponn'-ambala Guru.] pp. 3, 326. [*Madras*,] 1905. 8°. **14172. bb. 17.**

VĪRA-RĀGHAVĀCHĀRYAR, *M.* காங்கிரெஸ் வினாவிடை ௸ [Congress-vinā-viḍai. A catechetical history of the National Congresses in India.] Fourth edition. pp. 44. சென்னை [*Madras*,] 1890. 8°. **14170. k. 45.(2.)**

—— The Mysore Representative Assembly and the Indian National Congress. மைசூர்பிரதிநிதிசபையும் காங்கிரெஸ் சபையும். வினாவிடை. pp. 23. சென்னை [*Madras*,] 1891. 8°. **14170. g. 27.**

VĪRA-RĀGHAVĀCHĀRYAR, *Tiruvahīndrapuram.* *See* KŪRATT'-ĀṚVĀN. ஸ்ரீ . . . கூரேசவிஜயம் ௸ [Kūrēṣa-vijayam. Edited by Vīra-rāghavāchāryar.] [1892.] 8°. **14170. e. 44.**

VĪRA-RĀGHAVA MUDALIYĀR, *Andhaka-kavi.* சேயூர்முருகன் பிள்ளைத்தமிழ் [Ṣeyūr-murugan-piḷḷai-tamiṛ. A poem on the cult of Skanda at Cheyur. Edited with preface and biography of the poet by Kalkūḷam Kuppu-sāmi Mudaliyār.] pp. 12, i. xxviii. 88. *Madras*, 1902. 12°. **14172. a. 54.(1.)**

Forms no. 1 *of the* Nava-maṇi-mālai *Series.*

—— திருவாரூருலா. [Tiruvārūr-ulā. Ṣaiva verses. Edited with glossary by U. V. Sāminātha'-aiyar.] pp. 53, ii. 1905. *See* ACADEMIES, *etc.*—*Madura.* ["Ṣen-damiṛ" supplement.] no. 16. 1902, *etc.* 8°. **14172. i. 1.*(no. 16.)**

—— [19 occasional verses, with interpretation.] *See* TANI-PĀḌAL. (†தனிப்பாடற்றிரட்டு) [Tani-pādaṛ-ṭiraṭṭu.] pp. 179-188. [1892, *etc.*] 8°. **14172. c. 39.(5.)**

VĪRA-SVĀMI, *Madurai.* *See* Ēkāmbara Mudaliyār. மதுரைவீரஅலங்காரம். [Madurai-vīra-alaṅkāram.] 1892. 8°. **14172. b. 44.(2.)**

——— ००० மதுரைவீரசுவாமிகதை. [Madurai-vīra-svāmi-kathai. A poetical legend, purporting to be derived from the Kāṣi-khaṇḍam, of a general of a king of Madura who killed himself before the shrine of Ṣokka-nāthar at Madura, and is worshipped by annual sacrifices. Edited by T. Āru-muga Svāmi.] pp. 95. கஅஅக [*Madras,* 1881.] 16°. **14170. d. 18.(2.)**

VĪRĀ-SĀMI CHETṬIYĀR, *Ashṭāvadhānam, of Madras Presidency College.* Vinodarasamanjari, [a series of miscellaneous literary articles] edited [or rather reprinted] by A. Veerasawmy Chettiar . . . and originally published by the Rev. P. Percival . . . Second edition. To this are added the life of Auviyar and the Story of the Little Hunch Back. (*விநோதரசமஞ்சரி.) pp. ii. 428. *Madras,* 1891. 8°. **14170. k. 56.**

——— விநோதரசமஞ்சரி. [Vinōda-rasa-mañjari. A new and enlarged edition, with preface by K. Kuppu-sāmi Mudaliyār.] pp. i. ii. 536. சென்னை [*Madras,*] 1906. 8°. **14171. e. 14.**

Forms no. 1 *of the* Kathā-rasa-mañjari *Series.*

VĪRĀ-SĀMI MUDALIYĀR, *P. Ṣaḍaiy-appa.* சிற்பசிந்தாமணி. [Ṣirpa-chintāmaṇi. An astrological work on planetary influences upon the building of houses, *etc.*] pp. vii. 90. சென்னபட்டணம் [*Madras,*] 1887. 8°. **14170. k. 42.**

VĪRĀ-SĀMI NĀYUḌU, *of Chintadripet.* *See* Aruṇāchala Kavi-rāyar. ००० இராம நாடகம் ஓூ [Rāma-nāṭakam. Edited by Vīrā-sāmi.] 1893. 8°. **14170. l. 36.**

VĪRĀ-SĀMI PIḶḶAI, *M.* *See* Tiru-vaḷḷuvar. ००० திருக்குறள் ஓூ [Kuṛaḷ. Edited by Vīrā-sāmi.] [1875.] 8°. **14172. c. 10.**

VĪRĀ-SĀMI PIḶḶAI, *Ṣ.* *See* Strange (T. L.). ஹிந்துதர்மசாஸ்திரம். [Hindu-dharma-ṣāstram. A translation by Vīrā-sāmi.] 1857. 8°. **14170. g. 11.**

VĪRĀ-SĀMI UPĀDHYĀYAR, *Eṛumūr.* *See* Vīraṇa Pulavar. அருணசலகீர்த்தனை. [Aruṇāchala-kīrttanai. Edited by Vīrā-sāmi.] [1856.] 8°. **14172. b. 12.**

VĪRĀ-SĀMI UPĀDHYĀYAR, *Eṛumūr (continued).* ००० சிவசங்கர சதகம். [Ṣiva-ṣaṅkara-ṣatakam. A century of Ṣaiva verses.] pp. 16. 1906. *See* Rāma-sāmi Nāyuḍu, *K.* சதகத்திரட்டு. [Ṣataka-tiraṭṭu.] pt. 7. 1905-1906. 12°. **14170. dd. 10.**

VĪRĀ-SĀMI UPĀDHYĀYAR, *Kummadibūṇḍi.* கொந்திதேசத்தராசனுடைய மதிகெட்டா நாடகம். [Madigeṭṭā-nāṭakam. A romantic play.] pp. 140. சென்னை [*Madras,*] 1902. 8°. **14170. l. 60.**

VĪRA-ṢIṄGA UḌAIYĀR, *Nīrvēli Ṣ.* *See* Sāminātha Mudaliyār, *M. A.* தருமபுத்திரநாடகம். [Dharma-putra-nāṭakam. Edited by Vīra-ṣiṅga.] 1890. 8°. **14170. l. 16.**

VĪRAVANAM. வீரவனப்புராணம். [Vīravana-purāṇam. A poem on the sacred legends of Vīravanam, or Vīraiyūr, near Perundurai, translated into verse by Mīnākshi-sundaram Piḷḷai from the Sanskrit. Edited with notes by U. V. Sāminath'-aiyar.] pp. i. 2, ii. 107. சென்னபட்டணம் [*Madras,*] 1903. 8°. **14170. ee. 63.**

VĪRA-VANMAN. வீரவன்மன் வெற்றி. (Veeravanman Vetri [a romance] . . . Translated [from English] into Tamil by P. V. Sabapathy Moodaliar.) 2 vols. *Madras,* 1902. 8°. **14171. a. 54.**

Forms no. 2-3 *of the "Kathamanchari Series."*

VIRŪPĀKSHI LIṄG'-AIYAR. திருக்குமுளமென்னும் தென்திருப்பதிபுராணம் ஓூ [Ten-tirupadi-purāṇam, or Tiru-kumuḷa-purāṇam. The legends of the Vaishṇava sanctuary at South Tirupati, in verse. Followed by Ananta-nātha-svāmigaḷ-padigam, a hymn by the same author. Edited by G. Rāja-gōpāla Piḷḷai and T. Shaṇmukham Piḷḷai.] pp. 213, 4 ; 28 *plates.* சென்னை விக்ருதி [*Madras,* 1890.] 8°. **14170. e. 49.**

VIṢĀKHA-DATTA. *See* Naṭēṣa Ṣāstri, *Ṣ. M.* Mudrarakshasam : a tale . . . founded on the . . . drama by Visakhadatta, *etc.* 1885. 12°. **14170. k. 40.**

VIṢĀKHA PERU-MĀḶ AIYAR, *Tirutaṇigai.* *See* Māṇikka-vāchakar. ००० திருக்கோவையார். [Tiru-kōvaiyār. With interpretation by Viṣākha Perumāḷ.] [1897.] 12°. **14172. a. 46.**

VIṢĀKHA PERU-MĀḶ AIYAR, *Tirutaṇigai (continued). See* PAVAṆANDI. நன்னூல் மூ [Nan-nūl. With commentary by Viṣākha Peru-māḷ.] [1875.] 8°. **14172. f. 9.**

—— —— [1882.] 8°. **14172. e. 11.**

—— அணியிலக்கணம். [Aṇiy-ilakkaṇam. A manual of rhetoric. Edited by S. Anavarata-vināyakam Piḷḷai.] pp. 8, 68. சென்னை [*Madras*,] 1906. 12°. **14172. g. 3.(3.)**

—— பாலபோதவிலக்கணம். [Bāla-bōdhav-ilakkaṇam. An elementary Tamil grammar.] pp. ii. 288. சென்னபட்டணம் பரிதாபி [*Madras*, 1852.] 16°. **14172. g. 10.**

—— யாப்பிலக்கணம். [Yāpp'-ilakkaṇam. A manual of prosody. Edited by S. Anavarata-vināyakam Piḷḷai.] pp. vii. 46. சென்னை [*Madras*,] 1906. 12°. **14172. g. 3.(2.)**

VIṢĀLĀKSHI AMMĀḶ. கௌரீ. (Gowri ... Highly interesting Tamil novel.) pp. i. 95. *Madras*, 1906. 8°. **14171. e. 1.(3.)**

VISHṆU-CHITTAN. *See* PERIY-ĀṞVĀR.

VISTARINI (J.), *Monsignor, Missionary Apostolic. See* TAMB'-AIYĀ UPĀDHYĀYAR. ◦◦◦ பிரலாபகவிதை. [Pralāpa-kavitai. Verses on the death of Mgr. Vistarini.] 1896. 8°. **14170. c. 24.(11.)**

VIṢVA-BRAHMA-PURĀṆAM. விஸ்வபிரமபுராணம். [Viṣva-brahma-purāṇam. A treatise on origins, religious duties, *etc.* Metrically translated from the Sanskrit by Tiruvaiyāṟu A. Muttu-sāmi Bhāratiyār. With prose paraphrase by Mayilāḍuparam Kṛushṇ'-aiyar.] pt. i. pp. viii. xxiv. 383. சென்னை [*Madras*,] 1894. 8°. **14170. f. 16.**

VIṢVA-NĀTHA MUDALIYĀR, *M. S.* சந்திரவதனை அல்லது இரண்டுசகோதரர்கள். (Chandravadana, or The Two Brothers.) [A romantic drama.] pp. 87. *Madras*, 1898. 8°. **14170. l. 32.(7.)**

VIṢVA-NĀTHA PIḶḶAI, *D. C. See* CARROLL (D.).

VIṢVA-NĀTHA PIḶḶAI, *V. See* DEFOE (D.). The Life and Adventures of Robinson Crusoe. Translated ... by V. Visvanatha Pillai. 1906. 12°. **14171. d. 8.**

VIṢVA-NĀTHA ṢĀSTRI, *Arāli Nārāyaṇ'-aiyar.* நகுலமலைக்குறவஞ்சிநாடகம். [Nakula-malai-kuṟavañji-nāṭakam. A lyrical drama on the religious legend of the Nakula-malai or Mongoose Mountain. Edited by Ṣ. A. Kumāra-sāmi Piḷḷai.] pp. iv. 56. கொக்குவில் மன்மத [*Kokkuvil*, 1895.] 8°. **14170. l. 6.**

—— பரகிதம். [Para-hitam. A metrical tract on astrology, with prose paraphrase, *etc.* Edited by N. Ch. Raghu-nāth'-aiyar.] pp. 24. கொக்குவில் நந்தன [*Kokkuvil*, 1892.] 8°. **14170. i. 25.**

VIṢVA-NĀTHA SŪRI, *Kaḷamūr.* ◦◦◦ மணிப்பிரவாள விராடபர்வம். [Maṇi-pravāḷa-virāṭa-parvam. A metrical adaptation of the Virāṭa-parvam of the Mahā-bhāratam, in mixed Tamil and Sanskrit. Edited with notes by N. A. Gōpāla Dēṣikāchāryar.] pp. 96. சென்னை [*Madras*,] 1905. 8°. **14172. bb. 16.**

VIVĒKA-CHINTĀMAṆI. ◦◦◦ விவேகசிந்தாமணி [Vivēka-chintāmaṇi, called also Nīti-chintāmaṇi and Veḷḷai-chintāmaṇi. A collection of moral verses, according to the recension of Hari-hara-putra Upādhyāyar.] pp. 32. பிரமோதூத [*Madras*, 1871.] 16°. **14172. a. 13.(2.)**

VIVĒKĀNANDA, *Svāmi* [*i.e.* NARĒNDRA-NĀTHA DATTA.] ◦◦◦ பிரசங்கம். [Prasaṅgam. A lecture on theosophy delivered in Ceylon. Translated by A. Muttu-tambi Piḷḷai.] pp. 16. கொக்குவில் [*Kokkuvil*, 1897.] 8°. **14170. ee. 28.(2.)**

VIVĒKA-SĀGARAM. விவேகசாகரம். [Vivēka-sāgaram. A story illustrating the principles of ethics. Translated from the Persian by Riẓā Ḥusain Khān, and stylistically revised by Muḥyi al-Dīn Ḥusain. Edited by T. Shaṇmukha Kavi-rājar.] pp. i. iv. 178. பிங்கள [*Madras*, 1858.] 8°. **14172. c. 11.**

VIVĒKA-SĀRAM. வாசுதேவமனனம் என்னும் வழங்குகிற விவேகசாரம். [Vivēka-sāram, or Vāsudēva-mananam. A catechism of Advaita-Vēdānta philosophy. An edition based on that of Pāripākkam Muniy-appa Mudaliyār.] pp. ii. 170. சென்னை [*Madras*,] 1896. 8°. **14170. e. 68.**

VIVIDHA-PADĀRTHAM. விவிதபதார்த்தசஞ்சாயம் [Vividha-padārtha-ṣañjāyam. Conversations on familiar social topics.] pp. 40. [*Madras, n.d.*] 8°. **14172. h. 90.**

Without title-page and end.

VOCABULARIES. *See* Dictionaries.

VṚUTTĀCHALAM. சசிவர்ணன்சரித்திரம். [Ṣaṣivarṇan-charitram. A religious-philosophical story, purporting to be from the Vṛuttāchala-purāṇam.] *See* Rāma-sāmi Svāmi. நானாஜீவவாதக்கட்டளை ஞு [Nānā-jīva-vāda-kaṭṭaḷai, *etc.*] pp. 40-43. [1887.] 12°. **14170. d. 26.**

VYTHEANATHA MOODELIAR. *See* Vaidya-nātha Mudaliyār.

WALKER (J.). நீதிமொழித்திரட்டு. Nídimozhittirattu. A selection from the writings of Tamil moralists, [viz. from the Mūd'-urai, Nanneṟi, Nal-vaṟi, Nīti-neṟi-viḷakkam, Nāl-aḍiyār, and Aṟa-neṟi-chāram,] for the use of schools. pp. ii. i. 112. *Madras,* 1841. 8°. **14170. k. 35.**

WALKER (Thomas). *See* [Addenda] Bible.—New Testament.—*Epistles.* ◦ ◦ ◦ பிலிப்பியருக்கு . . . திருப ஞு [Philippians. With commentary *etc.* by T. Walker. Translated by the latter and J. David from the English.] 1908. 12°. **14170. bbb. 16.**

WALTHER (Christoph Theodosius). Historia Ecclesiastica. Cui adduntur Synchronismi Historiæ Exoticæ, præsertim Indicæ. Editio secunda. (*திருச்சபையினசரித்திரப பொஸ்தகம.) pp. 316, xxxiv. *Trangambariæ,* 1799. 8°. **14170. b. 60.**

WARD (Ferdinand D. W.). Practical Expositions of the Parables of Christ, and of the briefer Similes, employed by the Divine Teacher . . . உவமைகளும் ஒப்பனைகளும் ஞு. pp. vi. 332, 54. *Madras Tract and Book Society: Madras,* 1844. 12°. **14170. b. 47.**

WARD (William). The Salvation of the Soul . . . a translation of the Parent Society's tract Krishna Pal. ஆத்தும இரட்சிப்பு. Second edition. pp. 16. *Jaffna,* 1844. 12°. **14170. b. 1.(37.)**

WARING (Edward John). Remarks on the Uses of some Bazaar Medicines, and on a few of the common indigenous Plants of India, according to European Practice. [In English and Tamil.] (*சிலகடைஔஷதங்களுடையவும் . . . சிலபூண்டுகளுடையவும் பலங்களைபற்றிகாட்டிய குறிப்புகள்.) pp. xvii. 213. *Travancore,* 1860. 8°. **14170. i. 6.**

—— [Another copy.] **14170. i. 30.**

WASHBURN (George Thomas). *See* Hymnals. Tamil Christian Lyrics . . . from the lyrical compilations of . . . G. T. Washburn, *etc.* 1902. 12°. **14170. b. 30.**

WAY. The Temperate Way . . . a revision . . . of no. 38, of the Madras Tract Society's Miscellaneous publications . . . தெளிநெறி. Second edition. pp. 12. *Jaffna,* 1844. 12°. **14170. b. 1.(38.)**

—— True Way. மெய்வழி. [A Christian tract.] *See* Vēda-nāyaka Ṣāstri, *T. D.,* and Winslow (M.). Blind Way, *etc.* pp. 123-142. 1852. 32°. **14170. a. 3.**

WAYLAND (Francis), *the Elder.* Wayland's Moral Science. ஒழுக்கநூல். [Oṛukka-nūl. Translated by A. Barnes.] pp. 230. *Palamcottah,* 1859. 12°. **14172. h. 11.**

WEBB (Edward). *See* Hymnals. Tamil Christian Lyrics . . . from the lyrical compilations of . . . E. Webb, *etc.* 1902. 12°. **14170. b. 30.**

WERDIN (Johann Philipp). *See* Paulinus, *à Sancto Bartholomæo.*

WESLEY (Charles) and WESLEY (John). வெஸ்லியன் மெதொடிஸ்தர் என்னுஞ் சபையாரின் ஆதிப்பிரமாணங்கள். [The original Rules for Wesleyans.] pp. 8. [*Batticaloa,* 1893.] 12°. **14170. a. 49.(5.)**

WESLEY (John). [For the Service-book of the Wesleyan Methodists, adapted from the Book of Common Prayer of the Church of England by J. Wesley:] *See* Liturgies.—*Wesleyan Methodists.*

—— A collection of Hymns, for the use of the people called Methodists . . . With a new supplement. Translated into Tamil [by J. Kilner, D. P. Niles, and others. Edited by E. Rigg and others]. (*மெதொடிஸ்தர் . . . ஞானகீதங்கள்.) pp. vi. 936. *Batticaloa,* 1881. 12°. **14170. bbb. 10.**

—— ஞானபாடல்கள். Hymns translated from the collection by the Rev. J. Wesley. pp. 69, iii. *Madras,* 1825. 8°. **3437. g. 33.**

WESLEYAN METHODISTS. The Catechisms of the Wesleyan Methodists: compiled and published by order of the Conference . . . No. ii.—For children of seven years of age and upwards.

With an appendix, containing a short Catechism of Scripture History, and examples of prayer. Translated into Tamul. (*இரண்டாவது ஞானோபதேசம்.) pp. 114. *Madras*, 1827. 12°.
3504. bb. 16.

—— Second edition. [Without the appendix.] pp. 66. *Madras*, 1835. 12°. **3505. bbb. 36.**

—— The Catechism of the Wesleyan Methodists ... No. i. (ii.), for children of tender years ... with an appendix, containing a short catechism of scripture names, and prayers, *etc.* (*வேதசாரவினாவிடை.) 2 pts. *Madras*, 1850. 12°.
14170. b. 7-8.

—— *வெஸ்லியன் மெதொடிஸ்தரின் வேதசார வினாவிடை.* [Vēda-sāra-vinā-viḍai. The Wesleyan Methodist Scripture Catechism. Second edition.] 2 pts. *Batticaloa*, 1891-1892. 16° & 12°.
14170. a. 52.

WICKREMASINGHE (*Don* Martino de Zilva). Tamil Grammar Self-taught. In Tamil and Roman Characters. (Marlborough's Self-taught Series—no. 19.) pp. 120. *London*, 1906. 12°.
012902. eee.

WINFRED (S.). *See* Pañcha-tantram. Pancha Tantra. Translated ... by ... S. Winfred. 1873. 12°. **14170. k. 61.**

—— *See* Tamil Minor Poets. Tamil Minor Poets ... translated ... by ... S. Winfred, *etc.* 1872. 12°. **14172. c. 6.**

WINKEL (E.). A brief Commentary in Tamil on St. Paul's Epistle to the Galatians [chiefly based on the work of Philippi] ... *கலாத்தியருக்கு எழுதின நிருபத்தின் வியாக்கியானம்.* pp. 92. *Madras*, 1891. 8°. **14170. c. 36.**

WINSLOW (Miron). *See* Bible.—*Complete Bibles.* The Holy Bible ... [With the headings and chronology of the English version translated by M. Winslow.] 1844. 8°. **3070. i. 1.**

—— *See* Bible. — *Complete Bibles.* The Holy Bible ... revised [by M. Winslow and others], *etc.* 1850. 4°. **3070. d. 26.**

WINSLOW (Miron) (*continued*). *See* Knight (W.) and Winslow (M.). Spiritual Lamp. 1854. 16°.
14170. a. 33.(2.)

—— *See* Vēda-nāyaka Śāstri, *T.D.*, and Winslow (M.). Blind Way, *etc.* 1852. 32°. **14170. a. 3.**

—— —— 1861. 16°. **14170. a. 37.**

—— Conversion of the Taheitans ... *தகைத்தியக் தீவகத்தார் சரித்திரம்.* Second edition. pp. 12. *Jaffna*, 1843. 12°. **14170. b. 1.(8.)**

—— Good Counsel ... *நல்லறிவு.* Third edition. pp. 16. *Jaffna*, 1844. 12°. **14170. b. 1.(15.)**

—— Heavenly Way. Containing the history of a brahmin of Calcutta who became a convert to Christianity... *முத்திமார்க்கம்.* Fifth edition. pp. 8. *Jaffna*, 1843. 12°. **14170. b. 1.(1.*)**

—— The Means of Bliss ... *மோட்சகாரணம்.* Fifth edition. pp. 12. *Jaffna*, 1844. 12°.
14170. b. 1.(2.)

WINSLOW (Miron) and **ROBERTS** (Joseph). True Doctrine ... *மெய்யுபதேசபத்திரம்.* Third edition. pp. 8, 16. *Jaffna*, 1843. 12°. **14170. b. 1.(4.)**

WINSLOW (Miron) and **SCUDDER** (John). Attributes of the Hindu Triad ... *மும்மூர்த்திஇலட்சணம்.* Fifth edition. pp. 12. *Jaffna*, 1844. 12°.
14170. b. 1.(22.)

WOODWARD (Henry). *பரவருணீதி* [Parav-aruṇīti. An allegory on divine justice and mercy.] pp. 36. *Nellore*, 1833. 12°. **14170. b. 14.(1.)**

—— Divine Justice and Mercy ... *பரவருணீதி.* Second edition. pp. 34. *Jaffna*, 1842. 12°.
14170. b. 1.(28.*)

—— Good Opportunity ... *நற்சமயம்.* [A Christian tract.] Fourth edition. pp. 16. *Jaffna*, 1842. 12°. **14170. b. 1.(25.)**

—— Mercy and Justice ... *கருணாநீதி.* Second edition. pp. 27. *Jaffna*, 1845. 12°.
14170. b. 1.(59.)

YĀDAVA-GIRI. ∘ ∘ ∘ *சதுர்வேதி சரித்திர சங்கீர்த்தனை.* [Chatur-vēdi-charitra-saṅkīrttanai. An episode from the Yādava-giri-māhātmyam, on the legends of the Vaishṇava sanctuary near Melkote.

Translated into verse from the Sanskrit, with occasional prose paraphrases, on the basis of Gōpālāchārya Svāmi's rendering, by Tirupattūr R. K. Tiru-nārāyaṇa-dāsar, and edited by P. Appāsāmi Mudaliyār.] pp. 8, 32. திருப்பத்தூர் [*Tiruppattur*,] 1900. 8°. **14170. ee. 35.(4.)**

YĀJÑAVALKYA. ஶ்ரீயாஜ்ஞவல்க்ய ஸ்ம்ருதி: விஜ்ஞானேஶ்வரீய வ்யாக்யானஸஹிதா [Yājñavalkya-smruti. Sanskrit text, with Vijñānēṣvara's commentary Mitāksharā, and Tamil interpretation.] 1901, *etc.* *See* PERIODICAL PUBLICATIONS.—*Chidambaram.* ப்ரஹ்மவித்யா *etc.* [Brahma-vidyā.] vol. xv., no. 1, *etc.* 1886, *etc.* 4°. **14096. dd. 3.(vol. 15, etc.)**

YĀMUNĀCHĀRYAR (ĀḶAVANDĀR). ○○○ ஆளவந்தார்ஸ்தோத்ரம். [Āḷavandār-stōtram, or Stōtra-ratnam. A Sanskrit Vaishṇava hymn. With a Tamil commentary by Periyav-āchān Piḷḷai. Edited by Mahā-bhāshyam Raṅgāchāryar and Īchambāḍi Rāghavāchāryar.] pp. 78. *Madras*, 1878. 8°. **14028. c. 46.**

The Sanskrit text is given in Tamil characters.

—— శ్రీ ఆళవన్దార్ స్తోత్రము. [Āḷavandār-stōtram. Another edition, in Telugu character.] pp. 129. *Madras*, 1879. 12°. **14028. b. 52.**

—— சதுஃஶ்லோகீ [Chatuḥ-ṣlōkī. Four Sanskrit stanzas on the goddess Lakshmī. With Tamil version, analysis, and commentary.] *See* VARADĀCHĀRYAR, *Vātsya D.* ○○○ ப்ரபன்னபாரிஜாதம் ஆ [Prapanna-pārijātam.] pp. 143-154. [1895.] 8°. **14028. d. 55.**

—— ஸ்ரீமத்கீதார்த்த ஸங்க்ரஹம் [Gītārtha-saṅgraha. A Sanskrit epitome of the Bhagavad-gītā. Sanskrit text, with Tamil translation.] *See* MAHĀ-BHĀRATAM. ஸ்ரீபகவத்கீதை. [Bhagavad-gītā.] pp. 692-710. [1899.] 16°. **14065. b. 19.**

—— శ్రీ . . . ప్రమేయరత్నం . . . మాణిక్యమాలై. [Prameya-ratnam. A Vaishṇava theological tract. Followed by Periyav-āchān Piḷḷāi's Māṇikka-mālai. Edited by V. M. Ṣrīnivāsa Appaṅgār Svāmi.] pp. 61. చెన్నై ౧౯౦౪ [*Madras*, 1904.] 8°. **14170. ee. 6.(3.)**

—— తత్త్వభూషణము. [Tattva-bhūshaṇam. A treatise on the doctrines of Rāmānuja's school. Edited by Aṛagiya-maṇavāḷa Rāmānuja-jiyar Svāmi.] pp. 40. కంచి [*Conjevaram*,] 1902. 8°. **14170. ee. 6.(2.)**

YĀPP'-ARUṄGALAM. The Elements of Prosody. யாப்பருங்கலம். *See* POPE (G. U.). A larger Grammar of the Tamil Language, *etc.* pp. 335-358. 1858-1859. 8°. **14172. h. 81.**

YAṢŌDHARAN. Yasódhara-kāvyam (யசோதர காவியம்). [A narrative poem in 5 cantos, by an anonymous author, conveying Jain doctrine.] The first of the five Tamil minor epics. With argument in prose, &c., by T. Venkatarama Iyengar . . . With an English introduction by Arthur Davies. pp. 4, xxiv. i. xvii. lxvi. 79. *Madras*, 1908. 12°. **14172. a. 66.**

YATĪNDRA-PRAVAṆAR. *See* AṚAGIYA-MAṆAVĀḶA PERU-MĀḶ.

YATI-RĀJULU NĀYUḌU, *T.* *See* MORRIS (J. C.). Selections . . . to which are added a spelling and phraseology . . . by T. Eterajooloo Naidoo, Moonshee. 1848. 8°. **14172. h. 20.**

YŌGA. அட்டாங்க யோகக்குறள். வருத்தமறவுய்யும் வழி. [Aṭṭāṅga-yōga-kuṛaḷ. A poem in 59 *kuṛaḷ* distichs on the mystic exercises of the *ashṭāṅga-yōga*. Followed by Varutta-maṛav-uyyum vaṛi, 25 Ṣaiva stanzas. Edited by Ṣ. Subrahmaṇya Kavi-rāyar.] pp. 11. 1905. *See* ACADEMIES, *etc.*—*Madura.* ["Ṣen-damiṛ" supplement.] no. 10. 1902, *etc.* 8°. **14172. i. 1.*(no. 10.)**

YŌGA-VĀSISHṬHA-RĀMĀYAṆAM. *See* ĀḶAVANDĀR. ○○○ ஞானவாசிட்ட ஆ [Ñāna-vāṣiṭṭav-amala-rāmāyaṇam. A poem adapted and abridged from the Sanskrit Yōga-vāsishṭha-rāmāyaṇam.] [1851.] 4°. **14170. fff. 2.**

—— —— 1890. 8°. **14172. b. 41.**

—— *See* ĀḶAVANDĀR. ○○○ ஞானவாசிட்ட ஆ [Ñāna-vāṣiṭṭav-amala-rāmāyaṇam. A prose summary.] 1902. 8°. **14170. ee. 53.**

—— சீதாவிஜயவசனம். [Sītā-vijaya-vachanam. An episode of the Vāsishṭhōttara-rāmāyaṇam. Translated from the Sanskrit by T. Sundarāchāryar. Edited by Ṣ. K. Subba-rāya Mudaliyār.] pp. 43. கஅகசு [*Madras*, 1869.] 16°. **14170. d. 18.(1.)**

YŪSUF ibn MUḢAMMAD MUḢYI al-DĪN, *Maraik-kāyar, Nāgapaṭṭinam.* வணிகக்கணிதம். [Vaṇiga-gaṇitam. A mercantile ready-reckoner.] pp. i. 99, 4. *Madras,* 1891. 8°. **14170. i. 28.**

YŪSUF RAUTTAR ibn MADĀR ṠĀḢIB, *Mañjai-kollai.* Ready Reckoner. [In Tamil, English, Burmese, and Gujarati.] Containing reduction of weights by visses, lbs or by baskets. Edited by Broker M. Essoof Rawuther, *etc.* (*அளவுநிறை.) pp. 98. இரங்கோன் [*Rangoon,*] 1901. 16°. **14172. i. 21.**

ZABĪDĪ. *See* AḢMAD ibn AḢMAD.

ZAHN (FRANZ LUDWIG). *See* BIBLE.—*Abridgments and Selections.* வேதசரித்திரம். [Vēda-charitram. A translation of Zahn's Biblische Geschichten.] 1871-1873. 12°. **14170. b. 26, 27.**

ZAIDĀN (JURJĪ). *See* [Addenda] JURJĪ ZAIDĀN.

ẒĀMIN ÑĀNIYĀR, *Kamudaiyil, Saiyid.* *See* SUBB'-AIYA DĒṢIKAR, *P.* இஃது ... சையதுதாமின் ... பேரில் ... இயற்றப்பட்டு ௵ [Panegyrical verses upon Saiyid Ẓāmin.] 1900. 16°. **14172. a. 63.**

ZIEGENBALG (BARTHOLOMAEUS). *See* BIBLE.—*Complete Bibles.* Biblia Damulica ... libri ... opera B. Ziegenbalgii ... versi, *etc.* [1714]-1728. 4°. **3068. g. 6.**

—— *See* BIBLE —*Old Testament.* Librorum Sacrorum Veteris Testamenti ... editio secunda, *etc.* [From the version of Ziegenbalg and Schultze.] 1777-1796. 4°. **3068. g. 10.**

—— *See* BIBLE.—*New Testament.* Novum ... Testamentum ... in linguam damulicam versum opera ... B. Ziegenbalgii, *etc.* 1722. 12°. **1410. g. 1.**

—— *See* BIBLE.—New Testament.—*Gospels and Acts.* Quatuor Evangelia et Acta ... in linguam damulicam versa ... opera ... B. Ziegenbalg, & J. E. Grundler. 1714. 4°. **2. a. 4.**

—— *See* BIBLE. — New Testament. — *Gospels.* [*Matthew.*] Evangelium Matthaei ... [In Ziegenbalg's version], *etc.* 1739. 12°. **Grenville 20,059.**

—— [For editions of the translation of the Bible as revised by Fabricius and subsequent translators on the basis of Ziegenbalg's version :] *See* BIBLE.

—— *See* FREYLINGHAUSEN (J. A.). Theologia Thetica ... in lingua tamulica scripta a ... B. Ziegenbalg et J. E. Gründler. 1856. 8°. **3559. c. 13.**

—— *See* LUTHER (M.). மார்த்தின் லுத்தர் ... ஞானோபதேச ௵ [Martin Luther enbavarin ñānōpadēṣa - kuripp'- iḍattai vistarikkum vinā-viḍaigaḷ. Translated into Tamil by B. Ziegenbalg.] 1872. 12°. **14170. b. 20.**

ADDENDA.

'ABD al-ḲĀDIR LEBBAI (Kāmil Walī Daikkā), *Shaikh*. பன்னிரண்டுமாலை. [Pann'-irandu-mālai. 12 poems on themes of Muhammadan religion and ethics, from 'Abd al-Ḳādir's Sharī'at-mālai. Preceded by a metrical Munājāt by the editor, Vīra-ṣōṟam A. Shaikh Muḣammad.] pp. 40. இரங்கோன் [*Rangoon*,] 1907. 8°. **14173. b. 44.**

'ABD al-MAJĪD ibn MUḢAMMAD 'ABD al-KARĪM, *M.K.A.* கீர்த்தனமஜீது. [Kīrttana-majīd. Muhammadan lyrics.] pt. ii. pp. 16. கொழும்பு [*Colombo*,] 1907. 8°. **14173. b. 28.(8.)**

'ABD al-MASĪḢ. Abdool Messee, or The Jewel of Mercy . . . a translation [by Punari Mudaliyār] of the life of Abdool Messee, [formerly called Shaikh Sāliḣ, a convert from Muhammadanism and an agent of the Church Missionary Society, 1776-1827,] as published in one of the quarterly papers of the Church Missionary Society [viz. no. lxii., Midsummer, 1831]. கருணை நிதி. Third edition. pp. 20. *Jaffna*, 1844. 12°. **14170. b. 1.(36.)**

'ABD al-RAḢMĀN, *Nelliguppam*. *See* Muḣammad 'Ināyat Aḣmad. تلم الفرايض ['Ilm al-farā'iḍ. Translated into Tamil by 'Abd al-Raḣmān.] [1906.] 8°. **14173. b. 42.**

ABRAHAM PAṆḌITAR, *M., of Karuṇānidhi Medical Hall, Tanjore.* கருணாமிர்த சாகரத்திரட்டு [Karuṇāmirta-sāgara-tiraṭṭu. A manual of music for Christian schools, containing the notation and scoring of various hymns, *etc.*] சென்னை [*Madras*,] 1907, *etc.* 8°. **14171. h. 2.**

In progress.

ACADEMIES, *etc.*—Madras.—*University of Madras.* *See* [Addenda] Gōpālāchāryar, *K.Ṣ.*, and Mahādēva Mudaliyār, *V.* பொருநராற்றுப்படை ௵ (University of Madras. B.A. Examination of 1907. A critical Study of "Porunarattuppadai.") 1907. 12°. **14171. d. 2.(3.)**

ACADEMIES, *etc.*—Madras.—*University of Madras.* *See* Ṣelva-kēṣava-rāya Mudaliyār, *T.* University of Madras. F.A., 1908. Notes. Tamil Essays. 1907. 12°. **14172. g. 11.**

ACADEMIES, *etc.*—Trichinopoli. The Tamilian Antiquary. [In English and Tamil. Edited by D. Ṣavari-rāyan.] (The Tamilian Archaeological Society Series.) *Trichinopoly*, 1907, *etc.* 8°. **14172. m. 3.**

In progress.

ĀDI-VARĀHA KAVI. *See* [Addenda] Bāṇa. Kadambari in Tamil by Adivarahakavi († a Vaishnava Brahmin of the Chola kingdom who flourished 490 years ago), *etc.* 1907. 8°. **14171. e. 2.**

AGASTYAR. அகஸ்தியர் பள்ளு. [Agastyar-paḷḷu. A metrical treatise on medicine in 226 paragraphs, ascribed to Agastyar. Edited with prose paraphrase, *etc.*, by B. Muḣammad 'Abd Allāh Ṣāḣib.] pp. 17, 237. சென்னை [*Madras*,] 1907. 12°. **14171. g. 14.**

AGASTYAR. இலக்க சௌமியசாகரம் ௵ [Ilakka-saumya-sāgaram. A metrical handbook of medicine in 8 parts, ascribed to the legendary Agastyar, with prose commentary. Edited by B. Muḣammad 'Abd Allāh Ṣāḣib.] 4 vols. சென்னை [*Madras*,] 1907. 12°. **14171. g. 15.**

AGASTYAR. பஞ்சபட்சி சாஸ்திரம் . . . ஞானசரனுல் [*sic*] சாஸ்திரம் ௵ [Pañcha-pakshi-ṣāstram. A metrical work, ascribed to Agastyar, on divination from the flight, *etc.*, of the vulture, owl, crow, cock, and peacock; with paraphrase, *etc.*, by Ṣānta-liṅga Svāmi. Followed by 4 tracts,—viz. Ñāna-sara-nūl, Uyar-ñāna-sara-nūl, and Tirumeñ-ñāna-sara-nūl, on divination, and Dina-kramālaṅkāra-churukkam, on medical regimen.] pp. 82, 62. சென்னை [*Madras,*] 1907. 8°. **14170. i. 3.**

AHMAD ibn 'ABD ALLĀH. عباب الاخيار فى ترجمة لباب الاخبار [Lubāb al-akhbār. A collection of four hundred Traditions, or sayings of Muhammad, in Arabic. With a Tamil translation, entitled 'Ubāb al-akhyār, by Muhammad 'Abd al-Rahmān.] pp. iv. 132, *lith.* بمدراس ١٣٢٢ [*Madras,* 1904]. 8°. **14521. b. 31.**

AHMAD GHANĪ MARAIKKĀYAR, *Nāgūr K.* *See* [Addenda] JURJĪ ZAIDĀN. 'கஸ்ஸான் கன்னிகை ஶ்ரீ [Ghassān-kannigai-charitram. Translated from Zaidān's "Fatāt Ghassān" by Ahmad Ghanī.] 1908. 8°. **14170. k. 3.**

AKSHARA MUDALIYĀR, *T.P.* மகுடவல்லி. (Magudavalli. A highly interesting Tamil novel.) pp. i. 79. *Madras,* 1906. 8°. **14171. e. 18.**

ALEXIS, *Saint.* அர்ச். அலசம்மானை, விருத்தம். [Archya-ṣishṭa-alaṣ'-ammānai and °vṛuttam. The legend of St. Alexis, in both *ammānai* and *vṛuttam* metres, the latter by Santa-Cruz Pulavar.] pp. 72. யாழ்ப்பாணம் [*Jaffna,*] 1893. 12°. **14170. b. 59.**

ANANTĀCHĀRYAR, *Guṇakarambhāgam Ṣathakōpa.* *See* VĀLMĪKI. Sri Valmiki Ramayana . . . with Tamil translation and Sanskrit notes by . . . Ananthacharya. 1907. 8°. **14065. bbb. 15.**

ANAVARATA-VINĀYAKAM PIḶḶAI, *Ṣ.* *See* KAṆṆ'-UḌAIYA VAḶḶAL. ° ° ° ஒழிவிலொடுக்கம். [Oṛivil oḍukkam. With commentary. Edited by Anavarata-vināyakam.] 1906. 16°. **14170. dd. 14.**

ANB'-AMMĀḶ PAUL (*Mrs.* PAUL SOLOMON). Alagammal. A story of three families . . . அழகம்மாள் ஶ்ரீ. pp. i. 214. *Salem,* 1907. 8°. **14171. e. 23.(2.)**

ANTONY, *Saint.* St. Anthony of Padua. [Translated from the French] by F. J. Subhavakyam-pillay. . . . Revised by Revd. S. Gnanaprakasa Swamy. (பதுவை அர்ச். அந்தோனியார் சரித்திரம்.) pp. x. i. 275; 4 *plates.* *Jaffna,* 1907. 12°. **14170. bbb. 14.**

APPĀ-SĀMI CHEṬṬI, *Vaiṣya-kulam.* வாலிமோட்சநாடகம். [Vāli-mōksha-nāṭakam. A lyrical play on the epic legend of the destruction of the monkey-prince Vāli by Rāma. Edited by Ṣūḷai Muni-sāmi Mudaliyār.] pp. 88. சென்னை [*Madras,*] 1908. 8°. **14170. l. 30.(3.)**

AṚAGIYA-MAṆAVĀḶA PERU-MĀḶ, called MAṆAVĀḶA MĀ-MUNI, PERIYA-JĪYAR, and RAṄGA-NĀTHAN. [*Life.*] *See* PIḶḶAI LŌKĀCHĀRYAR. ° ° ° யதீந்த்ரப்ரவணப்ரபாவம். [Yatīndra-pravaṇa-prabhāvam.] 1907. 8°. **14170. ff. 23.**

AṚAGIYA-MAṆAVĀḶA PERU-MĀḶ, called MAṆAVĀḶA MĀ-MUNI, PERIYA-JĪYAR, and RAṄGA-NĀTHAN. *See* MAHĀ-BHĀRATAM. பகவத்கீதை ஶ்ரீ (Bhagavad Gita Venba.) [A poetical rendering by Aṛagiya-maṇavāḷar.] 1906-1907. 16°. **14172. a. 59.**

AṚAGIYA-MAṆAVĀḶA PERU-MĀḶ, called MAṆAVĀḶA MĀ-MUNI, PERIYA-JĪYAR, and RAṄGA-NĀTHAN. ° ° ° ஆசார்யஹ்ருதயம். இதற்கு . . . வ்யாக்யாநம். [Āchārya-hṛudayam. A digest of the Tiru-vāy-moṛi. With commentary ascribed to another Maṇavāḷa Mā-muni. Edited by T. Ṣrīnivāsa Rāghavāchāryar.] pp. iii. 416. சென்னை [*Madras,*] 1906. 8°. **14170. ff. 24.**

AṚAGIYA-MAṆAVĀḶA PERU-MĀḶ, called MAṆAVĀḶA MĀ-MUNI, PERIYA-JĪYAR, and RAṄGA-NĀTHAN. ° ° ° ஶ்ரீமணவாளமாமுநிகள் லோகோஜ்ஜீவனார்த்தமாகத் திருவாய்மலர்ந்தருளிய உபதேசரத்தினமாலை [Upadēṣa-ratna-mālai. With a commentary by Piḷḷai Lōkam-jīyar ("Lōkārya-jīyar"). Edited, with glossaries to the verses, by T. N. Ch. Kṛushṇam-āchārya Svāmi and Ṣ. Muttu-kṛushṇa Nāyuḍu.] pp. 173. சென்னை [*Madras,*] 1907. 8°. **14170. eee. 34.**

AṚAGIYA-MAṆAVĀḶA PERU-MĀḶ, called MAṆAVĀḶA MĀ-MUNI, PERIYA-JĪYAR, and RAṄGA-NĀTHAN. உபதேசரத்தினமாலை. [Upadēṣa-ratna-mālai. With interpretation, *etc.*] pp. 40. *See* [Addenda] ĀṚVĀRGAḶ.—Nāl-āyiram.—*Selections.* ° ° ° நித்யாநுசந்தாநம். [Nityānusandhānam.] 1907. 8°. **14170. eee. 31.**

ARNOLD (J. R.), also called ARUṆĀCHALAM SADĀṢIVAM PIḶḶAI. இயேசுநாயகர் திருச்சதகம். [Iyēṣu-nāyakar-tiru-ṣatakam.] . . . A poem of one hundred stanzas on the character of Christ, *etc.* pp. 114. *Manepy,* 1850. 32°. **14170. a. 2.**

ĀṞU-MUGA NĀYAKAR, *Kāñchīpuram.* வருண-தருப்பணம். [Varṇa-darpaṇam. An account of the Hindu caste-system, with especial reference to the identification of Vanniyars with Kshatriyas. With preface by P. Muni-sāmi Nāyakar.] pp. ii. iii. 24, ii. ix. ii. 6, 5, 394, 6, 4; 2 *plates.* சென்னை [*Madras,*] 1907. 8°. **14170. g. 13.**

ARUṆA-GIRI-NĀTHA SVĀMI, *Tiruvaṇṇāmalai.* ஸ்ரீ . . . திருப்புகழ் மூலம்-உரையும். [Tirupugaṛ. Edited with paraphrase by M. Vaḍi-vēlu Mudaliyār.] சென்னை [*Madras,*] 1906, *etc.* 12°. **14172. a. 61.**

In progress.

ĀṞVĀRGAḶ.—Nāl-āyiram.—*Selections.* ° ° ° நித்யாநுசந்தாநம். [Nityānusandhānam. Followed by the Upadēṣa-ratna-mālai. With interpretation and paraphrase by Māḍabhūshi Rāmānujāchāryar.] pp. 48, 14, 30, 72, 68, 40. சென்னை [*Madras,*] 1907. 8°. **14170. eee. 31.**

ĀṞVĀRGAḶ.—Nāl-āyiram.—*Mudal-āyiram.* Tirumâlai. [A religious poem ascribed to Toṇḍar-aḍi-poḍi, rendered into English blank verse, with notes.] pp. 32. 1906. *See* Periodical Publications.—*Srirangam.* The Viṣishtâdvaitin, *etc.* vol. i., no. 10. 1905, *etc.* 8°. **14170. eee. 11.(vol. 1.)**

ATṢARA. *See* Akshara.

AUVAIYĀR.—Supposititious Works. ஔவையார் . . . குறள் மூலமும்-உரையும். [Kuṛaḷ. Edited with glosses, paraphrases, and notes by M. Vaḍi-vēlu Mudaliyār.] pp. 112. [*Madras,*] 1906. 12°. **14172. a. 57.**

AUVAIYĀR.—Supposititious Works. உயர்ஞான சாரநூல். [Uyar-ñāna-sara-nūl. A tract on divination from the breath.] *See* [Addenda] Agastyar. பஞ்சபட்சி சாஸ்திரம் ௵ [Pañcha-pakshi-ṣā-stram.] pp. 37-46. 1907. 8°. **14170. i. 3.**

BĀDARĀYAṆA. ஸ்ரீநீலகண்டசிவாசாரியர் அருளிய பிரமசூத்திர சிவாத்துவித சைவபாடியம். [Brahma-sūtram. Sanskrit text, with a Tamil version of Ṣrī-kaṇṭha (Nīla-kaṇṭha) Ṣivāchāryar's Ṣivādvita-bhāshyam or monistic Ṣaiva exposition of the Sūtram, translated with prolegomena by Kāṣi-vāsi Ṣendināth'-aiyar.] திருமங்கலம் ௧௯௦௭ [*Tirumangalam, 1907, etc.*] 8°. **14049. bb. 22.**

In progress.

BĀLA-SUBRAHMAṆYA BRAHMA-SVĀMI, *Paramahaṃsa, of Madura.* காங்கிரெஸ் கீதை ௵ (Congress Gita. 23rd Session, Surat.) [A parody of the Bhagavad-gītā, ch. i.-ii., *etc.*, describing the political aims and methods of the 23rd Indian National Congress, in Sanskrit with Tamil commentary.] pp. 46. சென்னை [*Madras*, 1908.] *obl.* 32°. **14060. a. 16.**

BĀLA-SUBRAHMAṆYA KAVI-RĀYAR, *Tiruvāvinaṅguḍi, son of Periyavan Kavi-rāyar.* பழநித் தலபுராண வசனம். [Paṛani-tala-purāṇa-vachanam. A prose paraphrase by P. M. Kanda-sāmi Piḷḷai of the Paṛani-tala-purāṇam or sacred legend of Palni.] pp. xvi. 285, ii. சென்னை [*Madras,*] 1905. 12°. **14170. dd. 2.**

BĀṆA. Kadambari in Tamil [being part of a translation, in 1314 *vṛuttam* stanzas, of Bāṇa's Sanskrit romance "Kādambarī"] by Adivarahakavi († a Vaishnava Brahmin of the Chola kingdom who flourished 490 years ago). Edited by . . . P. R. Krishnamachariar. pp. i. i. 23. *Madura,* 1907. 8°. **14171. e. 2.**

BAṄKIM-CHANDRA CHAṬṬŌPĀDHYĀYA. ஆநந்தமடம். [Ānanda-maṭham. An historical novel. Translated from the Bengali by Mahēṣa-kumāra Ṣarmā. With a preface by G. Subrahmaṇya Aiyar.] pp. xvi. 251, vii. சென்னை [*Madras,*] 1908. 12°. **14171. d. 11.**

BAṄKIM-CHANDRA CHAṬṬŌPĀDHYĀYA. அந்தப்புரரகசியம் ௵ (Secrets of Zenana, or Anthappura Rahasyam. [A novel] by M. Ramalinga Mudalyar[, pt. i., or ch. 1-21, being adapted from Baṅkimchandra's Bengali novel Kapāla-kuṇḍalā, and pt. ii., or ch. 22-50, from Dāmōdara Mukhōpādhyāya's Mṛiṇmayī, a sequel to the latter].) pp. i. 180. சென்னை [*Madras,*] 1906. 8°. **14171. e. 20.**

BAṄKIM-CHANDRA CHAṬṬŌPĀDHYĀYA. பரிமளா. (Parimala. A highly interesting detective novel of Bankim Chandra Chatterjee. Translated [from Bengali into Tamil] by T. V. Krishnasawmy Sastri.) pp. x. 128. *Madras,* 1907. 8°. **14171. e. 3.**

Forms no. 2 of the Neethi Bothini Series.

BIBLE.—Old Testament.—*Psalms.* Book of Psalms. ஞானசங்கீதங்களின் புஸ்தகம். [In Fabricius' version.] pp. 138, 9. *Tranquebar,* 1907. 8°. **14170. b. 56.**

BIBLE.—New Testament.—*Epistles.* ○○○ பிலிப்பியருக்கு எழுதின நிருபத்தின்பேரில் . . . பாயிரமும் வியாக்கியானக் குறிப்புகளும். [Philippians. With commentary and introduction by T. Walker. Translated by the latter and J. David from the English.] pp. iii. 256; 1 *plate. S.P.C.K. Press: Vepery, Madras,* 1908. 12°. **14170. bbb. 16.**

BRĀHMA SAMĀJ. *See* [Addenda] Nara-simmalu Nāyuḍu. A brief History & Principles of the Southrn [*sic*] Indian Brama Samajams. 1908. 8°. **14170. eee. 33.**

CEYLON. History of Ceylon. இலங்கைச்சரித்திரம் . .˙. By a Brother of St. Joseph's, Colombogam. Second edition. pp. 204. *Jaffna,* 1907. 12°. **14172. g. 13.**

CHURCH MISSIONARY SOCIETY. *See* Jaffna.

DĀMŌDARA MUKHŌPĀDHYĀYA. *See* [Addenda] Baṅkim-chandra Chaṭṭōpādhyāya. அந்தப்புரரகசியம் ஆ (Secrets of Zenana . . . [A novel] by M. Ramalinga Mudalyar[, pt. i. being adapted from Baṅkim-chandra's Kapāla-kuṇḍalā, and pt. ii. from Dāmōdara's Mṛiṇmayī, a sequel to the latter].) 1906. 8°. **14171. e. 20.**

DAVID (Joseph), *of Mengnanapuram. See* [Addenda] Bible.—New Testament.—*Epistles.* ○○○ பிலிப்பியருக்கு . . . நிருப ஆ [Philippians. With commentary, *etc.*, by T. Walker. Translated by the latter and J. David from the English.] 1908. 12°. **14170. bbb. 16.**

DAVID (Joseph), *of Mengnanapuram. See* Indian Christians. Sketches of South Indian Christians . . . [Translated by J. David from the English.] 1896. 12°. **14171. a. 14.**

DAVID (Joseph), *of Mengnanapuram. See* Indian Christians. Sketches of Indian Christians, *etc.* 1897. 12°. **14171. a. 22.**

DHARMA-RĀJA DĪKSHITAR. ○○○ வேதாந்தபரிபாஷை. [Vēdānta-paribhāshai. An account of the principles of Vedantic monism. Translated from the Sanskrit of Dharma-rāja by Vishṇupuram Ş. Rāma-chandra Şāstri, and revised by G. Vaḍivēlu Cheṭṭi and M. Shaṇmukha Mudaliyār.] pp. i. iv. iv. 168. சென்னை [*Madras,*] 1907. 16°. **14170. dd. 18.**

ĒKĀMBARA MUDALIYĀR, *Şeñji.* சித்தர்ரஹஸ்யமென்னும் ஆரூட அலங்காரம் ஆ [Ārūḍha-alaṅkāram, or Siddhar-rahasyam. A compilation of verses on divination from the position of planets, flight of birds, *etc.*, ascribed to the legendary Siddhars, with prose interpretation.] pp. ii. 180. சென்னை [*Madras,*] 1907. 8°. **14171. g. 13.**

ĒKĀMBARA MUDALIYĀR, *Şeñji.* நளச்சக்ரவர்த்தி அம்மானை என்னும் தமயந்திமாலை. [Damayanti-mālai, or Naḷa-chakravartti-ammānai. A poem in *ammānai* metre on the epic legend of the loves of Nala and Damayantī. Edited by S. Şinna-sāmi Piḷḷai.] pp. 144. *Madras,* 1906. 8°. **14172. c. 26.**

EPHEMERIDES. A Tamil-English Cycle Calendar of 200 years, 1800 to 2000. By L. Rangasamy Raju . . . தமிழ்-இங்கிலீஷ் சைகில் காலண்டர். pp. ii. 32. *Madura,* 1907. 8°. **14172. i. 16.(3.)**

FABRICIUS (Johann Philipp). *See* [Addenda] Bible.—Old Testament.—*Psalms.* Book of Psalms, . . . [In Fabricius' version.] 1907. 8°. **14170. b. 56.**

GAṆA-PATI-DĀSAR. நெஞ்சறிவிளக்கம். [Neñj'-aṟi-viḷakkam. A poem on Şaiva theosophy, ascribed to a legendary Gaṇa-pati-dāsar.] pp. 12. *See* Siddhargaḷ. ○○○ பெரிய ஞானக்கோவை [Pęriya-ñāna-kōvai.] 1899. 12°. **14170. ee. 33.**

——— ——— pt. ii. 1906. 12°. **14170. dd. 12.**

GAṆA-PATI-DĀSAR. நெஞ்சறிவிளக்கம் மூலமும்-உரையும். [Neñj'-aṟi-viḷakkam. Edited with interpretation and commentary by M. Vaḍi-vēlu Mudaliyār.] pp. 46. மதருஸ் [*Madras,*] 1906. 8°. **14170. eee. 28.**

GAṆA-PATIYĀ PIḶḶAI, *Şivageṅgai P. See* Rāma-liṅgam Piḷḷai, *M. N.* ஸ்ரீ . . . ஸ்ரீராமர் வனவாசம். [Şrī-rāmar-vana-vāsam. Edited by Gaṇa-patiyā Piḷḷai.] 1907. 8°. **14172. bb. 24.**

GAṄGĀ-PRASĀD, *Mahā-rāj, son of Şiva-dās Tivārī. See* [Addenda] Kōka. Koga Sastiram . . . Translated and compiled from the Sanscrit by . . . Gangaprasad Pandit. 1907. 12°. **14171. f. 7.**

GNANAPRAKASA SWAMY. *See* Ñāna-prakāşa Svāmi.

GŌPĀLĀCHĀRYAR, *K. Śrīnivāsa*, and **MAHĀDĒVA MUDALIYĀR**, *V.* பொருநராற்றுப்படைப்பொருள்விளக்கம். (University of Madras. B.A. Examination of 1907. A critical Study of "Porunarattuppadai.") pp. i. i. 66. *Madras*, 1907. 12°. **14171. d. 2.(3.)**

HIPPOLYTE (J.), *O.M.I.* The Apostle of the Sacred Heart. திருவிருதய அப்போஸ்தலன் ... Edited by Revd. S. Gnana Prakasar. pp. v. 140. *Jaffna*, 1906. 12°. **14170. bbb. 13.**

IḶAIYA-TAMBI, *K.* A Code Mensuration for Training and Boarding Schools. First Stage. அளவைநூல் . . . By K. Iliatamby. pp. i. 37. *Batticaloa*, 1907. 8°. **14172. hh. 21.**

JURJĪ ZAIDĀN. 'கஸ்ஸான் கன்னிகை, சரித்திரம். [Ghassān-kannigai-charitram. Translated from Zaidān's "Fatāt Ghassān" by K. Aḥmad Ghanī Maraikkāyar, and recast into literary style by Taḷavāy M. Ṣinnavāppu Maraikkāyar.] pp. i. 183. சிங்கப்பூர் [*Singapore*,] 1908. 8°. **14170. k. 3.**

KAMBAN. *See* Rāma-liṅgam Piḷḷai, *M. N.* ஸ்ரீ . . . ஸ்ரீராமர் வனவாசம். [Śrī-rāmar-vana-vāsam. A poem based upon the Ayōdhyā-kāṇḍam of Kamban's Rāmāyaṇam.] 1907. 8°. **14172. bb. 24.**

KAMBAN. ஸ்ரீமத்: கம்பராமாயணம் கிஷ்கிந்தாகாண்டம் ஷ [Kamba-rāmāyaṇam, Kishkindhā-kāṇḍam. Edited with a commentary by Ṣ. N. Ponn'-ambala Piḷḷai.] . . . With a prefatory note in English by V. Coomaraswamy. *Jaffna*, 1907, *etc.* 8°. **14172. bb. 25.**

In progress.

KAMBAN. ஸ்ரீமத் கம்பராமாயண வசனம் ஷ [Kamba-rāmāyaṇa-vachanam. A prose paraphrase of Kamban's Rāmāyaṇam.] சென்னை [*Madras*,] 1907, *etc.* 8°. **14172. b. 55.**

In progress.

KANAKA-SABHAI KAVI-RĀYAR, *of Udaiyarpalayam.* திருப்புன்கூர்ப்புராணம். [Tirupunkūr-purāṇam. The legends of the Ṣaiva sanctuary of Tirupunkur, metrically adapted, with prose summaries, from Sanskrit and Tamil sources. Preceded by the local Dēvāram, *etc.*] pp. ii. vi. ix. 142, i. சிதம்பரம் [*Chidambaram*,] 1907. 8°. **14170. eee. 27.**

KANDAR. ° ° ° கந்தராரூடம் [Kandar-ārūḍham. A metrical treatise on astrological divination, purporting to have been conveyed by the god Subrahmaṇya to Agastyar. Pt. i., with an appendix called Kūpa-ṣāstram, on auspicious conditions for digging wells.] pt. i. pp. 42, 6. திருச்சிறுப்பள்ளி [*Trichinopoli*,] 1907. 8°. **14171. g. 17.**

KANDA-SĀMI KAVI-RĀYAR, *Uḍumalaipēṭṭai M. Rāma-sāmi, of Settur.* அரிமழத்தலபுராணம். மூலமும் குறிப்புரையும். [Arimaḻa-tala-purāṇam. The legends of the Ṣaiva sanctuary of Arimalam in verse, with glossary. Edited by Ṣ. R. Subrahmaṇya Kavi-rāyar.] pp. iv. i. i. 133, 24, 2. மதுரை [*Madura*,] 1907. 8°. **14170. eee. 32.**

KAṆṆA-DĀSAN. ஸ்ரீமகாபாரத ஆதிபர்வ ஓடம். [Ādi-parva-ōḍam. A poetical epitome of the Ādi-parvam of the Mahā-bhāratam in the form of an *ōḍam* or boat-song.] pp. 42. சென்னை [*Madras*,] 1907. 12°. **14172. a. 52.(3.)**

KANN'-AIYA NĀYUḌU, *Vēlūr.* காசிராமேஸ்வர மஜிலிக்கதை. [Kāṣi-rāmēṣvara-majili-kathai. A series of moral and religious stories interwoven into an account of Benares, Ramnad, and other holy places, for the instruction of pilgrims.] pp. 4, 224. *Madras*, 1908. 8°. **14171. e. 21.**

KANN'-AIYA NĀYUḌU, *Vēlūr.* பெரிய பொப்பிலிராஜன்கதை [Periya Bobbili-rājan-kathai. A poetical history of the Rajas of the *zamindari* of Bobbili. A Tamil version by Kann'-aiya from the Telugu.] pp. 100. *Madras*, 1907. 8°. **14171. a. 28.**

KĀṢI-VIṢVANĀTHA MUDALIYĀR, *Ṣaidāpuram.* மேகவெள்ளைக்கு மேலானபரிகாரம். [Mēha-veḷḷaikku mēl-āna parihāram. A tract on the cure of syphilitic diseases.] pp. 21. *Madras*, 1869. 16°. **14170. i. 2.(2.)**

KASTŪRI-RAṄG'-AYYAR, *A. Sītā-rāma.* ஸ்ரீ மஹாபாரதவினாவிடை. [Mahā-bhārata-vinā-viḍai. A catechism of the Mahā-bhāratam.] *Madras*, 1908, *etc.* 8°. **14171. e. 22.**

In progress.

KŌKA. Koga Sastiram. Or Treatment for barrenness in the womb. [In 8 chapters.] . . . Translated and compiled from the Sanscrit by Maharaj

Gangaprasad Pandit. (கோஹசாஸ்திரம்.) pp. 3, 4, 6, ii. xviii. 334; 1 plate. *Colombo*, 1907. 12°. **14171. f. 7.**

Ch. 2-8 *have each a separate roman pagination, beside the running Tamil numeration.*

KŌNĒRIY-APPA MUDALIYĀR, *Kāñchīpuram.* உபதேசகாண்டம். [Upadēṣa-kāṇḍam. An appendix in prose to Kachiy-appar's Kanda-purāṇam.] 1891. *See* ITIHĀSA-MAÑJARI. Ithihasa Manjari Series. [1888]-1894. 8°. **14172. d. 11.**

KṚUSHṆA AIYAR, *T. S., of St. Joseph's College, Trichinopoli.* The "District Geography" Series. In four parts. (*பூகோள சாஸ்திரம்.) *Trichinopoly,* 1908, *etc.* 8°. **14172. g. 14.**

In progress.

KṚUSHṆAM-ĀCHĀRYAR, *P. R.* *See* [Addenda] BĀṆA. Kadambari ... by Adivarahakavi. Edited by ... Krishnamachariar. 1907. 8°. **14171. e. 2.**

KṚUSHṆAM-ĀCHĀRYA SVĀMI, *Tirumalai Nallān Chakravartti.* *See* [Addenda] AḺAGIYA-MAṆAVĀḶA PERU-MĀḶ. ○ ○ ○ ஸ்ரீ . . . உபதேசரத்தினமாலை [Upadēṣa-ratna-mālai. Edited by Kṛushṇam-āchāryar.] 1907. 8°. **14170. eee. 34.**

KṚUSHṆA-SĀMI ṢĀSTRI, *T. V.* *See* [Addenda] BAṄKIM-CHANDRA CHAṬṬŌPĀDHYĀYA. பரிமளா. (Parimala ... Translated by T. V. Krishnasawmy Sastri.) 1907. 8°. **14171. e. 3.**

KUMĀRA-SVĀMI (*Sir* MUTTU). *See* MUTTU-KUMĀRA-SVĀMI, *Knight.*

KUMĀRA-SVĀMI MUDALIYĀR, *Ā. K., of Sorūpānanda Sabhā, Tirupattur.* *See* TIRU-TAKKA DĒVAR. ○ ○ ○ சீவக சிந்தாமணி ஸ்ரீ (Jeevaga Chinthamani, *etc.*) [A prose paraphrase by Kumāra-svāmi.] 1907. 8°. **14171. e. 23.(1.)**

KUMARĒṢAN (*Mrs. G.*), *of Govt. Hindu Girls' School, Salem.* Sundaravalli, a Tamil novel ... சுந்தரவல்லி ஸ்ரீ. pp. 216. *Madras,* 1907. 12°. **14171. d. 12.**

KŪPAM. கூபசாஸ்திரம். [Kūpa-ṣāstram. A tract on auspicious conditions for digging wells.] pp. 6. *See* [Addenda] KANDAR. ○ ○ ○ கந்தாரூடம் [Kandar-ārūḍham.] pt. i. 1907. 8°. **14171. g. 17.**

LADD (T. C.). *See* ṢELL'-AIYĀ PIḶḶAI, *M. T.*

LITURGIES.—ROME, *Church of.* ஞானாமிர்தம் ஸ்ரீ [Ñānāmirtam. A manual of Roman Catholic devotions, with Catechism.] pp. 201; 6 *plates.* புதுவை தூஅறூஅ [*Pondicherry,* 1858.] 16°. **14170. a. 22.**

LITURGIES.—ROME, *Church of.* ஞானாமிர்ததடாகம். [Ñānāmirta-taḍāgam. A book of Roman Catholic devotions, comprising lists of festivals, prayers for various occasions, Shorter Catechism, *etc.*] pp. xlix. 779; 4 *plates.* புதுவை தூஅாறூஅ [*Pondicherry,* 1858.] 16°. **14170. a. 30.**

Apparently translated or edited by P. Louis, a native priest; see Histoire des Missions Étrangères, vol. iv., p. 580. It includes most of the contents of the Ñānāmirtam.

LITURGIES.—ROME, *Church of.* Responses and Chants [in Latin]. For High Mass, Vespers, and Benediction. Transliterated into Tamil. பாடற் பூசை, மாலையாராதனை, ஆசிர்வாதம் இவைகளிலே லத்தீனிற் பாடுகின்ற பிரதியுத்தரங்களும் பாடல்களும். [With an appendix of devotions in Tamil.] pp. 128, iii. *Jaffna,* 1907. 16°. **14170. a. 50.**

LITURGIES.—ROME, *Church of.* செபரத்தினம். [Ṣeba-ratnam. Prayers and devotional readings. Edited by V. M. Lōpp'-aiyā. Second edition.] pp. 136. *Jaffna,* 1907. 32°. **14170. a. 63.**

LITURGIES.—WESLEYAN METHODISTS. உவெஸ்லியன் மெதொடிஸ்த சபையாரின் தேவாராதனைப் புத்தகம். Prayer and Service Book. pp. i. 103. *Batticaloa,* 1907. 8°. **14170. b. 58.**

LITURGIES.—WESLEYAN METHODISTS. உவெஸ்லியன் மெதொடிஸ்த சபையாரின் தேவாராதனைப் புத்தகம். [The Order for Morning Prayer and Lord's Supper.] pp. 29. *Batticaloa,* 1907. 8°. **14170. bb. 16.**

LŌPP'-AIYĀ, *V. M.* *See* [Addenda] LITURGIES.—Rome, *Church of.* செபரத்தினம். [Ṣeba-ratnam. Edited by Lōpp'-aiyā.] 1907. 32°. **14170. a. 63.**

MAHĀ-BHĀRATAM. *See* [Addenda] BĀLA-SUBRAHMAṆYA BRAHMA-SVĀMI. காங்கிரெஸ் கீதை ஸ்ரீ (Congress Gita, *etc.*) [A parody of the Bhagavad-gītā, describing the 23rd Indian National Congress.] [1908.] *obl.* 32°. **14060. a. 16.**

MAHĀ-BHĀRATAM. *See* [Addenda] KAṆṆA-DĀSAN. ஸ்ரீ . . . ஆதிபர்வ ஓடம். [Ādi-parva-ōḍam. A poetical epitome of the Ādi-parvam.] 1907. 12°. **14172. a. 52.(3.)**

MAHĀ-BHĀRATAM. *See* [Addenda] KASTŪRI-RANG'-AYYAR, *A. S.* ஸ்ரீ மஹாபாரத ஷ [Mahā-bhārata-vinā-vidai. A catechism of the Mahā-bhāratam.] 1908, *etc.* 8°. **14171. e. 22.**

MAHĀ-BHĀRATAM. *See* [Addenda] RĀGHAVA-MŪRTTI, *P.* விலாடபர்வ ஷ [Mādu-bidi-ṣandai, or Vilāḍa-parva-nāṭakam.] 1907. 8°. **14171. k. 6.**

MAHĀ-BHĀRATAM. ஸ்ரீகிருஷ்ணபகவான் திருவாய்மலர்ந்தருளிய அநுகீதை. [Anugītā. A supplement to the Bhagavad-gītā, forming ch. 16-51 of the Aṣva-mēdha-parva. Translated from the Sanskrit by Bāla-sarasvati Nārāyaṇa Sudarṣana.] pp. viii. iv. 216. சென்னை [*Madras,*] 1907. 16°. **14049. aa. 8.(1.)**

MAHĀ-BHĀRATAM. The Bhagavad Gita. A metrical translation into Tamil by S. Muthu Iyer ... ஸ்ரீ பகவத்கீதை வெண்பா. pp. 12, iii. 256. *Madras,* 1907. 12°. **14172. a. 67.**

MAHĀ-DĒVA MUDALIYĀR, *V.* *See* [Addenda] GŌPĀLĀCHĀRYAR, *K. Ṣ.*, and MAHĀ-DĒVA MUDALIYĀR, *V.* பொருநராற்றுப்படை ஷ (University of Madras ... A critical Study of "Porunarattup-padai.") 1907. 12°. **14171. d. 2.(3.)**

MAHĒṢA-KUMĀRA ṢARMĀ. *See* [Addenda] BAṄKIM-CHANDRA CHAṬṬŌPĀDHYĀYA. ஆநந்தமடம். [Ānanda-maṭham. Translated by Mahēṣa-kumāra.] 1908. 12°. **14171. d. 11.**

MAHĒṢA-KUMĀRA ṢARMĀ. *See* [Addenda] PRABHĀTA-KUMĀRA MUKHŌPĀDHYĀYA. நிர்மலா ஷ [Nirmalā. Translated by Mahēṣa-kumāra.] 1907. 12°. **14171. d. 1.(4.)**

MARAI-ÑĀNA-SAMBANDHAR, *Tiruvāvaḍuḍurai.* சைவசமய நெறி. [Ṣaiva-samaya-neri. An exposition of the Ṣaiva system of theology. With a commentary by Āru-muga Nāvalar. Second edition.] pp. 322, viii. சென்னபட்டணம் பவ [*Madras,* 1875.] 12°. **14172. a. 14.**

MASTĀN ṠĀHIB ('ABD al-KĀDIR), *Kuṇaṅguḍi.* ° ° ° மஸ்தான்சாகிபு அவர்கள் பாடல் [Pādal. With a paraphrase and commentary by M. Vaḍi-vēlu Mudaliyār.] pp. ii. 14, 451. மதருஸ் [*Madras,*] 1908. 8°. **14172. bb. 27.**

MOSES. Moses, the pious Negro ... விசுவாசபக்தி. [Translated from an American tract, reprinted by the London Tract Society as no. 257.] Second edition. pp. 8. *Jaffna,* 1844. 12°. **14170. b. 1.(21.)**

MṚUGĒṢA UPĀDHYĀYAR, *Ṣandiruppāy K.* *See* SĀMI-NĀTHA MUDALIYĀR, *M.A.* இராம நாடகம். [Rāma-nāṭakam. Edited by Mṛugēṣa.] 1896. 8°. **14170. l. 37.(1.)**

MUḌATTĀMA-KAṈṈIYĀR. *See* [Addenda] GŌPĀLĀCHĀRYAR, *K.Ṣ.*, and MAHĀ-DĒVA MUDALIYĀR, *V.* பொருநராற்றுப்படை ஷ (University of Madras ... A critical Study of "Porunarattuppadai.") 1907. 12°. **14171. d. 2.(3.)**

MUḤAMMAD 'ABD ALLĀH, *son of Bāburājapuram Bāwā Ṡāhib.* *See* [Addenda] AGASTYAR. அகஸ்தியர் பள்ளு. [Agastyar-paḷḷu. Edited with paraphrase by Muḥ. 'Abd Allāh.] 1907. 12°. **14171. g. 14.**

MUḤAMMAD 'ABD ALLĀH, *son of Bāburājapuram Bāwā Ṡāhib.* *See* [Addenda] AGASTYAR. இலக்க சௌமியசாகரம் ஷ [Ilakka-saumya-sāgaram. Edited by Muḥ. 'Abd Allāh.] 1907. 12°. **14171. g. 15.**

MUḤYI al-DĪN ibn ḤAMĪD MUḤYI al-DĪN, *K.M., of Nagur.* ஆலிமுல்பாஸிக்கீன் ஜாஹிலுல் முஷாயிக்கீன் ஷ ['Ālim al-fāsikīn jāhil al-mushā'ikhīn. Verses deriding certain worthless pretenders to learning.] pp. 8. கொழும்பு சென்னை [*Colombo, Madras* printed,] 1906. 8°. **14173. b. 28.(7.)**

MUḤYI al-DĪN ḤUSAIN ibn ZAIN al-'ĀBIDĪN. *See* VIVĒKA-SĀGARAM. விவேகசாகரம். [Vivēka-sāgaram. Stylistically revised by Muḥyi al-Dīn.] [1858.] 8°. **14172. c. 11**

MUNI-SĀMI MUDALIYĀR, *Ṣirumaṇavūr.* The Parimala Sastram ... சுகந்தபரிமளசாஸ்திரம் ஷ [Sugandha-parimaḷa-ṣāstram. A treatise on the preparation of perfumes and essences for food, toilette, and medicine.] சென்னை [*Madras,*] 1907, *etc.* 8°. **14171. g. 16.**
In progress.

MUNI-SĀMI MUDALIYĀR, *Ṣūlai.* *See* [Addenda] APPĀ-SĀMI CHEṬṬI. வாலிமோட்ச ஷ [Vāli-mōksha-nāṭakam. Edited by Muni-sāmi.] 1908. 8°. **14170. l. 30.(3.)**

MUNI-SĀMI MUDALIYĀR, *Ṣūḷai*. *See* [Addenda] Rāghava-mūrtti, *P*. மாடுபிடிசண்டை ஷூ [Māḍu-biḍi-ṣaṇḍai. Edited by Muui-sāmi.] 1907. 8°. **14171. k. 6.**

MUTTU AIYAR, *Tirunayam S*. *See* [Addenda] Mahā-bhāratam. The Bhagavad Gita. A metrical translation . . . by S. Muthu Iyer, *etc*. 1907. 12°. **14172. a. 67.**

MUTTU-KRUSHṆA NĀYUḌU, *Ṣ., of Triplicane*. *See* [Addenda] Aṟagiya-maṇavāḷa Peru-māḷ. ००० ஸ்ரீ . . . உபதேசரத்தினமாலை [Upadēṣa-ratna-mālai. Edited by Muttu-krushṇa.] 1907. 8°. **14170. eee. 34.**

MUTTU-KRUSHṆA NĀYUḌU, *Ṣ., of Triplicane*. *See* Vālmīki. அபயப்ரதாநஸார ஷூ [Tani-ṣlōkam. Edited by Muttu-krushṇa.] [1901.] 8°. **14065. bbb. 6.**

—— —— [1901.] 8°. **14065. bbb. 7.**

NACHINĀRKK'-INIYAR, *Bhāradvāji, of Madura*. *See* Tiru-takka Dēvar. ००० சீவகசிந்தாமணி ஷூ [Jīvaka-chintāmaṇi. With Nachinārkk'-iniyar's commentary.] 1907. 8°. **14172. bb. 28.**

ÑĀNA-PRAKĀṢA SVĀMI, *Ṣ., O.M.I.* *See* [Addenda] Antony, *St*. St. Anthony of Padua . . . Revised by . . . Gnanaprakasa Swamy. 1907. 12°. **14170. bbb. 14.**

ÑĀNA-PRAKĀṢA SVĀMI, *Ṣ., O.M.I.* *See* [Addenda] Hippolyte (J.). The Apostle of the Sacred Heart ... Edited by ... Gnana Prakasar. 1906. 12°. **14170. bbb. 13.**

ÑĀNA-PRAKĀṢA SVĀMI, *Ṣ., O.M.I.* Idolatry & Image-worship. விக்கிரகாராதனையும் சுரூப வணக்கமும். By Revd. S. Gnana Prakasar. (Catholic Tract no. 7.) pp. 14. *Jaffna*, [1906.] 8°. **14170. bb. 17.**

NARA-SIMMALU NĀYUḌU, *Sēlam Pagaḍāla*. A brief History and Principles of the Southrn [*sic*] Indian Brama Samajams (*தக்ஷிண இந்தியாவிலுள்ள பிரஹ்மசமாஜங்களின் சரித்திர சாரசங்கிரஹம்). pp. viii. 4, viii. x. 112. *Coimbatore*, 1908. 8°. **14170. eee. 33.**

NĀRĀYAṆA-DĀSAR, *Puduvai, disciple of Tirukōvalūr Ṣrīnivāsāchāryar*. *See* Veṅkaṭādri Svāmi, *A*. ஸ்ரீ . . . ஸ்ரீஹரிநாம ஷூ [Hari-nāma-saṅkīrt-tanaigaḷ. Translated by Nārāyaṇa-dāsar.] 1907. 12°. **14170. dd. 17.**

NĀRĀYAṈ'-AIYAṄGĀR, *T., of the Sētu-pati's Academy*. அநுமான விளக்கம். [Anumāna-viḷakkam. A tract on logical inference.] pp. 47. 1905. *See* Academies, *etc*.—*Madura*. ["Ṣen-damiṟ" supplement.] no. 9. 1902, *etc*. 8°. **14172. i. 1.*(no. 9.)**

NĀRĀYAṆA-SĀMI MUDALIYĀR, *C. K., of Ṣāradā-vilāsa Ṣen-damiṟ Saṅgham, Coimbatore*. பொய்யாமொழிப் புலவர் சரிதம். [Poyyā-moṟi-pulavar-charitam. A biographical and critical essay on Poyyā-moṟi Pulavar.] (தீஞ்சுவைப்பொக்கிஷம் இலக்கம். ௪.) pp. 18. சென்னை [*Madras*,] 1908. 8°. **14171. a. 53.(4.)**

NĀRĀYAṆA SUDARṢANA, *Kumbhaghōṇam* (Bāla-sarasvati). *See* [Addenda] Mahā-bhāratam. ஸ்ரீ . . . அநுகீதை. [Anugītā. Edited by Nārāyaṇa Sudarṣana.] 1907. 16°. **14049. aa. 8.(1.)**

PERCIVAL (Peter). Prayers for the use of Christian Families, with an essay on family religion, and a table of lessons for family worship. (*குடும்பப்பிரார்த்தனைமாலை.) pp. vii. 191, xiv. *Jaffna Religious Tract Society: Jaffna*, 1846. 8°. **14170. c. 19.**

PIḶḶAI LŌKAM-JĪYAR. *See* [Addenda] Aṟagiya-maṇavāḷa Peru-māḷ. ००० ஸ்ரீ . . . உபதேசரத்தினமாலை [Upadēṣa-ratna-mālai. With commentary by Piḷḷai Lōkam-jīyar ("Lōkārya-jīyar").] 1907. 8°. **14170. eee. 34.**

PONN'-AMBALA PIḶḶAI, *Ṣāvagachēri N*. *See* [Addenda] Kamban. ஸ்ரீமத் கம்பராமாயணம் ஷூ [Kamba-rāmāyaṇam, Kishkindhā-kāṇḍam. Edited with commentary by Ponn'-ambalar,] *etc*. 1907, *etc*. 8°. **14172. bb. 25.**

POYYĀ-MOṞI PULAVAR. [*Life*.] *See* [Addenda] Nārāyaṇa-sāmi Mudaliyār, *C.K.* பொய்யாமொழிப் புலவர் ஷூ [Poyyā-moṟi-pulavar-charitam.] 1908. 8°. **14171. a. 53.(4.)**

PRABHĀTA-KUMĀRA MUKHŌPĀDHYĀYA. நிர்மலா அல்லது ஒரு பத்திராசிரியரின் விடுமுறை. [Nirmalā. A story of modern life. Translated into Tamil by Mahēṣa-kumāra Ṣarmā from the Bengali.] pp. 21. சென்னை [*Madras*,] 1907. 12°. **14171. d. 1.(4.)**

RĀGHAVA-MŪRTTI, *Pāṇāmbaṭṭi.* விலாடபர்வ-நாடகமென்னும் மாடுபிடி சண்டை. [Māḍu-biḍi-ṣaṇḍai, or Vilāḍa-parva-nāṭakam. A drama on the episode of the cattle-raid in the Virāṭa-parvam of the Mahā-bhāratam, cantos xxv. foll. Edited by Ṣūḷai Muni-sāmi Mudaliyār.] pp. 120. சென்னை [*Madras,*] 1907. 8°. **14171. k. 6.**

RĀJA-RATNAM PILḶAI, *T. A., of Madras Christian College.* Panmanikkottu . . . A new Tamil poetical anthology . . . பன்மணிக்கொத்து . . . Compiled by T. A. Rajaruthnam Pillai. *Madras,* 1908, *etc.* 12°. **14172. a. 65.**

In progress.

RĀMA-CHANDRA ṢĀSTRI, *Vishṇupuram Ṣ.* *See* [Addenda] DHARMA-RĀJA DĪKSHITAR. ◦◦◦ வேதாந்தபரிபாஷை. [Vēdānta-paribhāshai. Translated by Rāma-chandra.] 1907. 16°. **14170. dd. 18.**

RĀMĀNUJĀCHĀRYAR, *Māḍabhūshi Tarka-tīrtha.* *See* [Addenda] ĀṚVĀRGAḶ.—Nāl-āyiram.—*Selections.* ◦◦◦ நித்யாநுசந்தாநம். [Nityānusandhānam. With interpretation *etc.* by Rāmānujāchāryar.] 1907. 8°. **14170. eee. 31.**

RĀMĀNUJĀCHĀRYAR, *Māḍabhūshi Tarka-tīrtha.* *See* VĀLMĪKI. அபயப்ரதாநஸார ஷ [Tani-ṣlōkam. With notes by Rāmānujāchāryar. Edited by the latter.] [1901.] 8°. **14065. bbb. 6.**

—— —— [1901.] 8°. **14065. bbb. 7.**

RĀMA-SĀMI NĀYUḌU, *Kāñchipuram.* *See* TIRU-MUṚAI.—*Dēvāram.* ◦◦◦ தேவார ஷ [Dēvāra-tiraṭṭu. Edited by Rāma-sāmi.] 1906. 8°. **14170. eee. 30.**

RAṄGA-SĀMI RĀJU, *L.* *See* [Addenda] EPHEMERIDES. A Tamil-English Cycle Calendar of 200 years . . . By L. Rangasamy Raju, *etc.* 1907. 8°. **14172. i. 16.(3.)**

ROBERTS (JOSEPH). True Doctrine, *etc.* 1843. 12°. *See* WINSLOW (M.) and ROBERTS (J.). **14170. b. 1.(4.)**

SAMBANDHA MUDALIYĀR, *T.* *See* TĀYUMĀNAVAR. தாயுமான . . . பாடல். [Tiru-pāḍaṯ-ṯiraṭṭu. With commentary *etc.* by Sambandha Mudaliyār.] 1891. 8°. **14172. c. 39.(vol. 1.)**

SĀMINĀTH'-AIYAR, *Uttamadānapuram V., of Madras Presidency College.* *See* TIRU-TAKKA DĒVAR. ◦◦◦ சீவகசிந்தாமணி ஷ. [Jīvaka-chintāmaṇi. Edited by Sāmināth'-aiyar.] 1907. 8°. **14172. bb. 28.**

SĀMINĀTH'-AIYAR, *Uttamadānapuram V., of Madras Presidency College.* *See* TOL-KĀPPIYA DĒVAR. ◦◦◦ திருப்பாதிரிப்புலியூர்க்கலம்பகம். [Tirupādiri-puliyūr-kalambakam. Edited by Sāmināth'-aiyar.] 1908. 8°. **14170. ee. 5.(3.)**

ṢARA-VAṆA PERU-MĀḶ AIYAR, *Tirutaṇigai Kandapp'-aiyar.* [For editions of the Kuṛaḷ followed by the Tiru-vaḷḷuva-mālai with Ṣara-vaṇa Peru-māḷ's commentary :] *See* TIRU-VAḶḶUVAR.

ṢENDINĀTH'-AIYAR, *Kāṣi-vāsi.* வைதிக சுத்தாத்துவித சைவசித்தாந்ததத்துவப்பட வினா-விடை. [Ṣaiva-siddhānta-tattva-paṭa-vinā-viḍai. A catechism of the Ṣuddhādvita system of Ṣaiva theology as synoptically represented in the author's Table of the latter.] pp. 87. திருமங்கலம் [*Tirumangalam,*] 1908. 8°. **14170. eee. 35.**

ṢENDINĀTH'-AIYAR, *Kāṣi-vāsi.* ஸ்ரீசீகாழிப் பெருவாழ்வின் சீவகாருண்ணியமாட்சி. [Ṣigāṛi-peruvāṛvin jīva-kāruṇya-māṭṣi. A defence of the Ṣaiva apostle Ñāna-sambandhar, who according to legend impaled 7000 Jains, against the charge of cruelty raised by a writer in the journal "Aṛivu-viḷakkam" of Trivandrum.] pp. 28. திருமங்கலம் ககூ௦ள [*Tirumangalam,* 1907.] 8°. **14170. c. 29.(3.)**

SHAKSPERE (WILLIAM). Shakespeare's Romeo and Juliet (*ரம்யனும் ஜொலியேத்தையும்). An adaptation in Tamil by S. V. Srinivasiar. pp. xiv. i. 116. *Madras,* 1908. 12°. **14171. i. 2.(3.)**

SOLOMON (*Mrs.* PAUL). *See* [Addenda] ANB'-AMMĀḶ PAUL.

ṢRĪNIVĀS'-AYYAR, *S. V., of Mailapur.* *See* [Addenda] SHAKSPERE (W.). Shakespeare's Romeo and Juliet. An adaptation . . . by S. V. Srinivasiar. 1908. 12°. **14171. i. 2.(3.)**

SUBRAHMAṆYA AIYAR, *Gaṇa-pati, Editor of "Svadēṣa-mitran."* Speeches & Essays of celebrated Indians on Swadesism and Swaraj. pp. 164. *Madras,* 1907. 12°. **14170. g. 29.**

CORRIGENDA.

Col.	Line
7	6 from top. After "R. Rāghav'-aiyaṅgār" add "and M. Rāghav'-aiyaṅgār."
10	8 from bottom. For "Vaidya-ratna-ṣurukkam" read "Vaidya-ratna-churukkam."
14	10 from bottom. For Ārāva-mud'-āchāryar read Ārāv'-amud'-āchāryar.
19	5 from bottom. Add after "king" the words "Kṛushṇa Rāya (died 1529)."
28	23 from top. Read **ĀRŌGYAM PIḶḶAI.**
30	13 from top. For "Ñāna-sambandhar" read "[Addenda] Maṟai-ñāna-sambandhar."
42	27 from top. Add the following footnote: Contains only the first 340 stanzas.
59	7 from top. Add: [by J. Evarts].
77	12 from bottom. Read "pp. 4, 4, ii. 6, 883, iv. சென்னை [*Madras*,] 1907. 8°." Delete footnote.
77	21-29 from top. Delete these two entries, and see col. 331 (**ṢIṬṬAMBALA-TAMBIRĀN SVĀMI**).
96	11-12 from top. Read "Theologia."
96	17 from top. Add: [Edited by H. Cordes and K. Graul.]
103	19 from top. Add to the list of headings *Ṣaṅkarāchāryar*.
109	4 from bottom. Add the following footnote: This edition of 1723 was the third. The first, containing 48 hymns, appeared in 1713, the second in 1721. The fourth edition, 1733, was edited by Pressier and Walther; the sixth appeared in 1779. The new hymnal of Fabricius (336 hymns) was first printed at Madras in 1774 (second edition 1797, third 1820, fourth 1825); an appendix (58 hymns) was printed at Tranquebar in 1786, another in 1787.
120	22 from top. This "poem of one hundred stanzas on the character of Christ" is by J. R. Arnold, and should therefore have been catalogued in col. 27. See Addenda (col. 448).
126	12 from top. Read Tiruvēṟkāḍu.
131	4 and 8 from bottom. Kaṇṇ'-aiya-dāsar is identical with Kaṇṇ'-aiya Nāyuḍu.
162	8 from top. Read "pp. 580, ii. *Madras*, 1907. 8°." Delete the following footnote.
175	23 from top. Read "J. M. N. Schwarz."
179	15 from bottom. For **MUDATTĀMA** read **MUḌATTĀMA.**
189	22-25. This article should be under the heading **MĀRKAṆḌA MUNI-SĀMI PIḶḶAI**, col. 170.
192	2 from top. For "no. 18" read "no. 14."
197	14 from top. For "1906, *etc.*" read "1907."
216	4-7 from bottom. This article should be under the heading **RICHMOND** (Legh).
225	17 and 18 from bottom. For "no. 10" read "no. 8."
229	6-8 from top. Delete this entry.
235	24 from top. Add "vol. i. 1—vol. xv. 7." In line 25 alter "1886, *etc.*" to "1886-1901." Delete the footnote on line 26. No more of this publication has been issued.
236	5 from top. Add: Edited by W. T. Satyanāthan.
241	11 from top. For [1899, *etc.*] read [1901.]
333	15 from top. For **14172** read **14170.**

INDEXES.

The references in this Index are to the names of authors or other headings under which the works are catalogued. Anonymous works catalogued under their titles are designated by the phrase in loco.

I. GENERAL INDEX OF TITLES.

[*The titles enclosed within square brackets are those in which the names of the works mentioned are transliterated literally, the consonants and sibilants being given in the hard and simple forms in which they are actually written in Tamil, without regard to the modifications that may occur in pronunciation.*]

II. SELECT SUBJECT-INDEX.

The classification is as follows:—

ARTS AND SCIENCES.

1. AGRICULTURE.

2. ASTRONOMY AND ASTROLOGY.

3. DECORATIVE ARTS.

4. MEDICINE, PHYSIOLOGY, SURGERY, AND HYGIENE.

5. MUSIC.

6. OCCULT ARTS, DIVINATION, ETC.

7. PHYSICAL SCIENCE AND NATURAL HISTORY.

8. OTHER ARTS AND SCIENCES.

Tamiẓ-ṣurukk'-eẓuttu (The Tamil Short-hand). Hari-kṛushṇa Paḍaiyāchi.

BIBLIOGRAPHY.

Alphabetical Index of Manuscripts. Madras, *City of.—Government Oriental MSS. Library.*

Catalogue ... of Oriental Manuscripts in the library of the late College, Fort St. George. Taylor (W.).

Classified Catalogue of Tamil printed Books. Murdoch (J.).

Classified Catalogue of the Public Reference Library. Madras, *City of.*

Examination and Analysis of the Mackenzie Manuscripts. Taylor (W.).

Manuscrits tamouls. Academies, *etc.—Paris.*

Report on a Search for ... Manuscripts. Madras, *Presidency of.*

CASTE AND ETHNOGRAPHY.

Balijavāru-purāṇam (Nāyaḍugāru-saṃsthāna-charitram). Nara-simmalu Nāyuḍu.

Caste (Jāti-vittiyāṣa-viḷakkam). Bower (H.).

Dēvāṅga-purāṇam. Dēvāṅgar.

History of the Sourashtras (Saurāshṭra-jātiyārin charitra-sāra-saṅgraham). Saurāshṭras.

Jāti-samayāchāra-viḷakkam. Ṣinn'-aiyā Mudaliyār.

Marapāḷa-purāṇam (Vēḷāḷa-p°.). Kanda-sāmi Piḷḷai, *V.Ṣ.*

Minute of the Madras Missionary Conference ... on ... Caste. Madras, *City of.*

Paḷḷigaḷ-vāyāppu. Shaṇmukha Grāmaṇi.

Pāṇḍiya-kula-viḷakkam. Ponnu-sāmi Nāḍār.

Paṛaiyar-uṛpatti-viḷakkam. Rāghava-mūrtti Piḷḷai.

Ṣeṅgunda-mannar-kula-dīpikai. Malaiy-appa Paṇḍitar.

Shanars are Kshatriyas. Ñāna-muttu Nāḍār.

Sūrya-chandra-vaṃṣa-paramparai-charitram. Shaṇmukha Grāmaṇi.

Vajra-sūchi. Aṣva-ghōsha.

Vannikula Vilakkam. Aiya-kannu Nāyakar.

Vanniyar-purāṇam. Vīra Piḷḷai.

Varṇa-chintāmaṇi. Kanaka-sabhai Piḷḷai, *K.*

Varṇa-darpaṇam. [Addenda] Āṟu-muga Nāyakar.

Yaduvaṃṣasthargaḷin kula-kāyam. Vēṅkaṭēṣa Piḷḷai.

COMPARATIVE PHILOLOGY.

Draviḍa-ṣabda-tattvam (Tamil Philology). Ṣēsha-giri Ṣāstri, *M.*

DRAMA.

Abhijñāna-ṣakuntalam. Kālidāsa.

'Alī-pādshā-nāṭakam. Vaṇṇa-kaḷañjiya Pulavar.

Alliy-araṣāṇi-nāṭakam. Kanda-sāmi Piḷḷai, *M.Ā.*

Arichandra. Hariṣchandra.

Bhōja-charitram. Nārāyaṇa Ṣāstri, *T.Ṣ.*

Chandravadanai (The Two Brothers). Viṣva-nātha Mudaliyār.

Chitrāṅgi-vilāsam. Appāvu Piḷḷai, *T.T.*

Comedy of Errors (Vibhrama-vilāsam). Shakspere (W.).

Damayanti. Praṇatārtihara Ṣivanār.

Damayanti-nāṭakam (Naḷa-n°.). Kṛushṇa-sāmi Piḷḷai, *Tañjai.*

Ḍambhāchāri-vilāsam. Kāṣi-viṣvanātha Mudaliyār.

Dēṣiṅgu-rājan-nāṭakam. Vīra-bhadra Aiyar.

Devadassi. Jacolliot (L.).

Dēva-sahāyam-piḷḷai-vāchaka-pā. Mutt'-aiyā Pulavar.

Dharma-putra-nāṭakam. Sāmi-nātha Mudaliyār.

Estākkiyār-nāṭakam. Tambi-muttu Piḷḷai.

Hariṣchandrōpākhyāna-nāṭakālaṅkāram (°kīrttanai). Nara-simm'-aiyar, *M.M.*

Hiraṇya-nāṭakam. Sōma-sundara Mudaliyār.

Hiraṇya-vilāsam. Kumāra-sāmi Upādhyāyar.

Iraṇḍu naṇbargaḷ (The Two Friends). Sambandha Mudaliyār.

Jānaki-pariṇayam. Muttu-subb'-aiya, *P.V.*

Jānakī-pariṇayam. Rāma-bhadra Dīkshitar.

Jana-manōllāsini. Ādi-nārāyaṇ'-aiyā.

Jīva-nāṭakam [anonymous]. Vālāmbāḷ.

Jōdi-mālai (Jyotimalai). Varadāchāryar, *Ṣ.*

Kalāvati. Sūrya-nārāyaṇa Ṣāstri.

Kalyāṇa-nāṭakam [*in loco*].

Kaṇḍi-rājā-nāṭakam (Kīrtti-ṣiṅga-mahā-rājan-charitram). Ṣiva-shaṇmukham Piḷḷai.

Karṇa-mahā-rājan-nāṭakam. Ēkāmbara Mudaliyār.

Kīchaka-vilāsam. Kaṇṇ'-ayya Nāyuḍu.

Kūlikku mār-aḍikkum kūttāḍichigaḷ-naḍippu. Kāṣi-viṣvanātha Mudaliyār.

Kuṣa-lava-nāṭakam. Aruṇāchala Kavi-rāyar, *Ṣ.*

Līlāvati-sulōchanai (Iraṇḍu sahōdarigaḷ). Sambandha Mudaliyār.

Madigeṭṭā-nāṭakam. Vīrā-sāmi Upādhyāyar, *K.*

Māḍu-biḍi-ṣandai (Vilāḍa-parva-nāṭakam). [Addenda] Rāghava-mūrtti.

Madurai-mīnākshiy-ammai-nāṭakam. Sundiram Piḷḷai.

Mahā-bhārata-nāṭakam (°kīrttanai). Subba-rāya Mudaliyār, *V.*, Mutti-rāma Kavi-rāyar, *G.*, and Kadir-vēl Kavi-rāja Paṇḍitar.

EDUCATION.

1. CLASSICAL GRAMMARS.

2. MODERN GRAMMARS AND READERS.

(i.) Grammars and Readers of Tamil.

(ii.) *Grammars and Readers of Tamil and other Languages.*

3. CLASSICAL DICTIONARIES OF TAMIL.

4. MODERN DICTIONARIES AND VOCABULARIES.

(i.) *Tamil.*

(ii.) *Tamil and other Languages.*

5. PROSODY (Yāppu) and STYLISTIC (Alaṅkāra).

6. MATHEMATICS.

7. MISCELLANEOUS.

ETHICS AND FABLES.

FICTION AND LEGEND.

Lalitāṅgi. NAṬA-RĀJA AIYAR, *M. V.*
Légendes Bouddhistes et Djainas. VINSON (É. H. J.).
Life and Adventures of Robinson Crusoe. DEFOE (D.).
Looking-glass for the Mind. VAIDYA-NĀTHA MUDALIYĀR, *T.*
Madana-kāma-rājan-kathai. MADANA-KĀMA-RĀJAN.
Madana-līlāvati. KUMĀRA-SĀMI MUDALIYĀR, *M.*
Madi geṭṭa manaivi (A Wife condoned). NAṬĒṢA ṢĀSTRI.
Mahā-bhārata-vachanam. VILLIPUTTŪRAR.
Mahā-bhārata-vinā-viḍai. [Addenda] KASTŪRI-RAṄG'-AYYAR, *A.S.*
Mahā-vindam. GŌVINDA PIḶḶAI, *V.*
Makuṭa-valli (Magudavalli). [Addenda] AKSHARA MUDALIYĀR.
Manav-ullāsa-kathai. NĀRĀYAṆA AIYAR.
Manō-rañjita-tiraṭṭu. ḢIKĀYĀT i LAṬĪF.
Mariyādai-rāman-kathai. MARIYĀDAI-RĀMAN.
Mati-mōsha-viḷakkam. RĀJA-GŌPĀLA BHŪPATI.
Mati-vāṇan. SŪRYA-NĀRĀYAṆA ṢĀSTRI.
Measure for Measure (Tann'-uyirai pōla maun'-uyirai ninai). NAṬĒṢA ṢĀSTRI.
Mediæval Tales of Southern India (Drāviḍa-madhya-kāla-kathaigaḷ). NAṬĒṢA ṢĀSTRI.
Mōhanāṅgi. ṢARA-VAṆA-MUTTU PIḶḶAI.
Mṛiṇmayī. [Addenda] DĀMŌDARA MUKHŌPĀDHYĀYA.
Mudrā-rākshasam. NAṬĒṢA ṢĀSTRI.
Muppatt'-iraṇḍu padumai-kathai. VIKRAMĀRKA-CHARITAM.
Nāgānandam. HARSHA-DĒVA.
Naḷa-chakravarttiyin charitram. NALAN.
Nālu-mantri-kathai (Aḷakēṣa-k°., The King and his four Ministers, Vier Geheimrath-Minister). NĀLU-MANTRI-KATHAI.
Ñāna-bhūshaṇi. NAṬA-RĀJA AIYAR, *M. V.*
Nan-neṟi-kathā-saṅgraham. ARNOLD (J. R.).
Nanṟiy-aṟiyā magan (The Ungrateful Son). ṢRĪNIVĀSA AIYAṄGĀR, *K.R.*
Nirmalā. NAṬA-RĀJA AIYAR, *M. V.*
——— [Addenda] PRABHĀTA-KUMĀRA MUKHŌPĀDHYĀYA.
Nīti-sāra-mañjari, Nīti-vinōda-kathā. MUḢAMMAD NIẒĀM MUḢYI al-DĪN.
Old Deccan Days. FRERE (M.).
Padmāvati-charitram. MĀDHAV'-AIYĀ.
Pakkā-kathai. ARABIAN NIGHTS.
Paṅkaja-valli-kathai. RĀMA-LIṄGA MUDALIYĀR, *T.*
Pann'-iraṇḍu-rājargaḷ-kathai. ṢĒSHĀCHALAM NĀYUḌU.
Paramārtha-guruvin kathai. BESCHI (C. G. E.).
Paṟa-moṟi-kathaigaḷ. RĀMA-LIṄGA MUDALIYĀR, *T.*
Parimaḷā. [Addenda] BAṄKIM-CHANDRA CHAṬṬŌPĀDHYĀYA.
Periya Bobbili-rājan-kathai. [Addenda] KANN'-AIYA NĀYUḌU.
Persian Stories. KEENE (H. G.).
Pleasing Tales (Inimaiy-āna kathaigaḷ). TALES.
Porteur de Sachet. NAṬĒṢA ṢĀSTRI.
Poṭṭoḍi. SUNDARAM PIḶḶAI, *G.*
Prabōdha-chandrōdaya-vachanam. KṚUSHṆA MIṢRA.
Pṛithulai. ṢRĪNIVĀSA AIYAṄGĀR, *K.R.*
Purāṇa-kathā-sāram. ṢRĪNIVĀSĀCHĀRYAR, *K. V.*
Raghu-vaṃṣam. KĀLIDĀSA.
Rāja-vaṃṣa-paramparai. MUNI-SĀMI MUDALIYĀR, *S.*
Rāmāyaṇam [*in loco*].
——— VĀLMĪKI.
Rāyar-appāji-kathai. APPĀJĪ.
Saguṇā. KṚUPAI SATYA-NĀTHAN.
Sahasra-mukha-rāvaṇan-kathai. RĀVAṆAN.
Sakala-kalā-bhūshaṇam. VIDYĀNANDA SVĀMI.
Sañjīvi-giri (Ṣeñji). VĒṄKAṬA-RĀMA ṢĀSTRI.
Ṣaṣi-varṇan-charitram. VṚUTTĀCHALAM.
Ṣata-mukha-rāvaṇan-kathai. RĀVAṆAN.
Sāvitri-charitai. SARASA-LŌCHANA CHEṬṬI.
Select Tamil Tales. NĀRĀYAṆA-SĀMI, *V.M.*
Sītā-vijaya-vachanam. YŌGA-VĀSISHṬHA-RĀMĀYAṆAM.
Son-in-law Abroad. RĀMA-CHANDRA RĀU, *P.*
Ṣrī-kṛushṇa-bōdhāmṛutam (Pann'-iraṇḍu-rājargaḷ-kathai). ṢĒSHĀCHALAM NĀYUḌU.
Ṣrī-māmi-goluv-irukkai (Mother-in-law in Council). NAṬĒṢA ṢĀSTRI.
Ṣrī-rāma-hṛudayam (Shaṭ-chakravarttigaḷin indra-jāla-kathaigaḷ). ṢĒSHĀCHALAM NĀYUḌU.
Ṣrī-rāmar-aṣva-mēdha-yāgam. BHĪMA KAVI-RĀYAR.
Suguṇa-sundari-charitram. VĒDA-NĀYAKAM PIḶḶAI.
Sundara-valli. [Addenda] KUMARĒṢAN (*Mrs.* G.).
Tales and Poems of South India. ROBINSON (E. J.).
Tales of Royar Appaji. APPĀJĪ.
Tales of the Sun. KINGSCOTE (G.), *Mrs.*, and NAṬĒṢA ṢĀSTRI.
Tennālu-rāman-kathai (Tales of Tennalirama). TENNĀLU-RĀMAN.
Tikk' aṭṭa iru-guṟandaigaḷ (The Two Orphans). NAṬĒṢA ṢĀSTRI.
Twelfth Night (Vayōlā-charitram). NAṬĒṢA ṢĀSTRI.
Ūṣōn-bālandai-kathai (Valentine and Orson). VALENTINE.
Uttara-kāṇḍa-kathai. VĀLMĪKI.
Vachana-chūḷāmaṇi (Tiviṭṭa-kumāran-kathai). TŌLĀ-MOṞI DĒVAR.
Vachana-sampradāya-kathai. MUTTU-KUṬṬI AYYĀ.
Vallāḷa-mahā-rājan-kathai. TIRU-VĒṄKAṬĀCHALA KAVI-RĀYAR.
Vālmīki-rāmāyaṇa-kiḷai-kathaigaḷ (Episodes from the Valmiki-ramayana). VĒṄKAṬA-RĀMA AIYAṄGĀR.
Vālmīki-rāmāyaṇa-vachanam. VĀLMĪKI.

GEOGRAPHY, TOPOGRAPHY, AND TRAVELS.

HISTORY.

I. GENERAL HISTORY AND ARCHÆOLOGY.

3. HISTORY OF LITERATURE.

LAW AND ADMINISTRATION.

LITERARY CRITICISM AND DRAMATURGY.

MISCELLANIES, COLLECTIONS, AND LITERARY PERIODICALS.

PHILOSOPHY AND THEOLOGY.

1. ṢAIVA SIDDHĀNTAM.

2. VAISHṆAVA SIDDHĀNTAM.

3. UPANISHADS AND ADVAITA-VĒDĀNTAM.

Vṛutti-prabhākaram, Vṛutti-ratnāvali. NIṢCHALA DĀSA.

4. NYĀYA AND VAIṢĒSHIKA.

Anumāna-viḷakkam. [Addenda] NĀRĀYAṈ'-AIYAṄGĀR, *T.*
Nyāya-prakāṣam. CHID-GHANĀNANDA GIRI.
Padārtha-dīpikai. MṚUGĒṢA PIḶḶAI, *Ṣ.P.*
Tarka-kaumudi. BHĀSKARA.
Tarka-viḷakkam (Aḷav'-iyal). SŌMA-SUNDARA PIḶḶAI.

5. YŌGA.

Cosmic Psychological Spiritual Philosophy. SABHĀPATI SVĀMI.
Haṭha-yōga-pradīpikā. SVĀTMĀRĀMA YŌGI.
Sitā-rāmāñjanēya-saṃvāda-sāra-saṅgraham. PARAṢU-RĀMA PANTULU.
Uttara-gītā [*in loco*].
Yōga-ñānānubhava-dīpikai. VĒṄKAṬA-RĀYA YŌGĪNDRAR.

6. ISLĀM.

Kimiyā i sa'ādat. MUHAMMAD ibn MUHAMMAD, *al-Ghazzālī.*
Miftāḥ al-raḥmān. MUHAMMAD ṢĀHIB.

7. MISCELLANEOUS SYSTEMS.

Advaita - dvaita - viṣishṭādvaita - siddhānta - sāra - saṅgraha-vinā-viḍai. NARA-SIMMALU NĀYUḌU.
Ārya - mata - siddhānta - saṅgraham. KUPPU - SĀMI AIYAR.
Brahma-sūtra-drāviḍa-bhāshyam. BĀDARĀYAṆA.
Daṣōpanishad-drāviḍa-bhāshyam. UPANISHADS.
Hinduism (Pūrva-hindu-samayam, Brahma-samaya-vinā-viḍai, Mata-vṛuksham). NARA-SIMMALU NĀYUḌU.
Light on the Path (Mārga-viḷakkam). COLLINS, afterwards COOK (M.).
Nijānanda-vilāsam. SUNDARA SVĀMI.
Prasaṅgam. VIVĒKĀNANDA.
Vivēka-chintāmaṇi. NIJA-GUṆA YŌGI.

POETRY.

I. CLASSICAL POETRY (NON-RELIGIOUS).

(i.) *Ethical Poetry.*

Āchāra-kōvai. PERU-VĀYIN MUḶḶIYĀR.
Aṟa-neṟi-chāram. MUNAI-PĀḌIYĀR.
Fleurs de l'Inde. INDIA.
Indische Sinnpflanzen und Blumen. GRAUL (K. F. L.).
Kapilar-agaval. KAPILAR.
Kuṟaṭ-saṅgraham. TIRU-VAḶḶUVAR.
Maṇavāḷa-nārāyaṇa-ṣatakam (Tiru-vēṅkaṭa-ṣ°.). NĀRĀYAṆA BHĀRATI.
Nal-vaḻi. AUVAIYĀR.
Nān-maṇi-ghaṭikai. VIḶAMBIYA-NĀGANĀR.
Nan-neṟi. ṢIVA-PRAKĀṢA DĒṢIKAR.
Nari-vṛuttam. TIRU-TAKKA DĒVAR.
Nīti-moḻi-tiraṭṭu. WALKER (J.).
Paḻa-moḻi. MUN-ṞUṞAIY-ARAIYAR.
Tamil Minor Poets (Nīti-nūṯ-ṯiraṭṭu). TAMIL MINOR POETS.
Tamil Wisdom. ROBINSON (E. J.).
Tiru-kuṟaḷ. AUVAIYĀR.—*Supposititious Works.*
Tri-kaṭukam. NALLĀDANĀR.
Vākk'-uṇḍām (Mūd'-urai). AUVAIYĀR.

(ii.) *Erotic, Romantic, and Panegyric Poetry.*

Abimannan-sundari-mālai. PUGAḺĒNDI.
Aindām battu. PARAṆAR.
Ain-diṇaiy-aim-badu. MĀṞAN POṞAIYANĀR.
Aiṅ-guṟu-nūṟu. KŪḌALŪR-KIḺĀR.
Alliy-araṣāni-mālai. PUGAḺĒNDI.
Āṟām battu. NACHEḶḶAIYĀR.
Bhāratam. NALLĀ PIḶḶAI.
Bhāratam (Bharata Venba). PERUN-DĒVANĀR.
Chūḷāmaṇi. TŌLĀ-MOḺI DĒVAR.
Ēḻām battu. KAPILAR.
Eṭṭām battu. ARIṢIL-KIḺĀR.
Hariṣchandra-purāṇam. VĪRA KAVI-RĀYAR.
Iniyadu nāṟ-padu. PŪDAṄ-ṢĒNDANĀR.
Iraṇḍām battu. KAṆṆANĀR.
Jīvaka-chintāmaṇi. TIRU-TAKKA DĒVAR.
Kadambari. [Addenda] BĀṆA.
Kāḷa-mēgha-pulavar . . . pāḍiyavai. KĀḶA-MĒGHAM.
Kaḷavaḻi. POYGAIYĀR.
Kaliṅgattu paraṇi. JAYAṄ-GOṆḌĀN.
Kali-togai. NALLANDUVANĀR.
Kamba-rāmāyaṇa-karu-poruḷ. KAMBAN.
Kamba-rāmāyaṇam. KAMBAN.
———— [Addenda] KAMBAN.
Kuriñji, Kuriñji-pāṭṭu. KAPILAR.
Madurai-kāñji. MARUDANĀR.
Mahā-bhāratam [*in loco*].
———— VILLIPUTTŪRAR.
Malai-baḍu-gaḍām (Kūttar-āṭṭu-paḍai). PERUṄ-KAUṢIKANĀR.
Maṇi-mēkhalai. ṢĀTTAN.
Marudam. ŌRAM-BŌGIYĀR.
Mullai. PĒYANĀR.
Mullai-pāṭṭu. NAPPŪDANĀR.
Mūnrām battu. GAUTAMANĀR.
Naiḍadam. ATIVĪRA-RĀMA PĀṆḌIYAN.
Naḷa-veṇ-bā. PUGAḺĒNDI.
Nalla-daṅgāḷ-kathai. PUGAḺĒNDI.
Nāṅgām battu. KĀPPIYANĀR.

(iv.) *Vaishṇava.*

Tiruv-ariyai-ṣilēdai-veṇ-bā-mālai, Tiruv-ariya-kuḍi-tirib'-antādi. KṚUSHṆAM-ĀCHĀRYAR, *Vēlāmūr.*
Tiru-vāy-moṛi. ĀṚVĀRGAḶ.
Tiru-vāy-moṛi-nūṭṭ'-antādi. AṚAGIYA-MAṆAVĀḶA PERU-MĀḶ.
Tiru-vēṅkaṭa-mālai. PIḶḶAI PERU-MĀḶ AIYAṄGĀR.
——————— RĀMAN CHEṬṬI.
Tiru-vēṅkaṭatt' antādi. PIḶḶAI PERU-MĀḶ AIYAṄGĀR.
Tiruv-evvuḷūr-tirib'-antādi. KṚUSHṆAM-ĀCHĀRYAR, *Vēlāmūr.*
Tukārām-svāmigaḷ-charitra-kīrttanai. GŌVINDA-DĀSAR.
Upadēṣa-ratna-mālai. AṚAGIYA-MAṆAVĀḶA PERU-MĀḶ.
——————— [Addenda] AṚAGIYA-MAṆAVĀḶA PERU-MĀḶ.
Vāna-mā-mala-rāmānuja-jīyar-svāmula-vāri maṭha-guru-parampara- (tiru-nakshatra-) taniyanlu (°vāṛi-tiru-nāmamulu). VĀNA-MĀ-MALAI RĀMĀNUJA-JĪYAR.
Vāṛi-tiru-nāmam. AP-PIḶḶAI.
Vishṇu-nāmāvaḷi (Mōksha-sūkshmam). RĀGHAVALU RĀMĀNUJA-DĀSAR.
Vishṇu-purāṇam. PURĀṆAS.
Yati-rāja-viṃṣati. AṚAGIYA-MAṆAVĀḶA PERU-MĀḶ.

(v.) *Other Cults.*

Kāṇūr-ṣelliy-amman-badigam. KANAKA-SABHAI PIḶḶAI, *V.*
Māriy-amman-tālāṭṭu. MĀRIY-AMMAN.
Muttu-māriy-amman-nava-ratnam. ṢELL'-AIYĀ PIḶḶAI, *Ṣ.*
Sarasvatiy-antādi. KAMBAN.
Siddhi-vighnēṣvara-ūñjal. VAIDYA-LIṄGA PIḶḶAI, *V.Ṣ.*
Vara-siddhi-vināyakar-pañcha-ratnam, *etc.* SĀMBA-ṢIVA KAVI-RĀYAR.
Vināyaka-pratishṭhai. NĀRĀYAṆA-SĀMI AIYAR, *of Periya-tirukōṇam.*
Vināyakar-agaval. AUVAIYĀR.—*Supposititious Works.*
——————— NAKKĪRA DĒVAR.

(vi.) *Advaita-vēdānti.*

Advaita-pāṭṭugaḷ. VĀLĀMBĀḶ.
Advitānubhavam. RĀMA KAVI.
Advita-rasa-mañjari. SADĀ-ṢIVA BRAHMĒNDRA.
Avirōta-vundiyār (Eclectic Vedantism, The Non-Controversialists' Dance). ṢĀNTA-LIṄGA SVĀMI, *T.*
Chin-maya-dīpikai. MUTT'-AIYA SVĀMI.
Daṣakam. ṢAṄKARĀCHĀRYAR. [*Doubtful and Supposititious Works.*]
Jīva-kāruṇya-viḷakkam. SACH-CHID-ĀNANDA SVĀMI.
Jīva-nāṭakam [anonymous]. VĀLĀMBĀḶ.
Kaivalya-nava-nītam. TĀṆḌAVA-RĀYA-MŪRTTI SVĀMI.
Lakshaṇā-vṛutti. ṢAṄKARĀCHĀRYAR. [*Doubtful and Supposititious Works.*]
Manīshā-pañchakam. ṢAṄKARĀCHĀRYAR. [*Doubtful and Supposititious Works.*]
Māyā-pralāpam. KAṆṆ'-UḌAIYA VAḶḶAL.
Mey-ñāna-viḷakkam. KṚUSHṆA MIṢRA.
Ñāna-vāṣiṭṭav-amala-rāmāyaṇam. ĀḶAVANDĀR, *V.*
Oṛivil oḍukkam. KAṆṆ'-UḌAIYA VAḶḶAL.
Prabōdha-chandrōdayam. KṚUSHṆA MIṢRA.
Ṛibhu-gītai-tiraṭṭu. ṢIVA-RAHASYAM.
Ṣaṣi-varṇa-bōdham. TATTVA-RĀYA SVĀMI.
Sōpāna-pañchakam, Sorūpānusandhāna-dudi. ṢAṄKARĀCHĀRYAR. [*Doubtful and Supposititious Works.*]
Svānubhūti-viḷakkam. SACH-CHID-ĀNANDA SVĀMI.
Vēdānta-paḷḷu. ĀVIḌAI AMMĀḶ.
Vēdānta-pāṭṭugaḷ. VĀLĀMBĀḶ.
Vivēka-shaṭkam. ṢAṄKARĀCHĀRYAR. [*Doubtful and Supposititious Works.*]

(vii.) *Jain.*

Dvādaṣānuprēkshai (Jīva-sambōdhanai). DĒVĒNDRA.
Tiru-nūṭṭ'-antādi. AVIRŌDHIY-ĀṚVĀR.

(viii.) *Yōga.*

Aṭṭāṅga-yōga-kuṛaḷ. YŌGA.
Yōga-vāsishṭha-rāmāyaṇam [*in loco*].

POLITICS AND SOCIETY.

Aiy-āyira-varsha-atiṣaya-rahasyam. SĀMI-NĀTHA PIḶḶAI, *Ch.A.*
Ārya-jana-aikyam (Congress-jana-sabhai). SUBRAH-MAṆYA AIYAR, *G.*
Congress-vinā-viḍai. VĪRA-RĀGHAVĀCHĀRYAR, *M.*
Dēṣābhimāni. PERIODICAL PUBLICATIONS.—*Madras.*
Dēṣōpakāri. PERIODICAL PUBLICATIONS.—*Madras.*
Hindu Nasen [*i.e.* Hindu-nēṣan]. PERIODICAL PUBLICATIONS.—*Penang.*
Mādar-mitri. PERIODICAL PUBLICATIONS.—*Madras.*
Manners and Customs of Native Christians (Kiṛista-vargaḷin āchāramum gurumār-bōdhakamum). MUTT'-AIYA PIḶḶAI, *E.*
Mysore Representative Assembly and the Indian National Congress. VĪRA-RĀGHAVĀCHĀRYAR, *M.*
Nāgai-paittiyam. RĀMA-SĀMI AIYAR, *Ṣ.*
Penang News (Pināṅgu-vartamāni). PERIODICAL PUBLICATIONS.—*Penang.*
Penang Standard (Pināṅgu-vijaya-kōtanan). PERIODICAL PUBLICATIONS.—*Penang.*
Peṇgaḷin charitram (History and Philosophy of the Female Sex). NARA-SIMMALU NĀYUḌU.

PROVERBS AND ADAGES.

RELIGION.

I. CHRISTIANITY.

(a) *Doctrinal Works and Tracts.*

(b) *Liturgies and Manuals.*

2. HINDUISM.

(i.) *Works on Hindu Doctrines, Cults, and Rituals.*

(ii.) *Anti-Christian Tracts.*

Kiṟistu-mata-khaṇḍanam. Madras, *City of.*

Kiṟistu-mata-tūla-vātūlam. Jaffna.—*Mlēchchha-mata-khaṇḍana-sabhai.*

Kiṟistu-samaya-bhēdam. Āṟu-muga Piḷḷai, *U.C.*

Māṃsa-bhōjana-vilakku. Jaffna.—*Kiṟistu-mata-khaṇḍana-sabhai.*

Mlēchchha-mata - khaṇḍana - sabhā - kākala - ghōsham. Jaffna.—*Mlēchchha-mata-khaṇḍana-sabhai.*

Ñāṉa-kummi. Muttu-kumāra Kavi-rājar.

Nikāra-nikāraṇam. Mlēchchha-matāndhakāra-bhāskaraṉ, *Pseud.*

Ṣaiva-dūshaṇa-parihāram. Jaffna.—*Ṣaiva-prakāṣa-sabhai.*

Viviliya-nūl-varalāṟu. Āṟu-muga Piḷḷai, *U.C.*

3. BRĀHMA SAMĀJ AND THEISM.

Brahma - samaya - vinā - viḍai. Nara - simmalu Nāyuḍu.

Dakshiṇa-indiyāvil uḷḷa brahma-samājaṅgaḷin charitra-sāra-saṅgraham (Brief History and Principles of the Southern Indian Brama Samajams). [Addenda] Nara-simmalu Nāyuḍu.

Hindu-mata-khaṇḍanam. Trincomali.

Kākala-ghōsha-dōsham. Trincomali.

Nikāra-nikāraṇa-nigraham. Trincomali.

Vēdam. Brāhma Samāj.

Vēdānta-sūryōdayam. Brāhma Samāj.

Vēda - poruḷ - sāra - saṅgraham. Nara - simmalu Nāyuḍu.

Vigraha-battikkun teyva-battikkuñ sambhāshaṇai. Roberts (W.).

4. ISLĀM.

Aḥkām al-ṣiyām. Aḥkām.

Asrār al-ṣalawāt ʻala khair al-bariyāt. ʻAbd al-Wahhāb ibn Muḥammad Hādī.

Bushra al-karīm. Ḥabīb Muḥammad, *al-Bakrī.*

Dajjāl nāmah. Dajjāl.

Dīn-neṟi-viḷakkam. Makhdūm Muḥammad ibn Makhdūm Piḷḷai.

al-Durar al-ḥisān. Muḥammad Yūsuf.

al-Durar fi ḥikāyāt al-ghurar (Ḳiṣaṣ al-auliyā). Nūḥ ibn ʻAbd al-Ḳādir.

Durrat al-mafākhir. Aḥmad ibn Muḥ. Ḥasan.

Fatḥ al-daiyān. Muḥammad ibn Aḥmad.

Fatḥ al-ṣamad fi asmā ahl al-Badr wa'l-Uḥud. Nūḥ ibn ʻAbd al-Ḳādir.

Fawā'id al-ḳur'ān. Shāh al-Ḥamīd ibn ʻAidarūs.

al-Fawā'id fi al-ṣalāt wa'l-ʻawā'id. Aḥmad ibn Aḥmad.

Futūḥ al-Miṣr wa'l-Bahnasā. Muḥammad ibn Muḥammad, *al-Muʻizz.*

al-Futūḥāt al-raḥmānīyat. Ḥabīb Muḥammad, *al-Bakrī.*

Futūḥāt al-salām. ʻAbd al-Ḳādir ibn Madār.

Ḥaḳīḳat al-islām (Īmān-uṇmai islām-nanmai). ʻAbd al-Ḳādir.

Hidāyat al-sālikīn. Muḥammad Ismāʻīl.

Irshād al-ʻibād [*in loco*].

Ḳur'ān [*in loco*].

Lubāb al-akhbār. [Addenda] Aḥmad ibn ʻAbd Allāh.

al-Nafaḥāt al-ʻiṭrīyah. Ṣadaḳat Allāh.

Ñāna - dīpa - saṃhāram. Ḥabīb Muḥammad ibn Nainā Muḥammad.

Naṣīḥat al-anām fi hidāyat al-islām. Muḥammad Ibrāhīm ibn ʻAbd al-Ghanī.

Nubẕat al-fawā'id. Muḥammad ʻAbd al-Ḳādir ibn Ādam.

Raḥmat al-mannān. Ḳur'ān.

Sair al-sālikīn. Muḥammad ʻAbd al-Ḳādir.

Ṣalāt al-arkān mālai. Sām Shihāb al-Dīn.

Shams al-īmān. Muḥammad Yūsuf.

Shams al-maʻrifat. Muḥammad ʻAbd al-Ḳādir ibn Ādam.

Talḳīn fī muhimmāt al-dīn. ʻAbd al-Majīd.

——— Muḥammad Ibrāhīm ibn ʻAbd al-Ghanī.

Ta'yīd al-raḥmān. Muḥammad ʻAbd al-Raḥmān ibn Ḳādir Mīrān.

Toṟugai-ḥaḳīḳat-viḷakkam. Vālai-bāva Ṣāḥib.

Tuḥfat al-aḥbāb. Muḥyī al-Dīn ibn Muḥammad.

——— Tamīm ibn Sulṭān.

Tuḥfat al-kirām. Nūḥ ibn ʻAbd al-Ḳādir.

ʻUbāb al-akhyār. [Addenda] Aḥmad ibn ʻAbd Allāh.

ʻUmdat al-nisā. Muḥammad Sharaf al-Dīn.

ʻUmdat al-ṣibyān. Muḥammad Tamīm.

Al-Waẓīfat al-Shāẕilīyah. ʻAlī ibn ʻAbd Allāh.

al-Witrīyah. Muḥammad ibn Abī Bakr.

al-Yāḳūtīyah. Muḥammad ibn Muḥammad, *al-Fāsī.*